학습계획표

학습계획표를 활용하여 학습 일정을 기록하고 계획하여 자신의 성적을 체크해 보세요.
스스로 실력을 확인하면서 공부하는 습관은 문제집을 끝까지 푸는 데 큰 도움이 됩니다.

Day	회차	학습 날짜	맞은 개수	틀린 개수	복습 날짜
Day 01	01회	월 일	개	개	월 일
Day 02	02회	월 일	개	개	월 일
Day 03	03회	월 일	개	개	월 일
Day 04	04회	월 일	개	개	월 일
Day 05	05회	월 일	개	개	월 일
Day 06	06회	월 일	개	개	월 일
Day 07	07회	월 일	개	개	월 일
Day 08	08회	월 일	개	개	월 일
Day 09	09회	월 일	개	개	월 일
Day 10	10회	월 일	개	개	월 일
Day 11	11회	월 일	개	개	월 일
Day 12	12회	월 일	개	개	월 일
Day 13	13회	월 일	개	개	월 일
Day 14	14회	월 일	개	개	월 일
Day 15	15회	월 일	개	개	월 일
Day 16	16회	월 일	개	개	월 일
Day 17	17회	월 일	개	개	월 일

취약 유형 체크표

정확히 이해하고 푼 문제에는 ∨를, 헷갈렸던 문제에는 △, 틀린 문제에는 ×표를 하고,
어떤 유형을 어려워하는지 확인하고, 복습할 때 활용해 보세요.

유형		목적	주제/의견	관계	그림 일치	할 일/부탁한 일	지불할 금액	이유 추론	언급 유무	담화 내용 일치	표 일치	짧은 대화 응답		긴 대화 응답		상황에 적절한 말	세트 문항	
회/번호		1	2	3	4	5	6	7	8	9	10	11	12	13	14	15	16	17
실전 모의고사 17회	01회																	
	02회																	
	03회																	
	04회																	
	05회																	
	06회																	
	07회																	
	08회																	
	09회																	
	10회																	
	11회																	
	12회																	
	13회																	
	14회																	
	15회																	
	16회																	
	17회																	
오답 문항 수																		

Listening ∞ master

BASIC

유형 탐구 13강

실전 모의고사 17회

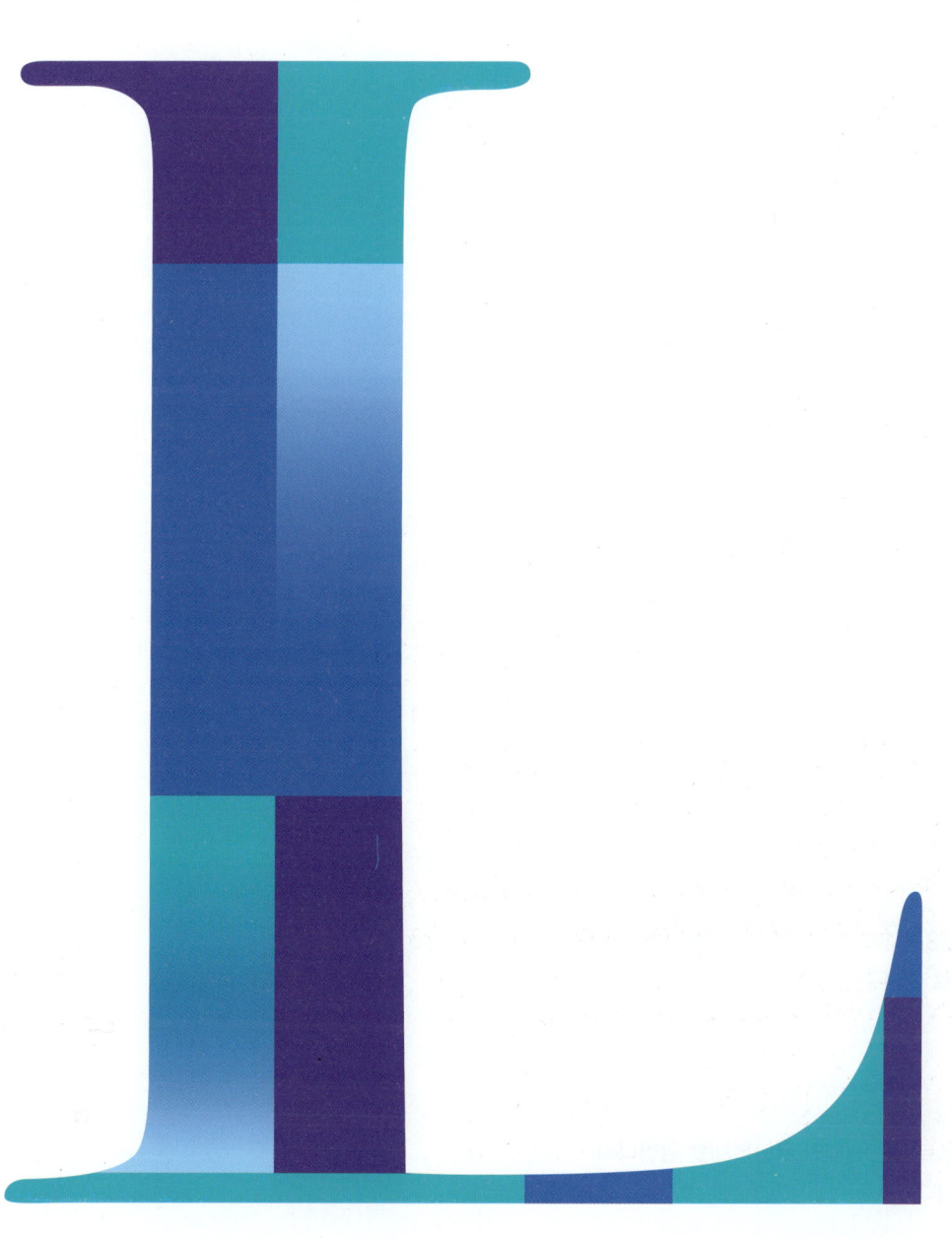

WRITERS

강소엽 김대성 육상태 장정근 조정훈 황선용

STAFF

발행인 정선욱
퍼블리싱 총괄 남형주
기획·개발 김태원 박하영 유희선
디자인 김정인 닷츠
유통·마케팅 서준성 김지희
제작 김한길 김경수

Listening Master BASIC ｜ 202012 제3판 1쇄 202511 제3판 7쇄
펴낸곳 이투스에듀(주) 서울시 서초구 남부순환로 2547
고객센터 1599-3225
등록번호 제2007-000035호
ISBN 979-11-6598-224-9[53740]

PREFACE

수능 영어듣기 만점 전략

전략 1 **수능 영어듣기 모의고사를 최대한 많이 풀어본다.**
많은 양의 실전 모의고사를 풀어보면서 수능 출제 경향 및 문제 유형을 파악하고, 다양한 소재를 접해봄으로써 수능 영어듣기 실전 감각을 높일 수 있습니다.

전략 2 **수능 영어듣기평가 녹음 속도보다 빠른 속도로 듣기 연습을 한다.**
수능 영어듣기평가 속도보다 빠른 속도로 듣는 것에 익숙해지면, 실제 시험에서의 속도가 편하게 느껴지고 영어듣기 실력은 향상될 것입니다.

전략 3 **수능 영어듣기평가 빈출 핵심표현을 암기한다.**
모르는 표현은 들어도 이해하기 어렵습니다. 따라서 수능 영어듣기평가에 자주 등장하는 어휘 및 표현은 평소에 꾸준히 암기하는 것이 좋습니다.

전략 4 **문제 풀이 후 다시 한 번 받아쓰기를 한다.**
다시 듣고 받아쓰면서 문제 해결의 단서를 이해하고 연음 및 주요 표현을 학습하며, 잘 들리지 않았던 부분을 확인할 수 있습니다. 이를 통해 수능 영어듣기평가의 철저한 대비가 가능합니다.

수능 영어듣기 교재 Check List

❶ **듣기 문항이 충분히 검증되었는가?**
Listening Master는 수능 및 모의평가 출제 위원이 집필한 문항으로 구성되었습니다.

❷ **학습 목표와 수준에 맞는 다양한 음원을 제공하는가?**
Listening Master는 실제 시험과 동일한 속도, 1.2배속, 문항별 음원을 제공하여 듣기 훈련을 할 수 있도록 하였습니다.

❸ **학습의 편의성을 고려하였는가?**
Listening Master는 회차별 듣기 필수표현 MASTER, 학습계획표, 취약 유형 체크표, 빠른 정답, 빠른 DICTATION 정답을 제공하여 효율적으로 학습할 수 있도록 하였습니다.

❹ **수능 영어듣기평가를 완벽 대비할 수 있는가?**
Listening Master는 BASIC, 영어듣기 모의고사 20회, 영어듣기 모의고사 40회의 3권으로 구성되어 유형부터 고난도 모의고사까지 체계적으로 학습하여 수능 영어듣기를 완전 정복할 수 있도록 하였습니다.

듣기를 학습하는 가장 쉽고 빠른 방법은?
시작하라, 수능 영어듣기 만점 전략
Listening Master로!

FEATURES

PART 1
유형 탐구

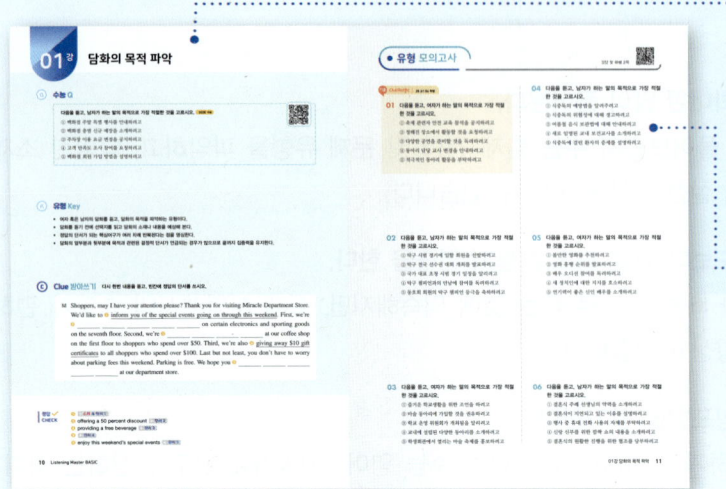

수능 Q에서 해당 유형 최신 수능 문제를 풀어본 후 유형 Key에서 유형 소개 및 전략에 대한 Tip을 제공합니다. Clue 받아쓰기를 통해 다시 한번 듣고, 정답의 단서가 되는 부분을 직접 써보며 유형의 특징을 파악할 수 있습니다.

유형 모의고사에서 방금 학습한 유형을 즉시 집중적으로 연습할 수 있고, 기출 Challenge 문항으로 최신 기출 문제를 풀어볼 수 있습니다.

PART 2
실전 모의고사

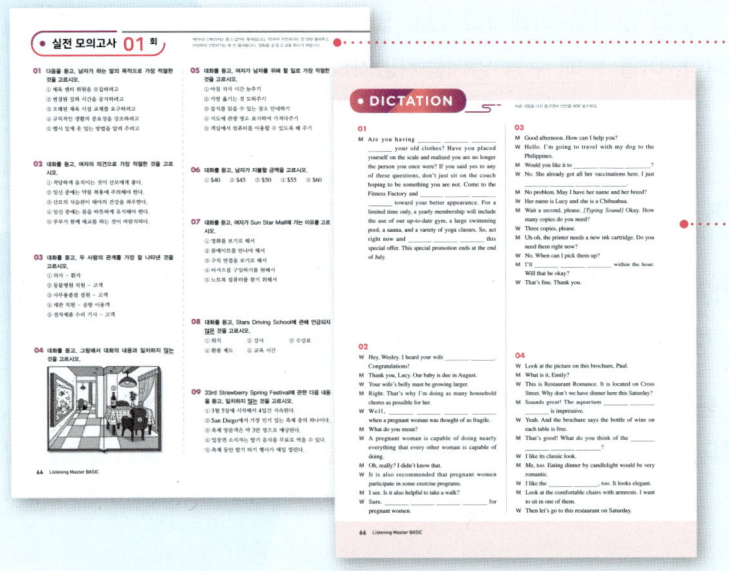

최신 수능과 모의평가를 철저히 분석하여 반영된 실전 모의고사 17회로, 수능 영어듣기 대비에 적합한 소재와 유형으로 구성되었습니다.

매회 모의고사 뒤에 수록되어 정답 단서, 핵심 표현, 연음·강세로 인해 잘 들리지 않는 어구의 빈칸을 받아쓰면서 대본의 전반적인 이해를 돕고 듣기 실력 또한 향상시킬 수 있습니다.

듣기 필수표현
MASTER

매회 대본에서 수능 영어듣기 핵심 표현들을 총정리하여 제공하여 학습 효과를 더욱 높일 수 있습니다.

수능 영어듣기 완벽 대비를 돕는
학습계획표 / 취약 유형 체크표 / 빠른 정답 & 빠른 DICTATION 정답

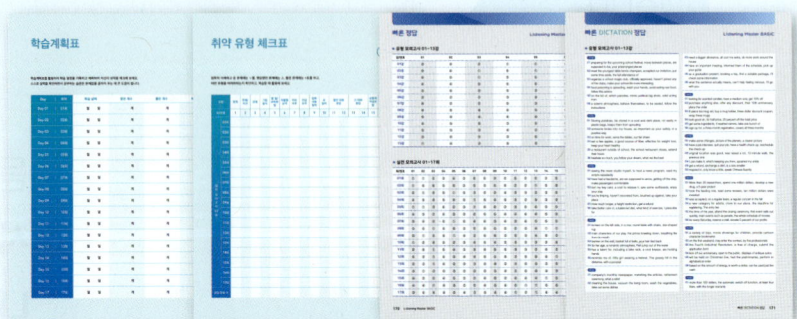

CONTENTS

PRESTUDY

● Listening Skills 발음편

우리말과 달리 영어 문장은 특정 단어가 다른 단어에 비해 강세를 받고, 강세를 받는 음절과 강세를 받지 않는 음절이 반복되면서 자연스러운 리듬이 발생한다. 문장에서 어떤 단어가 강세를 받는지를 이해하기 위해 기능어와 내용어를 알아야 한다. 기능어는 전치사, 접속사, 관사, 조동사, 대명사 등 문법적인 기능을 하는 단어이고, 내용어는 명사, 동사, 형용사, 부사처럼 그 단어가 의미를 가지고 있어 문장의 의미를 전달할 때 중요한 역할을 하는 단어이다. 그러므로 기능어는 약하게 발음되고, 내용어는 강하게 발음된다. 기능어를 듣지 못해도 문맥상 이해하는 데 어려움이 없기 때문에 내용어를 중심으로 들으며 의미를 추론하는 것이 필요하다.

01 연음 현상

발음을 쉽게 하기 위해 단어와 단어의 경계 없이 이어서 발음하는 것을 '연음'이라고 한다. 앞 단어가 자음으로 끝나고 뒤에 모음으로 시작하는 단어가 이어지면, 앞 자음이 뒤 모음에 연음된다.

> · does it / if you / check it out / hand it in / put it off / far away / wrap it up
>   think about / above it all / stop it / not at all / knock it off / win or lose

02 동화 현상

두 단어를 연달아 발음하기 어려운 경우 발음을 쉽게 하기 위해 '동화' 현상이 일어난다. 특히 발음하기 어려운 자음을 서로 비슷한 음으로 동화하여 부드럽게 발음한다.

> · [t]/[ts] + [j] → [tʃ]   want you / meet you / asked you / hates you
> · [d]/[dz] + [j] → [dʒ]   would you / could you / needs you / did you
> · [s] + [j] → [ʃ]   miss you / makes you / this university
> · [z] + [j] → [ʒ]   as you / knows you / how's your / use your

03 자음 생략 현상

두 단어의 사이에 유사하거나 동일 자음이 이어지는 경우 앞 자음이 생략되어 발음한다. 또한 자음 사이에 [t], [d], [p]가 오면 생략되거나 거의 발음되지 않는다. 더 나아가 empty, attempt, symptom 등과 같이 한 단어 안에 자음이 3개가 연속되는 경우에는 가운데 자음을 생략하여 발음한다.

> · [t+t] → [t] next time   [m+m] → [m] some money   [k+k] → [k] dark color
> · [v+b] → [b] I've been   [v+f] → [f] have fun   [d+t] → [t] include tax
> · first visit / last month / gold medal / remind me / old man / deep pot

04 축약 현상

I am을 I'm으로, is not을 isn't로 축약하여 발음하는 경우가 많다. 특히 부정어 not과 축약되면 끝소리 [t]가 잘 들리지 않을 수 있지만, 부정 축약형은 문장 강세를 받고 전후 문맥을 살펴 의미를 파악해야 한다. 이를 제외한 축약형은 문장의 의미를 파악하는 데 중요한 부분은 아니므로 약하고 빠르게 발음한다.

> · **We'll** come. / **They've** come. / **Where'd** you put it? / **Why'd** you call?
> · I **should've** left early. / She **could've** slept early.
> · **wasn't** / **weren't** / **doesn't** / **don't** / **didn't** / **won't** / **hasn't** / **haven't**

05 다양하게 변하는 [t] 발음

[t] 뒤에 [n]이 오는 경우 원래의 [튼]으로 발음되지 않고 '~은', '~흔'에 가까운 콧바람 소리와 유사하게 발음한다. 또한 [nt]가 모음 사이에 오거나 약하게 발음될 때 [t]는 [n] 발음에 동화되어 거의 발음되지 않는다.

> · button [버튼] → [버흔] / moutain [마운틴] → [마운흔] / cotton [코튼] → [코흔]
> · internet / center / twenty / interview / printout / percentage

06 [h] 생략

[h]는 강세가 있는 음절의 처음에 오는 경우를 제외하고는 주로 생략된다. 특히 [h]로 시작하는 대명사와 강세를 받지 않는 have, has, had에서 [h] 탈락 현상이 일어난다.

> · like **him** / what **happened** / tell **her** / give **her** / can **he** / ask **him** / respect **him**

07 묵음

단어의 철자에는 분명히 있지만 실제로는 발음되지 않는 것을 '묵음'이라고 한다. 단어의 철자만 익힌 상태에서 듣기를 할 경우 어려움을 줄 수도 있으므로 미리 알아두도록 한다.

> · **doubt** / **climb** / **thumb** / **handsome** / **budget** / **design**
> · **honest** / **hour** / **honor** / **knife** / **knock** / **kneel** / **knit** / **know**
> · **salmon** / **half** / **halves** / **calm** / **folk** / **psychology** / **receipt** / **cupboard**
> · **aisle** / **island** / **autumn** / **column** / **whistle** / **castle** / **hasten** / **fasten**

Listening Master

BASIC

유형 탐구

Q 수능 Q

다음을 듣고, 남자가 하는 말의 목적으로 가장 적절한 것을 고르시오. **2020 수능**

① 백화점 주말 특별 행사를 안내하려고
② 백화점 층별 신규 매장을 소개하려고
③ 주차장 이용 요금 변경을 공지하려고
④ 고객 만족도 조사 참여를 요청하려고
⑤ 백화점 회원 가입 방법을 설명하려고

K 유형 Key

- 여자 혹은 남자의 담화를 듣고, 담화의 목적을 파악하는 유형이다.
- 담화를 듣기 전에 선택지를 읽고 담화의 소재나 내용을 예상해 본다.
- 정답의 단서가 되는 핵심어구가 여러 차례 반복된다는 점을 명심한다.
- 담화의 앞부분과 뒷부분에 목적과 관련된 결정적 단서가 언급되는 경우가 많으므로 끝까지 집중력을 유지한다.

C Clue 받아쓰기   다시 한번 내용을 듣고, 빈칸에 정답의 단서를 쓰시오.

M Shoppers, may I have your attention please? Thank you for visiting Miracle Department Store. We'd like to ❶ <u>inform you of the special events going on through this weekend</u>. First, we're ❷ _____ _____ _____ _____ _____ on certain electronics and sporting goods on the seventh floor. Second, we're ❸ _____ _____ _____ _____ at our coffee shop on the first floor to shoppers who spend over $50. Third, we're also ❹ <u>giving away $10 gift certificates</u> to all shoppers who spend over $100. Last but not least, you don't have to worry about parking fees this weekend. Parking is free. We hope you ❺ _____ _____ _____ _____ _____ at our department store.

정답 ✓ CHECK
- ❶ 소재 & 단서 1
- ❷ offering a 50 percent discount 단서 2
- ❸ providing a free beverage 단서 3
- ❹ 단서 4
- ❺ enjoy this weekend's special events 단서 5

기출 Challenge | 20 고1 06 학평

01 다음을 듣고, 여자가 하는 말의 목적으로 가장 적절한 것을 고르시오.
① 축제 관련자 안전 교육 참석을 공지하려고
② 정해진 장소에서 활동할 것을 요청하려고
③ 다양한 공연을 준비할 것을 독려하려고
④ 동아리 담당 교사 변경을 안내하려고
⑤ 적극적인 동아리 활동을 부탁하려고

02 다음을 듣고, 남자가 하는 말의 목적으로 가장 적절한 것을 고르시오.
① 탁구 시범 경기에 임할 회원을 선발하려고
② 탁구 전국 선수권 대회 개최를 발표하려고
③ 국가 대표 초청 시범 경기 일정을 알리려고
④ 탁구 챔피언과의 만남에 참여를 독려하려고
⑤ 동호회 회원의 탁구 챔피언 등극을 축하하려고

03 다음을 듣고, 여자가 하는 말의 목적으로 가장 적절한 것을 고르시오.
① 즐거운 학교생활을 위한 조언을 하려고
② 마술 동아리에 가입할 것을 권유하려고
③ 학교 운영 위원회가 개최됨을 알리려고
④ 교내에 설립된 다양한 동아리를 소개하려고
⑤ 학생회관에서 열리는 마술 축제를 홍보하려고

04 다음을 듣고, 남자가 하는 말의 목적으로 가장 적절한 것을 고르시오.
① 식중독의 예방법을 알려주려고
② 식중독의 위험성에 대해 경고하려고
③ 여름철 음식 보관법에 대해 안내하려고
④ 새로 임명된 교내 보건교사를 소개하려고
⑤ 식중독에 걸린 환자의 증세를 설명하려고

05 다음을 듣고, 여자가 하는 말의 목적으로 가장 적절한 것을 고르시오.
① 볼만한 영화를 추천하려고
② 영화 흥행 순위를 발표하려고
③ 배우 오디션 참여를 독려하려고
④ 새 정치인에 대한 지지를 호소하려고
⑤ 연기력이 좋은 신인 배우를 소개하려고

06 다음을 듣고, 남자가 하는 말의 목적으로 가장 적절한 것을 고르시오.
① 결혼식 주례 선생님의 약력을 소개하려고
② 결혼식이 지연되고 있는 이유를 설명하려고
③ 행사 중 휴대 전화 사용의 자제를 부탁하려고
④ 신랑 신부를 위한 깜짝 쇼의 내용을 소개하려고
⑤ 결혼식의 원활한 진행을 위한 협조를 당부하려고

녹음 내용을 다시 들으면서 빈칸을 채워 넣으세요.

01

W Hello, students. This is vice principal Susan Lee. I know all of you are busy _____ _____ _____ _____ _____ _____. There are club activities going on in every part of our school building. You may want to _____ _____ _____ during activities. But I'd like to ask you to work in the place where you _____ _____ _____ _____. Your teachers want to make your safety the top priority. Once again, make sure to prepare for the festival in _____ _____ _____. Thank you for your cooperation.

02

M Hello, ping pong club members. I'm John Clement, your club leader. May 12th is going to be a very special day for our club. Everyone will _____ _____ _____ _____ _____ _____ in the national competition, Tom Clay. Tom is 14 years old — much, much younger than any of us — but he is the youngest table tennis player to ever win the national championship. It wasn't easy to bring him here, but he's finally _____ _____ _____. He is going to give us some demonstrations and afterwards there will be time for a short Q&A session. Don't forget to _____ _____ _____ _____ on May 12th for the meeting with this prodigy. I would appreciate _____ _____ _____ _____ all our members.

03

W Hi, students. This is Kate Brown, and I'm trying hard to _____ _____ _____ _____ _____. Finally, the magic club was _____ _____ by the school management committee last week. Now we just need members. If you _____ _____ _____ _____ _____ _____ yet, why don't you join the magic club? I'm sure being a member of the magic club will _____ _____ _____ _____ _____ _____ and exciting. Please visit the magic club office in the student union building if you're interested in magic. I hope to see you there.

04

M Hello, I'm David Kim, the school health teacher. As you know, _____ _____ _____ _____ now, and many people are afraid of getting infected. But don't worry too much. I'll tell you two simple ways to prevent getting the food poisoning. First, make sure to _____ _____ _____ before eating any kind of food. Second, try to _____ _____ _____ _____ such as fish or vegetables for the time being. The more you avoid raw food, the less likely you are to get food poisoning. I'm sure that if you _____ _____ _____, you won't have to worry too much about the threat of food poisoning.

05

W Hello, fellow club members. Today, I'd like to talk about *Spoken Out*. It's not well-known, and it's not _____ _____ _____ _____ top 30 movies at the box office. *Spoken Out* is a black comedy _____ _____ current political situations. It features actors Eric Dennis and Charlie Young, who _____ _____ _____ _____. It's a story about two future politicians who manage to escape from political embarrassment time and time again. The directing is fresh and the story is funny, and this should appeal to most adults who live a Monday-to-Friday working lifestyle. There are no special effects in this film, just _____ _____ _____ two promising stars. You'll have a wonderful time watching this black comedy.

06

M May I have your attention, please? I'd like to thank you for coming to the wedding of Peter Anderson and Mary Damon. Before the wedding ceremony starts, I'd like to tell you a couple of things. For us to maintain _____ _____ _____ in the wedding, please switch your cellphones to manner mode. For the same reason, please keep your eyes on your kids and make sure they _____ _____. And be sure _____ _____ _____ at least five minutes before the ceremony starts. We'll give an announcement when it's time. And during the ceremony, please _____ _____ _____ of the wedding director and give a big hand to the groom and the bride. Your consideration will make it much easier for us to have this wedding with a congratulatory mood. Thank you for your cooperation.

필수표현 NOTE

01 This is vice principal Susan Lee. 저는 교감 Susan Lee입니다.
Thank you for your cooperation. 협조해 주셔서 고맙습니다.

03 Why don't you join the magic club? 마술 동아리에 가입하는 것은 어떠세요?
I hope to see you there. 그곳에서 여러분을 만나기를 희망합니다.

04 Don't worry too much. 너무 많이 걱정하지 마십시오.

05 It features actors Eric Dennis and Charlie Young. 이 영화에는 Eric Dennis와 Charlie Young 배우들이 출연합니다.

06 We'll give an announcement when it's time. 시간이 되면 저희가 안내 방송을 할 것입니다.

02강 화자의 의견/대화의 주제 파악

Q 수능Q

대화를 듣고, 여자의 의견으로 가장 적절한 것을 고르시오. **2020 수능**

① 왼쪽 신체의 잦은 사용은 두뇌 활동을 촉진한다.
② 수면 시간과 심장 기능은 밀접한 관련이 있다.
③ 왼쪽으로 누워 자는 것은 건강에 도움이 된다.
④ 규칙적인 운동은 소화 불량 개선에 필수적이다.
⑤ 숙면은 정신 건강을 유지하는 데 중요한 요인이다.

K 유형Key

- 대화를 듣고, 화자의 의견이나 대화의 주제를 파악하는 유형이다.
- 의견 파악 유형인 경우 두 화자 중 누구의 의견을 묻는 것인지 확인하고 그 화자의 의견을 집중하여 듣는다.
- 대화에서 반복하여 언급되는 중심 소재를 파악하고 대화의 전체적인 흐름과 내용을 종합하여 의견과 주제를 추론한다.

C Clue 받아쓰기   다시 한번 내용을 듣고, 빈칸에 정답의 단서를 쓰시오.

W Hi, Sam. How are you?

M Fine. How about you, Christine?

W I feel really good.

M Wow! What happened to you? You usually say you're tired.

W Well, I ❶ <u>changed how I sleep</u>. I started sleeping on my left side, and it ❷ _____ _____ _____ _____.

M Really?

W Yeah. I've done it for a week, and ❸ _____ _____ _____ _____ _____.

M I didn't know how we sleep has something to do with digestion.

W It does. ❹ <u>Sleeping on your left side</u> helps the digestive process because your stomach is on the left.

M I can see that. But does improving digestion make you that much healthier?

W Sleeping on the left side does more than that. I think it's good for health because it also ❺ _____ _____ _____ _____ _____ _____.

M That makes sense. I guess I should try it.

정답 CHECK

❶ 소재
❷ has improved my health ▶ 단서 1
❸ my digestion has got better ▶ 단서 2
❹ 소재
❺ helps blood circulation to the heart ▶ 단서 3

01 대화를 듣고, 두 사람이 하는 말의 주제로 가장 적절한 것을 고르시오.
① 감자의 전파 과정
② 감자의 다양한 효능
③ 감자를 보관하는 방법
④ 감자를 이용한 요리법
⑤ 감자 재배 시 유의사항

02 대화를 듣고, 남자의 의견으로 가장 적절한 것을 고르시오.
① 휴가가 심신을 달래는 데 도움이 된다.
② 자신의 안전은 스스로가 책임져야 한다.
③ 자책하는 행위는 정신 건강에 좋지 않다.
④ 벌어진 일은 긍정적으로 보는 것이 좋다.
⑤ 집을 비울 때에는 문단속을 철저히 해야 한다.

03 대화를 듣고, 여자의 의견으로 가장 적절한 것을 고르시오.
① 각자 맡은 역할을 수행해야 한다.
② 아이들에게 독립심을 키워줘야 한다.
③ 어려운 점이 있으면 서로 도와야 한다.
④ 교대 시간을 탄력적으로 운영해야 한다.
⑤ 발생 가능한 문제점에 미리 대비해야 한다.

04 대화를 듣고, 두 사람이 하는 말의 주제로 가장 적절한 것을 고르시오.
① 맛있는 사과를 고르는 요령
② 건강을 유지하는 것의 중요성
③ 체중 조절에 효과가 있는 과일
④ 비타민 C와 비타민 K의 차이점
⑤ 사과 섭취가 건강에 미치는 이점

05 대화를 듣고, 남자의 의견으로 가장 적절한 것을 고르시오.
① 교내식당의 운영 시간이 연장되어야 한다.
② 교내식당의 음식 가격이 인하되어야 한다.
③ 학생을 위한 시간제 일자리가 늘어나야 한다.
④ 열심히 공부하면 누구나 수학을 잘할 수 있다.
⑤ 학생을 대상으로 하는 교내식당이 지어져야 한다.

06 대화를 듣고, 여자의 의견으로 가장 적절한 것을 고르시오.
① 지나치게 의무에 얽매이지 말아야 한다.
② 일을 서두르면 원하는 성과를 낼 수 없다.
③ 사람은 좋아하는 일을 해야 행복할 수 있다.
④ 돈은 인생을 좀 더 편안하게 살게 할 뿐이다.
⑤ 사업은 철저한 준비가 있어야 성공할 수 있다.

녹음 내용을 다시 들으면서 빈칸을 채워 넣으세요.

01

M Honey, where did you get all these potatoes?

W My friend Jennifer runs a potato farm, so she gave me some.

M This is a lot! Let's put them in the refrigerator.

W Oh, no. _____ _____ in a refrigerator gives them an unpleasant taste.

M Okay. Where should we keep them?

W They should _____ _____ _____ _____ _____ _____ _____ _____ _____.

M Then the basement would be good.

W That's perfect, but we also need to take the potatoes out of the plastic bag. Potatoes _____ _____ _____ _____ _____.

M I see. And I remember reading an article saying that storing potatoes with an apple _____ _____ _____ _____.

W Really? That's good to know.

M I'll bring an apple, and we can keep them together.

02

M Hi, Sally. I'm glad you're back!

W Hi, Thomas.

M How was your trip to Italy?

W It wasn't bad. But my house was.

M What do you mean?

W While I was on vacation, _____ _____ _____ _____ _____. They took almost everything.

M That's terrible! I'm sorry to hear that.

W I wish I hadn't taken the trip to Italy! It's all my fault.

M Well, it might have been a good thing that you weren't home when they broke in.

W What do you mean?

M You might have been hurt. Whatever you lost, it isn't _____ _____ _____ _____ _____.

W That's true. Maybe you're right.

M What is done cannot be undone. It's important to see that _____ _____ _____ _____.

03

W Isn't Jack here?

M Nope, not yet.

W Has he called or sent a text message?

M No, he hasn't.

W This is the second time this week. I think you need to do something to make sure that he's _____ _____ _____ _____.

M I'll talk to him about that.

W I have to pick up my children after school every afternoon. If he doesn't get here soon, I'll be late.

M Why don't you go? I can do the work by myself.

W No. You have your own job to do, and I can't let you _____ _____ _____. That's Jack's job.

M You're right. But if there is a problem, everyone helps out.

W Yeah, but if this becomes a regular occurrence, everyone will get tired and new problems will arise. We all need to do _____ _____ _____.

04

M Angela, I think you always look healthy.

W Do I? I'm happy to hear that.

M Do you have any special secret?

W Well, I _____ _____ _____ _____ almost every day, and I think that helps a lot.

M Eating apples every day?

W Yes. Apples are _____ _____ _____ _____ _____ and vitamins C and K. So eating them is very good for your health.

M I see. Ah, I think I've heard that eating apples is also _____ _____ _____ _____.

W Absolutely! They can also help _____ _____ _____ _____ if you eat them regularly.

M Wow, that's great! I've made up my mind to start eating apples from today.

05

W Math class is finally over.

M Yes. Why don't we go for lunch? It's already 1 o'clock.

W Sure. Let's go to the school restaurant.

M The school restaurant? How about going to _____ _____ _____ _____ _____?

W Why? The school restaurant's food is more delicious and cheaper than that of other restaurants.

M But as you know, _____ _____ _____ _____ at 1:30. 30 minutes is a bit short to enjoy lunch.

W Yeah, you're right.

M I think the school restaurant should _____ _____ _____ since there are lots of classes that end at 1 p.m.

W I agree. Otherwise, we can't have lunch there just like today. Why don't we ask the student council about it?

M That's a good idea.

06

W Honey, when are you going to open your restaurant?

M Well, I'm not sure yet. I don't even know if I should.

W What makes you _____ _____ _____?

M What if it's not successful? Then I'll lose all that money!

W Don't worry about that. It doesn't matter whether you make money or not. What's important is that _____ _____ _____ _____.

M But I have to make enough money to support my family.

W You'll be fine. You've been planning this for years.

M That's true. I've taken a lot of classes. This is something I've always wanted to do.

W Give it a try. We're behind you. Besides, nothing in life makes us happier than doing _____ _____ _____ _____.

M I guess you're right.

필수표현 NOTE

01 Where should we keep them? 우리가 감자를 어디에 보관해야 하죠?
That's good to know. 알아두면 좋네요.

04 Do you have any special secret? 무슨 특별한 비결이 있니?
I think that helps a lot. 그게 도움이 많이 되는 것 같아.
I've made up my mind to start eating apples from today. 나도 오늘부터 사과를 먹는 것을 시작하기로 결심했어.

05 Why don't we go for lunch? 점심 먹으러 갈래?
That's a good idea. 좋은 생각이야.

06 What if it's not successful? 실패하면 어떻게 해요?

Q 수능 Q

대화를 듣고, 두 사람의 관계를 가장 잘 나타낸 것을 고르시오. 2020 수능

① 곤충학자 – 학생
② 동물 조련사 – 사진작가
③ 농부 – 잡지기자
④ 요리사 – 음식 평론가
⑤ 독자 – 소설가

K 유형 Key

- 대화를 듣고, 두 사람의 관계를 파악하는 유형이다.
- 대화자의 직업이나 대화가 이루어지는 장소 및 상황에서 관계를 추론할 수 있는 단서를 파악한다.
- 대화에 등장한 직업이나 장소의 일부 표현만을 근거로 오답을 고르지 않도록 주의한다.

C Clue 받아쓰기 다시 한번 내용을 듣고, 빈칸에 정답의 단서를 쓰시오.

M Hello, I'm Ted Benson. You must be Ms. Brown.

W Hi, Mr. Benson. Thank you for ❶ <u>sparing time for this interview</u>. I've wanted to meet you since you won the "Best Rice Award."

M I'm honored. I'm ❷ _____ _____ _____ _____ _____ _____. The articles are very informative.

W Thank you. Can you tell me the secret to your success?

M I grow rice without using any chemicals to ❸ _____ _____ _____. It's organic.

W How do you do that?

M I put ducks into my fields, and they eat the insects.

W So that's how ❹ _____ _____ _____ _____ in the country. What a great idea!

M Yeah, that's the know-how I've got from my 30 years of farming life.

W Well, it's amazing. May I ❺ <u>take a picture of you</u> in front of your rice fields for my magazine article?

M Go ahead.

정답 CHECK ✓

❶ ▶ 단서 1
❷ a regular reader of your magazine ▶ 단서 2
❸ kill harmful insects ▶ 함정 1
❹ you grew the best rice ▶ 단서 3
❺ ▶ 함정 2

기출 Challenge | 20 고2 03 학평

01 대화를 듣고, 두 사람의 관계를 가장 잘 나타낸 것을 고르시오.
① 뉴스 제보자 – 기자
② 해외 특파원 – 방송 제작자
③ 동아리 담당 교사 – 방송 작가
④ 방송 광고 의뢰인 – 촬영 감독
⑤ 방송국 견학 학생 – 뉴스 진행자

02 대화를 듣고, 두 사람의 관계를 가장 잘 나타낸 것을 고르시오.
① 약사 – 환자
② 영화배우 – 팬
③ 직장 상사 – 직원
④ 식당 종업원 – 손님
⑤ 유람선 승무원 – 승객

03 대화를 듣고, 두 사람의 관계를 가장 잘 나타낸 것을 고르시오.
① 투숙객 – 호텔 직원
② 수강생 – 서핑 강사
③ 손님 – 열쇠 수리공
④ 요리사 – 식당 주인
⑤ 시민 – 분실물 센터 직원

04 대화를 듣고, 두 사람의 관계를 가장 잘 나타낸 것을 고르시오.
① 의사 – 환자
② 경찰관 – 행인
③ 코치 – 운동선수
④ 자전거 판매원 – 손님
⑤ 보험사 직원 – 보험 가입자

05 대화를 듣고, 두 사람의 관계를 가장 잘 나타낸 것을 고르시오.
① 버스 승객 – 버스 운전사
② 기차 승객 – 기차 승무원
③ 영화 관람객 – 매표소 직원
④ 경기 관람객 – 경기장 운영 요원
⑤ 놀이공원 방문객 – 놀이공원 직원

06 대화를 듣고, 두 사람의 관계를 가장 잘 나타낸 것을 고르시오.
① 교사 – 학생
② 의사 – 환자
③ 영양사 – 식당 직원
④ 수영 강사 – 수강생
⑤ 헬스 트레이너 – 고객

녹음 내용을 다시 들으면서 빈칸을 채워 넣으세요.

01

W Excuse me, Mr. Young. I'm Emma Baker.

M Oh, hi Emma. I've been waiting for you. Nice to meet you.

W Nice to meet you too.

M Is this your first visit to a broadcasting station?

W Yes, it is. I've been looking forward to _____ _____ _____ _____ _____.

M I see. You seem to be very interested in broadcasting.

W Yes, I'm the leader of my school's broadcasting club.

M Oh, you are? Today, you'll sit at a news desk and experience what it's like _____ _____ _____ _____ _____.

W Fantastic! I watch your news program every day. How can you deliver the news so effortlessly?

M I _____ _____ _____ _____ before I begin the broadcast.

W That's impressive. I really want to host a news program like you someday.

M I hope you will. Shall we go to the news studio now?

02

M You don't look so good. Is there anything wrong?

W I _____ _____ _____. Is there any place I can get some medicine?

M Yes. Do you know where the theater is?

W It's upstairs, isn't it?

M Right. There's a health center next to the theater, and you can get medicine there.

W I got it. When _____ _____ _____ _____ _____ at Mykonos Island Port?

M 7 : 20. We still have one hour to go.

W Well, I'd like to have dinner before _____ _____ _____ _____. Is the restaurant still open?

M Yes. You can use the restaurant as long as you're on the ship.

W Great. You're very kind.

M My pleasure. It's my job to _____ _____ _____.

03

W Excuse me. I _____ _____ _____ _____ at the restaurant.

M I'm sorry to hear that. I'll have it reissued.

W Is there _____ _____ _____ _____ _____?

M Yes, you need to pay $5 for it. Can you tell me your name and room number, please?

W Janice Hollins, and I'm staying in room 903.

M Thank you. *[Pause]* Here's your new key card.

W Thank you.

M Don't mention it. Is there anything else I can help you with?

W I _____ _____ _____ next to the lobby. Can I borrow one of them?

M Sure! They're for our guests.

W Great. When I go to the beach tomorrow, I'll borrow one.

M Okay. Please _____ _____ _____ with us.

04

M I see you're walking on the treadmill, Maria. How do you feel today?

W I feel much better, sir.

M That's good to hear, but it looks like _____ _____ a little bit.

W I think I'm okay.

M Listen, Maria. The doctor says you have to stay on the bench for at least one week.

W Oh, no. You know how important today's game is.

M I know, but you _____ _____ _____ the accident yet.

W It was only a small accident, sir. My bike just _____ _____ _____ the wall.

M Well, your left leg is still black and blue.

W It's just a bruise. It won't affect my performance in the game.

M Sorry. I can't let you play. Emily will _____ _____ _____ this time.

05

M Excuse me. Can I ask you a question?

W Oh, sure, sir.

M My son and I've been waiting for almost an hour, but there's still a long line of people ahead of us. _____ _____ _____ do we have to wait?

W Well, it will be another thirty minutes from here.

M Oh, no. It's not easy to ride the roller coasters here.

W Sorry for the inconvenience, but we get a lot of visitors on weekends.

M I see.

W By the way, is this your son?

M Yeah.

W There is _____ _____ _____ on this ride, and I'm afraid he is not tall enough.

M Oh, my... I didn't know that. Can I _____ _____ _____ on these tickets?

W Sure. Go to the ticket office over there, please.

06

W How do you feel nowadays, Mr. Miller?

M I don't feel any better. How are the test results?

W You have to _____ _____ _____ _____ your body. You're not as strong as you used to be.

M What should I do then?

W You need _____ _____ _____ and regular exercise.

M What do you mean by a balanced diet?

W You are lacking vitamin C. You have to eat more fresh fruits and vegetables.

M I see. And _____ _____ _____ _____ is good for me?

W I recommend swimming. You have to exercise at least three times a week.

M There are many things I need to do to stay healthy.

W And it's important to take the medicine _____ _____ _____ you.

M All right.

필수표현 NOTE

01 I've been waiting for you. 당신을 기다리고 있었어요.
Shall we go to the news studio now? 이제 뉴스 스튜디오로 갈까요?

02 Do you know where the theater is? 극장이 어디에 있는지 알고 있나요?
Is the restaurant still open? 식당이 아직 문을 열었나요?

03 Is there anything else I can help you with? 제가 도와드릴 수 있는 다른 일이 있나요?
Can I borrow one of them? 그것들 중 한 개를 빌릴 수 있나요?

04 You know how important today's game is. 오늘 경기가 얼마나 중요한지 아시잖아요.

04강 그림의 내용 일치 여부

Q 수능 Q

대화를 듣고, 그림에서 대화의 내용과 일치하지 <u>않는</u> 것을 고르시오. **2020 수능**

K 유형 Key

- 대화를 듣기 전에 선택지로 제시된 부분의 특징, 모양, 위치, 동작 등을 빠르게 살펴본다.
- 대화에서 선택지에 관한 내용이 순서대로 제시되므로 선택지의 모양, 위치 등에 유의하여 일치하지 않는 것을 고른다.

C Clue 받아쓰기   다시 한번 내용을 듣고, 빈칸에 정답의 단서를 쓰시오.

W What are you looking at, honey?

M Aunt Mary sent me a picture. She's already ❶ <u>set up a room for Peter.</u>

W Wow! She's excited for him to stay during the winter vacation, isn't she?

M Yes, she is. I like ❷ _____ _____ _____ _____ _____ _____ on the bed.

W I'm sure it must be very warm. Look at ❸ _____ _____ _____ _____ _____.

M It looks comfortable. He could sit there and read.

W Right. I guess that's why Aunt Mary ❹ _____ _____ _____ _____ _____.

M That makes sense. Oh, there's ❺ _____ _____ _____ _____ _____ _____.

W It looks real. I think it's a gift for Peter.

M Yeah, I remember she mentioned it. And do you see ❻ <u>the round mirror on the wall?</u>

W It's nice. It looks like the one Peter has here at home.

M It does. Let's show him this picture.

정답 CHECK

❶ ▶ 소재

❷ the blanket with the checkered pattern ▶ 단서 1

❸ the chair below the window ▶ 단서 2

❹ put the bookcase next to it ▶ 단서 3

❺ a toy horse in the corner ▶ 단서 4

❻ ▶ 단서 5

기출 Challenge | 20 고1 03 학평

01 대화를 듣고, 그림에서 대화의 내용과 일치하지 않는 것을 고르시오.

02 대화를 듣고, 그림에서 대화의 내용과 일치하지 않는 것을 고르시오.

03 대화를 듣고, 그림에서 대화의 내용과 일치하지 않는 것을 고르시오.

04 대화를 듣고, 그림에서 대화의 내용과 일치하지 않는 것을 고르시오.

05 대화를 듣고, 그림에서 대화의 내용과 일치하지 않는 것을 고르시오.

06 대화를 듣고, 그림에서 대화의 내용과 일치하지 않는 것을 고르시오.

녹음 내용을 다시 들으면서 빈칸을 채워 넣으세요.

01

W James, have you been to our new club room?

M Unfortunately, I haven't.

W I have a picture of it. Do you want to take a look?

M Sure. *[Pause]* Wow, I see _____ _____ _____ _____ _____ of the picture.

W Yes. We finally have our own lockers. Do you see the trophies on the lockers?

M Yeah. There are two trophies. Are they the ones we won in the National School Band Contest?

W Right. We won two years _____ _____ _____. I'm so proud of our band.

M Me, too. And the drums are under the clock.

W Yes. And on the right side of the picture is a _____ _____ _____ _____.

M Looks great. I also love the _____ _____ in front of the drums.

W I like it, too. We're really going to enjoy our new club room.

02

W Dan, how is your school play going?

M Mom, look at this picture. These are the _____ _____ _____ _____ _____.

W Okay. There is a big tree to the left.

M Do you see the boy's face in the tree? He took the role of a talking tree.

W I see. What does the bird sitting in the tree mean?

M The bird is a messenger between the prince and the princess.

W Oh, the princess on the left is holding a bunch of flowers.

M She's about to give it to _____ _____ _____ _____ before her.

W She must be blessing him.

M Right. He'll fight against the dragon on the right.

W The dragon is _____ _____ _____ _____ _____. I think the play will be exciting to see.

M Yes, it will be.

03

M How are your table tennis lessons going, Sandy?

W I'm doing my best. Here's a picture my friend took for me.

M Oh, the _____ _____ _____ _____ is very impressive. It says 'We Can Make It!'

W That's what the coach always says. There is a group photo of us under the banner. They are students who take lessons.

M All of them are smiling. Your coach is wearing a cap.

W Yeah. He loves wearing it. Do you see the _____ _____ _____ _____ on the table?

M Wow, do you hit all the balls at the lesson?

W Of course. I practice with two baskets of balls.

M Wow, that's great. You had _____ _____ _____ _____. Do you tie it for the lesson?

W Yes. I don't want my hair to cover my eyes.

M I see. Let's play table tennis together soon.

W That's a good idea, Dad.

04

M Julie, I took a very impressive picture yesterday.

W Did you? Let me take a look at it.

M Okay. Here it is.

W Is the young girl walking a dog your daughter?

M Yes. Her name's Sally, she's ten years old.

W She looks tall _____ _____ _____. The stream she is walking along is beautiful.

M It really is. That's why I like to take walks there.

W The arch-shaped bridge makes _____ _____ _____.

M I agree. I often watch fish swimming in the stream just like that young couple is doing.

W Wait a minute! What's the small thing over the stream?

M That's a fish. _____ _____ _____ _____ _____ _____ from time to time, and luckily, I captured one jumping.

W Wow, that's amazing! I thought it was a flying bird.

05

M What are you looking at, Laura?

W My son's drawing. I think he _____ _____ _____ _____ art.

M Let me see. It looks like he drew it from the veranda. He included a lot in his picture, _____ _____ _____ _____.

W Yes. He likes drawing details.

M All the cars are parked in the same direction.

W That's to protect plants and flowers from air pollution.

M I see. There are also some big trees.

W They provide shade in the summer. Do you see the open space between the two apartments? That's where _____ _____ _____ blows in.

M In the open space, a man and a woman _____ _____ _____ on a wooden bench.

W Yes. Sometimes I sit there and read books in my free time.

06

W Mr. Lee! Is that you?

M Yes. I took this picture over the weekend.

W You look like a good horse rider.

M I just posed for photographs.

W This picture _____ _____ _____ my childhood. I used to ride a horse. By the way, who is the man wearing sunglasses next to the horse?

M He is my cousin. He runs a business for tourists who want to experience the thrill of riding a horse.

W I see. Who is the _____ _____ _____ _____ _____ and a vest?

M She is my daughter Jane.

W She looks comfortable on a horse. _____ _____ _____ _____ _____ looks wonderful.

M It is. Do you see the girl _____ _____ _____? She is my niece. She made me a video of my daughter riding a horse on the hill.

W Really? I'd like to see the video, too.

필수표현 NOTE 📝

01 Have you been to our new club room? 우리 새 동아리실에 가 본 적 있니?

02 What does the bird sitting in the tree mean? 나무에 앉아 있는 새는 무엇을 의미하는 거니?
She must be blessing him. 그녀는 그에게 축복을 빌고 있음이 틀림없어.

03 I'm doing my best. 최선을 다하고 있어요.
That's what the coach always says. 그것은 코치님이 항상 하는 말이에요.

04 That's why I like to take walks there. 그것이 제가 거기서 산책하는 것을 좋아하는 이유예요.

05강 할 일/부탁한 일 고르기

대화를 듣고, 여자가 할 일로 가장 적절한 것을 고르시오. 2020 수능

① 간식 가져오기
② 책 기부하기
③ 점심 준비하기
④ 설거지하기
⑤ 세탁실 청소하기

K 유형 Key

- 대화를 듣고, 여자 또는 남자가 할 일이나 상대방에게 부탁한 일을 파악하는 유형이다.
- 과거에 한 일이나 상대방이 할 일 혹은 상대방이 부탁한 일 등으로 오답을 유도하는 경우가 있으므로 유의해야 한다.
- 주로 대화 후반부에 여자 또는 남자가 할 일이나 부탁한 일에 대한 결정적 단서가 등장한다.

C Clue 받아쓰기   다시 한번 내용을 듣고, 빈칸에 정답의 단서를 쓰시오.

M   Good morning, Jane.

W   Good morning, Mr. Smith.

M   Thanks for ❶ _____ _____ _____ _____ _____ _____ _____ _____ again.

W   I'm happy to help. And I ❷ brought some snacks for the elderly.

M   How considerate of you! Last time ❸ _____ _____ _____ _____. Everyone really enjoyed reading them.

W   It was my pleasure. So, what am I supposed to do today? Should I ❹ prepare lunch like I did before?

M   There are some other volunteers today, and they'll do that work.

W   Good. Then what would you like me to do?

M   Well, you could do the dishes or clean the laundry room.

W   I'm ❺ _____ _____ _____ _____. So I'll do that.

M   Great. We'll ❻ have someone else clean the laundry room.

정답 CHECK

❶ volunteering to work at our senior citizen's center   소재
❷   함정 1
❸ you donated some books   함정 2
❹   함정 3
❺ good at washing dishes   단서
❻   함정 4

01 대화를 듣고, 남자가 여자에게 부탁한 일로 가장 적절한 것을 고르시오.
① 퇴임식장 예약하기
② 사진 파일 보내주기
③ 점심 식사 주문하기
④ 행사 사진 촬영하기
⑤ 신문 기사 작성하기

02 대화를 듣고, 여자가 남자에게 부탁한 일로 가장 적절한 것을 고르시오.
① 음식 재료 씻기
② 화장실 청소하기
③ 샐러드 재료 사 오기
④ 찬장에서 접시 꺼내기
⑤ 진공청소기로 거실 청소하기

03 대화를 듣고, 남자가 여자에게 부탁한 일로 가장 적절한 것을 고르시오.
① 집안일 줄이기
② 용돈 올려 주기
③ 자유 시간 더 주기
④ 고등학생처럼 대하기
⑤ 아빠와 더 많은 시간 보내기

04 대화를 듣고, 남자가 할 일로 가장 적절한 것을 고르시오.
① 회의 참석하기
② 저녁 식사 준비하기
③ 공연 당일 일정 알리기
④ 동아리 공연장 예약하기
⑤ 수리점에서 기타 찾아오기

05 대화를 듣고, 여자가 할 일로 가장 적절한 것을 고르시오.
① 양복 구입하러 가기
② 졸업식 일정 확인하기
③ 여행사에 여행 상품 문의하기
④ 아들에게 원하는 선물 물어보기
⑤ 인터넷에서 여행 정보 확인하기

06 대화를 듣고, 남자가 여자를 위해 할 일로 가장 적절한 것을 고르시오.
① 한국어 번역해 주기
② 단어 뜻 조사해 주기
③ 한국어 선생님 소개해 주기
④ 한국어 수업 함께 들어주기
⑤ 선생님 연구실에 함께 가 주기

녹음 내용을 다시 들으면서 빈칸을 채워 넣으세요.

01

W Alex, let's go for lunch.

M Sorry, but I don't have time, Kate.

W What's keeping you so busy?

M I'm working on our _____ _____ _____.

W When's the deadline?

M Today. I'm doing the final job of _____ _____ _____ with the photos, but there's a problem.

W What is it?

M I don't have any photos of Mr. Williams' _____ _____.

W Really? I've got some photos I took at the ceremony with my digital camera.

M Oh, _____ _____ _____! Can you send me the photo files?

W Sure. I'll email them right after lunch.

M Thank you so much, Kate.

02

M Honey, when are your friends visiting us today?

W They're supposed to be here by five.

M Okay. We need to begin _____ _____ _____ now then.

W Yes. I already cleaned the bathroom this morning.

M Then I'll _____ _____ _____ _____ and organize the living room table.

W While you're at it, I'll _____ _____ _____ for the salad.

M I'm looking forward to your Italian salad. It's so delicious.

W I got vegetables from the grocery early this morning, so everything is fresh.

M Good. Is there anything else I can do?

W Oh, would you _____ _____ _____ _____ from the cupboard?

M No problem. I'll do that right away.

W Thank you.

03

M Mom, do you have a minute?

W Of course I do. What do you want to talk about?

M I think I _____ _____ _____ _____.

W You don't think we give you enough?

M Well, the amount was okay last year, but I'm in high school now. I'm involved in a lot of activities, which _____ _____ _____ _____.

W Is that all?

M I also think I deserve a bigger allowance, since I _____ _____ _____ _____ _____ these days.

W Do you? Like what?

M I shine Dad's shoes once a week, help Steve with his homework, and sometimes I help you with the dishes.

W Sounds like your request is quite reasonable. Let me discuss it with your father when he comes home.

04

W Chris, when did you say your guitar club will perform?

M We will perform for two days, on October 22nd and 23rd. I hope you come and see us, Mom.

W Don't worry. I'll go on the first day because I _____ _____ _____ _____ on October 23rd.

M Thank you, Mom.

W You reserved the community center for the performance, right?

M Yes. And I also _____ _____ _____ _____ _____ on the performance day.

W Great. Did you _____ _____ _____ _____ from the repair shop?

M I will go and get it now. I want my guitar back as soon as possible.

W While you do that, I'll make some stew for dinner.

M Thank you, Mom. I'm hungry.

W Be careful and see you in a bit.

05

M It's finally June.

W Time flies, doesn't it?

M Yes. It seems like only yesterday we congratulated Robin on graduating from high school.

W That's true. By the way, what should we buy him _____ _____ _____ _____?

M What about a suit?

W You know Robin doesn't like to wear a suit.

M Then why don't we ask him what he wants?

W Presents should be a surprise.

M Well, considering he studied to become an artist, what about _____ _____ _____ to Italy?

W That's a great idea. He always said that he wanted to visit Italy someday.

M Then a trip to Italy would be a meaningful experience for him.

W All right. I'll call a travel agency and _____ _____ _____ _____ for a future artist like Robin.

M Good idea. Go ahead and do that. _____ _____ _____ _____ on the Internet.

06

M Hi, Kelly. What are you up to?

W Hi, Josh. I can't understand this sentence.

M Let me see. Oh, it's written in Korean, isn't it?

W Yes. I think I know the meaning of every word, but it doesn't help me understand _____ _____ _____ _____ _____.

M Why don't you ask Mr. Kim, the Korean teacher?

W There are so many students in his class. It's not easy to ask questions during the lessons.

M Then you can go to his office after school.

W Well, I've never talked to him face-to-face, so I _____ _____ _____ _____ if I see him in his office.

M If that's the problem, _____ _____ _____ _____. What do you say?

W Thanks. Then let's go to see him after school today.

M Okay. No problem.

필수표현 NOTE

01 What's keeping you so busy? 무엇이 당신을 그렇게 바쁘게 하나요?
Can you send me the photo files? 사진 파일 좀 보내줄래요?

02 I'm looking forward to your Italian salad. 난 당신이 만든 이탈리안 샐러드가 기대돼요.

04 I want my guitar back as soon as possible. 제 기타를 가능한 한 빨리 돌려받고 싶어요.

06강 지불할 금액 파악

Q 수능 Q

대화를 듣고, 여자가 지불할 금액을 고르시오. `2020 수능`

① $72   ② $74   ③ $76   ④ $78   ⑤ $80

K 유형 Key

- 물건이나 입장권 등을 구매하는 상황에서 총액을 구하거나 할인 및 쿠폰을 사용하여 지불할 금액을 파악하는 유형이다.
- 대화의 후반부까지 여러 할인, 쿠폰, 추가 요금 등과 같은 조건이 제시되므로 끝까지 들은 후 계산해야 한다.

C Clue 받아쓰기   다시 한번 내용을 듣고, 빈칸에 정답의 단서를 쓰시오.

M Welcome to the Science and Technology Museum. How can I help you?

W Hi. I want to buy admission tickets.

M Okay. They're $20 for adults and $10 for children.

W Good. ❶ _____ _____ _____ _____ _____ _____ _____, please. And I'm a member of the National Robot Club. Do I get a discount?

M Yes. You get ❷ <u>10 percent off all of those admission tickets</u> with your membership.

W Excellent.

M We also have the AI Robot program. You can play games with the robots and take pictures with them.

W That sounds interesting. How much is it?

M It's just $5 per person. But the membership discount ❸ _____ _____ _____ _____ _____ _____.

W Okay. I'll ❹ _____ _____ _____.

M So ❺ <u>two adult and two child admission tickets, and four AI Robot program tickets</u>, right?

W Yes. Here are my credit card and membership card.

 정답 CHECK

❶ Two adult tickets and two child tickets ▶ 단서 1
❷ ▶ 단서 2
❸ does not apply to this program ▶ 단서 3
❹ take four tickets ▶ 단서 4
❺ ▶ 단서 5

기출 Challenge | 19 고1 11 학평

01 대화를 듣고, 남자가 지불할 금액을 고르시오.
① $40
② $45
③ $50
④ $54
⑤ $60

02 대화를 듣고, 여자가 지불할 금액을 고르시오.
① $110
② $117
③ $126
④ $130
⑤ $140

03 대화를 듣고, 남자가 지불할 금액을 고르시오.
① $26
② $28
③ $31
④ $34
⑤ $39

04 대화를 듣고, 여자가 지불할 금액을 고르시오.
① $325
② $395
③ $440
④ $550
⑤ $600

05 대화를 듣고, 남자가 지불할 금액을 고르시오.
① $42
② $43
③ $47
④ $50
⑤ $52

06 대화를 듣고, 여자가 지불할 금액을 고르시오.
① $250
② $270
③ $290
④ $320
⑤ $360

● DICTATION

녹음 내용을 다시 들으면서 빈칸을 채워 넣으세요.

01

W Welcome to Good Aroma Candle. How may I help you?

M Hi. I'm _____ _____ _____ _____ for my parents. They like flower scents.

W Come over here and try this flower scent.

M Thanks. *[Pause]* I like this rose scented candle. How much is it?

W Large candles and medium ones are on sale now. Large ones are $20 and medium ones are $10 each.

M Well then, I'll take two large candles.

W If you buy any three candles, we give you a soap for free.

M Great. Then I'll _____ _____ _____ _____ with the same scent as well. Did you say they're $10?

W Exactly. You're getting two large candles and one medium candle.

M That's right. Can I also use this mobile coupon?

W Of course, you _____ _____ _____ _____ the total price with that.

M Thank you. I'll pay by credit card.

02

M What are you doing on the Internet, honey?

W I'm going to buy an air fryer. What about this one? I think it's the best in terms of price and function.

M How much is it?

W It's $90. I'll put it in my shopping cart.

M Okay. Do you need to _____ _____ _____?

W Yes. I'll buy some pork to cook in the air fryer. A friend said air fryers do a great job cooking pork.

M Really? Let's try it.

W Oh, here are the pork ribs. I will buy 2 kg of ribs.

M They're $40. Not bad. Does this online shopping mall _____ _____ _____?

W Yes. We can get a 10 percent discount for _____ _____.

M That's good. We get the 10 percent discount on the air fryer and the pork ribs, right?

W Yes, it's on the total. I'll _____ _____ _____ with my credit card.

03

W Can I help you?

M Yes, please. I'm looking for some tea mugs.

W Okay. Would you look at these mugs? I recommend this _____ _____ _____ _____.

M Oh, I like these white mugs.

W It's one of the most popular sets these days. The set of 6 pieces costs $25.

M I'll take one set. And I want to _____ _____ _____ _____.

W What about this one in the shape of a tree? It's $6.

M That looks practical. I'll take it. Can I use this _____ _____ _____ here?

W Yes, Oh, you can use it. I'll take that off the total.

M Great. I'll use it. Here's my credit card.

W Thank you. Would you wait a second while I _____ _____ _____ for you?

M Sure.

04

M What are you browsing the Internet for?

W I'm looking at watches.

M Are you planning to buy watches for Jenny and Jack on Children's Day?

W Yes. Do you see any watches you like on this site?

M The pink watch with the small dial would _____ _____ _____ Jenny. How much is it?

W It costs $400, but it's on sale right now. So we can get it _____ _____ _____.

M Great. Let's order it. What if we buy this silver metal watch for Jack?

W I like the design. It costs $350.

M Look at this banner. It says we can get a coupon code for _____ _____ _____ _____ _____ _____ in celebration of Children's Day.

W Wonderful. I'll order both watches and I'll use the coupon code.

M Okay. They'll be happy with the watches.

05

W Good morning, sir. How may I help you?

M Hello. I'm here to _____ _____ _____ to make fruit and vegetable juice.

W Then I'd like to recommend some carrots and apples. They match well with each other.

M Okay. How much are they?

W You can get unwashed carrots for $2 and washed ones for $3. For apples, I'll give you a basket of them for $10.

M I'd like _____ _____ _____ and 3 baskets of apples.

W Alright. Is there anything else you need?

M Do you sell bananas, too? They are also healthy snacks.

W Sure. It's $5 for a bunch of bananas.

M Alright. I'll just _____ _____ _____ _____ bananas. Here is the money.

06

M Hello, ma'am. How may I help you?

W I'm here to _____ _____ _____ yoga classes. How much do they cost?

M They are $100 a month.

W What if I take yoga classes for three months? I heard there is a special discount for _____ _____ _____.

M That's right. We offer a 10 percent discount.

W Cool. Then I'll sign up for three months.

M What about our towel service? Are you interested in using that?

W How much do I have to pay for it?

M Those who register for three months can use the service for $20. That fee _____ _____ _____ _____.

W That sounds good. I'll use that, too. Here's my credit card.

필수표현 NOTE

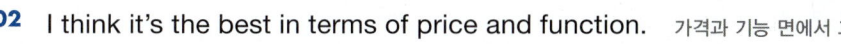
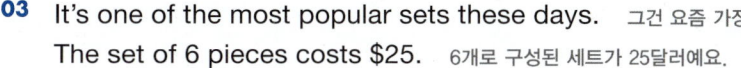

02 I think it's the best in terms of price and function. 가격과 기능 면에서 그것이 최고라고 생각해요.

03 It's one of the most popular sets these days. 그건 요즘 가장 인기 있는 세트 중 하나예요.
The set of 6 pieces costs $25. 6개로 구성된 세트가 25달러예요.

06 How much do I have to pay for it? 그것은 얼마인가요?

07강 이유 추론

Q 수능 Q

대화를 듣고, 남자가 요리 대회 참가를 포기한 이유를 고르시오. **2020 수능**

① 다친 팔이 낫지 않아서
② 조리법을 완성하지 못해서
③ 다른 대회와 일정이 겹쳐서
④ 입학시험 공부를 해야 해서
⑤ 대회 전에 유학을 떠나야 해서

K 유형 Key

- 대화의 초반부에 두 사람이 나누는 대화의 소재와 주제를 파악한다.
- 대화의 후반부에서 주로 이유에 해당하는 단서가 등장하므로 끝까지 듣고 답을 골라야 한다.
- 대화에서 부분적으로 언급된 정보를 포함한 선택지를 성급하게 고르지 않도록 유의한다.

C Clue 받아쓰기   다시 한번 내용을 듣고, 빈칸에 정답의 단서를 쓰시오.

W Hi, Michael.

M Hi, Sarah. Did you apply for the cooking contest?

W I did. I've already finished developing a recipe.

M That's great. Actually, I ❶ _____ _____ _____ in it.

W Why? Is ❷ your arm still hurt?

M No, it's fully healed.

W Is ❸ _____ _____ _____ _____ yet?

M I already created a unique recipe for the contest.

W Then, what made you give up the contest?

M You know I've planned to study abroad. ❹ The cooking school in Italy just informed me that I've been accepted. The problem is I have to ❺ _____ _____ _____ _____ _____.

W I'm sorry you'll miss the contest. But it's good for you since you've always wanted to study in Italy.

M I think so, too. I wish you luck in the contest.

W Thanks. I'll do my best.

정답 ✔ CHECK
❶ gave up participating [소재]
❷ [함정 1]
❸ your recipe not ready [함정 2]
❹ [단서 1]
❺ leave before the contest begins [단서 2]

기출 Challenge | 19 고1 03 학평

01 대화를 듣고, 남자가 발표 자료를 수정해야 하는 이유를 고르시오.
① 최신 자료가 아니어서
② 발표 일정이 바뀌어서
③ 명칭 표기에 오류가 있어서
④ 그림 자료가 선명하지 않아서
⑤ 발표할 내용의 순서가 틀려서

02 대화를 듣고, 여자가 동창회에 참석할 수 없는 이유를 고르시오.
① 가족 모임이 있어서
② 건강 검진을 받아야 해서
③ 프로젝트 마감 작업이 있어서
④ 새 직장 취업을 위한 면접이 있어서
⑤ 추수감사절 식사 준비를 해야 해서

03 대화를 듣고, Orion 벼룩시장이 열리는 장소가 변경된 이유를 고르시오.
① 주차장 시설이 없어서
② 장소 임대료가 인상되어서
③ 부스 배열 공간이 협소해서
④ 지하철이 닿지 않는 곳이어서
⑤ 주변 지역의 다리 공사가 있어서

04 대화를 듣고, 남자가 이번 주말에 등산을 갈 수 없는 이유를 고르시오.
① 등산 장비가 없어서
② 할 일이 밀려 있어서
③ 등산을 좋아하지 않아서
④ 아르바이트를 해야 해서
⑤ 조깅하다 발목을 다쳐서

05 대화를 듣고, 여자가 옷을 교환하려는 이유를 고르시오.
① 얼룩이 있어서
② 색상이 어두워서
③ 더 작은 치수를 원해서
④ 가격이 더 싼 것을 원해서
⑤ 디자인이 마음에 들지 않아서

06 대화를 듣고, 남자가 여자를 채용할 수 없는 이유를 고르시오.
① 면접에 응하지 않아서
② 회계 분야 경력이 없어서
③ 중국어 구사력이 부족해서
④ 이미 다른 지원자를 선택해서
⑤ 대학 전공이 직무와 맞지 않아서

DICTATION

녹음 내용을 다시 들으면서 빈칸을 채워 넣으세요.

01

W Tony, are you ready for your science presentation tomorrow?

M Yes, Ms. Woods, thanks to your help. I've already printed out the presentation material.

W Can I take a look at it? Hmm. I'm afraid you need to _____ _____ _____.

M Why? Are there any errors in the date or the names? I've checked them twice.

W No, they're correct.

M Did I use old data?

W No, you used the latest data. But this _____ _____ _____ _____ is not clear.

M Oh, my! I'll change it to _____ _____ _____.

W Okay. I'm sure you'll do well tomorrow.

M Thank you, Ms. Woods.

02

M Lisa. What are you doing here?

W Oh, David. I _____ _____ _____ _____ at Duo Technology today. Do you work here in this building?

M Yes. Did you _____ _____ _____ at the bank?

W Not yet, but I'll quit next month after I finish a project.

M I hope you get the job at Duo. By the way, are you coming to the high school reunion the day before Thanksgiving Day?

W I'm afraid I can't.

M Why not? Do you have plans with your family?

W No. I _____ _____ _____ _____ scheduled for that day.

M That's too bad. Everybody will miss you.

W I'm sorry, but it's really hard to _____ _____ _____.

M Okay. I hope you can make it to our next reunion.

03

W Honey, why don't we go to the Orion Flea Market this weekend?

M That's a good idea. It's on Palm Street, right?

W Oh, don't you know? It moved to a new location last month.

M Where is it held now?

W In the area beside the Ron Bridge.

M Why was the market moved? The _____ _____ _____ _____ because it had a wide area for many booths.

W As I know, the rent for the market place _____ _____ _____ _____, so the sellers had no choice but to find a new spot.

M I see. Is the transportation to the new place convenient?

W Yes, it's just about a _____ _____ from the subway station.

M Is there a parking lot?

W There is, but it's not as large as _____ _____ _____.

M Okay. We'd better take the subway then.

04

W Jack, do you have a few minutes?

M Sure, Laura. Is there anything I can do for you?

W My friends and I are planning to climb Mt. Seorak this weekend. Will you join us?

M I wish I could, but I don't think _____ _____ _____ _____.

W Is it because you don't have equipment for climbing?

M No. I like to go hiking and I have a lot of basic equipment.

W Then, _____ _____ _____ _____ climbing the mountain with us?

M I _____ _____ _____ while I was jogging a few days ago.

W Oh, I'm sorry to hear that. I hope you get well soon.

M Thanks. I wish I could join you.

05

W Hi, John. Where are you going?

M I'm going to the Garden Mall to _____ _____ _____ for a shirt I bought yesterday.

W Why? You don't like the design?

M It's very nice, but my brother told me that I could buy it for half the price online.

W No wonder you want a refund. By the way, I was thinking about going to the mall to _____ _____ _____.

M Really? Is there a problem with the skirt?

W No, but I'd rather have one that _____ _____ _____ _____.

M Then, shall we go there together?

W Why don't you go first? I'll catch up with you soon.

M All right.

06

M Ms. Anderson. Thanks for coming to the job interview today.

W You're welcome. If you have any questions about me, I'll answer them the best I can.

M Alright. According to your résumé, you _____ _____ business administration back in college.

W That's correct. I also studied economics as a minor.

M Great. What about work experience in the field of accounting?

W I've worked as an accountant at Brighton Electronics for 2 years.

M Outstanding. How fluently can you speak Chinese?

W To be honest with you, I _____ _____ _____ _____.

M Hmm. I'm looking for an accounting expert to work at our Chinese branch. Unless you _____ _____ _____, I can't hire you.

W I understand.

필수표현
NOTE

01 Can I take a look at it? 내가 그것을 봐도 될까?
Are there any errors in the date or the names? 날짜나 이름에 오류가 있나요?

02 Do you have plans with your family? 가족과 계획이 있니?

03 Is the transportation to the new place convenient? 새로운 장소로의 교통은 편리한가요?

04 Do you have a few minutes? 시간 좀 있니?

05 I'll catch up with you soon. 금방 따라갈게.

08강 언급되지 않은 것 고르기

ⓠ 수능 Q

대화를 듣고, Ten Year Class Reunion Party에 관해 언급되지 <u>않은</u> 것을 고르시오. 2020 수능

① 장소   ② 날짜   ③ 회비
④ 음식   ⑤ 기념품

ⓚ 유형 Key

- 대화에서 언급되지 않은 것을 고르는 유형으로 세부 내용을 파악하는 유형이다.
- 지시문과 선택지를 통해 대화의 소재와 내용을 미리 파악한다.
- 선택지의 순서대로 대화가 진행되므로 대화를 끝까지 듣고 언급되지 않은 선택지를 고른다.

ⓒ Clue 받아쓰기   다시 한번 내용을 듣고, 빈칸에 정답의 단서를 쓰시오.

W   Hi, Ross. How's everything going for our Ten Year Class Reunion Party?

M   I think we're done, Jennifer.

W   Then let's go over what we've prepared.

M   I already booked the ❶ _____ _____ _____ _____ _____ _____.

W   Good. It must have been very difficult to get a reservation because our party is on ❷ _____ _____.

M   Yeah, we were lucky.

W   What food will they serve?

M   Their ❸ steak, spaghetti, and pizza are famous, so that's what I ordered.

W   Sounds delicious. And the ❹ _____ _____ _____ _____ _____ _____, too.

M   You ordered mugs for souvenirs, right?

W   Yes, I did. I'll bring them that day.

M   Perfect. It's going to be a great party.

정답 CHECK

❶ Silver Corral Restaurant for the party ▶ 단서 1
❷ December 24th ▶ 단서 2
❸ ▶ 단서 3
❹ souvenirs for the party are ready ▶ 단서 4

기출 Challenge │ 20 고2 03 학평

01 대화를 듣고, Dream Bio Research Project에 관해 언급되지 **않은** 것을 고르시오.
① 연구원 수
② 예산 규모
③ 연구 목적
④ 연구 장소
⑤ 연구 기간

02 대화를 듣고, 영화 *A Night in Paradise*에 관해 언급되지 **않은** 것을 고르시오.
① 감독
② 주연 배우
③ 영화평
④ 투자금
⑤ 상영 시간

03 대화를 듣고, Youth Chamber Orchestra에 관해 언급되지 **않은** 것을 고르시오.
① 신입 단원의 수
② 총 단원의 수
③ 정기 연습 요일
④ 지휘자의 수
⑤ 정기 공연 일정

04 대화를 듣고, Dolphin Swimming Competition에 관해 언급되지 **않은** 것을 고르시오.
① 신설된 부문
② 개최 장소
③ 참가 신청 기한
④ 참가 신청 방법
⑤ 참가비

05 대화를 듣고, Norton Film Festival에 관해 언급되지 **않은** 것을 고르시오.
① 기간
② 상영관의 수
③ 폐막식
④ 주요 행사
⑤ 패키지 관람권

06 대화를 듣고, Weekly Market에 관해 언급되지 **않은** 것을 고르시오.
① 개최 요일
② 개최 장소
③ 판매 방식
④ 물품 가격
⑤ 수익금 기부

녹음 내용을 다시 들으면서 빈칸을 채워 넣으세요.

01

M Hello, Dr. Peterson. How are you doing these days?

W Hello, Dr. Collins. Good, I'm working on the Dream Bio Research Project.

M You mean the medical research project sponsored by the government?

W That's right. _____ _____ _____ _____ are involved in the project and I'm the head researcher.

M Wow, you're in charge of a really big job. How big is the budget for the project?

W We're allowed to _____ _____ _____ _____ on the project.

M That's a really huge amount. It's a project to _____ _____ _____ _____ for lung cancer, isn't it?

W That's right.

M How long will the research project last?

W It's _____ _____ _____. I hope we can develop the drug within this period.

M I wish you success, Dr. Peterson.

W Thank you, Dr. Collins.

02

M Jane, have you seen the movie, *A Night in Paradise*?

W Not yet, but I'm going to see it tomorrow. I like Ted Nolan, the director of the movie.

M Who _____ _____ _____ _____ in the movie?

W Neil Young took it. He often appears in Ted's movies.

M He's a great actor. I _____ _____ _____ about the movie, and they were all very positive about the director's work.

W Yes. He also tends to produce movies that require a large budget.

M I heard that more than _____ _____ _____ _____ _____ in this movie.

W Wow, the computer graphics must be great. I can't wait to see it.

03

M Mom, I _____ _____ to the Youth Chamber Orchestra.

W Congratulations, Mark. You've been wanting to join it.

M Yes. They added ten members through this audition.

W How many members are there in the orchestra?

M There are 35 members including the new members.

W That's a lot.

M Right. We meet and practice on Tuesdays and Thursdays _____ _____ _____ _____.

W I see. Do you know if the orchestra has any plan for performances?

M We'll perform at a nursing home in two months, and then have _____ _____ _____ _____ _____ _____.

W I'm looking forward to seeing you perform.

M I'm excited about it too.

04

W Honey, the announcement on this year's Dolphin Swimming Competition is posted on their website.

M Really? Is there anything different from last year's competition?

W Yes. There's _____ _____ _____ _____ _____ in their twenties.

M Let me see. *[Pause]* Oh, the competition place has also changed to the Olson Swimming Center this year.

W That's good for Tom. The center is _____ _____ _____ _____.

M Yeah. We'd better tell Tom the news.

W I will. When is _____ _____ _____ for the competition?

M It's October 10th.

W _____ _____ _____ of 20 dollars is the same as last year, right?

M Yes. I hope Tom does well in the competition.

W Same here.

05

M Sandra, this year's Norton Film Festival will open soon.

W Right. It's held around _____ _____ _____ _____ _____. What are the dates for this year?

M It runs from July 7th to July 13th.

W Oh, I'm available then.

M Great. Let's see some movies together. The films will be shown at 20 theaters around the City of Breen.

W Okay. I'd really like to _____ _____ _____ _____.

M Then, you need to reserve a ticket early because _____ _____ _____ _____ _____.

W I will. What are main events?

M There are _____ _____ _____ _____ _____ and talking with directors.

W That'd be great.

M Why don't we check _____ _____ _____ _____ _____ on the Internet?

W That's a good idea.

06

W Kevin, look at this advertisement.

M What's it about?

W It's about Weekly Market, a nonprofit charity organization.

M Sounds like we can go there and sell the items we don't use any more. When is it held?

W It's scheduled _____ _____ _____. This week, it will be held at the Central Plaza.

M Great! The plaza isn't far from here. How can we sell our items?

W According to the ad, we have to _____ _____ _____. It says there will be 120 stalls.

M I see.

W The great thing about this organization is that we can help others.

M What do you mean?

W We have to _____ _____ _____ _____ _____ _____ to UNICEF.

M What a good cause! Let's quickly reserve a stall before they're all taken.

필수표현 NOTE

02 I can't wait to see it. 빨리 그것을 보고 싶어.

03 Do you know if the orchestra has any plan for performances?
관현악단이 공연에 대한 어떤 계획이 있는지 알고 있니?

04 Is there anything different from last year's competition? 작년 대회와 다른 점이 있나요?

05 It runs from July 7th to July 13th. 그건 7월 7일부터 7월 13일까지 열려.

09강 담화의 내용 일치 여부

Q 수능 Q

Green Ocean 영화 시사회에 관한 다음 내용을 듣고, 일치하지 않는 것을 고르시오. **2020 수능**

① 100명을 초대할 예정이다.
② 다음 주 토요일 오후 4시에 시작할 것이다.
③ 영화 출연 배우와 사진을 찍을 수 있다.
④ 입장권을 우편으로 보낼 예정이다.
⑤ 초대받은 사람은 극장에서 포스터를 받을 것이다.

K 유형 Key

- 담화를 듣고, 선택지의 내용과 일치하거나 일치하지 않는 것을 파악하는 유형이다.
- 담화를 듣기 전 지시문과 선택지를 통해 소재와 세부 내용을 미리 파악한다.
- 담화 내용의 순서대로 선택지가 구성되어 있으므로, 내용과 선택지가 일치하는지 차례대로 확인한다.

C Clue 받아쓰기   다시 한번 내용을 듣고, 빈칸에 정답의 단서를 쓰시오.

W Hello, listeners. Welcome to Good Day Movie. We'd like to let you know about a great chance to see the preview of the movie *Green Ocean* by Feather Pictures. ❶ _____ _____ _____ _____ _____ _____ to the event. It'll begin at the Glory Theater ❷ at 4 p.m. next Saturday. After watching the movie, you can meet and ❸ _____ _____ _____ _____ _____ of the movie. If you're interested, apply for admission tickets on the *Green Ocean* homepage, and the tickets will be sent ❹ _____ _____ _____ to the first 100 people who apply. ❺ Those who are invited will be given a poster at the theater. Hurry up and don't miss this chance to watch *Green Ocean* in advance. Now we'll be back after the commercial break. So stay tuned.

정답 CHECK
❶ One hundred people will be invited ▶ 단서 1
❷ ▶ 단서 2
❸ take pictures with the actors ▶ 단서 3
❹ by text message ▶ 단서 4
❺ ▶ 단서 5

기출 Challenge | 19 고1 11 학평

01 Dream Children's Library에 관한 다음 내용을 듣고, 일치하지 않는 것을 고르시오.
① 6학년까지의 어린이를 대상으로 한다.
② 도서뿐 아니라 다양한 장난감이 있다.
③ 특별 독서 토론 프로그램을 운영한다.
④ 주말에 어린이들을 위해 영화를 상영한다.
⑤ 개관일에 만화 캐릭터 엽서를 제공한다.

02 Orion Youth Film Festival에 관한 다음 내용을 듣고, 일치하지 않는 것을 고르시오.
① 11월 첫째 주말에 개최될 것이다.
② Orion 지역 고등학교 학생들만 참여할 수 있다.
③ 작품 상영 시간은 30분 이내이어야 한다.
④ 작품은 현지의 영화학과 교수 5명이 심사한다.
⑤ 신청 마감일은 10월 20일이다.

03 Blue Technology Programs에 관한 다음 내용을 듣고, 일치하지 않는 것을 고르시오.
① 4차 산업혁명의 미래에 관한 것이다.
② 2주 동안 운영된다.
③ 대학 기숙사에서 지내게 된다.
④ 숙박료 외에는 무료이다.
⑤ 신청서를 온라인으로 제출해야 한다.

04 H&Q Motors Three-Day Celebration에 관한 다음 내용을 듣고, 일치하지 않는 것을 고르시오.
① 75주년을 기념한다.
② 무료 열기구 탑승을 시작으로 한다.
③ 유명한 카레이서의 사인회를 가진다.
④ 마지막 날에는 직원 대상 연회를 갖는다.
⑤ 3일 내내 골동품 자동차들이 전시된다.

05 17th Welton High Choir Competition에 관한 다음 내용을 듣고, 일치하지 않는 것을 고르시오.
① 성탄절 전날 개최될 것이다.
② 예선을 통과한 8개 팀이 본선에 참가한다.
③ 오후 1시부터 3시까지 강당에서 열린다.
④ 참가 순서는 제비뽑기로 결정된다.
⑤ 수상자는 대회 직후에 발표될 것이다.

06 Eco-Point Program에 관한 다음 내용을 듣고, 일치하지 않는 것을 고르시오.
① 온실 가스 배출량 감소를 목표로 한다.
② 사용한 에너지양에 따라 인센티브를 준다.
③ 6개월간 전기 사용량을 10% 이상 줄이면 15점을 준다.
④ 1점은 1달러의 가치를 지닌다.
⑤ 포인트는 현금처럼 사용할 수 있다.

녹음 내용을 다시 들으면서 빈칸을 채워 넣으세요.

01

W Hello, listeners! I'm happy to introduce you to the first children's library in our town. It's the Dream Children's Library. Our library is for children in the sixth grade and younger. We have _____ _____ _____ _____ as well as books for different ages of children. There are special reading discussion programs for your children. Also, we offer _____ _____ _____ _____ every weekend. We're excited to tell you our library is now ready to open. Our opening day is November 24th. On opening day, we'll _____ _____ _____ _____ to all the visitors. Don't miss it! For more information, visit our website www. dreamchildrenslibrary.org.

02

M Hello. My name is Ethan Lupien, the president of a movie making club in the Orion region. I'm happy to announce information on the Orion Youth Film Festival. The contest will be held _____ _____ _____ _____ of November at the Madison Bridge Center. Only high school students from the Orion region _____ _____ _____ _____. Participants should submit works which are limited to a running time of 30 minutes. They will be judged _____ _____ _____ in the local film industry. The registration deadline is October 20th, so sign up today!

03

W Good morning. I want to tell you about Blue Technology Programs. Blue Technology University will have a two-week, academic camp to inform high school students about the future of _____ _____ _____ _____. It'll be held for two weeks from August 5th to 18th at Blue Technology University, and students will stay in the university dormitories. The camp _____ _____ _____ _____. You must fill out and _____ _____ _____ _____ online. All applications are due by May 30th. For more information or to submit your application, visit the school homepage.

04

M Hello, everyone. Come and help us celebrate our 75th anniversary. H&Q Motors will be turning 75 on May 1st, making us the oldest car dealership in Nevada. We will be having a three-day celebration. On May 1st, we will _____ _____ _____ _____ with free hot-air balloon rides at 6 p.m. On May 2nd, we will have a famous car racer, John Smith, signing autographs from 2 to 4 p.m. On May 3rd, we will have a picnic _____ _____ _____ _____ at 5:30 in the afternoon. During all three days, there will be _____ _____ _____ _____ and carnival rides for the children.

05

W Hello, students. This is your vice principal, Anita Adams. This announcement is to inform you that the 17th Welton High Choir Competition _____ _____ _____ _____ _____ _____.
At the beginning of the year, we accepted teams who were willing to compete, and a total of 18 teams registered to enter. Since only eight teams will be performing in the final competition, we _____ _____ _____ last week and carefully chose the top eight groups. The competition will be held in the auditorium between 1 and 3 p.m., and all students are asked to be seated before it begins. The participating teams will _____ _____ _____ _____, and the winners will be announced right after the competition.

06

M Hello. My name is Jacob Turner, and I'm from the community service center. Today, I'd like to introduce you all to our Eco-Point program. This program aims to reduce the amount of greenhouse gas emissions. It provides incentives _____ _____ _____ _____ _____ _____ you use. If you decrease your usage of both electricity and city gas by more than 10 percent over the course of 6 months, you'll be awarded 50 points. Each point _____ _____ _____ _____, and the points _____ _____ _____ _____ _____ _____ at places like supermarkets and restaurants. Please sign up and become an active citizen who cares about the environment.

필수표현 NOTE

01 We're excited to tell you our library is now ready to open.
이제 저희 도서관이 개관할 준비가 되었음을 알려 드리게 되어 기쁩니다.
Don't miss it! 놓치지 마세요!

03 All applications are due by May 30th. 모든 지원서는 5월 30일까지 마감됩니다.

06 This program aims to reduce the amount of greenhouse gas emissions.
이 프로그램은 온실 가스 배출량 감소를 목표로 합니다.

10강 표의 내용 파악

Q 수능 Q

다음 표를 보면서 대화를 듣고, 여자가 구매할 도마를 고르시오. **2019 수능**

Cutting Boards at Camilo's Kitchen

	Model	Material	Price	Handle	Size
①	A	plastic	$25	X	medium
②	B	maple	$35	○	small
③	C	maple	$40	X	large
④	D	walnut	$45	○	medium
⑤	E	walnut	$55	○	large

K 유형 Key

- 주어진 표를 보면서 대화를 듣고, 대화에서 등장한 정보를 바탕으로 화자가 선택할 대상을 고르는 유형이다.
- 대화를 들으면서 화자가 제시한 조건을 충족하지 않는 항목들은 지운다.
- 대화를 끝까지 들은 후에 제시된 항목 중에서 모든 조건을 충족하는 항목을 최종 선택한다.

C Clue 받아쓰기 다시 한번 내용을 듣고, 빈칸에 정답의 단서를 쓰시오.

M Welcome to Camilo's Kitchen.

W Hello. ❶ I'm looking for a cutting board.

M Let me show you our five top-selling models, all at affordable prices. Do you have a preference for any material? We have plastic, maple, and walnut cutting boards.

W I don't want the plastic one because I think plastic isn't ❷ _____ _____.

M I see. What's your budget range?

W ❸ No more than $50.

M Okay. Do you prefer one with or without a handle?

W I think a cutting board with a handle is easier to use. So I'll take ❹ _____ _____ _____ _____.

M Then, which size do you want? You have two models left.

W Hmm. A small-sized cutting board ❺ _____ _____ when I cut vegetables. I'll buy the other model.

M Great. Then this is the cutting board for you.

정답 ✓ CHECK

❶ 소재
❷ environmentally friendly ▶ 단서 1
❸ ▶ 단서 2
❹ one with a handle ▶ 단서 3
❺ isn't convenient ▶ 단서 4

기출 *Challenge* | 19 고2 09 학평

01 다음 표를 보면서 대화를 듣고, 두 사람이 구매할 Air Fryer를 고르시오.

Air Fryer

	Model	Price	Automatic Switch Off	Capacity (liters)	Warranty
①	A	$59	X	2	1 year
②	B	$68	○	2	1 year
③	C	$84	○	4	1 year
④	D	$95	○	4	2 years
⑤	E	$109	X	5	2 years

02 다음 표를 보면서 대화를 듣고, 남자가 예약할 항공편을 고르시오.

Flights to Toronto

	Flight	Type of Flight	Time of Departure	Price
①	A	Non-stop	09:05	$700
②	B	Stopover	15:35	$550
③	C	Non-stop	18:30	$750
④	D	Stopover	17:50	$500
⑤	E	Non-stop	20:20	$650

03 다음 표를 보면서 대화를 듣고, 여자가 구매할 텐트를 고르시오.

Camping Tents

	Model	Price	Color	Weight
①	A	$85	Darkgray	2kg
②	B	$75	Yellow	2.5kg
③	C	$70	Darkbrown	2.5kg
④	D	$60	Black	3kg
⑤	E	$75	Green	2kg

04 다음 표를 보면서 대화를 듣고, 두 사람이 구매할 생일 파티 세트를 고르시오.

Birthday Party Set

	Set	Balloon	Banner	Party Hat	Cake
①	A	○	X	○	X
②	B	X	X	○	○
③	C	○	○	X	X
④	D	○	○	○	X
⑤	E	○	○	X	○

05 다음 표를 보면서 대화를 듣고, 두 사람이 등록할 로봇 프로그램을 고르시오.

Community Center Robot Programs

	Program	Topic	Day	Fee	Free Gift
①	A	Soccer Robot	Wednesday	$40	None
②	B	Soccer Robot	Friday	$45	Soccer ball
③	C	Dancing Robot	Wednesday	$50	None
④	D	Dancing Robot	Friday	$60	None
⑤	E	Dancing Robot	Friday	$65	Soccer ball

06 다음 표를 보면서 대화를 듣고, 남자가 구매할 탁상시계를 고르시오.

Digital Desk Clocks

	Model	Melody	Backlight	Shape	Color
①	A	X	○	Rectangular	Gray
②	B	X	X	Round	Blue
③	C	○	○	Round	Gray
④	D	○	X	Rectangular	Blue
⑤	E	○	○	Rectangular	Blue

녹음 내용을 다시 들으면서 빈칸을 채워 넣으세요.

01

M Honey, what are you looking at?

W A website that sells air fryers. I want one so we can cook more healthily.

M Good idea. We can fry foods using less oil if we buy one. How much do you think we should spend?

W Well, I don't want to spend _____ _____ _____ _____.

M Okay. Then how about these models?

W Hmm... it's safer to buy one that will turn off if it gets too hot.

M You're right. Let's choose one with _____ _____ _____ _____ _____.

W What about capacity? My friend bought one that could only hold two liters. She regretted not buying a bigger one.

M In that case, we should get one with a capacity of _____ _____ _____ _____. Now we have these two to choose from.

W They both look good. But I think the one _____ _____ _____ _____ is better.

M I agree. Let's order this one.

02

W Hello. How can I help you?

M Hi. I want to book a flight to Toronto next Wednesday, September 29th.

W Okay. Do you want a non-stop flight or a stopover?

M First, I'll ask you a question. _____ _____ _____ _____ _____ to make a stopover?

W It takes about eight hours.

M Really? It takes quite a long time for a stopover. Then, I'll _____ _____ _____ _____.

W Non-stop flights depart almost in the afternoon, when do you want to depart?

M I would like a flight departing after 6 p.m.

W Then there are two left. Which of these do you prefer?

M Well, this one is quite late, but it's cheaper. I'll _____ _____ _____ _____ _____.

W Okay. I'll make a reservation for this flight, then.

M Yes, thank you.

03

M Good afternoon. Can I help you find something?

W Yes. As you know, it's the perfect season for camping these days. I'm _____ _____ _____ _____ for two people.

M Well, look at the catalog here. There are tents for you on the left.

W I have a hard time making decisions. Could you please help me choose?

M Of course. First of all, what is your budget?

W Well, I _____ _____ _____ _____ _____ _____.

M I see. And which of these five colors do you like?

W Well, I really don't want a dark color. Other colors are okay _____ _____ _____ _____.

M Then there are two to choose from. I recommend the lighter one.

W Okay. I'll take that one. Here's my credit card.

04

M Honey, next Friday is Betty's birthday. We need to decorate our house for the party.

W Right. Let's order a set of decorations online.

M Good! Betty likes balloons, so we'll definitely _____ _____ _____ _____.

W Yeah. How about a banner? If we have a banner on the wall, the pictures will _____ _____.

M Yeah. Do we need party hats, too?

W Last year, Betty felt uncomfortable wearing a party hat. This time, let's _____ _____ _____.

M Okay. What about the cake?

W Why don't we _____ _____ _____ _____ _____ _____ near our house?

M Great. The bakery has a lot of wonderful cakes.

W Okay. Let's order this set then.

05

W Daniel, what are you looking at?

M I'm looking at the Community Center Robot Programs. I'd like to take one of them next month.

W That sounds interesting! I'd love to join you.

M I'm interested in either the soccer robot or the dancing robot. What do you think?

W Both sound like fun! But I'd prefer _____ _____ _____ _____.

M Okay. Which day are you free after school next month, Wednesday or Friday?

W Friday _____ _____ _____ _____. I have a piano and violin class after school on Wednesday.

M Then we can choose one of these two programs.

W This program offers a soccer ball _____ _____ _____ _____, but costs $5 more.

M Why don't we choose _____ _____ _____? I don't need a soccer ball.

W Okay. Let's sign up.

06

W What are you doing on your computer, Jake?

M I'm looking for a digital clock for my desk, but I don't know what to choose. Can you help me?

W Sure. Well, what kind of alarm do you want?

M Hmm... I'd like _____ _____ _____.

W Then you can choose one of these three clocks. How about the backlight function?

M I think _____ _____ _____ _____. I'll be able to see the clock in the dark.

W Okay. Now you have to decide on the shape. Which do you prefer, _____ _____ _____?

M Either would be okay, but the color is what really matters to me. I'd like a blue one.

W Okay. Then this model is the best for you.

M I'll get it. Thanks.

필수표현 NOTE

01 What are you looking at? 뭘 보고 있어요?
How about these models? 이 모델들은 어때요?
03 Could you please help me choose? 고르는 것을 좀 도와주시겠어요?
What is your budget? 예산은 어떻게 되나요?
06 Either would be okay, but the color is what really matters to me. 둘 다 괜찮지만, 나한테는 색상이 정말 중요해.
Then this model is the best for you. 그러면 이 모델이 네게 딱 맞네.

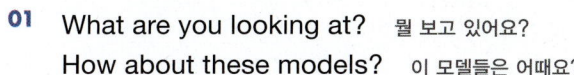

10강 표의 내용 파악 **49**

11강 응답 추론(짧은 대화, 긴 대화)

Q 수능 Q

대화를 듣고, 남자의 마지막 말에 대한 여자의 응답으로 가장 적절한 것을 고르시오. **2020 수능**

Woman: _____

① Definitely! This book isn't as interesting as yours.
② Terrific! I'll check right away if there are any nearby.
③ Never mind. I won't take that course next semester.
④ Really? I didn't know you have a degree in philosophy.
⑤ Why not? You can join my philosophy discussion group.

K 유형 Key

- 짧은 대화나 긴 대화를 듣고, 마지막 말에 대한 적절한 응답을 찾는 유형이다.
- 선택지가 영어로 제시되므로 대화가 나오기 전 미리 읽고 의미를 해석해 본다.
- 마지막 말에 대한 단순한 응답이 아닌 대화의 전반적인 흐름을 파악하여 종합적인 추론을 한다.

C Clue 받아쓰기   다시 한번 내용을 듣고, 빈칸에 정답의 단서를 쓰시오.

M Amy, what are you reading?

W Dad, it's ❶ <u>a book for my philosophy course</u>.

M Let me take a look. Wow! It's a book by Kant.

W Yeah. It's very difficult to understand.

M You're right. His books take a lot of effort to read since they include his deep knowledge and thoughts.

W I think so, too. Do you have any ideas for me to understand the book better, Dad?

M Well, why don't you ❷ <u>join a philosophy discussion group</u>? You can find one in our area.

W Are there discussion groups for philosophy? That sounds interesting.

M Yeah. You can ❸ _____ _____ _____ _____ in the group about the book you're reading.

W You mean I can understand Kant's book more clearly by discussing it?

M Absolutely. Plus, you can ❹ _____ _____ _____ _____ in the group as well.

W [_____]

정답 ✓
CHECK
❶ [소재 1]
❷ [소재 2]
❸ share ideas with others [단서 1]
❹ develop critical thinking skills [단서 2]

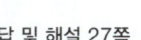

기출 Challenge | 20 고1 03 학평

01 대화를 듣고, 여자의 마지막 말에 대한 남자의 응답으로 가장 적절한 것을 고르시오.

① Really? I should have seen her.
② No way. I'm going to miss you a lot.
③ No. I didn't go to the bookstore that day.
④ I'm sorry. I'm not interested in her writing.
⑤ Yes. I can't believe I'm going to see her in person.

02 대화를 듣고, 남자의 마지막 말에 대한 여자의 응답으로 가장 적절한 것을 고르시오.

① Sorry, but I lost your wireless earphones.
② Right. Your drone is much faster than mine.
③ Actually, the science club needs more drones.
④ Don't worry. I'll show you how to fly a drone.
⑤ Good. I'll enter the competition and hopefully win.

03 대화를 듣고, 여자의 마지막 말에 대한 남자의 응답으로 가장 적절한 것을 고르시오.

① It's seven thirty now.
② I need to wake up at six.
③ I don't have time tomorrow.
④ I'd like a single room, please.
⑤ I'm sorry. I don't have a watch.

04 대화를 듣고, 남자의 마지막 말에 대한 여자의 응답으로 가장 적절한 것을 고르시오.
Woman: _____
① Let me help you repair your bicycle.
② I'm going to send the package for you.
③ I'm going to wear a helmet just in case.
④ I'll call City Hall to request road repairs.
⑤ I'll drop by a drugstore on my way home.

05 대화를 듣고, 여자의 마지막 말에 대한 남자의 응답으로 가장 적절한 것을 고르시오.
Man: _____
① No. Your work experience is good enough.
② No, I don't. If you hire me, I'll do my best.
③ Yeah. I quit working at the Italian restaurant.
④ Right. All the questions were hard to answer.
⑤ Well, I don't want to work as a chef any more.

06 대화를 듣고, 남자의 마지막 말에 대한 여자의 응답으로 가장 적절한 것을 고르시오.
Woman: _____
① Yeah. That's what insurance is for.
② You're right. You can get a full refund.
③ I don't think so. You should leave tomorrow.
④ Okay. You can choose whatever bags you want.
⑤ Of course. It is not easy to reserve flight tickets.

녹음 내용을 다시 들으면서 빈칸을 채워 넣으세요.

01

W Did you hear that Golden Bookstore will _____ _____ _____ _____ _____ for Lora Johnson?

M Oh, she is _____ _____ _____ _____ _____. I've read all of her novels. When is it?

W This Sunday afternoon. Do you want to come with me?

M

02

M Did you hear that the science club will _____ _____ _____ _____?

W A drone competition? When is it? I'm interested.

M November 10th. You know, _____ _____ _____ _____ _____ _____ a brand-new wireless earphones.

W

03

W Good afternoon, sir. How can I help you?

M Could you _____ _____ _____ _____ _____ tomorrow morning? I'm staying in room 801.

W Certainly. _____ _____ would you like it?

M

04

M I'm back, Mom.

W Oh, Jack. You're limping. What happened?

M I twisted my ankle when I _____ _____ _____ _____ on my way home.

W Let me see. *[Pause]* Oh, it's a bit swollen. You'd better see a doctor.

M It's not serious. I'll just wrap some bandages around it and get some rest.

W Okay. I'll get the bandages for you. By the way, where did the accident happen?

M In front of the post office. The road was bumpy.

W Oh, I know _____ _____ _____ _____ _____ for several weeks.

M I don't understand why the city government doesn't do anything about it.

W I _____ _____ _____ so this doesn't happen again.

M What are you going to do?

W

05

W Have a seat here, please.

M Thank you. It's nice to meet you.

W Let me ask you a few things. _____ _____ _____ _____ _____ _____ _____ before?

M Yes, I have. I worked at an Italian restaurant on Lake Street last year.

W Good. What did you do there and how long did you work?

M I worked _____ _____ _____ for almost six months.

W I think that's enough experience to work here.

M Thank you. By the way, can you _____ _____ _____ _____ _____?

W It's $10 and you'll get additional $2 during the weekend.

M Great! I worked for only $7 an hour at my previous workplace.

W Okay. Do you have _____ _____ _____ regarding this job?

M ▓▓▓▓▓▓▓▓▓▓▓▓▓▓▓▓

06

W Hi, Michael. You look excited. What's up?

M Remember when I _____ _____ _____ _____ to France and England? I'm leaving tomorrow.

W Wow, great! This will be your first time _____ _____, right?

M Yeah. I can't wait to go.

W Do you _____ _____ _____?

M I think so. I've made hotel reservations and I've finished packing my bags.

W Did you _____ _____ _____?

M No, I didn't. Is it a must?

W Sure. What if you get injured or have your wallet stolen while traveling?

M Oh, I see. You mean I have to be prepared just in case, right?

W ▓▓▓▓▓▓▓▓▓▓▓▓▓▓▓▓

필수표현
NOTE

01 Do you want to come with me? 나랑 같이 갈래?

04 You'd better see a doctor. 병원에 가는 게 좋겠다.

05 Let me ask you a few things. 몇 가지를 물어볼게요.

06 What if you get injured or have your wallet stolen while traveling?
만약 네가 여행 중에 다치거나 지갑을 도난당하면 어떻겠어?

12강 상황에 적절한 말 추론

Q 수능 Q

다음 상황 설명을 듣고, Brian의 어머니가 Brian에게 할 말로 가장 적절한 것을 고르시오. 2020 수능

Brian's mother: _____

① Make sure to call me whenever you go somewhere new.
② School trips are good opportunities to make friends.
③ I believe traveling broadens your perspective.
④ How about carrying the luggage on your own?
⑤ Why don't you pack your bag by yourself for the trip?

K 유형 Key

- 담화를 듣고, 주어진 상황에서 특정 화자가 할 말로 가장 적절한 것을 추론하는 유형이다.
- 담화를 들으면서 주요 인물 간의 관계와 어떤 상황에 처해 있는지를 파악해야 한다.
- 담화 후반부에 상대방에게 말하고자 하는 바가 드러나는 부분에 집중하여 듣고 이를 바탕으로 정답을 유추한다.
- 대화 상대방이 할 법한 말이 오답 선택지로 나오는 경우가 있으므로 유의해야 한다.

C Clue 받아쓰기   다시 한번 내용을 듣고, 빈칸에 정답의 단서를 쓰시오.

W Brian is a high school student. He has only traveled with his family before. Until now his mother has always taken care of his travel bag, so he doesn't have any experience preparing it himself. This weekend, Brian is supposed to ❶ go on a school trip with his friends. He asks his mother to ❷ _____ _____ _____ _____ _____ _____ this time, too. However, she believes Brian is old enough to prepare what he needs, and she thinks this time is a great opportunity for him to ❸ _____ _____ _____ _____ _____. So, she wants to tell Brian that he should get his things ready and put them in his bag ❹ _____ _____ _____. In this situation, what would Brian's mother most likely say to Brian?

Brian's mother

정답 ✓
CHECK
❶ 소재
❷ get his stuff ready for his trip 단서 1
❸ learn to be more independent 단서 2
❹ without her help 단서 3

기출 Challenge | 19 고1 09 학평

01 다음 상황 설명을 듣고, Jina가 어머니에게 할 말로 가장 적절한 것을 고르시오.

Jina: _____

① Please help me choose a nice flower pot.
② Would you come with me to the Market Day?
③ Can I take this flower pot for a school event?
④ I'm not sure if I can plant my flowers in this pot.
⑤ Why don't we look for an item to sell at the market?

02 다음 상황 설명을 듣고, John이 Juliet에게 할 말로 가장 적절한 것을 고르시오.

John: _____

① Right. You'll be able to get better.
② Good. You can rely on me about it.
③ Okay. I will give you a day off tomorrow.
④ Thanks. I'm very satisfied with your work.
⑤ Sorry. I don't want to work anymore today.

03 다음 상황 설명을 듣고, Angela가 Jim에게 할 말로 가장 적절한 것을 고르시오.

Angela: _____

① It's time for you to go to bed.
② It's not a good habit to sit up all night.
③ You're not allowed to watch TV at this time.
④ I'm very pleased that you've done it for me today.
⑤ You'd better go wash your face and brush your teeth.

04 다음 상황 설명을 듣고, Sam이 여자에게 할 말로 가장 적절한 것을 고르시오.

Sam: _____

① Could you please give up your seat?
② You should be careful not to miss your stop.
③ I'm getting off soon, so you can have my seat.
④ The subway might not be able to leave on time.
⑤ Leaning against the door can be pretty dangerous.

05 다음 상황 설명을 듣고, Kelly가 Tom에게 할 말로 가장 적절한 것을 고르시오.

Kelly: _____

① It's hard for me to sleep at night these days.
② Can you ignore the noise and focus on your work?
③ I apologize for all the noise I have been making.
④ I think it's best to let your children feel comfortable.
⑤ Could you please keep it down so I can get some sleep?

06 다음 상황 설명을 듣고, Nathan이 직원에게 할 말로 가장 적절한 것을 고르시오.

Nathan: _____

① Will you have it repaired by next week?
② I am to blame for the crack on the screen.
③ Can you please tell me what's wrong with it?
④ I'd like to know if I have to pay for the repairs.
⑤ I don't understand why it stops working suddenly.

• DICTATION

녹음 내용을 다시 들으면서 빈칸을 채워 넣으세요.

01

M Jina is a high school student. Her school is hosting a Market Day to _____ _____ _____ _____ _____ in the neighborhood. Jina's teacher says that students who want to take part in the event should _____ _____ _____ _____ to school. Jina wants to participate in the school market, so as soon as she gets home, she starts looking for items she can sell at the school Market Day. Finally, she finds her mother's old flower pot in the basement. Now, she wants to ask her mother for permission to _____ _____ _____ _____ _____. In this situation, what would Jina most likely say to her mother?

Jina

02

W Juliet has been working as a secretary for a trading company for 10 years. She is _____ _____ and she has never been late. She has never made a mistake in arranging a meeting or managing schedules. Her boss, John, is very _____ _____ _____ _____ _____. People around her are particularly impressed with her positive personality, and they always praise her for her satisfactory work. John decides to _____ _____ _____ _____ _____ to work. In this situation, what would John most likely say to Juliet?

John

03

M Angela's five-year-old son, Jim, is watching TV in the living room now. It's 9 o'clock, and it's time _____ _____ _____ _____. Angela tells him to turn off the TV and get ready for bed. Hearing her, Jim turns off the TV and goes to his room _____ _____ _____ _____ or brushing his teeth. Angela goes to his room and sees him lying in the bed. Now, She wants to tell him that _____ _____ _____ _____ _____. In this situation, what would Angela most likely say to Jim?

Angela

04

W Sam gets on the subway after a long day from school. On the subway car, there is _____ _____ _____ _____. Luckily, Sam gets to sit there. He starts to doze off as soon as the subway leaves the station. About ten minutes later, he gets woken up by the rattling sound of the subway car. Sam sees _____ _____ _____ _____ _____ _____ to an old lady. The woman seems really tired as she leans against the pole. Since he has just two stops left _____ _____ _____, he thinks he might as well give up his seat. In this situation, what would Sam most likely say to the woman?

Sam

56 Listening Master BASIC

05

M Kelly works as a nurse at a general hospital. Once a week, she works the night shift from 10 p.m. to 6 a.m. After she finishes her work at dawn, she always feels exhausted and _____ _____ _____ _____. One day, as she goes to bed after her night shift, she _____ _____ _____ _____ and kids yelling. It's coming from the apartment above her. Her upstairs neighbor is Tom, and he has two children. Kelly tries to ignore the noise, but _____ _____ _____ _____ _____. As she finds it impossible to sleep, she decides to go upstairs to talk to Tom. In this situation, what would Kelly most likely say to Tom?

Kelly ▟▟▟▟▟▟▟▟▟▟▟▟▟▟▟▟▟▟▟▟

06

W Nathan bought himself a smartphone about a year ago. Last Sunday, he _____ _____ _____ while walking, and afterwards he noticed a small crack on the screen. Ever since that day, the phone _____ _____ _____ _____. The phone freezes whenever he runs certain applications. In addition, the battery seems to run out faster than before. He needs to charge it twice a day. Nathan decides to _____ _____ _____ _____ _____. The clerk at the service center says it will take about a week before the work is done. Nathan wonders if the repair is _____ _____ _____. In this situation, what would Nathan most likely say to the clerk?

Nathan ▟▟▟▟▟▟▟▟▟▟▟▟▟▟▟▟▟▟▟▟

**필수표현
NOTE**

01 As soon as she gets home, she starts looking for items she can sell at the school Market Day.
집에 오자마자, 학교 Market Day에 팔 수 있는 물건을 찾기 시작합니다.

04 The woman seems really tired as she leans against the pole.
그 여자는 기둥에 기대어 매우 피곤해 보입니다.

05 Once a week, she works the night shift from 10 p.m. to 6 a.m.
일주일에 한 번, 그녀는 오후 10시부터 오전 6시까지 야간 근무를 합니다.

06 In addition, the battery seems to run out faster than before.
게다가, 배터리가 전보다 더 빨리 닳는 것 같습니다.

He needs to charge it twice a day.   그는 그것을 하루에 두 번 충전해야 합니다.

Q 수능 Q

다음을 듣고, 물음에 답하시오. `2019 수능`

01 여자가 하는 말의 주제로 가장 적절한 것은?

① why traditional foods are popular
② misconceptions about organic foods
③ unexpected origins of common foods
④ when foods spread across countries
⑤ importance of eating fresh foods

02 언급된 음식이 아닌 것은?

① Caesar salad
② bagels
③ kiwis
④ potatoes
⑤ buffalo wings

K 유형 Key

- 비교적 긴 담화를 듣고, 주제를 묻는 문항과 언급 유무 문항이 세트로 구성된 유형이다.
- 담화의 초반에 주로 주제나 목적이 언급되는 경우가 많고, 언급 유무 문항의 선택지는 담화의 순서대로 제시되므로 언급되는 선택지를 차례대로 지워 나간다.
- 담화를 두 번 들려주므로 두 번째 들을 때 놓친 부분을 확인하고 정답을 점검한다.

C Clue 받아쓰기   다시 한번 내용을 듣고, 빈칸에 정답의 단서를 쓰시오.

W Hello, students. Previously, we discussed traditional foods in different countries. Today, I'll talk about ❶ <u>surprising birthplaces of everyday foods</u>. First, people believe the Caesar salad is named after a Roman emperor. But a well-known story is that the name ❷ _____ _____ _____ _____ _____ _____. He created it by putting together some basic ingredients when running out of food. Second, bagels are a famous New York food. But they're likely from central Europe. A widely repeated story says that ❸ _____ _____ _____ _____ in Vienna to celebrate the defeat of an invading army. Third, many people think kiwis are from New Zealand. It's probably because a small flightless bird from New Zealand has the same name. In fact, ❹ _____ _____ _____ _____ _____. Last, if there's any country known for potatoes, it's Ireland. That's because crop failures of this food caused extreme hunger in Ireland in the 19th century. However, the food is believed to come ❺ _____ _____ _____. Now, we'll watch a short video about these foods.

정답 CHECK

❶ ▶ 소재
❷ came from a chef in Mexico ▶ 단서 1
❸ they were first made ▶ 단서 2
❹ the food is from China ▶ 단서 3
❺ from South America ▶ 단서 4

[01~02] 다음을 듣고, 물음에 답하시오.

01 여자가 하는 말의 주제로 가장 적절한 것은?
① home appliances made smarter with technology
② ways of upgrading smart home appliances
③ how to buy smart home appliances online
④ benefits of energy-efficient home appliances
⑤ negative impacts of AI technologies on humans

02 언급된 가전제품이 아닌 것은?
① washing machines　② refrigerators
③ speakers　④ air conditioners
⑤ vacuum cleaners

[03~04] 다음을 듣고, 물음에 답하시오.

03 남자가 하는 말의 주제로 가장 적절한 것은?
① activities that make you feel good
② the impact of gardening on psychology
③ how to deal with psychological problems
④ vegetables that are good for growing in the garden
⑤ relationship between outdoor activity and mental illness treatment

04 언급된 심리 상태가 아닌 것은?
① depression　② comfort
③ stress　④ accomplishment
⑤ delight

[05~06] 다음을 듣고, 물음에 답하시오.

05 여자가 하는 말의 주제로 가장 적절한 것은?
① commonly used objects in Egyptian paintings
② the importance of a frontal view in Egyptian paintings
③ the improvement of Egyptian painters' social status
④ the influence of political situations on the Egyptian arts
⑤ the Egyptian painting style for representing human figures

06 언급된 신체 부위가 아닌 것은?
① legs　② arms
③ chest　④ faces
⑤ shoulders

녹음 내용을 다시 들으면서 빈칸을 채워 넣으세요.

01 ~ 02

W Hello, everyone. With technologies like Artificial Intelligence, it is possible to digitize homes. Today, I'd like to introduce to you _____ _____ _____ _____ with the help of technology. First are smart washing machines. Smart washers with AI techniques can _____ _____ _____ _____ _____ _____ so they regulate the washing strength and detergent. They can even send an alert when detergent is out of stock. Next are smart refrigerators. They allow the user to monitor food items inside. They can even _____ _____ _____ that can be made with those items. There are also smart speakers. Speakers controlled by voice commands can do various tasks such as creating a play list and searching the Internet. Lastly, robotic vacuum cleaners can automatically clean the tight and usually overlooked spaces that are _____ _____ _____ _____ _____ _____. Now, let's watch a video about these smart home appliances.

03 ~ 04

M Hello. Let's talk about gardening. Gardening is more than just shoveling dirt and watering plants. It is a way for you to relax without being a couch potato. Did you know that spending just 30 minutes a day in your garden _____ _____ _____ _____? I'll give you some examples. Gardening is a great way to _____ _____ _____ _____ _____. It has a calming effect on the human psyche. Studies have shown that exposure to sunlight makes people feel _____ _____ _____ _____. Gardening can also reduce stress. While doing garden work, you can free yourself from the thoughts that complicate your life. Lastly, gardens give you _____ _____ _____ _____ that is nearly unrivaled. If you have a garden, why don't you plant vegetables in your garden?

05 ~ 06

W Hello, everyone. I'd like to talk about Egyptian paintings today. What do you think of the Egyptian paintings in this picture? Do the figures look realistic to you? No, of course they don't. Egyptian painters followed _____ _____ _____ of their own. The painters used multiple points of view to show _____ _____ _____ _____ _____ on flat surfaces. The legs, arms and faces of people are drawn from a side view, while the shoulders are facing front. The human body is twisted _____ _____ _____ _____. The shoulder faces the viewer but the waist and legs face sideways. Egyptian artists also had their own way of _____ _____ _____ _____ _____.

It was based on the person's social status. In the next picture, you can see ordinary people were generally drawn as much smaller than gods, pharaohs, and other important people. Now let's watch some video clips to help you understand better.

필수표현 NOTE

01~02 They can even send an alert when detergent is out of stock.
그것은 세제가 비어 갈 때 경보를 보낼 수도 있습니다.

03~04 It is a way for you to relax without being a couch potato.
그것은 소파에 누워 TV만 보며 시간을 보내지 않고도 휴식을 취할 수 있는 방법입니다.

It has a calming effect on the human psyche. 그것은 인간의 정신에 진정 효과가 있습니다.

05~06 I'd like to talk about Egyptian paintings today.
오늘 저는 이집트 그림에 대해서 이야기하고 싶습니다.

What do you think of the Egyptian paintings in this picture?
이 사진에 있는 이집트 그림들에 대해서 여러분은 어떻게 생각하십니까?

Listening Master

BASIC

실전 모의고사

● 실전 모의고사 **01** 회

1번부터 17번까지는 듣고 답하는 문제입니다. 1번부터 15번까지는 한 번만 들려주고, 16번부터 17번까지는 두 번 들려줍니다. 방송을 잘 듣고 답을 하시기 바랍니다.

01 다음을 듣고, 남자가 하는 말의 목적으로 가장 적절한 것을 고르시오.

① 체육 센터 회원을 모집하려고
② 변경된 강좌 시간을 공지하려고
③ 오래된 체육 시설 교체를 요구하려고
④ 규칙적인 생활의 중요성을 강조하려고
⑤ 맵시 있게 옷 입는 방법을 알려 주려고

02 대화를 듣고, 여자의 의견으로 가장 적절한 것을 고르시오.

① 적당하게 움직이는 것이 산모에게 좋다.
② 임신 중에는 약물 복용에 주의해야 한다.
③ 산모의 식습관이 태아의 건강을 좌우한다.
④ 임신 중에는 몸을 따뜻하게 유지해야 한다.
⑤ 부부가 함께 태교를 하는 것이 바람직하다.

03 대화를 듣고, 두 사람의 관계를 가장 잘 나타낸 것을 고르시오.

① 의사 – 환자
② 동물병원 직원 – 고객
③ 사무용품점 점원 – 고객
④ 세관 직원 – 공항 이용객
⑤ 전자제품 수리 기사 – 고객

04 대화를 듣고, 그림에서 대화의 내용과 일치하지 <u>않는</u> 것을 고르시오.

05 대화를 듣고, 여자가 남자를 위해 할 일로 가장 적절한 것을 고르시오.

① 아침 식사 시간 늦추기
② 가방 옮기는 것 도와주기
③ 잡지를 읽을 수 있는 장소 안내하기
④ 지도에 관광 명소 표시하여 가져다주기
⑤ 객실에서 컴퓨터를 이용할 수 있도록 해 주기

06 대화를 듣고, 남자가 지불할 금액을 고르시오.

① $40   ② $45   ③ $50   ④ $55   ⑤ $60

07 대화를 듣고, 여자가 Sun Star Mall에 가는 이유를 고르시오.

① 영화를 보기로 해서
② 룸메이트를 만나야 해서
③ 구직 면접을 보기로 해서
④ 티셔츠를 구입하기를 원해서
⑤ 노트북 컴퓨터를 찾기 위해서

08 대화를 듣고, Stars Driving School에 관해 언급되지 <u>않은</u> 것을 고르시오.

① 위치   ② 강사   ③ 수강료
④ 환불 제도   ⑤ 교육 시간

09 33rd Strawberry Spring Festival에 관한 다음 내용을 듣고, 일치하지 <u>않는</u> 것을 고르시오.

① 3월 5일에 시작해서 4일간 지속된다.
② San Diego에서 가장 인기 있는 축제 중의 하나이다.
③ 축제 방문객은 약 3만 명으로 예상된다.
④ 입장권 소지자는 딸기 음식을 무료로 먹을 수 있다.
⑤ 축제 동안 딸기 따기 행사가 매일 열린다.

10 다음 표를 보면서 대화를 듣고, 두 사람이 예약할 방을 고르시오. [3점]

Lambert Hotel

	Room	View	Charge (per night)	Internet Access	In-room Safe
①	A	garden view	$120	X	X
②	B	ocean view	$150	X	X
③	C	ocean view	$250	X	○
④	D	ocean view	$400	○	○
⑤	E	ocean view	$500	○	○

11 대화를 듣고, 남자의 마지막 말에 대한 여자의 응답으로 가장 적절한 것을 고르시오.

① That's because I don't like it.

② I go to a gym near my house.

③ It's very nice of you to say so.

④ Sounds great. Let's practice it together.

⑤ It is helpful in training my body and spirit.

12 대화를 듣고, 여자의 마지막 말에 대한 남자의 응답으로 가장 적절한 것을 고르시오.

① I'm sorry. But these gloves are too big for me.

② This way, please. Gloves for rock climbing are here.

③ Right. You only have to buy either a helmet or gloves.

④ No problem. Let's go rock climbing this Saturday.

⑤ If I were you, I'd buy the black gloves, not the white ones.

13 대화를 듣고, 남자의 마지막 말에 대한 여자의 응답으로 가장 적절한 것을 고르시오.

Woman: _____

① If I were you, I wouldn't rent the house.

② Right. I want to work at the real estate agency.

③ Good. Your house looks much better than mine.

④ Don't worry. I'll lend you money for the monthly fee.

⑤ Great! No wonder you said you found the perfect house.

14 대화를 듣고, 여자의 마지막 말에 대한 남자의 응답으로 가장 적절한 것을 고르시오.

Man: _____

① That's great! I'll take the pink one.

② I see. I won't check out those items.

③ Okay. Then I'll try on this shirt first.

④ I'm sorry, but I want to get a refund.

⑤ Don't worry. I can have it delivered to you.

15 다음 상황 설명을 듣고, David가 점원에게 할 말로 가장 적절한 것을 고르시오. [3점]

David: _____

① Excuse me. Can I use your cellphone?

② How long do I have to wait to get a table?

③ I didn't know the restaurant is closed today.

④ I'm sorry, but you've dialed the wrong number.

⑤ Can you hold onto my cellphone? I'll be there soon.

[16~17] 다음을 듣고, 물음에 답하시오.

16 여자가 하는 말의 주제로 가장 적절한 것은? [3점]

① how to choose animals for animal testing

② cosmetic products that require animal testing

③ the uselessness of animal testing in cosmetics

④ the decrease in animal testing in the cosmetics industry

⑤ why animal testing is necessary in many industries

17 언급된 동물이 아닌 것은?

① mice   ② dogs   ③ cats

④ rabbits   ⑤ chickens

녹음 내용을 다시 들으면서 빈칸을 채워 넣으세요.

01

M Are you having _____ _____ _____ _____ your old clothes? Have you placed yourself on the scale and realized you are no longer the person you once were? If you said yes to any of these questions, don't just sit on the couch hoping to be something you are not. Come to the Fitness Factory and _____ _____ _____ _____ toward your better appearance. For a limited time only, a yearly membership will include the use of our up-to-date gym, a large swimming pool, a sauna, and a variety of yoga classes. So, act right now and _____ _____ _____ this special offer. This special promotion ends at the end of July.

02

W Hey, Wesley. I heard your wife _____ _____. Congratulations!

M Thank you, Lucy. Our baby is due in August.

W Your wife's belly must be growing larger.

M Right. That's why I'm doing as many household chores as possible for her.

W Well, _____ _____ _____ _____ when a pregnant woman was thought of as fragile.

M What do you mean?

W A pregnant woman is capable of doing nearly everything that every other woman is capable of doing.

M Oh, really? I didn't know that.

W It is also recommended that pregnant women participate in some exercise programs.

M I see. Is it also helpful to take a walk?

W Sure. _____ _____ _____ _____ for pregnant women.

03

M Good afternoon. How can I help you?

W Hello. I'm going to travel with my dog to the Philippines.

M Would you like it to _____ _____ _____?

W No. She already got all her vaccinations here. I just _____ _____ _____ _____.

M No problem. May I have her name and her breed?

W Her name is Lucy and she is a Chihuahua.

M Wait a second, please. *[Typing Sound]* Okay. How many copies do you need?

W Three copies, please.

M Uh-oh, the printer needs a new ink cartridge. Do you need them right now?

W No. When can I pick them up?

M I'll _____ _____ _____ within the hour. Will that be okay?

W That's fine. Thank you.

04

W Look at the picture on this brochure, Paul.

M What is it, Emily?

W This is Restaurant Romance. It is located on Cross Street. Why don't we have dinner here this Saturday?

M Sounds great! The aquarium _____ _____ _____ is impressive.

W Yeah. And the brochure says the bottle of wine on each table is free.

M That's good! What do you think of the _____ _____ _____ _____?

W I like its classic look.

M Me, too. Eating dinner by candlelight would be very romantic.

W I like the _____ _____, too. It looks elegant.

M Look at the comfortable chairs with armrests. I want to sit in one of them.

W Then let's go to this restaurant on Saturday.

05

W Welcome to Queensland Hostel! What can I do for you?

M Hi. My name is Chris Jackson. I made a reservation three days ago.

W Okay. Let me see. *[Typing Sound]* You _____ _____ _____ _____ for two days, right?

M That's right.

W Your room is 202. Here's the key. Breakfast is served from 7:00 to 8:30 in the dining hall.

M Thank you. Can you tell me where I can use a computer?

W There is a lounge at the end of this aisle. You can use computers and read magazines there.

M Thank you. And can you recommend any tourist attractions around here?

W Sure. I'll bring you a city map after I _____ _____ _____ _____ on it.

M Thank you. Then I'll take my bags upstairs now.

W Okay. I'll _____ _____ _____ _____ in ten minutes.

06

W Good morning. How can I help you?

M I'm _____ _____ _____ _____ for my daughter. Can you recommend one?

W Sure. What do you think of this gray one? It's 35 dollars.

M Well, I like the design, but I don't think she'll like that color.

W Then how about choosing one of these pink ones?

M They look good. How much is this one?

W The list price is 50 dollars, but it's _____ _____ _____ now.

M Good. I'll take it. And how much is this doll? It's very cute.

W It's 10 dollars, but if you buy a purse, you can _____ _____ _____ _____ _____.

M Okay. Then I'll take the purse and the doll. Here is my credit card.

W Thank you.

07

M Hi, Alice! Where are you going?

W Hi, Jake. I'm going to the Sun Star Mall.

M What a coincidence! I'm going there, too. Let's go together.

W Okay. Are you _____ _____ _____ _____?

M No. I'll meet my roommate, Jack, and see a movie with him.

W Then you have to go to the cinema on the top floor, don't you?

M Right. What about you? What are you going there for?

W To get my notebook computer. I _____ _____ _____ _____ _____ when I bought a T-shirt in the afternoon.

M You should have been more careful. By the way, how was your job interview yesterday?

W Not bad. I think _____ _____ _____ _____ _____.

M I really hope so.

08

[Cellphone rings.]

M Hi, Emily. What's up?

W I heard you _____ _____ _____ _____. Congratulations!

M Thanks. You know how hard it is to get by without one.

W You're right. That's why I called you. Can you recommend a driving school?

M Sure. I went to Stars Driving School on Kingston Street. It isn't far from your house.

W What made you choose that school?

M It has kind instructors and new cars. And most of all, the classes _____ _____ _____ other schools.

W How much are they?

M Four hundred dollars, _____ _____. Ah, there is one more thing.

W What is it?

M You _____ _____ _____ _____ if you pass the driving test on your first attempt.

09

W Now let me tell you about the 33rd Strawberry Spring Festival. The festival, which is held at Olympic Park, starts on March 5th and _____ _____ _____ _____. One of the most popular festivals in San Diego, the festival _____ _____ _____ every year. Last year, about 30,000 people visited the festival and about 50,000 are expected to visit this year. Tickets for the festival cost $20 per person. _____ _____ _____ _____ _____ the various foods made from strawberries, such as strawberry cake and strawberry juice, free of charge. What's better, _____ _____ _____ _____ _____ _____ every day during the festival. For more information, visit the festival website.

10

M Look at this brochure, Monica. I'm going to reserve a hotel room for our honeymoon.

W Well, I want us to have _____ _____ _____ the whole beach.

M So do I. How about this room?

W Well, I think $500 is _____ _____ _____ _____. Our quality time together is what's important.

M I see. Then how about _____ _____?

W Justin, we are supposed to be getting away from it all and having time for ourselves.

M I know what you mean. We won't have to spend as much money on our hotel room.

W No. And I won't bring many valuables, so there's no need _____ _____ _____.

M Okay. Then let me reserve this room.

W Thank you, Justin. I can't wait for our trip.

11

M What's your _____ _____?

W Most of all, I love to practice Taekwondo in my free time.

M Interesting! I'd like to know _____ _____ _____ _____.

W

12

W Hi, I'd like to _____ _____ _____ _____ _____ _____. Do you have a helmet?

M Sorry, we don't have any rock climbing helmets in stock at the moment.

W I'm sorry to hear that. Then _____ _____ _____?

M

13

M Ms. Brown, I think I've finally _____ _____

_____ _____ _____ _____.

W That's great news! Is it located near an elementary school?

M Yes, it's located only five minutes' walk from Lincoln Elementary School.

W How about the number of bedrooms? As I told you, I need at least three bedrooms.

M It has _____ _____ _____ _____

_____.

W Oh, really? Very good.

M But there's even _____ _____ _____

_____ about the house.

W One more wonderful thing? What is it? I'm curious.

M _____ _____ _____ is only $700.

W

14

W Good afternoon, sir. What can I do for you?

M Can I see the shirt in the shop window?

W You mean the pink shirt with a white collar?

M Yes, but I'd like one with a different color.

W No problem. This shirt _____ _____ a variety of colors. We keep them on this shelf.

M Wow, impressive! There are so many colors.

W They are popular items. Take your time and pick what you like most.

M Well, I'd like to choose either the blue, gray, or light brown one. Can I _____ _____ _____ now?

W Of course. The fitting room is right over there.

M Thank you.

W Oh, wait a minute, sir! You can only _____

_____ _____ _____ at a time.

M

15

M David has to work late in his office today. It is seven o'clock in the evening and he feels hungry, so he goes to a nearby fast food restaurant to _____ _____ _____ _____. He buys a sandwich and a carton of milk and comes back to his office. But he soon realizes that he doesn't have his cellphone in his pocket. He remembers that he _____ _____ _____ the checkout counter while taking some money out of his wallet. He _____ _____ _____ and a clerk from the restaurant answers the phone. In this situation, what would David most likely say to the clerk?

David

16~17

W As most of you know, many animals _____

_____ _____ _____ new medicines, paints, and even food. But do you also know that more than 33 animals die in laboratories each second worldwide? It's a real tragedy for many animals including mice, dogs, and cats. But, now I've got hopeful news for them, especially rabbits. They have been largely used in the cosmetics industry, but recently, the industry began to _____ _____ _____. This is a surprising change for the industry that tested nearly all its products on animals 20 years ago. Back in 1980s, eye irritation tests on rabbits were the subject of the protest against animal testing. Since then, many cosmetics companies have put considerable money and effort into _____ _____ _____ animal testing. As a result, the animal use in the industry _____ _____ _____ _____.

실전 모의고사 **02** 회

1번부터 17번까지는 듣고 답하는 문제입니다. 1번부터 15번까지는 한 번만 들려주고, 16번부터 17번까지는 두 번 들려줍니다. 방송을 잘 듣고 답을 하시기 바랍니다.

01 다음을 듣고, 여자가 하는 말의 목적으로 가장 적절한 것을 고르시오.

① 카메라를 광고하려고
② 착시 현상을 설명하려고
③ 전자제품 수리를 요청하려고
④ 자연보호의 중요성을 강조하려고
⑤ 예술 작품 감상법에 대해 조언하려고

02 대화를 듣고, 남자의 의견으로 가장 적절한 것을 고르시오.

① 자주 웃으면 면역력이 높아진다.
② 소리 내어 웃는 것은 다이어트에 좋다.
③ 웃음과 두뇌 발달은 밀접한 관계가 있다.
④ 웃음을 통해 인간관계를 개선할 수 있다.
⑤ 억지웃음은 기분이 나아지는 데 도움이 된다.

03 대화를 듣고, 두 사람의 관계를 가장 잘 나타낸 것을 고르시오.

① 의사 – 환자
② 의사 – 간호사
③ 영양사 – 상담 고객
④ 스포츠 감독 – 선수
⑤ 헬스클럽 직원 – 고객

04 대화를 듣고, 그림에서 대화의 내용과 일치하지 않는 것을 고르시오.

05 대화를 듣고, 남자가 여자를 위해 할 일로 가장 적절한 것을 고르시오.

① 의상 수선하기
② 마녀 모자 만들기
③ 의상 대여점에 가기
④ 흡혈귀 복장 만들기
⑤ 여동생에게 모자 빌리기

06 대화를 듣고, 여자가 지불할 금액을 고르시오. [3점]

① $33 ② $43 ③ $48 ④ $50 ⑤ $53

07 대화를 듣고, 남자가 오늘 저녁에 축구를 보러 갈 수 없는 이유를 고르시오.

① 무료입장권을 잃어버려서
② 입장권을 예매하지 못해서
③ 도서관에서 공부를 해야 해서
④ 시간제 일자리 일을 해야 해서
⑤ 룸메이트 생일 파티에 참석해야 해서

08 대화를 듣고, 학교 설문 조사에 관해 언급되지 않은 것을 고르시오.

① 체육관 ② 교사 ③ 도서관
④ 화장실 ⑤ 역사

09 Wild Flower Tour에 관한 다음 내용을 듣고, 일치하지 않는 것을 고르시오. [3점]

① 투어 참가자는 오전 8시에 호텔을 떠난다.
② 투어 참가자는 약 100종의 야생화를 볼 수 있다.
③ 12세 어린이의 참가비는 40달러이다.
④ 점심과 물 한 병이 참가비에 포함되어 있다.
⑤ 참가 신청은 호텔 프런트 데스크에서 이루어진다.

10 다음 표를 보면서 대화를 듣고, 두 사람이 볼 영화를 고르시오.

Springfield Cinema

	Movie	Genre	Screen Time	Film Rate
①	Rush in Time	Action	09:30–11:30	7 or older
②	A Cat in the Wall	Horror	10:00–11:50	13 or older
③	Travel to the Past	Science Fiction	11:00–13:30	7 or older
④	Rainbow on the Hill	Drama	10:00–11:50	13 or older
⑤	Wildlife in Africa	Drama	10:30–12:30	7 or older

11 대화를 듣고, 여자의 마지막 말에 대한 남자의 응답으로 가장 적절한 것을 고르시오.

① Math is always too difficult for us.

② I've studied really hard for the test.

③ You should have studied math hard.

④ I'm not interested in math anymore.

⑤ It was because you are good at math.

12 대화를 듣고, 남자의 마지막 말에 대한 여자의 응답으로 가장 적절한 것을 고르시오.

① I worked late last night.

② I went through a red light.

③ I was caught in a traffic jam.

④ I reserved a ticket on the Internet.

⑤ I took the subway instead of a bus.

13 대화를 듣고, 여자의 마지막 말에 대한 남자의 응답으로 가장 적절한 것을 고르시오.

Man: _____

① Okay. Just let me know your address.

② Good choice! Your son will like the gray shirt.

③ Do you want to pay in cash or with a credit card?

④ Since you bought a blue shirt, you get a gray one free.

⑤ I'll have it ready when you come back tomorrow.

14 대화를 듣고, 남자의 마지막 말에 대한 여자의 응답으로 가장 적절한 것을 고르시오.

Woman: _____

① I'm sure you'll get better day by day.

② It's not your fault that you got infected.

③ That's why I told you to go see the movie.

④ You should go see an eye doctor right now.

⑤ Please avoid sharing items with anyone until you're cured.

15 다음 상황 설명을 듣고, Jenny가 Robert에게 할 말로 가장 적절한 것을 고르시오.

Jenny: _____

① I'll help you write the report.

② You can use my printer anytime.

③ Can you print out my report file?

④ Why don't you repair the printer?

⑤ When will you submit your report?

[16~17] 다음을 듣고, 물음에 답하시오.

16 여자가 하는 말의 주제로 가장 적절한 것은? [3점]

① desert animals that have a long lifespan

② the reason why camels can go without water

③ measuring the water intake of desert animals

④ animals that can go without water for a long time

⑤ how giraffes find leaves with high water content

17 언급된 동물이 <u>아닌</u> 것은?

① camels　　② giraffes　　③ Fennec foxes

④ lizards　　⑤ kangaroo rats

녹음 내용을 다시 들으면서 빈칸을 채워 넣으세요.

01

W People say the most important part of digital images is to show greener grass, a bluer sky, or a brighter sun than they see on earth. They may be right, but our approach is different. We _____ _____ _____, natural lines, and natural colors. From capture to connection to output, our digital technology shows you the world as you see it. In addition, the size is just right and you can comfortably keep it in your pocket. _____ _____ _____ _____, you don't have to be an expert to operate this camera. You only have to _____ _____ _____ _____ and you can store all of your memories easily.

02

M You look unhappy. What's the matter?

W I've been getting a lot of stress because of my studies.

M Well, how about laughing instead of making a face?

W Are you kidding? I don't feel like laughing at all.

M Just _____ _____ _____ _____ for one minute. According to a study, forced laughter helps improve your mood.

W Oh, really? I'm not sure it will work for me.

M In the study, most people _____ _____ _____ after just 60 seconds of forced laughter.

W I don't understand how that would work.

M Our body releases hormones that make us happy because it doesn't know the laughter is fake.

W You mean just laughing can _____ _____ _____?

M Yeah. It's worth trying.

W Okay. I'll give it a shot.

03

M Good morning. How can I help you?

W Yes, I'd like to start an exercise program.

M Wonderful. Let me ask you a few questions first. Are you _____ _____ _____?

W No, I'm not.

M Do you have any health conditions I should know about, such as shortness of breath or dizziness?

W No, I'm pretty healthy.

M Good. What is your goal in _____ _____ _____ _____? For example, are you trying to improve in a sport, such as tennis or golf?

W No, I'd just like to _____ _____ _____. What kind of exercise do you recommend?

M You should do some aerobics. We have aerobics classes on Tuesdays and Fridays.

W Great. I'd like to get started as soon as possible.

04

W Did you go to Michael's housewarming party?

M Yes. He moved to a new house with a large garden. I took a picture of the garden with my cellphone. Take a look.

W Wow! Michael has an outdoor table _____ _____ _____.

M Yeah. We had lunch there.

W The big tree next to the table has many leaves. It goes well with the garden.

M What do you think about the swing _____ _____ _____ the tree? Michael said he made it himself.

W It's great! And I like the pond in front of the tree.

M Me, too. There were many fish in the pond.

W _____ _____ _____ _____ the swing is for his two sons, right?

M Yeah. They like to play basketball.

05

W Hi, David. Where are you going now?

M I'm going to a costume rental shop for the Halloween party.

W What costume do you have in mind this year?

M I'll borrow a vampire costume. What about you, Sharon?

W I'm going to be a witch. I've been working on _____ _____ _____ _____.

M Wow! I didn't know you have talent for making clothes.

W I'm just trying. The problem is that I might not have enough time to make a witch's hat.

M Well, my little sister, Cindy, has a black one. If you want, I'll ask her _____ _____ _____ it to you.

W Oh, thank you. A black hat will _____ _____ _____ my costume.

M She's not going to wear it because she wants to be a princess this time.

W That's good. I'm sure she'll make a beautiful princess.

06

M Good afternoon. How can I help you?

W I'd like to buy some roses for my husband. Tomorrow is his 30th birthday.

M How many roses would you like to buy?

W I'd like 30 roses. What kinds of roses do you have?

M Take a look _____ _____ _____. We have red ones and yellow ones.

W How much are they?

M Red roses cost one dollar each, and yellow ones are _____ _____ _____ _____ dollars each.

W Then I'll take ten red ones and twenty yellow ones.

M Ten red ones and twenty yellow ones, right?

W Yes. Can you _____ _____ _____ _____ a ribbon wrapped around it?

M Sure, but it'll cost an extra three dollars. Will that be okay?

W Yes, that's fine.

07

W Hi, Peter. Where are you going?

M Hi, Alice. I'm going to the school library. I have a part-time job there.

W What time do you _____ _____ today?

M Four o'clock. Why?

W Listen, you know there is a soccer match between the LA Tigers and the Seattle Giants this evening, don't you?

M Yeah. The LA Tigers is my favorite soccer team.

W I have _____ _____ _____ for the match. Why don't you come to the game with me this evening?

M Oh, I'd love to go with you, but I can't. Today is my roommate's birthday, and there's _____ _____ _____ _____ _____ _____.

W That's too bad. Well, I'll have to ask another friend.

08

W What are you reading, James?

M I'm reading an article from our school newspaper.

W What is it about?

M It's about a survey that asked students to _____ _____ _____ provided by our school.

W Interesting! Tell me about the results.

M Eighty-five percent said our school gym was excellent and seventy-nine percent said we had good teachers.

W Was there anything the students were not satisfied with?

M Yes. Only twenty percent thought our school lunches were good, and twenty-five percent said the _____ _____ _____ _____ enough.

W I agree. I also think the restrooms are too dirty.

M Nevertheless, seventy-two percent of the students said they were proud of our school.

W That may be because our school has _____ _____ _____ than other schools.

● DICTATION

09

M Hi, everyone. Before you go back to your rooms, I'd like to tell you about the Wild Flower Tour the day after tomorrow. _____ _____ _____ _____ the hotel at 8 a.m. for Mount Green. There, they will experience beautiful nature and see about 100 beautiful wild flowers. The tour cost is $80 per person, and children under the age of 13 can _____, _____ _____ _____ _____.

Lunch and a bottle of water are included in the cost. If you want to join this tour, please _____ _____ _____ _____ at the tour office next to the hotel front desk by 8 p.m. this evening. That's all. I hope all of you have a relaxing evening.

10

M There are lots of movies to choose from, honey.

W Anything is okay for me _____ _____ the horror movie.

M What do you think of seeing an action movie then?

W You mean *Rush in Time*? It's nine forty now.

M Oh, I didn't know that. Then how about watching a science fiction movie?

W It must be exciting, but our children _____ _____ _____ _____ wait for over an hour to see the movie. What do you think of *Rainbow on the Hill*?

M Our daughter can't see the movie because she is _____ _____ _____ _____.

W I see. Then we have only one choice left.

M Okay. I think our children will also like it.

W Good. Let's watch that one.

11

W Tomorrow is _____ _____ _____ _____. Are you ready for it?

M Yes! I'm sure I'll get a good grade this time.

W Are you? What _____ _____ _____ _____?

M

12

M What's up, Rachel? You look irritated.

W Well, I _____ _____ _____ by the police on my way to work.

M _____ _____? What did you do?

W

13

M Good afternoon. How can I help you?

W Can I exchange this brown shirt for a larger one?

M Sure. Do you have the receipt?

W Here it is. I bought this shirt for my son last Sunday, but it's a little bit _____ _____ _____.

M I see. Let me check for a moment. *[Pause]* Uh-oh, I'm afraid the larger ones in the same color _____ _____ _____.

W Would you check if any of your other locations have the size I need?

M Wait a second. *[Typing Sound]* Well, the shop in Kingstown has the size.

W Kingstown? That's too far.

M If it's okay with you, we can _____ _____ _____ _____. It'll take three days.

W That would be great.

M ▒▒▒▒▒▒▒▒▒▒▒▒▒▒▒▒▒▒▒▒▒▒▒▒

14

W Okay, I've finished examining your eyes.

M Are my eyes infected?

W Yes, they are. But fortunately it's _____ _____ _____. Have you been to any crowded places recently?

M Well, I went to the movies a few days ago.

W You might have got infected there.

M Maybe, but I _____ _____ _____ before and after the show.

W I'll give you these eye drops. Put one or two drops into your eyes every two hours for the next three days.

M Okay. Is there anything else I should do?

W Well, it's important for you _____ _____ _____ _____ _____.

M Of course. _____ _____ _____ _____ then?

W ▒▒▒▒▒▒▒▒▒▒▒▒▒▒▒▒▒▒▒▒▒▒▒▒

15

M Jenny gets homework to write _____ _____ _____ _____ _____ _____ at geography class. Jenny goes to a study café with her classmate Robert and they write the report on their own notebook computers. About two hours later, they _____ _____ _____ and save the report files on their USB sticks. Now they only have to print out the files. But Jenny remembers that her printer is out of order. She wants Robert to _____ _____ _____ _____ _____.

In this situation, what would Jenny most likely say to Robert?

Jenny ▒▒▒▒▒▒▒▒▒▒▒▒▒▒▒▒▒▒▒▒▒▒▒▒

16~17

W Good morning, students. Yesterday, you learned about various plants living in the desert, remember? Let me start today's lesson by asking you a question. What animal do you think can _____ _____ _____ for a long time? Many of you probably guessed camels, and you are right. They can last for several weeks without water. But do you know there are other animals that can _____ _____ without water than camels? They are giraffes, Fennec foxes and kangaroo rats. A giraffe eats about 75 pounds of leaves and fruit a day. Thanks to the _____ _____ _____ in them, giraffes can go several months without drinking water. Kangaroo rats are even more amazing. They can go up to 3 to 5 years without taking a single sip of water. They _____ _____ _____ and they get enough water from them.

실전 모의고사 **03** 회

1번부터 17번까지는 듣고 답하는 문제입니다. 1번부터 15번까지는 한 번만 들려주고, 16번부터 17번까지는 두 번 들려줍니다. 방송을 잘 듣고 답을 하시기 바랍니다.

01 다음을 듣고, 여자가 하는 말의 목적으로 가장 적절한 것을 고르시오.

① 습득된 분실물을 안내하려고
② 불편 사항 신고를 요청하려고
③ 할인 판매 행사를 공지하려고
④ 어린이 놀이방 이용 방법을 설명하려고
⑤ 웹사이트 주소가 변경되었음을 알려 주려고

02 대화를 듣고, 남자의 의견으로 가장 적절한 것을 고르시오.

① 수돗물을 믿고 마셔도 된다.
② 생수 가격을 낮출 필요가 있다.
③ 플라스틱 병을 재활용해야 한다.
④ 수도 정화 시설을 현대화해야 한다.
⑤ 물을 마시는 것은 건강에 도움이 된다.

03 대화를 듣고, 두 사람의 관계를 가장 잘 나타낸 것을 고르시오.

① 극작가 – 배우
② 의사 – 코미디언
③ 사진작가 – 배우
④ 연출자 – 연기자
⑤ 매니저 – 코미디언

04 대화를 듣고, 그림에서 대화의 내용과 일치하지 <u>않는</u> 것을 고르시오.

05 대화를 듣고, 여자가 남자에게 부탁한 일로 가장 적절한 것을 고르시오.

① 추천서 쓰기
② 이력서 검토하기
③ 지원 연장 요청하기
④ 박물관 가는 길 알려 주기
⑤ 인턴 연수 프로그램 정보 제공하기

06 대화를 듣고, 남자가 지불할 금액을 고르시오. [3점]
① $17   ② $27   ③ $34   ④ $37   ⑤ $44

07 대화를 듣고, 여자가 Taste of Sun Restaurant에 지원하지 <u>않는</u> 이유를 고르시오.

① 일이 너무 힘들어서
② 시간당 임금이 적어서
③ 주말에 공부를 해야 해서
④ 집에서 먼 곳에 위치해서
⑤ 부모님이 허락하지 않아서

08 대화를 듣고, 아파트에 관해 두 사람이 언급하지 <u>않은</u> 것을 고르시오.

① 침실 개수   ② 건축 연도
③ 가구 비치 여부   ④ 커튼 유무 여부
⑤ 층수

09 Water Rocket Competition에 관한 다음 내용을 듣고, 일치하지 <u>않는</u> 것을 고르시오.

① 교내 축제 첫날에 개최될 것이다.
② 1, 2, 3학년생 모두가 참가할 수 있다.
③ 참가 신청은 온라인으로 이루어질 것이다.
④ 이번 주 월요일부터 참가 신청을 할 수 있다.
⑤ 1등은 새 태블릿 PC를 받는다.

10 다음 표를 보면서 대화를 듣고, 남자가 구입할 장난감을 고르시오.

Toys for Babies

	Toy	Recommended Age	Material
①	baby drum	over 1-year-old	plastic
②	baby drum	over 1-year-old	wood
③	color block	over 6-month-old	plastic
④	color block	over 6-month-old	wood
⑤	princess doll	over 6-month-old	cotton

11 대화를 듣고, 여자의 마지막 말에 대한 남자의 응답으로 가장 적절한 것을 고르시오.

① Sure! I'll work at the restaurant.

② Sorry. But I've already had lunch.

③ Do you? Okay, let's go there for lunch.

④ Really? Your spaghetti is always delicious.

⑤ Okay. Let me cook seafood spaghetti for you.

12 대화를 듣고, 남자의 마지막 말에 대한 여자의 응답으로 가장 적절한 것을 고르시오.

① Yes. I did it on my own.

② No, thanks. I don't feel good today.

③ Sure. I practice yoga every morning.

④ I'm really sorry. I couldn't make it in time.

⑤ Really? I'd also like to enjoy some live music.

13 대화를 듣고, 여자의 마지막 말에 대한 남자의 응답으로 가장 적절한 것을 고르시오.

Man: _____

① No. The interview was not that difficult.

② You should. I really hope you get the job.

③ Don't worry. I'll drive you to the company.

④ ACE Company? Do you want to work there?

⑤ Then, can you help me prepare for the interview?

14 대화를 듣고, 남자의 마지막 말에 대한 여자의 응답으로 가장 적절한 것을 고르시오. [3점]

Woman: _____

① I'm sorry. I don't know how to drive.

② Me too. I prefer the checkered patterns.

③ I know, but it's better to be safe than sorry.

④ I don't think so. I'm afraid you were overcharged.

⑤ That's a good idea. I want to learn how it works.

15 다음 상황 설명을 듣고, Charlie가 호텔의 접수 담당자에게 할 말로 가장 적절한 것을 고르시오.

Charlie: _____

① I lost the keys to my room.

② I'd like to stay for another night.

③ I need a wake-up call tomorrow morning.

④ I have an important meeting here tonight.

⑤ I'm afraid I left my wristwatch in the room.

[16~17] 다음을 듣고, 물음에 답하시오.

16 남자가 하는 말의 주제로 가장 적절한 것은?

① new usages of money

② various forms of money

③ the unfair distribution of wealth

④ the influence of money on society

⑤ the evolution of the world economy

17 언급된 것이 <u>아닌</u> 것은? [3점]

① rice   ② tobacco   ③ salt

④ corn   ⑤ seashell

녹음 내용을 다시 들으면서 빈칸을 채워 넣으세요.

01

W Good afternoon, everybody. Thank you for visiting Tailor's Mart. For better customer service, we've decided to _____ _____ _____ _____ _____. Please let us know if you have any problems or inconveniences at any of our facilities including the sales sections, the lost and found centers, and the playrooms for children. You can text us at 1400–777 or post a message on our website at www.TailorsMart.com starting this Sunday. We'll select the best 10 customers and give _____ _____ _____ _____ to each of them at the end of this month. We're looking forward to your _____ _____. Thank you.

02

W I'm thirsty, Jeff.

M I have some water. Here you go.

W Thanks. *[Pause]* Wow! It tastes really good. Where did you buy this water?

M I didn't buy it. It's tap water. I'm just reusing the bottle.

W You drink tap water? Is it safe?

M Our tap water _____ _____ _____, so it's clean enough to drink.

W Really? But I still don't feel like drinking tap water.

M Recently, I read a newspaper article that our city received an award for _____ _____ _____ _____.

W Did it? I didn't know that.

M The quality of our tap water is just as good as bottled water. You can _____ _____ it.

W I see. Thanks for letting me know.

03

W Good afternoon, Mr. Anderson. I really enjoyed your comedy show yesterday.

M Thank you for saying so.

W How do you feel today?

M I'm afraid I _____ _____ _____ _____.

W Are you still busy then?

M Yes. I feel like I spend all day in front of cameras trying to _____ _____ _____.

W I like your acting, but I want you to have enough rest.

M I try to, but it's easier said than done.

W I understand. Then, did you regularly _____ _____ _____ _____ _____?

M I couldn't. My busy schedule doesn't allow me to take it every eight hours.

W Oh, no! You should keep in mind that this is not a minor disease.

M I see.

04

[Cellphone rings.]

W Hey, Fred. Where are you now?

M I'm afraid I'll be a little bit late. Did you finish _____ _____ _____ _____?

W Yeah. We're almost done. We put the banner on the stage wall.

M You mean the banner that says "10TH ANNIVERSARY"?

W Yeah. We placed it in the middle of the wall. And we made a rainbow _____ _____ _____ _____.

M Good! Where did you put the chairs for the violinists?

W We put two chairs at the left side of the stage.

M Great! Where did you put the piano?

W We put it on the right side of the stage.

M How about microphones?

W We set up two microphones _____ _____ _____ _____ the stage.

M Thanks, Rachel.

05

W   Excuse me, Professor Smith. Can I come in?

M   Sure, Jane. What brings you here?

W   Well, I'm here to _____ _____ _____ _____.

M   Tell me about it, Jane.

W   I want to _____ _____ the internship program at the City Museum.

M   Good for you! It will give you precious experience. So, what do you want me to do?

W   In order to apply, a résumé, a transcript, and a letter of recommendation are required.

M   I see. Do you have everything ready?

W   I only have to prepare a recommendation letter. Would you _____ _____ _____ for me by next Friday?

M   Of course not. I'll have it ready no later than next Monday.

W   Thank you, sir.

06

M   Hi, I'd like to buy dog shampoo.

W   This way, please. How about this one made by Happy Pet? It's very _____ _____ _____ _____ _____ _____.

M   How much is it?

W   It's $20, and it's one of the most popular dog shampoos at the moment.

M   I think the bottle is a bit small. Do you have _____ _____ _____?

W   Sure! This big one is $10 more expensive, but there's twice as much shampoo as in the small one.

M   Okay. I'll buy this big one. I'd also like to _____ _____ _____.

W   I see. This one is also made by Happy Pet, and it's only $7 a tube.

M   Then can I buy two dog toothpaste?

W   So one big dog shampoo and _____ _____ _____ _____, right?

M   Yes. Here is my credit card.

07

M   Sera, I heard that you _____ _____ _____ _____ _____ _____.

W   Yeah, that's right. Working there was too demanding. I'm looking for a new part-time job.

M   Then why don't you apply to the Taste of Sun Restaurant?

W   The Taste of Sun Restaurant? It's located on Lincoln Street, isn't it?

M   Right. It's close to your house. What's better, _____ _____ _____ is $10.

W   Ten dollars? That'd be great! What are the working hours?

M   From 5 p.m. to 8 p.m. including weekends.

W   Including weekends? Well, I guess I won't apply there.

M   Why not? _____ _____ _____ _____ you to work part-time on weekends?

W   They do, but I have to _____ _____ _____.

M   Well, then you'll have to find another one.

08

[Telephone rings.]

W   Hello?

M   Hello. I'm calling about the apartment you're advertising.

W   Okay. What would you like to know?

M   Well, first I want to know _____ _____ _____ there are.

W   There are three bedrooms.

M   And _____ _____ _____ _____?

W   Yes. It has a refrigerator, an air conditioner, a new sofa and a set of reclining chairs in the living room.

M   What about curtains?

W   There are curtains on all the windows. They've just been dry cleaned.

M   I see. And does the apartment have a nice view?

W   Sure. It's _____ _____ _____ _____, so it has a fantastic view.

M   I see. Would it be possible for me to stop by around 7 p.m. this evening?

W   No problem.

09

M Hi, students. Let me tell you about our _____
_____ _____. The school science club will
hold a Water Rocket Competition on the first day
of the school festival. The competition is open to
first and second graders only. _____ _____
_____ _____ _____ on the science club
website, and the application period is from this
Monday until the end of this month. The first
prize winner will be given a brand-new tablet PC
_____ _____ _____ _____. I hope
many of you will participate in this contest.

10

W What are you doing on the computer, honey?

M I'm searching for a toy to give to Mary.

W Why don't you buy her a pretty doll?

M Girls don't have to _____ _____ _____
all the time.

W Oh, you're right. Then how about buying a baby
drum for her?

M Mary is just 8 months old. I think we have to buy
_____ _____ _____ for her age. What do
you think of this color block?

W That looks nice. Which material do you think is
okay for her?

M I think wood _____ _____ _____ plastic.
You know how she puts everything around her into
her mouth.

W Yeah, I know. Well, this _____ _____ _____
wood and appropriate for her age.

M Great. I'll buy it for her.

11

W Why don't _____ _____ _____ _____?
It's already 12 o'clock.

M Why not? Is there anything in particular you want to
eat for lunch?

W How about seafood spaghetti? I know _____
_____ _____ _____ behind our office.

M ▓▓▓▓▓▓▓▓▓▓▓▓▓▓▓▓▓▓▓▓▓▓▓▓▓▓▓▓▓▓▓

12

M You always _____ _____ and energetic, Mrs.
Brown.

W Thank you for saying so, Mr. Anderson.

M I really envy you. Can you tell me _____ _____?

W ▓▓▓▓▓▓▓▓▓▓▓▓▓▓▓▓▓▓▓▓▓▓▓▓▓▓▓▓▓▓▓

13

M Hi, Stella!

W Hi, David. How are you?

M _____ _____. By the way, you look very happy now.

W Do I? Actually, I got a text message from ACE Company that I _____ _____ _____ _____ _____.

M Really? Congratulations! When is the interview going to be held?

W Next Friday.

M And if you pass the interview, _____ _____ _____ by ACE Company, right?

W Yes. Oh, I'm already quite nervous.

M Don't worry. With your ability and experience, you'll do great at the interview.

W Thank you. Well, I have to start _____ _____ _____ _____ right away.

M

14

M Hey, Anna. Let's get in the car and start our trip.

W Wait a minute, Henry! Did you check the oil?

M No, I didn't.

W What about the tire pressure?

M Well, I didn't check that, either. Why do you ask?

W You have to _____ _____ _____ _____ the car before you drive a long distance.

M Don't worry. My car is as good as new. It's only two years old.

W I think we should _____ _____ _____ _____ _____ before we set out.

M Come on, honey. We don't have enough time to do that. If we don't leave now, we may _____ _____ _____ a traffic jam.

W But you should know safety is more important.

M It sounds like you don't trust me. I'm _____ _____ _____.

W

15

W Charlie _____ _____ New York on a business trip for two days because he has a couple of important meetings. On the day of his arrival, he participates in a meeting. The meeting ends late at night, and he stays at a nearby hotel. The next morning, he gets up early and checks out. While he is on his way to the next meeting, however, he realizes that he _____ _____ _____ in the hotel room. Fortunately, he has enough time to get it back. He _____ _____ _____ the desk clerk, and she asks how she can help him. In this situation, what would Charlie most likely say to the desk clerk?

Charlie

16~17

M Good afternoon, everyone. What comes to your mind when you think of money? Bills or coins? In fact, many objects _____ _____ _____ _____ money throughout history. In the early days of America, tobacco was used as money, but so many people grew tobacco that it became worthless as a means of exchange. Roman soldiers once received part of their pay _____ _____, which is the origin of our word *salary*, or payment for one's work. Early Egyptians used _____ _____ wheat and corn as money, while the native people on the island of Fiji used whale's teeth. Perhaps the _____ _____ _____ used as money was the seashell. Seashells were used in many parts of Africa, and American Indians had been using them as money before Columbus came to the continent.

실전 모의고사 **04** 회

1번부터 17번까지는 듣고 답하는 문제입니다. 1번부터 15번까지는 한 번만 들려주고, 16번부터 17번까지는 두 번 들려줍니다. 방송을 잘 듣고 답을 하시기 바랍니다.

01 다음을 듣고, 여자가 하는 말의 목적으로 가장 적절한 것을 고르시오.

① 화재 예방 방법을 설명하려고
② 소방 시설 점검을 촉구하려고
③ 주차장 확장 공사를 공지하려고
④ 비상 대피 훈련 실시를 안내하려고
⑤ 재난 복구 자원봉사자를 모집하려고

02 대화를 듣고, 두 사람이 하는 말의 주제로 가장 적절한 것을 고르시오.

① 자녀 양육의 어려움
② 아이들의 효과적인 학습 전략
③ 미술 성적을 올릴 수 있는 방법
④ 아이들을 위한 좋은 미술 수업 찾기
⑤ 미술 학습이 아이들에게 미치는 이점

03 대화를 듣고, 두 사람의 관계를 가장 잘 나타낸 것을 고르시오.

① 의사 – 환자
② 면접관 – 구직자
③ 전화 상담원 – 고객
④ 라디오 진행자 – 청취자
⑤ 경찰관 – 교통사고 목격자

04 대화를 듣고, 그림에서 대화의 내용과 일치하지 <u>않는</u> 것을 고르시오.

05 대화를 듣고, 남자가 할 일로 가장 적절한 것을 고르시오.

① 회의실 청소하기
② 마이크 설치하기
③ 프로젝터 연결하기
④ 발표 자료 출력하기
⑤ David에게 연락하기

06 대화를 듣고, 여자가 지불할 금액을 고르시오.

① $12   ② $13   ③ $14   ④ $15   ⑤ $16

07 대화를 듣고, 남자가 여자에게 전화를 건 이유를 고르시오.

① 장난감의 부품을 잃어버려서
② 장난감의 상태가 좋지 않아서
③ 장난감의 사용 방법을 몰라서
④ 장난감 대여를 연장하기 위해서
⑤ 장난감 반납 일자를 확인하기 위해서

08 대화를 듣고, giant armadillo에 관해 언급되지 <u>않은</u> 것을 고르시오. [3점]

① 서식지   ② 생김새   ③ 먹이
④ 수명   ⑤ 천적 종류

09 5th Wilson High School Hiking Day에 관한 다음 내용을 듣고, 일치하지 <u>않는</u> 것을 고르시오. [3점]

① Hanes 국립 공원의 북쪽 입구에서 출발한다.
② 도보 여행은 약 세 시간이 걸린다.
③ 휴식 지역에서 간식과 음료수가 제공된다.
④ 남쪽 입구에서 학급별 단체 사진을 찍을 기회가 주어진다.
⑤ 버스는 오후 12시 30분에 학생들을 태울 것이다.

10 다음 표를 보면서 대화를 듣고, 두 사람이 고용하기로 결정한 사람을 고르시오.

Job Applicants

	Name	Age	Years of Experience	A Command of Foreign Language
①	Paul Wilson	45	15 years	Spanish
②	Joe Anderson	62	26 years	French
③	Frank Simpson	29	none	French, Spanish
④	James Smith	37	6 years	none
⑤	Kurt Gordon	43	12 years	French

11 대화를 듣고, 여자의 마지막 말에 대한 남자의 응답으로 가장 적절한 것을 고르시오.

① I'm sorry. I forgot to order a pizza.

② Thanks a lot. You're a really good chef.

③ No problem. You can eat the leftover pizza.

④ That's right. You shouldn't have ordered pizza.

⑤ Really? Then let me cook something for you now.

12 대화를 듣고, 남자의 마지막 말에 대한 여자의 응답으로 가장 적절한 것을 고르시오.

① I have a slight fever today.

② Summer is my favorite season.

③ Let me check the weather forecast.

④ We also had too much rain last year.

⑤ I'm afraid I can't make it there in time.

13 대화를 듣고, 여자의 마지막 말에 대한 남자의 응답으로 가장 적절한 것을 고르시오.

Man: _____

① Good idea. Let's fly to Korea next month.

② Right. You're sure to be a good tour guide.

③ As you said, traveling always makes us happy.

④ Sorry. I can't go to the language school with you.

⑤ Sure! I'm looking forward to my new life in Korea.

14 대화를 듣고, 남자의 마지막 말에 대한 여자의 응답으로 가장 적절한 것을 고르시오. [3점]

Woman: _____

① No way. The doctor said you need more rest.

② Don't be late. The party begins at seven o'clock.

③ Okay. I'll drop by the hospital on my way to the party.

④ I'm sorry. I'm afraid I can't make it to your birthday party.

⑤ No problem. I can take you to the hospital tomorrow morning.

15 다음 상황 설명을 듣고, Susan이 관리자에게 할 말로 가장 적절한 것을 고르시오.

Susan: _____

① Can I have another bottle of water?

② I can't get my change from the machine.

③ Do you have change for a one-dollar bill?

④ I'd like to get a refund on this bottle of water.

⑤ Can you tell me where a vending machine is?

[16~17] 다음을 듣고, 물음에 답하시오.

16 여자가 하는 말의 주제로 가장 적절한 것은?

① ways of adjusting to school life

② how to choose a club for freshmen

③ advantages of joining a club at school

④ difficulties of promoting a club to freshmen

⑤ differences between high school life and middle school life

17 언급된 동아리가 아닌 것은?

① classic guitar   ② computer   ③ magic

④ math   ⑤ science

01

W Attention, please. A disaster can happen anywhere and at any moment. That's why it is very important to know how to respond in disaster situations. As part of our office safety program, an emergency _____ _____ _____ _____ _____ in our company building on June 21st at 2 p.m. When the fire alarm sounds, all the workers will have to _____ _____ _____ and move promptly to the outdoor parking lot. You must not use the elevators. The entire exercise will not _____ _____ _____ 30 minutes. We're sorry to cause any inconveniences, but the safety is most important. Thank you.

02

M What are you looking at on the Internet, honey?

W I'm looking at some art lessons for our children.

M Are you going to sign Lucy up for one of them?

W Yeah. She's interested in fine art these days.

M Good. I heard children can _____ _____ _____ through art.

W Right. This website says it helps children develop basic skills like reasoning, making decisions, and solving problems.

M One of my friends said his son _____ _____ _____ _____ after taking art lessons.

W I also heard that learning fine art can increase a child's _____ _____.

M You mean it is also helpful for schoolwork?

W Yeah. According to a study, students who participated in art lessons got higher test scores in other subjects.

03

M Hello. Could you introduce yourself?

W Sure. My name is Helen, and I'm from San Francisco.

M It's nice to talk to you, Helen. What do you do for a living?

W I'm a web designer.

M Good. What would you like to request?

W "My Heart Will Go On" by Celine Dion.

M Okay. Who do you want to _____ _____ _____ _____?

W My friend, Eric Baker. He is in the hospital. He was injured in an accident.

M Oh, I hope he'll get better soon. _____ _____ _____ _____ _____ to tell him.

W Yeah. I want to tell him that my heart will go on forever.

M Wow, that's the name of the song you requested. I'll _____ _____ _____ for you. Thanks for calling.

04

M What are you doing on the computer, honey?

W I'm getting some ideas about bathroom decorations from a website.

M Let me see. *[Pause]* Well, I like the three round lights.

W What do you think of the _____ _____?

M I think our children will like it. And the toothbrush holder _____ _____ _____ is practical, isn't it?

W Yeah. It saves space because it is attached to the wall.

M The shelf in the left corner is also a good idea.

W Right. We can put shampoo bottles on it. What do you think of the toilet seat?

M It doesn't _____ _____ _____ _____ it. Why don't we buy one with flowers?

W That sounds good.

05

[Cellphone rings.]

W Hey, Jake. Where are you now?

M I'm on my way. I'll be there in fifteen minutes.

W Oh, no! We've got only thirty minutes before the presentation.

M That's why I called you. Can you _____ _____ _____ _____ in the conference room?

W I already did. What about the presentation files? Don't you need to _____ _____ _____?

M I'll _____ _____ _____ it as soon as I get there.

W Ah, there's one more thing! How about the microphones?

M Don't worry. I asked David to set them up.

W Good. Is there anything else I can help you with?

M Well, if you've got time, go to the conference room and help David, please.

W No problem.

06

M Cookies! Homemade cookies are on sale now!

W Excuse me. I'd like to buy some cookies for my son's birthday.

M Great! We have several kinds of cookies. _____ _____ _____ _____ before you make a choice.

W He likes chocolate chip cookies and almond cookies.

M Those are many children's favorites, too. Chocolate chip cookies are one dollar and almond cookies are _____ _____ _____.

W I'll take five chocolate chip cookies and four almond cookies, please.

M Five chocolate chip cookies and four almond cookies, right?

W Yes. And can you _____ _____?

M No problem, ma'am. But it'll _____ _____ _____ _____ dollars.

W Okay. I'll take them wrapped, please.

M Thank you. Wait a minute, please.

07

[Telephone rings.]

W This is Teddy's Toy Library. How can I help you?

M Hi. I _____ _____ _____ _____ for my son yesterday, but I have a problem with one of them.

W May I have your name, please?

M It's John Hamilton.

W Let me see. *[Typing Sound]* You checked out a toy car and a set of blocks, right?

M Yeah, but I'm afraid one wheel _____ _____ from the car.

W You mean you lost it?

M I'm afraid so. My son _____ _____ _____ _____ somewhere. I'm wondering what I should do about that.

W You only have to pay the cost of the part when you return the toys.

M I see. The toys are due next Tuesday, right?

W That's right.

08

M Laura, come here and look at these animals.

W Oh, they look weird, Dad. I've never seen them before.

M They're giant armadillos. They live in South America.

W They look like they're _____ _____ over their necks and backs.

M Yeah. And they _____ _____ _____ on their forefeet.

W Wow, the claws look powerful.

M They use them to dig burrows. And they also dig to find food or to escape from predators.

W What do they _____ _____?

M They prefer termites as prey, and they _____ _____ _____ _____ for 12 to 15 years.

W I see. Why don't we take some pictures? I want to show them to my friends.

M Okay.

09

M Good morning, students. I'm very happy to announce that the 5th Wilson High School Hiking Day will start soon. We are at the northern entrance of Hanes National Park. Our hike will start here at 9 a.m. and it should _____ _____ _____ _____. We'll provide snacks and soft drinks for each of you at the rest area. And you will be given a chance to _____ _____ _____ for each class at the rest area. The school buses will _____ _____ _____ at 12:30 p.m. at the southern entrance. So be sure to arrive at the southern entrance before then. If you have any questions, ask your homeroom teacher.

10

W How many people applied for the security guard's job?

M There are five applicants. We have to choose one of them.

W Let me see. This applicant is the youngest, but he _____ _____ _____.

M You're right. We need a security guard with at least five years of experience.

W What do you think of Paul Wilson? He has fifteen years of experience.

M I'm afraid he _____ _____ _____. You know we have many visitors from France.

W Oh, right. Then, what do you think of this person? He has the most experience.

M Don't you think he is _____ _____ _____ be a security guard?

W I guess so. Well, this applicant satisfies all the qualifications, right?

M Yeah. Let's hire him.

11

W Dad, I _____ _____ _____ _____. Is there anything to eat?

M Check in the refrigerator. There should be some leftover pizza.

W _____ _____? I already ate that in the afternoon.

M ▓▓▓▓▓▓▓▓▓▓▓▓▓▓▓▓▓▓▓▓▓▓▓▓▓▓▓▓▓▓

12

M It _____ _____ _____ day by day, isn't it?

W You're right. Summer is coming. Do you like summer?

M No. I don't like it because I _____ _____ _____. What about you?

W ▓▓▓▓▓▓▓▓▓▓▓▓▓▓▓▓▓▓▓▓▓▓▓▓▓▓▓▓▓▓

13

W Patrick, I heard that you'll go to Korea next year.

M Right. I have a plan to quit working here and start a new life in Korea.

W Wow, great! So what _____ _____ _____ _____ _____ _____ in Korea?

M A tour guide.

W Really? Since you're outgoing, working as a tour guide will be suitable for you.

M Absolutely! I'll be a good tour guide and _____ _____ _____ _____ _____ in Korea.

W How about Korean? Won't you need Korean skills to work in Korea?

M Don't worry. _____ _____ _____ _____ at a language school for a few months.

W Have you? I think you are preparing well to be a tour guide.

M ▨▨▨▨▨▨▨▨▨▨▨▨▨▨▨▨▨▨▨▨▨▨▨▨

14

[Cellphone rings.]

W Hi, Raymond. What's up?

M Oh, Julia. Can you do me a favor?

W Sure. What is it?

M I'm afraid I can't make it to Jane's birthday party tomorrow. Can you _____ _____ _____ _____ her?

W Of course I can. But do you have any other problems?

M Well, actually, I'm in the hospital. I _____ _____ _____ _____ a couple of days ago.

W Oh, my.... What happened?

M I was hit by a bicycle and fell to the ground. The doctor said I have to _____ _____ _____ _____ for a week.

W Oh, that's too bad. What hospital are you in?

M I'm in Smith County Hospital on Franklin Avenue.

W ▨▨▨▨▨▨▨▨▨▨▨▨▨▨▨▨▨▨▨▨▨▨▨▨

15

M Susan is a high school student. She is studying in the library to prepare for a midterm exam. While she is studying, she feels thirsty so she goes out and _____ _____ _____ _____ in the lobby. She _____ _____ _____ _____ into the machine for a bottle of water, which costs 70 cents. She gets the water and she waits for the _____ _____ _____ _____. But nothing happens. She finds the phone number of the manager on the left side of the machine and calls him. The manager answers and asks her what the problem is. In this situation, what would Susan most likely say to the manager?

Susan ▨▨▨▨▨▨▨▨▨▨▨▨▨▨▨▨▨▨▨

16~17

W Hello, freshmen. I am Stella Brown, principal of Green High School. How was your first day of high school? I hope all of you will quickly _____ _____ _____ _____ _____. To do that, I recommend you join a school club. _____ _____ _____ _____ will offer many benefits. First, you can meet seniors and make new friends. Take the classic guitar club for example. The club has many senior members, and they will help you _____ _____ _____ _____ _____ _____. Second, you can improve your knowledge of the field you're interested in. If you _____ _____ _____ _____, join the computer club. Finally, joining some clubs can actually help you pass the college entrance exam. If you _____ _____ _____ _____ _____ _____, you will soon understand how helpful it can be.

● 실전 모의고사 **05** 회

1번부터 17번까지는 듣고 답하는 문제입니다. 1번부터 15번까지는 한 번만 들려주고, 16번부터 17번까지는 두 번 들려줍니다. 방송을 잘 듣고 답을 하시기 바랍니다.

01 다음을 듣고, 남자가 하는 말의 목적으로 가장 적절한 것을 고르시오.

① 육아용품을 홍보하려고
② 음악의 중요성을 강조하려고
③ 유아 교육 방법을 설명하려고
④ 상품 환불 방법을 알려 주려고
⑤ 소음 공해의 실태를 고발하려고

02 대화를 듣고, 여자의 의견으로 가장 적절한 것을 고르시오.

① 수업 중에 노트북 사용을 자제해야 한다.
② 컴퓨터 소음을 줄일 수 있는 기술이 필요하다.
③ 학교에서 인터넷 연결이 원활할 수 있도록 해야 한다.
④ 정기적인 업데이트를 통해 컴퓨터의 성능을 유지해야 한다.
⑤ 수업 내용을 잘 기억하기 위해서 손으로 필기하는 것이 좋다.

03 대화를 듣고, 두 사람의 관계를 가장 잘 나타낸 것을 고르시오.

① 화가 – 모델
② 배우 – 분장사
③ 관람객 – 사진작가
④ 극작가 – 연출가
⑤ 면접관 – 자원봉사 지원자

04 대화를 듣고, 그림에서 대화의 내용과 일치하지 <u>않는</u> 것을 고르시오.

05 대화를 듣고, 남자가 여자를 위해 할 일로 가장 적절한 것을 고르시오.

① 과일 씻기
② 주스 사 오기
③ 저녁 준비하기
④ 약국에 다녀오기
⑤ 병원 진료 예약하기

06 대화를 듣고, 여자가 지불할 금액을 고르시오. [3점]

① $135
② $150
③ $165
④ $180
⑤ $195

07 대화를 듣고, 남자가 수영 캠프에 참가할 수 <u>없는</u> 이유를 고르시오.

① 서핑을 배워야 해서
② 시간제 일을 해야 해서
③ 삼촌을 도와드려야 해서
④ 하와이를 여행해야 해서
⑤ 기말고사 공부를 해야 해서

08 대화를 듣고, 남자에 관한 내용으로 언급되지 <u>않은</u> 것을 고르시오.

① 경력
② 자원봉사
③ 지원 동기
④ 자격증
⑤ 사는 곳

09 Komodo dragon에 관한 다음 내용을 듣고, 일치하지 <u>않는</u> 것을 고르시오. [3점]

① 세계에서 가장 큰 도마뱀이다.
② 날카로운 발톱을 가지고 있다.
③ 몸이 비늘로 덮여 있다.
④ 1년에 20번에서 30번 정도 알을 낳는다.
⑤ 새끼는 30인치만큼 자라면 나무에서 내려온다.

10 다음 표를 보면서 대화를 듣고, 두 사람이 구입할 자동차를 고르시오.

Used Cars

	Model	Color	Mileage (miles)	Transmission	Price
①	A	White	120,000	Automatic	$4,000
②	B	Green	70,000	Automatic	$5,000
③	C	White	88,000	Automatic	$7,000
④	D	Green	65,000	Manual	$6,500
⑤	E	Black	80,000	Automatic	$7,500

11 대화를 듣고, 여자의 마지막 말에 대한 남자의 응답으로 가장 적절한 것을 고르시오.

① No, I don't want to buy the black bike.

② Sure. You can ride my bike anytime you want.

③ Thanks to you, I could learn how to ride a bike.

④ Don't worry. I'll lend you money to fix the bike.

⑤ Okay. Then you will be able to ride your bike home.

12 대화를 듣고, 남자의 마지막 말에 대한 여자의 응답으로 가장 적절한 것을 고르시오.

① No. I don't feel good, either.

② Sure. She thinks the price is reasonable.

③ Yes. It's a good idea to have some fresh fruit.

④ Of course. I'm looking forward to meeting her, too.

⑤ Yeah. She's worked overtime for three days in a row.

13 대화를 듣고, 여자의 마지막 말에 대한 남자의 응답으로 가장 적절한 것을 고르시오.

Man: _____

① Well, I'm not interested in chemistry anymore.

② Okay. Let's study both chemistry and biology.

③ Right. You have to go to Patricia Jackson's office.

④ Take chemistry, and you won't have any regrets.

⑤ Me too. Biology is easier to study than chemistry.

14 대화를 듣고, 남자의 마지막 말에 대한 여자의 응답으로 가장 적절한 것을 고르시오. [3점]

Woman: _____

① Why don't you apply for the company once again?

② I'm sorry to say that you are not qualified for the job.

③ How about making a contract with the company?

④ I'm sure you can do whatever the company asks you to do.

⑤ I know a very competent lawyer. Let's contact him right away.

15 다음 상황 설명을 듣고, Michael이 어머니에게 할 말로 가장 적절한 것을 고르시오.

Michael: _____

① I'm sorry. I already have plans today.

② Sounds great. I want to play computer games.

③ Do you really think so? I don't agree with you.

④ No, thank you. I prefer playing with a toy robot.

⑤ I'm sure I can go without computer games for a while.

[16~17] 다음을 듣고, 물음에 답하시오.

16 여자가 하는 말의 주제로 가장 적절한 것은?

① body gestures as a language

② body gestures in different cultures

③ how to express feelings effectively

④ the definition of good communication

⑤ difficulties of understanding body gestures

17 언급된 신체 부위가 아닌 것은?

① head   ② arm   ③ leg

④ shoulder   ⑤ nose

● DICTATION

녹음 내용을 다시 들으면서 빈칸을 채워 넣으세요.

01

M Are you tired from taking care of your baby? Don't worry about it anymore! Modern electronics are here to help you. This new _____ _____ _____ when it hears a baby crying. The secret is the sensor hidden in the cradle. _____ _____ the voice-recognition technology, this sensor does not respond to everyday noises, but only recognizes the sound of a baby crying. In addition, the cradle can record your voice and replay it while it's rocking. At the same time, it can also play music babies feel comfortable with. Call us now for _____ _____ _____ _____. For more information, visit our website at www.autocradle.co.uk.

02

M What's wrong, Stella? You look upset.

W I couldn't concentrate on the lecture because of some noisy students.

M Really? Were they chatting during the lecture?

W No. The problem was the _____ _____ _____ _____ on their laptop.

M Were the sounds really that loud?

W They were loud enough to disturb other students.

M But they were probably searching for information they didn't understand, weren't they?

W You know what? Some students were just surfing the Internet for fun.

M Oh, that's not good.

W In addition, most of them rarely made eye contact with the professor. They just looked at their computer screens.

M There seems to be many _____ _____ _____ _____ laptops during the class.

W You can say that again! Our professor should _____ _____ _____ _____ laptops in class.

03

W Excuse me. Aren't you Richard Taylor?

M Yes, I am.

W I'm a big fan of your work, Mr. Taylor. I've always wanted to meet you.

M Thank you. It's always a pleasure to see people who _____ _____ _____.

W The pictures at _____ _____ are amazing. I think they're your best yet.

M I'm glad you like them. I paid close attention to facial expressions of the Africans this time.

W In what area of Africa did you _____ _____ _____?

M I took this picture in Liberia, West Africa. I still cannot forget the pale black eyes of this boy.

W When I paid the admission price, I was told that you _____ _____ _____ _____ African aid groups.

M Yes. I want to raise people's consciousness on Africa through my work.

W I'm really happy to contribute to the donation.

M Thank you very much. I hope you have a good time here.

04

W What's this picture, Minjun?

M That was taken at my son's first birthday party.

W Wow! This little child _____ _____ _____ must be your son, right?

M Yeah. He is so cute, isn't he?

W He is adorable. And you also look great _____ _____ _____ _____.

M Thank you. I wore a necktie like my son.

W Is this your wife lifting the teddy bear _____ _____ _____?

M Yes, that's her. And the girl _____ _____ _____ is Hana, my first daughter.

W She is so pretty. She has grown so much since I saw her last time.

M You know what? The cake on the table was made by my wife.

W Wow! She did a great job!

05

M Mom, I'm home. Uh-oh, what's wrong with you?

W I think I _____ _____ _____.

M Why don't you go see a doctor?

W Today is Sunday and all the hospitals are closed around our neighborhood.

M Then I'll go get some medicine. The pharmacy on May Street is open on Sundays.

W I've already _____ _____ _____, but I don't feel any better.

M I heard vitamin C is good for a cold.

W Well, can you go and buy some juice? I'm _____ _____ _____ _____.

M I think fresh fruit would be better than juice.

W I feel like eating grapes, but they are out of season now.

M Then I'll go _____ _____ _____ _____ grape juice. I'll be back in a minute.

W Thanks, James.

06

M Hello. How may I help you?

W I'd like to rent a compact car _____ _____ _____.

M We have a blue one and a gray one available now. They're both the latest model.

W Great. I'll take the blue one. How much is the rental fee?

M It's fifty dollars a day, but if you join our membership program, you can _____ _____ _____ _____.

W Good. Then I'd like to become a member.

M Fill out this form, please. And I strongly recommend you _____ _____ _____ just in case. It's ten dollars per day.

W All right. I'll buy it. Oh, I need a GPS navigation system, too.

M No problem. The fee for that is five dollars a day.

W Okay. Here is my credit card.

M Thanks.

07

W Oh, at last the final exams are over!

M Right. Now we can enjoy summer vacation from next week.

W Great! By the way, will you _____ _____ _____ _____ _____ _____ during the vacation?

M I'd love to, but I can't.

W Why not? Because of your part-time job?

M No. I'll go to Hawaii during the camp.

W Ah, your uncle is in Hawaii, _____ _____ _____. You went there to help him on the winter vacation, didn't you?

M Right. But this time I'm not going to help him. I'm going to _____ _____ _____ _____.

W Learn to surf? Sounds exciting.

M Yes! I'm really looking forward to my vacation in Hawaii.

08

W Well, Mr. Lee. I see from your résumé that you had a lot of experience working in a shoe store.

M Yes. My father _____ _____ _____ _____, and I helped him there after school.

W What kind of _____ _____ have you done?

M I taught basketball at Wellington Orphanage.

W I see. Can I ask why you are thinking of _____ _____ _____ _____?

M Well, I like counseling, but I miss sports. This job would give me a chance to do both of them.

W So you think you're ready to live in Chicago?

M Sure. _____ _____ _____ _____ Columbus, but I've always wanted to live in a big city.

W Okay. I'll let you know the results in a few days or so.

M Thank you.

09

M Good morning, everyone. Have you ever heard of Komodo dragons? Look at this picture. They are the largest lizard in the world. As you see in this picture, they have powerful legs, _____ _____, and a long tail. Round, brownish-black _____ _____ _____ _____, and their mouth has sharp teeth. Komodo dragons use their tongue to pick up chemical signals to locate injured prey. They lay around 20 to 30 eggs _____ _____ _____. To avoid predators, the young spend much of their first few years in trees, but move to the ground once _____ _____ _____ _____ in total length.

10

W What are you looking at on the computer, honey?

M I'm searching for a used car.

W Have you found any good ones?

M There are five that caught my attention. What color do you like?

W Well, any color is okay _____ _____.

M Then how about this white one?

W Uh-oh, look at the mileage. It's _____ _____ one hundred thousand miles. That's a bad sign.

M Then I bet you'll like this green one. The mileage is the lowest among these five cars.

W Honey, have you forgotten that I can't drive cars _____ _____ _____?

M Oh, I'm sorry. Then what do you think of this other white one?

W Well, I'm _____ _____ _____ the price. I prefer this green one. I think its price is reasonable.

M That's good. Let's contact the dealer right now.

11

W Hi. I've _____ _____ _____ _____. Can you fix it?

M Sure, but it'll take about 30 minutes. I have two bicycles to fix ahead of yours.

W No problem. _____ _____ _____ _____ with you and be back in 30 minutes.

M

12

M Hey, Mary. Look at Jane standing over there. She _____ _____ _____, doesn't she?

W Well, it's _____ _____ that she looks exhausted.

M Do you know the reason?

W

13

M Sarah, have you decided ________ ________ ________ ________ between chemistry and biology next semester?

W Not yet. What about you, John?

M I'll take the chemistry course. Why don't you take it with me?

W But don't you think chemistry is ________ ________ ________ ________?

M Not at all. Once you understand the basic concepts of chemistry, it'll be much easier to study than biology.

W Really? Who's ________ ________ ________?

M Patricia Jackson. Every student says she's one of the best science teachers in our school.

W That's right. ________ ________ ________, too.

M ______________________________

14

W Hey, Stuart. You don't look very good. What's wrong with you?

M Well, I ________ ________ ________ my job last week. That's why I'm in such a bad mood.

W I can't believe that. Why did they dismiss you?

M They said I wasn't ________ ________ ________ ________.

W That's not true. I remember you won the top employee prize last year.

M That's right. I think my age is the real reason they fired me.

W They can't do that. It's totally unfair. I think you should ________ ________ ________ ________ the company.

M Do you really think I can win?

W Of course. Age discrimination is definitely ________ ________ ________.

M I see. Then what should I do?

W ______________________________

15

W Michael is an elementary school student. He likes to play computer games. His mother is very concerned about him because he is ________ ________ ________ computer games that he doesn't go outside to play with his friends. One day, Michael's mother gets a good idea. She decides to ________ ________ ________ not playing computer games. She knows he also likes toy robots, so she tells him that if he doesn't play computer games for a week, she will buy him a toy robot. Michael ________ ________ ________ ________ and is excited about it. In this situation, what would Michael most likely say to his mother?

Michael ______________________________

16 ~ 17

W Hello, everyone. It's nice to meet you again. Last week, I talked about how to communicate effectively to express feelings. Today I'd like to talk about ________ ________ ________ ________. Do you think communication is done only in language? I'm sure all of you don't think so. Your gestures can also ________ ________ ________ ________ to the other as language. If you don't like an opinion, you will move your head sideways. ________ ________ ________ also means you're not satisfied with something. If you've done something you're proud of, you can ________ ________ ________. Do you want to know if someone is lying? Make sure that person touches his nose. Many people ________ ________ ________ ________ ________. Now watch the television in front. I'm going to show you a movie clip of various body languages from all over the world.

1번부터 17번까지는 듣고 답하는 문제입니다. 1번부터 15번까지는 한 번만 들려주고, 16번부터 17번까지는 두 번 들려줍니다. 방송을 잘 듣고 답을 하시기 바랍니다.

01 다음을 듣고, 여자가 하는 말의 목적으로 가장 적절한 것을 고르시오.
① 체형에 맞는 운동 종목을 추천해 주려고
② 운동을 중도에 포기하지 않도록 조언하려고
③ 체육관 벽에 거울이 있는 이유를 설명하려고
④ 운동 중에 거울을 보지 않도록 주의를 주려고
⑤ 운동 전후에 하는 스트레칭의 중요성을 강조하려고

02 대화를 듣고, 두 사람이 하는 말의 주제로 가장 적절한 것을 고르시오. [3점]
① 1인 가구의 생활 수준
② 1인 가구의 소비 행태
③ 1인 가구가 증가하는 이유
④ 1인 가구를 위한 사회 정책
⑤ 1인 가구를 겨냥한 마케팅 전략

03 대화를 듣고, 두 사람의 관계를 가장 잘 나타낸 것을 고르시오.
① 우체국 직원 – 고객
② 배달원 – 물품 수령인
③ 웨딩 플래너 – 예비 신부
④ 예식장 직원 – 결혼식 하객
⑤ 신용카드 회사 직원 – 신용카드 신청인

04 대화를 듣고, 그림에서 대화의 내용과 일치하지 <u>않는</u> 것을 고르시오.

05 대화를 듣고, 남자가 할 일로 가장 적절한 것을 고르시오.
① 청소 검사하기
② 교실 청소하기
③ 쓰레기통 비우기
④ 감사의 말 전하기
⑤ 급우에게 전화하기

06 대화를 듣고, 여자가 지불할 금액을 고르시오. [3점]
① $20   ② $50   ③ $80   ④ $90   ⑤ $100

07 대화를 듣고, 남자가 내일 오전에 휴가를 내려고 하는 이유를 고르시오.
① 심한 감기를 앓고 있어서
② 어머니를 보살펴 드려야 해서
③ 정기 건강 검진을 받아야 해서
④ 야근 업무에 피로가 누적되어서
⑤ 수술로 인한 회복 시간이 필요해서

08 대화를 듣고, 마술 쇼에 관해 언급되지 <u>않은</u> 것을 고르시오.
① 장소
② 참가 마술사 수
③ 입장료
④ 공연 시작일
⑤ 공연 시간

09 Short Marathon에 관한 다음 내용을 듣고, 일치하지 <u>않는</u> 것을 고르시오.
① 목적은 개교 30주년을 축하하는 것이다.
② 학년에 관계없이 모든 학생이 참가할 수 있다.
③ 세 개의 달리기 코스로 이루어져 있다.
④ 참가 신청서 작성은 학교 웹사이트에서 이루어진다.
⑤ 모든 참가자가 기념품과 메달을 받는다.

10 다음 표를 보면서 대화를 듣고, 남자가 결혼식장으로 갈 방법을 고르시오. [3점]

Ways to Holland Wedding Hall

	Transportation	Time	Fare (per person)	Number of Transfer
①	Car	About 180 mins	$10	0
②	Subway	About 120 mins	$3.0	0
③	Direct Bus	About 70 mins	$7.0	0
④	Bus & Subway	About 80 mins	$4.0	2
⑤	Bus & Subway	About 90 mins	$4.0	1

11 대화를 듣고, 여자의 마지막 말에 대한 남자의 응답으로 가장 적절한 것을 고르시오.

① Don't worry. I'll find a good hotel.

② No, the hotel didn't open yesterday.

③ Don't go to the beach. It's still cold.

④ I like it. Let's book the hotel right now.

⑤ Sure! You'll enjoy the trip to Jeju Island.

12 대화를 듣고, 남자의 마지막 말에 대한 여자의 응답으로 가장 적절한 것을 고르시오.

① You can get on any ride you want.

② Children under six can't ride this one.

③ It's less crowded early in the morning.

④ Some cost two tickets, and others cost one.

⑤ Roller coasters are most popular among teens.

13 대화를 듣고, 여자의 마지막 말에 대한 남자의 응답으로 가장 적절한 것을 고르시오.

Man: _____

① I'm not good at reading maps.

② He's been absent for a week now.

③ Don't worry. You're being so sensitive.

④ Why not? I'll meet you here after school.

⑤ He lives with his mom and grandparents.

14 대화를 듣고, 남자의 마지막 말에 대한 여자의 응답으로 가장 적절한 것을 고르시오.

Woman: _____

① Sorry. It's hard to find a seafood restaurant.

② Good. Let's go to the cooking class with her.

③ Okay. I'll clean the fridge after watching the movie.

④ Sure! My grandmother really enjoyed your spaghetti.

⑤ Don't worry. Let me go buy some seafood right now.

15 다음 상황 설명을 듣고, Fred가 손님에게 할 말로 가장 적절한 것을 고르시오.

Fred: _____

① It's not your fault. Don't worry about it.

② You're here again. I'm happy to see you.

③ I forgot to give you the change yesterday. Here it is.

④ Stay in line and wait for your turn. It won't be long.

⑤ You left your purse here. Try to be more careful.

[16~17] 다음을 듣고, 물음에 답하시오.

16 남자가 하는 말의 주제로 가장 적절한 것은?

① a series of eye-catching world news

② reasons why television news is popular

③ the world's most popular sporting events

④ influences of advertisements on viewing rates

⑤ the popularity of sports in the world of advertising

17 언급된 광고가 아닌 것은?

① television   ② billboard   ③ slogan

④ uniform   ⑤ sponsorship

● DICTATION

녹음 내용을 다시 들으면서 빈칸을 채워 넣으세요.

01

W Hello, exercise lovers. As you've probably noticed, almost all gyms have mirrors of various sizes on the walls. Those mirrors help make the gym look bigger. But be careful! Mirrors can be one of the main reasons why you decide to _____ _____ _____ the gym. You may not believe it, but it's true. If you look at your reflection during a workout, you feel more tired and _____ _____. It's because you are likely to have negative thoughts about yourself by _____ _____ _____ _____. So don't look at yourself in the mirror when you work out.

02

W Ross, have you decided on the topic for your social studies assignment?

M Yes. My topic is about the decrease in family size, especially single-person households in New York.

W Why did you choose New York?

M New York _____ _____ _____ _____ _____ single-person households in the U.S.

W Why are there so many single-person households?

M _____ _____ _____ _____ in homes that they once shared with their spouses.

W I see. The divorce rate is very high these days. I think young people are waiting longer to get married and that may be another reason for the increase.

M Right. Besides, those who earn high incomes _____ _____ _____ _____ _____ _____ with roommates.

W Are there any other factors?

M I haven't finished my assignment yet, but I'll let you know later.

03

M Excuse me.

W Yes? What can I do for you?

M I _____ _____ _____ for Alice Brewer.

W Alice Brewer? Wow! That must be the wedding gown.

M Really? Congratulations! I hope you have a great wedding.

W Oh, I wish it were for me.

M Then who's the lucky girl? I need her to come out and sign for this.

W She's my coworker, but she's not here right now. She won't be back for another hour.

M I'm afraid I can't wait that long. Could you receive it and _____ _____ _____?

W Sure. That won't be a problem.

M Thank you. I've got a lot of other deliveries _____ _____ _____.

W Where do I have to sign?

M Right here, please.

04

W Hi, Tom. Thank you for sending me the picture yesterday.

M Hi, Grace. Did you have a look at it?

W Sure. I saved it in my cellphone here. Look, this wooden structure is really impressive.

M Yeah, it looks like _____ _____ _____, right?

W Yes. Where was the picture taken?

M On the top of a mountain in a suburban area.

W I guessed so, since you _____ _____ _____ _____ in your hand. The old pine tree behind the wooden building makes it look more attractive.

M Yeah. What's more interesting is that the structure was built _____ _____ _____.

W You must have been afraid when you were standing there.

M How did you know that?

W You were _____ _____ the wooden column.

05

W Wow! You did a good job. The classroom is perfectly clean.

M Thanks. I'm good at cleaning.

W I see. Oh, look at the waste bin. It's almost full.

M Ted _____ _____ _____ _____ that.

W Where is Ted?

M Maybe he already left. I saw him packing his school bag a while ago. Should I call him and tell him to come back?

W You don't have to do that. Maybe he forgot.

M Well, I _____ _____ _____ _____ for him.

W Will you do that? I'm sure Ted will do _____ _____ _____ you later.

M Probably. But it doesn't really matter to me.

W You're such a nice boy!

06

W These pictures came out really well.

M Yes, they sure did. Why don't you frame some of them?

W That's exactly what I was thinking. I like those heart-shaped frames over there. How much are they?

M Normally they are ten dollars each, but I will _____ _____ _____ _____ _____.

W That's still too expensive. Can you _____ _____ _____ a little more? I had five rolls of film developed here.

M Well, that's why I offered you ten percent off. How many pictures are you going to frame?

W I'd like to frame two pictures from _____ _____ _____ _____.

M So a total of ten pictures, right? In that case, I will give you an _____ _____ _____ _____ _____ _____.

W Okay. That sounds more reasonable. I'll pay by credit card.

07

M Ms. Donovan, can I talk to you for a second?

W Sure, Mr. Williams! Come on in and have a seat.

M Thank you.

W So, what's this about?

M Would you mind if I _____ _____ _____ _____ tomorrow?

W Of course not. I hear the flu is going around. Are you feeling okay?

M I'm fine. It's just my mom. She is _____ _____ _____ tomorrow morning.

W Oh, no! I'm sorry to hear that. I didn't know she was sick.

M Well, it's a fairly routine operation, but I think I _____ _____ _____ _____ her.

W I hope it isn't serious. And I think you should take the entire day off, not just the morning.

M Thanks a lot. You are so understanding.

W Don't mention it. That's how I should be.

08

W Kevin, look at the ad.

M Oh, a magic show will be held at the Royal Culture Center.

W Right. It says _____ _____ _____ _____ _____, including Jack Hunters.

M Jack Hunters is my favorite magician. Why don't we see this show?

W I'd like to, but the tickets are $20. Don't you think it's expensive?

M A bit. But I'm sure it'll _____ _____ _____ _____.

W Okay. Let's go. The show starts on May 10th and lasts 5 days. When do want to see the show?

M _____ _____, the better. Let's see it on the first day.

W The first day? I love it. _____ _____ _____ _____ _____ the performance.

M Me, too.

● DICTATION

09

M Hello, students. Please give me your attention for a minute. Let me tell you about the Short Marathon, which will be held on the 1st of next month. The purpose of _____ _____ _____ _____ _____ the school's 30th anniversary and the marathon is open to all students _____ _____ _____. The marathon consists of three running courses: 5 km, 7 km, and 10 km, so you can sign up for the distance that is _____ _____ _____ _____ _____. You can complete an entry form for the marathon on the school's website. Souvenirs will be offered to all participants, and _____ _____ _____ _____ _____ will receive a medal. I hope many students who are interested in marathons participate.

10

W What are you looking at?

M I'm looking for the best way to get to Holland Wedding Hall.

W Who's getting married?

M My cousin, Gerald. I'm going to accompany my parents to the wedding hall.

W Then you will drive your car there, won't you?

M I'd rather not. There's usually _____ _____ _____ _____. Last time, it took me almost 3 hours to drive there, so I missed the wedding.

W Then are you going to take the subway?

M _____ _____ _____ _____ there. Mom can't stand taking the subway for longer than one hour.

W Then the direct bus is a good option.

M Well, the fare is expensive for the amount of time we save, so I'd _____ _____ _____ it.

W Then you have two options, the one with a longer time and one transfer and the one with a shorter time and two transfers.

M I'll take the one with _____ _____ _____.

11

W Honey, _____ _____ _____ the Rainbow Hotel for our trip to Jeju Island?

M I'd like to stay at a hotel near the beach. Is it located near the beach?

W Yes, it is. And it opened just last month, so _____ _____ _____ are in very good condition.

M ▨▨▨▨▨▨▨▨▨▨▨▨▨▨▨▨▨▨▨▨

12

M Hi! How much are the tickets?

W They're _____ _____ _____, or fifteen tickets for ten dollars.

M Can you tell me _____ _____ _____ we have to spend for each ride?

W ▨▨▨▨▨▨▨▨▨▨▨▨▨▨▨▨▨▨▨▨

13

M Hello, Mrs. Williams. You wanted to see me, right?

W Yes, Nick. Come on in and have a seat.

M Thank you.

W How's your school life?

M It's as good as ever.

W I'm glad to hear that. Actually, I hear you're doing very well.

M It's all thanks to you. I know ________ ________ ________ to put me in the right direction.

W No, no. You made the choice to go in the right direction. By the way, have you seen Jack recently?

M No. We're ________ ________ ________ now.

W But you know where he lives, don't you?

M Yes, I do.

W So can you ________ ________ ________ this afternoon?

M ________________________________

14

M Jenny, are you busy now?

W No. I'm just watching a movie on my smartphone. Why?

M Then will you ________ ________ ________ and help me for a minute?

W Sure! What should I do, Dad?

M You know your grandmother is coming this evening, don't you?

W Yes, I do. ________ ________ ________ ________ ________ for about a week.

M That's right. So I'm thinking about making the seafood spaghetti that she likes.

W Great. I also like your seafood spaghetti.

M But the problem is that there's ________ ________ ________ in the fridge.

W ________________________________

15

W Fred comes from a big family. His parents always put emphasis on honesty. To save his parents the burden of paying his tuition, Fred works part-time at a nearby supermarket. Yesterday, he ________ ________ ________ ________ to a female customer. He only realized that after the customer had left, so he felt bad. Today, Fred sees the same customer waiting in line to pay for the groceries. He feels grateful that he can ________ ________ ________ his mistake. Right now she stands before the check-out counter, ready to pay. Fred wants to ________ ________ ________ and give the change back to her. In this situation, what would Fred most likely say to the customer?

Fred ________________________________

16 ~ 17

M What kinds of television programs are popular varies depending on age, gender, region, and culture. However, global audiences gather to watch television for two reasons. They are huge news stories such as the explosion of an airplane by a missile and sporting events. Then which of the two ________ ________ ________? Needless to say, it's sporting events. Sports may be the best advertising vehicle ever invented. It fills much of the prime time when the highest advertisement rates are guaranteed. Other than hours of television time, you can create more profits by ________ ________ around the grandstands, painting slogans on the fields, and getting the players to wear uniforms with corporate logos. Marketers realized that sports has generated and will ________ ________ ________ ________. In fact, advertising during the 2020 Super Bowl is known to have cost $6,000,000 for a 30-second spot.

실전 모의고사 **07** 회

1번부터 17번까지는 듣고 답하는 문제입니다. 1번부터 15번까지는 한 번만 들려주고, 16번부터 17번까지는 두 번 들려줍니다. 방송을 잘 듣고 답을 하시기 바랍니다.

01 다음을 듣고, 여자가 하는 말의 목적으로 가장 적절한 것을 고르시오.

① 물놀이의 위험성을 경고하려고
② 지역 농산물 애용을 촉구하려고
③ 다양한 지역 축제를 소개하려고
④ 가족 여행의 장점을 알려 주려고
⑤ 휴가를 보낼 만한 곳을 추천하려고

02 대화를 듣고, 남자의 의견으로 가장 적절한 것을 고르시오. [3점]

① 제목으로 책의 내용을 미리 속단해서는 안 된다.
② 좋은 책은 주변 사람들에게 적극적으로 추천해야 한다.
③ 원작 영화는 책을 읽고 나서 봐야 감동이 제대로 전달된다.
④ 책에 담긴 감동적인 내용은 책으로 읽을 때 비로소 느낄 수 있다.
⑤ 원작을 바탕으로 만든 영화는 원작의 인기를 더욱 높여 줄 수 있다.

03 대화를 듣고, 두 사람의 관계를 가장 잘 나타낸 것을 고르시오.

① 팬 – 코치
② 에이전트 – 운동 선수
③ 감독 – 배우
④ 의사 – 환자
⑤ 리포터 – 작가

04 대화를 듣고, 그림에서 대화의 내용과 일치하지 <u>않는</u> 것을 고르시오.

05 대화를 듣고, 여자가 남자에게 부탁한 일로 가장 적절한 것을 고르시오.

① 집까지 데려다 주기
② 공항에 태워다 주기
③ 여분의 열쇠 만들기
④ 보험 회사에 전화하기
⑤ 공항에서 여자의 사촌 데려오기

06 대화를 듣고, 남자가 지불할 금액을 고르시오.

① $45   ② $50   ③ $55   ④ $60   ⑤ $66

07 대화를 듣고, 여자가 John과 통화하고자 하는 이유를 고르시오.

① 약속 날짜를 변경하기 위해서
② 메일 주소를 알아보기를 원해서
③ 모임 날짜의 변경을 알리기 위해서
④ 모임에 참여 여부를 확인하기 위해서
⑤ 수영 수업에 관해 물어보기 위해서

08 대화를 듣고, 남자가 할 일에 관해 언급되지 <u>않은</u> 것을 고르시오.

① 나무 손질하기   ② 개에게 밥 주기
③ 꽃에 물 주기   ④ 분리수거하기
⑤ 우편물 확인하기

09 Jeju Teddy Bear Museum에 관한 다음 내용을 듣고, 일치하지 <u>않는</u> 것을 고르시오.

① 2019년 4월에 개관하였다.
② 역사관과 예술관을 갖추고 있다.
③ 폐관 시간 2시간 전에 입장권 판매를 중단한다.
④ 음식이나 음료를 박물관에 가지고 들어갈 수 없다.
⑤ 야외에 제주 해변이 보이는 정원을 갖추고 있다.

10 다음 표를 보면서 대화를 듣고, 두 사람이 예약할 객실을 고르시오.

Sun Star Hotel

	Room Type	View	Room Rate (a day)	Breakfast
①	Deluxe	Ocean	$270	X
②	Deluxe	Mountain	$250	○
③	Standard	Mountain	$230	X
④	Premium	Ocean	$290	○
⑤	Executive	Ocean	$340	○

11 대화를 듣고, 여자의 마지막 말에 대한 남자의 응답으로 가장 적절한 것을 고르시오.

① Right. You should stop feeding them.

② If I were you, I would buy the goldfish.

③ Once a day. It's not difficult to raise them.

④ I think so. You shouldn't have paid $10.

⑤ Don't worry. I'll take care of the goldfish.

12 대화를 듣고, 남자의 마지막 말에 대한 여자의 응답으로 가장 적절한 것을 고르시오.

① I'd like to get a refund for this skirt.

② It's my daughter's eleventh birthday.

③ That's too expensive for a teenage girl.

④ She really wants a new cellphone case.

⑤ I wonder how much she'll like my present.

13 대화를 듣고, 여자의 마지막 말에 대한 남자의 응답으로 가장 적절한 것을 고르시오.

Man: _____

① You don't have to order the yoga mats.

② You shouldn't have practiced yoga here.

③ Let me check the customer bulletin board.

④ It's not difficult to get a job at a yoga center.

⑤ I think you're the best worker at our yoga center.

14 대화를 듣고, 남자의 마지막 말에 대한 여자의 응답으로 가장 적절한 것을 고르시오. [3점]

Woman: _____

① I've heard nothing from him since then.

② He has every reason to respond like that.

③ I have nothing good to say about his friend.

④ If I were you, I would not see him any longer.

⑤ Well, I have no idea what kind of a person he is.

15 다음 상황 설명을 듣고, Olivia가 Dustin에게 할 말로 가장 적절한 것을 고르시오.

Olivia: _____

① I asked you not to come home late.

② I forgot to buy candles. What should I do?

③ Hurry up! Hot chocolate is waiting for you.

④ Do you know where the chili pepper bottle is?

⑤ Can you drop by the store and buy chili pepper?

[16~17] 다음을 듣고, 물음에 답하시오.

16 남자가 하는 말의 주제로 가장 적절한 것은? [3점]

① difficulties of raising children

② how to take care of stressed children

③ the importance of expressing emotion

④ effects of colors on children's emotion

⑤ reasons children like to draw a painting

17 언급된 색이 <u>아닌</u> 것은?

① red   ② green   ③ white

④ blue   ⑤ yellow

01

W Are you looking for _____ _____ _____ _____ your holiday? A place to provide you with a variety of water activities and a valuable experience with your family? Well, what about Paradise Springs? Paradise Springs is a fairly small town, but it offers _____ _____ _____ _____. Water sports are by far the most popular. You can enjoy your day outside rafting or swimming in the sun. You can also try your luck at fishing in peaceful surroundings. Or maybe you would prefer to pick some wild strawberries that grow along the roadsides. Also, there are lovely campgrounds where you can _____ _____ _____ with your family. You can enjoy shopping at the open market where _____ _____ _____ _____ grown in their gardens. If you want to have a nice holiday, you are welcome to visit Paradise Springs.

02

M Have you read *Captain Jackson's Destiny*?

W No, but I read about it in the paper. It said a movie will be made _____ _____ the book.

M I've heard that, too. Anyways, I'd like to recommend this book to you. It's really touching.

W Well, the title doesn't sound like my sort of thing.

M The story is different from what you would expect from the title. It's the best thing I've read in ages. I'm sure you'll like it.

W Really? Then when the movie _____ _____, I'll watch it.

M Well, I don't think that's a good idea.

W How come?

M The movie _____ _____ _____ as much as the book.

W Do you really think so?

M Of course. Touching stories often fail to _____ _____ _____ _____ in the form of a movie.

03

W Hi, Hank. You've been doing pretty well.

M Thank you, Lisa. Yeah, I'm satisfied with my recent performance. What's up, anyway?

W I have some good news and bad news for you.

M It's about my contract, right?

W Yes. The good news is that the Angels have offered you a three-year, 10 million dollar contract.

M A three-year, 10 million dollar contract? That's awesome. What's the bad news?

W You have to _____ _____ a special medical test, not just a routine physical exam. That is, you have to prove there is _____ _____ _____ your shoulder.

M Isn't my recent performance enough to prove that my shoulder is strong?

W I am afraid that they want to make sure about your shoulder.

M Well, _____ _____ _____ _____, it's understandable. I'll sleep on it. Thanks, Lisa.

04

W Look! I've finally _____ _____ _____ _____ _____ for the Christmas party.

M Great! I like the Merry Christmas banner on the center wall.

W Thanks. And I placed _____ _____ _____ _____ _____ next to the fireplace.

M I like it there. In particular, the star-shaped decoration on top of the tree looks very impressive.

W Thanks.

M Oh, you _____ _____ _____ _____ on each side of the fireplace.

W Yes. One is for our son, and the other is for our daughter.

M Good. What are the _____ _____ _____ on the round table?

W They are gift boxes. I'll put the kids' gifts there.

M They will be very happy to open them.

05

M Linda, is that you?

W Oh, Mark. Hi.

M What are you doing outside your car in this hot weather?

W Can you believe this? I _____ _____ _____ _____ the car.

M Really? Did you call an insurance company?

W Yes. But the _____ _____ _____ _____ for the past ten minutes.

M It sounds like there's a high demand for their services right now.

W Mark, will you do me a favor?

M Sure. What is it?

W I have to go to the airport to pick up my cousin. He's supposed to arrive at 4 p.m.

M Sounds like you need to hurry.

W Yes. Can you _____ _____ _____ right now? I have a spare key there.

M Sure. I can drive you back here again.

W Thanks a million.

06

M Excuse me.

W Yes. Is there anything you need?

M Yeah, I think there is _____ _____ _____ this check.

W Really? What is it, sir?

M Look at this. It says here the steak dinner costs $60, not $50.

W Oh, it was $50 _____ _____ the end of August. But because of the rising cost of beef, we raised the price by 20 percent at the beginning of September.

M Oh, you did? I didn't know that. What about the tax and service charges?

W The tax _____ _____ _____ the price of the meal and the service charge is 10 percent of the total. As you can see, your total is $60.

M I see. Here's my credit card.

W Thank you, sir.

07

[Cellphone rings.]

M Hello, Laura! How are you?

W Hi, Jason. Fine, thanks. Listen! I'm going to _____ _____ _____ _____ _____. Would you like to join us?

M A study group? Sure, I'd love to. Who else do you have in mind?

W Tony and Julia both said yes. Which time is good for you, Thursday evening or Friday evening?

M Thursday evening is better for me.

W Good. What's your e-mail address? I am going to send you the details.

M My e-mail address is Jason@naver.com.

W Okay. And I am trying to reach John, but I can't _____ _____ _____ _____ him. You're in swimming class with him, aren't you?

M Yes. Is John going to be a member of the study group?

W That's what I _____ _____ _____ him. Can you tell him to call me?

M No problem.

08

M Good morning, honey.

W Good morning. Did you sleep well last night?

M Yes, I did. When do you think breakfast will be ready?

W In half an hour.

M Then I'll _____ _____ _____ in the garden.

W Thanks. And can you feed Poppy? Our lovely dog needs some breakfast, too.

M Sure. I'll also _____ _____ _____.

W Thank you, Ted. Oh, one more thing. I forgot to _____ _____ _____ yesterday. Would you do that, too?

M No problem. I'm sure to work up an appetite doing all of those chores.

W Well, you'll be rewarded with a delicious breakfast.

09

M Welcome to the Jeju Teddy Bear Museum. Here you will find everything you want to know about teddy bears! The museum opened on April 24th, 2019. It has a history gallery and an art gallery. We are open from 9 a.m. to 7 p.m. throughout most of the year. But from July 16th to August 25th, we stay open until 10 p.m. Tickets are on sale _____ _____ _____ _____ the closing time. No food or drinks may be _____ _____ the museum. Our museum also has a gift shop, with over 1,000 products for sale. There you will find stuffed teddy bears of all sizes, jewelry, T-shirts, cups, and much more. During your visit, be sure to stop by the _____ _____ — it has a perfect view of Jeju Beach.

10

M Honey, let's look at the Sun Star Hotel reservation site and decide which room to stay in for our trip next month.

W Okay. Is there _____ _____ _____ _____ _____?

M Any room is okay, except for a standard room. It's our once-in-a-lifetime honeymoon.

W Yes. What about the view?

M I want to _____ _____ _____ _____ _____ and see the ocean.

W Me, too. An ocean view is better than a mountain view.

M Now we have to think about the room rate.

W Well, although it's our honeymoon, I think more than $300 a day is too expensive.

M I agree. Um... now _____ _____ _____ _____ _____.

W Don't you think this room with breakfast is _____ _____ _____ _____ _____?

M Yes, I do. Okay, let's book this room.

11

W Oh, _____ _____ _____ look really cute. I'll buy five of them.

M Thank you. That's $10 in total.

W Here's $10. Ah, how often do I have to _____ _____ _____?

M

12

M May I help you, ma'am?

W Yes. I'm _____ _____ _____ _____ for my daughter.

M Okay. What do you _____ _____ _____?

W

13

M Cindy, did you read the new post on _____

_____ _____ _____ _____?

W No, I didn't. What's it about?

M The shower room.

W The shower room? Is it about the water temperature?

M Yes, right. Someone complained that _____

_____ _____ _____ _____ _____

to take a shower after practicing yoga.

W I _____ _____ _____ last night. You don't

have to worry about it.

M Oh, really? That was really fast.

W I also ordered _____ _____ _____ _____

_____ yesterday.

M Good. You always work hard.

W _____ _____. I'm just doing my job.

M ▮▮▮▮▮▮▮▮▮▮▮▮▮▮▮▮▮▮▮▮▮▮

14

W Hi, Greg. Can you spare a few minutes to talk to me?

M Sure. What do you want to talk about?

W It's about Bob. I don't know _____ _____

_____ _____ him or not.

M What happened? You've been seeing him for months.

W Do you remember the other day when his idea

_____ _____ _____?

M Yes. He looked a bit disappointed.

W That evening, he said almost nothing.

M He might have been shocked. He had probably worked on his idea for days.

W Maybe, but he went too far. And the day before yesterday, his best friend fell off a bicycle. When he heard the news, guess what he said.

M Beats me. What did he say?

W He said it _____ _____ _____.

M Well, Bob might have had a reason to be angry at him at that time.

W ▮▮▮▮▮▮▮▮▮▮▮▮▮▮▮▮▮▮▮▮▮▮

15

W Olivia and Dustin got married exactly one year ago, and today is their first wedding anniversary. _____ _____ _____ _____, they decide to have a small party at home. Olivia is now making hot chocolate. It's the drink she and Dustin had on their first date. Dustin is going to arrive about ten minutes later. Putting a cake with candles on the table, she speeds up to get the hot chocolate ready in time for his arrival. Now all she has to do is put chili pepper into the hot chocolate. She opens the cupboard and finds the chili pepper bottle _____ _____. She wants to ask Dustin to _____ _____ _____ _____. She calls Dustin on his cellphone and he answers it. In this situation, what would Olivia most likely say to Dustin?

Olivia ▮▮▮▮▮▮▮▮▮▮▮▮▮▮▮▮▮▮▮▮▮▮

16 ~ 17

M Hello everyone and thanks for coming. I'm Jim Brown, a child education expert. Over the next three weeks, I will talk about _____ _____ _____ _____ _____ _____. Today, I'll start by talking about colors. As there are many colors in the world, each color affects children's emotions in many ways. First, red, the most intense color, can _____ _____ _____ _____ such as anger in children, so red isn't a good color for children who get angry easily. On the other hand, a stressed or irritated child may feel calm and comfortable when they _____ _____ _____ _____ _____ _____. Does your child feel depressed? Then show your child yellow things such as yellow tulips. Yellow is _____ _____ _____ _____ on the color scale, so your child will feel much better after looking at yellow tulips. Are there any questions so far?

1번부터 17번까지는 듣고 답하는 문제입니다. 1번부터 15번까지는 한 번만 들려주고, 16번부터 17번까지는 두 번 들려줍니다. 방송을 잘 듣고 답을 하시기 바랍니다.

01 다음을 듣고, 남자가 하는 말의 목적으로 가장 적절한 것을 고르시오.
① 수질 오염에 대한 대책을 발표하려고
② 주민 회의에 참석할 것을 권장하려고
③ 배수로 청소에 적극적인 동참을 호소하려고
④ 쓰레기 투기 기업에 대한 불매 운동을 선언하려고
⑤ 수질 오염 방지를 위한 탄원서에 서명을 요청하려고

02 대화를 듣고, 여자의 의견으로 가장 적절한 것을 고르시오.
① 외국어는 실생활에서 배워야 한다.
② 스페인어는 속도가 빨라 이해하기 어렵다.
③ 스페인어의 국제적 위상이 커져 가고 있다.
④ 외국어를 배우려면 원어민 친구를 사귀어야 한다.
⑤ 외국어를 처음 배울 때에는 핵심어에 집중해야 한다.

03 대화를 듣고, 두 사람의 관계를 가장 잘 나타낸 것을 고르시오.
① 기자 – 작가
② 경찰 – 목격자
③ 바리스타 – 손님
④ 영화배우 – 감독
⑤ 서점 주인 – 직원

04 대화를 듣고, 그림에서 대화의 내용과 일치하지 않는 것을 고르시오.

05 대화를 듣고, 여자가 할 일로 가장 적절한 것을 고르시오.
① 나무에 물 주기
② 세탁기 속 살펴보기
③ 음성 메시지 남기기
④ 휴대전화에 전화하기
⑤ 버스 회사에 전화하기

06 대화를 듣고, 남자가 지불할 금액을 고르시오. [3점]
① $72   ② $108   ③ $180
④ $220   ⑤ $240

07 대화를 듣고, 여자가 Forest Campsite에서 캠핑을 하기를 원하지 않는 이유를 고르시오.
① 시설이 낡아서
② 이용 요금이 비싸서
③ 물놀이 시설이 없어서
④ 집에서 멀리 떨어져서
⑤ 캠핑객들이 너무 많아서

08 대화를 듣고, Mara Island에 관해 언급되지 않은 것을 고르시오.
① 면적   ② 위치   ③ 주민 수
④ 날씨   ⑤ 교통

09 Korean Food Cooking Contest에 관한 다음 내용을 듣고, 일치하지 않는 것을 고르시오. [3점]
① 크리스마스이브에 개최된다.
② 아마추어와 직업 요리사 부문으로 나뉜다.
③ 신문사와 백화점으로부터 후원을 받는다.
④ 대회의 전 과정이 인터넷으로 생중계된다.
⑤ 참가 등록은 12월 5일까지이다.

10 다음 표를 보면서 대화를 듣고, 두 사람이 예약할 방을 고르시오.

Restaurant Rooms

	Room	Floor	Capacity (People)	Dinner Type	Price
①	A	3rd	80	Set Menu	$40
②	B	2nd	80	Buffet	$35
③	C	2nd	100	Set Menu	$35
④	D	1st	120	Buffet	$30
⑤	E	1st	120	Set Menu	$30

11 대화를 듣고, 남자의 마지막 말에 대한 여자의 응답으로 가장 적절한 것을 고르시오.

① Good. Your complaint finally worked.

② Right. I don't want to work at the fruit store.

③ Yes, you should have bought more apples than now.

④ Absolutely! Apples are more delicious than oranges.

⑤ Sure! We must ask them to exchange these for fresh ones.

12 대화를 듣고, 여자의 마지막 말에 대한 남자의 응답으로 가장 적절한 것을 고르시오.

① My grandfather stays there.

② It's not my idea. It was yours.

③ Well, it's demanding but it's worth it.

④ Washing, drying, and those sorts of things.

⑤ Don't get me wrong. I'm trying to help you.

13 대화를 듣고, 남자의 마지막 말에 대한 여자의 응답으로 가장 적절한 것을 고르시오. [3점]

Woman: _____

① I agree. Don't feel too bad about the letter.

② Sure. Call me when you are ready to leave.

③ I am fed up with getting useless spam mails.

④ Well, I think I should write a letter to my dad.

⑤ That's right. I'm not used to saying "I love you."

14 대화를 듣고, 여자의 마지막 말에 대한 남자의 응답으로 가장 적절한 것을 고르시오.

Man: _____

① I'm sure you'll get your bike back soon.

② Please catch the man who stole my bike.

③ Thanks to you, I learned how to ride a bike.

④ I'm also happy to hear you bought a good bike.

⑤ I'll park my bike in the public bike parking area.

15 다음 상황 설명을 듣고, Nick이 학생에게 할 말로 가장 적절한 것을 고르시오.

Nick: _____

① It was nice of you to yield your seat to him.

② Thanks, but this bag isn't as heavy as it looks.

③ Why don't you give your seat to the old man?

④ It's a really good habit to read on the subway.

⑤ You can have this seat. I'll get off at the next stop.

[16~17] 다음을 듣고, 물음에 답하시오.

16 여자가 하는 말의 주제로 가장 적절한 것은?

① difficulties of playing group sports

② how to play individual sports better

③ positive effects of playing sports on kids

④ reasons children like to play group sports

⑤ differences between adults and children in playing sports

17 언급된 스포츠가 아닌 것은?

① soccer　　② swimming　　③ marathon

④ baseball　　⑤ table tennis

녹음 내용을 다시 들으면서 빈칸을 채워 넣으세요.

01

M Hello, Grand City residents! We're here today _____ _____ _____ _____ _____. It's not for us, but for all of our residents, including our children and our grandchildren. Now, more than half of the rivers, lakes, and streams in our city are polluted. Doing water activities like swimming, rafting, and fishing in these polluted waters may entail serious health risks. At this moment, we _____ _____ _____ _____ the government to do more to clean up our waterways and to improve water quality standards. We also need to urge big companies to stop dumping waste and polluting our waters. For all of these reasons, we need you _____ _____ _____ _____. Please take a little time and help save our bodies of water.

02

W Hey, Henry. How's the Spanish course going?

M It's pretty tough.

W Tough? Why?

M Our teacher is using a lot of _____ _____. He even tapes conversations with his friends and uses them in class.

W That sounds very helpful. So, _____ _____ _____ _____ for you to learn Spanish?

M Well, the speed, for a start. They just talk so fast that I can't understand which word or phrase they use.

W Maybe you shouldn't try to understand every word and phrase in the initial stage of learning a foreign language.

M What do you mean?

W You should just listen for _____ _____ _____. I mean the most important words.

M But how do I know what they are?

W They're usually the words _____ _____ _____ _____.

03

M Hi! It's nice to see you.

W Hi! Have a seat here, please. Would you drink a cup of coffee?

M No thanks. First of all, congratulations on winning the Writer of the Month award.

W I really _____ _____ _____ _____ who love my new novel, *Police Life*.

M I also read it _____ _____ _____ _____. It's really realistic.

W Well, I interviewed more than 100 policemen to write it.

M I heard that some movie directors want to _____ _____ _____ _____ _____ _____.

W That's right. Once it's decided, I'll let you know first.

M Really? Then can I write an article about it?

W Of course, you can.

M Thank you. Your fans will be _____ _____ _____ _____ _____.

04

W At last, _____ _____ _____ _____ is starting.

M Look at the two girls playing drums in front.

W And the two boys are passing by waving the American flag just behind them.

M Both the girls and boys are very cute, aren't they?

W Yes, they are. Look behind them. Can you see the woman with a big hat _____ _____ _____ _____ _____?

M That's a really big flag. What do you think about the old man with the beard?

W You mean the old man riding on a bicycle and waving?

M Yes. Let's wave at him, too.

W Why not? Look! There's _____ _____ _____ _____ _____ _____ following the old man.

M Everyone in the carriage is really enjoying the parade.

05

W Liam! Where are you?

M I'm in the yard. I just finished watering the plants. What's up?

W Where is the jacket I wore yesterday?

M It's in the washing machine. Why?

W Oh, my! I think my cellphone is in the pocket.

M No. I checked every pocket before putting it in.

W Then, where is my phone? I can't find it anywhere. I'm sure I _____ _____ _____ _____ _____ after I used it on the bus.

M Why don't you call your cellphone?

W I already did, but I just heard a recorded voice saying _____ _____ _____ .

M Maybe your cellphone _____ _____ _____ your jacket. _____ _____ _____ the bus company?

W Okay. I really hope they have my phone.

06

W What can I do for you?

M I'd like to _____ _____ _____ flute lessons. How much are they per month?

W They're $120.

M Not too expensive. _____ _____ _____ my ten-year-old son to learn how to play the flute. How much are the lessons for him?

W They're $80 for children under 13.

M That's _____ _____ . Then can you sign both of us up for flute lessons?

W Sure. And since you and your son are family, we'll discount 10 percent off the total cost.

M Wow! That's a really good deal.

W That's not all. We'll give you both a cleaning set _____ _____ , which is a $20 value.

M Thank you. Here's my credit card.

W Hold on.

07

M Samantha, I think I _____ _____ _____ _____ for our camping trip next weekend.

W Did you? What's the name of the campsite?

M Forest Campsite near Wellington Mountain.

W Oh, then it's not that far from here.

M The fee is only $20 a day per tent. It's really cheap.

W Well, I think it must be popular with campers like us.

M For sure, so we have to _____ _____ _____ _____ .

W Um... I don't want to go camping in a crowded place.

M But it's also _____ _____ _____ _____ _____ . You said you wanted to play in the water.

W I do. But what I want more is to _____ _____ _____ _____ _____ _____ .

M Well, then I'll look for another campsite.

08

M Stella, I heard that you're going to take a trip to Jeju Island this weekend.

W Yes. You know, it's my first trip since I started working here in Seoul.

M What are you going to do on Jeju Island?

W First, I'll visit Mara Island.

M Mara Island? Isn't that _____ _____ _____ in Korea?

W No, it isn't. It has an area of about 0.3 km².

M Ah, I must be confused with another island. It's _____ _____ _____ _____ _____ of Korea, isn't it?

W That's right. I heard there are about 100 residents _____ _____ _____ _____ .

M How about the weather there?

W It should be good. Since the island _____ _____ _____ _____ just like Seoul, it's very sunny now.

M Great. I hope you'll have a wonderful trip.

09

W Hi, Korean food lovers. I'm going to tell you some good news. The Korean Food Cooking Contest is going to be held at the Olympic Convention Center on Christmas Eve. _____ _____ _____ _____ _____ can participate in this contest. There are two different categories: amateur and professional chefs. The entry fee is $30 per person, and _____ _____ _____ _____ _____ will receive a $1,000 prize and a round-trip ticket to Seoul, Korea. The contest is sponsored by Fact Newspaper and Star Department Store, and the entire event will _____ _____ _____ on the Internet. Registration for participation is from December 5th to December 15th. I hope many of you who love Korean food participate.

10

W Let's look at this pamphlet and choose a room for your father's seventieth birthday party.

M Okay. Wow! This restaurant is three stories tall.

W It specializes in _____ _____, company luncheons, and all kinds of group dining.

M I see. Which room do you think is the most suitable?

W Well, many guests are your father's age, so walking up to the third floor isn't easy for them.

M I agree.

W And almost one hundred friends of your parents' came to our wedding last year, right?

M Yes. We need a room that can _____ _____ _____ 100 people.

W You're right. And you said most of them _____ _____ the buffet.

M Yes, that's what I heard. Let's make the dinner a set menu.

W Then we have two choices left.

M Well, I think the _____ _____ _____ _____ _____, although it's a little more expensive.

W Then let's reserve that room.

11

M Honey, look. More than half of _____ _____ _____ _____. Where did you buy them?

W At Green's Fruit Store. I can't understand how they sold such bad apples.

M Let's go there right now. We have to _____ _____ _____.

W ▓▓▓▓▓▓▓▓▓▓▓▓▓▓▓▓▓▓▓▓▓

12

W I heard you _____ _____ _____ every Sunday.

M Yeah, I go to the senior community and _____ _____ _____.

W Oh, it must be _____ _____, right?

M ▓▓▓▓▓▓▓▓▓▓▓▓▓▓▓▓▓▓▓▓▓

13

W Hi, Austin. You look happy today.

M Hi, Molly. I _____ _____ _____ _____ look so.

W Really? What happened?

M I got a hand-written letter from my mother.

W A hand-written letter? Why? Did she go somewhere?

M No, she's at home with us _____ _____.

W Then why did she send you a letter? What did she want to say?

M Nothing special. She just wanted me to know that she loves me.

W Doesn't she ever tell you that at home?

M Of course, she does.

W Then why did she send you a letter to tell you that?

M I have no idea, but I think the letter is very special. I had a _____ _____ _____ than getting an ordinary text message.

W ▨▨▨▨▨▨▨▨▨▨▨▨▨▨▨▨▨▨▨▨▨

14

W Officer! Please help me.

M Calm down, please. What's the problem?

W Somebody _____ _____ _____ _____.

M Did you lock it?

W Yes, I did. I think he broke my bike lock and took my bike.

M Where did you park your bike?

W _____ _____ _____ _____ _____ _____ in front of the post office on Lake Street.

M There's a CCTV nearby that shows that area. By checking it, we should be able to find out who took your bike.

W Really? I'm _____ _____ _____ _____.

M ▨▨▨▨▨▨▨▨▨▨▨▨▨▨▨▨▨▨▨▨▨

15

M Nick is a high school teacher. Today is the first day he starts teaching at Winsley High School. Now he _____ _____ _____ to school. It's early in the morning, but all the seats _____ _____. A student wearing a high school uniform is reading a book in the seat in front of him. At the next stop, an old man gets on the subway. He looks like he's in his seventies. He searches for _____ _____ _____. At that time, the student finds the old man, stands up, and _____ _____ _____ to him. Now the student is standing next to Nick. _____ _____ _____ him, Nick wants to praise him. In this situation, what would Nick most likely say to the student?

Nick ▨▨▨▨▨▨▨▨▨▨▨▨▨▨▨▨▨▨▨▨▨

16~17

W Hello, everyone. Welcome to my YouTube channel. I'm sports columnist Jane Fonda. Today, I'm going to talk about children and sports. _____ _____ _____ both adults and children many benefits. Playing team sports such as soccer and basketball can improve _____ _____ _____ _____ _____. If your children enjoy individual sports such as swimming or marathon, it'll also have a positive effect on them. Studies show that children who participate in these sports _____ _____ _____ than those who don't. Do you think your children _____ _____? Then have them play table tennis or tennis. They will need to hit the ball accurately, and learning this skill will _____ _____ _____. That's all for today's video. See you next time.

● 실전 모의고사 **09** 회

1번부터 17번까지는 듣고 답하는 문제입니다. 1번부터 15번까지는 한 번만 들려주고, 16번부터 17번까지는 두 번 들려줍니다. 방송을 잘 듣고 답을 하시기 바랍니다.

01 다음을 듣고, 여자가 하는 말의 목적으로 가장 적절한 것을 고르시오.
① 웹사이트 운영 방식의 변화를 안내하려고
② 저축을 통한 재산 관리 방법을 소개하려고
③ 실내 적정 온도 유지의 중요성을 알리려고
④ 계절에 맞추어 출시된 신상품을 광고하려고
⑤ 절약 정보를 담고 있는 웹사이트를 소개하려고

02 대화를 듣고, 남자의 의견으로 가장 적절한 것을 고르시오.
① 힘든 시기를 현명하게 대처해야 한다.
② 인생의 목표를 확실하게 설정해야 한다.
③ 모든 직업에는 좋은 점과 나쁜 점이 있다.
④ 학창 시절에 다양한 경험을 해 보아야 한다.
⑤ 결과에 연연하지 말고 과정을 중시해야 한다.

03 대화를 듣고, 두 사람의 관계를 가장 잘 나타낸 것을 고르시오.
① 사건 의뢰인 – 탐정
② 성우 – 만화 영화 감독
③ 시나리오 작가 – 배우
④ 범죄 신고인 – 경찰관
⑤ 영화 평론가 – 방송 진행자

04 대화를 듣고, 그림에서 대화의 내용과 일치하지 <u>않는</u> 것을 고르시오.

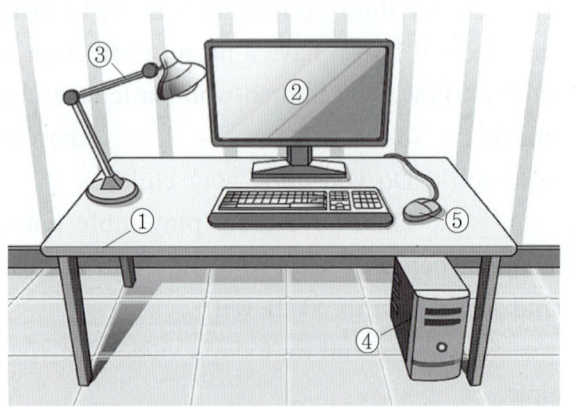

05 대화를 듣고, 남자가 할 일로 가장 적절한 것을 고르시오.
① 레벨 테스트 보기
② 국적 기재 확인하기
③ 이름 철자 수정하기
④ 무료 수업 참관하기
⑤ 한 시간 동안 대기하기

06 대화를 듣고, 여자가 지불할 금액을 고르시오. [3점]
① $300   ② $320   ③ $340
④ $360   ⑤ $400

07 대화를 듣고, 남자가 은행에 전화를 건 이유를 고르시오.
① 투자 상담을 받으려고
② 휴대전화를 돌려주려고
③ 채용 여부를 확인하려고
④ 저축 계좌를 개설하려고
⑤ 은행의 위치를 알아보려고

08 대화를 듣고, 여자의 출장 경유지로 언급되지 <u>않은</u> 것을 고르시오.
① 하와이   ② 도쿄   ③ 방콕
④ 타이베이   ⑤ 부산

09 Crystal Forest Concerts에 관한 다음 내용을 듣고, 일치하지 <u>않는</u> 것을 고르시오.
① 7월 한 달 동안 매주 토요일에 열린다.
② 10팀의 밴드가 공연을 할 예정이다.
③ 접이식 의자나 담요를 가지고 올 수 있다.
④ 콘서트 내내 푸드 트럭을 이용할 수 있다.
⑤ 18세 미만 청소년의 입장료는 10달러이다.

10 다음 표를 보면서 대화를 듣고, 두 사람이 예약할 오토 캠핑장을 고르시오.

Auto Camping Sites

	Site	Capacity (m²)	Electricity	Hot Water	Deck
①	A	8	○	X	○
②	B	12	X	X	X
③	C	13	X	○	○
④	D	13	○	X	○
⑤	E	15	X	○	X

11 대화를 듣고, 여자의 마지막 말에 대한 남자의 응답으로 가장 적절한 것을 고르시오.

① Yes. He's old enough to sleep alone.

② Please don't make him fall off the bed.

③ You're right. He needs to get some sleep.

④ Actually, I've been with him all day long.

⑤ I'll go and make him calm down right away.

12 대화를 듣고, 남자의 마지막 말에 대한 여자의 응답으로 가장 적절한 것을 고르시오.

① Don't blame yourself.

② You can do better next time.

③ Thanks. That's very kind of you.

④ You should have been more careful.

⑤ Oh, that's not mine. Thanks, anyway.

13 대화를 듣고, 여자의 마지막 말에 대한 남자의 응답으로 가장 적절한 것을 고르시오.

Man: _____

① Okay. Let me buy some medicine right away.

② Right. I was also troubled by the cold for a few days.

③ I agree. It's most important to cure a cold quickly.

④ I see. You choose to relax enough without medicine.

⑤ Well, I'd like you to recommend a doctor's clinic nearby.

14 대화를 듣고, 남자의 마지막 말에 대한 여자의 응답으로 가장 적절한 것을 고르시오. [3점]

Woman: _____

① I never would have guessed he is a painter.

② He doesn't know what it's like to have a baby.

③ He sees his paintings as a means of gaining fame.

④ He draws more paintings than any female painter.

⑤ He seems to use fixed gender roles in his paintings.

15 다음 상황 설명을 듣고, Matt가 사장에게 할 말로 가장 적절한 것을 고르시오.

Matt: _____

① I put my cellphone on manner mode.

② Well, I like my coworkers for one thing.

③ Sorry to say this. I am afraid I have to quit.

④ Come to my restaurant. I'll treat you to lunch.

⑤ My father is okay now. I'll go back to work soon.

[16~17] 다음을 듣고, 물음에 답하시오.

16 여자가 하는 말의 주제로 가장 적절한 것은? [3점]

① musical instruments that kids want to learn

② considerations when buying musical instruments

③ importance of teaching kids music from an early age

④ differences between string and keyboard instruments

⑤ benefits of teaching kids to play musical instruments

17 언급된 악기가 <u>아닌</u> 것은?

① piano   ② flute   ③ guitar

④ violin   ⑤ cello

• DICTATION

녹음 내용을 다시 들으면서 빈칸을 채워 넣으세요.

01

W What if you can save $100 a year simply by replacing your five most-used light bulbs? What if you can save another $100 by using a programmable thermostat? You can also save more if you keep window shades and curtains closed during summer and open in daylight hours during winter. And you can save money if you only run your bathroom fan for 15 minutes. These are just _____ _____ _____ _____ you can find on our website, www.savebysmallthings.com. Together, these tips could _____ _____ _____ _____ from your annual household bills. Join our website and use it. The website is free, updated seasonally, so keep _____ _____ _____.

02

M You have finally become an actress.

W It's all thanks to you.

M I don't think so. It's because of your constant effort. What's it like to _____ _____ _____ in different movies?

W It's a lot of fun, but sometimes it's very tiring.

M What makes you so tired?

W Quite often I have to _____ _____ _____ _____.

M Nothing in life is easy, especially if you want to make something special happen.

W I agree. And it's really hard to memorize all those lines. Sometimes I think I don't have a life of my own.

M Sounds like you're having a hard time now. But remember — those who deal with _____ _____ _____ _____ are successful.

W Yeah, that's what you used to say to us in my school days.

M I still say that. That's what matters in life.

W I'll keep that in mind and do my best. Thanks, Mr. Jeter.

03

M Good morning, Ms. Willson.

W Good morning, Mr. Jenkins.

M I'm happy to work with you again. Thank you for asking me.

W You deserve it. Furthermore, your voice is proper for the boy in my animation.

M Am I _____ _____ _____ _____ _____ _____?

W Yes. A boy detective is the main character. He's solving a crime in the movie.

M I can't wait to read the whole script.

W Here's the script. After you read it, I'll explain _____ _____ _____ about the animation.

M Okay. While reading it, I'll _____ _____ _____ for the boy.

W Please make your voice sound cheerful. The boy has a very positive personality.

M Okay. I'll be sure to do that.

04

M I heard you bought a computer and a computer desk.

W Yes. My parents bought them for me. Would you like to see the photo I took of my computer desk?

M Sure. Show me the picture.

W Hold on. Here it is.

M Wow! Your computer desk is quite simple. No bookshelves, and no drawers!

W Yes, the desk only _____ _____ _____.

M It looks good. I see you placed the monitor and keyboard _____ _____ _____ _____ the desk.

W Yeah, and I put the desk lamp _____ _____ the monitor.

M That's a good idea. But don't turn it on for too long.

W Of course, I won't. What do you think about keeping the computer _____ _____ _____?

M Great. Mine is next to the monitor. I'd better move it under the desk, too. _____ _____ _____ in front of the monitor looks very convenient.

05

W Welcome to YST English Institute. What can I do for you?

M I'm here to _____ _____ _____ an English course.

W Okay. What's your name, please?

M Daniel Baggio.

W Sounds like you are from Italy.

M No, I'm Argentinian. But people always think I'm Italian because of my name.

W I see. What course are you thinking of taking?

M I'd like to take _____ _____ _____. I took an intermediate course in Canada last year, so I think I'll be able to handle an advanced course here.

W You have to _____ _____ _____ _____ first to take an advanced course. It's our policy.

M Okay, I'll take the test. How long will it take?

W It takes about one hour to find out whether you're ready or not.

M All right.

06

M May I help you?

W Yes, please. I'm here to buy a dinner table.

M Great. How many people is the table for?

W I'd like to buy one for four people. *[Pause]* Oh, I like this table here.

M That's one of _____ _____ _____ _____ these days. That's $300, without the chairs.

W How much is it with the four chairs?

M It's $400.

W Hmm. Is there any way for me to _____ _____ _____? I really like the table, but it's quite expensive.

M Fortunately, we're _____ _____ _____ _____. You can get a 10 percent discount on the total price.

W That sounds great. I'll buy the table and four chairs. Here's my credit card.

M Okay. Would you write down your home address?

W Sure.

07

[Telephone rings.]

W Hello. You've reached Morgan Bank. How may I help you?

M Yes, I'd like to talk to Ian Kennedy. Is he working there?

W Just a moment. I'm sorry he's _____ _____ _____ _____ another customer. Would you like to hold, or should I ask him to call you back?

M Could you ask him to call his cellphone?

W Call his cellphone? Do you have his phone?

M Yes. I found it on the subway. While I was looking _____ _____ _____ _____ return it, I pushed number one long enough to contact you.

W Okay. I'll tell him what you said. He'll probably give you useful advice in return about investments and savings accounts. That's his field of expertise.

M Good to hear that. I need that kind of advice.

W Oh, I think he can talk to you now. I'll _____ _____ _____ _____ to him.

M Thanks, and it was nice talking to you.

W You're welcome.

08

M Welcome back from your _____ _____! Where did you go this time?

W I went to Hawaii, but I only stayed there for one night.

M How was it?

W The weather was great, and the beach was beautiful, but my schedule was _____ _____ _____ _____ either of them.

M Where did you go next?

W I flew to Tokyo, where I stayed for three nights.

M And you didn't have time to do anything else, right?

W Yes. Then I went to Bangkok, but I _____ _____ _____ in Taipei for three hours.

M How was Bangkok?

W Wonderful. I have a friend there, so we had dinner together.

M Great. Then you _____ _____ _____ San Francisco from Bangkok?

W Right. I got home last night.

M So, where are you going next?

W I'm going to fly to Incheon next Monday.

09

M Why don't you spend your summer Saturday evenings attending Crystal Forest Concerts? These concerts will be held from six to nine in the evening every Saturday in July. _____ _____ _____ will perform their beautiful songs. You can _____ _____ _____ _____ _____ or blanket to enjoy our live music under the forest trees. A food truck will be available throughout the concerts. The entrance fee is $10 per adult and it's _____ _____ _____ _____ _____. We strongly recommend the whole family to come and enjoy the concerts. It's a great chance to make an unforgettable memory with your family.

10

M Now we have to decide on which auto camping site to reserve.

W I think we need a campsite _____ _____ 9 square meters. Anything else would be too small.

M You're right. What about electricity?

W I don't think we need electricity. It may disturb our view when we try to see stars in the sky.

M I agree. It won't be that uncomfortable to _____ _____ _____ for a couple of days.

W Do you think we need hot water?

M I don't care either way, but Jamie won't _____ _____ _____ without hot water.

W I'm with him. I don't like to take showers with cold water, either.

M Now we have to decide on a deck.

W We _____ _____ one. With a deck, we don't have to worry about snakes or a little rain.

M You're right. Then let's reserve this auto camping site.

11

W Honey, Henry is crying in his room.

M Okay. I'll go and _____ _____ _____.

W He must _____ _____ because he woke up alone in his room.

M

12

M Oh, dear. Are you okay?

W Yeah, I'm fine. The floor is _____ _____.

M Yes, it really is. Can I _____ _____ _____?

W

13

M Sophie, you don't look good today. What's wrong?

W Oh, Brian. I think I _____ _____ _____.

M Then why don't you go see a doctor?

W No, I won't.

M Why not? The doctor will help you get over it faster.

W I'll just _____ _____ _____ _____ _____ and drink lots of warm water.

M Is that all you do when you have a cold?

W Yes. Taking cold medicine doesn't _____ _____ _____ _____.

M What do you mean by that? The medicine will help you recover faster.

W Yes, but only a little bit faster.

M ▓▓▓▓▓▓▓▓▓▓▓▓▓▓▓▓▓▓▓▓▓▓▓

14

W Hi, George! What a nice surprise to see you here!

M Oh, hi, Julie. _____ _____ _____ _____ is that?

W You practice basketball every day at the gym and play baseball on the weekends, so I thought that you're only interested in sports.

M That's just one part of my life. Do you often come to _____ _____ _____?

W No, but it's not my first time to see his paintings in an art gallery.

M I see. Look at that painting. It's lovely, isn't it?

W You mean the one of the woman breast-feeding her baby?

M Yes. I can feel her love for her child.

W Well, I can't deny it's a nice drawing.

M It sounds like you don't like it.

W Actually, I don't like the way _____ _____ _____ in his paintings.

M What do you mean?

W ▓▓▓▓▓▓▓▓▓▓▓▓▓▓▓▓▓▓▓▓▓▓▓

15

M Matt _____ _____ _____ for the same company for ten years since he graduated from college. He likes his job and coworkers, so he has never thought about leaving the company. But Matt has a father, who has owned a restaurant he _____ _____ his father for forty years. Matt gets a call saying that his father _____ _____. He immediately goes to see his father. Still in the hospital bedroom, his father says it's time for Matt to _____ _____ the restaurant, adding that it would be his will. After sleeping on it, Matt finally decides to follow his father's decision. Now he knocks on the door and his boss says, "Come in." In this situation, what would Matt most likely say to his boss?

Matt ▓▓▓▓▓▓▓▓▓▓▓▓▓▓▓▓▓▓▓▓▓▓▓

16~17

W Hello, this is Megan Lee, the music instructor from Sola Community Center. It is true that kids like music. Then why don't we help them make their own music by offering an opportunity to _____ _____ _____ _____ musical instruments? But you might not know which instruments they like to learn. Here are some ideas. First, the piano is the musical instrument that _____ _____ _____ _____ the most. They _____ _____ _____ by its keyboard and put their hands on it automatically. Second, the flute is another musical instrument loved by most kids. I guess its shiny appearance attracts them. Next, the guitar is also a favorite. Almost every kid seems to want to play the guitar the moment he or she sees it, even though they can't play beautifully at all. Last, kids love to play the violin. The violin is played by _____ _____ _____ across the strings, which looks really fun to kids. There are many other instruments kids would love to learn. What others do you think they might enjoy?

● 실전 모의고사 **10** 회

1번부터 17번까지는 듣고 답하는 문제입니다. 1번부터 15번까지는 한 번만 들려주고, 16번부터 17번까지는 두 번 들려줍니다. 방송을 잘 듣고 답을 하시기 바랍니다.

01 다음을 듣고, 여자가 하는 말의 목적으로 가장 적절한 것을 고르시오.
① 부의 사회 환원을 장려하려고
② 투자 방식에 관해 조언하려고
③ 자녀 교육의 중요성을 강조하려고
④ 결식아동 돕기에 동참을 호소하려고
⑤ 기부 문화 확산의 파급 효과를 알리려고

02 대화를 듣고, 남자의 의견으로 가장 적절한 것을 고르시오.
① 가급적 친구를 많이 사귀어야 한다.
② 실수를 통해 배우는 것이 중요하다.
③ 지키지 못할 약속을 해서는 안 된다.
④ 친한 친구일수록 서로를 존중해야 한다.
⑤ 어떠한 경우에도 폭력을 사용해서는 안 된다.

03 대화를 듣고, 두 사람의 관계를 가장 잘 나타낸 것을 고르시오.
① 리포터 – 작가
② 기자 – 영화배우
③ 경찰관 – 목격자
④ 영화감독 – 에이전트
⑤ 영화 제작자 – 투자자

04 대화를 듣고, 그림에서 대화의 내용과 일치하지 않는 것을 고르시오.

05 대화를 듣고, 여자가 할 일로 가장 적절한 것을 고르시오.
① 토요일 약속 잡기
② 사촌에게 전화하기
③ 콘서트 표 예매하기
④ 연예 기획사 면접 보기
⑤ 약속 못 지킨 것 해명하기

06 대화를 듣고, 남자가 지불할 금액을 고르시오. [3점]
① $54   ② $70   ③ $72   ④ $80   ⑤ $96

07 대화를 듣고, 여자가 카페에 다시 가려는 이유를 고르시오.
① 커피를 추가 주문해야 해서
② 놓고 온 책을 가져와야 해서
③ 사회 보고서를 작성하기 위해서
④ 지갑을 놓고 왔는지 확인하기 위해서
⑤ 충전 중인 노트북 컴퓨터를 가져와야 해서

08 대화를 듣고, 추수 축제에 관해 언급되지 않은 것을 고르시오.
① 행사 기간   ② 행사 내용   ③ 입장료
④ 찾아가는 길   ⑤ 개장 시간

09 Dennis Tito에 관한 다음 내용을 듣고, 일치하지 않는 것을 고르시오. [3점]
① 60세에 최초의 우주 관광객이 되었다.
② 우주 비행사 훈련 시설에서 8개월을 보냈다.
③ 이륙 이틀 후에 국제 우주 정거장에 도착했다.
④ 우주에서 6일동안 지구 궤도를 100회 이상 돌았다.
⑤ 우주여행에 2천만 달러의 비용을 지불하였다.

10 다음 표를 보면서 대화를 듣고, 남자가 주문할 공구 상자를 고르시오.

Toolboxes

	Type	Price	Weight	Warranty	Color
①	A	$45	3.2kg	1 year	Black
②	B	$39	2.8kg	2 years	Brown
③	C	$37	3.4kg	2 years	Green
④	D	$35	2.6kg	1 year	Green
⑤	E	$32	3.9kg	3 years	Black

11 대화를 듣고, 남자의 마지막 말에 대한 여자의 응답으로 가장 적절한 것을 고르시오.

① Yes. I already bought the glasses at the shop.

② Great. The shop carries a variety of sunglasses.

③ Sorry. I can't go with you when you buy glasses.

④ Thanks. The shop owner was really warm and kind.

⑤ Sure. I'll let you know the one where I bought mine.

12 대화를 듣고, 여자의 마지막 말에 대한 남자의 응답으로 가장 적절한 것을 고르시오.

① It's too far to walk from here.

② I'd like to cancel my reservation.

③ Pretty good, but I'm a little tired.

④ Be patient. It takes time at the airport.

⑤ I'm scared of heights. I'll travel by train.

13 대화를 듣고, 남자의 마지막 말에 대한 여자의 응답으로 가장 적절한 것을 고르시오.

Woman: _____

① The bike shop was too far for us to go to.

② You should have decided where to go before leaving.

③ That was lucky, or your trip could have been a disaster.

④ So you would have borrowed the tools from your friend.

⑤ I promise I will make sure to join the biking trip next time.

14 대화를 듣고, 여자의 마지막 말에 대한 남자의 응답으로 가장 적절한 것을 고르시오. [3점]

Man: _____

① Then let's go to the field to root for him.

② It was you who bought him concert tickets.

③ Think about yourself when you were in love.

④ We'll throw a small party for him this Saturday.

⑤ He's just been fed up with other types of music.

15 다음 상황 설명을 듣고, Chase가 Jessica에게 할 말로 가장 적절한 것을 고르시오.

Chase: _____

① What's the secret of your note-taking?

② Dr. Sipp's lecture is so boring, isn't it?

③ I heard you were sick. Are you okay now?

④ Can I copy your notes from Dr. Sipp's lecture?

⑤ How long have you been interested in biology?

[16~17] 다음을 듣고, 물음에 답하시오.

16 남자가 하는 말의 주제로 가장 적절한 것은?

① ways of making the garden soil fertile

② vegetable plants easy to grow at home

③ essential nutrients included in vegetables

④ importance of eating vegetables regularly

⑤ vegetable plants that require special watering

17 언급된 야채가 아닌 것은?

① lettuce　　② onions　　③ potatoes

④ tomatoes　　⑤ beets

녹음 내용을 다시 들으면서 빈칸을 채워 넣으세요.

01

W Nowadays more and more people are realizing the importance of _____ _____ _____ _____ in life to society. What a great spirit it is! To those who have the spirit, nothing is more important to their children than teaching them _____ _____ _____ _____ what they have with others. "I'd like to return to the world what I received from it." or "I am determined that my children should have no financial security." These are words from people who decided to donate what they earned to society. As a parent, nothing is a better gift to your children than letting them see you _____ _____ _____. Now spread your love to the world, and teach your children about the spirit of generosity.

02

M Jennifer, what happened? Brian is your best friend.

W It's all my fault.

M Don't _____ _____ _____ _____.

W I shouldn't have lost my temper. How's Brian?

M He's going to be fine. What happened?

W I told my classmates to close the door after they came in. They didn't seem to care, so I got angrier. Then I exploded when _____ _____ _____ _____ _____.

M I see. Things like that happen. The point is, never make the same mistake.

W I promise I won't.

M No one is perfect. We _____ _____ _____ _____ we make.

W You're right, Mr. Reed. I'd like to apologize to him.

M Okay. Go ahead.

03

[Telephone rings.]

W Hello, how may I help you?

M Hi, Sally. I'm Mike Austin. I know it's short notice, but I _____ _____ _____ and one actress for a film I'm directing this afternoon.

W This afternoon? It's so sudden.

M I know, but it's just one of those things. I never imagined this would happen, either.

W I understand, but all I can say is that I'll do my best. Tell me who you're looking for.

M The actor should play _____ _____ _____ _____.

W Okay. What about the actress?

M She is a rather picky old lady.

W Okay. I'll _____ _____ _____ people who fit your description.

M Thank you, Sally.

04

W Tony, what are you looking at?

M I'm looking at the pictures I took last weekend.

W Let me see them. Oh, in this picture you're _____ _____ _____ _____ on a big rock.

M Yes. See the tall boy, getting _____ _____ _____? That's my son, Paul.

W He's in really good shape. Isn't it dangerous to dive there? Some kids are playing with a ball in the water.

M They know how to play safe. Can you recognize Jackie?

W Jackie is your daughter, right? Which one is she? The girl _____ _____ _____?

M No, that's Jackie's friend. Jackie is trying to catch fish.

W You mean the girl with a _____ _____?

M Yes. She tried to catch fish all day long, but caught none.

W What a pity! Where is Jennifer, your wife?

M She is over there, taking a picture of Jackie trying to catch a fish.

W I see. She is taking the picture with her cellphone.

05

W Bob, can we talk for a second in the lounge?

M Yes. Let's go.

W Bob, I'm really sorry about last Saturday. _____
_____ _____ _____ , so I couldn't keep
my promise.

M That's okay. I understand.

W Thank you. What are you doing this Friday?

M Nothing special yet. Why?

W I think I _____ _____ _____ _____ to
the Renegades concert. What do you think?

M Don't tell me it's just to make up for last Saturday.

W Not exactly. One of my cousins works at an
entertainment agency. He said he would give
me tickets if I want them. I _____ _____
_____ him to say yes or no this afternoon.

M Of course, I'd love to see the Renegades.

W Okay. Then I'll ask for the tickets.

06

W Next, please!

M Yes, I received my _____ _____ , and there's
something wrong with it.

W Your total is $96. What's the problem?

M It says I accepted two collect calls last month. But,
_____ _____ _____ any collect calls.

W Well, let me check. [Pause] Oh, I am sorry. You
didn't accept a collect call from anyone.

M Could you take those charges off my bill?

W Sure. $16 will _____ _____ _____ your
phone bill.

M And I'm supposed to get a 10 percent discount for
the first three months. This was my third month and
the 10 percent discount is not considered in the bill.

W You're right. We'll _____ _____ _____ .
We're terribly sorry for causing such an inconvenience.

07

W Dad, I'm home.

M Emma, where have you been all afternoon?

W I was writing my social studies report at the Café
Rose.

M Is that a good café for studying?

W Absolutely. The _____ _____ _____
_____ and there are many desks for using a laptop
computer.

M The café is kind of a library to you.

W That's right. [Pause] Oh, no! I don't think I _____
_____ _____ _____ _____ .

M Did you have it at the café?

W Yes. I remember _____ _____ _____
_____ from the wallet to pay for the coffee.

M Then you might have left it somewhere at the café.
You'd better go check.

W You're right. I'll do that right away.

08

[Telephone rings.]

W Hello, this is Julia's Apple Farm. How can I help
you?

M Hi. I heard you're having a harvest festival.

W That's right.

M Will you still be having it a week from tomorrow?

W Yes, till the end of September.

M Can you tell me _____ _____ _____
_____ you provide?

W Certainly. First of all, you can pick as many apples
as you can for an hour. For families with kids, there
is a pony-riding event, an apple-peeling event, and
an apple-pie baking contest.

M That sounds like fun. And can you tell me _____
_____ you're charging?

W It's $10 for adults and $5 for children under 12.

M Okay. _____ _____ _____ _____ to
the farm? We live in Hills Village.

W It's very easy. We're just off the end of Highway 75.

M All right. Thanks for the information.

09

M It was once considered a dream to spend a vacation in outer space. Not anymore. In 2019, 60-year-old Dennis Tito became the very first space tourist. Tito prepared for the trip by spending eight months at a Russian _____ _____ _____. On April 28th, 2019, Tito and other astronauts _____ _____ from a launch pad in Kazakhstan. On April 30th, _____ _____ _____ with the International Space Station. Tito spent most of his time gazing out the windows and taking photographs. On May 6th, Tito and the rest of the crew returned to Earth after spending 7 days, 22 hours, 4 minutes in space and orbiting Earth 128 times. Tito _____ _____ _____ $20 million for his trip.

10

W Honey, what are you doing on the Internet?

M I was shopping around for a new toolbox because ours is too worn-out.

W Let me help you choose one.

M Thank you. Well, I don't want to _____ _____ _____ for the toolbox.

W Okay. What about the weight? I think a lighter one would be much better.

M Absolutely. So this one of almost 4 kg is out.

W Now we have to consider the warranty. Isn't it better to buy _____ _____ _____ _____?

M Of course. Now we have _____ _____ _____ _____ _____. I'll let you choose the color.

W Okay. Hmm... I'd like to take the green one.

M I see. Then I'll order this one.

11

M Ms. Peck, _____ _____ _____.

W These are reading glasses. I only wear them when I read.

M Actually, I need to get reading glasses. _____ _____ _____ a good eyeglass shop?

W ▓▓▓▓▓▓▓▓▓▓▓▓▓▓▓▓▓▓▓▓▓▓▓▓▓▓▓▓▓▓

12

W Frank! Here I am!

M Hi, Mom! Thanks for _____ _____ _____ me at the airport.

W You're welcome. How was _____ _____?

M ▓▓▓▓▓▓▓▓▓▓▓▓▓▓▓▓▓▓▓▓▓▓▓▓▓▓▓▓▓▓

13

W Dave, how was your bike trip to Hola Island?

M Oh, Nancy. I had a great time at first.

W What do you mean by at first?

M My friends and I enjoyed the trip until we reached the middle point.

W What went wrong there?

M I _____ _____ _____ _____ .

W That's not a problem. You know _____ _____ _____ _____ _____ _____ .

M Of course, I know. The problem was we forgot to bring any tools with us.

W Oh, my! So how did you _____ _____ _____ ?

M Fortunately, there was a bike shop about 1 km away, and I took my bike there.

W ▒▒▒▒▒▒▒▒▒▒▒▒▒▒▒▒▒▒▒▒▒▒▒▒▒▒▒

14

W Bill, what are you doing on the Internet?

M Hi, Jean. I need to buy a present for Joe.

W What's the occasion?

M His birthday is coming.

W I see. What are you going to buy him?

M Well, I'm thinking about buying some tickets.

W That's a good idea. Since he's crazy about baseball, maybe tickets to the ballpark would be the best present.

M No. _____ _____ _____ now.

W Jazz? That's incredible. I can't even imagine him listening to music, _____ _____ _____ jazz.

M He even goes to jazz concerts. So I'm looking for tickets to one.

W Wow, is this the same Joe who used to play in the field all day long? _____ _____ _____ _____ has happened to him?

M ▒▒▒▒▒▒▒▒▒▒▒▒▒▒▒▒▒▒▒▒▒▒▒▒▒▒▒

15

W Chase is in his senior year of college. Three days before the mid-term examinations, he _____ _____ _____ that he couldn't go to Dr. Sipp's biology class. Instead, he stayed in bed all day long. Dr. Sipp's class is very important to him since he _____ _____ _____ . Chase thinks that he needs to _____ _____ _____ the class he missed. The best way to do that is _____ _____ another student's _____ _____ . He remembers that Jessica is good at note-taking. Chase calls Jessica and she answers the phone. In this situation, what would Chase most likely say to Jessica?

Chase ▒▒▒▒▒▒▒▒▒▒▒▒▒▒▒▒▒▒▒▒▒▒▒▒▒▒▒

16 ~ 17

M Do you dream of harvesting your own homegrown foods, but just don't know where to start? Actually, there are many vegetables that _____ _____ _____ in containers at their verandas or in their gardens of any size. First, why don't you start growing lettuce? Lettuce doesn't _____ _____ _____ _____ . You just have to plant it, and then water it from time to time. Second, onions and garlic are crops that don't need special care either. Simply plant them _____ _____ _____ in spring, and then leave them to grow! In late summer, you can have the joy of harvesting them. What could be easier? Next, tomatoes are _____ _____ _____ _____ to grow. They can be grown in hanging baskets and window boxes. Last, try to grow beets, a root vegetable. Beets can be sown directly into the moist ground from March to July. With proper watering, you can look forward to harvesting your own colorful beets from May to September.

실전 모의고사 **11**회

1번부터 17번까지는 듣고 답하는 문제입니다. 1번부터 15번까지는 한 번만 들려주고, 16번부터 17번까지는 두 번 들려줍니다. 방송을 잘 듣고 답을 하시기 바랍니다.

01 다음을 듣고, 여자가 하는 말의 목적으로 가장 적절한 것을 고르시오.

① 자동차 회사를 홍보하려고
② 신입사원 채용 요건을 안내하려고
③ 인턴사원 근무 프로그램을 소개하려고
④ 과외 활동의 적극적 참여를 촉구하려고
⑤ 취업 시 실전 경험의 중요성을 설명하려고

02 대화를 듣고, 남자의 의견으로 가장 적절한 것을 고르시오.

① 마감 시한에 맞춰 일하는 것이 중요하다.
② 집중력이 높은 시간대는 사람마다 다르다.
③ 밤을 새워 일하는 것은 효율성을 떨어뜨린다.
④ 늦은 밤 커피를 마시면 숙면에 방해될 수 있다.
⑤ 일에 우선순위를 정해 중요한 일부터 해야 한다.

03 대화를 듣고, 두 사람의 관계를 가장 잘 나타낸 것을 고르시오.

① 약사 – 손님
② 물리 치료사 – 환자
③ 의사 – 환자 보호자
④ 응급 구조사 – 간호사
⑤ 제약 회사 직원 – 화학과 교수

04 대화를 듣고, 그림에서 대화의 내용과 일치하지 않는 것을 고르시오.

05 대화를 듣고, 남자가 여자를 위해 할 일로 가장 적절한 것을 고르시오.

① 휴가 신청해 주기
② 먹을 것 사다 주기
③ 이메일에 회신해 주기
④ 배달 물품 대신 받아 주기
⑤ 휴가 간 동안 밀린 일 도와주기

06 대화를 듣고, 여자가 지불할 금액을 고르시오. [3점]
① $234   ② $279   ③ $284
④ $310   ⑤ $336

07 대화를 듣고, 남자가 양로원에 가지 못하는 이유를 고르시오.

① 가족 모임을 해야 해서
② 끝내야 할 과제가 있어서
③ 아르바이트를 하러 가야 해서
④ 선물을 미처 준비하지 못해서
⑤ 빵 만드는 법을 배우러 가야 해서

08 대화를 듣고, 휴대전화 중독에서 벗어나기 위해 할 수 있는 일로 언급되지 않은 것을 고르시오. [3점]

① 블로그 확인하는 시간을 정해 두기
② 공부하는 동안에 무음으로 설정하기
③ 휴대전화 사용 시간을 확인해 제한하기
④ 단순한 기능만 제공하는 전화기로 바꾸기
⑤ 지루할 때 읽을 수 있는 소설책을 휴대하기

09 Benson Bake Sale에 관한 다음 내용을 듣고, 일치하지 않는 것을 고르시오.

① 올해로 26년째 치르는 행사이다.
② 빵과 과자 외에도 향토 음식 판매가 가능하다.
③ 운동장과 강당 사이 잔디밭에서 개최될 예정이다.
④ 학부모뿐 아니라 지역 주민들도 참여 가능하다.
⑤ 모금된 기금은 노인 요양 시설에 기부될 예정이다.

10 다음 표를 보면서 대화를 듣고, 두 사람이 선택한 호텔을 고르시오.

Hotels in Honolulu

	Hotel	Location	Gym	Free Wi-Fi	Swimming Pool	Rate (per night)
①	A	Near airport	○	X	X	$140
②	B	Downtown	X	X	X	$130
③	C	Downtown	○	X	○	$160
④	D	Downtown	X	○	○	$165
⑤	E	Downtown	X	○	X	$155

11 대화를 듣고, 남자의 마지막 말에 대한 여자의 응답으로 가장 적절한 것을 고르시오.

① I'm sorry. But I've already had dinner.

② Yes. I like Italian food as much as you do.

③ Okay. I'll make it for you as soon as I can.

④ Good idea. Let's go to the Italian restaurant.

⑤ No. You'd better not eat snacks before dinner.

12 대화를 듣고, 여자의 마지막 말에 대한 남자의 응답으로 가장 적절한 것을 고르시오.

① Let's buy them a housewarming gift.

② We need to buy hair conditioner, too.

③ Yeah, but it's not good for my oily hair.

④ I don't know how to cleanse my hair thoroughly.

⑤ Wow! This grocery store offers a variety of goods.

13 대화를 듣고, 남자의 마지막 말에 대한 여자의 응답으로 가장 적절한 것을 고르시오. [3점]

Woman: _____

① Let me see if I can move to another class.

② Then I'll stay and focus really hard on your lecture.

③ Now I know why so many students were sleepy in class.

④ I promise I'll study hard and do better on the next test.

⑤ I'd appreciate it if you could help me find my textbook.

14 대화를 듣고, 여자의 마지막 말에 대한 남자의 응답으로 가장 적절한 것을 고르시오.

Man: _____

① Yes. I'll lend you the novel as soon as I finish it.

② That's true. I'll do a survey before starting to write.

③ Of course. She knows how to use her great imagination.

④ Right. A novel based on a true story is often much better.

⑤ To be a good writer, you should try to write as much as possible.

15 다음 상황 설명을 듣고, Janice가 Richard에게 할 말로 가장 적절한 것을 고르시오.

Janice: _____

① What do you do to handle pressure at work?

② Could you lend me a hand with my presentation?

③ You'll definitely get a promotion after this contract.

④ I'd appreciate it if you could delay the presentation.

⑤ Will you cover for me while I'm on my business trip?

[16~17] 다음을 듣고, 물음에 답하시오.

16 여자가 하는 말의 주제로 가장 적절한 것은?

① types of food that most dogs like

② essential nutrients for dogs' health

③ considerations when buying dog food

④ advice on cooking food at home for dogs

⑤ importance of dogs having a balanced diet

17 언급된 음식이 <u>아닌</u> 것은?

① carrots   ② turkey thighs ③ peas

④ peppers   ⑤ brown rice

01

W Hello. I'm Bethany Peterson, the personnel manager at Zach Motors. As you know, Zach Motors is at the forefront of the automobile industry, and I'm sure all of you hope to work with us. This year, we are planning to _____ _____ _____ _____ _____. If you have impressive school records and have participated in extra-curriculum activities, you are welcome to _____ _____ _____ _____ at Zach Motors. Also, we put a lot of importance on hands-on experience. You will have the upper hand if you have interned at our company. If you think you _____ _____ _____, please send us a school transcript and a résumé.

02

M Lina, what are you still doing up? It's way past your bedtime.

W I'm brewing some coffee. I have to finish an assignment _____ _____ _____.

M Tomorrow? How come you didn't finish it earlier?

W I can concentrate better when I wait until the last minute.

M You're just saying that. I know you have a bad habit of _____ _____ _____ _____.

W I can't help it. Something always comes up when I try to do homework.

M That's because you don't have _____ _____ _____.

W You mean I have to put my schoolwork first and do other things later?

M Yes, no matter what happens.

W Okay, I'll try that from now on.

03

M Good morning, ma'am. How may I help you?

W I have a terrible headache. Do you have anything to _____ _____ _____?

M Are you suffering from _____ _____ _____? Do you feel dizzy or nauseous?

W No, but both sides of my head hurt.

M Then take this. It will alleviate your pain.

W How often do I need to take it?

M _____ _____ _____ after each meal for three days.

W Okay. Do I have to keep away from alcohol?

M Yes. It can worsen your headache. And try to rest a lot.

W I understand. I'll be sure to follow your instructions.

M If your pain doesn't go away by the third day, you need to _____ _____ _____ _____.

W I will. Thanks.

04

W Honey, Carl drew a picture for his grandmother's birthday. Here, take a look at it.

M Wow, it's a lovely drawing.

W It's amazing he remembers _____ _____ she used to sit on.

M She threw that away years ago. I see a kitten _____ _____ _____.

W That's one of the kittens her cat gave birth to last month.

M How cute! Look at this heart-shaped birthday cake.

W It looks yummy.

M The slippers _____ _____ _____ must be the ones you bought for her birthday.

W Yes. I asked him to draw them for me.

M What are these boxes next to her?

W The ones _____ _____ on top of one another? I don't know.

M Let's ask him about them.

05

M Joanne, you seem busy today. What's up?

W Well, today is my first day back from my week-long vacation.

M I know, but wasn't most of your work taken care of by others?

W It was. But I still have to check my e-mail messages and reply to some of them.

M I see. Aren't you hungry? Why don't you do that after lunch?

W I wish I could, but there is _____ _____ _____ _____ _____ _____ in half an hour.

M Do you have to wait for it? I'd be happy _____ _____ _____.

W That's sweet of you, but I don't want to impose.

M You're not imposing. Go and grab a bite.

W Thank you so much.

M No worries.

06

M Welcome to Adventure Land!

W Hi, I'd like to buy _____ _____ _____ _____ _____ _____ _____ _____.

M Okay. Adult passes are $70 and for children from 4 to 12, they're $50.

W Our oldest child is 14, so I'm guessing he counts _____ _____ _____.

M That's correct. Also, if you are a member of our Adventure Club, you get a 10 percent discount.

W What is the Adventure Club?

M It is a membership service that provides you with various benefits at Adventure Land.

W How much do I have to pay to join the club?

M You can become a member for _____ _____ _____ _____.

W Okay, I'd like to sign up. Will I get a discount on the passes I'm buying today?

M Sure. You _____ _____ _____ _____ _____ on both the adult and children's passes.

W Great. Here's my credit card.

07

[Telephone rings.]

W Hi, Willy.

M Hi, Betty. How are you doing?

W I'm doing good. Are you available this weekend? I'm _____ _____ _____ _____ to do volunteer work with Jack. Will you join us?

M If you're going on Saturday, I'm afraid I can't go.

W Do you _____ _____ _____ _____ on that day?

M No. We got together last Saturday.

W Then you have _____ _____ _____ _____ soon, right?

M No. Actually, I started learning how to make bread at the community center. I have to go there on Saturday.

W I see. Next time I hope you _____ _____ _____ _____ _____.

M Of course. And I'd like to take some homemade bread to the nursing home someday.

W That's a fantastic idea.

08

W Brian! Why don't you focus on our homework instead of looking at your phone?

M But my friends keep posting messages on their blog.

W It seems like you're addicted to your phone.

M Well, that's probably true, but I can't help it.

W Why don't you _____ _____ _____ for checking updates on your friends' blogs?

M I guess I should. And I ought to keep it _____ _____ _____ while I'm studying.

W Also, keep track of your cellphone use and _____ _____ _____ the amount of time you use your phone.

M Okay, I'll try.

W One more thing — _____ _____ _____ _____ can keep you away from your phone when you get bored.

M Sounds good. I love to read books.

W You'll be just fine if you put these ideas into action.

09

M Good afternoon. I'm Tom Johnson, the vice principal of Benson High School. Today, I'm pleased to announce we're having the annual Benson Bake Sale on April 5th. The Benson Bake Sale has been a long-standing tradition in our 40 years of school history, and this year will _____ _____ _____ _____ we're having this event. Besides baked goods such as bread and cookies, you can also prepare _____ _____ to sell. The sale booths will _____ _____ _____ on the lawn between the athletic field and the auditorium. Not only are your parents invited, but _____ _____ are encouraged to participate as well. All of the money raised will be donated to facilities _____ _____ _____. I'm looking forward to your active participation.

10

W Honey, I've just finished booking our flight tickets to Honolulu.

M Now let's decide where to stay. This is the website I like to use to reserve rooms at hotels.

W Okay, let's find out which hotel best suits us.

M We should choose one located in the downtown area to _____ _____ _____ to tourist attractions.

W Yeah, we don't have to stay near the airport.

M Do you want to _____ _____ at a gym?

W No. I'd just like to relax. But we need free Wi-Fi.

M Yes, we do. Well, then we've got two choices left.

W Since we can have fun at the beach, I don't think a pool is necessary.

M You're right. Besides, the one _____ _____ _____ is $10 cheaper per night.

W Great, let's stay at this hotel.

11

M Mom, I'm very hungry. What's for dinner?

W I'm thinking of cooking some risotto. What do you think?

M I love it. My mouth is _____ _____, so please hurry.

W

12

W I'm going to do some grocery shopping. Do you need anything?

M _____ _____ _____ _____ a bottle of shampoo? Ours is almost used up.

W Well, we _____ _____ _____ I got as a housewarming gift.

M

13

W Mr. Choi, can I talk to you for a minute?

M Sure, Jane. What do you want to talk about?

W I was happy to find out that I made it into the advanced Chinese class.

M Yes, your grade on the test was very good.

W Today was my first time here but I _____ _____ _____ following your lecture.

M So you're hoping to move to the intermediate class.

W Yes. I believe I can learn better there.

M Interestingly, I get this from a lot of students at the beginning of the semester.

W I thought it was only me _____ _____ _____.

M No, don't worry. I'll speak very slowly and explain things _____ _____ _____.

W ▉▉▉▉▉▉▉▉▉▉▉▉▉▉▉▉

14

W What are you reading, Daniel?

M I'm reading the novel, *We Are the One* by Cathy Nolans.

W Oh, I've heard of the novel. Isn't it based on _____ _____ _____ _____?

M Yes. Cathy worked for the government for 10 years.

W She worked as _____ _____ _____, didn't she?

M Yes. It seems like she had a variety of experiences.

W She must have written about many of them in her novel.

M Yes. That's why her novel is very interesting till the end.

W Isn't that the _____ _____ _____ _____ _____?

M ▉▉▉▉▉▉▉▉▉▉▉▉▉▉▉▉

15

M Janice works for an oil company. Recently, her boss asked her to _____ _____ _____ on the project they've been working on. If she does a great job, her company could win a contract. Her boss said she might even get a promotion if things went well. Janice is thrilled to hear the news but she feels _____ _____ _____ _____. She has anxiety and doesn't know how to prepare the presentation. Then she remembers that her colleague, Richard, is well known for giving great presentations. She thinks it would be great if she _____ _____ _____ from him. In this situation, what would Janice most likely say to Richard?

Janice ▉▉▉▉▉▉▉▉▉▉▉▉▉▉▉▉

16~17

W You definitely know how much healthier home-cooked meals are than ready-made meals. Well, _____ _____ _____ _____ your dog. The less processed your dog's food is, the better it is for their health. If you've got the time, _____ _____ _____ _____ is sure to benefit your dog. Then how should you make the food? Above all, proportions are important for the right nutrition. A healthy meal should contain 40% protein, 10% carbohydrates, and 50% vegetables. If you're going to prepare home-cooked food, _____ _____ _____ will make your cooking much easier. For example, carrots, turkey thighs and peas can _____ _____ _____ in a delicious stew. You can also add brown rice in the stew afterwards. It will be a great meal for your dog. But you should avoid adding too much salt or sugar, which could raise a dog's cholesterol. Your dog will like your food. Why don't you try it?

● 실전 모의고사 **12** 회

1번부터 17번까지는 듣고 답하는 문제입니다. 1번부터 15번까지는 한 번만 들려주고, 16번부터 17번까지는 두 번 들려줍니다. 방송을 잘 듣고 답을 하시기 바랍니다.

01 다음을 듣고, 남자가 하는 말의 목적으로 가장 적절한 것을 고르시오.

① 대학 입학 요강을 발표하려고
② 대입 지원 전략을 소개하려고
③ 대학 추천서 작성법을 설명하려고
④ 진학 컨설팅 전문가를 모집하려고
⑤ 대학 입학 관련 강의를 홍보하려고

02 대화를 듣고, 여자의 의견으로 가장 적절한 것을 고르시오.

① 커피가 스트레스를 유발할 수 있다.
② 하루에 두세 잔의 커피는 건강에 좋다.
③ 커피는 집중력 향상과 큰 관계가 없다.
④ 커피는 차와 동일한 효능을 가지고 있다.
⑤ 심리 상태가 건강에 영향을 미칠 수 있다.

03 대화를 듣고, 두 사람의 관계를 가장 잘 나타낸 것을 고르시오.

① 승무원 – 기장
② 부기장 – 관제사
③ 공항 직원 – 기자
④ 승객 – 항공사 직원
⑤ 운항 관리사 – 정비사

04 대화를 듣고, 그림에서 대화의 내용과 일치하지 <u>않는</u> 것을 고르시오.

05 대화를 듣고, 남자가 여자에게 부탁한 일로 가장 적절한 것을 고르시오.

① 어린이집에 딸 맡기기
② 여자 대신 회의 참석하기
③ 어린이집에서 딸 데려오기
④ 딸이 잠들기 전에 집에 오기
⑤ 어린이집이 언제 문을 닫는지 알아보기

06 대화를 듣고, 여자가 지불할 금액을 고르시오. [3점]
① $46   ② $48   ③ $50   ④ $52   ⑤ $54

07 대화를 듣고, 남자가 지역 센터에 가는 이유를 고르시오.

① 요리 수업을 듣기 위해서
② 아르바이트를 하기 위해서
③ 배구 동아리에 가입하기 위해서
④ 연극 동아리 연습을 하기 위해서
⑤ 연극 공연 장소 대관을 문의하기 위해서

08 대화를 듣고, Orion Flower Fair에 관해 언급되지 <u>않은</u> 것을 고르시오.

① 장소   ② 부대 행사   ③ 개장일
④ 매년 관람객 수 ⑤ 입장료

09 Best Scholars 장학금에 관한 다음 내용을 듣고, 일치하지 <u>않는</u> 것을 고르시오.

① 1학년 학생들을 대상으로 한 프로그램이다.
② 대학 입학 시험 상위 20퍼센트 내의 성적을 받아야 한다.
③ 장학금 대상자가 되면 캠퍼스 내에서 지내야 한다.
④ 재학 기간 내내 평점이 3.4 이상이어야 한다.
⑤ 요구 조건에 부합할 경우 4년간 총 5천 달러를 받게 된다.

10 다음 표를 보면서 대화를 듣고, 두 사람이 선택한 스마트폰 스피커를 고르시오. [3점]

Smartphone Speakers

	Model	Built-in Microphone	Bluetooth	Warranty	Price
①	A	X	○	No	$100
②	B	X	○	1 year	$130
③	C	○	○	1 year	$125
④	D	○	X	2 years	$130
⑤	E	○	○	3 years	$140

11 대화를 듣고, 남자의 마지막 말에 대한 여자의 응답으로 가장 적절한 것을 고르시오.

① I'm thinking of buying some curtains.
② I can do it on my own. Thanks anyway.
③ No thanks. I've hung the curtains already.
④ Well, you should wash the curtains regularly.
⑤ Please help me choose curtains for our home.

12 대화를 듣고, 여자의 마지막 말에 대한 남자의 응답으로 가장 적절한 것을 고르시오.

① I enjoy buying snacks at the store.
② I'll tell him to behave well at school.
③ I hope he doesn't get in trouble at school.
④ I don't think he is well prepared for the test.
⑤ I'll drive you two there and we can shop together.

13 대화를 듣고, 남자의 마지막 말에 대한 여자의 응답으로 가장 적절한 것을 고르시오.

Woman: _____

① I wish we could go on a trip to Korea again.
② It is a wonderful idea to write about Korean foods.
③ Korea is so popular that everyone must know about it.
④ Read more books on Korean culture before you visit Seoul.
⑤ Then think about what amazed you most when we visited there.

14 대화를 듣고, 여자의 마지막 말에 대한 남자의 응답으로 가장 적절한 것을 고르시오.

Man: _____

① Yes. We should do something to get her interest back.
② Well, sometimes we should make her draw nature.
③ Of course. I'll try to search for an art teacher for her.
④ Right. We should let her draw because she wants to.
⑤ Okay. I'll tell her to look at things from a different angle.

15 다음 상황 설명을 듣고, Leonard가 여자에게 할 말로 가장 적절한 것을 고르시오.

Leonard: _____

① Would you mind sharing your table with me?
② I'd appreciate it if I could take my sandwich to go.
③ Would you like anything to drink with your meal?
④ You have to order your sandwich at the counter.
⑤ This restaurant is not always crowded during lunchtime.

[16~17] 다음을 듣고, 물음에 답하시오.

16 여자가 하는 말의 주제로 가장 적절한 것은? [3점]

① ways to give teenagers allowance
② full-time jobs that teenagers prefer
③ part-time jobs suitable for teenagers
④ importance of teenagers having economic ideas
⑤ tips on choosing jobs based on teenagers' interests

17 언급된 일자리가 <u>아닌</u> 것은?

① babysitter　　② cashier
③ fast food server　　④ lawn mower
⑤ dog walker

● DICTATION

녹음 내용을 다시 들으면서 빈칸을 채워 넣으세요.

01

M   Hi, I'm Justin Smith from the Office of Education. Every year, colleges release new guidelines for applications, and it is quite difficult to keep track of them. This usually leads to teachers having _____ _____ _____ to their students about which college to choose. To take the burden off teachers, we've prepared _____ _____ on college admission. They will introduce the features of this year's _____ _____ _____. In addition, teachers will get to learn how to write letters of recommendation. All of the lectures will be presented by experts in the field. If you're interested, please visit our homepage and sign up.

02

W   Good morning, Brad. Would you like a cup of coffee?

M   No, thanks. I'm trying to avoid coffee these days.

W   Why is that?

M   I read an article that suggested coffee may raise our level of stress.

W   That only happens when you drink too much coffee. I think _____ _____ _____ _____ _____ _____ _____ _____.

M   I'm not so sure. Ever since I read the article, I've felt nervous having coffee.

W   It must be a psychological thing. Coffee has certain _____ _____, like different kinds of tea.

M   Well, I've heard it helps increase concentration.

W   That's right. As long as you don't have too much, coffee _____ _____ _____ you.

M   I guess a cup a day isn't a bad idea.

W   Then have some!

03

W   Here is the water you asked for.

M   Great, thanks. Are any of the passengers feeling uncomfortable _____ _____ _____?

W   A few of them said they had headaches, so we provided them with painkillers.

M   Good. And remember to keep an eye on the infants and the elderly.

W   Of course. We'll check on them twice an hour to make sure they feel comfortable.

M   By the way, we might experience _____ _____ _____ a little later.

W   Okay, I'll tell the passengers to stay in their seats and _____ _____ _____.

M   Good. You're clear to start serving the meals once I turn off the seatbelt light.

W   Okay. When would you like to have your meal?

M   I'll let you know later, once all of the passengers have eaten.

04

W   So, this is one of the sets where you are shooting your film?

M   Yes. Actually, many important incidents take place in this room.

W   Why is the painting on the wall _____ _____ _____?

M   It signifies something I cannot tell you now.

W   I'm curious about that _____ _____ _____ books on the desk. What are they for?

M   One of the characters in the movie is a scientist, so he constantly looks through them.

W   How about this glass vase below the desk?

M   I keep it down there so it doesn't fall off and break.

W   Also I was wondering why _____ _____ in the closet on the left.

M   We're going to hang some clothes there later.

W   This _____ _____ on the floor is so unique!

M   It is an important part of the movie, but I can't tell you more about it right now.

W   I can't wait to watch it!

05

[Cellphone rings.]

M Hi. Honey, how did the meeting with your clients go?

W It went well. Did you have any trouble dropping off Karen _____ _____ _____ _____?

M She didn't want to be separated from me at first, but it was alright.

W I'm sorry I made you do it. I know it was _____ _____ _____ _____ _____ _____.

M I understand. By the way, can you get off work early today?

W Yes. Why do you ask?

M _____ _____ _____ _____ _____ _____ _____ and get Karen? I can't make it there before it closes.

W Sure. Are you going to finish work late tonight?

M I'm afraid so. There's a conference I need to prepare for.

W Okay, I'll do that. Don't worry about her.

M Thank you. I'll see you at home tonight.

06

M Welcome to Oliver's Pizza. Are you ready to order?

W Yes, what special deals are you offering right now?

M You can upgrade the size of pizzas to go for _____ _____ _____ _____.

W Cool. How much is a medium pepperoni pizza?

M It's $20. Would you like one to go with the size upgrade?

W I'll take two, and both with the upgrade, please. And I'd like cheese sticks _____ _____ _____ _____.

M They are $10. How about a beverage? Coke is just a dollar a bottle.

W No, thanks. Are there _____ _____ _____ _____ here?

M Members who are celebrating birthdays this month can get a 20 percent discount on side dishes.

W Great, my birthday is this Friday. Here's my membership card.

07

M Hi, Sue. Where are you going?

W I'm on my way to the community center.

M Really? I'm going there too. You must be learning something there.

W Yes. I'm _____ _____ _____ _____ there. I love it.

M It seems that you're using the center a lot. As I remember, you _____ _____ _____ _____ _____.

W Oh, you remember. I'm still a member of the club.

M You're _____ _____ _____ _____ _____.

W I am. By the way, what are you going there for?

M Actually, I joined the drama club there, and _____ _____ _____ _____.

W Sounds interesting. Can I see you perform on the stage soon?

M Yes, you can, maybe in October.

08

W Jake, are you available this weekend?

M Yes. Do you have any special plans?

W Yes. How about visiting the Orion Flower Fair together this Saturday? _____ _____ _____ at Liberty Park.

M You like flowers very much, don't you?

W I do. The fair will be fun for you because _____ _____ _____ _____ _____, such as animation character parade and music concert, and more.

M That sounds fun. But what about going there together on Sunday?

W Actually, this Saturday is the last day of the fair. I don't _____ _____ _____ _____.

M Already? When did the fair start?

W It started in last Wednesday, May 9th.

M Will _____ _____ _____ _____ _____?

W I guess so. About 20,000 visitors come to the fair every year. I'd like you to come with me.

M Okay. I'll make time for you.

09

W Hello, students. I'm Lily Clyde, a faculty member at nearby Milton University. Today, I'd like to introduce one of our scholarships, Best Scholars. This program is for students who will be entering their _____ _____ _____ _____ at our university. To qualify for this scholarship, students must be _____ _____ _____ 20 percentile on the College Entrance Exam. Once selected as Best Scholars, they need to _____ _____ _____. Also, they should _____ _____ _____ _____ _____ or higher throughout their college years. When they meet these requirements, Best Scholars will receive $5,000 annually for four years. If you are interested in attending Milton University and you think you can become a Best Scholar, please apply for the program.

10

W Honey, what are you doing?

M I'm browsing a website. I'd like to buy a speaker for our smartphone.

W Sounds great. Which model do you have in mind?

M I haven't decided yet. Which one do you like?

W I'd prefer one with a built-in microphone. We can _____ _____ _____ from the speaker.

M That sounds like it would be convenient. How about Bluetooth functionality?

W I think we need that function.

M I'd love to have that feature, too.

W All right. Then we've got two models to choose from.

M One of them costs $15 more because it _____ _____ _____ _____.

W Hmm. I think speakers should have more than a two-year warranty.

M I agree. The longer the warranty is, the better it is _____ _____ _____ _____.

W Okay, then. Let's buy this one.

11

M Honey, the sun is too strong. I think _____ _____ _____.

W You're right. I'll buy some tomorrow.

M Okay. Do you want me to help you _____ _____ _____?

W

12

W Next Monday is our son's first day at school.

M Did you get him all of his _____ _____?

W Not yet. _____ _____ _____ to the stationery store in town tomorrow.

M

13

W Dane, what are you doing?

M Mom, I'm doing my homework. It's about _____ _____ _____ _____ and its culture.

W That sounds interesting. Which country did you choose?

M I chose Korea because you took me to Seoul last year.

W Korea is a wonderful country and I'm glad you decided to _____ _____ _____ _____ .

M The thing is there are so many things to write about that I can't pick just one.

W Hmm. Why don't you write about Korean food?

M I thought about it, but Korean food is already well-known.

W Do you want to write about less popular aspects of Korean culture?

M Yes, I do. I want to choose things that _____ _____ _____ my classmates.

W ▒▒▒▒▒▒▒▒▒▒▒▒▒▒▒▒▒▒▒▒▒▒▒▒▒▒▒

14

W Honey, look at this picture.

M The girl in the picture looks just like our Sophie.

W Exactly. Sophie _____ _____ _____ in her art class today. Isn't it surprising?

M Yeah. She must have artistic talent.

W You're right. In addition, she loves drawing very much.

M We must do something to help her develop her talent. What should we do?

W I think we should not _____ _____ _____ _____ a picture.

M That makes sense. Forcing her would not help her develop.

W If she were forced, she might even _____ _____ _____ _____ _____ . I think voluntary atmosphere is important.

M ▒▒▒▒▒▒▒▒▒▒▒▒▒▒▒▒▒▒▒▒▒▒▒▒▒▒▒

15

M Leonard is a college student. On campus, there are several dining establishments and his favorite one is a place that serves sandwiches. It is a type of restaurant where people have to place an order at the counter and take the food to their table by themselves. One day, after finishing his morning classes, Leonard feels hungry and goes to the restaurant. Placing an order, he looks around and notices that all the tables _____ _____ _____ . Among them, there's one table where _____ _____ _____ is having her meal. When his sandwich is ready, Leonard takes it and walks up to her. He wants to know if he can _____ _____ _____ _____ and eat his sandwich. In this situation, what would Leonard most likely say to the woman?

Leonard ▒▒▒▒▒▒▒▒▒▒▒▒▒▒▒▒▒▒▒▒▒▒▒▒▒▒▒

16~17

W Good morning, I'm Nora Dun from Happy Youth Center. You teenagers may want to take the financial responsibility in some parts of your life. How can you do it? As you already might have guessed, _____ _____ _____ is one of the best ways to handle it. Let me share some _____ _____ _____ _____ _____ _____ .

First, you can easily find a job as a babysitter because almost everyone in the neighborhood will need a babysitter. Second, grocery stores are always looking for _____ _____ _____ . You can work after school and on weekends. Next, you can also work as a _____ _____ _____ . Fast food restaurants usually want to hire teenagers. Last, a dog walker is another good job for teenagers because there must be some dog owners who need someone to _____ _____ _____ . There are many other jobs. Let's talk about them.

● 실전 모의고사 **13** 회

1번부터 17번까지는 듣고 답하는 문제입니다. 1번부터 15번까지는 한 번만 들려주고, 16번부터 17번까지는 두 번 들려줍니다. 방송을 잘 듣고 답을 하시기 바랍니다.

01 다음을 듣고, 여자가 하는 말의 목적으로 가장 적절한 것을 고르시오.

① 연례 청소에 대한 협조를 구하려고
② 엘리베이터 정기 점검을 공지하려고
③ 노후화된 시설 정비의 필요성을 강조하려고
④ 효율적인 엘리베이터 관리 방법을 소개하려고
⑤ 고층 사무실 근무자들에게 계단 사용을 촉구하려고

02 대화를 듣고, 남자의 의견으로 가장 적절한 것을 고르시오.

① 아이가 정해진 시간 동안 책을 읽도록 지도해야 한다.
② 아이의 나이에 이해하기 적합한 책을 읽도록 해야 한다.
③ 아이가 책을 이해했는지를 반드시 짚고 넘어가야 한다.
④ 아이가 가능한 한 많은 종류의 책을 접하도록 해야 한다.
⑤ 아이가 책 내용에 관한 질문을 자유롭게 하도록 해야 한다.

03 대화를 듣고, 두 사람의 관계를 가장 잘 나타낸 것을 고르시오.

① 배관공 – 집주인
② 부동산 중개인 – 임대인
③ 인테리어 업자 – 의뢰인
④ 주방용품점 주인 – 손님
⑤ 생수 배달원 – 카페 주인

04 대화를 듣고, 그림에서 대화의 내용과 일치하지 않는 것을 고르시오.

05 대화를 듣고, 남자가 여자를 위해 할 일로 가장 적절한 것을 고르시오.

① 아침 식사 준비하기
② 교복 상의 단추 달기
③ 학교에 늦겠다고 연락하기
④ 학교까지 차로 데려다주기
⑤ 과학 과제를 이메일로 제출하기

06 대화를 듣고, 여자가 지불할 금액을 고르시오. [3점]

① $214   ② $230   ③ $278
④ $294   ⑤ $310

07 대화를 듣고, 남자가 내일 공항에 갈 수 없는 이유를 고르시오.

① 친구와 약속이 있어서
② 마무리할 학교 숙제가 있어서
③ 동아리 담당 교사를 만나야 해서
④ 동아리를 위한 동영상 촬영이 있어서
⑤ 동아리 홍보 동영상 편집을 해야 해서

08 대화를 듣고, Willmar Family Day 행사에 관해 언급되지 않은 것을 고르시오.

① 행사 장소   ② 주최 단체
③ 새로운 게임   ④ 참가자 기념품
⑤ 개장 시간

09 T. S. Eliot에 관한 다음 내용을 듣고, 일치하지 않는 것을 고르시오. [3점]

① 미국 중산층 가정의 막내로 태어났다.
② 어린 시절 신체적인 제약으로 체육에 참여하지 못했다.
③ 대학에서 철학을 전공해 3년 만에 학위를 받았다.
④ 대학 졸업 후 프랑스로 가서 귀화하였다.
⑤ 1948년에 노벨 문학상을 수상하였다.

10 다음 표를 보면서 대화를 듣고, 두 사람이 구입할 오븐을 고르시오.

Ovens

	Model	Microwave Function	Auto-cooking Menu	Heat Source	Price
①	A	○	X	Electric	$250
②	B	X	○	Steam	$295
③	C	X	○	Electric	$310
④	D	X	X	Steam	$270
⑤	E	X	○	Steam	$330

11 대화를 듣고, 남자의 마지막 말에 대한 여자의 응답으로 가장 적절한 것을 고르시오.

① I'm sorry, but there are no printer shops nearby.

② I left my presentation document with the closer one.

③ The printer shop is close, so you can walk there.

④ It's located next to the gas station on King Street.

⑤ The printer shop opens at 10 o'clock in the morning.

12 대화를 듣고, 여자의 마지막 말에 대한 남자의 응답으로 가장 적절한 것을 고르시오.

① I'm concerned that my eyes are failing.

② I've always assumed you had good eyes.

③ I'm planning to have my eyes examined.

④ It might be dangerous to have the surgery.

⑤ I always wear contact lenses when I go out.

13 대화를 듣고, 남자의 마지막 말에 대한 여자의 응답으로 가장 적절한 것을 고르시오.

Woman: _____

① I agree. This gym is always full of people.

② That's because I couldn't stick to my workout routine.

③ You're right. We offer various yoga and boxing classes.

④ Let me check if we have other fitness programs.

⑤ Don't worry. We'll motivate you to keep working out.

14 대화를 듣고, 여자의 마지막 말에 대한 남자의 응답으로 가장 적절한 것을 고르시오.

Man: _____

① Okay. I will drive myself to work.

② Right. I'll enjoy a leisurely commute.

③ You're right. Now I'll leave home earlier.

④ Yeah. I was impressed by the beautiful bridge.

⑤ Of course. I've been reading while commuting.

15 다음 상황 설명을 듣고, Coach가 Kevin에게 할 말로 가장 적절한 것을 고르시오.

Coach: _____

① I wish I could have an ace player like you.

② Will you spend more time with your family?

③ Could you ask your team members to work harder?

④ I want you to be in charge of this training session.

⑤ If you don't train hard enough, you won't succeed.

[16~17] 다음을 듣고, 물음에 답하시오.

16 남자가 하는 말의 주제로 가장 적절한 것은? [3점]

① unique habits of night-active animals

② reasons the moon makes animals eat less

③ importance of understanding habits of animals

④ some animals to be influenced by lunatic cycle

⑤ efforts some night-active animals make for survival

17 언급된 동물이 아닌 것은?

① badgers   ② cats   ③ coyotes

④ lions   ⑤ scorpions

녹음 내용을 다시 들으면서 빈칸을 채워 넣으세요.

01

W Hi, I'm Kelly Howard from the maintenance office. I'd like to thank you all for being cooperative during the annual cleaning of the building last week. Now, let me make another announcement regarding our facilities. Starting June 1st, _____ _____ _____ in our company building will _____ _____ _____ _____ for one week. The elevators that go to odd-numbered floors will be checked for the first two days, and the next two days are for the ones that stop at even-numbered floors. The elevators that have access to all floors _____ _____ _____ for the rest of the week. During this period, those of you whose offices are located on lower levels are encouraged to take the stairs. Thank you in advance for your cooperation.

02

W Jack, do you have time to talk?

M Sure. What can I help you with?

W I need to ask about children's reading needs. You have _____ _____ _____ _____.

M What's the matter? Hmm, your child is about nine, right?

W That's right. I want to do something to _____ _____ _____. What should I do?

M I'd like you to recommend books so that he doesn't waste time reading.

W Waste time? I don't understand what you mean.

M You need to find books that are _____ _____ _____ _____.

W Yes, that is important.

M If he tries reading books _____ _____ _____ _____, he's likely to lose interest in reading.

W Then he'll waste his time, right?

M That's right.

W Thank you. I'll follow your advice.

03

M Good morning, Ms. Morton.

W Oh, you're Mr. Taylor, right?

M Yes. You gave me a call yesterday.

W The water in the kitchen sink _____ _____. Come on in. *[Pause]* This _____ _____ _____ _____.

M Let me check pipes under the sink first.

W I hope it won't be a big problem.

M Don't worry, Ms. Morton. Usually, it's a simple problem caused by a _____ _____ _____ _____.

W I hope so. Is there anything I can do while you are working at it?

M Well, would you bring me a glass of water?

W No problem.

04

M Mom, would you look at my poster? I'm going to submit it to the Environment Poster Contest.

W I like how you wrote 'Love Trees' in the middle at the top.

M Thanks. I tried to convey the message that we _____ _____ _____ _____.

W Okay. Two birds in the tree to the left look cute.

M The birds are there to show that if we preserve trees, birds will benefit as well.

W That's a good message. You did a good job with the man and the woman.

M See the potted plant the man is holding? That expresses the idea that we need to care for plants.

W The woman is _____ _____ _____ _____. That means the same, right?

M Exactly. And what do you think of the message 'It's up to you.' at the bottom of the poster?

W That's a great way to tell everyone that _____ _____ _____ _____.

M Yeah. That's what I want everyone to think about.

W Your poster is very symbolic. I really like it.

05

M Amelia, it's time for breakfast.

W Okay, Dad. Let me finish this first.

M What are you doing on your computer?

W I have to turn in my science assignment by email. It was due last night.

M How many times have I told you to finish things in time?

W I was trying to, but this one took longer than I thought.

M Hurry up or you'll _____ _____ _____ _____.

W Okay, all I need to do is click the send button. *[Pause]* It's all done.

M Now get changed into your school uniform.

W Oh, I almost forgot. _____ _____ _____ _____ on my jacket is missing.

M And you're telling me that now? Okay, I'll quickly _____ _____ _____ _____ _____.

W Thank you so much, Dad.

06

M Hello, ma'am. How may I help you?

W I'd like to buy some clothes for my mother's birthday.

M Okay. Feel free to browse and tell me if you need any help.

W I like _____ _____ _____. I'm sure it would look great on her.

M This skirt is $150. It's one of our best-selling items.

W Great. I'll take it. And I'd like to buy something that goes well with it.

M We have _____ _____ _____ _____ that will go great with the skirt.

W Let me take a look at them. Oh, these blouses are really pretty.

M Originally, they were $80, but they are _____ _____ _____ _____.

W Great. I'll _____ _____ _____ _____ — one in ivory and the other in sky blue.

M Okay. Would you like to pay by cash or credit card?

W I'll pay by credit card.

07

W Tony, you look very busy.

M Oh, Mom. I'm _____ _____ _____ for my movie club.

W What is it for?

M This is for _____ _____ _____. I filmed it myself.

W Great. By the way, are you available tomorrow afternoon?

M No, I'm not. Why do you ask?

W Grandma will visit us for three days. She'll arrive at William Airport and I'd like you to join me for _____ _____ _____.

M I want to see Grandma as soon as possible. But I can't go there with you.

W Do you have _____ _____ _____ _____ or meet with your friend?

M No. I'm supposed to meet with my club teacher tomorrow.

W Okay.

08

W Honey, why don't we go to Willmar Family Day Event this Saturday?

M That's a good idea. Is it held in the Olsen Park as usual?

W Yes. And the Love Community Center will _____ _____ _____ this year. As you know, the hosting organization is different every year.

M I'd like to _____ _____ _____. We had fun there last year.

W Yes. Especially, our kids loved the games for kids.

M Are there _____ _____ _____ _____ _____ _____?

W According to this flyer, they prepared some games that parents and kids do together.

M Great. That'll be fun.

W Yes. The event _____ _____ _____ in the morning. Keep that in mind, honey.

M Okay. I'm sure our kids will enjoy it.

09

M Thomas Stearns Eliot was born into a middle-class family in the United States _____ _____ _____ _____ _____ _____. He had to overcome physical limitations in his early years. This meant he could not participate in physical activities as a child. As he spent time alone reading, his love of literature deepened. He later studied philosophy at Harvard University and _____ _____ _____ _____ after three years. After that, he moved to France, where he continued to study philosophy. He later moved to the United Kingdom and _____ _____ _____ _____ at age 39. He received attention for his poem The Love Song of J. Alfred Prufrock, which was considered a modern masterpiece. In 1948, he was awarded the Nobel Prize in Literature.

10

W I think we're pretty much done purchasing home appliances.

M Yes, we bought a refrigerator, a laundry machine.... Oh, how about an oven?

W I almost forgot. I brought a flyer back from the store. Ovens are on sale this week.

M Wonderful. Do you like this one with the _____ _____?

W No, I don't think that would be useful.

M Okay, how about one with an auto-cooking menu?

W I would love that feature. You just press a button and the oven _____ _____ the food.

M I like that, too. Would you prefer an electric or _____ _____?

W I heard steam-cooked foods maintain more of their flavor and fewer nutrients are lost.

M Steam ovens sound much better. Let's buy one.

W Good. And I'd like to spend less than $300.

M Okay. Well, there's only one model that's perfect for us.

W Great. Let's go to the store and buy it.

11

M Shelly, do you know _____ _____ _____ _____?

W Yes. Actually there are two shops around here.

M Then would you tell me where _____ _____ _____ _____?

W

12

W Do you have any special plans for winter vacation?

M I have poor eyesight, so _____ _____ _____ getting laser eye surgery.

W But I've never seen you _____ _____.

M

13

W Hi. How may I help you?

M I'd like to know what your gym has to offer.

W We have yoga classes every day and boxing classes on Friday evenings.

M Are they all included in the gym membership?

W Yes. Is this your first time _____ _____ _____?

M No, I joined two different gyms before, but I quit both after a couple of months.

W Could you tell me why you left?

M One had _____ _____ _____, and the other was much too crowded.

W We have clean facilities and our gym is never packed with people.

M Well, there was another reason. I _____ _____ _____ to keep exercising.

W I see. That happens to many people.

M I'm afraid I might quit this gym after a few months, too.

W ▩▩▩▩▩▩▩▩▩▩▩▩▩▩▩▩▩▩▩▩

14

M Alley, the news said the bridge will finally open.

W What bridge do you mean, Ryan?

M I mean the bridge over the Gen River. I've been waiting for it.

W You sound excited. When does it open?

M It'll open this Saturday. My commuting time will be _____ _____ _____ _____ _____.

W Congratulations. You've been complaining about a _____ _____ _____.

M Soon I'll just drive across the bridge to work.

W So how much time will it save you?

M My commute will be about 20 minutes shorter.

W 20 minutes? Now you won't _____ _____ _____ _____.

M ▩▩▩▩▩▩▩▩▩▩▩▩▩▩▩▩▩▩▩▩

15

W Kevin is the starting quarterback on his school's football team. Everyone says he's an ace and talks about how great his play is. However, these days Kevin spends more time _____ _____ _____ his friends and less time practicing football. He's even _____ _____ _____, where every member on the team is required to participate. His coach _____ _____ _____ Kevin believes in his abilities so much that he is neglecting his training. The coach thinks hard work is as important as talent and there won't be any growth when Kevin is content with his ability and does not make an effort to improve. In this situation, what would the coach most likely say to Kevin?

Coach ▩▩▩▩▩▩▩▩▩▩▩▩▩▩▩▩▩▩▩▩

16 ~ 17

M Hello, everyone. Have you ever heard that _____ _____ _____ _____ _____ _____ have been linked to the lunar cycle? For example, a full moon can scare normally night-active animals into the darkness. Here are some of the most unexpected ways the moon affects animal behavior. First, European badgers tend to raise their leg up as they pee more often when the moon is between the Earth and sun. The badgers use this move to _____ _____ _____. Second, cats and dogs seem to get injured more often during the full moon. We don't know why they are less careful during this time. Next, lions usually hunt at night, but they will sometimes hunt during the day, especially after a full moon. For some reason, lions eat less food during moonlit nights. To _____ _____ _____ _____ _____ _____, they hunt during the following day. Last, the moonlight makes scorpions glow in the dark. The brighter they become, the deeper scorpions try to hide.

01 다음을 듣고, 여자가 하는 말의 목적으로 가장 적절한 것을 고르시오.
① 새 도서관 개관을 홍보하려고
② 책 포장 봉사 활동을 소개하려고
③ 책 기부 행사 참여를 독려하려고
④ 책 읽기 캠페인에 대해 안내하려고
⑤ 아프리카 아이들을 위한 기금을 마련하려고

02 대화를 듣고, 두 사람이 하는 말의 주제로 가장 적절한 것을 고르시오.
① 환경을 살리는 등반
② 히말라야 등반의 어려움
③ 효과적인 원정대 조직 방법
④ 등반 시 지켜야 할 안전 수칙
⑤ 기후 변화로 인한 생태계 파괴

03 대화를 듣고, 두 사람의 관계를 가장 잘 나타낸 것을 고르시오.
① 면접관 – 지원자
② 제과점 주인 – 점원
③ 식료품 가게 주인 – 손님
④ 축제 진행 요원 – 방문객
⑤ 제빵 학원 강사 – 수강생

04 대화를 듣고, 그림에서 대화의 내용과 일치하지 않는 것을 고르시오.

05 대화를 듣고, 남자가 여자를 위해 할 일로 가장 적절한 것을 고르시오.
① 방 청소해 주기   ② 차 만들어 주기
③ 약 가져다주기   ④ 선생님에게 전화하기
⑤ 저녁 식사 차려 주기

06 대화를 듣고, 여자가 지불할 금액을 고르시오. [3점]
① $90   ② $105   ③ $123   ④ $142   ⑤ $145

07 대화를 듣고, 남자가 학교 캠핑 여행에 갈 수 없는 이유를 고르시오.
① 할머니 댁을 방문해야 해서
② 어머니의 병간호를 해야 해서
③ 캠핑 장비를 준비하지 못해서
④ 끝내야 할 학교 숙제가 있어서
⑤ 할머니가 집에 방문할 예정이어서

08 대화를 듣고, Whitney Gym에 관해 언급되지 않은 것을 고르시오.
① 위치   ② 예약 시스템   ③ 사용료
④ 샤워 시설   ⑤ 운영 시간

09 One-Dollar Store에 관한 다음 내용을 듣고, 일치하지 않는 것을 고르시오.
① 20,000종 이상의 생활용품을 판매한다.
② 냉동식품과 화분에 심는 식물도 취급한다.
③ 전국적으로 900개 이상의 가맹점이 있다.
④ 현재 미국 생활용품 시장 점유율이 60퍼센트이다.
⑤ 가맹점 가입을 위한 별도의 예치금은 없다.

10 다음 표를 보면서 대화를 듣고, 두 사람이 주문할 의자를 고르시오.

Chairs for Sale

	Type	Price	Armrest	Headrest	Color
①	A	$142	X	X	Red
②	B	$165	○	○	Black
③	C	$150	○	X	Black
④	D	$135	○	X	Red
⑤	E	$140	○	○	Red

11 대화를 듣고, 남자의 마지막 말에 대한 여자의 응답으로 가장 적절한 것을 고르시오.

① Of course. Dogs like to have a friend.

② Oh, the puppies all look like the same.

③ Yes. I'll teach you how to care for dogs.

④ Thank you. My baby will like the toy dog.

⑤ That'd be great. I finally have my own dog.

12 대화를 듣고, 여자의 마지막 말에 대한 남자의 응답으로 가장 적절한 것을 고르시오.

① You should talk to him in a clear and loud voice.

② I've been busy all day taking care of the sales report.

③ Don't be irritated. Just finish the report that I asked for.

④ You also need to complete the accounting report soon.

⑤ I'll make sure a problem like this never happens again.

13 대화를 듣고, 남자의 마지막 말에 대한 여자의 응답으로 가장 적절한 것을 고르시오.

Woman: _____

① That's right. It was a big help for me.

② Yes. Let's go buy a new notebook together.

③ I'm sorry. That's not what I want to borrow.

④ No problem. I'll go and get it from my locker.

⑤ Of course. I brought the notebook I borrowed.

14 대화를 듣고, 여자의 마지막 말에 대한 남자의 응답으로 가장 적절한 것을 고르시오. [3점]

Man: _____

① I'm sorry, but you can't study at school after 7 p.m.

② I hope you'll come earlier and study much harder.

③ Okay. I'll encourage other students to come early too.

④ No problem. I'll talk about your situation to the school janitor.

⑤ Why don't you ask your parents to give you a ride to school?

15 다음 상황 설명을 듣고, Mr. Parker가 직원에게 할 말로 가장 적절한 것을 고르시오.

Mr. Parker: _____

① Can you give me a city map for the city tour?

② I'd like to reserve a baby carriage for tomorrow.

③ I'm sorry, but can I return this carriage after 6:00?

④ Thanks for letting me use the carriage for an extra hour.

⑤ Is there an additional charge for using two baby carriages?

[16~17] 다음을 듣고, 물음에 답하시오.

16 남자가 하는 말의 주제로 가장 적절한 것은?

① the cause of indoor air pollution

② air pollution's influence on our bodies

③ ways to measure the indoor air quality

④ the correlation of indoor air pollutants and diseases

⑤ indoor air pollution-related diseases and their management

17 언급된 오염 물질이 <u>아닌</u> 것은? [3점]

① dust ② toxic gas ③ bacteria

④ virus ⑤ mold

녹음 내용을 다시 들으면서 빈칸을 채워 넣으세요.

01

W Hello, students. This is the school librarian, Hannah Simpson. To help Africans living in extreme poverty, our school library _____ _____ _____ _____ and donating them to poor children in Africa. If you have books you don't feel like reading again, bring them to the school library. We'll wrap them with the help of student council members and send them to the African Librarian Council. If you want to _____ _____ _____ _____, you can bring them to the school library during lunch time. _____ _____ _____ _____ _____ _____, you'll share the joy your beloved books have brought you with African children and help fight illiteracy in Africa.

02

W Hey, John. What are you reading now?

M I'm reading a newspaper article about Himalayan expeditions.

W Is it about professional climbers _____ _____ _____ high peaks?

M No. It's about _____ _____ _____ on Mt. Everest.

W Oh, I once heard about that. It's a kind of ecotourism, right?

M Yeah. Climbers _____ _____ _____ _____ _____ _____ to the peak.

W That's interesting. Tell me more about it.

M According to the article, they aim to remove 7 tons of trash this year.

W Wow! That'll help a lot _____ _____ _____ _____.

M I agree. You know what? I'm going to write about the expeditions for my science class.

W That sounds like a great idea. Good luck!

03

W Good morning, Leo.

M Good morning, Ms. Carter.

W We'll have a busy day because there's a festival nearby.

M A lot of people might visit us. How can we make use of this chance?

W We need to set up a stand outside of our store and _____ _____ _____ _____ _____.

M That's a good idea. The bakery might be too crowded for some customers to come in.

W Yes. Would you take care of the outside stand today?

M Sure. I'll _____ _____ _____ right away and move some bread outside.

W Thank you. It's been almost a year since you began to _____ _____ _____ _____. You've worked very hard.

M Thank you for saying so. I enjoy working here.

W Thanks to you, _____ _____ _____ _____ a lot.

04

M Jessie, how was your family trip to the Bronx Castle?

W It was a new experience to me. Would you _____ _____ _____ _____ some photos?

M Sure.

W Here's my favorite. [Pause] The castle at the back is Bronx Castle.

M I see a flag on top of the castle, and it _____ _____ _____ _____ _____.

W That's the symbol of the Bronx family. And my family took this wagon drawn by two horses.

M That must have been a great experience.

W Yes. And this _____ _____ _____ _____ was very kind.

M Was the sun very strong at that time? You're wearing a hat in the picture.

W Yes, it was. Thanks to the hat, I didn't get a sunburn.

05

W Dad, I'm home.

M Hi, Isabella. You don't seem to have any energy. Didn't you have anything to eat?

W No. I had _____ _____ _____, so I skipped lunch.

M My poor girl! Did you see the school nurse?

W I tried to. But there was a long line of students waiting in the nurse's office, so I went back to class.

M Why don't we see a doctor tomorrow? I'll call your homeroom teacher and tell her that you're sick.

W No, that's okay. Couldn't I just _____ _____ _____ instead?

M Sure, we have some in the _____ _____. How about drinking some hot tea before you take the medicine?

W No, Dad. I don't really feel like having any.

M Alright. Go to your room and get some rest. I'll bring you some medicine in a few minutes.

W Thanks, Dad.

06

[Telephone rings.]

M This is Albright Lighting. How may I help you?

W Hello, this is Serena Jones speaking. I'd like to _____ _____ _____ for some light bulbs.

M Okay. Which type of light bulbs do you need?

W Do you manufacture LED bulbs?

M Sure, we do. Our 5-watt LED bulbs cost $5 and our 7-watt bulbs cost $8.

W Great. I need some 5-watt and 7-watt bulbs. _____ _____ _____, to be exact.

M We have enough 5-watt bulbs in stock, but I'm afraid we have just five 7-watt bulbs.

W Then I'll _____ _____ _____ of the 7-watt bulbs. And can I get them delivered by tomorrow afternoon?

M If you use an express delivery service, you can receive them by tomorrow morning. But you'll have to pay a charge of _____ _____ _____ _____ _____.

W That's fine. I'll use the express delivery service.

M Alright. Please tell me your address.

07

W Henry, you're going on the school camping trip this weekend, right?

M I'm sorry I can't.

W Why not? Do you have an _____ _____ _____?

M No, I don't.

W You were excited about it the other day, saying you _____ _____ _____ _____ _____.

M Right. But my mom is sick. She needs a helping hand.

W You're a good son. But your father can help her while you're at camp.

M Unfortunately, he is visiting my Grandma at her home. He'll be back next Monday.

W That's too bad. So you should _____ _____ _____ _____ for the weekend.

M That's right.

W I hope your mom can _____ _____ _____.

M Thank you.

08

W Joseph, do you know that Whitney Gym will open this Friday?

M Of course, Mom. I've been looking forward to it.

W It's on Cherry Street, so it's very close to our home. You can even walk there.

M Right. I'll play basketball with my friends at the gym this Friday.

W Then did you _____ _____ _____ already? I heard they have a reservation system.

M Sure. The reservation system is _____ _____, _____ _____.

W How much is to play basketball?

M It's 10 dollars per hour. We _____ _____ _____ _____ _____ _____.

W Does the fee include using the shower facilities?

M Of course. I saw pictures, and the shower facilities look great.

W I hope you have a good time at the new gym.

09

M If you've always imagined running your own business someday, the One-Dollar Store can make your dreams a reality. The One-Dollar Store _____ _____ _____ _____ _____ , including frozen foods and potted plants, all for a uniform price — just one dollar. And it retains _____ _____ _____ nationwide to provide easy access to customers. According to the latest US economic report, the One-Dollar Store currently holds _____ _____ _____ _____ _____ of household items in the United States and continues to increase its competitive strength each year. If you want to become the owner of a One-Dollar Store franchise, you are required to make a minimum _____ _____ _____ $60,000 in advance and submit the request form to our website, www.one-dollarstore.com.

10

M Honey, what are you looking at on the Internet?

W I'm shopping for a chair for Sue. Her chair is very worn-out.

M Let's pick one together. _____ _____ _____ do you have in mind?

W I don't want to _____ _____ _____ _____ on the chair.

M Okay. What about an armrest? I think she needs one.

W Of course. And a headrest too?

M Well, I don't think so. It's necessary only for those who work at their desks for a long time.

W I see. Then we'd better choose one _____ _____ .

M Yes. Now we have _____ _____ _____ _____ _____ . What color would Sue like?

W She'd like red.

M Then this is the chair for Sue. Let's order it now.

W Okay.

11

M Do you _____ _____ _____ ?

W No, I don't. But I'd like to have one someday.

M Actually, my dog _____ _____ _____ two baby dogs. Do you want one?

W

12

W How are you doing on the sales report I asked for this morning?

M Oh, I'm really sorry, director. I _____ _____ _____ while I was doing other work.

W Richard, _____ _____ in you. It seems like you didn't pay attention to what I said.

M

13

M Alice, do you know the scope of the _____ _____ _____?

W Yes. We should study from chapter 1 to 5.

M Thank you. I didn't hear it because I _____ _____ _____ _____ due to the flu.

W Are you okay now?

M Fortunately, yes. I think I need to study a lot more material than I expected.

W Yeah. We need to put a lot of time into preparing for the exam.

M I'm a little worried about _____ _____ _____ _____.

W Don't worry. You can do it if you start preparing it right away.

M Do you really think so?

W Absolutely. Do you want me to _____ _____ _____ _____?

M Yes, please. Can I borrow it now?

W ▓▓▓▓▓▓▓▓▓▓▓▓▓▓▓▓▓▓▓▓▓▓

14

M Good morning, Tina. You came to school early today.

W Good morning, Mr. Roberts. Actually, I usually get to school around 7 o'clock.

M Really? Is there any special reason you've become _____ _____ _____ _____?

W At the start of my senior year, I _____ _____ _____ _____ to wake up early and study for an extra hour in the morning.

M It's nice to see a student _____ _____ _____ _____ _____ _____.

W Thanks. By the way, could you do me a favor, Mr. Roberts?

M Sure. What can I do for you?

W Sometimes when I arrive at school early, I can't get inside.

M How come?

W If I get here too early, the front door _____ _____ _____. Could you ask someone to open it before 7 o'clock?

M ▓▓▓▓▓▓▓▓▓▓▓▓▓▓▓▓▓▓▓▓▓▓

15

W Mr. Parker is staying at the Pacific Guam Hotel and is planning to go on a city tour today with his wife and little daughter. He expects to walk quite a distance around the city with his daughter, so he decides to use the _____ _____ _____ _____, which is freely given to guests of the hotel. Dropping by the baby carriage rental office, he asks if there are any baby carriages _____ _____. Luckily, the clerk says there are many carriages available to Mr. Parker and he can use one until 6 o'clock. But Mr. Parker _____ _____ _____ _____ _____ _____ _____ and he thinks he won't be able to return the baby carriage on time. In this situation, what would Mr. Parker most likely say to the clerk?

Mr. Parker ▓▓▓▓▓▓▓▓▓▓▓▓▓▓▓▓▓

16~17

M As many people are now _____ _____ _____, skin problems, and various kinds of allergies inside buildings, they are gradually becoming more aware of _____ _____ _____. So today I'd like to talk about what sick building syndrome is and _____ _____ _____ _____ it. Sick building syndrome refers to a number of diseases that occur as a result of exposure to harmful air pollutants at a home or work building. Artificial pollutants such as dust, construction materials, chemical compounds, and toxic gases can all deteriorate indoor air quality. _____ _____ _____ are "natural," but they are also major biological pollutants in the indoor air. If these indoor air pollutants are not carefully managed, they can cause sick building syndrome. To deal with this problem, you should improve the quality of air in your buildings by ventilating them well, using natural air fresheners and cleansers against indoor air pollutants, and growing live plants.

● 실전 모의고사 **15**회

1번부터 17번까지는 듣고 답하는 문제입니다. 1번부터 15번까지는 한 번만 들려주고, 16번부터 17번까지는 두 번 들려줍니다. 방송을 잘 듣고 답을 하시기 바랍니다.

01 다음을 듣고, 여자가 하는 말의 목적으로 가장 적절한 것을 고르시오.
① 건강에 좋은 다이어트 식품을 소개하려고
② 몸에서 음식물이 소화되는 과정을 설명하려고
③ 저녁 식사량을 줄여야 하는 이유를 알려 주려고
④ 끼니마다 균형 잡힌 식사를 할 것을 당부하려고
⑤ 영양의 결핍이 신체에 미치는 영향을 경고하려고

02 대화를 듣고, 남자의 의견으로 가장 적절한 것을 고르시오.
① 기술 혁신을 통해 노동 비용을 줄여야 한다.
② 회사 재정난 해결을 위해 모두가 분담해야 한다.
③ 자금난을 해결하기 위해 직원들을 정리해고 해야 한다.
④ 부족한 회사 자금을 메우기 위해 은행 대출이 필요하다.
⑤ 회사 발전을 위해 직원들의 복지에 더욱 신경 써야 한다.

03 대화를 듣고, 두 사람의 관계를 가장 잘 나타낸 것을 고르시오.
① 교사 – 학부모
② 보건교사 – 학생
③ 상담사 – 의뢰인
④ 병원 직원 – 간호사
⑤ 의사 – 환자 보호자

04 대화를 듣고, 그림에서 대화의 내용과 일치하지 않는 것을 고르시오.

05 대화를 듣고, 남자가 여자에게 부탁한 일로 가장 적절한 것을 고르시오.
① 같이 공부하기
② 복사 카드 빌려주기
③ 한국사 가르쳐 주기
④ 역사책 대출하기
⑤ 복사물 주기

06 대화를 듣고, 여자가 지불할 금액을 고르시오. [3점]
① $235
② $270
③ $450
④ $500
⑤ $540

07 대화를 듣고, 남자의 축구 동아리 연습이 취소된 이유를 고르시오.
① 축구 골대를 교체해야 해서
② 비가 온다는 예보가 있어서
③ 코치 선생님이 결근을 해서
④ 동아리 회원들이 적게 나와서
⑤ 운동장 잔디를 교체해야 해서

08 대화를 듣고, Wonder Circus에 관해 언급되지 않은 것을 고르시오.
① 공연 주제
② 객석 규모
③ 입장료
④ 공연장 위치
⑤ 공연 기간

09 Science Book Report Contest에 관한 다음 내용을 듣고, 일치하지 않는 것을 고르시오.
① 저명한 물리학자의 탄생을 기념하는 대회이다.
② 3학년은 대회 참가가 불가능하다.
③ 대회 중간에 책을 참조할 수 없다.
④ 6월 15일에 개최될 예정이다.
⑤ 인터넷을 통해 참가 신청서를 작성해야 한다.

10 다음 표를 보면서 대화를 듣고, 두 사람이 선택한 수업을 고르시오. [3점]

After-school Class Schedule

	Class	Teacher	Day	Time
①	Swimming	Andrew	Monday	6–7 p.m.
②	Yoga	Stephanie	Tuesday	6–7 p.m.
③	Pilates	James	Wednesday	6–7 p.m.
④	Boxing	Matthew	Thursday	7–8 p.m.
⑤	English	Maria	Friday	6–7 p.m.

11 대화를 듣고, 남자의 마지막 말에 대한 여자의 응답으로 가장 적절한 것을 고르시오.

① Mark anniversaries on your desk calendar.

② If you remember them, others will appreciate it.

③ Give me a call when you want to know about it.

④ Give me your cellphone, and I'll show you how.

⑤ Take your time. Someday you will remember them.

12 대화를 듣고, 여자의 마지막 말에 대한 남자의 응답으로 가장 적절한 것을 고르시오.

① You should've come a little earlier.

② I'm sorry, but I don't think I can fix it.

③ You should buy a new watch tomorrow.

④ I'll give you a call when I'm done with it.

⑤ You can take it back at our service center.

13 대화를 듣고, 남자의 마지막 말에 대한 여자의 응답으로 가장 적절한 것을 고르시오.

Woman: _____

① I agree. You always need to do the right thing.

② Alright. Let's donate the money to a worthwhile cause.

③ I don't think so. You deserve to share the money with me.

④ Okay. I'll go to the police station and ask if anyone is looking for it.

⑤ No way. I think moral judgment changes according to the situation.

14 대화를 듣고, 여자의 마지막 말에 대한 남자의 응답으로 가장 적절한 것을 고르시오.

Man: _____

① It might be easier with her help.

② Without your help, I couldn't do it.

③ How about giving her some vegetables?

④ It's hard to be a good farmer, but you can do it.

⑤ Our vegetables in the garden already grew a lot.

15 다음 상황 설명을 듣고, Mr. Johnson이 학생들에게 할 말로 가장 적절한 것을 고르시오. [3점]

Mr. Johnson: _____

① Unfortunately, our picnic has been postponed until next month.

② We'll go on a picnic to the amusement park unless otherwise noted.

③ The principal is worried about our picnic, so you should be very careful.

④ If you have a reason for not joining the picnic, please let me know by today.

⑤ Due to an accident at the amusement park, we should abandon our plan to go there.

[16~17] 다음을 듣고, 물음에 답하시오.

16 남자가 하는 말의 주제로 가장 적절한 것은?

① various common cold symptoms

② various causes of catching a cold

③ misconceptions about cold treatments

④ effective ways to treat the common cold

⑤ a home remedy for the prevention of colds

17 언급된 것이 <u>아닌</u> 것은?

① vitamin　　② herbal tea　　③ honey

④ steam　　⑤ antibiotic

01

W The most common saying about eating meals healthily is "Eat like a king at breakfast, a prince at lunch and a beggar at dinner." This saying may be based on the fact the amount of calories you consume from each meal should balance with the amount of your activity. In other words, because you become less active and burn fewer calories as the day goes by, you should control your weight by gradually lessening the intake of food. But unfortunately, _____ _____ _____. Your body _____ _____ _____ day and night — even while you sleep. So I recommend you not to follow this common saying. You should eat the same amount of nutritionally dense foods at each meal _____ _____ _____ _____.

02

M Oh, no. According to these figures, our company's _____ _____ _____ _____ soon.

W I think it's time to make a big decision.

M What decision are you talking about?

W We need to reduce the size of the company.

M Do you mean that we should lay off some of our employees to solve our financial problems?

W Unfortunately, yes. Because labor costs are so high, we need to cut down on them urgently.

M But the employees at this company are like a family. We should stay together.

W I know how you feel. But if our company goes bankrupt, they will all lose their jobs.

M What if all employees agree to _____ _____ _____ to save the company?

W Isn't that too idealistic?

M I don't think so. If we _____ _____ _____ _____ _____ _____ _____ together, we can keep our company profitable.

03

[Knocking Sound]

W Come in. *[Pause]* Oh, you must be Mr. Cruise, Tom's father.

M That's right. Thank you for meeting with me.

W You're welcome. It's part of my job.

M Tom likes you a lot.

W Oh, really? I like him too. He's very funny.

M Thank you for saying so.

W His nurse said he doesn't cry any longer when _____ _____ _____ _____.

M Good for him. Well, Tom said that he will be able to go home soon. Is that right?

W That's right. He's much better. I think I can _____ _____ _____ _____ this Friday.

M Sounds great. I'd _____ _____ _____ now. Thanks for this good news.

W No problem. I'll see you again soon.

04

W Steve, I heard you spent a summer vacation at Pearl Island. How was it?

M It was great. Take a look at this picture. *[Pause]* Isn't it beautiful?

W The _____ _____ _____ _____ is very tall.

M The lighthouse is _____ _____ _____ on the island.

W The seagulls in the sky are cute. The scenery looks very impressive.

M Right. Do you see the small house next to the lighthouse?

W Is it for the lighthouse worker?

M Yes. Look at the chairs down the hill. My wife and I spent so much time _____ _____ _____ _____ _____.

W Sounds great. The tree _____ _____ _____ _____ makes the scenery look even better.

M I think so, too. I'll never forget the time on the island.

W I hope I can go there on vacation in the future.

05

W   Keith! Long time, no see.

M   Hi, Jane. What are you doing in the library?

W   I'm here to copy some pages from the history book I borrowed.

M   Do you know you need a copy card to use the copy machine in this library?

W   No, I didn't. Can I borrow yours if you have one?

M   Sure, here it is. Anyway, what is the topic of the book you're studying?

W   It's _____ _____ _____ stories of those who fought for Korean independence from Japanese colonial rule.

M   Sounds interesting. Can you _____ _____ _____ _____ of the stories for me?

W   No problem. I'll _____ _____ _____ for you in a few minutes.

M   I appreciate it.

06

M   Welcome to Hafa Tours. How may I help you?

W   I'd like to reserve a hotel room on Emerald Island.

M   Alright. _____ _____ _____ _____ are you going to stay?

W   I'll arrive on August 15th and stay for two nights.

M   Do you have a particular hotel in mind?

W   No. I just want a hotel room with a nice ocean view.

M   Then, the Keytings Hotel would be perfect for you. It's right on the beach.

W   Good. How much is _____ _____ _____?

M   A room with meals provided costs $300 a night. Without meals, it's just $250 a night.

W   Please reserve a room _____ _____ _____. Here's my credit card.

M   Oh, you have a card associated with our company. You can get a _____ _____ _____ _____ the total price.

W   That's fantastic.

07

M   Mom, I'm home.

W   Oh, Dave. You are home early. Didn't you say you'd be late because of _____ _____ _____ _____?

M   I did. Unfortunately, it was cancelled.

W   Oh, you must have been disappointed.

M   Yes, I was.

W   You were excited about practicing _____ _____ _____ _____ _____ on the grass field.

M   That's right. Furthermore, it's a perfect day for practice today.

W   Yes. So what was the matter?

M   _____ _____ _____ _____ today. He got the flu.

W   That's too bad. I hope he'll get well soon.

M   He will. He promised he'd make sure not to cancel next week's practice.

W   I hope so.

08

W   Mark, have you seen the Wonder Circus?

M   Several times. Actually, I'm a _____ _____ _____ _____ _____.

W   I heard they have a new theme every year.

M   That's right. This year's theme is *The Sons of the Sun*.

W   Then the circus will feature songs, dances, and performances based on that theme?

M   Yes. The performance is incredible.

W   I also heard that the circus is famous for _____ _____ _____ of about 1,000 seats and a big stage.

M   Yes. If you see it in person, you'll be impressed.

W   I want to see it. Well, the _____ _____ _____ _____ _____. It's 70 dollars for an adult.

M   I agree with you, but it's worth seeing.

W   Do you know the performance dates for this year?

M   It'll start on June 10th and _____ _____ _____ _____.

W   I'll make sure to see the circus this year.

● DICTATION

09

M Hello, I'm Harvey Smith, your science teacher. I'm going to make a brief announcement about the 18th annual Science Book Report Contest. Our high school holds this writing contest every year _____ _____ _____ Dr. Sparrow's birthday. I'm sure most of you have heard of Dr. Sparrow — he was one of the most influential physicists in the history of our country. All students _____ _____ _____ _____ can participate in the contest. Participants should read a science book in advance, and on the day of the contest they'll write a book report. Students will _____ _____ _____ _____ to the book while they are writing. The contest will be held on the morning of June 15th in the school library. After the contest we'll choose the winners and display their names on the school bulletin board on June 20th. If you want to take part in the contest, please _____ _____ _____ _____ and fill out the application form.

10

W John, look at this schedule. Why don't we take an after-school class together?

M Okay. Do you have any class in mind?

W Well, I want to take a class to get _____ _____ _____.

M I heard Andrew gives wonderful lessons. He's well-liked by many students. What do you say to taking his class?

W Sorry, but I'm a little _____ _____ _____.

M Then, what about the boxing class? I'm sure you would get a lot of exercise.

W It sounds interesting, but I _____ _____ a class that ends at 8 p.m.

M Why is that?

W I go to a math academy at 8 p.m. every day, and it takes me about fifteen minutes to walk there.

M Alright. But I have to _____ _____ _____ at 6 p.m. every Wednesday.

W Then we have no other option but one. Let's sign up for it.

M Alright.

11

M Honey, it's hard for me to _____ _____.

W How about _____ _____ _____ on your cellphone?

M Sounds like a good way, but I don't know how to do it.

W

12

W My watch has suddenly stopped. Can you fix it?

M No problem, ma'am. Please fill out this _____ _____ and leave your watch here with us.

W Okay. Then, _____ _____ _____ _____ _____ to get it?

M

13

W Nick, can I talk to you? It'll just take a moment.

M Sure, what's up?

W I found a hundred-dollar bill _____ _____ _____ to school.

M Really? What are you going to do with the money?

W I'd like to _____ _____ _____ _____ _____.

M If I were you, I would spend it all on myself.

W Wouldn't it be dishonest to use it like that?

M Haven't you ever heard the phrase "Finders keepers"?

W But _____ _____ _____ me I should send the money back to where it came from.

M If your heart points you in that direction, just follow it.

W ▩▩▩▩▩▩▩▩▩▩▩▩▩▩▩▩▩

14

M Honey, where are these vegetables from?

W Ms. Taylor gave them to me. She grew them in her garden.

M I think she's a good farmer. All her vegetables are very fresh.

W Yes. I'll _____ _____ _____ _____ _____ for dinner.

M Sounds great.

W Why don't we _____ _____ _____ _____ _____?

M I'd like to, but we need to realize that it's a lot of work.

W Still, I want to try it.

M Well, it would be good to grow and eat our own vegetables.

W Yeah. Ms. Taylor said that she'd _____ _____ _____ _____.

M ▩▩▩▩▩▩▩▩▩▩▩▩▩▩▩▩▩

15

W Mr. Johnson is a teacher at Jimmy Carton High School. He and his students have planned a school picnic to Dream Land, the biggest amusement park in the state, and have been _____ _____ _____ _____ it for the past week. The picnic is scheduled for next Monday, but Mr. Johnson has just received some bad news. The principal mentioned that there was a big accident in that amusement park several days ago, and after a meeting with school board members, he decided to _____ _____ _____ to Dream Land. The principal now wants Mr. Johnson to _____ _____ _____ to his class. In this situation, what would Mr. Johnson most likely say to the students?

Mr. Johnson ▩▩▩▩▩▩▩▩▩▩▩▩▩▩▩▩

16~17

M We have a variety of beliefs about the common cold, but the fact is, most of them are wrong. So, today I'd like to talk about the _____ _____ _____ _____ _____ _____ _____ _____ on a cold. Many people believe taking vitamins or drinking herbal tea will make a cold _____ _____ _____. However, studies haven't proven either one to make an existing cold go away faster. What about steam? Although many think inhaling steam may temporarily relieve symptoms of a dry nose and sore throat, experts agree that this is not a cure. Another myth about the common cold is that _____ _____ _____ _____ as a treatment. Antibiotics kill bacteria, but the common cold is caused by a virus. Therefore, antibiotics will have no effect on viral organisms that cause the common cold.

실전 모의고사 **16** 회

1번부터 17번까지는 듣고 답하는 문제입니다. 1번부터 15번까지는 한 번만 들려주고, 16번부터 17번까지는 두 번 들려줍니다. 방송을 잘 듣고 답을 하시기 바랍니다.

01 다음을 듣고, 여자가 하는 말의 목적으로 가장 적절한 것을 고르시오.
① 눈 축제의 일정과 세부 활동을 알려 주려고
② 눈 축제 장소 변경에 대해 양해를 구하려고
③ 눈 축제 자원봉사자들의 노고에 감사하려고
④ 눈 축제를 위한 자원봉사자 모집을 공지하려고
⑤ 성공적인 눈 축제를 위한 부서별 협조를 구하려고

02 대화를 듣고, 남자의 의견으로 가장 적절한 것을 고르시오.
① 바쁘더라도 충분한 식사 시간을 가지는 것이 좋다.
② 음식 맛을 모르며 식사하는 것은 건강에 좋지 않다.
③ 함께 식사하는 것이 혼자보다 음식 맛을 좋게 만든다.
④ 음식 맛을 제대로 느끼려면 앉아서 식사를 해야 한다.
⑤ 오래 서서 식사하는 것은 소화 불량을 초래할 수 있다.

03 대화를 듣고, 두 사람의 관계를 가장 잘 나타낸 것을 고르시오.
① 관람객 – 조각가
② 건물 관리인 – 입주민
③ 여행객 – 관광 안내원
④ 박물관장 – 유물 기증자
⑤ 고고학자 – 골동품 수집가

04 대화를 듣고, 그림에서 대화의 내용과 일치하지 <u>않는</u> 것을 고르시오.

05 대화를 듣고, 여자가 할 일로 가장 적절한 것을 고르시오.
① 주차 스티커 발급하기
② 주차 위반 스티커 떼기
③ 자동차 등록증 가져오기
④ 차량 주차 위치 말해 주기
⑤ 차 유리창에 주차 스티커 붙이기

06 대화를 듣고, 남자가 지불할 금액을 고르시오. [3점]
① $70   ② $75   ③ $80   ④ $88   ⑤ $90

07 대화를 듣고, 여자가 전화를 받을 수 <u>없었던</u> 이유를 고르시오.
① 도서관에 가야 해서
② 뮤지컬 관람 중이어서
③ 집에 물건을 찾으러 가서
④ 도서관 열람실 안이어서
⑤ 수업 중 발표를 하고 있어서

08 대화를 듣고, Aram Gallery 단체 관람에 관해 언급되지 <u>않은</u> 것을 고르시오.
① 최소 인원   ② 해설사   ③ 개장 시간
④ 관람 비용   ⑤ 사전 예약

09 7th Sammamish Day Camp에 관한 다음 내용을 듣고, 일치하지 <u>않는</u> 것을 고르시오.
① 1~6학년 여학생이 대상이다.
② 자원봉사자에 의해 운영된다.
③ 총 5일간 진행된다.
④ 노래 부르기, 공예품 만들기 등의 활동을 한다.
⑤ 등록은 7월 5일 오전 9시부터 할 수 있다.

10 다음 표를 보면서 대화를 듣고, 남자가 선택한 마이크를 고르시오. [3점]

Microphones

	Model	Portability	Voice Direction	Battery Life	Price
①	A	Wired	Omnidirectional	6 years	$500
②	B	Wired	Unidirectional	8 years	$650
③	C	Wireless	Omnidirectional	6 years	$550
④	D	Wireless	Unidirectional	6 years	$600
⑤	E	Wireless	Unidirectional	8 years	$750

11 대화를 듣고, 여자의 마지막 말에 대한 남자의 응답으로 가장 적절한 것을 고르시오.

① Right. I borrowed the suit from a friend.

② Thanks. You were really a big help for me.

③ Actually, I don't think the suit matches you well.

④ Sure. Let's go to the department store right now.

⑤ Yeah, it's important to make a good first impression.

12 대화를 듣고, 남자의 마지막 말에 대한 여자의 응답으로 가장 적절한 것을 고르시오.

① Right. I really practiced a lot.

② This time I want to win the game.

③ I had no idea about the opposing team.

④ I am so happy that you're going to stay with me.

⑤ Don't blame yourself so much for making mistakes.

13 대화를 듣고, 여자의 마지막 말에 대한 남자의 응답으로 가장 적절한 것을 고르시오.

Man: _____

① Yeah. Practice makes perfect.

② Thanks. That's really encouraging.

③ I'd like to, but I'm busy on that day.

④ If you take that class, you can learn it.

⑤ I'm sorry. I've never tried programming.

14 대화를 듣고, 남자의 마지막 말에 대한 여자의 응답으로 가장 적절한 것을 고르시오.

Woman: _____

① Can you please help me to meet your boss?

② When did you start preparing the presentation?

③ Are there any people for me to get help from?

④ Have you and our boss ever worked together before?

⑤ How about a new Italian restaurant that opened downtown?

15 다음 상황 설명을 듣고, Dave가 남자에게 할 말로 가장 적절한 것을 고르시오. [3점]

Dave: _____

① No thanks. I'll pay for it.

② That's right. I was in you class.

③ That's okay. Think nothing of it.

④ How lucky I am! Nice to meet you.

⑤ I'm sorry. I took you for my friend.

[16~17] 다음을 듣고, 물음에 답하시오.

16 여자가 하는 말의 주제로 가장 적절한 것은?

① ways to keep fruits fresh

② how to recycle fruit peels

③ necessity for us to eat fruit peels

④ importance of regular fruit intake

⑤ difficulties in growing summer fruits

17 언급된 과일이 아닌 것은?

① banana　　② grape　　③ watermelon

④ orange　　⑤ kiwi

녹음 내용을 다시 들으면서 빈칸을 채워 넣으세요.

01

W Hello, citizens. It's almost time to announce the fifth Sap Snow Festival. It's a festival of snow and ice held at Sap Park and other sites in the city of Sap. But first we need _____ _____ _____ _____.
You can learn all the details on the different tasks by checking the Sap Snow Festival website. If you are _____ _____ _____, please submit your application online. Your application will be viewed by the team leaders of the teams you wish to volunteer for. We can't have a successful festival without _____ _____ _____ _____.
We're looking forward to hearing from you.

02

M I know that you're busy today, but why are you eating while standing?
W I'm so busy that I don't have time to sit and eat properly.
M You know what? Posture is very important in order to properly taste food.
W In what posture should I eat?
M You have to sit and eat _____ _____ _____ _____.
W Tell me in more detail.
M In a study, baked brownies were _____ _____ _____ _____ and then tasted. As a result, the group who sat down and ate brownies evaluated that they were more delicious than the group who ate them standing up.
W That sounds interesting.
M Yes. The research team recommended _____ _____ _____ _____ if you want to enjoy eating properly.
W I see. From now on, I should not eat while standing.

03

M Wow, amazing! I bet you're really proud of yourself.
W Sure, I am.
M The works are really better _____ _____ _____.
W Thank you. Other visitors all agreed with that.
M Is there any reason you've been working with soap?
W It's a good material to _____ _____ _____ _____ _____.
M Now I understand why most of your works are reproductions of ancient remains.
W Right. Just like the ancient remains, my works won't lose their value even if they're damaged.
M You chose the right material. And I saw some people _____ _____ _____ _____ _____. Are you selling them?
W Yes. You can buy them in the gift shop.
M Okay, great. I'll buy some on my way out. And once again, I love your works.
W Thanks so much.

04

[Cellphone rings.]
W Oh, Mr. Smith. What's up?
M How's a next stage _____ _____ _____ _____ _____ _____ going?
W It's just finished. You can check it.
M Okay. Did you hang a picture of a sunflower on the wall?
W Of course. And I put a sofa under the picture.
M Good job. Is there a round table _____ _____ _____ _____ _____?
W Yes. And I put a long, straight living room lamp on the left side of the sofa.
M I think it's not easy to get a lamp like that.
W No, it isn't.
M Finally, on the right side of the sofa, did you put a flower pot with a tree _____ _____ _____?
W Of course.

05

M Good morning. How can I help you?

W Good morning. I came here with _____ _____ _____ _____ on my car.

M It's our policy to attach a parking violation sticker on any unauthorized vehicles.

W Well, I just moved in 505 yesterday.

M You must not have received _____ _____ _____ _____ yet. You need to display that on your car.

W No, I haven't gotten it yet. What should I do?

M First, we need _____ _____ _____ _____ _____ _____.

W Hang on a second. I have my car registration in my car. I'll be right back.

M Okay.

06

W Hello. Can I help you?

M Yes. I'm looking for a cutting board to take camping.

W Let me see. *[Pause]* Yes, these wooden cutting board and plastic cutting board _____ _____ _____ _____.

M That's good. Oh, I like both. How much are they?

W The wooden cutting board is $40, and _____ _____ _____ _____ is $30.

M I'll buy the plastic cutting board. I think it's lighter than the wooden one. And I need a camping knife, too.

W Of course. For camping knives, this one is popular. What do you think?

M I like it. How much is it?

W It's $50, and since you're buying a cutting board, I can _____ _____ _____ _____ _____ _____ _____.

M Really? That's great. Here's my credit card.

W Thank you.

07

M Where were you, Andrea? I called you several times, but you didn't answer the phone.

W Really? Sorry. Why did you call me?

M After class, I went to the library _____ _____ _____.

W Did you borrow the books I asked for? *Musical History* and *Sound & Stage*.

M Actually, that's what I was calling about. I borrowed my books and went to borrow the ones you asked for, but I _____ _____ _____ _____ of one.

W Didn't I write them down on a Post-It?

M Yes, you did. But I left it at home because I thought I could remember them.

W So you were only able to borrow one of them? Which one?

M No. Surprisingly, I remembered the other before I left the library.

W What a relief! I couldn't answer the phone because I _____ _____ _____ _____ during the class.

M I see. Well, I have your books here.

08

[Telephone rings.]

W Good afternoon. This is Aram Gallery. How can I help you?

M Yes. I'd like to know about _____ _____.

W Okay. First of all, groups must have at least 20 people.

M I see. Can we get help from a docent?

W Yes, it's _____ _____ _____.

M What time is the museum open? Can we visit there at 10 a.m.?

W Sure. We are open between 10 a.m. to 3 p.m.

M Do I have to _____ _____ _____ _____ _____?

W Yes. Groups must make a reservation a week before your visit.

M I see. Thank you for your information.

09

M Welcome to our 7th Sammamish Day Camp. As you know, our camp is ________ ________ ________ ________ going into first through the sixth grades in the fall. The camp is run one hundred percent by volunteers from our community. The camp runs 9:00 a.m.–4:00 p.m., ________ ________ ________ for one week. It's filled with a wide range of great activities. Campers will also sing songs, ________ ________ ________, participate in the community service projects and much more! Registration opens at 10 a.m. on July 5th. Thank you.

10

W Good afternoon. Can I help you?

M Yes. I'm looking for a microphone for my son's birthday present.

W Okay. Please take a look at this brochure.

M Thanks. I think a wireless one would be better. That way he can be ________ ________ ________ ________.

W Yes. What about the voice direction?

M Could you tell me more about it?

W Omnidirectional is best for group singing and unidirectional is great for singing alone.

M He ________ ________ ________ ________, so I'll take unidirectional.

W All right. Last, what about the battery life? Of course the longer, the better, right?

M You're right, but unfortunately, it's not ________ ________ ________ ________.

W I see. Then I think this one is also good.

M Okay. I'll take the cheaper one. Here's my credit card.

11

W Mike, are you ready for your interview tomorrow?

M I'm not sure. As you know, this is ________ ________ ________ ________, so I'm really nervous.

W Don't worry. You'll do fine. Oh, did you ________ ________ ________ for the interview?

M

12

M Congratulations on winning. It was a really cool dance.

W Thank you. It was ________ ________ ________ ________. The opponent in the final was one of the best.

M I know. Now I see how hard ________ ________ ________ ________.

W

13

M Jessica, I heard that you were taking a computer programing class. Do you like it?

W At first, I was really excited to take it, but it's not _____ _____ _____.

M Really? How's that?

W Programing is way more difficult than I thought. I don't know how you're so good at it.

M You're right, it's difficult. It just requires _____ _____ _____ _____ _____ _____.

W That's for sure. But I think it's too hard for me.

M It's brand-new to you right now. It'll get easier over time.

W That's what my instructor says.

M Come on! Give it time. You'll get really _____ _____ _____!

W Do you really think so?

M ▨▨▨▨▨▨▨▨▨▨▨▨▨▨▨▨

14

M It was a great presentation, Susan.

W Thank you. I sure hope the boss also liked it.

M I think he liked your idea. He took notes when you _____ _____ _____ _____ _____.

W Really? That was an important part of my presentation. It took more than a month to _____ _____ _____.

M I know. We went to visit some companies together. Don't you remember?

W Sure. How could I forget? I couldn't have done it without your help.

M I didn't do anything. I just went with you.

W I'd like to _____ _____ _____ _____ _____. How about this evening?

M All right. Do you have any restaurant in mind?

W ▨▨▨▨▨▨▨▨▨▨▨▨▨▨▨▨

15

M One summer day, Dave goes to the local shopping mall to buy some summer clothes. After _____ _____ _____ _____, he feels tired. So he decides to take a coffee break at a café in the mall. While drinking his coffee, Dave sees a familiar face passing by in front of the café. Dave is sure it's James, a guy who _____ _____ _____ _____ in high school. They lost contact with each other over 5 years ago. Dave hurries out of the café and _____ _____ _____ _____ James' shoulder, and he looks back. At that moment, Dave realizes that the man is not James. In this situation, what would Dave most likely say to the man?

Dave ▨▨▨▨▨▨▨▨▨▨▨▨▨▨▨▨▨▨▨▨▨▨

16~17

W Hello, everyone. When you eat fruits, do you eat even the skin? Most probably won't do that. However, various studies indicate that _____ _____ _____ _____ _____ _____ _____ because it contains _____ _____ _____ _____ in it. Today, I'm going to give you some examples. First, banana peels are rich in dietary fiber and lutein, which is good for anti-aging of the eyes. Grape skin contains substances that activate the longevity gene. And it helps to keep blood sugar from rising after eating. Pineapple peel _____ _____ _____ such as manganese and copper. Orange peel contains twice as much vitamins A and C than flesh, and apple peel contains 3 to 8 times more antioxidants than flesh, and kiwi peel contains hemocyanin, which helps sleep. What do you think? From now on, do you _____ _____ _____ _____ _____ when you eat the fruits?

● 실전 모의고사 **17** 회

1번부터 17번까지는 듣고 답하는 문제입니다. 1번부터 15번까지는 한 번만 들려주고, 16번부터 17번까지는 두 번 들려줍니다. 방송을 잘 듣고 답을 하시기 바랍니다.

01 다음을 듣고, 남자가 하는 말의 목적으로 가장 적절한 것을 고르시오.
① 기침 치료에 좋은 약을 홍보하려고
② 기침의 생리학적 과정을 설명하려고
③ 기침을 할 때 지켜야 할 것에 대해 조언하려고
④ 기침을 멎게 하는 효과적인 방법을 소개하려고
⑤ 증세에 따른 기침의 종류와 치료법을 알려 주려고

02 대화를 듣고, 여자의 의견으로 가장 적절한 것을 고르시오.
① 냉장고 청소는 주기적으로 자주 하는 것이 좋다.
② 냉장고 문을 너무 오랫동안 열어 두지 말아야 한다.
③ 냉장고에 너무 많은 음식을 넣어 두는 것은 좋지 않다.
④ 냉장고에 보관하는 음식의 유효 기간을 꼭 지켜야 한다.
⑤ 음식 목록을 작성하는 것이 냉장고 정리에 도움이 된다.

03 대화를 듣고, 두 사람의 관계를 가장 잘 나타낸 것을 고르시오.
① 감독 – 마라톤 선수
② 의사 – 호흡기 환자
③ 자동차 정비사 – 고객
④ 구조대원 – 구조 요청자
⑤ 관리소 직원 – 건물 입주자

04 대화를 듣고, 그림에서 대화의 내용과 일치하지 <u>않는</u> 것을 고르시오.

05 대화를 듣고, 여자가 할 일로 가장 적절한 것을 고르시오.
① 식당 예약하기
② 대기표 받아 오기
③ 요리법 설명하기
④ 식당 앞에서 줄 서기
⑤ 식당 위치 알아보기

06 대화를 듣고, 남자가 지불할 금액을 고르시오. [3점]
① $100
② $110
③ $120
④ $130
⑤ $140

07 대화를 듣고, 여자의 심경이 불안한 이유를 고르시오.
① 검사 결과가 좋지 않을 것 같아서
② 동생의 수술 시간이 점점 임박해서
③ 합격 여부를 알리는 전화가 오지 않아서
④ 시험에 떨어진 것을 부모님께서 들킬 것 같아서
⑤ 제시간에 면접 장소에 도착하지 못할 것 같아서

08 대화를 듣고, Milk Up Festival에 관해 언급되지 <u>않은</u> 것을 고르시오.
① 개최 목적
② 프로그램
③ 후원
④ 신청 방법
⑤ 참가 비용

09 3rd Ballet Festival에 관한 다음 내용을 듣고, 일치하지 <u>않는</u> 것을 고르시오. [3점]
① 5시간 동안 진행된다.
② 시립 발레단이 초청된다.
③ 발레 수업 비용은 25달러이다.
④ 참가자 전원에게 장학금이 주어진다.
⑤ 등록 마감일은 7월 20일이다.

10 다음 표를 보면서 대화를 듣고, 두 사람이 신청할 프로그램을 고르시오.

Summer Kids Programs

	Program	Period	Location	Fee
①	Cooking	July 10–16	Eastside Community Center	$200
②	Computer Coding	June 15–28	Technical College	$150
③	Forest Exploration	June 22–29	Sandburg Forest	$100
④	Scuba Diving	July 13–19	Middle View Pool	$150
⑤	Fishing	August 1–7	Lake Windsor	$250

11 대화를 듣고, 남자의 마지막 말에 대한 여자의 응답으로 가장 적절한 것을 고르시오.

① As you know, I really want to pass.

② I'll tell you how to do it after practice.

③ In fact, I need you to help me practice.

④ So now I'm just waiting for the test result.

⑤ Practicing more will help you get your black belt.

12 대화를 듣고, 여자의 마지막 말에 대한 남자의 응답으로 가장 적절한 것을 고르시오.

① Sorry. I'm too busy to teach you now.

② Don't worry. I can teach you if you want.

③ Thanks. You always make me feel pleasant.

④ Come on. I really want to see you play the guitar.

⑤ Right. Playing the guitar isn't a thing you can learn easily.

13 대화를 듣고, 남자의 마지막 말에 대한 여자의 응답으로 가장 적절한 것을 고르시오.

Woman: _____

① Okay, Dad. Thanks for your advice.

② Really? Now I see why you're upset.

③ I'm sorry. I broke your heart so much.

④ Good point. She needs to learn how to apologize.

⑤ Okay. Then, keep it a secret that I apologized to her.

14 대화를 듣고, 여자의 마지막 말에 대한 남자의 응답으로 가장 적절한 것을 고르시오. [3점]

Man: _____

① No problem. I can take care of them.

② I know. I thought you didn't like to volunteer.

③ I'm sorry. I have another appointment on that day.

④ Why not? Everyone in the center will welcome you.

⑤ Right. We should be more concerned about the elderly.

15 다음 상황 설명을 듣고, Jenny가 David에게 할 말로 가장 적절한 것을 고르시오.

Jenny: _____

① That's too bad. I think I can help you, then.

② Sorry, I'm too busy to go to the library now.

③ Well, I want you to check if there's the book.

④ Then, can you return my books to the library?

⑤ Don't worry. I'll be able to lend you the books.

[16~17] 다음을 듣고, 물음에 답하시오.

16 남자가 하는 말의 주제로 가장 적절한 것은?

① simple habits for staying healthy

② reasons to get a good night's sleep

③ the effect of regular exercise on sleep

④ effective measures when you can't sleep

⑤ the importance of sleeping in the right posture

17 언급된 활동이 아닌 것은?

① walking ② exercise ③ reading

④ nap ⑤ shower

01

M Hello, students. I'm your school nurse Connor Evans. It's cold season again, so it's that time of year when it's important to protect yourself and the people around you. So I'd like to remind you of _____ _____ _____ _____ _____ when you have to cough. First, make sure to cover your mouth and nose whenever you cough. If possible, _____ _____ _____ to cover your mouth or nose instead of handkerchief, and dispose of it immediately. If a cough suddenly sneaks up on you and no tissue is available, cough into your upper sleeve, not into your hands. This _____ _____ _____ _____ into the air. Please keep these tips in mind.

02

W Hi, Peter! It's been a while!

M Hello, Angela. Come on in. I'm _____ _____ _____.

W Oh, are you going to throw out those stuff over there?

M Yeah. I didn't realize that there was so much to throw away in there.

W You mean you can't use any of it?

M Everything is bad or expired. I forgot to check the dates for a long time.

W I see. How about _____ _____ _____ _____ _____ in the refrigerator?

M A list of items?

W Yes. You can put the list of all the food on the refrigerator.

M I get it. That way I can easily see what's in the fridge and what I don't have.

W Right. Then you can also _____ _____ _____ you don't need.

M Okay. I'll try that. Thanks for the advice.

03

M Hello in there! How are you doing?

W It couldn't be worse! Hey, please _____ _____ _____ _____.

M Okay. We'll find the problem quickly and let you come out.

W Thank you, but please hurry. I can't stand being stuck in here anymore.

M I know. Just _____ _____ _____ _____ _____ for another few minutes.

W But I am having trouble breathing. I am knocking myself out. You've got to get me out of here!

M Now, you'll be just fine. Try to relax.

W But _____ _____ this elevator crashes?

M You don't have to worry about that. That kind of thing will never happen. The cables are safe and secure.

W Okay. I'll trust you.

04

[Cellphone rings.]

W Hi, Justin. I texted you a picture of the poster I made for our concert a few minutes ago. Did you get it?

M Yeah. I like it.

W That's good. Should I _____ _____ _____ _____, "Guitar & Songs," at the top?

M Yeah. It looks good there.

W Okay. What do you think of the girl playing the guitar?

M I think it's perfect. And I like the musical notes _____ _____ _____.

W Thanks. And I drew those three birds on the musical notes.

M That _____ _____ _____ in our concert, right?

W That's right.

M And I like how you put the time and place below the musical notes. Great job!

W Really? Thank you for saying so.

05

M Here we are. This is the restaurant I told you about.

W There are so many people in front of the restaurant!

M As far as I know, there's always _____ _____ _____.

W Have you eaten here before?

M No, I haven't been there, but I wanted to come because I liked the reviews.

W I see. By the way, why is this restaurant so famous?

M I don't know, but they say there are special foods that _____ _____ _____ _____ _____ _____.

W Okay. Why don't we wait in line over there?

M Oh, Look. It says that you have to _____ _____ _____ _____ at the counter first.

W Right. I'll go and pick up the ticket, so stay in line here.

M Okay.

06

W Hi. Can I help you?

M Yes. I saw an advertisement for a discount sale on the door.

W Yeah, we're offering discounts of more than fifty percent.

M Great! *[Pause]* How much are these boots? I like their design.

W Their regular price is $100, but they're _____ _____ _____ _____ _____ _____ right now.

M Wow, I'll take them. And how about these sneakers?

W They're $20 _____ _____ _____ _____.

M Wow, that's so cheap. I'll take them, too. And how about these shoes over here? Are they also _____ _____?

W Yes. They're $60.

M I'll have to buy them, too. Here's my credit card.

W Thanks.

07

M How did the result come out? Were you accepted?

W No. Not yet. I didn't get a call from them.

M Why don't you call them first? They may _____ _____ _____ _____ _____.

W No, I wasn't allowed to.

M Isn't it right that if you pass the exam, they will call you?

W Sure. I think it is about time _____ _____ _____.

M If they don't call by 12 o'clock, what happens?

W It means I'm not hired.

M We've got just 30 minutes until 12 o'clock.

W Right. That's why I'm so anxious.

M What else can you do _____ _____ _____ _____ _____?

W I never knew waiting could be so painful!

08

M What are you going to do this weekend?

W I'm going to participate in the Milk Up Festival.

M Milk Up Festival? What is it?

W It's a festival held to _____ _____ _____ _____ _____.

M I see. So what do you usually do at that festival?

W There are various programs such as exhibitions and performances, so I plan to _____ _____ _____.

M Who is sponsoring the program?

W It's run by the city hall.

M That sounds great. I'll also have to take my kids this weekend.

W You need to _____ _____ _____ _____ _____.

M Okay. I'll access the website right now.

09

W Hello. We are proud to announce our 3rd Ballet Festival. The festival _____ _____ _____ _____ from 11 a.m. to 4 p.m. on August 20th. The festival will be held in the main hall of the city hall, and the City Ballet will be invited to perform. Participants can _____ _____ _____, and the cost of it is $25. _____ _____ _____ _____ City Hall scholarships. The registration deadline is July 20th. We are extremely excited about the third annual Ballet Festival and look forward to seeing you there.

10

M Honey, can you help me choose a summer kids programs for Josh?

W Sure.

M Which program are you thinking?

W Do you think he'd like to _____ _____?

M Probably not. He never wants to go hiking.

W Ah, you're right. Then, how about computer coding? He's interested in computer programing.

M Sure, but he's got _____ _____ _____ _____ _____. I think he'd like this program.

W Cooking? Yeah, he'd like that, but that's all the way on the east side.

M Right. That's too far away.

W But these two aren't far. I'm sure Josh would like both. Which of them do you think would be better?

M This one. It's cheaper. Spending $250 would be _____ _____.

W Then let's sign him up for that program.

11

M Are you just getting back from your Taekwondo practice, Barbara? You look tired.

W Yes, Grandpa. I practiced longer today _____ _____ _____ _____ my Taekwondo test next week.

M Oh, that's good. You've _____ _____ _____ _____ for it.

W ████████████████████████████████████

12

W Jacob, you're really good at playing the guitar.

M Thanks. Why don't you learn _____ _____ _____ _____ _____? It can make you feel good.

W I'd love to, but I've _____ _____ _____.

M ████████████████████████████████████

13

M Is something wrong, Jennifer? You look upset.

W I am, Dad. I had an argument with my friend Linda.

M Really? Did you _____ _____ _____ _____?

W Why me? She was at fault, too.

M I understand that. But it's always a good idea for you to apologize first.

W What do you mean?

M If both of you _____ _____ _____ _____ _____, you might never be able to recover your friendship.

W Oh, you think so?

M Yeah. If you _____ _____ _____ with her, you'd better act first.

W ░░░░░░░░░░░░░░░░░░░░░░░░░░

14

W Hello, Oliver. Where are you going?

M Hello, Margaret. I'm going to the community center.

W Why are you going there?

M Didn't I tell you about it? I've _____ _____ there since last month.

W Really? What kind of volunteer work do you do?

M Well, I _____ _____ _____ _____ _____.

W You mean helping to prepare lunch boxes?

M Yeah, that's right.

W What do you do with the packed lunch boxes?

M We deliver them to the elderly living alone in the neighborhood.

W Really? Can I join you and _____ _____ _____?

M ░░░░░░░░░░░░░░░░░░░░░░░░░░

15

W Jenny is going to the local library to return the books she had checked out. She's going to come back home right after returning the books because her family _____ _____ _____ _____ _____ _____. On the way to the library, she meets David by chance. Jenny asks him where he is going. He says he is going to the library to _____ _____ _____ for the social assignment. Jenny asks him which library it is, and she learns he's going to the same library. Jenny wants to ask David if he can _____ _____ _____ for her. In this situation, what would Jenny most likely say to David?

Jenny ░░░░░░░░░░░░░░░░░░░░░░░░░░

16~17

M Hello, everybody. Perhaps many of you have struggled with being unable to sleep at night. Today I'm going to give you some tips for dealing with it. First of all, try to get enough sunlight during the day. If you get enough sunlight during the day, you can _____ _____ _____ because a large amount of melatonin is released at night. Try to walk for at least an hour a day right away. Never exercise at night. Exercising in the evening or late at night _____ _____ _____ _____ _____ _____, so you should finish exercising 5–6 hours before bedtime. When you exercise, your blood pressure _____ _____ _____. Also, do not try to force yourself to fall asleep. If you can't sleep after 20 minutes of lying down, sit on a sofa or chair and read a book or watch TV. Lastly, if you take a cool shower 2 hours before bed, it is _____ _____ _____ _____. When your body temperature goes down, you can get a good night's sleep. Thank you for listening.

듣기 **필수표현** MASTER

01 회

- Our baby is due in August.　　아기는 8월 출산 예정이에요.
- Can you tell me where I can use a computer?　　어디서 컴퓨터를 사용할 수 있는지 말씀해 주시겠습니까?
- What a coincidence!　　우연의 일치구나!
- You should have been more careful.　　좀 더 조심했어야지.
- What made you choose that school?　　그 학원을 선택한 이유가 뭐야?
- Take your time and pick what you like most.　　천천히 보시고 가장 마음에 드시는 것을 고르세요.

02 회

- It's worth trying.　　그것은 해 볼 만한 가치가 있어.
- What kind of exercise do you recommend?　　어떤 종류의 운동을 추천하시나요?
- Was there anything the students were not satisfied with?　　학생들이 만족하지 않은 것이 있었니?
- Can I exchange this brown shirt for a larger one?　　이 갈색 셔츠를 더 큰 것으로 교환할 수 있을까요?
- Would you check if any of your other locations have the size I need?　　제가 필요한 사이즈가 다른 지점에 있는지 확인해 주시겠어요?
- You might have got infected there.　　거기서 감염됐을지도 모르겠네요.

03 회

- What brings you here?　　여기는 무슨 일로 왔니?
- Do you have everything ready?　　모든 것이 준비되었니?
- Would it be possible for me to stop by around 7 p.m. this evening?　　제가 오늘 저녁 7시쯤에 들러도 될까요?
- When is the interview going to be held?　　면접은 언제 실시될 예정이야?
- With your ability and experience, you'll do great at the interview.　　네 능력과 경험이면, 너는 면접을 잘할 거야.
- My car is as good as new.　　내 차는 새것이나 다름없어요.

04 회

- What do you do for a living?　　무슨 일을 하세요?
- That's why I called you.　　그래서 제가 당신에게 전화한 거예요.
- Is there anything to eat?　　먹을 게 있나요?
- I'm afraid I can't make it to Jane's birthday party tomorrow.　　내일 Jane의 생일 파티에 갈 수 없을 것 같아.
- Be sure to arrive at the southern entrance before then.　　반드시 그 전에 남쪽 입구에 도착하도록 하십시오.
- Won't you need Korean skills to work in Korea?　　한국에서 일을 하려면 한국어 실력이 필요하지 않을까?

05 회

- [ ] Are you tired from taking care of your baby?
- [ ] You can say that again!
- [ ] I feel like eating grapes, but they are out of season now.
- [ ] Have you found any good ones?
- [ ] We have a blue one and a gray one available now.

아기를 돌보느라 지치셨나요?
바로 그거야!
포도를 먹고 싶지만, 지금은 제철이 아니구나.
좋은 것을 발견했어요?
지금 파란색과 회색을 이용하실 수 있습니다.

06 회

- [ ] You must have been afraid when you were standing there.
- [ ] Should I call him and tell him to come back?
- [ ] You are so understanding.
- [ ] That's exactly what I was thinking.
- [ ] Don't mention it.

네가 그곳에 서 있을 때 무서웠나 보네.
전화해서 다시 오라고 해야 할까요?
널리 헤아려 주시는군요.
그게 바로 제가 생각하고 있었던 거예요.
천만에요.

07 회

- [ ] One is for our son, and the other is for our daughter.
- [ ] Will you do me a favor?
- [ ] Who else do you have in mind?
- [ ] He went too far.
- [ ] It's the drink she and Dustin had on their first date.
- [ ] You don't have to worry about it.

하나는 우리 아들, 다른 하나는 우리 딸의 것이에요.
부탁 좀 하나 들어줄래?
달리 누구를 염두에 두고 있니?
그는 정도가 지나쳤어.
그것은 그녀와 Dustin이 첫 데이트 때 마셨던 음료입니다.
이것에 대해서는 걱정하지 않으셔도 됩니다.

08 회

- [ ] Would you drink a cup of coffee?
- [ ] How much are they per month?
- [ ] What's the name of the campsite?
- [ ] This restaurant is three stories tall.
- [ ] Which room do you think is the most suitable?

커피 한 잔 할래요?
한 달에 얼마인가요?
캠핑장 이름이 뭐야?
이 식당은 3층짜리 건물이네요.
어느 방이 가장 적절할 것 같아요?

09 회

- [ ] What makes you so tired?
- [ ] How long will it take?
- [ ] That's his field of expertise.
- [ ] I can't deny it's a nice drawing.
- [ ] I'll keep that in mind and do my best.
- [ ] I can't wait to read the whole script.

무엇 때문에 그렇게 피곤하니?
얼마나 걸릴까요?
그것이 그의 전문 분야거든요.
그것이 멋진 그림이라는 것을 부인할 수는 없지.
그 말씀 명심하고 최선을 다할게요.
빨리 전체 대본을 읽고 싶어요.

10 회

- I shouldn't have lost my temper.
  제가 이성을 잃지 말았어야 했어요.
- Isn't it dangerous to dive there?
  저기서 다이빙하는 것은 위험하지 않나요?
- Could you take those charges off my bill?
  청구서에서 그 요금들을 빼 줄 수 있나요?
- Where have you been all afternoon?
  오후 내내 어디 있었니?
- The problem was we forgot to bring any tools with us.
  문제는 우리가 어떠한 도구도 가져오는 것을 잊었다는 것이었어.

11 회

- It's way past your bedtime.
  취침 시간이 훨씬 지났잖아.
- How come you didn't finish it earlier?
  어째서 미리 끝내지 않았니?
- That's because you don't have your priorities straight.
  그건 네가 우선순위들을 제대로 세우지 않기 때문이야.
- Are you suffering from any other symptoms?
  또 다른 증상에 시달리고 계신가요?
- Do I have to keep away from alcohol?
  술은 멀리해야 하나요?
- It seems like you're addicted to your phone.
  넌 네 휴대전화에 중독된 것 같아.
- She must have written about many of them in her novel.
  그녀는 자신의 소설 속에 그것 중 많은 것에 대해 분명 썼음이 틀림없어.

12 회

- Ever since I read the article, I've felt nervous having coffee.
  그 기사를 읽은 이후에는 커피를 마시는 것이 걱정이 돼.
- It must be a psychological thing.
  그건 심리적인 것임이 틀림없어.
- How did the meeting with your clients go?
  고객들과의 회의는 어떻게 됐어요?
- What special deals are you offering right now?
  지금 제공하는 특가가 무엇인가요?
- Are you available this weekend?
  이번 주말에 시간 있니?
- The longer the warranty is, the better it is regardless of the price.
  품질 보증 기간이 더 길수록, 가격에 상관없이 더 좋아요.
- Would you like one to go with the size upgrade?
  사이즈 업그레이드로 하나 포장해 가시겠어요?

13 회

- I hope it won't be a big problem.
  큰 문제가 아니기를 바라요.
- How many times have I told you to finish things in time?
  제때에 일을 끝내라고 얼마나 많이 말했니?
- Feel free to browse and tell me if you need any help.
  편히 둘러보시고 도움이 필요하시면 제게 말씀해 주세요.
- I'm supposed to meet with my club teachers tomorrow.
  내일 동아리 선생님과 만나기로 되어 있어요.
- That happens to many people.
  많은 사람들이 그렇죠.

14^회

- How can we make use of this chance? 이 기회를 어떻게 활용할 수 있을까요?
- Can I get them delivered by tomorrow afternoon? 내일 오후까지 받을 수 있을까요?
- It's necessary only for those who work at their desks for a long time. 그것은 책상에서 오래 일하는 사람들에게만 필요해요.
- We need to put a lot of time into preparing for the exam. 우리는 시험 준비에 많은 시간을 쏟아야 할 필요가 있어.
- How come? 왜지?
- Does the fee include using the shower facilities? 사용료에는 샤워 시설을 이용하는 것도 포함되어 있니?

15^회

- It's time to make a big decision. 중요한 결정을 내려야 할 때입니다.
- Isn't that too idealistic? 너무 이상적이지 않나요?
- What is the topic of the book you're studying? 그런데 네가 공부하고 있는 책의 주제가 뭐니?
- What do you say to taking his class? 그분 수업을 들어 보는 게 어때?
- Then we have no other option but one. 그러면 우리는 한 수업 외에는 선택의 여지가 없네.
- If I were you, I would spend it all on myself. 내가 너라면, 그냥 나를 위해 쓸 텐데.

16^회

- Tell me in more detail. 좀 더 자세히 말해 봐.
- I bet you're really proud of yourself. 틀림없이 스스로가 정말로 자랑스러우시겠어요.
- Is there any reason you've been working with soap? 비누로 작업해 온 이유가 있나요?
- What a relief! 다행이다!
- Give it time. 시간을 가져.
- I couldn't have done it without your help. 당신의 도움 없이는 못했을 거예요.

17^회

- Make sure to cover your mouth and nose whenever you cough. 기침할 때마다 반드시 입과 코를 가리도록 하세요.
- I can't stand being stuck in here anymore. 더 이상 여기 갇혀있는 것을 견딜 수가 없어요.
- What do you think of the girl playing the guitar? 기타를 치고 있는 소녀는 어때?
- Have you eaten here before? 당신은 전에 여기서 드셔 본 적이 있나요?
- Why is this restaurant so famous? 이 식당은 왜 그렇게 유명한가요?
- Which of them do you think would be better? 그것들 중 어느 것이 더 낫다고 생각하세요?
- What kind of volunteer work do you do? 무슨 자원봉사를 하는데?
- How did the result come out? 결과는 어떻게 됐니?

● 유형 모의고사 01~13강

강/번호	01	02	03	04	05	06
01강	②	④	②	①	①	⑤
02강	③	④	①	⑤	①	③
03강	⑤	⑤	①	③	⑤	②
04강	④	④	⑤	⑤	⑤	⑤
05강	②	④	②	⑤	③	⑤
06강	②	②	②	③	③	③
07강	④	②	②	⑤	③	③
08강	④	⑤	④	④	⑤	④
09강	⑤	④	④	④	④	③
10강	④	⑤	⑤	③	④	⑤
11강	⑤	⑤	②	④	④	①
12강	③	④	⑤	③	⑤	④
13강	①	④	②	⑤	⑤	③

● 실전 모의고사 01~17회

회/번호	01	02	03	04	05	06	07	08	09	10	11	12	13	14	15	16	17
01회	①	①	②	③	④	③	⑤	⑤	③	②	⑤	②	⑤	③	⑤	④	⑤
02회	①	⑤	⑤	⑤	⑤	②	⑤	③	⑤	⑤	②	②	①	⑤	③	④	④
03회	②	①	②	⑤	①	⑤	③	②	②	④	③	③	②	③	⑤	②	①
04회	④	⑤	④	⑤	④	⑤	①	⑤	④	⑤	⑤	②	⑤	③	②	③	③
05회	①	①	③	④	②	③	①	④	④	②	⑤	⑤	④	⑤	⑤	①	③
06회	④	③	②	⑤	③	④	②	⑤	⑤	④	④	④	④	⑤	③	⑤	⑤
07회	⑤	④	⑤	⑤	①	⑤	④	④	④	④	③	④	⑤	⑤	⑤	④	③
08회	⑤	⑤	①	⑤	⑤	②	⑤	⑤	⑤	③	⑤	③	⑤	①	①	③	④
09회	⑤	①	②	⑤	①	④	②	⑤	⑤	③	⑤	③	④	⑤	③	①	⑤
10회	①	②	④	⑤	②	③	④	⑤	④	③	⑤	③	③	③	④	②	③
11회	②	⑤	①	⑤	④	③	⑤	④	⑤	⑤	③	③	②	④	②	④	④
12회	⑤	②	①	④	③	④	④	⑤	⑤	⑤	②	⑤	⑤	④	①	③	④
13회	②	②	①	④	②	③	③	④	④	②	④	⑤	②	⑤	⑤	④	③
14회	③	①	②	⑤	③	②	②	⑤	④	④	②	④	④	③	⑤	④	④
15회	④	②	⑤	④	⑤	④	③	④	⑤	②	④	④	④	①	⑤	③	③
16회	④	④	①	④	③	②	⑤	④	⑤	⑤	②	①	⑤	⑤	⑤	④	④
17회	③	⑤	④	④	②	④	③	⑤	④	④	①	②	①	④	④	④	④

● 유형 모의고사 01~13강

01강

01 preparing for the upcoming school festival, move between places, are supposed to be, your prearranged places
02 meet the youngest table tennis champion, accepted our invitation, put some time aside, the full attendance of
03 organize a school magic club, officially approved, haven't joined any of the clubs, make your school life more interesting
04 food poisoning is spreading, wash your hands, avoid eating raw food, follow this advice
05 on the list of, which parodies, mimic political big shots, solid acting from
06 a solemn atmosphere, behave themselves, to be seated, follow the instructions

02강

01 Storing potatoes, be stored in a cool and dark place, rot easily in plastic bags, keeps them from sprouting
02 someone broke into my house, as important as your safety, in a positive way
03 on time for work, serve the tables, our fair share
04 eat a few apples, a good source of fiber, effective for weight loss, keep your heart healthy
05 a restaurant outside of school, the school restaurant closes, extend their hours
06 hesitate so much, you follow your dream, what we like best

03강

01 seeing the news studio myself, to host a news program, read my scripts repeatedly
02 have had a headache, are we supposed to arrive, getting off the ship, make passengers comfortable
03 lost my key card, a cost to reissue it, saw some surfboards, enjoy your stay
04 you're limping, haven't recovered from, brushed up against, take your place
05 How much longer, a height restriction, get a refund
06 take better care of, a balanced diet, what kind of exercise, I prescribe for

04강

01 lockers on the left side, in a row, round table with chairs, star-shaped rug
02 main characters of our play, the prince kneeling down, breathing fire from its mouth
03 banner on the wall, basket full of balls, your hair tied back
04 for her age, a romantic atmosphere, Fish jump out of the water
05 has a talent for, including a bike rack, a cool breeze, are holding hands
06 reminds me of, little girl wearing a helmet, The grassy hill in the distance, with a ponytail

05강

01 company's monthly newspaper, matching the articles, retirement ceremony, what a relief
02 cleaning the house, vacuum the living room, wash the vegetables, take out some dishes
03 need a bigger allowance, all cost me extra, do more work around the house
04 have an important meeting, informed them of the schedule, pick up your guitar
05 as a graduation present, booking a trip, find a suitable package, I'll check some information
06 what the sentence actually means, can't help feeling nervous, I'll go with you

06강

01 looking for scented candles, have a medium one, get 10% off
02 purchase anything else, offer any discount, their 10th anniversary, place the order
03 6-piece tea mug set, buy a mug holder, three-dollar discount coupon, wrap these mugs
04 look good on, for half price, 20 percent off the total price
05 get some ingredients, 4 washed carrots, take one bunch of
06 sign up for, a three-month registration, covers all three months

07강

01 make some changes, picture of the planets, a clearer picture
02 have a job interview, quit your job, have a health check-up, reschedule the check-up
03 original location was good, was raised a lot, 10-minute walk, the previous one
04 I can make it, what's keeping you from, sprained my ankle
05 get a refund, exchange a skirt, is a size smaller
06 majored in, only know a little, speak Chinese fluently

08강

01 More than 20 researchers, spend one million dollars, develop a new drug, a 5-year project
02 took the leading role, read some reviews, ten million dollars were invested
03 was accepted, on a regular basis, a regular concert in the fall
04 a new category for adults, close to our place, the deadline for registering, The entry fee
05 this time of the year, attend the closing ceremony, that event sells out quickly, main events such as parade, the whole schedule of movies
06 for every Saturday, reserve a stall, donate 5 percent of our profits

09강

01 a variety of toys, movie showings for children, provide cartoon character bookmarks
02 on the first weekend, may enter the contest, by five professionals
03 the Fourth Industrial Revolution, is free of charge, submit the application form
04 kick off our anniversary, open to the public, displays of antique autos
05 will be held on Christmas Eve, had the preliminaries, perform in alphabetical order
06 based on the amount of energy, is worth a dollar, can be used just like cash

10강

01 more than 100 dollars, the automatic switch off function, at least four liters, with the longer warranty

02 How long will it take, take a non-stop flight, take the cheaper flight
03 looking for a tent, can't spend more than 80 dollars, if it's not dark
04 need plenty of them, look better, just skip them, buy a cake from the bakery
05 the dancing robot program, is better for me, as a free gift, the cheaper program
06 one with melodies, it's a great feature, rectangular or round

11강

01 hold a book signing event, one of my favorite writers
02 hold a drone competition, the first prize winner will receive
03 give me a wake-up call, What time
04 fell off my bike, the road has been bumpy, should do something
05 Have you ever worked at a restaurant, as a server, tell me the hourly wage, any other questions
06 was planning a trip, traveling abroad, have everything ready, buy travel insurance

12강

01 raise money for the homeless, bring their own items, take the flower pot to school
02 very hardworking, pleased with her job performance, praise Juliet for her ability
03 for him to go to bed, without washing his face, he should wash himself clean
04 only one seat left, a woman giving up her seat, before getting off
05 needs to sleep soundly, hears balls bouncing around, the sounds only get louder
06 dropped the phone, has been acting strangely, take it in for repairs, free of charge

13강

01~02 household appliances made smarter, sense the different types of fabric, show relevant recipes, hard to access in traditional ways
03~04 greatly affect your mood, relieve any feelings of depression, more comfortable and brighter, a feeling of accomplishment
05~06 a certain pattern, every aspect of a figure, in an awkward position, calculating the size of figures

● 실전 모의고사 01~17회

01회

01 difficulty in fitting into, take the first step, take advantage of
02 was pregnant, gone are the days, Moderate exercise is good
03 get some vaccinations, need her medical records, have them ready
04 on the wall, candlestick on the table, checkered tablecloth
05 reserved a single room, mark some good places, bring it to you
06 looking for a purse, 10 percent off, get it for 5 dollars
07 planning on buying something, left it there by mistake, I might get the job
08 got a driver's license, are cheaper than, including tax, get twenty dollars back
09 lasts for four days, attracts many visitors, A ticket holder can enjoy, a strawberry picking event will be held
10 a view overlooking, too much per night, Internet access, for a safe
11 favorite pastime, why you enjoy it
12 buy some equipment for rock climbing, how about gloves
13 found the perfect house for you, three bedrooms and two bathrooms, one more wonderful thing, The monthly rent
14 comes in, try these on, take in one item

15 get something to eat, put it on, dials his cellphone
16~17 are used to test, stop animal testing, finding alternatives to, has dropped quite dramatically

02회

01 pursue natural textures, Last but not least, press the green button
02 force yourself to laugh, reported feeling better, boost our mood
03 taking any medication, starting a fitness program, lose some weight
04 with a parasol, that's hanging from, The basketball hoop beside
05 making a witch costume, if she'll lend, go well with
06 at our selection, one and a half, make a bouquet with
07 finish work, two free tickets, no way I can miss his party
08 rate the services, restrooms were not clean, a longer history
09 Tour participants will leave, join for half the price, sign up for it
10 except for, won't be able to, only eight years old
11 our big math test, makes you think so
12 was pulled over, How come
13 tight on him, are sold out, have the item delivered
14 not that serious, washed my hands, not to infect anyone else, What should I do
15 a report on desert and climates, finish writing it, print out her report file
16~17 go without water, last longer, high water content, mainly eat seeds

03회

01 start listening to your suggestions, a 100-dollar gift certificate, active participation
02 is strictly monitored, its water purification system, count on
03 don't feel any better, make people laugh, take the medicine I prescribed
04 setting up the stage, out of colorful balloons, in the center of
05 ask you a favor, apply for, mind writing it
06 effective for removing dirt and bacteria, a bigger one, buy dog toothpaste, two tubes of toothpaste
07 quit working at the amusement park, their hourly wage, Don't your parents allow, study on weekends
08 how many bedrooms, is the apartment furnished, on the 10th floor
09 Water Rocket Competition, Applications will be made online, along with a medal
10 play with dolls, an appropriate toy, is safer than, is made of
11 we go to lunch, a good spaghetti restaurant
12 look lively, the secret
13 Just existing, passed the written interview test, you'll be hired, preparing for the interview
14 check every inch of, get the car checked thoroughly, get caught in, an experienced driver
15 flies to, left his wristwatch, goes back to
16~17 have been used as, in salt, grains of, most common object

04회

01 evacuation drill will be conducted, leave the building, take more than
02 develop their creativity, showed less negative behavior, attention span
03 dedicate the song to, I bet you have something, play the song
04 frog showerhead, beside the mirror, have a pattern on
05 set up the projector, print them out, take care of
06 Take a good look, two dollars each, wrap them, cost an extra three
07 checked out some toys, is missing, must have put it
08 wearing armor, have large claws, feed on, are known to live
09 take about three hours, take group photos, pick you up
10 is not qualified, doesn't speak French, too old to
11 feel a bit hungry, Leftover pizza

12 is getting hotter, sweat too much
13 will you do for a living, have a more satisfying life, I've been studying it
14 deliver my gift to, broke my left anklebone, stay in the hospital
15 finds a vending machine, puts a one-dollar bill, change to be returned
16~17 adjust to high school life, Joining a school club, make your school life more enjoyable, are interested in computers, join the math or science club

05회

01 cradle automatically rocks, Combined with, a free fifteen-day trial
02 typing and clicking sounds, side effects of using, think twice before allowing
03 appreciate my work, this exhibition, take this picture, donate all profits to
04 holding a pencil, with a necktie on, over her head, holding a balloon
05 caught a cold, taken some pills, feeling a little thirsty, buy a bottle of
06 for three days, get a twenty-percent discount, get full-coverage insurance
07 take part in the swimming camp, running a guesthouse, learn how to surf
08 runs a shoe store, volunteer work, leaving your present job, I've been living in
09 sharp claws, scales cover their body, once a year, they've reached 30 inches
10 except black, well over, with manual transmissions, not satisfied with
11 got a flat tire, I'll leave my bike
12 looks really tired, no wonder
13 which course to take, more difficult than biology, the chemistry teacher, I've heard that
14 was fired from, performing my duties adequately, file a lawsuit against, against the law
15 so hooked on, reward him for, agrees to her proposal
16~17 communication through body gestures, convey as much meaning, Crossing your arms, shrug your shoulders, touch their noses while lying

06회

01 stop going to, less relaxed, looking at your reflection
02 has the highest number of, Many divorced people remain, don't need to share their rooms
03 have a delivery, sign for her, to deal with
04 an old pavilion, had a walking stick, on a rock, leaning against
05 was supposed to empty, can do his work, something to repay
06 give you ten percent off, lower the price, each roll of film, extra one dollar off per frame
07 have the morning off, having an operation, have to be with
08 seven famous magicians will perform, be worth that much, The earlier, I can't wait to see
09 the marathon is to celebrate, regardless of grade, appropriate for your running ability, those who complete their course
10 an awful traffic jam, Not all the way, rather not ride, the shorter time
11 how about booking, all the facilities
12 a dollar each, how many tickets
13 what you've done, not as close, take me there
14 stop watching it, She will stay with us, not enough seafood
15 failed to give change, make up for, admit his mistake
16~17 attracts more advertisements, placing billboards, continue to generate revenue

07회

01 a place to spend, much for your amusement, share memorable experiences, local folks sell produce
02 based on, comes out, won't move you, stir their intended emotions
03 go through, nothing wrong with, considering my injury history
04 finished decorating the living room, the Christmas tree you bought, hung a big sock, two square boxes
05 locked my keys in, lines have been busy, drive me home
06 something wrong with, up until, is included in
07 make a weekly study group, get a hold of, want to ask
08 trim the trees, water the flowers, check the mailbox
09 until one hour before, brought into, outside garden
10 any room type you'd prefer, wake up in the morning, there are two rooms left, better than the cheaper one
11 these yellow goldfish, feed the goldfish
12 looking for a present, have in mind
13 our website's customer bulletin board, the water is not hot enough, already fixed it, the yoga mats you mentioned, My pleasure
14 whether to continue dating, was turned down, served him right
15 Instead of eating out, almost empty, pick up the ingredient
16~17 various factors that affect children's emotions, create a negative emotion, are exposed to green or blue, the most joyful color

08회

01 to ask for your help, need to strongly ask, to sign our petitions
02 authentic material, what makes it difficult, the key words, with the most stress
03 appreciate all the readers, to write an article, make your novel into a movie, happy to read the news
04 the Independence Day parade, waving a big American flag, a carriage drawn by two horses
05 put it in my jacket, it's turned off, dropped out of, What about calling
06 sign up for, I'd also like, quite reasonable, for free
07 found a good campsite, hurry and book it, equipped with water play facilities, spend a peaceful time in nature
08 the smallest island, located in the southernmost part, living on the island, has four distinct seasons
09 Anyone who loves Korean food, the winner of each category, be broadcast live
10 family gatherings, hold at least, complained about, second floor would be better
11 the apples are rotten, complain about it
12 do volunteer work, help bathe them, hard work
13 have every reason to, as usual, totally different feeling
14 just stole my bike, In the public bike parking area, relieved to hear that
15 takes the subway, are taken, an empty seat, yields his seat, Feeling proud of
16~17 Playing sports offers, children's teamwork and communication skills, have better endurance, lack concentration, improve their concentration

09회

01 some of the tips, cut hundreds of dollars, returning and saving
02 live different lives, shoot through the night, the hardest times wisely
03 taking the role of a boy, my directing plan, practice voice acting
04 has four legs, in the middle of, next to, under the desk, The wireless mouse
05 sign up for, an advanced course, take a level test
06 the most popular ones, get a discount, celebrating our 10th anniversary
07 on the line with, for a way to, put you right through
08 business trip, too tight to enjoy, had a stopover, flew back to
09 Ten different bands, bring your own lawn chair, free for youth under 18
10 bigger than, live without electricity, take a shower, definitely need
11 check on him, be scared
12 very slippery, help you up
13 caught a cold, get some rest at home, make that much difference

14 What kind of greeting, this artist's exhibits, he depicts gender
15 has been working, inherited from, suddenly collapsed, take over
16~17 learn how to play, kids want to learn, are usually fascinated, rubbing the bow

10회

01 donating what they have, the value of sharing, giving to others
02 blame yourself too much, Brian didn't close the door, should learn from the mistakes
03 need one actor, a rather tough role, start looking for
04 sitting on a mat, ready to dive, with the bucket, dragonfly net
05 Something urgent came up, can get two tickets, need to call
06 telephone bill, I never received, be deducted from, reissue your bill
07 atmosphere is very quiet, have my wallet with me, taking out some money
08 what kinds of activities, how much, How can I get
09 astronaut training facility, blasted off, the spacecraft docked, paid a reported
10 spend over $40, one with longer warranty, two options to choose from
11 you're wearing glasses, Would you recommend
12 coming to meet, the flight
13 got a flat tire, how to fix a flat tire, handle the problem
14 He's into jazz, not to mention, What in the world
15 was so sick, majors in biology, catch up with, to copy, lecture notes
16~17 beginners can grow, require any special care, on well-drained soil, the ideal easy vegetable

11회

01 recruit hundreds of new employees, apply for a job, meet our qualifications
02 that's due tomorrow, putting important things off, your priorities straight
03 relieve the pain, any other symptoms, Take two pills, go see a specialist
04 the armchair, on her lap, under the table, piled up
05 a delivery that's supposed to arrive, to receive it
06 two passes for adults and two for kids, as an adult, only $50 a year, get a 10 percent discount
07 going to the nursing home, have a family gathering, some assignment to finish, make sure to join us
08 set aside time, in silent mode, try to limit, having a novel handy
09 mark the 26th time, local foods, be set up, local residents, for the disabled
10 have easy access, work out, without a pool
11 already watering
12 Could you pick up, still have some
13 had a problem, who got discouraged, in more detail
14 the writer's real life, an intelligence agent, power from the true story
15 make a presentation, a lot of pressure, gets some tips
16~17 the same goes for, making dog food yourself, mixing some ingredients, be cooked together

12회

01 difficulty giving advice, free lectures, college admission process
02 a couple of cups a day are fine, health benefits, is good for
03 with the altitude, some minor turbulence, fasten their seatbelts
04 covered by cloth, tall stack of, there's nothing, rectangular carpet
05 at the daycare center, my turn to drop her off, Could you drive to the daycare center
06 only two extra dollars, as a side dish, any benefits for members
07 taking a cooking class, joined the center's volleyball club, leading a very active life, we will practice today

08 It's being held, there are many other activities, want to miss it, the fair be crowded
09 first year of study, in the top, live on campus, maintain a GPA of 3.4
10 answer calls directly, has a longer warranty, regardless of the price
11 we need curtains, hang the curtains
12 school supplies, I'll take him
13 introducing a foreign country, write about its culture, are unfamiliar to
14 drew her portrait, push her into drawing, lose her interest in drawing
15 are already taken, only one woman, have a seat there
16~17 doing part-time jobs, good jobs for you to do, cashiers and baggers, fast food server, walk their dogs

13회

01 all the elevators, go through regular inspections, will be examined
02 experience of raising children, improve his reading, appropriate for his age, that he can't understand
03 doesn't drain, sink is troubling me, blockage in the pipes
04 need to preserve trees, watering a small plant, they have a choice
05 be late for school, One of the buttons, sew a new one on
06 this brown skirt, a variety of blouses, 20 percent off now, take two of them
07 editing a video clip, advertising our club, picking her up, an assignment to do
08 host the event, thank hosting organizations, new games for this year's event, starts at nine
09 as the last of six children, earned his bachelor's degree, became a British citizen
10 microwave function, automatically cooks, steam oven
11 a printer shop nearby, the closer one is
12 I'm thinking about, wearing glasses
13 joining a gym, unsanitary shower facilities, wasn't determined enough
14 much shorter with the bridge, long commuting time, be pressed for time
15 hanging out with, skipped training sessions, is concerned that
16~17 strange patterns of some animal behavior, mark their territory, make up for this less eating

14회

01 is collecting old books, donate your old books, By participating in this book donation
02 who have conquered, a cleanup expedition, gather trash on their way up, to restore the environment
03 display our bread on it, set it up, work for my bakery, sales have gone up
04 take a look at, has a shield on it, horseman with a beard
05 a terrible stomachache, take some medicine, first-aid kit
06 place an order, Ten of each, just order five, one dollar for each bulb
07 assignment to finish, had the camping gear ready, take care of mom, get well soon
08 make a reservation, a first-come, first-served basis, rented a court for two hours
09 sells over 20,000 household items, over 900 franchises, a 60 percent market share, cash deposit of
10 What price range, spend more than $160, without a headrest, two options to choose from
11 have a dog, gave birth to
12 forgot about it, I'm disappointed
13 history mid-term exam, missed the previous class, studying five whole chapters, lend you my notebook
14 such an early bird, made up my mind, with such a good work ethic, is usually locked
15 baby carriage rental office, available now, is planning to come back after dinner

16~17 suffering from headaches, sick building syndrome, how we should handle, Bacteria and mold

15회

01 that isn't true, continuously burns calories, in a balanced way
02 going to be bankrupt, a salary reduction, share the burden of this financial crisis
03 he gets a shot, let him go home, better get going
04 lighthouse on the hill, a tourist attraction, sitting on these two chairs, next to the chairs
05 a collection of, make an extra copy, have them ready
06 When and how long, the nightly rate, without the meals, 10 percent discount off
07 your soccer club practice, with the new soccer goalpost, Our coach was absent
08 big fan of that circus, its large scale, tickets are a little expensive, last for two months
09 in celebration of, except for 3rd graders, be unable to refer, come to my office
10 a good workout, afraid of water, can't attend, do volunteer work
11 remember anniversaries, using an app
12 request form, when should I come back
13 on my way, return it to the owner, my conscience tells
14 make a salad with these, have our own vegetable garden, give me many tips
15 eagerly looking forward to, cancel the picnic, announce the news
16~17 myths relating to cold treatments and their real effects, go away quicker, antibiotics can be used

16회

01 volunteers for various tasks, interested in volunteering, the volunteers like you
02 in a proper posture, served to be eaten, eating in a sitting position
03 than I expected, express the passage of time, carrying around bars of soap
04 setting for the living room scene, in front of the sofa, with many leaves
05 a parking violation sticker, a parking permit sticker, a copy of your car registration
06 are suitable for camping, the plastic cutting board, give you 10 percent off the knife
07 to borrow books, couldn't remember the title, was giving a presentation
08 group visits, possible on request, make a reservation in advance
09 open to all girls, Monday through Friday, create amazing crafts
10 free to move around, likes to sing alone, within my $700 budget
11 my first job interview, buy that suit
12 a really tough competition, you have been practicing
13 what I expected, a lot of patience and time, good at it
14 presented the part on company management, prepare that part, buy you dinner in return
15 several hours of shopping, was in his class, puts his hand on
16~17 you need to eat fruit with its skin, a lot of nutrients, contains many minerals, feel like eating the peels

17회

01 some simple tips to follow, use a tissue, prevents spreading cold germs
02 cleaning the refrigerator, making a list of items, stop buying food
03 get me out quickly, keep calm and be patient, what if
04 keep the concert title, beside the guitar, represents the songs
05 a long line, are sold only at this restaurant, get a waiting ticket
06 on sale for 50 percent off, at a discounted price, on sale
07 let you know the result, they called me, except waiting for the call

08 save the declining dairy industry, take the kids, register first on their website
09 is scheduled to run, take ballet class, Participants can audition for
10 explore forests, a full schedule in June, too much
11 to get ready for, been practicing a lot
12 how to play the guitar, never played it
13 apologize to her first, wait too long to apologize, value your friendship
14 been volunteering, work for packing lunch boxes, do the work
15 is supposed to have dinner together, get some materials, return her books
16~17 easily fall asleep, delays the time you fall asleep, tends to rise, good to sleep well

MEMO

10개년 기출의 핵심만 모은 **수능 국어 기본서**

국어 상위 1%는 기본 무게 부터 다르다!
GYM

문법

문학

독서

모든 문제 적용 가능한
필수 문법 개념 100

- - - - - - - - - - - - - - - -

예문 분석 및
집중 적용 연습

필수 **문학 개념 100**
교재 및 **영상 학습**

- - - - - - - - - - - - - - - -

실전 지문 풀이로
개념 원리 반복 학습

원리 독해로 지문을
읽는 방법 학습

- - - - - - - - - - - - - - - -

주제 독해로 영역별
배경지식 습득

Listening master

BASIC

정답 및 해설

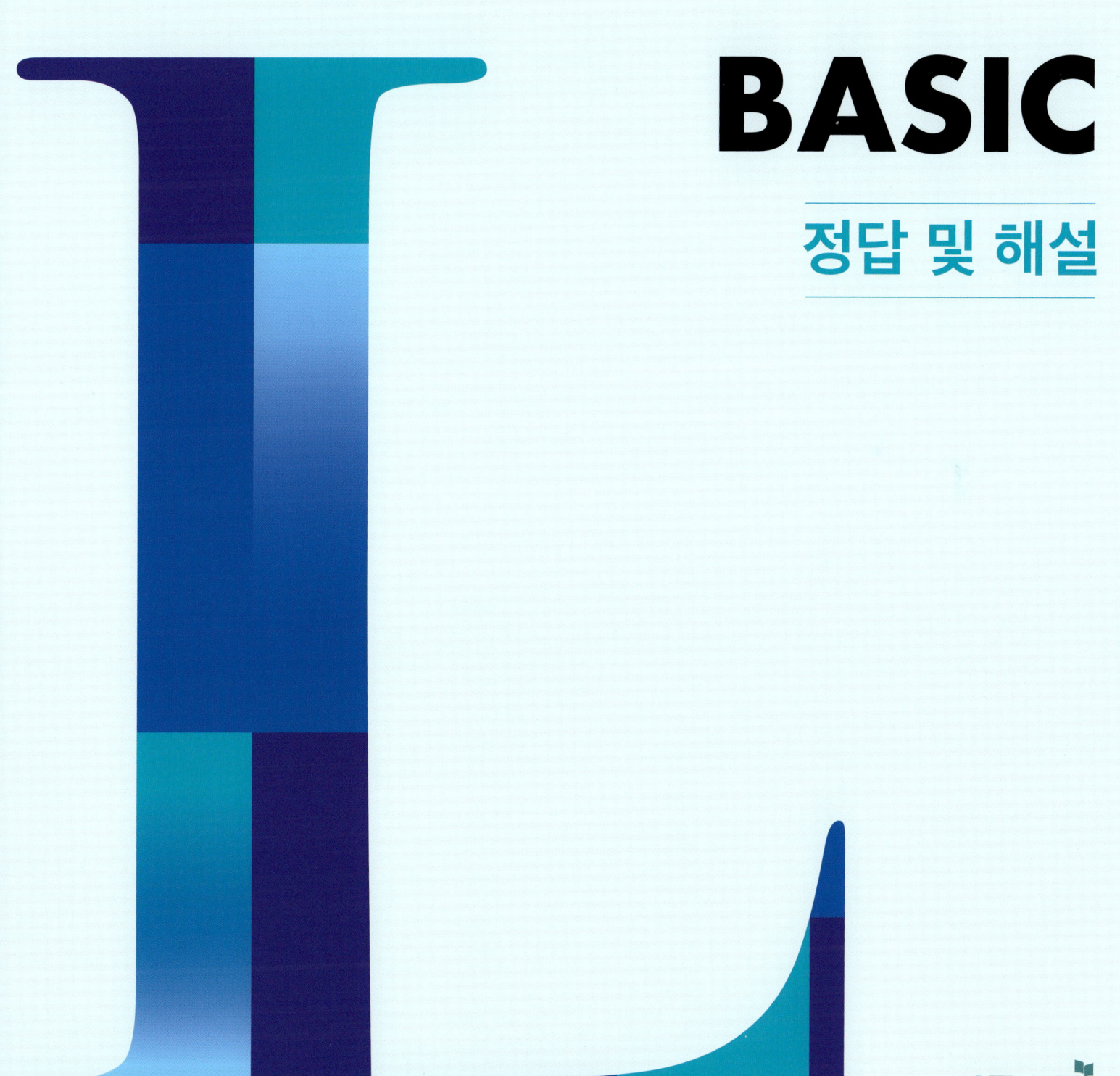

이투스북

Listening ∞ master

BASIC

정답 및 해설

01강 담화의 목적 파악
본문 10쪽

수능 Q
정답 ①

남 고객 여러분, 주목해 주시겠습니까? Miracle 백화점을 방문해 주셔서 감사합니다. 이번 주말 내내 계속되는 특별 행사에 대해 여러분에게 알려드리고 싶습니다. 먼저, 7층에서 특정 전자 제품과 스포츠 용품에 대한 50퍼센트 할인을 제공하고 있습니다. 둘째, 50달러 넘게 지출하시는 고객님께 1층에 있는 커피숍에서 무료 음료를 제공하고 있습니다. 셋째, 100달러 넘게 지출하시는 모든 고객님께 10달러의 상품권을 또한 드리고 있습니다. 마지막으로, 이번 주말에는 주차 요금을 걱정하실 필요가 없습니다. 주차가 무료입니다. 저희 백화점에서 이번 주말에 열리는 이 특별 행사를 즐기시기 바랍니다.

Solution

남자는 Miracle 백화점에 있는 고객들에게 이번 주말에 진행하는 특별 행사에 대해 알려드리겠다고 하면서, 그 내용을 구체적으로 언급하고 있으므로 남자가 하는 말의 목적으로 가장 적절한 것은 ①이다.

Words

inform ~ of ... ~에게 …를 알리다 offer 제공하다(= provide)
electronics 전자 제품 goods 상품 gift certificate 상품권
last but not least 마지막으로 don't have to ~할 필요가 없다
parking fee 주차 요금

유형 모의고사
본문 11쪽

01 ② 02 ④ 03 ② 04 ① 05 ① 06 ⑤

01 정답 ②

Script

W Hello, students. This is vice principal Susan Lee. I know all of you are busy preparing for the upcoming school festival. There are club activities going on in every part of our school building. You may want to move between places during activities. But I'd like to ask you to work in the place where you are supposed to be. Your teachers want to make your safety the top priority. Once again, make sure to prepare for the festival in your prearranged places. Thank you for your cooperation.

여 안녕하세요, 학생 여러분. 저는 교감 Susan Lee입니다. 여러분 모두 다가오는 학교 축제를 준비하느라 바쁘다는 것을 알고 있습니다. 학교 건물 모든 곳에서 동아리 활동이 한창입니다. 이러한 활동을 하는 동안에 여러분은 장소들을 이동하고 싶을지도 모릅니다. 하지만 저는 여러분이 있어야 하는 장소에서 활동하기를 요청드립니다. 여러분의 선생님은 여러분의 안전을 최우선으로 삼고자 합니다. 다시 말씀드리면, 반드시 여러분의 미리 정해진 장소에서 축제를 준비해 주십시오. 협조해 주셔서 고맙습니다.

Solution

여자는 학교 축제를 위한 동아리 활동에 바쁜 학생들에게 미리 정해진 장소에서 활동할 것을 요청하고 있으므로 여자가 하는 말의 목적으로 가장 적절한 것은 ②이다.

Words

vice principal 교감 be busy -ing ～하느라 바쁘다
upcoming 다가오는 be supposed to ～하기로 되어 있다
top priority 최우선 (과제) make sure to 반드시 ～하다
prearranged 미리 정해진 cooperation 협조, 협동

02 정답 ④

Script

M Hello, ping pong club members. I'm John Clement, your club leader. May 12th is going to be a very special day for our club. Everyone will meet the youngest table tennis champion in the national competition, Tom Clay. Tom is 14 years old — much, much younger than any of us — but he is the youngest table tennis player to ever win the national championship. It wasn't easy to bring him here, but he's finally accepted our invitation. He is going to give us some demonstrations and afterwards there will be time for a short Q&A session. Don't forget to put some time aside on May 12th for the meeting with this prodigy. I would appreciate the full attendance of all our members.

남 안녕하세요, 탁구 동호회 회원 여러분. 저는 동호회 회장인 John Clement입니다. 5월 12일은 우리 동호회에 아주 특별한 날이 될 것입니다. 여러분 모두는 전국 대회 최연소 탁구 우승자인 Tom Clay를 만나게 될 것입니다. Tom은 14세로 우리들 누구보다도 훨씬 훨씬 더 어립니다만 전국 선수권 대회에서 우승을 차지한 역대 최연소 탁구 선수입니다. 그를 여기에 초청하기가 쉽지 않았지만 마침내 우리의 초대를 수락했습니다. 그는 몇 차례 우리에게 시범을 보여줄 것이며 그 후에 간단한 질의응답 시간을 가질 예정입니다. 이 신동과의 만남을 위해 5월 12일에 시간을 따로 떼어놓는 것을 잊지 마시기 바랍니다. 우리 회원 모두가 전부 참석해 주시면 감사하겠습니다.

Solution

남자는 전국 대회 최연소 탁구 우승자를 초청하여 시범 및 질의응답 시간을 가질 예정이니 모두 빠짐없이 참석해 달라고 독려하고 있으므로 남자가 하는 말의 목적으로 가장 적절한 것은 ④이다.

Words

championship 선수권 대회; 우승 demonstration 시범
session 시간, 기간 put aside 따로 떼어놓다 prodigy 신동, 천재
attendance 참석, 출석

03 정답 ②

Script

W Hi, students. This is Kate Brown, and I'm trying hard to organize a school magic club. Finally, the magic club was officially approved by the school management committee last week. Now we just need members. If you haven't joined any of the clubs yet, why don't you join the magic club? I'm sure being a member of the magic club will make your school life more interesting and exciting. Please visit the magic club office in the student union building if you're interested in magic. I hope to see you there.

여 안녕하세요, 학생 여러분. 저는 Kate Brown이고, 교내 마술 동아리를 조직하기 위해 열심히 노력하고 있습니다. 마침내, 마술 동아리가 지난주 학교 운영 위원회에서 공식적으로 승인을 받았습니다. 이제 우리는 단지 회원을 필요로 합니다. 여러분이 아직 어떤 동아리에도 가입하지 않았다면, 마술 동아리에 가입하는 것은 어떠세요? 여러분이 마술 동아리 부원이 되면 학교생활이 더 재미있고 흥미진진해질 것이라고 저는 확신합니다. 마술에 관심이 있다면 학생 회관 건물에 있는 마술 동아리실을 방문해 주십시오. 그곳에서 여러분을 만나기를 희망합니다.

Solution

여자는 지난주 학교 운영 위원회로부터 마술 동아리가 공식적으로 승인을 받았다고 하면서 학생들에게 마술 동아리에 가입할 것을 권유하고 있으므로 여자가 하는 말의 목적으로 가장 적절한 것은 ②이다.

Words

organize 조직하다 officially 공식적으로 approve 승인하다
school management committee 학교 운영 위원회
student union 학생 회관

04 정답 ①

Script

M Hello, I'm David Kim, the school health teacher. As you know, food poisoning is spreading now, and many people are afraid of getting infected. But don't worry too much. I'll tell you two simple ways to prevent getting the food poisoning. First, make sure to wash your hands before eating any kind of food. Second, try to avoid eating raw food such as fish or vegetables for the time being. The more you avoid raw food, the less likely you are to get food poisoning. I'm sure that if you follow this advice, you won't have to worry too much about the threat of food poisoning.

남 안녕하세요, 저는 교내 보건교사 David Kim입니다. 여러분이 아시다시피, 현재 식중독이 퍼지고 있으며, 많은 사람들이 감염되는 것을 두려워하고 있습니다. 하지만 너무 많이 걱정하지 마십시오. 식중독에 걸리는 것을 막을 수 있는 두 가지 간단한 방법을 여러분에게 말씀드리겠습니다. 먼저, 그 어떤 음식이라도 먹기 전에는 반드시 손을 씻으십시오. 둘째, 당분간 생선 또는 채소와 같은 익히지 않은 음식을 먹는 것을 피하려고 하십시오. 여러분이 익히지 않은 음식을 피하면 피할수록, 식중독에 걸릴 가능성은 더 줄어듭니다. 여러분이 이 조언을 따르면 식중독의 위협에 대해 너무 많이 걱정할 필요가 없을 것이라고 확신합니다.

Solution

남자는 교내 보건교사로서 식중독을 예방할 수 있는 두 가지 간단한 방법을 구체적으로 언급하고 있으므로 남자가 하는 말의 목적으로 가장 적절한 것은 ①이다.

Words

food poisoning 식중독 spread 퍼지다 get infected 감염되다

prevent 막다, 방지하다 make sure to 반드시 ~하다 avoid 피하다
raw 익히지 않은, 날것의 threat 위협

05 정답 ①

Script

W Hello, fellow club members. Today, I'd like to talk about *Spoken Out*. It's not well-known, and it's not on the list of top 30 movies at the box office. *Spoken Out* is a black comedy which parodies current political situations. It features actors Eric Dennis and Charlie Young, who mimic political big shots. It's a story about two future politicians who manage to escape from political embarrassment time and time again. The directing is fresh and the story is funny, and this should appeal to most adults who live a Monday-to-Friday working lifestyle. There are no special effects in this film, just solid acting from two promising stars. You'll have a wonderful time watching this black comedy.

여 안녕하세요, 동료 회원 여러분. 오늘 저는 'Spoken Out'에 관해 말씀드리고 싶습니다. 이 영화는 잘 알려져 있지 않으며, 흥행 성적도 30위권 안에 있지 않습니다. 'Spoken Out'은 현재의 정치적 상황을 희화화한 블랙코미디입니다. 이 영화에는 정치계 거물들을 모방하는 Eric Dennis와 Charlie Young 배우들이 출연합니다. 이것은 몇 번이고 계속해서 정치적으로 곤란한 상황을 겨우 빠져나가는 두 명의 미래 정치인들에 관한 이야기입니다. 연출이 신선하고 이야기가 재미있어서 이것은 월요일부터 금요일까지 일하는 생활 방식으로 살고 있는 대부분의 성인들의 관심을 끌 것입니다. 이 영화에는 특수 효과가 없고 단지 두 명의 유망한 배우들의 탄탄한 연기력이 있을 뿐입니다. 여러분은 이 블랙코미디를 시청하면서 멋진 시간을 보내게 될 것입니다.

Solution

여자는 잘 알려져 있지는 않지만 재미있는 블랙코미디 영화를 소개하면서 이 영화를 보면 멋진 시간을 보내게 될 것이라고 추천하고 있으므로 여자가 하는 말의 목적으로 가장 적절한 것은 ①이다.

Words

box office 매표 성적; 매표소 feature 출연하다 mimic 모방하다
big shot 거물 embarrassment 곤란한 상황; 난처함
time and time again 몇 번이나 appeal to ~의 관심을 끌다
promising 유망한

06 정답 ⑤

Script

M May I have your attention, please? I'd like to thank you for coming to the wedding of Peter Anderson and Mary Damon. Before the wedding ceremony starts, I'd like to tell you a couple of things. For us to maintain a solemn atmosphere in the wedding, please switch your cellphones to manner mode. For the same reason, please keep your eyes on your kids and make sure they behave themselves. And be sure to be seated at least five minutes before the ceremony starts. We'll give an announcement when it's time. And during the ceremony, please follow the instructions of the wedding director and give a big hand to the groom and the bride. Your consideration will make it much easier for us to have this wedding with a congratulatory mood. Thank you for your cooperation.

남 주목해 주시겠습니까? Peter Anderson과 Mary Damon의 결혼식에 와 주셔서 감사드리고 싶습니다. 결혼식이 시작되기 전에 몇 가지 드릴 말씀이 있습니다. 저희가 이 결혼식을 엄숙한 분위기로 유지할 수 있도록 여러분의 휴대전화를 매너 모드로 전환해 주시기 바랍니다. 같은 이유로 여러분의 자녀들을 잘 살펴봐 주시고, 그들이 얌전히 행동하도록 확실하게 해 주십시오. 그리고 결혼식이 시작되기 적어도 5분 전에는 반드시 착석해 주십시오. 시간이 되면 저희가 안내 방송을 할 것입니다. 그리고 식이 진행되는 동안 사회자의 지시에 따라 주시고 신랑과 신부에게 큰 박수를 보내 주시기를 부탁드립니다. 여러분의 배려가 저희가 이 결혼식을 축하하는 분위기에서 진행하는 것을 한결 수월하도록 해 줄 것입니다. 여러분의 협조에 감사합니다.

Solution

남자는 결혼식에 앞서서 결혼식이 엄숙하고 축하하는 분위기 속에서 진행될 수 있도록 몇 가지 사항을 당부하고 있으므로 남자가 하는 말의 목적으로 가장 적절한 것은 ⑤이다.

Words

solemn 엄숙한, 경건한
behave oneself 얌전하게 굴다, 예의 바르게 행동하다
give a big hand 큰 박수를 보내다 groom 신랑 bride 신부
congratulatory 축하의

 02강 화자의 의견/대화의 주제 파악 본문 14쪽

수능 Q 정답 ③

여 안녕, Sam. 어떻게 지내니?
남 잘 지내. 너는 어때, Christine?
여 정말로 좋아.
남 와! 무슨 일이 있었니? 대체로 피곤하다고 말하잖아.
여 음, 내가 잠자는 방식을 바꿨어. 왼쪽으로 누워서 자기 시작했는데, 그게 내 건강을 개선해 줬어.
남 정말이야?
여 그래. 일주일 동안 이렇게 잤는데, 소화가 점점 더 잘됐어.
남 잠자는 방식이 소화와 관련이 있는 줄은 몰랐어.
여 관련이 있어. 왼쪽으로 누워 자면 소화 작용을 도와주는데, 이는 네 위가 왼쪽에 있기 때문이야.
남 이해할 수 있겠어. 그런데 소화가 잘 되면 네가 그렇게까지 훨씬 더 건강해지니?
여 왼쪽으로 누워 자는 것은 그 이상의 효과가 있어. 나는 그것이 심장으로의 혈액 순환도 도와주기 때문에 건강에 좋다고 생각해.
남 그게 일리가 있네. 나도 시도해 봐야겠다.

Solution

여자가 왼쪽으로 누워 잔 이후부터 건강이 좋아졌다면서, 왼쪽으로 누워 자는 것의 장점을 열거하고 있으므로 여자의 의견으로 가장 적절한 것은 ③이다.

Words

digestion 소화 have something to do with ～와 관련이 있다
stomach 위; 복부 blood circulation 혈액 순환

유형 모의고사 본문 15쪽

01 ③ **02** ④ **03** ① **04** ⑤ **05** ① **06** ③

01 정답 ③

Script

M Honey, where did you get all these potatoes?
W My friend Jennifer runs a potato farm, so she gave me some.
M This is a lot! Let's put them in the refrigerator.
W Oh, no. Storing potatoes in a refrigerator gives them an unpleasant taste.
M Okay. Where should we keep them?
W They should be stored in a cool and dark place.
M Then the basement would be good.
W That's perfect, but we also need to take the potatoes out of the plastic bag. Potatoes rot easily in plastic bags.
M I see. And I remember reading an article saying that storing potatoes with an apple keeps them from sprouting.
W Really? That's good to know.
M I'll bring an apple, and we can keep them together.

남 여보, 이 감자들을 어디서 얻었나요?
여 친구 Jennifer가 감자 농장을 운영하고 있어서, 감자를 약간 주었어요.

남 정말 많아요! 그것들을 냉장고에 넣어요.

여 오, 안 돼요. 감자를 냉장고에 저장하면 감자의 맛이 이상해져요.

남 알겠어요. 우리가 감자를 어디에 보관해야 하죠?

여 차갑고 어두운 장소에 감자를 보관해야 해요.

남 그러면 지하실이 좋겠어요.

여 완벽하지만, 우리는 또한 비닐 봉투에서 감자를 꺼내야 해요. 감자는 비닐 봉투에서 쉽게 썩어요.

남 알았어요. 그리고 사과와 함께 감자를 보관하면 감자에 싹이 나는 것을 막아준다고 언급하는 기사를 읽은 게 기억나요.

여 정말요? 알아두면 좋네요.

남 내가 사과를 가져올 테니 그것들을 함께 두면 돼요.

두 사람은 감자를 지하실에 보관하고, 비닐 봉투에서 꺼내어 사과와 함께 두어야 하는 등 어떻게 감자를 보관해야 하는지 열거하고 있으므로 두 사람이 하는 말의 주제로 가장 적절한 것은 ③이다.

Words

rot 썩다 article 기사 sprout 싹이 나다

02 정답 ④

Script

M Hi, Sally. I'm glad you're back!

W Hi, Thomas.

M How was your trip to Italy?

W It wasn't bad. But my house was.

M What do you mean?

W While I was on vacation, someone broke into my house. They took almost everything.

M That's terrible! I'm sorry to hear that.

W I wish I hadn't taken the trip to Italy! It's all my fault.

M Well, it might have been a good thing that you weren't home when they broke in.

W What do you mean?

M You might have been hurt. Whatever you lost, it isn't as important as your safety.

W That's true. Maybe you're right.

M What is done cannot be undone. It's important to see that in a positive way.

남 안녕, Sally. 네가 돌아와서 기뻐!

여 안녕, Thomas.

남 이탈리아 여행은 어땠어?

여 여행은 나쁘지 않았어. 그렇지만 집은 그랬어.

남 무슨 말이야?

여 내가 휴가 중에 누군가가 우리 집에 침입했어. 거의 모든 것을 가져갔어.

남 그런 끔찍한 일이! 정말 안됐다.

여 이탈리아 여행을 가지 않았더라면 좋았을 텐데! 다 내 잘못이야.

남 음, 도둑들이 침입했을 때 네가 집에 없었던 것이 좋은 일이었을 수도 있어.

여 무슨 말이니?

남 네가 다쳤을지도 모를 일이었잖아. 네가 뭘 잃어버렸든, 너의 안전만큼 중요하지는 않아.

여 맞아. 네 말이 맞을지도 몰라.

남 벌어진 일은 어떻게 할 수 없잖아. 그것을 긍정적인 방식으로 보는 것이 중요해.

여자는 휴가 중에 집에 도둑이 들어 속상해하고 있고 남자는 다치지 않은 것

이 다행이라고 하며 이미 벌어진 상황을 긍정적으로 보는 것이 중요하다고 말하고 있으므로 남자의 의견으로 가장 적절한 것은 ④이다.

Words

break into 침입하다

What is done cannot be undone. 이미 저지른 일은 돌이킬 수 없다.(엎질러진 물이다.)

03 정답 ①

Script

W Isn't Jack here?

M Nope, not yet.

W Has he called or sent a text message?

M No, he hasn't.

W This is the second time this week. I think you need to do something to make sure that he's on time for work.

M I'll talk to him about that.

W I have to pick up my children after school every afternoon. If he doesn't get here soon, I'll be late.

M Why don't you go? I can do the work by myself.

W No. You have your own job to do, and I can't let you serve the tables. That's Jack's job.

M You're right. But if there is a problem, everyone helps out.

W Yeah, but if this becomes a regular occurrence, everyone will get tired and new problems will arise. We all need to do our fair share.

여 Jack이 안 왔니?

남 응, 아직 안 왔어.

여 그가 전화를 하거나 문자 메시지를 보냈니?

남 아니, 안 했어.

여 이번 주에 두 번째야. 내 생각에는 그가 시간에 맞추어 일하러 오는 것을 확실히 하기 위해서 네가 뭔가를 해야 해.

남 그것에 관해 그와 얘기해 볼게.

여 나는 매일 오후 방과 후에 아이들을 데리러 가야 해. 그가 곧 오지 않으면 나는 늦을 거야.

남 가보지 그러니? 내가 혼자서 그 일을 할 수 있어.

여 아니. 너는 네 할 일이 있으니까 내가 너에게 서빙하는 일을 하게 할 수는 없어. 그것은 Jack의 일이야.

남 네 말이 맞아. 하지만 문제가 있으면 모두들 도와야지.

여 맞아, 하지만 이것이 주기적으로 발생하면 모두들 피곤해질 거고 새로운 문제점들이 생겨날 거야. 우리 모두 공평한 각자의 몫을 할 필요가 있어.

남자는 Jack의 일을 대신 해주겠다고 하였지만, 여자는 그 일은 Jack의 일이고 모두 공평하게 각자의 몫을 수행해야 한다고 말하고 있으므로 여자의 의견으로 가장 적절한 것은 ①이다.

Words

on time 시간에 맞추어, 정각에 occurrence 발생

04 정답 ⑤

Script

M Angela, I think you always look healthy.

W Do I? I'm happy to hear that.

M Do you have any special secret?

W Well, I eat a few apples almost every day, and I think that helps a lot.

M Eating apples every day?

W Yes. Apples are a good source of fiber and vitamins C and K. So eating them is very good for your health.

M I see. Ah, I think I've heard that eating apples is also effective for weight loss.

W Absolutely! They can also help keep your heart healthy if you eat them regularly.

M Wow, that's great! I've made up my mind to start eating apples from today.

- -

남 Angela, 너는 항상 건강해 보여.

여 내가? 그 말을 들으니 좋네.

남 무슨 특별한 비결이 있니?

여 음, 나는 거의 매일 사과를 몇 개씩 먹는데, 그게 도움이 많이 되는 것 같아.

남 매일 사과를 먹는다고?

여 응. 사과는 섬유소와 비타민 C와 K의 좋은 공급원이야. 그래서 그것을 먹는 것이 네 건강에 아주 좋아.

남 알았어. 아, 사과를 먹는 것이 체중 감소에도 효과적이라고 들은 것 같아.

여 물론이지! 네가 사과를 정기적으로 먹으면 네 심장을 건강하게 유지하는 데도 도움을 줄 수 있어.

남 와, 대단하다! 나도 오늘부터 사과를 먹는 것을 시작하기로 결심했어.

Solution

두 사람은 여자의 건강 비결인 사과 섭취의 장점에 대해 구체적으로 열거하고 있으므로 두 사람이 하는 말의 주제로 가장 적절한 것은 ⑤이다.

Words

healthy 건강한 special secret 비결 source 공급원, 원천
fiber 섬유소 effective 효과적인 make up one's mind 결심하다

05 정답 ①

Script

W Math class is finally over.

M Yes. Why don't we go for lunch? It's already 1 o'clock.

W Sure. Let's go to the school restaurant.

M The school restaurant? How about going to a restaurant outside of school?

W Why? The school restaurant's food is more delicious and cheaper than that of other restaurants.

M But as you know, the school restaurant closes at 1:30. 30 minutes is a bit short to enjoy lunch.

W Yeah, you're right.

M I think the school restaurant should extend their hours since there are lots of classes that end at 1 p.m.

W I agree. Otherwise, we can't have lunch there just like today. Why don't we ask the student council about it?

M That's a good idea.

- -

여 수학 수업이 드디어 끝났어.

남 응. 점심 먹으러 갈래? 벌써 1시야.

여 그래. 교내식당에 가자.

남 교내식당? 학교 밖에 있는 식당에 가는 것은 어때?

여 왜? 교내식당의 음식이 다른 식당들보다 더 맛있고 더 저렴하잖아.

남 하지만 너도 알다시피, 교내식당은 1시 30분에 문을 닫아. 점심을 즐기기에 30분은 약간 부족해.

여 그래, 네 말이 맞아.

남 1시에 끝나는 수업이 많으니까 교내식당이 운영 시간을 연장해야 할 것 같아.

여 동의해. 그렇지 않으면, 꼭 오늘처럼 우리는 교내식당에서 점심을 먹을 수 없어. 학생회에 이것에 대해 요청해 보는 게 어때?

남 좋은 생각이야.

Solution

여자는 교내식당에서 점심을 먹자고 하였으나 남자는 시간이 부족하다며 1시에 끝나는 수업이 많으므로 교내식당의 운영 시간이 연장되어야 한다고 말하고 있으므로 남자의 의견으로 가장 적절한 것은 ①이다.

Words

extend 연장하다, 늘리다 otherwise 그렇지 않으면
student council 학생회

06 정답 ③

Script

W Honey, when are you going to open your restaurant?

M Well, I'm not sure yet. I don't even know if I should.

W What makes you hesitate so much?

M What if it's not successful? Then I'll lose all that money!

W Don't worry about that. It doesn't matter whether you make money or not. What's important is that you follow your dream.

M But I have to make enough money to support my family.

W You'll be fine. You've been planning this for years.

M That's true. I've taken a lot of classes. This is something I've always wanted to do.

W Give it a try. We're behind you. Besides, nothing in life makes us happier than doing what we like best.

M I guess you're right.

- -

여 여보, 언제 식당을 개업할 거예요?

남 글쎄, 아직 잘 모르겠어요. 심지어 개업을 해야 할지도 모르겠어요.

여 무엇 때문에 그렇게 많이 주저하는 거예요?

남 실패하면 어떻게 해요? 그러면 그 돈을 다 날릴 텐데요!

여 그런 걱정은 하지 말아요. 당신이 돈을 버는지 그렇지 않은지는 중요하지 않아요. 중요한 것은 당신의 꿈을 따라가는 것이에요.

남 하지만 가족을 부양할 충분한 돈을 벌어야 하잖아요.

여 당신은 잘할 거예요. 이 일을 수년 동안 계획해 왔잖아요.

남 사실이에요. 수업을 많이 들었지요. 이건 내가 늘 해 보고 싶어 했던 것이고요.

여 시도해 보세요. 우리가 당신을 응원하고 있어요. 게다가 인생에서 우리가 가장 좋아하는 일을 하는 것보다 우리를 더 행복하게 만드는 것은 없어요.

남 당신 말이 맞는 것 같아요.

Solution

남자는 개업을 망설이고 있고, 여자는 한번 시도해 보라며 좋아하는 일을 해야 행복할 수 있다고 하였으므로 여자의 의견으로 가장 적절한 것은 ③이다.

Words

hesitate 주저하다 matter 중요하다
give it a try 한번 해보다, 시도하다 be behind ~을 응원하다

수능 Q 정답 ③

남 안녕하세요, 저는 Ted Benson입니다. Brown 씨이시죠.
여 안녕하세요, Benson 씨. 이 인터뷰를 위해 시간을 내주셔서 감사합니다. '최고의 쌀 상'을 수상하신 이후 뵙고 싶었습니다.
남 영광입니다. 저는 귀 잡지의 정기 독자예요. 기사들이 매우 유익해요.
여 감사합니다. 성공 비결을 말씀해 주시겠어요?
남 저는 해충을 죽이기 위한 어떠한 화학 물질도 사용하지 않고 쌀을 재배합니다. 유기농이죠.
여 어떻게 그렇게 하시나요?
남 저는 논에 오리들을 넣고, 오리가 해충을 먹습니다.
여 그것이 우리나라에서 최고의 쌀을 재배하신 방법이군요. 정말 좋은 생각이에요!
남 네, 그것이 제가 30년 동안 농사를 지으면서 얻은 비결입니다.
여 음, 놀라워요. 제가 저의 잡지 기사에 쓰도록 논 앞에서 당신 사진을 찍어도 될까요?
남 그럼요.

Solution

두 사람이 서로 인사를 나눈 뒤에 여자는 인터뷰를 위해 시간을 내준 것에 감사하다고 말했고, 남자는 여자가 만든 잡지의 정기 독자라고 했으며, 이후 남자의 쌀농사 짓는 방법에 관해 이야기를 나눈 후, 잡지 기사에 쓸 사진을 촬영한 것으로 보아 두 사람의 관계를 가장 잘 나타낸 것은 ③이다.

Words

spare 할애하다, 내다 regular reader 정기 독자 informative 유익한 chemical 화학 물질 harmful insect 해충 organic 유기농의 know-how 비결, 노하우

유형 모의고사 본문 19쪽

01 ⑤ **02** ⑤ **03** ① **04** ③ **05** ⑤ **06** ②

01 정답 ⑤

Script

W Excuse me, Mr. Young. I'm Emma Baker.
M Oh, hi Emma. I've been waiting for you. Nice to meet you.
W Nice to meet you too.
M Is this your first visit to a broadcasting station?
W Yes, it is. I've been looking forward to seeing the news studio myself.
M I see. You seem to be very interested in broadcasting.
W Yes, I'm the leader of my school's broadcasting club.
M Oh, you are? Today, you'll sit at a news desk and experience what it's like to host a news program.
W Fantastic! I watch your news program every day. How can you deliver the news so effortlessly?
M I read my scripts repeatedly before I begin the broadcast.
W That's impressive. I really want to host a news program like you someday.

M I hope you will. Shall we go to the news studio now?

여 안녕하세요, Young 씨. 저는 Emma Baker입니다.
남 오, 안녕하세요, Emma. 당신을 기다리고 있었어요. 만나서 반가워요.
여 저도 만나서 반갑습니다.
남 방송국에 온 것은 이번이 처음인가요?
여 네, 맞아요. 뉴스 스튜디오를 직접 보는 것을 기대하고 있었어요.
남 그렇군요. 방송에 매우 관심이 많은 것 같군요.
여 네, 저는 교내 방송 동아리 회장이에요.
남 오, 그래요? 오늘, 당신은 뉴스 데스크 자리에 앉아서 뉴스 프로그램을 진행하는 것이 어떤 것인지 경험할 거예요.
여 멋져요! 저는 매일 당신의 뉴스 프로그램을 시청하고 있어요. 어떻게 그렇게 쉽게 뉴스를 전달할 수 있으세요?
남 방송을 시작하기 전에 뉴스 대본을 반복적으로 읽어요.
여 인상적이네요. 저는 정말로 언젠가 당신처럼 뉴스 프로그램을 진행하고 싶어요.
남 그렇게 되기를 바라요. 이제 뉴스 스튜디오로 갈까요?

Solution

여자가 뉴스 스튜디오를 직접 보는 것을 기대하고 있고, 뉴스 데스크에 앉아 뉴스 진행을 경험해 보기로 하였으며, 남자에게 남자가 진행하는 뉴스를 시청한다고 하면서 뉴스를 쉽게 전달하는 방법에 대해 묻자, 남자는 뉴스 시작 전 반복적으로 대본을 읽는다고 답변한 것으로 보아 두 사람의 관계를 가장 잘 나타낸 것은 ⑤이다.

Words

broadcasting station 방송국 effortlessly 쉽게, 힘들이지 않고 impressive 인상적인 host 진행하다, 주최하다

02 정답 ⑤

Script

M You don't look so good. Is there anything wrong?
W I have a headache. Is there any place I can get some medicine?
M Yes. Do you know where the theater is?
W It's upstairs, isn't it?
M Right. There's a health center next to the theater, and you can get medicine there.
W I got it. When are we supposed to arrive at Mykonos Island Port?
M 7:20. We still have one hour to go.
W Well, I'd like to have dinner before getting off the ship. Is the restaurant still open?
M Yes. You can use the restaurant as long as you're on the ship.
W Great. You're very kind.
M My pleasure. It's my job to make passengers comfortable.

남 안 좋아 보이세요. 무슨 문제가 있나요?
여 머리가 아프네요. 약을 얻을 수 있는 곳이 있나요?
남 네. 극장이 어디에 있는지 알고 있나요?
여 위층에 있죠, 그렇지 않나요?
남 맞아요. 극장 옆에 보건 센터가 있어요. 그리고 거기서 약을 구할 수 있습니다.
여 알겠습니다. Mykonos 섬 항구에는 언제 도착할 예정인가요?
남 7시 20분이요. 아직 한 시간을 더 가야 합니다.
여 음, 배에서 내리기 전에 저녁을 먹고 싶은데요. 식당이 아직 문을 열었나요?

남 네. 배를 타고 있는 동안에는 식당을 이용하실 수 있습니다.
여 좋아요. 아주 친절하시네요.
남 천만에요. 승객들을 편안하게 모시는 것이 제 일인 걸요.

Solution

여자는 남자에게 약을 구할 수 있는 곳, 항구 도착 시간과 식당 영업 여부 등을 물어보았고, 남자는 모두 친절하게 답변하며 승객을 편하게 해주는 것이 자신의 일이라고 했으므로 두 사람의 관계를 가장 잘 나타낸 것은 ⑤이다.

Words

be supposed to ~하기로 되어 있다 get off 내리다
as long as ~하는 한

03 정답 ①

Script

W Excuse me. I lost my key card at the restaurant.
M I'm sorry to hear that. I'll have it reissued.
W Is there a cost to reissue it?
M Yes, you need to pay $5 for it. Can you tell me your name and room number, please?
W Janice Hollins, and I'm staying in room 903.
M Thank you. *[Pause]* Here's your new key card.
W Thank you.
M Don't mention it. Is there anything else I can help you with?
W I saw some surfboards next to the lobby. Can I borrow one of them?
M Sure! They're for our guests.
W Great. When I go to the beach tomorrow, I'll borrow one.
M Okay. Please enjoy your stay with us.

여 실례합니다. 제가 식당에서 키 카드를 잃어버렸어요.
남 유감입니다. 제가 재발급해 드리겠습니다.
여 키 카드를 재발급하는 데 비용이 드나요?
남 네, 5달러를 지불하셔야 합니다. 이름과 객실 번호를 말씀해 주시겠어요?
여 Janice Hollins이고, 903호에 머물고 있습니다.
남 고맙습니다. [잠시 후] 새로운 키 카드가 여기 있습니다.
여 고마워요.
남 천만에요. 제가 도와드릴 수 있는 다른 일이 있나요?
여 로비 옆에 서핑 보드 몇 개를 봤어요. 그것들 중 한 개를 빌릴 수 있나요?
남 물론이죠! 서핑 보드는 투숙객들을 위한 것이니까요.
여 아주 좋아요. 내일 해변에 갈 때, 한 개를 빌릴게요.
남 알겠습니다. 즐거운 시간 되십시오.

Solution

여자는 키 카드를 잃어버려 재발급을 받으면서 서핑 보드를 빌릴 수 있냐고 물었고, 남자는 투숙객을 위해 비치된 것이므로 빌릴 수 있다고 한 것으로 보아 두 사람의 관계를 가장 잘 나타낸 것은 ①이다.

Words

key card 키 카드 reissue 재발급하다 surfboard 서핑 보드

04 정답 ③

Script

M I see you're walking on the treadmill, Maria. How do you feel today?

W I feel much better, sir.
M That's good to hear, but it looks like you're limping a little bit.
W I think I'm okay.
M Listen, Maria. The doctor says you have to stay on the bench for at least one week.
W Oh, no. You know how important today's game is.
M I know, but you haven't recovered from the accident yet.
W It was only a small accident, sir. My bike just brushed up against the wall.
M Well, your left leg is still black and blue.
W It's just a bruise. It won't affect my performance in the game.
M Sorry. I can't let you play. Emily will take your place this time.

남 러닝머신 위에서 걷고 있는 게 보이는구나, Maria. 오늘은 기분이 어떠니?
여 훨씬 나아졌어요, 선생님.
남 그렇다니 다행이구나, 하지만 약간 다리를 절고 있는 것 같은데.
여 저는 괜찮은 것 같아요.
남 잘 들어라, Maria. 의사가 말하기를 너는 최소한 일주일은 벤치에 있어야 한다고 하더구나.
여 아, 안 돼요. 오늘 경기가 얼마나 중요한지 아시잖아요.
남 알고 있지만, 너는 그 사고로부터 아직 회복되지 않았단다.
여 그건 단지 작은 사고였어요, 선생님. 제 자전거가 벽에 살짝 스쳤을 뿐이라고요.
남 음, 네 왼쪽 다리가 아직도 시퍼렇게 멍이 들었잖니.
여 그건 단지 타박상일 뿐이에요. 그건 제가 경기하는 것에 영향을 주지는 않을 거예요.
남 미안하다. 나는 네가 (경기를) 뛰게 할 수 없구나. 이번에는 Emily가 너를 대신할 거다.

Solution

남자는 다리를 절고 있는 여자에게 벤치에서 쉬어야 한다고 하였고, 여자는 단지 타박상이라며 중요한 경기에 출전하고 싶어 하지만, 남자는 여자가 경기에 뛰는 것을 만류한 것으로 보아 두 사람의 관계를 가장 잘 나타낸 것은 ③이다.

Words

limp 다리를 절다 brush up against ~에 살짝 스치다
black and blue 시퍼렇게 멍이 든 bruise 타박상

05 정답 ⑤

Script

M Excuse me. Can I ask you a question?
W Oh, sure, sir.
M My son and I've been waiting for almost an hour, but there's still a long line of people ahead of us. How much longer do we have to wait?
W Well, it will be another thirty minutes from here.
M Oh, no. It's not easy to ride the roller coasters here.
W Sorry for the inconvenience, but we get a lot of visitors on weekends.
M I see.
W By the way, is this your son?
M Yeah.

W There is a height restriction on this ride, and I'm afraid he is not tall enough.

M Oh, my... I didn't know that. Can I get a refund on these tickets?

W Sure. Go to the ticket office over there, please.

남 실례합니다. 질문 하나 해도 될까요?

여 아, 물론이죠, 손님.

남 제 아들과 제가 거의 한 시간 동안 계속 기다렸는데, 아직도 우리 앞에 사람들 줄이 길어요. 얼마나 더 오래 기다려야 하나요?

여 음, 여기서부터 30분은 더 기다리셔야 합니다.

남 아, 이런. 여기서 롤러코스터 타기가 쉽지 않네요.

여 불편을 끼쳐드려서 죄송합니다만, 주말에는 방문객이 많습니다.

남 알겠습니다.

여 그런데, 이 아이가 아드님입니까?

남 네.

여 이 놀이기구는 신장 제한이 있는데요, 아드님이 충분히 크지 않은 것 같습니다.

남 아, 이런… 그걸 몰랐네요. 이 표들을 환불받을 수 있을까요?

여 물론이죠. 저쪽에 있는 매표소로 가 주세요.

남자는 롤러코스터를 타기 위해 얼마나 더 기다려야 하는지 물었고, 여자는 30분 더 기다려야 한다고 하면서, 이 놀이기구는 신장 제한이 있는데 남자의 아들의 키가 충분하지 않은 것 같다고 한 것으로 보아 두 사람의 관계를 가장 잘 나타낸 것은 ⑤이다.

ride 타다; 놀이기구 inconvenience 불편 restriction 제한
get a refund 환불받다

06 정답 ②

W How do you feel nowadays, Mr. Miller?

M I don't feel any better. How are the test results?

W You have to take better care of your body. You're not as strong as you used to be.

M What should I do then?

W You need a balanced diet and regular exercise.

M What do you mean by a balanced diet?

W You are lacking vitamin C. You have to eat more fresh fruits and vegetables.

M I see. And what kind of exercise is good for me?

W I recommend swimming. You have to exercise at least three times a week.

M There are many things I need to do to stay healthy.

W And it's important to take the medicine I prescribe for you.

M All right.

여 요즘은 기분이 어떠세요, Miller 씨?

남 기분은 나아진 것 같지 않습니다. 검사 결과는 어떤가요?

여 몸을 더 잘 돌보셔야겠습니다. 예전만큼 튼튼하지 않으세요.

남 그러면 제가 무엇을 해야 하나요?

여 균형 잡힌 식단과 규칙적인 운동이 필요합니다.

남 균형 잡힌 식단이라는 건 무슨 말씀이시죠?

여 비타민 C가 부족합니다. 신선한 과일과 채소를 더 드셔야 합니다.

남 알겠습니다. 그리고 어떤 종류의 운동이 제게 좋은가요?

여 수영을 추천합니다. 일주일에 적어도 세 번은 운동하셔야 합니다.

남 건강을 유지하기 위해 제가 해야 할 일이 많군요.

여 그리고 제가 처방해 드리는 약을 드시는 것이 중요합니다.

남 알겠습니다.

여자가 남자의 검사 결과에 대해 말하면서, 균형 잡힌 식단과 규칙적인 운동을 강조하고 있고, 남자에게 처방해 주는 약을 거르지 말라고 한 것으로 보아 두 사람의 관계를 가장 잘 나타낸 것은 ②이다.

result 결과 balanced 균형 잡힌 diet 식단 lack ~이 부족하다
prescribe 처방하다

수능Q   정답 ④

여 무엇을 보고 있어요, 여보?

남 Mary 아주머니가 내게 사진을 보내셨어요. 그분은 벌써 Peter를 위한 방을 꾸미셨어요.

여 와! 그분은 그가 겨울 방학 동안 머물게 되어서 들떠 계시네요. 그렇지 않나요?

남 네, 맞아요. 나는 침대 위에 체크무늬가 있는 담요가 마음에 들어요.

여 분명히 매우 따뜻할 거예요. 창문 아래 의자를 보세요.

남 안락해 보여요. 그는 그곳에 앉아서 독서를 할 수 있겠네요.

여 맞아요. 그래서 Mary 아주머니가 책장을 옆에 두셨나 봐요.

남 말이 되네요. 오, 구석에 장난감 말이 있어요.

여 그것이 진짜 같아요. Peter에게 줄 선물인 것 같네요.

남 네, 그녀가 그것에 대해 말씀하셨던 것이 기억나요. 그리고 벽에 둥근 거울이 보이죠?

여 좋아요. Peter가 여기 집에서 쓰는 것과 비슷하게 보여요.

남 그러네요. 그에게 이 사진을 보여주자고요.

Solution

구석에 장난감 말이 있다고 했지만 그림에서는 곰인형이 있으므로 대화의 내용과 일치하지 않는 것은 ④이다.

Words

checkered pattern 체크무늬   bookcase 책장   mention 언급하다

유형 모의고사   본문 23쪽

01 ④   02 ④   03 ⑤   04 ⑤   05 ⑤   06 ⑤

01 정답 ④

Script

W James, have you been to our new club room?

M Unfortunately, I haven't.

W I have a picture of it. Do you want to take a look?

M Sure. *[Pause]* Wow, I see lockers on the left side of the picture.

W Yes. We finally have our own lockers. Do you see the trophies on the lockers?

M Yeah. There are two trophies. Are they the ones we won in the National School Band Contest?

W Right. We won two years in a row. I'm so proud of our band.

M Me, too. And the drums are under the clock.

W Yes. And on the right side of the picture is a round table with chairs.

M Looks great. I also love the star-shaped rug in front of the drums.

W I like it, too. We're really going to enjoy our new club room.

여 James, 우리 새 동아리실에 가 본 적 있니?

남 유감스럽게도, 가 본 적이 없어.

여 그곳의 사진이 있어. 한번 볼래?

남 그럴게. *[잠시 후]* 와, 사진 왼쪽에 사물함이 보이네.

여 응. 드디어 사물함이 생겼어. 사물함 위에 있는 트로피 보여?

남 응. 두 개의 트로피가 있네. 그것들은 우리가 전국 학교 밴드 경연대회에서 탄 것들인가?

여 맞아. 우리는 2년 연속으로 우승을 했어. 나는 우리 밴드가 정말 자랑스러워.

남 나도 그래. 그리고 드럼은 시계 아래에 있구나.

여 응. 그리고 사진 오른쪽에는 의자가 있는 둥근 탁자가 있어.

남 멋져 보인다. 나는 드럼 앞에 놓인 별 모양의 깔개도 맘에 들어.

여 나도 좋아. 우리는 새 동아리실을 정말 즐길 거야.

Solution

오른쪽에 둥근 탁자가 있다고 했지만 그림에서는 직사각형의 탁자가 있으므로 대화의 내용과 일치하지 않는 것은 ④이다.

Words

in a row 연속으로, 계속해서   star-shaped 별 모양의   rug 깔개

02 정답 ④

Script

W Dan, how is your school play going?

M Mom, look at this picture. These are the main characters of our play.

W Okay. There is a big tree to the left.

M Do you see the boy's face in the tree? He took the role of a talking tree.

W I see. What does the bird sitting in the tree mean?

M The bird is a messenger between the prince and the princess.

W Oh, the princess on the left is holding a bunch of flowers.

M She's about to give it to the prince kneeling down before her.

W She must be blessing him.

M Right. He'll fight against the dragon on the right.

W The dragon is breathing fire from its mouth. I think the play will be exciting to see.

M Yes, it will be.

여 Dan, 학교 연극은 어떻게 되어가고 있니?

남 엄마, 이 사진 좀 보세요. 이들이 우리 연극의 주인공들이에요.

여 그래. 왼쪽에 큰 나무가 있구나.

남 나무에 있는 소년의 얼굴이 보이세요? 그 애가 말하는 나무의 역할을 맡았어요.

여 그렇구나. 나무에 앉아 있는 새는 무엇을 의미하는 거니?

남 그 새는 왕자와 공주 사이의 전령이에요.

여 오, 왼쪽에 있는 공주는 꽃다발을 들고 있구나.

남 그녀는 자기 앞에 무릎을 꿇고 있는 왕자에게 그것을 주려고 해요.

여 그녀는 그에게 축복을 빌고 있음이 틀림없어.

남 맞아요. 그는 오른쪽에 있는 용과 싸울 것이거든요.

여 용이 입에서 불을 뿜고 있네. 그 연극은 보기에 흥미진진할 것 같구나.

남 네, 그럴 거예요.

Solution

무대 중앙에 있는 왕자가 무릎을 꿇고 있다고 했지만 그림에서는 서 있으므로 대화의 내용과 일치하지 않는 것은 ④이다.

03 정답 ⑤

Script

M How are your table tennis lessons going, Sandy?

W I'm doing my best. Here's a picture my friend took for me.

M Oh, the banner on the wall is very impressive. It says 'We Can Make It!'

W That's what the coach always says. There is a group photo of us under the banner. They are students who take lessons.

M All of them are smiling. Your coach is wearing a cap.

W Yeah. He loves wearing it. Do you see the basket full of balls on the table?

M Wow, do you hit all the balls at the lesson?

W Of course. I practice with two baskets of balls.

M Wow, that's great. You had your hair tied back. Do you usually tie it for the lesson?

W Yes. I don't want my hair to cover my eyes.

M I see. Let's play table tennis together soon.

W That's a good idea, Dad.

남 Sandy, 탁구 수업은 잘 되어가니?

여 최선을 다하고 있어요. 여기 제 친구가 저를 위해 찍은 사진이에요.

남 오, 벽에 걸린 현수막이 매우 인상적이야. '우리는 해낼 수 있어!'라고 적혀 있구나.

여 그것은 코치님이 항상 하는 말이에요. 현수막 밑에 있는 단체 사진이 있어요. 그 애들은 수업을 듣는 학생들이에요.

남 모두가 웃고 있구나. 네 코치는 모자를 쓰고 있네.

여 네. 그는 그것을 쓰는 것을 좋아해요. 탁구대 위에 공이 가득한 바구니가 보이죠?

남 와, 수업 때에 모든 공을 다 치니?

여 물론이죠. 공 두 바구니를 가지고 연습해요.

남 와, 대단해. 너는 머리를 뒤로 묶었구나. 수업을 위해 머리를 묶니?

여 네. 제 머리가 눈을 가리는 것을 원하지 않으니까요.

남 그렇구나. 조만간 함께 탁구를 치자.

여 그거 좋은 생각이에요, 아빠.

Solution

여자가 머리를 뒤로 묶었다고 했지만 그림에서는 여자가 단발머리를 하고 있으므로 대화의 내용과 일치하지 않는 것은 ⑤이다.

Words

banner 현수막 make it 해내다, 성공하다 tie 묶다

04 정답 ⑤

Script

M Julie, I took a very impressive picture yesterday.

W Did you? Let me take a look at it.

M Okay. Here it is.

W Is the young girl walking a dog your daughter?

M Yes. Her name's Sally, she's ten years old.

W She looks tall for her age. The stream she is walking along is beautiful.

M It really is. That's why I like to take walks there.

W The arch-shaped bridge makes a romantic atmosphere.

M I agree. I often watch fish swimming in the stream just like that young couple is doing.

W Wait a minute! What's the small thing over the stream?

M That's a fish. Fish jump out of the water from time to time, and luckily, I captured one jumping.

W Wow, that's amazing! I thought it was a flying bird.

남 Julie, 어제 제가 아주 인상적인 사진을 찍었어요.

여 그랬어요? 제가 한번 볼게요.

남 알겠어요. 여기 있어요.

여 개를 산책시키는 여자아이가 당신의 딸인가요?

남 네. 이름은 Sally이고, 열 살이에요.

여 나이에 비해 키가 커 보이는군요. 그 애가 따라 걷고 있는 냇가가 아름답네요.

남 정말 그래요. 그것이 제가 거기서 산책하는 것을 좋아하는 이유예요.

여 아치 모양의 다리가 낭만적인 분위기를 만들어 주네요.

남 동의해요. 저는 저 젊은 커플이 하는 것처럼 냇가에서 물고기가 헤엄치는 것을 종종 봐요.

여 잠깐만요! 냇가 위에 있는 저 조그만 것은 뭐죠?

남 물고기예요. 물고기들이 물 밖으로 종종 뛰어오르는데 운이 좋게도 제가 한 마리가 뛰어오르는 것을 포착했어요.

여 와, 놀라워요! 저는 날아가는 새로 생각했어요.

Solution

물고기가 뛰어오르는 장면을 포착했다고 했지만 그림에서는 날아가는 새가 있으므로 대화의 내용과 일치하지 않는 것은 ⑤이다.

Words

arch-shaped 아치 모양의 atmosphere 분위기

05 정답 ⑤

Script

M What are you looking at, Laura?

W My son's drawing. I think he has a talent for art.

M Let me see. It looks like he drew it from the veranda. He included a lot in his picture, including a bike rack.

W Yes. He likes drawing details.

M All the cars are parked in the same direction.

W That's to protect plants and flowers from air pollution.

M I see. There are also some big trees.

W They provide shade in the summer. Do you see the open space between the two apartments? That's where a cool breeze blows in.

M In the open space, a man and a woman are holding hands on a wooden bench.

W Yes. Sometimes I sit there and read books in my free time.

남 무엇을 보고 있어요, Laura?

여 제 아들의 그림이요. 그 애가 미술에 소질이 있는 것 같아요.

남 어디 봅시다. 베란다에서 그린 것 같군요. 자전거 고정대를 포함해서 그림에 많은 것을 담았네요.

여 네. 그 애는 세세한 것을 그리는 걸 좋아해요.
남 모든 차들이 같은 방향으로 주차되어 있네요.
여 그것은 식물과 꽃들을 공기 오염으로부터 보호하기 위해서예요.
남 그렇군요. 큰 나무들도 있네요.
여 그 나무들이 여름철에 그늘을 만들어 줘요. 두 아파트 사이에 트인 공간이 보이죠? 그곳이 시원한 바람이 불어오는 곳이에요.
남 그 트인 공간에 남자와 여자가 손을 잡고 나무 벤치에 앉아 있네요.
여 네. 저는 여가 시간에 가끔씩 거기에 앉아서 책을 읽어요.

Solution

남자와 여자가 손을 잡고 나무 벤치에 앉아 있다고 했지만 그림에서는 남자 혼자 앉아 있으므로 대화의 내용과 일치하지 않는 것은 ⑤이다.

Words

have a talent for ~에 재능이 있다 bike rack 자전거 고정대

06 정답 ⑤

Script

W Mr. Lee! Is that you?
M Yes. I took this picture over the weekend.
W You look like a good horse rider.
M I just posed for photographs.
W This picture reminds me of my childhood. I used to ride a horse. By the way, who is the man wearing sunglasses next to the horse?
M He is my cousin. He runs a business for tourists who want to experience the thrill of riding a horse.
W I see. Who is the little girl wearing a helmet and a vest?
M She is my daughter Jane.
W She looks comfortable on a horse. The grassy hill in the distance looks wonderful.
M It is. Do you see the girl with a ponytail? She is my niece. She made me a video of my daughter riding a horse on the hill.
W Really? I'd like to see the video, too.

여 Lee 씨! 이게 당신이에요?
남 네. 주말에 이 사진을 찍었어요.
여 말을 잘 타는 기수처럼 보여요.
남 그냥 사진을 찍으려고 포즈를 취한 거였어요.
여 이 사진을 보니 제 어린 시절이 떠오르네요. 저도 승마를 했었어요. 그건 그렇고, 말 옆에 선글라스를 쓰고 있는 남자는 누구예요?
남 제 사촌이에요. 그는 말을 타는 짜릿함을 경험하길 원하는 관광객들을 위한 사업을 하고 있어요.
여 그렇군요. 헬멧을 쓰고 조끼를 입고 있는 저 어린 여자아이는 누구예요?
남 제 딸 Jane이에요.
여 말 위에 있는 것이 편안해 보이네요. 먼발치에 있는 풀로 덮인 낮은 산이 멋져 보여요.
남 그것은 그래요. 머리를 하나로 묶은 여자아이 보이시죠? 제 조카예요. 그 아이는 제 딸이 언덕에서 말을 타고 있는 것을 비디오로 찍어 주었어요.
여 정말이요? 그 비디오도 보고 싶은데요.

Solution

여자아이가 머리를 하나로 묶고 있다고 했지만 그림에서는 머리를 풀고 있고 곱슬머리이므로 대화의 내용과 일치하지 않는 것은 ⑤이다.

Words

remind 생각나게 하다 in the distance 저 멀리, 먼 곳에

05강 할 일/부탁한 일 고르기 본문 26쪽

수능Q 정답 ④

남 좋은 아침이에요, Jane.
여 좋은 아침이에요, Smith 씨.
남 우리 노인 센터에서 다시 자원봉사를 하기로 해줘서 감사합니다.
여 도움을 드려서 제가 기뻐요. 그리고 어르신들을 위해 간식을 조금 가져왔어요.
남 정말 사려 깊으시군요! 지난번에 당신이 몇 권의 책을 기부했죠. 모든 이가 정말 그것들을 즐겁게 읽었어요.
여 그건 제가 기뻐서 한 일이에요. 그러면 저는 오늘 무슨 일을 해야 하나요? 전에 했던 것처럼 점심을 준비해야 하나요?
남 오늘은 다른 봉사자들이 계셔서, 그분들이 그 일을 할 거예요.
여 잘되었군요. 그럼 제가 무엇을 했으면 하시나요?
남 음, 설거지를 하거나 세탁실 청소를 하셨으면 합니다.
여 제가 설거지를 잘해요. 그러니 그것을 할게요.
남 좋아요. 다른 사람에게 세탁실 청소를 시킬게요.

Solution

노인 센터에 봉사활동을 하러 온 여자는 자신이 무엇을 해야 하는지 물었고, 남자가 설거지나 세탁실 청소를 하면 좋겠다고 하자, 여자는 설거지를 하겠다고 말했으므로 정답은 ④이다.

Words

the elderly 어르신들 considerate 사려 깊은 donate 기부하다
laundry room 세탁실

유형 모의고사 본문 27쪽

01 ②   02 ④   03 ②   04 ⑤   05 ③   06 ⑤

01 정답 ②

Script

W Alex, let's go for lunch.
M Sorry, but I don't have time, Kate.
W What's keeping you so busy?
M I'm working on our company's monthly newspaper.
W When's the deadline?
M Today. I'm doing the final job of matching the articles with the photos, but there's a problem.
W What is it?
M I don't have any photos of Mr. Williams' retirement ceremony.
W Really? I've got some photos I took at the ceremony with my digital camera.
M Oh, what a relief! Can you send me the photo files?
W Sure. I'll email them right after lunch.
M Thank you so much, Kate.

여 Alex, 점심 먹으러 가죠.
남 미안하지만, 난 시간이 없어요, Kate.
여 무엇이 당신을 그렇게 바쁘게 하나요?

남 나는 우리 회사의 월간 신문 작업을 하고 있어요.
여 마감일이 언제죠?
남 오늘이에요. 기사와 사진을 연결시키는 최종 작업을 하고 있는데 문제가 생겼어요.
여 그게 뭐죠?
남 Williams 씨의 내가 그 행사에서 사진이 전혀 없어요.
여 정말요? 내가 그 행사에서 내 디지털 카메라로 찍은 사진 몇 장을 가지고 있어요.
남 아, 다행이에요! 사진 파일 좀 보내줄래요?
여 물론이죠. 점심 후에 바로 이메일로 보낼게요.
남 정말 고마워요, Kate.

Solution

남자는 Williams 씨의 은퇴식 사진이 없는 문제를 여자에게 말하는데, 여자는 자신에게 디지털 카메라로 찍은 사진이 몇 장 있다고 하였고 남자는 여자에게 사진 파일을 보내 달라고 부탁하였으므로 정답은 ②이다.

Words

monthly 월간의 deadline 마감일, 마감 시간 match 연결시키다
retirement 은퇴, 퇴임 relief 안도, 안심

02 정답 ④

Script

M Honey, when are your friends visiting us today?
W They're supposed to be here by five.
M Okay. We need to begin cleaning the house now then.
W Yes. I already cleaned the bathroom this morning.
M Then I'll vacuum the living room and organize the living room table.
W While you're at it, I'll wash the vegetables for the salad.
M I'm looking forward to your Italian salad. It's so delicious.
W I got vegetables from the grocery early this morning, so everything is fresh.
M Good. Is there anything else I can do?
W Oh, would you take out some dishes from the cupboard?
M No problem. I'll do that right away.
W Thank you.

남 여보, 당신 친구들이 오늘 언제 우리를 방문하나요?
여 5시까지 여기에 오기로 되어 있어요.
남 알았어요. 그러면 지금 집을 청소하기 시작할 필요가 있네요.
여 네. 오늘 아침에 벌써 화장실을 청소했어요.
남 그럼 난 거실을 진공청소기로 청소하고 거실 탁자를 정리할게요.
여 당신이 그 일을 하는 동안, 난 샐러드에 들어갈 채소를 씻을게요.
남 난 당신이 만든 이탈리안 샐러드가 기대돼요. 아주 맛있어요.
여 오늘 아침 일찍 식료품점에서 채소를 사 와서 모든 것이 신선해요.
남 좋아요. 내가 할 수 있는 다른 어떤 일이 있을까요?
여 아, 찬장에서 접시 좀 꺼내줄래요?
남 그럴게요. 지금 바로 할게요.
여 고마워요.

Solution

남자는 거실을 진공청소기로 청소하고 거실 탁자를 정리하고 다른 어떤 일을 하면 좋을지 물었고, 여자는 찬장에서 접시를 꺼내 달라고 부탁하였으므로 정답은 ④이다.

Words

vacuum 진공청소기로 청소하다 organize 정리하다 cupboard 찬장

03 정답 ②

Script

M Mom, do you have a minute?
W Of course I do. What do you want to talk about?
M I think I need a bigger allowance.
W You don't think we give you enough?
M Well, the amount was okay last year, but I'm in high school now. I'm involved in a lot of activities, which all cost me extra.
W Is that all?
M I also think I deserve a bigger allowance, since I do more work around the house these days.
W Do you? Like what?
M I shine Dad's shoes once a week, help Steve with his homework, and sometimes I help you with the dishes.
W Sounds like your request is quite reasonable. Let me discuss it with your father when he comes home.

남 엄마, 잠시 시간 있으세요?
여 당연히 있지. 무슨 말을 하고 싶은 거니?
남 저 용돈이 더 많이 필요한 것 같아요.
여 너에게 충분히 주고 있지 않다고 생각하니?
남 음, 작년까지는 그 액수가 괜찮았지만, 지금은 고등학생이에요. 많은 활동에 참여하고 있는데, 모두 돈이 추가로 들어요.
여 그게 다니?
남 또한 요즈음 집안일을 더 많이 거들고 있기 때문에 용돈을 더 받을 자격이 있다고 생각해요.
여 그래? 예를 들어보자면?
남 아빠 구두를 일주일에 한 번씩 닦아 드리고, Steve 숙제를 도와주며, 가끔씩 엄마 설거지도 도와드리고 있어요.
여 듣고 보니 네 요구가 꽤 타당하구나. 아빠가 집에 오시면 논의해 보도록 하마.

Solution

남자는 고등학생이 되면서 활동이 늘었고, 집안일도 더 많이 거들고 있다고 말하면서 여자에게 용돈을 올려줄 것을 부탁하고 있으므로 정답은 ②이다.

Words

allowance 용돈 deserve ~할 자격이 있다 reasonable 타당한

04 정답 ⑤

Script

W Chris, when did you say your guitar club will perform?
M We will perform for two days, on October 22nd and 23rd. I hope you come and see us, Mom.
W Don't worry. I'll go on the first day because I have an important meeting on October 23rd.
M Thank you, Mom.
W You reserved the community center for the performance, right?
M Yes. And I also informed them of the schedule on the performance day.
W Great. Did you pick up your guitar from the repair shop?
M I will go and get it now. I want my guitar back as soon as possible.

W While you do that, I'll make some stew for dinner.
M Thank you, Mom. I'm hungry.
W Be careful and see you in a bit.

- -

여 Chris. 네 기타 동아리가 언제 공연할 거라고 했지?
남 10월 22일과 23일 이틀 동안 공연할 거예요. 우리를 보러 오셨으면 좋겠어요. 엄마.
여 걱정하지 마. 10월 23일에 중요한 회의가 있어서 첫날에 갈게.
남 감사해요. 엄마.
여 공연을 위한 문화 센터를 예약했지, 그렇지?
남 네. 그리고 공연 당일 일정도 그쪽에 알렸어요.
여 잘했구나. 수리점에서 네 기타를 찾아왔니?
남 지금 가서 가져올 거예요. 제 기타를 가능한 한 빨리 돌려받고 싶어요.
여 네가 그렇게 하는 동안 난 저녁으로 스튜를 좀 만들게.
남 고마워요. 엄마. 배고프네요.
여 조심하고 조금 이따 보자.

Solution

여자는 수리점에서 기타를 찾아왔는지 물었고 남자는 지금 가서 그것을 찾아오겠다고 말하였으므로 정답은 ⑤이다.

Words

perform 공연하다 inform 알리다

05 정답 ③

Script

M It's finally June.
W Time flies, doesn't it?
M Yes. It seems like only yesterday we congratulated Robin on graduating from high school.
W That's true. By the way, what should we buy him as a graduation present?
M What about a suit?
W You know Robin doesn't like to wear a suit.
M Then why don't we ask him what he wants?
W Presents should be a surprise.
M Well, considering he studied to become an artist, what about booking a trip to Italy?
W That's a great idea. He always said that he wanted to visit Italy someday.
M Then a trip to Italy would be a meaningful experience for him.
W All right. I'll call a travel agency and find a suitable package for a future artist like Robin.
M Good idea. Go ahead and do that. I'll check some information on the Internet.

- -

남 마침내 6월이네요.
여 시간 참 빠르죠, 그렇지 않나요?
남 그래요. Robin의 고등학교 졸업을 축하할 때가 불과 어제 같은데 말이에요.
여 맞아요. 그건 그렇고, 졸업 선물로 그 애에게 무엇을 사주어야 할까요?
남 양복은 어때요?
여 당신도 알다시피 Robin은 양복 입는 것을 좋아하지 않아요.
남 그러면 그 애에게 원하는 것을 물어보는 건 어때요?
여 선물은 깜짝 놀라게 해 주는 것이어야죠.

남 음, 그 애가 예술가가 되기 위해 공부했다는 것을 감안해서 이탈리아로 가는 여행을 예약해 주는 게 어때요?
여 그거 좋은 생각이에요. 그 애는 언젠가 이탈리아를 방문하고 싶다고 항상 말했어요.
남 그러면 이탈리아 여행이 그 애에게는 의미 있는 경험이 될 거예요.
여 알겠어요. 여행사에 전화해서 Robin과 같은 미래의 예술가를 위한 적합한 여행 상품이 있는지 찾아볼게요.
남 좋은 생각이에요. 그렇게 해요. 인터넷에서 정보를 좀 찾아볼게요.

Solution

여자는 Robin의 졸업 선물을 고민하고 있고, 남자가 미래 예술가를 꿈꾸는 Robin에게 이탈리아 여행을 예약해 주자고 하자, 여자는 좋은 아이디어라며 여행사에 전화해 보겠다고 하였고 남자는 인터넷에서 정보를 찾아보겠다고 하였으므로 정답은 ③이다.

Words

congratulate 축하하다 suit 양복 suitable 적합한

06 정답 ⑤

Script

M Hi, Kelly. What are you up to?
W Hi, Josh. I can't understand this sentence.
M Let me see. Oh, it's written in Korean, isn't it?
W Yes. I think I know the meaning of every word, but it doesn't help me understand what the sentence actually means.
M Why don't you ask Mr. Kim, the Korean teacher?
W There are so many students in his class. It's not easy to ask questions during the lessons.
M Then you can go to his office after school.
W Well, I've never talked to him face-to-face, so I can't help feeling nervous if I see him in his office.
M If that's the problem, I'll go with you. What do you say?
W Thanks. Then let's go to see him after school today.
M Okay. No problem.

- -

남 안녕, Kelly. 뭐 하고 있니?
여 안녕, Josh. 이 문장이 이해가 안 돼.
남 어디 좀 볼까. 오, 한국어로 쓰여 있는 거네. 아니니?
여 맞아. 모든 단어의 뜻을 알고 있는데, 그게 그 문장이 실제로 무엇을 의미하는지 이해하는 데 도움이 안 돼.
남 한국어 선생님이신 김 선생님께 여쭤보지 그러니?
여 그분 수업에 학생들이 많아. 수업 시간에 질문을 하는 것이 쉽지 않아.
남 그럼 방과 후에 그분의 연구실로 가면 되잖아.
여 음, 그분과 대면하여 이야기를 나눠본 적이 없어서 연구실에서 그분을 뵙게 되면 나는 긴장될 수밖에 없어.
남 그게 문제라면 내가 함께 가 줄게. 어때?
여 고마워. 그러면 오늘 방과 후에 선생님을 뵈러 가자.
남 그래. 문제될 것 없어.

Solution

여자는 개인적으로 이야기를 나눠본 적이 없는 한국어 선생님을 연구실에서 뵙는 것이 긴장된다고 하였고, 남자는 함께 가 주겠다고 하였으므로 정답은 ⑤이다.

Words

face-to-face 대면하여 can't help -ing ~할 수밖에 없다

06강 지불할 금액 파악

본문 30쪽

수능 Q

정답 ②

남 과학기술 박물관에 오신 것을 환영합니다. 어떻게 도와드릴까요?
여 안녕하세요. 입장권을 사고 싶습니다.
남 알겠습니다. 어른은 20달러이고 어린이는 10달러입니다.
여 좋습니다. 어른 입장권 두 장과 어린이 입장권 두 장을 주세요. 그리고 저는 국립 로봇 클럽의 회원입니다. 제가 할인을 받나요?
남 네. 손님의 회원권으로 모든 입장권에 10퍼센트 할인을 받습니다.
여 아주 좋군요.
남 저희 박물관에는 AI 로봇 프로그램도 있습니다. 로봇들과 게임을 하고 사진을 같이 찍을 수 있습니다.
여 그거 재미있겠군요. 얼마인가요?
남 1인당 5달러밖에 안 합니다. 그런데 그 회원 할인은 이 프로그램에 적용되지 않습니다.
여 알겠습니다. 티켓 네 장을 살게요.
남 그럼 어른 입장권 두 장과 어린이 입장권 두 장, 그리고 AI 로봇 프로그램 티켓 네 장이지요, 맞나요?
여 네. 여기 제 신용카드와 회원증입니다.

Solution

여자는 20달러인 어른 입장권 두 장과 10달러인 어린이 입장권 두 장을 구입하면서 국립 로봇 클럽 회원이라서 10퍼센트 할인을 받았고, 1인당 5달러인 AI 로봇 프로그램 티켓 네 장을 할인 적용 없이 구입하기로 했으므로, 여자가 지불할 금액은 ② '74달러'이다.

Words

admission ticket 입장권 apply to ~에 적용되다

유형 모의고사

본문 31쪽

01 ② **02** ② **03** ② **04** ③ **05** ③ **06** ③

01 정답 ②

Script

W Welcome to Good Aroma Candle. How may I help you?
M Hi. I'm looking for scented candles for my parents. They like flower scents.
W Come over here and try this flower scent.
M Thanks. *[Pause]* I like this rose scented candle. How much is it?
W Large candles and medium ones are on sale now. Large ones are $20 and medium ones are $10 each.
M Well then, I'll take two large candles.
W If you buy any three candles, we give you a soap for free.
M Great. Then I'll have a medium one with the same scent as well. Did you say they're $10?
W Exactly. You're getting two large candles and one medium candle.
M That's right. Can I also use this mobile coupon?
W Of course, you get 10 percent off the total price with that.
M Thank you. I'll pay by credit card.

여 Good Aroma Candle에 오신 것을 환영합니다. 어떻게 도와드릴까요?
남 안녕하세요. 부모님께 드릴 향초를 찾고 있어요. 그들은 꽃 향을 좋아하세요.
여 이쪽으로 오셔서 이 꽃 향을 맡아 보세요.
남 감사합니다. *[잠시 후]* 저는 이 장미꽃 향이 좋네요. 이것은 얼마인가요?
여 큰 양초와 중간 크기의 양초는 지금 할인 중입니다. 큰 양초는 개당 20달러이고 중간 크기의 양초는 개당 10달러입니다.
남 음 그럼. 저는 큰 양초 두 개를 살게요.
여 양초를 세 개를 구입하시면, 무료로 비누를 드립니다.
남 좋네요. 그럼 같은 향으로 중간 크기도 하나 할게요. 10달러라고 하셨나요?
여 맞습니다. 그럼 두 개의 큰 양초와 한 개의 중간 크기의 양초네요.
남 맞아요. 제가 이 모바일 쿠폰도 사용할 수 있나요?
여 물론이죠. 그 쿠폰으로 총 가격에서 10퍼센트 할인됩니다.
남 감사합니다. 신용카드로 지불할게요.

Solution

남자는 개당 20달러인 큰 양초 두 개와 10달러인 중간 크기의 양초 한 개를 구입하기로 하였고, 10퍼센트 할인이 되는 쿠폰을 사용한다고 하였으므로 남자가 지불할 금액은 ② '45달러'이다.

Words

candle 양초 scented ~의 냄새가 나는, 향기로운 for free 무료로

02 정답 ②

Script

M What are you doing on the Internet, honey?
W I'm going to buy an air fryer. What about this one? I think it's the best in terms of price and function.
M How much is it?
W It's $90. I'll put it in my shopping cart.
M Okay. Do you need to purchase anything else?
W Yes. I'll buy some pork to cook in the air fryer. A friend said air fryers do a great job cooking pork.
M Really? Let's try it.
W Oh, here are the pork ribs. I will buy 2 kg of ribs.
M They're $40. Not bad. Does this online shopping mall offer any discount?
W Yes. We can get a 10 percent discount for their 10th anniversary.
M That's good. We get the 10 percent discount on the air fryer and the pork ribs, right?
W Yes, it's on the total. I'll place the order with my credit card.

남 여보, 인터넷으로 무엇을 하고 있어요?
여 에어 프라이어를 하나 사려고요. 이건 어때요? 가격과 기능 면에서 그것이 최고라고 생각해요.
남 얼마인가요?
여 90달러예요. 내 쇼핑 카트에 넣을게요.
남 알았어요. 다른 어떤 것을 구매해야 되나요?
여 네. 에어 프라이어에 넣어 요리할 돼지고기를 살 거예요. 친구 말로는 에어 프라이어가 돼지고기 요리를 잘 한대요.
남 정말요? 한번 해 보죠.
여 오, 여기 돼지갈비가 있네요. 갈비 2킬로그램을 살게요.
남 40달러군요. 나쁘지 않은데요. 이 온라인 쇼핑몰에서 할인을 제공해 주

나요?

여 네. 이곳의 10주년 기념일이라서 10퍼센트 할인을 받을 수 있어요.

남 좋군요. 에어 프라이어랑 돼지갈비에 대해 10퍼센트 할인을 받는 거죠, 맞죠?

여 네, 그것은 총액에 대한 거예요. 제 신용카드로 주문을 할게요.

Solution

여자는 90달러인 에어 프라이어와 40달러인 돼지갈비를 사기로 하였고, 쇼핑몰에서 제공하는 10퍼센트 할인을 받으므로 여자가 지불할 금액은 ② '117달러'이다.

Words

in terms of ~의 관점에서 function 기능 purchase 구매하다
pork rib 돼지갈비 anniversary 기념일

03 정답 ②

Script

W Can I help you?

M Yes, please. I'm looking for some tea mugs.

W Okay. Would you look at these mugs? I recommend this 6-piece tea mug set.

M Oh, I like these white mugs.

W It's one of the most popular sets these days. The set of 6 pieces costs $25.

M I'll take one set. And I want to buy a mug holder.

W What about this one in the shape of a tree? It's $6.

M That looks practical. I'll take it. Can I use this three-dollar discount coupon here?

W Yes, you can use it. I'll take that off the total.

M Great. I'll use it. Here's my credit card.

W Thank you. Would you wait a second while I wrap these mugs for you?

M Sure.

- -

여 도와드릴까요?

남 네, 그래 주세요. 저는 티 머그잔을 좀 찾고 있어요.

여 알겠습니다. 이 머그잔들을 보시겠어요? 여기 6개로 구성된 티 머그 세트를 추천드려요.

남 아, 이 하얀 머그잔들이 마음에 들어요.

여 그건 요즘 가장 인기 있는 세트 중 하나예요. 6개로 구성된 세트가 25달러예요.

남 한 세트를 살게요. 그리고 머그 걸이를 사고 싶어요.

여 나무 모양의 이건 어떠세요? 그건 6달러예요.

남 그거 실용적으로 보이네요. 그것을 살게요. 여기서 이 3달러 할인 쿠폰을 사용할 수 있을까요?

여 네, 사용하실 수 있어요. 총액에서 그 금액을 빼드릴게요.

남 좋아요. 그것을 사용할게요. 여기 제 신용카드입니다.

여 감사합니다. 이 머그잔들을 포장하는 동안 잠시 기다려 주시겠어요?

남 그러죠.

Solution

남자는 25달러인 티 머그 세트 한 개와 6달러인 머그 걸이를 한 개 사기로 하였고, 3달러 할인 쿠폰을 사용하기로 하였으므로 남자가 지불할 금액은 ② '28달러'이다.

Words

practical 실용적인 take off (표시된 금액 등에서) ~을 빼다
wrap 포장하다

04 정답 ③

Script

M What are you browsing the Internet for?

W I'm looking at watches.

M Are you planning to buy watches for Jenny and Jack on Children's Day?

W Yes. Do you see any watches you like on this site?

M The pink watch with the small dial would look good on Jenny. How much is it?

W It costs $400, but it's on sale right now. So we can get it for half price.

M Great. Let's order it. What if we buy this silver metal watch for Jack?

W I like the design. It costs $350.

M Look at this banner. It says we can get a coupon code for 20 percent off the total price in celebration of Children's Day.

W Wonderful. I'll order both watches and I'll use the coupon code.

M Okay. They'll be happy with the watches.

- -

남 인터넷에서 무엇을 보고 있어요?

여 시계를 살펴보고 있어요.

남 어린이날에 Jenny와 Jack을 위한 시계를 살 계획인가요?

여 그래요. 이 사이트에서 마음에 드는 시계가 있어요?

남 작은 문자반의 그 분홍색 시계는 Jenny에게 잘 어울릴 것 같아요. 얼마예요?

여 400달러인데, 지금 할인 중이에요. 그래서 절반 가격에 살 수 있어요.

남 아주 좋네요. 그것을 주문합시다. Jack에게는 이 은색 금속 시계를 사주면 어떨까요?

여 디자인이 마음에 들어요. 350달러네요.

남 이 배너 광고 좀 봐요. 어린이날 기념으로 전체 가격의 20퍼센트를 할인해 주는 쿠폰을 사용할 수 있다고 되어 있어요.

여 아주 좋네요. 내가 시계를 두 개 주문하고 그 쿠폰을 사용할게요.

남 그래요. 아이들이 시계를 보면 행복해할 거예요.

Solution

여자는 반값 할인을 하는 400달러인 분홍색 시계와 350달러인 은색 금속 시계를 구매하기로 하였고, 전체 금액에서 20퍼센트를 할인해 주는 쿠폰을 사용하기로 했으므로 여자가 지불할 금액은 ③ '440달러'이다.

Words

dial (시계 등의) 문자반[눈금판]

05 정답 ③

Script

W Good morning, sir. How may I help you?

M Hello. I'm here to get some ingredients to make fruit and vegetable juice.

W Then I'd like to recommend some carrots and apples. They match well with each other.

M Okay. How much are they?

W You can get unwashed carrots for $2 and washed ones for $3. For apples, I'll give you a basket of them for $10.

M I'd like 4 washed carrots and 3 baskets of apples.

W Alright. Is there anything else you need?
M Do you sell bananas, too? They are also healthy snacks.
W Sure. It's $5 for a bunch of bananas.
M Alright. I'll just take one bunch of bananas. Here is the money.

여 좋은 아침입니다. 손님. 어떻게 도와드릴까요?
남 안녕하세요. 과일과 채소 주스를 만들 재료를 좀 사러 왔어요.
여 그러면 당근과 사과를 추천해 드려요. 서로 잘 어울리거든요.
남 좋습니다. 얼마인가요?
여 세척되지 않은 당근은 하나에 2달러이고, 세척된 것은 3달러예요. 사과는 한 바구니에 10달러에 드릴게요.
남 세척된 당근 네 개 주시고, 사과는 세 바구니 주세요.
여 알겠습니다. 다른 더 필요한 거 있으세요?
남 바나나도 판매하시나요? 그것들도 매우 건강에 좋은 간식이거든요.
여 물론이죠. 바나나 한 송이에 5달러예요.
남 좋아요. 바나나는 한 송이만 살게요. 여기 돈입니다.

Solution

남자는 세척된 당근 네 개, 사과 세 바구니, 바나나 한 송이를 구매하고자 하는데, 세척된 당근은 개당 3달러, 사과는 한 바구니에 10달러, 바나나는 한 송이에 5달러이므로 남자가 지불할 금액은 ③ '47달러'이다.

Words

ingredient 재료 match with ~와 어울리다 a bunch of 한 송이[다발/묶음]의

06 정답 ③

Script

M Hello, ma'am. How may I help you?
W I'm here to sign up for yoga classes. How much do they cost?
M They are $100 a month.
W What if I take yoga classes for three months? I heard there is a special discount for a three-month registration.
M That's right. We offer a 10 percent discount.
W Cool. Then I'll sign up for three months.
M What about our towel service? Are you interested in using that?
W How much do I have to pay for it?
M Those who register for three months can use the service for $20. That fee covers all three months.
W That sounds good. I'll use that, too. Here's my credit card.

남 안녕하세요, 손님. 어떻게 도와드릴까요?
여 요가 수업을 등록하러 왔습니다. 얼마인가요?
남 한 달에 100달러입니다.
여 3개월 동안 요가 수업을 수강하면 어떻게 되나요? 3개월 등록하면 특별 할인이 있다고 들었어요.
남 맞아요. 10퍼센트 할인을 제공합니다.
여 좋네요. 그러면 3개월간 등록할게요.
남 수건 대여 서비스는 어떻게 하시겠어요? 그것을 사용하시는데 관심이 있으신가요?
여 그것은 얼마인가요?
남 3개월 등록을 하신 분들은 그 서비스를 20달러에 이용하실 수 있어요. 그 비용은 3개월 전체 비용입니다.

여 좋아요. 그것도 이용할게요. 여기 제 신용카드입니다.

Solution

여자는 한 달 수강료가 100달러인 요가 수업을 3개월간 등록하면서 10퍼센트 할인을 받고, 3개월간 20달러인 수건 대여 서비스도 이용한다고 하였으므로 여자가 지불할 금액은 ③ '290달러'이다.

Words

sign up for ~에 등록하다 registration 등록

수능 Q
정답 ⑤

여 안녕, Michael.
남 안녕, Sarah. 요리 대회에 참가 신청했니?
여 했어. 나는 이미 조리법 개발을 끝냈어.
남 잘됐다. 사실 나는 그것에 참가하는 것을 포기했어.
여 왜? 팔이 아직도 아프니?
남 아니, 완전히 나았어.
여 조리법이 아직 준비가 안 됐니?
남 난 이미 그 대회를 위한 독특한 조리법을 만들었어.
여 그렇다면, 무엇 때문에 그 대회를 포기한 거야?
남 너도 알다시피, 내가 유학 가는 것을 계획했잖아. 이탈리아의 요리 학교에서 내가 합격했다고 막 알려왔어. 문제는 내가 그 대회가 시작되기 전에 떠나야 한다는 거야.
여 네가 그 대회를 놓치게 되어 유감이다. 하지만 네가 이탈리아에서 공부하기를 항상 원했기 때문에 네게 좋은 일이야.
남 나도 그렇게 생각해. 대회에서 행운을 빌게.
여 고마워. 최선을 다할게.

Solution
두 사람이 요리 대회 참가 신청에 대해 대화를 나누고 있다. 남자는 대회 참가를 포기하겠다고 하였고, 여자가 그 이유를 묻자 남자는 이탈리아의 요리 학교에 합격되어 대회 시작 전 떠나야 한다고 답변했으므로 정답은 ⑤이다.

Words
apply for ~에 지원하다 recipe 조리법 give up ~을 포기하다
abroad 외국으로 inform 알리다

유형 모의고사
본문 35쪽

01 ④ 02 ② 03 ② 04 ⑤ 05 ③ 06 ③

01 정답 ④

Script

W Tony, are you ready for your science presentation tomorrow?
M Yes, Ms. Woods, thanks to your help. I've already printed out the presentation material.
W Can I take a look at it? Hmm. I'm afraid you need to make some changes.
M Why? Are there any errors in the date or the names? I've checked them twice.
W No, they're correct.
M Did I use old data?
W No, you used the latest data. But this picture of the planets is not clear.
M Oh, my! I'll change it to a clearer picture.
W Okay. I'm sure you'll do well tomorrow.
M Thank you, Ms. Woods.

- -

여 Tony. 내일 과학 발표는 준비됐니?

남 네, Woods 선생님. 선생님 덕분이에요. 이미 발표 자료를 프린트했어요.
여 내가 그것을 봐도 될까? 음. 좀 바꿔야 할 것 같은데.
남 왜요? 날짜나 이름에 오류가 있나요? 저는 그것들을 두 번이나 확인했어요.
여 아니, 그것들은 정확해.
남 제가 오래된 자료를 사용했나요?
여 아니, 최신 자료를 사용했어. 그런데 행성에 대한 이 사진이 선명하지 않아.
남 오, 이런! 그것을 좀 더 선명한 사진으로 바꿀게요.
여 좋아. 넌 내일 틀림없이 잘 할 거야.
남 고마워요, Woods 선생님.

Solution
여자는 남자의 발표 자료를 본 뒤 행성 사진이 선명하지 않음을 알려주었고, 남자를 그것을 좀 더 선명한 사진으로 바꾸겠다고 말하였으므로 정답은 ④이다.

Words
material 자료 latest 최신의

02 정답 ②

Script

M Lisa. What are you doing here?
W Oh, David. I have a job interview at Duo Technology today. Do you work here in this building?
M Yes. Did you quit your job at the bank?
W Not yet, but I'll quit next month after I finish a project.
M I hope you get the job at Duo. By the way, are you coming to the high school reunion the day before Thanksgiving Day?
W I'm afraid I can't.
M Why not? Do you have plans with your family?
W No. I have a health check-up scheduled for that day.
M That's too bad. Everybody will miss you.
W I'm sorry, but it's really hard to reschedule the check-up.
M Okay. I hope you can make it to our next reunion.

- -

남 Lisa. 여기는 무슨 일이야?
여 오, David. 나는 오늘 Duo Technology에서 취업 면접이 있어. 너는 여기 이 건물에서 일하니?
남 응. 은행의 일자리는 그만뒀어?
여 아직은 아니지만, 프로젝트를 끝낸 후 다음 달에 그만둘 거야.
남 네가 Duo에서 일자리를 구했으면 좋겠어. 그런데, 추수감사절 전날에 있는 고등학교 동창회에 오는 거지?
여 갈 수 없을 것 같아.
남 왜 못 오니? 가족과 계획이 있니?
여 아니. 난 그날에 예정된 건강 검진이 있어.
남 그거 안됐다. 모두가 너를 보고 싶어 할 거야.
여 미안하지만 건강 검진 일정을 다시 잡는 것이 정말 힘들어.
남 알았어. 다음 동창회에는 네가 올 수 있기를 바라.

Solution
남자는 여자에게 추수감사절 전날에 있는 고등학교 동창회에 오는지 물었고, 여자는 그날 건강 검진이 예정되어 있어서 참석할 수 없다고 하였으므로 정답은 ②이다.

Words
high school reunion 고등학교 동창회 health check-up 건강 검진
scheduled 예정된

03 정답 ②

W Honey, why don't we go to the Orion Flea Market this weekend?

M That's a good idea. It's on Palm Street, right?

W Oh, don't you know? It moved to a new location last month.

M Where is it held now?

W In the area beside the Ron Bridge.

M Why was the market moved? The original location was good because it had a wide area for many booths.

W As I know, the rent for the market place was raised a lot, so the sellers had no choice but to find a new spot.

M I see. Is the transportation to the new place convenient?

W Yes, it's just about a 10-minute walk from the subway station.

M Is there a parking lot?

W There is, but it's not as large as the previous one.

M Okay. We'd better take the subway then.

여 여보, 우리 이번 주말에 Orion 벼룩시장에 가는 게 어때요?

남 좋은 생각이에요. 그건 Palm 가에 있지요, 맞죠?

여 아, 몰라요? 그곳은 지난달에 새로운 장소로 옮겼어요.

남 지금은 어디서 열리나요?

여 Ron 다리 옆의 지역에서요.

남 왜 시장이 옮겨졌나요? 원래 위치는 많은 부스를 수용할 넓은 면적이 있어서 좋았어요.

여 내가 알기로는, 그 시장의 장소 임대료가 많이 올라서 판매자들이 새로운 장소를 찾을 수밖에 없었어요.

남 그렇군요. 새로운 장소로의 교통은 편리한가요?

여 네, 지하철역에서 걸어서 10분 정도 거리예요.

남 주차장이 있나요?

여 있긴 한데, 이전 주차장만큼 크진 않아요.

남 알았어요. 그럼 우리가 지하철을 타는 게 좋겠네요.

Solution

남자는 Orion 벼룩시장이 열리던 예전 위치가 부스 공간이 커서 좋다고 말하며 왜 시장이 옮겨졌는지 물었고, 여자는 그곳의 장소 임대료가 많이 인상되어 새로운 장소로 옮길 수밖에 없었다고 했으므로 정답은 ②이다.

Words

flea market 벼룩시장 raise 올리다, 인상하다
have no choice but to ~하는 수밖에 없다

04 정답 ⑤

Script

W Jack, do you have a few minutes?

M Sure, Laura. Is there anything I can do for you?

W My friends and I are planning to climb Mt. Seorak this weekend. Will you join us?

M I wish I could, but I don't think I can make it.

W Is it because you don't have equipment for climbing?

M No. I like to go hiking and I have a lot of basic equipment.

W Then, what's keeping you from climbing the mountain with us?

M I sprained my ankle while I was jogging a few days ago.

W Oh, I'm sorry to hear that. I hope you get well soon.

M Thanks. I wish I could join you.

여 Jack, 시간 좀 있니?

남 물론이야, Laura. 내가 뭐 도와줄 수 있는 일 있니?

여 내 친구들과 내가 이번 주말에 설악산을 등반할 계획이야. 함께 할래?

남 그러고 싶은데, 그럴 수 없을 것 같아.

여 등산 장비가 없어서 그러니?

남 아니. 난 등산 가는 것을 좋아해서 기본 장비는 많이 가지고 있어.

여 그럼, 왜 우리와 등산을 못 가는데?

남 며칠 전에 조깅하다가 발목을 삐었어.

여 오, 유감이다. 빨리 회복하기를 바랄게.

남 고마워. 너와 함께 갈 수 있다면 좋을 텐데.

Solution

여자는 이번 주말에 설악산 등반을 함께 가자고 제안했고, 남자는 조깅을 하다가 발목을 삐어서 등산을 함께 갈 수 없다고 하였으므로 정답은 ⑤이다.

Words

sprain one's ankle 발목을 삐다 get well 회복하다

05 정답 ③

Script

W Hi, John. Where are you going?

M I'm going to the Garden Mall to get a refund for a shirt I bought yesterday.

W Why? You don't like the design?

M It's very nice, but my brother told me that I could buy it for half the price online.

W No wonder you want a refund. By the way, I was thinking about going to the mall to exchange a skirt.

M Really? Is there a problem with the skirt?

W No, but I'd rather have one that is a size smaller.

M Then, shall we go there together?

W Why don't you go first? I'll catch up with you soon.

M All right.

여 안녕, John. 어디에 가니?

남 어제 산 셔츠를 환불하러 Garden Mall에 가는 길이야.

여 왜? 디자인이 맘에 안 드니?

남 디자인은 아주 좋은데, 내 남동생이 인터넷에서 그것을 반값에 살 수 있다고 했거든.

여 네가 환불을 원하는 것도 당연하겠네. 그런데, 나도 치마를 교환하러 쇼핑몰에 갈 생각이었어.

남 정말? 치마에 무슨 문제가 있니?

여 아니, 하지만 그냥 한 치수 더 작은 것을 원해.

남 그럼, 우리 거기 같이 갈까?

여 먼저 가는 게 어때? 금방 따라갈게.

남 알겠어.

Solution

남자가 어제 산 셔츠를 환불하러 Garden Mall에 가는 길에 여자도 치마를 교환하러 간다고 하자 무슨 문제가 있냐고 물었고, 여자는 한 치수 더 작은 사이즈를 원한다고 하였으므로 정답은 ③이다.

Words

exchange 교환하다 catch up with ~를 따라잡다

06 정답 ③

Script

M Ms. Anderson. Thanks for coming to the job interview today.

W You're welcome. If you have any questions about me, I'll answer them the best I can.

M Alright. According to your résumé, you majored in business administration back in college.

W That's correct. I also studied economics as a minor.

M Great. What about work experience in the field of accounting?

W I've worked as an accountant at Brighton Electronics for 2 years.

M Outstanding. How fluently can you speak Chinese?

W To be honest with you, I only know a little.

M Hmm. I'm looking for an accounting expert to work at our Chinese branch. Unless you speak Chinese fluently, I can't hire you.

W I understand.

남 Anderson 씨. 오늘 면접에 와주셔서 감사합니다.

여 천만에요. 저에 대해 궁금하신 점이 있으시면 최선을 다해 답하겠습니다.

남 좋습니다. 이력서에 따르면, 대학 때 경영학을 전공하셨네요.

여 맞습니다. 또한 경제학을 부전공으로 공부했습니다.

남 아주 좋습니다. 회계 분야에 경력은 어떤가요?

여 Brighton Electronics 사에서 2년간 회계사로 일했습니다.

남 훌륭하군요. 중국어는 얼마나 유창하게 하실 수 있나요?

여 솔직히 말씀드리면, 조금 압니다.

남 음. 저는 중국 지사에서 일할 회계 전문가를 찾고 있어요. 중국어가 유창하지 않는 한, 채용할 수가 없습니다.

여 알겠습니다.

Solution

남자는 중국어 구사 능력을 물어보았고, 여자가 조금밖에 알지 못한다고 하자 남자는 중국 지사에서 일할 회계 전문가를 찾고 있어서 중국어를 유창하게 구사하지 못하면 채용할 수 없다고 하였으므로 정답은 ③이다.

Words

major in ~을 전공하다 business administration 경영학
economics 경제학 minor 부전공 accounting 회계
accountant 회계사 fluently 유창하게

 08강 언급되지 않은 것 고르기 본문 38쪽

수능Q 정답 ③

여 안녕, Ross. 우리 10주년 동창회 파티 준비는 어떻게 되어 가고 있어?

남 준비가 다 된 것 같아, Jennifer.

여 그럼 우리가 준비한 것을 검토해 보자.

남 나는 이미 파티를 위해 Silver Corral 식당을 예약했어.

여 좋아. 우리 파티가 12월 24일이라서 예약하기가 무척 어려웠겠다.

남 맞아, 운이 좋았어.

여 그 식당이 어떤 음식을 제공할 거니?

남 그 식당의 스테이크, 스파게티, 그리고 피자가 유명해서 그걸로 주문했어.

여 맛있겠다. 그리고 파티 기념품도 준비되어 있어.

남 네가 기념품으로 머그잔을 주문했지, 그렇지?

여 맞아, 주문했어. 그건 그날 내가 가져올게.

남 완벽해. 멋진 파티가 될 거야.

Solution

장소(Silver Corral Restaurant), 날짜(December 24th), 음식(Their steak, spaghetti, and pizza), 기념품(mugs for souvenirs)은 언급되었으나 ③ '회비'에 대해서는 언급되지 않았다.

Words

reunion 동창회 go over ~을 검토하다 souvenir 기념품

유형 모의고사 본문 39쪽

01 ④	02 ⑤	03 ④	04 ④	05 ⑤	06 ④

01 정답 ④

Script

M Hello, Dr. Peterson. How are you doing these days?

W Hello, Dr. Collins. Good, I'm working on the Dream Bio Research Project.

M You mean the medical research project sponsored by the government?

W That's right. More than 20 researchers are involved in the project and I'm the head researcher.

M Wow, you're in charge of a really big job. How big is the budget for the project?

W We're allowed to spend one million dollars on the project.

M That's a really huge amount. It's a project to develop a new drug for lung cancer, isn't it?

W That's right.

M How long will the research project last?

W It's a 5-year project. I hope we can develop the drug within this period.

M I wish you success, Dr. Peterson.

W Thank you, Dr. Collins.

남 안녕하세요, Peterson 박사님. 요즘 어떻게 지내세요?

여 안녕하세요, Collins 박사님. 잘 지내요, 저는 Dream Bio 연구 프로젝트에 대해 연구하고 있어요.
남 정부가 후원하는 의학 연구 프로젝트를 말씀하시는 건가요?
여 맞아요. 20명 이상의 연구자들이 이 프로젝트에 참여하고 있고, 저는 수석 연구원이에요.
남 와, 정말 큰일을 맡으셨군요. 그 프로젝트의 예산은 얼마나 큰가요?
여 우리는 그 프로젝트에 백만 달러를 쓸 수 있어요.
남 정말 엄청난 액수네요. 그것은 폐암을 위한 신약을 개발하는 프로젝트죠, 그렇지 않나요?
여 맞아요.
남 그 연구 프로젝트는 얼마나 지속될까요?
여 그것은 5년간의 프로젝트예요. 우리가 이 기간 내에 그 약을 개발할 수 있기를 희망해요.
남 성공을 빌어요, Peterson 박사님.
여 감사합니다, Collins 박사님.

Solution

연구원 수(More than 20 researchers), 예산 규모(spend one million dollars on the project), 연구 목적(develop a new drug for lung cancer), 연구 기간(It's a 5-year project.)은 언급되었으나, ④ '연구 장소'는 언급되지 않았다.

Words

medical 의학의 sponsor 후원하다 involve 참여시키다
head researcher 수석 연구원 budget 예산 lung cancer 폐암
last 지속되다 period 기간

02 정답 ⑤

Script

M Jane, have you seen the movie, *A Night in Paradise*?
W Not yet, but I'm going to see it tomorrow. I like Ted Nolan, the director of the movie.
M Who took the leading role in the movie?
W Neil Young took it. He often appears in Ted's movies.
M He's a great actor. I read some reviews about the movie, and they were all very positive about the director's work.
W Yes. He also tends to produce movies that require a large budget.
M I heard that more than ten million dollars were invested in this movie.
W Wow, the computer graphics must be great. I can't wait to see it.

- -

남 Jane, 영화 'A Night in Paradise'를 봤니?
여 아직 못 봤어. 하지만, 내일 보러 갈 거야. 나는 그 영화의 감독인 Ted Nolan을 좋아해.
남 그 영화에서 누가 주연을 맡았니?
여 Neil Young이 맡았어. 그는 Ted의 영화에 종종 출연해.
남 그는 훌륭한 배우야. 영화에 대한 몇몇 평을 읽었는데, 그것들 모두는 감독의 작품에 대해 아주 긍정적이었어.
여 그래. 그는 또한 큰 예산이 요구되는 영화를 제작하는 경향이 있어.
남 이번 영화에 천만 달러 이상이 투자되었다고 들었어.
여 와, 컴퓨터 그래픽이 정말 멋지겠구나. 빨리 그것을 보고 싶어.

Solution

감독(Ted Nolan, the director of the movie), 주연 배우(Neil Young took it.), 영화평(they were all very positive about the director's work), 투자금(more than ten million dollars were invested)은 언

급되었으나, ⑤ '상영 시간'은 언급되지 않았다.

Words

leading role 주연 invest 투자하다

03 정답 ④

Script

M Mom, I was accepted to the Youth Chamber Orchestra.
W Congratulations, Mark. You've been wanting to join it.
M Yes. They added ten members through this audition.
W How many members are there in the orchestra?
M There are 35 members including the new members.
W That's a lot.
M Right. We meet and practice on Tuesdays and Thursdays on a regular basis.
W I see. Do you know if the orchestra has any plan for performances?
M We'll perform at a nursing home in two months, and then have a regular concert in the fall.
W I'm looking forward to seeing you perform.
M I'm excited about it too.

- -

남 엄마, 제가 Youth 실내 관현악단에 합격했어요.
여 축하해, Mark. 넌 그곳에 들어가고 싶어 했잖아.
남 맞아요. 이번 오디션을 통해 10명의 단원들이 추가되었어요.
여 관현악단에는 몇 명의 단원이 있니?
남 새로운 단원을 포함해서 35명이 있어요.
여 수가 많구나.
남 맞아요. 우리는 화요일과 목요일에 정기적으로 만나서 연습을 해요.
여 그렇구나. 관현악단이 공연에 대한 어떤 계획이 있는지 알고 있니?
남 두 달 후에 양로원에서 공연을 한 다음, 가을에 정기 공연을 할 거예요.
여 네가 공연하는 것을 보는 것이 기대돼.
남 저도 흥분이 돼요.

Solution

신입 단원의 수(They added ten members through this audition.), 총 단원의 수(35 members including the new members), 정기 연습 요일(practice on Tuesdays and Thursdays on a regular basis), 정기 공연 일정(have a regular concert in the fall)은 언급되었으나, ④ '지휘자의 수'는 언급되지 않았다.

Words

on a regular basis 정기적으로 nursing home 양로원

04 정답 ④

Script

W Honey, the announcement on this year's Dolphin Swimming Competition is posted on their website.
M Really? Is there anything different from last year's competition?
W Yes. There's a new category for adults in their twenties.
M Let me see. *[Pause]* Oh, the competition place has also changed to the Olson Swimming Center this year.
W That's good for Tom. The center is close to our place.
M Yeah. We'd better tell Tom the news.

W I will. When is the deadline for registering for the competition?
M It's October 10th.
W The entry fee of 20 dollars is the same as last year, right?
M Yes. I hope Tom does well in the competition.
W Same here.

여 여보, 올해 돌고래 수영 대회에 관한 공지가 웹사이트에 게재되었어요.
남 그래요? 작년 대회와 다른 점이 있나요?
여 네. 이십 대 성인을 위한 새로운 부문이 있네요.
남 어디 봐요. [잠시 후] 아, 대회 장소도 올해 Olson 수영장으로 바뀌었네요.
여 그건 Tom에게 잘됐네요. 그 센터는 우리 집에서 가까우니까요.
남 네. 우리는 Tom에게 그 소식을 말하는 것이 좋겠어요.
여 내가 할게요. 대회 등록 마감일이 언제인가요?
남 10월 10일이에요.
여 20달러의 참가비는 작년과 같아요, 그렇죠?
남 네. Tom이 대회에서 잘하면 좋겠어요.
여 나도 그래요.

Solution

신설된 부문(a new category for adults in their twenties), 개최 장소(the Olson Swimming Center), 참가 신청 기한(It's October 10th.), 참가비(The entry fee of 20 dollars)는 언급되었으나, ④ '참가 신청 방법'은 언급되지 않았다.

Words

announcement 공지, 발표 competition 대회 category 부문, 범주 deadline 마감일 register 등록하다 entry fee 참가비

05 정답 ⑤

Script

M Sandra, this year's Norton Film Festival will open soon.
W Right. It's held around this time of the year. What are the dates for this year?
M It runs from July 7th to July 13th.
W Oh, I'm available then.
M Great. Let's see some movies together. The films will be shown at 20 theaters around the City of Breen.
W Okay. I'd really like to attend the closing ceremony.
M Then, you need to reserve a ticket early because that event sells out quickly.
W I will. What are main events?
M There are main events such as parade and talking with directors.
W That'd be great.
M Why don't we check the whole schedule of movies on the Internet?
W That's a good idea.

남 Sandra, 올해 Norton 영화제가 곧 열릴 거야.
여 맞아. 그건 연중 이맘때 열리지. 올해의 날짜는 언제지?
남 그건 7월 7일부터 7월 13일까지 열려.
여 아, 난 그때 시간이 있어.
남 잘됐다. 우리 영화 몇 편을 같이 보자. 영화는 Breen 시 전역의 20개 극장에서 상영될 거야.
여 알았어. 난 폐막식에 정말로 참석하고 싶어.
남 그럼, 그 행사는 빨리 매진되니까 너는 일찍 표를 예매해야 해.

여 그렇게. 주요 행사는 뭐가 있지?
남 퍼레이드와 감독과의 대화와 같은 주요 행사가 있어.
여 그거 멋지겠는걸.
남 인터넷으로 영화들의 전체 일정을 확인해 보는 게 어때?
여 그거 좋은 생각이야.

Solution

기간(It runs from July 7th to July 13th.), 상영관의 수(20 theaters), 폐막식(the closing ceremony), 주요 행사(parade and talking with directors)는 언급되었으나, ⑤ '패키지 관람권'은 언급되지 않았다.

Words

closing ceremony 폐막식 sell out 매진되다

06 정답 ④

Script

W Kevin, look at this advertisement.
M What's it about?
W It's about Weekly Market, a nonprofit charity organization.
M Sounds like we can go there and sell the items we don't use any more. When is it held?
W It's scheduled for every Saturday. This week, it will be held at the Central Plaza.
M Great! The plaza isn't far from here. How can we sell our items?
W According to the ad, we have to reserve a stall. It says there will be 120 stalls.
M I see.
W The great thing about this organization is that we can help others.
M What do you mean?
W We have to donate 5 percent of our profits to UNICEF.
M What a good cause! Let's quickly reserve a stall before they're all taken.

여 Kevin, 이 광고를 봐.
남 무엇에 관한 것인데?
여 비영리 자선 단체인 Weekly Market에 관한 거야.
남 들어 보니 우리가 그곳에 가서 더 이상 사용하지 않는 물건을 팔 수 있네. 언제 열려?
여 매주 토요일에 열릴 예정이야. 이번 주에는 Central Plaza에서 열릴 거야.
남 잘됐네! 그 광장은 여기서 멀지않아. 우리 물건을 어떻게 팔 수 있지?
여 광고에 따르면 가판대를 예약해야 해. 120개의 가판대가 있을 거라고 해.
남 그렇구나.
여 그 단체에 관해 훌륭한 점은 우리가 다른 사람을 도울 수 있다는 거야.
남 무슨 말이야?
여 수익의 5퍼센트를 UNICEF에 기부해야 해.
남 좋은 취지네! 다 예약되기 전에 서둘러 가판대를 예약하자.

Solution

개최 요일(every Saturday), 개최 장소(at the Central Plaza), 판매 방식(reserve a stall), 수익금 기부(donate 5 percent of our profits to UNICEF)는 언급되었으나, ④ '물품 가격'은 언급되지 않았다.

Words

nonprofit charity organization 비영리 자선 단체 stall 가판대, 좌판 donate 기부하다 cause 대의명분; 원인

수능 Q   정답 ④

여 안녕하세요, 청취자 여러분. Good Day Movie에 오신 것을 환영합니다. Feather Pictures가 제작한 영화 'Green Ocean'의 시사회를 볼 멋진 기회에 관해 알려 드리고 싶습니다. 100명이 그 행사에 초대될 것입니다. 그 행사는 다음 주 토요일 오후 4시에 Glory 극장에서 시작할 것입니다. 영화 관람 후에 영화 출연 배우들을 만나고 그들과 사진을 찍을 수 있습니다. 관심이 있으시면 'Green Ocean' 홈페이지에서 입장권을 신청하세요. 그러면 먼저 신청하는 100명에게 문자 메시지로 입장권이 발송될 것입니다. 초대받은 분들은 극장에서 포스터를 받으실 겁니다. 서둘러서 'Green Ocean'을 미리 볼 수 있는 이 기회를 놓치지 마세요. 자, 저희는 광고 시간 후에 돌아오겠습니다. 그러니 채널을 고정하세요.

Solution

입장권은 문자 메시지로 발송될 것이라고 했으므로 ④가 담화의 내용과 일치하지 않는다.

Words

preview 시사회 apply for ~을 신청하다 text message 문자 메시지
in advance 미리, 사전에 commercial break 광고 시간
stay tuned 채널을 고정하다

유형 모의고사   본문 43쪽

01 ⑤   **02** ④   **03** ④   **04** ④   **05** ④   **06** ③

01 정답 ⑤

Script

W Hello, listeners! I'm happy to introduce you to the first children's library in our town. It's the Dream Children's Library. Our library is for children in the sixth grade and younger. We have a variety of toys as well as books for different ages of children. There are special reading discussion programs for your children. Also, we offer movie showings for children every weekend. We're excited to tell you our library is now ready to open. Our opening day is November 24th. On opening day, we'll provide cartoon character bookmarks to all the visitors. Don't miss it! For more information, visit our website www.dreamchildrenslibrary.org.

여 안녕하세요, 청취자 여러분! 우리 마을 최초의 어린이 도서관을 소개하게 되어 기쁩니다. 꿈 어린이 도서관입니다. 저희 도서관은 6학년 이하 어린이를 위한 것입니다. 저희는 다양한 연령대의 어린이를 위한 도서는 물론 다양한 장난감도 보유하고 있습니다. 여러분의 자녀를 위한 특별 독서 토론 프로그램이 있습니다. 또한 주말마다 어린이들을 위한 영화 상영을 제공합니다. 이제 저희 도서관이 개관할 준비가 되었음을 알려 드리게 되어 기쁩니다. 개관일은 11월 24일입니다. 개관일에는 모든 방문객에게 만화 캐릭터 책갈피를 제공할 예정입니다. 놓치지 마세요! 더 많은 정보를 위해서는 저희 웹사이트 www.dreamchildrenslibrary.org를 방문

하십시오.

Solution

개관일에는 모든 방문객에게 만화 캐릭터 책갈피를 제공한다고 말했으므로 ⑤가 담화의 내용과 일치하지 않는다.

Words

a variety of 다양한 showing 상영 bookmark 책갈피

02 정답 ④

M Hello. My name is Ethan Lupien, the president of a movie making club in the Orion region. I'm happy to announce information on the Orion Youth Film Festival. The contest will be held on the first weekend of November at the Madison Bridge Center. Only high school students from the Orion region may enter the contest. Participants should submit works which are limited to a running time of 30 minutes. They will be judged by five professionals in the local film industry. The registration deadline is October 20th, so sign up today!

남 안녕하세요. 제 이름은 Ethan Lupien이고 Orion 지역 영화 제작 동아리 회장입니다. Orion 청소년 영화제에 관한 정보를 알려 드리게 되어 기쁩니다. 영화제는 11월 첫째 주말에 Madison Bridge 센터에서 개최될 것입니다. 오직 Orion 지역의 고등학생들만이 대회에 참가할 수 있습니다. 참가자들은 30분의 상영 시간으로 제한된 작품을 제출해야 합니다. 그것들은 현지 영화 산업에 종사하는 5명의 전문가들에 의해 심사될 것입니다. 신청 마감일은 10월 20일이니 오늘 신청하세요!

Solution

출품작은 현지 영화 산업에 종사하는 5명의 전문가들에 의해 심사될 것이라고 했으므로 ④가 담화의 내용과 일치하지 않는다.

Words

region 지역 announce 알리다, 발표하다 participant 참가자
running time 상영 시간

03 정답 ④

Script

W Good morning. I want to tell you about Blue Technology Programs. Blue Technology University will have a two-week, academic camp to inform high school students about the future of the Fourth Industrial Revolution. It'll be held for two weeks from August 5th to 18th at Blue Technology University, and students will stay in the university dormitories. The camp is free of charge. You must fill out and submit the application form online. All applications are due by May 30th. For more information or to submit your application, visit the school homepage.

여 안녕하세요. Blue Technology Programs에 대해 말씀드리고 싶습니다. Blue Technology 대학교는 고등학교 학생들에게 4차 산업혁명의 미래에 관해 알려 주기 위해 2주간의 학술 캠프를 운영합니다. 8월 5일부터 18일까지 2주 동안 Blue Technology 대학교에서 진행될 것이고 학생들은 대학 기숙사에서 지내게 될 것입니다. 캠프는 무료입니다. 여러분들은 신청서를 작성하여 온라인으로 제출해야 합니다. 모든 지원

서는 5월 30일까지 마감됩니다. 정보를 더 알고 싶거나 신청서를 제출하려면, 학교 홈페이지를 방문해 주세요.

04 정답 ④

Script

M Hello, everyone. Come and help us celebrate our 75th anniversary. H&Q Motors will be turning 75 on May 1st, making us the oldest car dealership in Nevada. We will be having a three-day celebration. On May 1st, we will kick off our anniversary with free hot-air balloon rides at 6 p.m. On May 2nd, we will have a famous car racer, John Smith, signing autographs from 2 to 4 p.m. On May 3rd, we will have a picnic open to the public at 5:30 in the afternoon. During all three days, there will be displays of antique autos and carnival rides for the children.

남 안녕하세요, 여러분. 오셔서 저희의 75주년 기념일을 축하하는 것을 도와주세요. H&Q Motors는 5월 1일에 75주년이 될 것이고, 그것은 Nevada에서 가장 오래된 자동차 대리점이 될 것입니다. 우리는 3일 간의 축하 행사를 할 것입니다. 5월 1일에는 오후 6시에 무료 열기구 탑승으로 기념일을 시작합니다. 5월 2일에는 오후 2시부터 4시까지 유명한 카레이서인 John Smith의 사인회가 있을 것입니다. 5월 3일에는 오후 5시 30분에 대중에게 개방된 피크닉을 열 예정입니다. 3일 동안 어린이들을 위해 골동품 자동차 전시와 카니발 놀이기구가 있을 것입니다.

Solution

행사의 마지막 날인 5월 3일 오후 5시 30분에는 대중에게 개방된 피크닉을 연다고 했으므로 ④가 담화의 내용과 일치하지 않는다.

Words

dealership (자동차) 대리점 kick off ~을 시작하다
autograph (유명인의) 사인 antique 골동품(인)

05 정답 ④

Script

W Hello, students. This is your vice principal, Anita Adams. This announcement is to inform you that the 17th Welton High Choir Competition will be held on Christmas Eve. At the beginning of the year, we accepted teams who were willing to compete, and a total of 18 teams registered to enter. Since only eight teams will be performing in the final competition, we had the preliminaries last week and carefully chose the top eight groups. The competition will be held in the auditorium between 1 and 3 p.m., and all students are asked to be seated before it begins. The participating teams will perform in alphabetical order, and the winners will be announced right after the competition.

여 안녕하세요, 학생 여러분. 교감 Anita Adams입니다. 이 발표는 여러

분에게 제17회 Welton High Choir 대회가 성탄절 전날에 개최된다는 것을 알리고자 함입니다. 연초에 저희는 기꺼이 참가하고자 하는 팀을 접수받았고, 총 18개의 팀이 대회에 참가하겠다고 등록했습니다. 오직 8팀만이 본선에서 공연하게 되므로, 지난주에 예선전을 가졌고 상위 8팀을 신중하게 선택하였습니다. 대회는 오후 1시부터 3시 사이에 강당에서 열리며, 모든 학생들은 대회가 시작되기 전에 착석하기 바랍니다. 참가 팀은 알파벳 순서로 공연할 것이고, 수상자들은 대회 직후 발표될 것입니다.

Solution

참가 팀은 알파벳 순서대로 공연한다고 했으므로 ④가 담화의 내용과 일치하지 않는다.

Words

vice principal 교감 choir 합창단 willing to 기꺼이 ~하는
preliminary 예선전 auditorium 강당

06 정답 ③

Script

M Hello. My name is Jacob Turner, and I'm from the community service center. Today, I'd like to introduce you all to our Eco-Point program. This program aims to reduce the amount of greenhouse gas emissions. It provides incentives based on the amount of energy you use. If you decrease your usage of both electricity and city gas by more than 10 percent over the course of 6 months, you'll be awarded 50 points. Each point is worth a dollar, and the points can be used just like cash at places like supermarkets and restaurants. Please sign up and become an active citizen who cares about the environment.

남 안녕하세요. 제 이름은 Jacob Turner이며, 주민 센터에서 나왔습니다. 오늘 저는 여러분 모두에게 Eco-Point 프로그램을 소개하고 싶습니다. 이 프로그램은 온실 가스 배출량 감소를 목표로 합니다. 여러분이 사용하는 에너지양을 토대로 인센티브를 제공해 줍니다. 만약 6개월 동안 전기와 도시가스 둘 다의 사용량을 10퍼센트 이상 줄인다면 50점을 받게 됩니다. 1점은 1달러의 가치를 가지며, 포인트는 슈퍼마켓과 식당 같은 곳에서 현금처럼 사용할 수 있습니다. 신청하셔서 환경에 관심을 가지는 적극적인 시민이 되십시오.

Solution

전기와 도시가스 둘 다의 사용량을 6개월간 10퍼센트 이상 줄였을 때 50점을 준다고 했으므로 ③이 담화의 내용과 일치하지 않는다.

Words

aim 목표로 하다 emission 배출 based on ~에 근거하여
worth ~의 가치를 가진 care about ~에 관심을 가지다

수능 Q   정답 ④

남 Camilo's Kitchen에 오신 것을 환영합니다.

여 안녕하세요. 저는 도마를 찾고 있습니다.

남 저희 가게에서 가장 잘 팔리는, 가격이 모두 적당한 다섯 개 모델들을 보여 드리겠습니다. 어떤 선호하는 특별한 재질이 있으신가요? 플라스틱, 단풍나무, 호두나무 도마가 있습니다.

여 플라스틱은 환경친화적이 아니라고 생각해서 플라스틱 도마는 원치 않습니다.

남 알겠습니다. 예산 범위가 어떻게 되시나요?

여 50달러를 넘지 않았으면 해요.

남 좋습니다. 손잡이가 있는 것 혹은 없는 것 중 어떤 것을 선호하시나요?

여 손잡이가 있는 도마가 더 사용하기 쉬울 것 같습니다. 그래서 손잡이가 있는 것을 사겠어요.

남 그러면 어떤 크기를 원하시나요? 두 가지 모델이 남았습니다.

여 음. 작은 크기의 도마는 채소를 자를 때 편리하지 않아요. (나머지) 다른 모델을 사겠습니다.

남 좋습니다. 그렇다면 이것이 손님에게 맞는 도마네요.

Solution

여자는 재질이 플라스틱이 아니며, 가격이 50달러를 넘지 않고, 손잡이가 있는 것으로, 작지 않은 크기의 도마를 사겠다고 했으므로, 여자가 구매할 도마는 ④이다.

Words

cutting board 도마 affordable (가격이) 적당한 preference 선호 material 재질, 소재 range 범위

유형 모의고사   본문 47쪽

01 ④   02 ⑤   03 ⑤   04 ③   05 ④   06 ⑤

01 정답 ④

Script

M Honey, what are you looking at?

W A website that sells air fryers. I want one so we can cook more healthily.

M Good idea. We can fry foods using less oil if we buy one. How much do you think we should spend?

W Well, I don't want to spend more than 100 dollars.

M Okay. Then how about these models?

W Hmm... it's safer to buy one that will turn off if it gets too hot.

M You're right. Let's choose one with the automatic switch off function.

W What about capacity? My friend bought one that could only hold two liters. She regretted not buying a bigger one.

M In that case, we should get one with a capacity of at least four liters. Now we have these two to choose from.

W They both look good. But I think the one with the longer warranty is better.

M I agree. Let's order this one.

남 여보, 뭘 보고 있어요?

여 에어 프라이어를 판매하는 웹사이트요. 우리가 더 건강하게 요리할 수 있어서 그것을 원해요.

남 좋은 생각이에요. 그것을 사면 기름을 덜 사용해서 음식을 튀길 수 있어요. 우리가 얼마를 써야 한다고 생각해요?

여 음. 100달러보다 더 많이 쓰고 싶지 않아요.

남 좋아요. 그렇다면 이 모델들은 어때요?

여 음… 과열되면 꺼지는 것을 사는 것이 더 안전해요.

남 맞아요. 자동 꺼짐 기능이 있는 것을 선택합시다.

여 용량은 어때요? 제 친구는 2리터밖에 안 되는 것을 샀어요. 그녀는 더 큰 것을 사지 않은 것을 후회했어요.

남 그렇다면 우리는 적어도 4리터의 용량을 가진 것을 사야 해요. 이제 이 두 가지 중에서 선택할 수 있어요.

여 둘 다 좋아 보여요. 하지만 보증 기간이 더 긴 것이 더 낫다고 생각해요.

남 동의해요. 이걸로 주문합시다.

Solution

두 사람은 100달러를 넘지 않고, 자동 꺼짐 기능이 있고, 적어도 4리터 용량이며 보증 기간이 더 긴 것을 사겠다고 했으므로, 두 사람이 구매할 에어 프라이어는 ④이다

Words

automatic 자동의 function 기능 capacity 용량 warranty (품질 등의) 보증

02 정답 ⑤

Script

W Hello. How can I help you?

M Hi. I want to book a flight to Toronto next Wednesday, September 29th.

W Okay. Do you want a non-stop flight or a stopover?

M First, I'll ask you a question. How long will it take to make a stopover?

W It takes about eight hours.

M Really? It takes quite a long time for a stopover. Then, I'll take a non-stop flight.

W Non-stop flights depart almost in the afternoon, when do you want to depart?

M I would like a flight departing after 6 p.m.

W Then there are two left here. Which of these do you prefer?

M Well, this one is quite late, but it's cheaper. I'll take the cheaper flight.

W Okay. I'll make a reservation for this flight, then.

M Yes, thank you.

여 안녕하세요. 어떻게 도와드릴까요?

남 안녕하세요. 다음 주 수요일인 9월 29일 토론토행 항공편을 예약하고 싶어요.

여 알겠습니다. 직항을 원하세요, 아니면 경유를 원하세요?

남 먼저 하나 여쭤 볼게요. 경유하는 데 시간이 얼마나 걸릴까요?

여 여덟 시간 정도 걸립니다.

남 정말요? 경유하는 데 시간이 꽤 오래 걸리네요. 그럼 직항편으로 할게요.

여 직항은 거의 오후에 출발하는데, 언제 출발하고 싶으신가요?
남 오후 6시 이후에 출발하는 항공편을 이용하고 싶습니다.
여 그럼 여기 두 편이 남네요. 이 중에 어느 것이 더 나으신가요?
남 음, 이것이 매우 늦기는 하지만 더 저렴하군요. 더 저렴한 항공편을 이용할게요.
여 알겠습니다. 그러면 이 항공편으로 예약해 드리겠습니다.
남 네, 감사합니다.

남자는 직항이고, 오후 6시 이후에 출발하고, 요금이 더 싼 것을 선택했으므로, 남자가 예약할 항공편은 ⑤이다.

non-stop 직항 stopover 경유, 단기 체류 depart 출발하다

03 정답 ⑤

M Good afternoon. Can I help you find something?
W Yes. As you know, it's the perfect season for camping these days. I'm looking for a tent for two people.
M Well, look at the catalog here. There are tents for you on the left.
W I have a hard time making decisions. Could you please help me choose?
M Of course. First of all, what is your budget?
W Well, I can't spend more than 80 dollars.
M I see. And which of these five colors do you like?
W Well, I really don't want a dark color. Other colors are okay if it's not dark.
M Then there are two to choose from. I recommend the lighter one.
W Okay. I'll take that one. Here's my credit card.

남 안녕하세요. 무언가를 찾고 계신 걸 도와드릴까요?
여 네. 아시다시피, 요즘 캠핑하기 완벽한 계절이잖아요. 2인용 텐트를 찾고 있어요.
남 그럼, 여기 카탈로그를 보세요. 왼쪽 편에 손님을 위한 텐트들이 있습니다.
여 결정하기가 어렵네요. 고르는 것을 좀 도와주시겠어요?
남 물론이지요. 우선, 예산은 어떻게 되나요?
여 음, 80달러 넘게 쓸 수는 없어요.
남 그러시군요. 그리고 이 다섯 가지 색상 중 좋아하는 색상은요?
여 음, 전 정말 어두운 색은 싫어요. 어둡지 않으면 다른 색들은 괜찮아요.
남 그럼 두 개의 선택할 것이 남네요. 저는 더 가벼운 것을 추천합니다.
여 좋아요. 저것을 살게요. 여기 제 신용카드입니다.

여자는 80달러가 넘지 않고, 어두운 색이 아닌 것을 원하고, 무게는 가벼운 것을 선택했으므로, 여자가 구매할 텐트는 ⑤이다.

recommend 추천하다

04 정답 ③

M Honey, next Friday is Betty's birthday. We need to decorate our house for the party.

W Right. Let's order a set of decorations online.
M Good! Betty likes balloons, so we'll definitely need plenty of them.
W Yeah. How about a banner? If we have a banner on the wall, the pictures will look better.
M Yeah. Do we need party hats, too?
W Last year, Betty felt uncomfortable wearing a party hat. This time, let's just skip them.
M Okay. What about the cake?
W Why don't we buy a cake from the bakery near our house?
M Great. The bakery has a lot of wonderful cakes.
W Okay. Let's order this set then.

남 여보, 다음 주 금요일이 Betty의 생일이에요. 파티를 위해 집을 장식해야 해요.
여 맞아요. 온라인으로 장식품 세트를 주문합시다.
남 좋아요! Betty가 풍선을 좋아하니까 그것들은 분명 많이 필요해요.
여 네. 현수막은 어때요? 벽에 현수막을 붙이면 사진이 더 잘 나올 거예요.
남 그래요. 파티 모자도 필요한가요?
여 작년에 Betty가 파티 모자 쓰는 것을 불편해했어요. 이번에는 그것을 생략하죠.
남 좋아요. 케이크는 어때요?
여 우리 집 근처의 빵집에서 케이크를 사는 게 어때요?
남 훌륭해요. 그 빵집에 멋진 케이크가 많아요.
여 그래요. 그러면 이 세트를 주문해요.

두 사람은 풍선과 현수막이 있고, 파티 모자와 케이크를 포함하지 않는 것을 선택했으므로 두 사람이 구매할 생일 파티 세트는 ③이다.

decorate 장식하다 definitely 분명히 banner 현수막 skip 생략하다

05 정답 ④

W Daniel, what are you looking at?
M I'm looking at the Community Center Robot Programs. I'd like to take one of them next month.
W That sounds interesting! I'd love to join you.
M I'm interested in either the soccer robot or the dancing robot. What do you think?
W Both sound like fun! But I'd prefer the dancing robot program.
M Okay. Which day are you free after school next month, Wednesday or Friday?
W Friday is better for me. I have a piano and violin class after school on Wednesday.
M Then we can choose one of these two programs.
W This program offers a soccer ball as a free gift, but costs $5 more.
M Why don't we choose the cheaper program? I don't need a soccer ball.
W Okay. Let's sign up.

여 Daniel, 무엇을 보고 있니?
남 주민 센터 로봇 프로그램들을 보고 있어. 다음 달에 그것들 중 하나를 수

강하고 싶어.

여 재미있을 것 같네! 나도 너와 같이 하고 싶어.

남 나는 축구 로봇이나 춤추는 로봇에 관심이 있어. 너는 어떻게 생각하니?

여 둘 다 재미있을 것 같아! 하지만 나는 춤추는 로봇 프로그램이 더 마음에 들어.

남 좋아. 다음 달에는 방과 후에 어느 요일이 한가하니, 수요일 아니면 금요일?

여 금요일이 나는 더 좋아. 수요일에는 방과 후에 피아노와 바이올린 수업이 있어.

남 그러면 이 두 프로그램 중 하나를 선택할 수 있겠다.

여 이 프로그램은 무료 선물로 축구공을 주는데, 5달러 더 비싸네.

남 더 저렴한 것을 선택하는 게 어때? 나는 축구공이 필요하지 않아.

여 그래. 등록하자.

Solution

두 사람은 춤추는 로봇 프로그램이고, 금요일에 열리고, 축구공은 필요하지 않아 더 저렴한 것을 선택했으므로, 두 사람이 등록할 로봇 프로그램은 ④이다.

Words

prefer 더 좋아하다

06 정답 ⑤

Script

W What are you doing on your computer, Jake?

M I'm looking for a digital clock for my desk, but I don't know what to choose. Can you help me?

W Sure. Well, what kind of alarm do you want?

M Hmm... I'd like one with melodies.

W Then you can choose one of these three clocks. How about the backlight function?

M I think it's a great feature. I'll be able to see the clock in the dark.

W Okay. Now you have to decide on the shape. Which do you prefer, rectangular or round?

M Either would be okay, but the color is what really matters to me. I'd like a blue one.

W Okay. Then this model is the best for you.

M I'll get it. Thanks.

- - - - - - - - - - - - - - - - - - - -

여 컴퓨터로 뭐 하고 있니, Jake?

남 내 책상에 둘 디지털 탁상시계를 찾고 있는데, 무엇을 선택해야 할지 모르겠어. 나를 도와줄 수 있니?

여 물론이지. 자, 어떤 종류의 알람을 원해?

남 음… 멜로디가 있는 것을 원해.

여 그러면 이 세 개의 시계 중에서 하나를 선택할 수 있겠네. 배경 조명 기능은 어때?

남 그것은 아주 좋은 기능이라고 생각해. 어둠 속에서 시계를 볼 수 있잖아.

여 좋아. 이제 모양을 선택해야겠다. 직사각형이나 둥근 것 중 어느 것이 더 좋니?

남 둘 다 괜찮지만, 나한테는 색상이 정말 중요해. 나는 파란색이 좋아.

여 좋아. 그러면 이 모델이 네게 딱 맞네.

남 그것을 사야겠어. 고마워.

Solution

남자는 멜로디가 있는 알람 기능과 배경 조명 기능을 원하고, 모양은 신경 쓰지 않지만 파란색을 원한다고 했으므로, 남자가 구매할 탁상시계는 ⑤이다.

Words

backlight 배경 조명 rectangular 직사각형의 matter 중요하다

수능Q 정답 ②

남 Amy, 무엇을 읽고 있니?

여 아빠, 철학 강의를 위한 책이에요.

남 어디 한번 보자. 와! Kant의 책이구나.

여 네. 그것은 이해하기가 매우 어려워요.

남 맞아. 그의 책은 읽는 데 많은 노력이 필요한데, 왜냐하면 그것에는 그의 깊은 지식과 사고가 담겨 있기 때문이지.

여 저도 그렇게 생각해요. 제가 그 책을 더 잘 이해하기 위한 무슨 아이디어가 있으세요, 아빠?

남 음, 철학 토론 모임에 가입하지 그러니? 우리 지역에서 하나를 찾을 수 있어.

여 철학을 위한 토론 모임이 있다고요? 흥미로운데요.

남 그래. 네가 읽고 있는 책에 관하여 모임 내의 다른 사람들과 생각을 공유할 수 있지.

여 아빠 말씀은, 토론을 통해 Kant의 책을 더 분명히 이해할 수 있다는 거죠?

남 바로 그거지. 게다가, 너는 모임에서 비판적 사고 능력 또한 계발할 수 있어.

여 아주 좋아요! 당장 근처에 모임이 있는지 확인해 볼게요.

Solution

남자는 철학 토론 모임의 장점을 설명하였고 여자는 흥미를 보이고 있는 상황이다. 남자가 마지막에 토론 모임의 추가적인 장점을 설명하고 있고, 여자는 이에 대한 적극적인 관심과 동의를 표현하는 것이 자연스러우므로 ②가 여자의 응답으로 가장 적절하다.

① 맞아요! 이 책은 아빠의 책만큼 재미있지 않아요.

③ 걱정 하지 마세요. 저는 다음 학기에는 그 강의를 수강하지 않을 거예요.

④ 정말요? 저는 아빠가 철학 학위를 가지고 있다는 것을 몰랐어요.

⑤ 왜 안 되겠어요? 아빠는 제 철학 토론 모임에 가입할 수 있어요.

Words

philosophy 철학 critical 비판적인

유형 모의고사 본문 51쪽

| 01 ⑤ | 02 ⑤ | 03 ② | 04 ④ | 05 ② | 06 ① |

01 정답 ⑤

Script

W Did you hear that Golden Bookstore will hold a book signing event for Lora Johnson?

M Oh, she is one of my favorite writers. I've read all of her novels. When is it?

W This Sunday afternoon. Do you want to come with me?

M Yes. I can't believe I'm going to see her in person.

- - - - - - - - - - - - - - - - - - - -

여 Golden 서점에서 Lora Johnson의 책 사인회가 열린다는 것을 들었니?

남 오, 그녀는 내가 가장 좋아하는 작가 중 한 명이야. 그녀의 소설을 다 읽었어. 그게 언제니?

여 이번 주 일요일 오후야. 나랑 같이 갈래?

남 응. 내가 그녀를 직접 보게 된다니 믿기지 않아.

여자가 Golden 서점에서 Lora Johnson의 책 사인회가 열린다고 하였고 남자는 자신이 가장 좋아하는 작가 중 한 명이라며 흥미를 보이고 있는 상황이다. 여자가 같이 가자고 제안하였고, 이에 대한 동의를 표현하는 것이 자연스러우므로 ⑤가 남자의 응답으로 가장 적절하다.

① 정말? 내가 그녀를 봤어야 했는데.
② 안 돼. 네가 많이 그리울 거야.
③ 아니. 나는 그날 그 서점에 가지 않았어.
④ 미안해. 나는 그녀의 글에 관심이 없어.

signing event 사인회 novel 소설

02 정답 ⑤

M Did you hear that the science club will hold a drone competition?
W A drone competition? When is it? I'm interested.
M November 10th. You know, the first prize winner will receive a brand-new wireless earphones.
W Good. I'll enter the competition and hopefully win.

남 과학 동아리가 드론 대회를 열 것이라는 소식을 들었니?
여 드론 대회? 그게 언제야? 나 관심이 있어.
남 11월 10일. 있잖아, 1등은 최신형 무선 이어폰을 받게 될 거야.
여 좋은데. 그 대회에 출전해서 우승을 하고 싶어.

남자는 여자에게 과학 동아리에서 드론 대회를 개최한다고 하였고 여자는 흥미를 보이고 있는 상황이다. 남자가 1등에게는 무선 이어폰을 준다고 하였고, 이에 대한 적극적인 관심을 표현하는 것이 자연스러우므로 ⑤가 여자의 응답으로 가장 적절하다.

① 미안하지만, 네 무선 이어폰을 잃어버렸어.
② 맞아. 네 드론이 내 것보다 훨씬 더 빨라.
③ 사실, 과학 동아리는 더 많은 드론이 필요해.
④ 걱정 마. 네게 드론을 날리는 법을 보여 줄게.

brand-new 최신의 wireless 무선의

03 정답 ②

W Good afternoon, sir. How can I help you?
M Could you give me a wake-up call tomorrow morning? I'm staying in room 801.
W Certainly. What time would you like it?
M I need to wake up at six.

여 안녕하세요, 손님. 어떻게 도와드릴까요?
남 내일 아침에 모닝콜을 해 주실 수 있나요? 저는 801호에 묵고 있습니다.
여 물론입니다. 몇 시에 해 드리면 될까요?
남 저는 여섯 시에 일어나야 합니다.

남자는 내일 아침에 모닝콜을 해 줄 수 있는지 물었고, 여자는 가능하다고 하

면서 몇 시에 모닝콜을 원하는지 물었으므로, ②가 남자의 응답으로 가장 적절하다.

① 지금은 7시 30분입니다.
③ 저는 내일 시간이 없습니다.
④ 저는 1인실을 원합니다.
⑤ 죄송합니다. 저는 시계가 없습니다.

wake-up call (호텔 등에서의) 모닝콜

04 정답 ④

M I'm back, Mom.
W Oh, Jack. You're limping. What happened?
M I twisted my ankle when I fell off my bike on my way home.
W Let me see. [Pause] Oh, it's a bit swollen. You'd better see a doctor.
M It's not serious. I'll just wrap some bandages around it and get some rest.
W Okay. I'll get the bandages for you. By the way, where did the accident happen?
M In front of the post office. The road was bumpy.
W Oh, I know the road has been bumpy for several weeks.
M I don't understand why the city government doesn't do anything about it.
W I should do something so this doesn't happen again.
M What are you going to do?
W I'll call City Hall to request road repairs.

남 다녀왔습니다, 엄마.
여 아, Jack. 절뚝거리고 있구나. 무슨 일이 있었니?
남 집에 오는 길에 자전거에서 떨어져서 발목을 삐었어요.
여 어디 보자. [잠시 후] 아, 약간 부었구나. 병원에 가는 게 좋겠다.
남 심각하지는 않아요. 그 주변에 붕대를 좀 감고 휴식을 취할게요.
여 그래. 네게 붕대를 가져다줄게. 그런데 어디서 그 사고가 일어났니?
남 우체국 앞에서요. 길이 울퉁불퉁했어요.
여 아, 그 길이 몇 주 동안 울퉁불퉁했다는 것을 나도 알고 있어.
남 시 당국이 왜 그것에 대해 아무 일도 하지 않는지 이해할 수 없어요.
여 이런 일이 다시 일어나지 않도록 내가 무언가를 해야겠다.
남 무엇을 하실 건데요?
여 시청에 전화해서 도로 보수를 요청할 거야.

남자는 우체국 앞 울퉁불퉁한 길에서 자전거에서 떨어져 발목을 삐었고, 그 도로에 대해 시 당국이 왜 아무런 조치를 하지 않는지 이해할 수 없다고 하였으며, 여자도 그 문제를 인지하여 무언가를 하겠다고 한 상황이다. 남자가 무엇을 할 것인지 묻고, 여자는 이에 대해 구체적으로 언급하는 것이 자연스러우므로 ④가 여자의 응답으로 가장 적절하다.

① 네 자전거 고치는 것을 내가 도와줄게.
② 너를 위해 내가 그 소포를 보낼게.
③ 만약을 위해서 나는 헬멧을 착용할 거야.
⑤ 집에 오는 길에 약국에 들를게.

limp 절뚝거리다 twist (발목·손목 등을) 삐다. 접질리다 ankle 발목
swollen 부어오른 bandage 붕대 bumpy 울퉁불퉁한

05 정답 ②

Script

W Have a seat here, please.

M Thank you. It's nice to meet you.

W Let me ask you a few things. Have you ever worked at a restaurant before?

M Yes, I have. I worked at an Italian restaurant on Lake Street last year.

W Good. What did you do there and how long did you work?

M I worked as a server for almost six months.

W I think that's enough experience to work here.

M Thank you. By the way, can you tell me the hourly wage?

W It's $10 and you'll get additional $2 during the weekend.

M Great! I worked for only $7 an hour at my previous workplace.

W Okay. Do you have any other questions regarding this job?

M No, I don't. If you hire me, I'll do my best.

여 여기 앉으세요.

남 고맙습니다. 만나서 반갑습니다.

여 몇 가지를 물어볼게요. 전에 식당에서 일해본 적이 있으세요?

남 네, 있습니다. 작년에 Lake 가에 있는 이탈리안 식당에서 일했어요.

여 좋아요. 그곳에서 무슨 일을 했고 얼마나 오랫동안 일을 했나요?

남 거의 6개월 동안 종업원으로 일을 했습니다.

여 그 정도면 여기서 일을 하기에 충분한 경력인 것 같아요.

남 고맙습니다. 그런데, 시간당 임금을 알려 주실 수 있나요?

여 시간당 10달러이고 주말에는 2달러를 추가로 더 받을 거예요.

남 좋아요! 이전 직장에서는 시간당 7달러만 받고 일했거든요.

여 그래요. 이 직무와 관련해서 다른 질문이 있나요?

남 아니요, 없습니다. 저를 채용하신다면, 최선을 다하겠습니다.

Solution

두 사람은 구직 면접 중으로 여자는 지원자인 남자에게 이전 직무 경력에 대해 물었고, 남자도 여자에게 시간당 임금에 대해 물어보았으며, 이전 직장보다 시간당 임금이 높은 것에 관심을 표현하였다. 여자는 마지막에 남자에게 일과 관련한 다른 질문이 있는지 물었고, 남자는 이에 대한 대답과 함께 지원자로서 적극적인 구직 의지를 표현하는 것이 자연스러우므로 ②가 남자의 응답으로 가장 적절하다.

① 아니요. 당신의 근무 경력이면 충분히 좋아요.
③ 그래요. 저는 이탈리안 식당에서 일하는 것을 그만두었어요.
④ 맞아요. 모든 질문이 대답하기 어려웠어요.
⑤ 음, 더 이상 요리사로 일하고 싶지 않아요.

Words

hourly wage 시간당 임금 additional 추가의 previous 이전의
regarding ~에 관하여

06 정답 ①

Script

W Hi, Michael. You look excited. What's up?

M Remember when I was planning a trip to France and England? I'm leaving tomorrow.

W Wow, great! This will be your first time traveling abroad, right?

M Yeah. I can't wait to go.

W Do you have everything ready?

M I think so. I've made hotel reservations and I've finished packing my bags.

W Did you buy travel insurance?

M No, I didn't. Is it a must?

W Sure. What if you get injured or have your wallet stolen while traveling?

M Oh, I see. You mean I have to be prepared just in case, right?

W Yeah. That's what insurance is for.

여 안녕, Michael. 너 들떠 보여. 무슨 일 있니?

남 내가 프랑스와 영국으로 여행 계획을 세우고 있었던 거 기억해? 내일 떠나.

여 와, 좋겠다! 이번이 네가 처음으로 해외 여행 가는 거잖아, 맞지?

남 응. 빨리 가고 싶어.

여 준비는 다 했니?

남 그런 것 같아. 호텔을 예약했고 가방 꾸리는 것을 끝냈어.

여 여행 보험은 들었니?

남 아니, 안 들었어. 그거 꼭 해야 하는 거니?

여 물론이지. 만약 네가 여행 중에 다치거나 지갑을 도난당하면 어떻겠어?

남 아, 알겠어. 만약을 위해서 대비해야 한다는 말이구나, 그렇지?

여 응. 그게 보험이 있는 이유지.

Solution

여자는 해외 여행을 떠나는 남자에게 여행 중 부상이나 도난에 대비하여 여행 보험에 가입할 것을 권유하고 있고, 남자는 만약을 위해서 대비해야 하는 것임을 물었으므로, 여자는 이에 대한 동의를 표현하는 것이 자연스러우므로 ①이 여자의 응답으로 가장 적절하다.

② 맞아. 너는 전액 환불받을 수 있어.
③ 나는 그렇게 생각하지 않아. 너는 내일 떠나야 해.
④ 좋아. 너는 네가 원하는 어떤 가방이든지 선택할 수 있어.
⑤ 물론이지. 항공권을 예약하는 것은 쉽지 않아.

Words

insurance 보험 must 반드시 해야 하는 것
just in case 만약을 위해서

수능 Q   정답 ⑤

여 Brian은 고등학생입니다. 그는 전에 오직 가족하고만 여행을 해 보았습니다. 지금까지 그의 어머니가 항상 그의 여행 가방을 챙겨 주었으므로, 그는 여행 가방을 직접 준비한 경험이 없습니다. 이번 주말에 Brian은 자기 친구들과 수학여행을 가기로 되어 있습니다. 그는 이번에도 어머니에게 여행에 필요한 물건을 준비해 달라고 부탁합니다. 하지만, 어머니는 Brian이 자신에게 필요한 것을 준비할 수 있는 충분한 나이가 되었다고 믿고, 이번이 Brian이 보다 자립적이 되는 법을 배울 수 있는 좋은 기회라고 생각합니다. 그래서 어머니는 Brian에게 어머니의 도움 없이 자신의 물건들을 준비해서 그것들을 가방에 꾸려야 한다고 말하고 싶어 합니다. 이런 상황에서 Brian의 어머니는 Brian에게 뭐라고 말할 것 같은가요?

Brian's mother 여행을 위한 가방을 스스로 꾸리는 게 어떻겠니?

Solution

Brian의 어머니는 Brian에게 자립심을 길러 주기 위해서 이번에는 여행 가방을 스스로 꾸리라고 말하고 싶어 하는 상황이므로, 이러한 상황에서 Brian의 어머니가 Brian에게 할 말로 가장 적절한 것은 ⑤이다.

① 새로운 곳에 갈 때마다 꼭 나에게 전화해라.
② 수학여행은 친구를 사귈 좋은 기회야.
③ 나는 여행이 네 시야를 넓혀 준다고 믿는다.
④ 짐을 너 스스로 옮기는 게 어떻겠니?

Words

school trip 수학여행   stuff 물건   opportunity 기회
independent 자립적인, 독립적인

유형 모의고사   본문 55쪽

01 ③   02 ④   03 ⑤   04 ③   05 ⑤   06 ④

01 정답 ③

Script

M Jina is a high school student. Her school is hosting a Market Day to raise money for the homeless in the neighborhood. Jina's teacher says that students who want to take part in the event should bring their own items to school. Jina wants to participate in the school market, so as soon as she gets home, she starts looking for items she can sell at the school Market Day. Finally, she finds her mother's old flower pot in the basement. Now, she wants to ask her mother for permission to take the flower pot to school. In this situation, what would Jina most likely say to her mother?

Jina Can I take this flower pot for a school event?

남 Jina는 고등학생입니다. 그녀의 학교는 동네 노숙자를 위한 기금을 마련하기 위해 Market Day를 개최할 것입니다. Jina의 선생님은 행사에 참여하고 싶은 학생들이 자신의 물건을 학교에 가져와야 한다고 말합니다. Jina는 학교 시장에 참여하고 싶어서, 집에 오자마자, 학교 Market Day에 팔 수 있는 물건을 찾기 시작합니다. 마침내, 그녀는 지하실에서 어머니의 오래된 화분을 발견합니다. 지금 그녀는 어머니에게 그 화분을 학교에 가져갈 수 있도록 허락을 요청하고 싶습니다. 이런 상황에서 Jina는 어머니에게 뭐라고 말할 것 같은가요?

Jina 제가 이 화분을 학교 행사에 가져가도 되나요?

Solution

Jina는 학교에서 개최하는 Market Day에 가져갈 물건으로 어머니의 오래된 화분을 발견하고 그것을 가져갈 수 있는지를 물어보려는 상황이므로, 이러한 상황에서 Jina가 어머니에게 할 말로 가장 적절한 것은 ③이다.

① 멋진 화분을 하나 고르는 것을 도와주세요.
② Market Day에 저와 함께 가 주실 수 있나요?
④ 이 화분에 제 꽃을 심을 수 있는지 잘 모르겠어요.
⑤ 시장에 팔 물건을 찾아보는 건 어때요?

Words

host 개최하다   raise (자금 등을) 모으다; 올리다
the homeless 노숙자들   take part in ~에 참여하다

02 정답 ④

Script

W Juliet has been working as a secretary for a trading company for 10 years. She is very hardworking and she has never been late. She has never made a mistake in arranging a meeting or managing schedules. Her boss, John, is very pleased with her job performance. People around her are particularly impressed with her positive personality, and they always praise her for her satisfactory work. John decides to praise Juliet for her ability to work. In this situation, what would John most likely say to Juliet?

John Thanks. I'm very satisfied with your work.

여 Juliet은 무역 회사에서 10년 동안 비서로 일하고 있습니다. 그녀는 부지런히 일하고 지각을 한 적이 없습니다. 그녀는 회의 소집이나 일정 관리에 있어서는 실수를 한 적이 없습니다. 그녀의 상사인 John은 그녀의 업무 수행에 매우 만족하고 있습니다. 그녀 주위의 사람은 특별히 그녀의 긍정적인 성격을 인상 깊어 하고, 그들은 항상 그녀의 만족스러운 업무를 칭찬합니다. John은 Juliet의 업무 능력에 대해 칭찬해 주겠다고 결심합니다. 이런 상황에서 John은 Juliet에게 뭐라고 말할 것 같은가요?

John 고마워요. 나는 당신의 업무에 매우 만족하고 있어요.

Solution

Juliet은 10년 동안 비서로 근무하며 부지런하고 지각을 한 적이 없으며 맡은 업무에 실수도 없어 Juliet의 상사인 John은 Juliet의 업무 능력에 대해 칭찬하기로 한 상황이므로, 이러한 상황에서 John이 Juliet에게 할 말로 가장 적절한 것은 ④이다.

① 맞아요. 더 잘할 수 있을 거예요.
② 좋아요. 그것에 관해 저를 믿어도 돼요.
③ 좋아요. 당신에게 하루 휴가를 드릴게요.
⑤ 죄송해요. 오늘은 더 이상 일하고 싶지 않아요.

Words

secretary 비서   trading 무역   praise 칭찬하다
satisfactory 만족스러운

03 정답 ⑤

Script

M Angela's five-year-old son, Jim, is watching TV in the living room now. It's 9 o'clock, and it's time for him to go to bed. Angela tells him to turn off the TV and get ready for bed. Hearing her, Jim turns off the TV and goes to his room without washing his face or brushing his teeth. Angela goes to his room and sees him lying in the bed. Now, she wants to tell him that he should wash himself clean. In this situation, what would Angela most likely say to Jim?

Angela You'd better go wash your face and brush your teeth.

남 Angela의 5살된 아들 Jim은 지금 거실에서 TV를 보고 있습니다. 9시이고, 그가 자러 가야 할 시간입니다. Angela는 그에게 TV를 끄고 잘 준비를 하라고 말합니다. 그녀의 말을 듣고, Jim은 TV를 끄고 세수나 양치질을 하지 않고 자기 방으로 갑니다. Angela는 그의 방에 가서 그가 침대에 누워 있는 것을 봅니다. 지금 그녀는 그에게 씻어야 한다고 말하기를 원합니다. 이런 상황에서 Angela는 Jim에게 뭐라고 말할 것 같은가요?

Angela 가서 세수하고 양치해야 한단다.

Solution

Angela는 Jim에게 자러 가야 할 시간이라고 말하였고, Jim은 세수와 양치질을 하지 않고 방으로 들어갔으므로 Angela는 그에게 씻으라고 말하려는 상황이므로, 이러한 상황에서 Angela가 Jim에게 할 말로 가장 적절한 것은 ⑤이다.

① 자러 갈 시간이구나.
② 밤을 새우는 것은 좋은 습관이 아니란다.
③ 이 시간에 TV를 보는 것은 안 된단다.
④ 오늘 나를 위해 네가 그것을 해 주어서 매우 기쁘구나.

Words

sit up all night 밤을 꼬박 새우다

04 정답 ③

Script

W Sam gets on the subway after a long day from school. On the subway car, there is only one seat left. Luckily, Sam gets to sit there. He starts to doze off as soon as the subway leaves the station. About ten minutes later, he gets woken up by the rattling sound of the subway car. Sam sees a woman giving up her seat to an old lady. The woman seems really tired as she leans against the pole. Since he has just two stops left before getting off, he thinks he might as well give up his seat. In this situation, what would Sam most likely say to the woman?

Sam I'm getting off soon, so you can have my seat.

여 Sam은 학교에서의 긴 하루를 끝내고 지하철을 탑니다. 지하철에는 한 자리만 남아 있습니다. 운 좋게도, Sam이 그 자리에 앉게 됩니다. 지하철이 역을 떠나자마자 그는 졸기 시작합니다. 약 10분 뒤에, 그는 지하철의 덜컹거리는 소리에 잠에서 깹니다. Sam은 한 여자가 한 할머니에게 자신의 자리를 양보하는 것을 봅니다. 그 여자는 기둥에 기대어 매우 피곤해 보입니다. 내리기까지 두 정거장만 남았기 때문에 그는 자신의 자

리를 양보하는 게 좋겠다고 생각합니다. 이런 상황에서 Sam은 여자에게 뭐라고 말할 것 같은가요?

Sam 저는 곧 내리니 제 자리에 앉으셔도 돼요.

Solution

Sam은 할머니에게 자리를 양보한 한 여자가 기둥에 기대어 매우 피곤해하는 것을 보고, 내릴 정거장이 두 정거장만 남았기 때문에 자리를 양보하려는 상황이므로, 이러한 상황에서 Sam이 여자에게 할 말로 가장 적절한 것은 ③이다.

① 자리를 양보해 주시겠어요?
② 내릴 역을 놓치지 않도록 조심해야 해요.
④ 지하철이 제시간에 출발하지 못할지도 몰라요.
⑤ 문에 기대는 것은 꽤 위험할 수 있어요.

Words

doze off 졸다   rattling 덜컹거리는   lean against ~에 기대다
get off 내리다   might as well ~하는 게 낫다

05 정답 ⑤

Script

M Kelly works as a nurse at a general hospital. Once a week, she works the night shift from 10 p.m. to 6 a.m. After she finishes her work at dawn, she always feels exhausted and needs to sleep soundly. One day, as she goes to bed after her night shift, she hears balls bouncing around and kids yelling. It's coming from the apartment above her. Her upstairs neighbor is Tom, and he has two children. Kelly tries to ignore the noise, but the sounds only get louder. As she finds it impossible to sleep, she decides to go upstairs to talk to Tom. In this situation, what would Kelly most likely say to Tom?

Kelly Could you please keep it down so I can get some sleep?

남 Kelly는 종합병원에서 간호사로 근무합니다. 일주일에 한 번, 그녀는 오후 10시부터 오전 6시까지 야간 근무를 합니다. 새벽에 일을 마치고 나면 그녀는 항상 기진맥진하여 숙면을 필요로 합니다. 어느 날, 그녀가 야간 근무를 마치고 잠자리에 들 때, 그녀는 공이 여기저기로 튀고 아이들이 소리 지르는 것을 듣습니다. 그것은 그녀의 아파트 위층에서 나는 것입니다. 그녀의 위층 이웃은 Tom이고, 그에게는 두 명의 아이들이 있습니다. Kelly는 그 소음을 무시하려고 애썼으나, 그 소리는 커지기만 합니다. 잠 드는 것이 불가능하다는 것을 알고서, 그녀는 Tom에게 말하기 위해 위층으로 올라가기로 결심합니다. 이런 상황에서 Kelly는 Tom에게 뭐라고 말할 것 같은가요?

Kelly 제가 잠을 좀 잘 수 있게 조용히 해 주시겠어요?

Solution

Kelly는 야간 근무 후 피곤한 상태에서 위층 이웃인 Tom의 아이들이 내는 소리로 잠을 잘 수 없어서 위층에 올라가서 Tom에게 말하기로 한 상황이므로, 이러한 상황에서 Kelly가 Tom에게 할 말로 가장 적절한 것은 ⑤이다.

① 요즘 제가 밤에 잠을 자는 것이 힘들어요.
② 소음을 무시하고 일에 집중할 수 있으신가요?
③ 제가 소음을 낸 것에 대해 사과드려요.
④ 당신의 아이들이 편안하다고 느끼도록 하는 게 최선이라고 생각해요.

Words

night shift 야간 근무   dawn 새벽   soundly (잠이 든 모양이) 깊이[곤히]
bounce 튀다   ignore 무시하다   keep down (소리 등을) 낮추다

06 정답 ④

W Nathan bought himself a smartphone about a year ago. Last Sunday, he dropped the phone while walking, and afterwards he noticed a small crack on the screen. Ever since that day, the phone has been acting strangely. The phone freezes whenever he runs certain applications. In addition, the battery seems to run out faster than before. He needs to charge it twice a day. Nathan decides to take it in for repairs. The clerk at the service center says it will take about a week before the work is done. Nathan wonders if the repair is free of charge. In this situation, what would Nathan most likely say to the clerk?

Nathan I'd like to know if I have to pay for the repairs.

여 Nathan은 약 1년 전에 스마트폰을 구입했습니다. 지난주 일요일에, 그는 걷다가 전화기를 떨어뜨렸고, 이후에 그는 화면에 작은 금이 간 것을 발견했습니다. 그날 이후로, 전화기가 이상하게 작동하기 시작했습니다. 그가 특정 앱을 실행시킬 때마다 전화기는 작동을 멈춥니다. 게다가, 배터리가 전보다 더 빨리 닳는 것 같습니다. 그는 그것을 하루에 두 번 충전해야 합니다. Nathan은 그것을 수리 맡기로 결심합니다. 서비스 센터 직원은 수리가 완료될 때까지 대략 일주일 정도 걸릴 거라고 말합니다. Nathan은 수리가 무료인지 궁금합니다. 이런 상황에서 Nathan은 직원에게 뭐라고 말할 것 같은가요?

Nathan 제가 수리비를 지불해야 하는지 알고 싶습니다.

Solution

Nathan은 지난주에 전화기를 떨어뜨린 후 전화기가 이상하게 작동하기 시작하여 서비스 센터에 수리를 맡기려고 하면서 그 수리가 무료인지 궁금한 상황이므로, 이러한 상황에서 Nathan이 직원에게 할 말로 가장 적절한 것은 ④이다.

① 다음 주까지 수리를 해 주시겠어요?
② 화면에 금이 간 것은 제 책임이에요.
③ 그것에 무슨 문제가 있는지 알려 주시겠어요?
⑤ 그것이 갑자기 작동을 멈추는 이유를 모르겠어요.

Words

crack 금 freeze 작동을 멈추다, 정지하다

13강 세트 문항
본문 58쪽

수능 Q
정답 01 ③ 02 ⑤

여 학생 여러분, 안녕하세요. 이전에 우리는 여러 다른 나라의 전통 음식에 대해 논의했습니다. 오늘 저는 일상 음식의 놀라운 탄생지에 대해 이야기하겠습니다. 첫째, 사람들은 시저 샐러드가 로마 황제의 이름을 따서 지은 것이라고 믿습니다. 하지만 유명한 이야기에 따르면 그 이름은 멕시코의 한 요리사에게서 유래했다고 합니다. 그는 음식이 부족할 때 몇 가지 기본적인 재료들을 모아 그것을 만들었습니다. 둘째, 베이글은 유명한 뉴욕 음식입니다. 하지만 그것은 중부 유럽에서 유래한 것 같습니다. 널리 반복되는 이야기에 의하면 그것은 Vienna에서 침략군의 격퇴를 기념하기 위해 처음 만들어졌다고 합니다. 셋째, 많은 사람들은 키위가 뉴질랜드에서 유래했다고 생각합니다. 그것은 아마도 뉴질랜드의 작은 날지 못하는 새가 똑같은 이름을 가지고 있기 때문일 겁니다. 사실, 그 음식은 중국에서 유래했습니다. 마지막으로, 감자로 알려진 나라가 있다면, 그것은 아일랜드입니다. 그것은 이 음식의 흉작이 19세기에 아일랜드에서 극심한 기아를 일으켰기 때문입니다. 하지만 그 음식은 남아메리카에서 유래한 것으로 여겨집니다. 이제 이 음식들에 대한 짧은 비디오를 보도록 하겠습니다.

Solution

01

사람들이 잘못 알고 있는 일상 음식의 유래에 대한 내용이므로, 여자가 하는 말의 주제로 가장 적절한 것은 ③ '일상 음식의 뜻밖의 유래'이다.

① 왜 전통 음식이 인기가 있는가
② 유기농 식품에 관한 오해
④ 언제 음식이 여러 나라로 퍼지는가
⑤ 신선한 음식을 먹는 것의 중요성

02

시저 샐러드, 베이글, 키위, 감자는 언급되었지만, ⑤ '버펄로 윙(향료 소스와 함께 제공되는 기름에 튀긴 닭 날개 요리)'은 언급되지 않았다.

Words

birthplace 탄생지 emperor 황제 ingredient (요리의) 재료
run out of ~을 다 써 버리다 celebrate 기념하다, 축하하다
flightless (새가) 날지 못하는 crop failure 흉작 hunger 기아, 기근

유형 모의고사
본문 59쪽

| 01 ① | 02 ④ | 03 ② | 04 ⑤ | 05 ⑤ | 06 ③ |

01 정답 ①   02 정답 ④

W Hello, everyone. With technologies like Artificial Intelligence, it is possible to digitize homes. Today, I'd like to introduce to you household appliances made smarter with the help of technology. First are smart washing machines. Smart washers with AI techniques can sense the different types of fabric so they regulate the washing strength and detergent. They can even send an alert when detergent is out of stock. Next are smart refrigerators.

They allow the user to monitor food items inside. They can even show relevant recipes that can be made with those items. There are also smart speakers. Speakers controlled by voice commands can do various tasks such as creating a play list and searching the Internet. Lastly, robotic vacuum cleaners can automatically clean the tight and usually overlooked spaces that are hard to access in traditional ways. Now, let's watch a video about these smart home appliances.

여 안녕하세요, 여러분. 인공 지능과 같은 기술을 사용하면, 가정을 디지털화할 수 있습니다. 오늘은 기술의 도움으로 더욱 똑똑해진 가전제품을 소개하고자 합니다. 첫 번째는 스마트 세탁기입니다. AI 기술이 접목된 스마트 세탁기는 다양한 유형의 직물을 감지할 수 있어 세탁 강도와 세제를 조절합니다. 그것은 세제가 비어 갈 때 경보를 보낼 수도 있습니다. 다음은 스마트 냉장고입니다. 그것은 사용자로 하여금 내부의 식품을 모니터링할 수 있도록 합니다. 해당 물품(재료)들로 만들 수 있는 관련 조리법도 알려 줄 수 있습니다. 스마트 스피커도 있습니다. 음성 명령으로 제어되는 스피커는 재생 목록 생성, 인터넷 검색 등 다양한 작업을 수행할 수 있습니다. 마지막으로 로봇 진공청소기는 기존 방식으로 접근하기 어려운 비좁고 일반적으로 간과되는 공간을 자동으로 청소할 수 있습니다. 이제 이러한 스마트 가전제품에 대한 비디오를 보겠습니다.

Solution

01
기술의 도움으로 더욱 스마트해진 가전제품을 소개하는 내용이므로, 여자가 하는 말의 주제로 가장 적절한 것은 ① '기술로 더 똑똑해진 가전제품'이다.

② 스마트 가전제품을 업그레이드하는 방법
③ 온라인으로 스마트 가전제품을 사는 방법
④ 에너지 효율이 좋은 가전제품의 이점
⑤ AI 기술이 인간에게 미치는 부정적인 영향

02
세탁기, 냉장고, 스피커, 진공청소기는 언급되었지만, ④ '에어컨'은 언급되지 않았다.

Words

artificial 인공의 intelligence 지능 digitize 디지털화하다
household appliance 가전제품 fabric 직물, 섬유
regulate 조절하다 detergent 세제 alert 경보 relevant 관련된
command 명령 task 과업 overlook 간과하다 access 접근하다

03 정답 ②   ## 04 정답 ⑤

Script

M Hello. Let's talk about gardening. Gardening is more than just shoveling dirt and watering plants. It is a way for you to relax without being a couch potato. Did you know that spending just 30 minutes a day in your garden greatly affect your mood? I'll give you some examples. Gardening is a great way to relieve any feelings of depression. It has a calming effect on the human psyche. Studies have shown that exposure to sunlight makes people feel more comfortable and brighter. Gardening can also reduce stress. While doing garden work, you can free yourself from the thoughts that complicate your life. Lastly, gardens give you a feeling of accomplishment that

is nearly unrivaled. If you have a garden, why don't you plant vegetables in your garden?

남 안녕하세요. 정원 가꾸기에 대해 이야기하겠습니다. 정원 가꾸기는 단지 삽으로 땅을 파고 식물에 물을 주는 것 이상입니다. 그것은 소파에 누워 TV만 보며 시간을 보내지 않고도 휴식을 취할 수 있는 방법입니다. 정원에서 하루에 단 30분의 시간만 보내도 기분에 큰 영향을 준다는 것을 알고 계셨나요? 몇 가지 예를 들어 보겠습니다. 정원 가꾸기는 우울감을 완화하는 좋은 방법입니다. 그것은 인간의 정신에 진정 효과가 있습니다. 연구에 따르면 햇빛에 노출되면 사람들이 더 편안하고 밝은 느낌을 갖는다고 합니다. 정원 가꾸기는 또한 스트레스를 줄일 수 있습니다. 정원 일을 하는 동안 여러분의 삶을 복잡하게 하는 생각에서 벗어날 수 있습니다. 마지막으로 정원은 거의 비할 데 없는 성취감을 선사합니다. 정원이 있다면, 정원에 채소를 심어 보는 것은 어떻습니까?

Solution

03
정원 가꾸기가 심리에 큰 영향을 준다는 내용이므로, 남자가 하는 말의 주제로 가장 적절한 것은 ② '정원 가꾸기가 심리에 미치는 영향'이다.

① 기분을 좋게 만드는 활동들
③ 심리적인 문제를 다루는 방법
④ 정원에 재배하기 좋은 채소
⑤ 야외 활동과 정신 질환 치료와의 관계

04
우울, 편안함, 스트레스, 성취는 언급되었지만 ⑤ '기쁨'은 언급되지 않았다.

Words

shovel 삽으로 파다 relieve 누그러뜨리다 depression 우울
psyche 정신, 심리 reduce 줄이다 complicate 복잡하게 하다
accomplishment 성취 unrivaled 비할 데 없는

05 정답 ⑤   ## 06 정답 ③

W Hello, everyone. I'd like to talk about Egyptian paintings today. What do you think of the Egyptian paintings in this picture? Do the figures look realistic to you? No, of course they don't. Egyptian painters followed a certain pattern of their own. The painters used multiple points of view to show every aspect of a figure on flat surfaces. The legs, arms and faces of people are drawn from a side view, while the shoulders are facing front. The human body is twisted in an awkward position. The shoulder faces the viewer but the waist and legs face sideways. Egyptian artists also had their own way of calculating the size of figures. It was based on the person's social status. In the next picture, you can see ordinary people were generally drawn as much smaller than gods, pharaohs, and other important people. Now let's watch some video clips to help you understand better.

여 안녕하세요, 여러분. 오늘 저는 이집트 그림에 대해서 이야기하고 싶습니다. 이 사진에 있는 이집트 그림들에 대해서 여러분은 어떻게 생각하십니까? 그 모습들이 여러분에게 사실적으로 보입니까? 물론 아닙니다. 이집트 화가들은 자신들만의 특정 방식을 따랐습니다. 그 화가들은 평평한 표면 위에 인물의 모든 면을 보여 주기 위해 다중 시점을 사용했습니다. 사람의 다리, 팔, 그리고 얼굴이 옆면에서 그려진 반면, 어깨는 앞을 향하고 있습니다. 인간의 몸은 어색한 자세로 뒤틀려 있습니다. 어깨는 그림을

보는 사람을 향하고 있지만, 허리와 다리는 옆을 향하고 있습니다. 이집트의 화가들은 또한 인물의 크기를 계산하는 데 있어서도 자신들만의 방법이 있었습니다. 그것은 사람의 사회적인 지위에 근거를 두었습니다. 다음 사진에서 평민들은 일반적으로 신, 파라오, 그리고 다른 중요한 사람들보다 훨씬 더 작게 그려져 있는 것을 볼 수 있습니다. 이제 여러분들의 더 나은 이해를 돕고자 몇 가지 비디오 클립을 보도록 하겠습니다.

05

이집트 그림에서는 다중 시점을 사용하여 인간의 몸을 뒤틀리게 그렸고, 인물의 크기도 사회적인 지위에 근거를 둔다는 내용이므로, 여자가 하는 말의 주제로 가장 적절한 것은 ⑤ '인간의 모습을 표현하는 이집트의 화풍'이다.

① 이집트 그림에서 가장 흔하게 사용된 사물들
② 이집트 그림에서 정면의 중요성
③ 이집트 화가의 사회적 지위의 향상
④ 정치적인 상황이 이집트 예술에 미친 영향

06

다리, 팔, 얼굴, 어깨는 언급되었지만, ③ '가슴'은 언급되지 않았다.

figure 인물, 모습 realistic 사실적인 multiple 다중의
point of view 시점 aspect 면, 측면 twist 비틀다, 뒤틀다
awkward 어색한 calculate 계산하다 social status 사회적 지위

실전 모의고사 01회

본문 64쪽

01 ①	02 ①	03 ②	04 ③	05 ④
06 ③	07 ⑤	08 ⑤	09 ③	10 ②
11 ⑤	12 ②	13 ⑤	14 ③	15 ⑤
16 ④	17 ⑤			

01 정답 ①

Script

M Are you having difficulty in fitting into your old clothes? Have you placed yourself on the scale and realized you are no longer the person you once were? If you said yes to any of these questions, don't just sit on the couch hoping to be something you are not. Come to the Fitness Factory and take the first step toward your better appearance. For a limited time only, a yearly membership will include the use of our up-to-date gym, a large swimming pool, a sauna, and a variety of yoga classes. So, act right now and take advantage of this special offer. This special promotion ends at the end of July.

남 오래된 옷이 꼭 맞는 데 어려움이 있으십니까? 체중계에 올라가서 더 이상 예전의 자신이 아니라는 것을 알아차린 적이 있습니까? 만약 이 질문들 중 어느 것에라도 그렇다고 대답하셨다면 자신이 아닌 것이 되기를 바라면서 그저 소파에 앉아만 계시지 마십시오. Fitness Factory에 오셔서 더 나은 외모를 향한 첫걸음을 내디디십시오. 한정된 기간 동안만 연간 회원권에 최신식의 체육관, 넓은 수영장, 사우나, 그리고 여러 가지의 요가 강좌 이용이 포함될 것입니다. 그러니 지금 당장 실행에 옮기셔서 이 특별한 제안을 활용하십시오. 이 특별 행사는 7월 말에 끝납니다.

Solution

Fitness Factory라는 체육 센터의 연회원이 되면 체육관, 수영장, 사우나, 요가 강좌를 이용할 수 있으며, 이 특별 행사가 7월 말에 끝난다고 했으므로 남자가 하는 말의 목적으로 가장 적절한 것은 ①이다.

Words

fit into ~에 꼭 들어맞다 place 놓다, 두다 scale 체중계, 저울
appearance 외모 up-to-date 최신식의
take advantage of ~을 활용하다 promotion (판촉) 행사

02 정답 ①

Script

W Hey, Wesley. I heard your wife was pregnant. Congratulations!
M Thank you, Lucy. Our baby is due in August.
W Your wife's belly must be growing larger.
M Right. That's why I'm doing as many household chores as possible for her.
W Well, gone are the days when a pregnant woman was thought of as fragile.
M What do you mean?
W A pregnant woman is capable of doing nearly everything that every other woman is capable of doing.
M Oh, really? I didn't know that.
W It is also recommended that pregnant women participate in some exercise programs.
M I see. Is it also helpful to take a walk?
W Sure. Moderate exercise is good for pregnant women.

여 이봐요, Wesley. 당신의 아내가 임신했다고 들었어요. 축하해요!
남 고마워요, Lucy. 아기는 8월 출산 예정이에요.
여 당신 아내의 배가 틀림없이 점점 더 커지고 있겠군요.
남 맞아요. 그래서 아내를 위해 가능한 한 많은 집안일을 내가 하고 있어요.
여 음, 임신부가 연약하다고 생각되던 때는 지났어요.
남 무슨 말이에요?
여 임신부는 모든 다른 여자들이 할 수 있는 거의 모든 일을 할 수 있어요.
남 아, 정말이요? 그걸 몰랐네요.
여 임신부가 몇몇 운동 프로그램에 참여하는 것 또한 권장되고 있어요.
남 알겠어요. 산책을 하는 것도 도움이 되나요?
여 물론이죠. 적당한 운동은 임신부에게 좋아요.

Solution

임신한 아내를 위해 가능한 한 많은 집안일을 하고 있다는 남자에게 여자는 임신부가 다른 여자들이 할 수 있는 일들을 거의 모두 할 수 있고 임신부가 적당한 운동 프로그램에 참여하는 것도 권장되고 있다고 했으므로 여자의 의견으로 가장 적절한 것은 ①이다.

Words

pregnant 임신한 due (출산) 예정인 belly 배
household chores 집안일 fragile 연약한, 부서지기 쉬운
capable ~을 할 수 있는 participate in ~에 참여하다
moderate 적당한 be good for ~에 좋다

03 정답 ②

Script

M Good afternoon. How can I help you?
W Hello. I'm going to travel with my dog to the Philippines.
M Would you like it to get some vaccinations?
W No. She already got all her vaccinations here. I just need her medical records.
M No problem. May I have her name and her breed?
W Her name is Lucy and she is a Chihuahua.
M Wait a second, please. *[Typing Sound]* Okay. How many copies do you need?
W Three copies, please.
M Uh-oh, the printer needs a new ink cartridge. Do you need them right now?
W No. When can I pick them up?
M I'll have them ready within the hour. Will that be okay?
W That's fine. Thank you.

남 안녕하세요. 어떻게 도와드릴까요?
여 안녕하세요. 저는 제 강아지와 함께 필리핀으로 여행을 가려고 합니다.

남 강아지에게 예방 접종을 시키려고 하십니까?
여 아니요. 이미 여기서 모든 예방 접종을 했어요. 단지 제 강아지의 진료 기록이 필요합니다.
남 문제없습니다. 강아지의 이름과 품종을 말씀해 주시겠습니까?
여 강아지의 이름은 Lucy이고, 품종은 치와와입니다.
남 잠깐만 기다려 주세요. [자판 두드리는 소리] 좋습니다. 복사본이 몇 부 필요하십니까?
여 세 부를 부탁드립니다.
남 이런, 지금 프린터에 새 잉크 카트리지가 필요해요. 지금 당장 필요하십니까?
여 아니요. 언제 그것들을 가져갈 수 있을까요?
남 한 시간 안에 그것들을 준비해 놓겠습니다. 괜찮으시겠습니까?
여 좋습니다. 감사합니다.

강아지를 데리고 필리핀으로 여행을 가려는 여자가 남자에게 강아지의 진료 기록을 요청하고, 남자는 여자의 강아지에 대해 확인한 후 진료 기록을 준비해 두겠다고 했으므로, 두 사람의 관계를 가장 잘 나타낸 것은 ②이다.

vaccination 예방 접종 medical record 진료 기록 breed 품종
copy 복사(본) ink cartridge (프린터의) 잉크 카트리지
right now 지금 당장

04 정답 ③

W Look at the picture on this brochure, Paul.
M What is it, Emily?
W This is Restaurant Romance. It is located on Cross Street. Why don't we have dinner here this Saturday?
M Sounds great! The aquarium on the wall is impressive.
W Yeah. And the brochure says the bottle of wine on each table is free.
M That's good! What do you think of the candlestick on the table?
W I like its classic look.
M Me, too. Eating dinner by candlelight would be very romantic.
W I like the checkered tablecloth, too. It looks elegant.
M Look at the comfortable chairs with armrests. I want to sit in one of them.
W Then let's go to this restaurant on Saturday.

여 이 안내 책자의 그림을 봐, Paul.
남 그게 뭐야, Emily?
여 이곳은 Restaurant Romance야. Cross 거리에 위치하고 있어. 이번 주 토요일에 여기서 저녁을 먹는 게 어때?
남 그거 멋지다! 벽에 있는 수조가 인상적이야.
여 응. 그리고 안내 책자에 따르면 식탁 위에 있는 와인 한 병은 무료라고 해.
남 괜찮은데! 식탁 위에 있는 촛대는 어떻게 생각해?
여 고풍스러운 외관이 마음에 들어.
남 나도 그래. 촛불을 켜고 저녁을 먹는다는 건 매우 낭만적일 거야.
여 체크무늬의 식탁보도 마음에 들어. 우아해 보여.
남 팔걸이가 있는 편안한 의자들을 봐. 그것들 중 하나에 앉고 싶어.
여 그러면 이번 주 토요일에 이 식당으로 가자.

식탁 위에는 촛대가 놓여 있다고 했지만 그림에서는 꽃병이 놓여 있으므로 대화의 내용과 일치하지 않는 것은 ③이다.

brochure 안내 책자 aquarium 수조 impressive 인상적인
candlestick 촛대 romantic 낭만적인 checkered 체크무늬의
tablecloth 식탁보 elegant 우아한 armrest 팔걸이

05 정답 ④

W Welcome to Queensland Hostel! What can I do for you?
M Hi. My name is Chris Jackson. I made a reservation three days ago.
W Okay. Let me see. [Typing Sound] You reserved a single room for two days, right?
M That's right.
W Your room is 202. Here's the key. Breakfast is served from 7:00 to 8:30 in the dining hall.
M Thank you. Can you tell me where I can use a computer?
W There is a lounge at the end of this aisle. You can use computers and read magazines there.
M Thank you. And can you recommend any tourist attractions around here?
W Sure. I'll bring you a city map after I mark some good places on it.
M Thank you. Then I'll take my bags upstairs now.
W Okay. I'll bring it to you in ten minutes.

여 Queensland 호스텔에 오신 것을 환영합니다! 무엇을 도와드릴까요?
남 안녕하세요. 제 이름은 Chris Jackson입니다. 3일 전에 예약을 했습니다.
여 알겠습니다. 어디 봅시다. [자판 두드리는 소리] 1인실을 이틀 동안 예약하셨군요, 그렇죠?
남 맞습니다.
여 손님의 방은 202호입니다. 여기 열쇠가 있습니다. 조식은 7시에서 8시 30분에 식당에서 제공됩니다.
남 감사합니다. 어디서 컴퓨터를 사용할 수 있는지 말씀해 주시겠습니까?
여 이 복도 끝에 휴게실이 있습니다. 그곳에서 컴퓨터를 사용하고 잡지를 읽으실 수 있습니다.
남 감사합니다. 그리고 이 주변의 관광 명소를 좀 추천해 주시겠습니까?
여 물론이죠. 제가 시내 지도에 좋은 장소들을 표시하여 가져다 드리겠습니다.
남 감사합니다. 그러면 이제 저는 제 가방을 위층으로 옮기겠습니다.
여 알겠습니다. 10분 후에 그것을 가져다 드리겠습니다.

남자는 호스텔에서 체크인을 하며 직원인 여자에게 관광 명소를 추천해 달라고 했고 이에 여자가 지도에 좋은 장소를 표시하여 가져다 주겠다고 했으므로 정답은 ④이다.

make a reservation 예약하다(= reserve) dining hall 식당
lounge 휴게실 aisle 복도, 통로 tourist attraction 관광 명소
mark 표시하다

06 정답 ③

Script

W Good morning. How can I help you?

M I'm looking for a purse for my daughter. Can you recommend one?

W Sure. What do you think of this gray one? It's 35 dollars.

M Well, I like the design, but I don't think she'll like that color.

W Then how about choosing one of these pink ones?

M They look good. How much is this one?

W The list price is 50 dollars, but it's 10 percent off now.

M Good. I'll take it. And how much is this doll? It's very cute.

W It's 10 dollars, but if you buy a purse, you can get it for 5 dollars.

M Okay. Then I'll take the purse and the doll. Here is my credit card.

W Thank you.

여 안녕하세요. 어떻게 도와드릴까요?

남 제 딸에게 줄 지갑을 찾고 있습니다. 하나 추천해 주시겠습니까?

여 물론이죠. 이 회색 지갑은 어떻게 생각하세요? 35달러입니다.

남 음, 그 디자인이 마음에 들지만, 제 딸이 그 색상을 좋아할 것 같지 않아요.

여 그러면 이 분홍색 지갑들 중에서 하나를 선택하시는 것이 어떨까요?

남 괜찮아 보이네요. 이것은 얼마입니까?

여 정가는 50달러입니다만, 지금 10퍼센트 할인됩니다.

남 좋습니다. 그것을 사겠습니다. 그리고 이 인형은 얼마입니까? 아주 귀엽네요.

여 그것은 10달러입니다만, 지갑을 구입하시면 5달러에 구입하실 수 있습니다.

남 알겠습니다. 그러면 그 지갑과 그 인형을 구입하겠습니다. 여기 제 신용 카드입니다.

여 감사합니다.

Solution

정가 50달러짜리 지갑을 10퍼센트 할인받으면 45달러이고, 지갑을 구입하면 10달러짜리 인형을 5달러에 구입할 수 있으므로 남자가 지불할 금액은 ③ '50달러'이다.

Words

purse 지갑 recommend 추천하다 list price 정가

07 정답 ⑤

Script

M Hi, Alice! Where are you going?

W Hi, Jake. I'm going to the Sun Star Mall.

M What a coincidence! I'm going there, too. Let's go together.

W Okay. Are you planning on buying something?

M No. I'll meet my roommate, Jack, and see a movie with him.

W Then you have to go to the cinema on the top floor, don't you?

M Right. What about you? What are you going there for?

W To get my notebook computer. I left it there by mistake when I bought a T-shirt in the afternoon.

M You should have been more careful. By the way, how was your job interview yesterday?

W Not bad. I think I might get the job.

M I really hope so.

남 안녕, Alice! 어디 가니?

여 안녕, Jake. Sun Star Mall에 가는 길이야.

남 우연의 일치구나! 나도 거기에 가는데. 같이 가자.

여 그래. 뭔가 살 계획이니?

남 아니. 내 룸메이트 Jack을 만나서 같이 영화를 볼 거야.

여 그러면 제일 위층에 있는 극장에 가야겠구나, 그렇지 않니?

남 맞아. 넌 어때? Sun Star Mall에 왜 가니?

여 노트북 컴퓨터를 찾으러. 오후에 티셔츠를 샀을 때 실수로 그곳에 노트북 컴퓨터를 두고 왔거든.

남 좀 더 조심했어야지. 그런데, 어제 본 구직 면접은 어땠어?

여 나쁘지 않았어. 일자리를 얻을 것 같아.

남 정말로 그러길 바라.

Solution

Sun Star Mall에 왜 가느냐는 남자의 물음에 여자는 실수로 두고 온 노트북 컴퓨터를 찾으러 간다고 말했으므로 정답은 ⑤이다.

Words

What a coincidence! 우연의 일치구나! by mistake 실수로
job interview 구직 면접

08 정답 ⑤

Script

[Cellphone rings.]

M Hi, Emily. What's up?

W I heard you got a driver's license. Congratulations!

M Thanks. You know how hard it is to get by without one.

W You're right. That's why I called you. Can you recommend a driving school?

M Sure. I went to Stars Driving School on Kingston Street. It isn't far from your house.

W What made you choose that school?

M It has kind instructors and new cars. And most of all, the classes are cheaper than other schools.

W How much are they?

M Four hundred dollars, including tax. Ah, there is one more thing.

W What is it?

M You get twenty dollars back if you pass the driving test on your first attempt.

[휴대전화가 울린다.]

남 안녕, Emily. 무슨 일이야?

여 너 운전면허 땄다는 소식 들었어. 축하해!

남 고마워. 운전면허 없이 그럭저럭 살기가 얼마나 힘든지 너도 알잖아.

여 맞아. 그래서 내가 네게 전화한 거야. 운전 학원 추천해 줄 수 있니?

남 물론이지. 나는 Kingston Street에 있는 Stars 운전 학원에 다녔어. 네 집에서 멀지 않아.

여 그 학원을 선택한 이유가 뭐야?

남 친절한 강사와 새 자동차들이 있어. 그리고 무엇보다도, 수업이 다른 학

원보다 더 저렴해.
여 얼마인데?
남 세금을 포함해서 400달러야. 아, 한 가지 더 있어.
여 그게 뭔데?
남 첫 응시에 운전 시험에 통과하면 20달러를 돌려받아.

위치, 강사, 수강료, 환불 제도는 언급되었으나 ⑤ '교육 시간'은 언급되지 않았다.

get by 그럭저럭 살아가다 instructor 강사 tax 세금 attempt 시도

09 정답 ③

W Now let me tell you about the 33rd Strawberry Spring Festival. The festival, which is held at Olympic Park, starts on March 5th and lasts for four days. One of the most popular festivals in San Diego, the festival attracts many visitors every year. Last year, about 30,000 people visited the festival and about 50,000 are expected to visit this year. Tickets for the festival cost $20 per person. A ticket holder can enjoy the various foods made from strawberries, such as strawberry cake and strawberry juice, free of charge. What's better, a strawberry picking event will be held every day during the festival. For more information, visit the festival website.

여 이제 제33회 딸기 봄 축제에 대해 말씀드리겠습니다. 올림픽 공원에서 열리는 이 축제는 3월 5일에 시작해서 4일 동안 계속됩니다. San Diego에서 가장 인기 있는 축제 중의 하나인 이 축제는 해마다 많은 방문객을 끌어 모으고 있습니다. 작년에는 약 3만 명이 이 축제를 방문했고, 올해에는 약 5만 명이 방문할 것으로 예상됩니다. 축제 입장료는 일인당 20달러입니다. 입장권 소지자는 딸기 케이크와 딸기 주스 같은 딸기로 만들어진 다양한 음식을 무료로 즐길 수 있습니다. 게다가, 딸기 따기 행사가 축제 동안 매일 열릴 것입니다. 더 많은 정보를 원하시면, 축제 웹사이트를 방문해 주십시오.

작년 축제의 방문객 수가 약 3만 명이었고, 올해에는 약 5만 명이 방문할 것으로 예상된다고 했으므로 ③이 담화의 내용과 일치하지 않는다.

be held 열리다 last 계속되다, 지속하다 attract 끌다, 끌어 모으다
ticket holder 입장권 소지자

10 정답 ②

M Look at this brochure, Monica. I'm going to reserve a hotel room for our honeymoon.
W Well, I want us to have a view overlooking the whole beach.
M So do I. How about this room?
W Well, I think $500 is too much per night. Our quality time together is what's important.
M I see. Then how about Internet access?

W Justin, we are supposed to be getting away from it all and having time for ourselves.
M I know what you mean. We won't have to spend as much money on our hotel room.
W No. And I won't bring many valuables, so there's no need for a safe.
M Okay. Then let me reserve this room.
W Thank you, Justin. I can't wait for our trip.

남 Monica, 이 안내 책자 좀 봐요. 우리 신혼여행에 묵을 호텔 방을 예약하려고 해요.
여 음, 난 우리가 전체 해변을 내려다보는 전망을 갖길 원해요.
남 나도 그래요. 이 방은 어때요?
여 음, 하룻밤에 500달러는 너무 많다고 생각해요. 우리가 함께하는 소중한 시간이 중요한 거잖아요.
남 알겠어요. 그럼 인터넷 접속은 어때요?
여 Justin, 우리는 모든 것을 떠나 잠시 쉬며 우리만을 위한 시간을 가져야 하잖아요.
남 무슨 말인지 알겠어요. 호텔 방에 그렇게 많은 돈을 쓸 필요가 없겠군요.
여 그럼요. 그리고 난 귀중품을 많이 가지고 가지도 않아서 금고도 필요 없어요.
남 좋아요. 그럼 이 방으로 예약을 할게요.
여 고마워요, Justin. 여행을 빨리 가고 싶어요.

두 사람은 신혼여행에서 묵을 호텔 방으로 우선 해변이 보여야 하고, 하룻밤에 500달러 이하이며, 인터넷과 금고는 필요 없다고 했으므로, 두 사람이 예약할 방은 ②이다.

brochure 안내 책자, 소책자 overlook ~을 내려다보다
quality time 소중한(가치 있는) 시간 access 접속
get away from it all 모든 것을 떠나 잠시 쉬다
valuables 귀중품 safe 금고

11 정답 ⑤

M What's your favorite pastime?
W Most of all, I love to practice Taekwondo in my free time.
M Interesting! I'd like to know why you enjoy it.
W It is helpful in training my body and spirit.

남 네가 가장 좋아하는 여가 활동은 무엇이니?
여 무엇보다도, 나는 여가 시간에 태권도 연습하는 것을 좋아해.
남 흥미롭구나! 네가 왜 그것을 좋아하는지 알고 싶어.
여 그것은 내 몸과 마음을 단련하는 데 도움이 돼.

여가 활동으로 태권도를 연습하는 여자에게 남자는 그것을 좋아하는 이유를 묻고 있으므로, 이에 대한 여자의 응답으로 가장 적절한 것은 ⑤ '그것은 내 몸과 마음을 단련하는 데 도움이 돼.'이다.

① 그건 내가 그것을 좋아하지 않기 때문이야.
② 나는 집 근처에 있는 체육관에 가.
③ 그렇게 말해 주다니 정말 고마워.
④ 좋은 생각이야. 함께 그것을 연습하자.

pastime 여가 활동, 심심풀이 most of all 무엇보다도

12 정답 ②

Script

W Hi, I'd like to buy some equipment for rock climbing. Do you have a helmet?

M Sorry, we don't have any rock climbing helmets in stock at the moment.

W I'm sorry to hear that. Then how about gloves?

M This way, please. Gloves for rock climbing are here.

여 안녕하세요. 암벽 등반용 장비를 좀 사고 싶은데요. 헬멧이 있나요?
남 미안하지만, 현재 암벽 등반용 헬멧은 재고가 없어요.
여 아쉽네요. 그러면 장갑은 어때요?
남 이리 오세요. 암벽 등반용 장갑은 이쪽에 있습니다.

Solution

암벽 등반용 장비를 사러 온 여자는 헬멧이 없다는 남자의 말에 장갑은 있는지 물었으므로, 이에 대한 남자의 응답으로 가장 적절한 것은 ② '이리 오세요. 암벽 등반용 장갑은 이쪽에 있습니다.'이다.

① 미안합니다. 하지만 이 장갑은 나에게 너무 커요.
③ 맞아요. 당신은 헬멧이나 장갑을 사기만 하면 돼요.
④ 괜찮아요. 이번 주 토요일에 암벽 등반을 하러 가요.
⑤ 내가 당신이라면, 흰색 장갑이 아니라 검은색 장갑을 살 거예요.

Words

equipment 장비 rock climbing 암벽 등반
in stock 재고의, 비축되어 at the moment 현재

13 정답 ⑤

Script

M Ms. Brown, I think I've finally found the perfect house for you.

W That's great news! Is it located near an elementary school?

M Yes, it's located only five minutes' walk from Lincoln Elementary School.

W How about the number of bedrooms? As I told you, I need at least three bedrooms.

M It has three bedrooms and two bathrooms.

W Oh, really? Very good.

M But there's even one more wonderful thing about the house.

W One more wonderful thing? What is it? I'm curious.

M The monthly rent is only $700.

W Great! No wonder you said you found the perfect house.

남 Brown 씨, 마침내 당신을 위한 완벽한 집을 찾은 것 같아요.
여 아주 좋은 뉴스군요! 그 집이 초등학교 근처에 위치해 있나요?
남 네, Lincoln 초등학교에서 걸어서 5분 거리에 위치해 있어요.
여 침실의 개수요? 말씀드렸다시피, 침실이 적어도 세 개는 있어야 해요.
남 이 집에는 침실 세 개와 욕실 두 개가 있습니다.
여 오, 정말이요? 아주 좋아요.
남 하지만 이 집에 관해 심지어 한 가지 더 멋진 점이 있어요.
여 한 가지 더 멋진 점이라고요? 그게 뭐죠? 궁금해요.
남 월 임대료가 불과 700달러예요.
여 굉장하네요! 당신이 완벽한 집을 찾았다고 말한 것이 당연해요.

Solution

남자가 여자에게 여자가 원하는 조건을 갖춘 완벽한 집을 찾았다고 하면서 이에 대해 자세하게 말하자 여자는 매우 좋아하고, 남자가 이 집의 멋진 점이 한 가지 더 있다고 하면서 월 임대료가 불과 700달러밖에 하지 않는다고 말했으므로, 이에 대한 여자의 응답으로 가장 적절한 것은 ⑤ '굉장하네요! 당신이 완벽한 집을 찾았다고 말한 것이 당연해요.'이다.

① 내가 당신이라면, 이 집을 빌리지 않을 거예요.
② 그래요. 나는 부동산 사무실에서 일하고 싶어요.
③ 좋아요. 당신의 집이 내 집보다 훨씬 더 좋아 보여요.
④ 걱정 마세요. 당신에게 월 임대료를 내기 위한 돈을 빌려줄게요.

Words

be located 위치하다 at least 적어도 curious 궁금한
monthly rent 월 임대료 no wonder ~하는 것도 당연하다

14 정답 ③

Script

W Good afternoon, sir. What can I do for you?

M Can I see the shirt in the shop window?

W You mean the pink shirt with a white collar?

M Yes, but I'd like one with a different color.

W No problem. This shirt comes in a variety of colors. We keep them on this shelf.

M Wow, impressive! There are so many colors.

W They are popular items. Take your time and pick what you like most.

M Well, I'd like to choose either the blue, gray, or light brown one. Can I try these on now?

W Of course. The fitting room is right over there.

M Thank you.

W Oh, wait a minute, sir! You can only take in one item at a time.

M Okay. Then I'll try on this shirt first.

여 안녕하세요, 손님. 무엇을 도와드릴까요?
남 진열장에 있는 셔츠를 볼 수 있을까요?
여 흰 칼라의 분홍색 셔츠 말씀입니까?
남 네, 하지만 저는 다른 색의 셔츠를 원합니다.
여 문제없습니다. 그 셔츠는 다양한 색상으로 나왔습니다. 그것들은 이 선반 위에 있습니다.
남 와, 인상적이에요! 아주 많은 색상이 있군요.
여 그것들은 인기 있는 품목들입니다. 천천히 보시고 가장 마음에 드시는 것을 고르세요.
남 음, 저는 파란색, 회색, 또는 밝은 갈색 셔츠 중에서 하나를 고르고 싶습니다. 지금 이것들을 입어 봐도 될까요?
여 물론이죠. 탈의실은 바로 저쪽에 있습니다.
남 감사합니다.
여 아, 잠깐만요, 손님! 한 번에 한 품목씩만 가지고 들어가실 수 있습니다.
남 알겠습니다. 그러면 이 셔츠를 먼저 입어 보겠습니다.

Solution

셔츠를 여러 벌 입어 보고 그 중에 하나를 구입하려는 남자에게 여자는 한 번에 한 품목씩만 탈의실에 가지고 들어갈 수 있다고 말하고 있으므로, 이에 대한 남자의 응답으로 가장 적절한 것은 ③ '알겠습니다. 그러면 이 셔츠를 먼저 입어 보겠습니다.'이다.

① 잘됐군요! 저는 분홍색 셔츠를 구입하겠습니다.

② 알겠습니다. 그 품목들을 계산하지 않겠습니다.
④ 죄송합니다만, 저는 환불받고 싶습니다.
⑤ 걱정 마세요. 그것을 당신에게 배달해 드릴 수 있습니다.

Words

take one's time 천천히 하다 fitting room 탈의실

15 정답 ⑤

Script

M David has to work late in his office today. It is seven o'clock in the evening and he feels hungry, so he goes to a nearby fast food restaurant to get something to eat. He buys a sandwich and a carton of milk and comes back to his office. But he soon realizes that he doesn't have his cellphone in his pocket. He remembers that he put it on the checkout counter while taking some money out of his wallet. He dials his cellphone and a clerk from the restaurant answers the phone. In this situation, what would David most likely say to the clerk?

David Can you hold onto my cellphone? I'll be there soon.

남 David는 오늘 사무실에서 늦게까지 근무해야 합니다. 시간은 저녁 7시이고, 그는 배가 고파서 먹을 것을 사기 위해 근처에 있는 패스트푸드 식당에 갑니다. 그는 샌드위치 하나와 우유 한 통을 사서 그의 사무실로 돌아옵니다. 하지만, 그는 주머니에 자신의 휴대전화가 없다는 것을 곧 깨닫습니다. 그는 지갑에서 돈을 꺼내는 동안 계산대 위에 그것을 두었던 것을 기억합니다. 그는 자신의 휴대전화로 전화를 걸고, 그 식당의 한 점원이 전화를 받습니다. 이런 상황에서, David는 그 점원에게 뭐라고 말할 것 같은가요?

David 제 휴대전화를 보관해 주시겠습니까? 거기로 곧 가겠습니다.

Solution

David가 패스트푸드 식당에 두고 온 자신의 휴대전화로 전화를 걸자 그 식당의 점원이 전화를 받은 상황이므로, 이러한 상황에서 David가 점원에게 할 말로 가장 적절한 것은 ⑤ '제 휴대전화를 보관해 주시겠습니까? 거기로 곧 가겠습니다.'이다.
① 실례합니다. 당신의 휴대전화를 사용할 수 있을까요?
② 자리를 얻으려면 얼마나 오래 기다려야 하나요?
③ 그 식당이 오늘 문을 닫는지 몰랐습니다.
④ 죄송합니다만, 전화를 잘못 거셨습니다.

Words

carton 상자, 곽 realize 깨닫다 checkout counter 계산대
wallet 지갑 dial 전화를 걸다 clerk 점원

16 정답 ④   17 정답 ⑤

Script

W As most of you know, many animals are used to test new medicines, paints, and even food. But do you also know that more than 33 animals die in laboratories each second worldwide? It's a real tragedy for many animals including mice, dogs, and cats. But, now I've got hopeful news for them, especially rabbits. They have been largely used in the cosmetics industry, but recently, the industry began to stop animal testing. This is a surprising change for the industry that tested nearly all its products on animals 20 years ago. Back in 1980s, eye irritation tests on rabbits were the subject of the protest against animal testing. Since then, many cosmetics companies have put considerable money and effort into finding alternatives to animal testing. As a result, the animal use in the industry has dropped quite dramatically.

여 여러분 대부분이 알고 있듯이, 많은 동물들이 신약, 페인트, 그리고 심지어 음식을 실험하는 데에 사용됩니다. 하지만 전 세계적으로 1초에 33마리 이상의 동물이 실험실에서 죽는다는 사실도 아십니까? 그것은 쥐, 개, 그리고 고양이를 포함한 많은 동물들에게는 대단한 비극입니다. 하지만 이제 그것들에게, 특히 토끼에게 희망적인 소식이 있습니다. 그것들은 화장품 업계에서 주로 사용되어 왔지만, 최근에 그 업계는 동물 실험을 중단하기 시작했습니다. 이는 20년 전만 해도 거의 모든 제품을 동물에게 실험했던 그 업계로서는 놀라운 변화입니다. 1980년대로 돌아가 보면, 토끼에 대한 눈의 염증 실험은 동물 실험을 반대하는 항의의 주제였습니다. 그때 이후로, 많은 화장품 회사들은 상당한 돈과 노력을 동물 실험의 대안을 찾는 데에 쏟아부었습니다. 그 결과, 그 업계의 동물 사용은 아주 급격히 감소했습니다.

Solution

16
1980년대에 동물 실험을 반대하는 항의 이후로 화장품 업계에서 많은 돈과 노력을 대안을 찾는 데 들여 동물 실험을 줄였다는 내용이다. 따라서 여자가 하는 말의 주제로 가장 적절한 것은 ④ '화장품 업계에서의 동물 실험의 감소'이다.
① 동물 실험을 위한 동물 선택 방법
② 동물 실험을 필요로 하는 화장품
③ 화장품에서의 동물 실험의 무익함
⑤ 많은 산업에서 동물 실험이 필요한 이유

17
쥐, 개, 고양이, 토끼는 언급되었지만, ⑤ '닭'은 언급되지 않았다.

Words

tragedy 비극 cosmetics 화장품 irritation 염증
subject 주제, 대상 protest 항의 considerable 상당한
alternative 대안 drop 감소하다 dramatically 급격히

01 ①	02 ⑤	03 ⑤	04 ⑤	05 ⑤
06 ②	07 ⑤	08 ③	09 ⑤	10 ⑤
11 ②	12 ②	13 ①	14 ⑤	15 ③
16 ④	17 ④			

01 정답 ①

Script

W People say the most important part of digital images is to show greener grass, a bluer sky, or a brighter sun than they see on earth. They may be right, but our approach is different. We pursue natural textures, natural lines, and natural colors. From capture to connection to output, our digital technology shows you the world as you see it. In addition, the size is just right and you can comfortably keep it in your pocket. Last but not least, you don't have to be an expert to operate this camera. You only have to press the green button and you can store all of your memories easily.

여 디지털 이미지의 가장 중요한 부분은 땅에서 관찰하는 것보다 더 푸른 잔디나 더 파란 하늘, 또는 더 밝은 태양을 보여 주는 것이라고 사람들은 말합니다. 그들이 옳을지도 모릅니다만 저희 접근법은 다릅니다. 저희는 자연스러운 질감, 자연스러운 선, 그리고 자연스러운 색깔을 추구합니다. 포착하는 순간부터 출력 연결을 하기까지, 저희의 디지털 기술은 여러분이 보는 그대로의 세상을 여러분에게 보여 줍니다. 게다가 크기는 딱 알맞아서 여러분은 그것을 주머니 안에 편안하게 넣을 수 있습니다. 마지막으로 덧붙일 중요한 말은, 여러분은 이 카메라를 조작하기 위해 전문가가 될 필요는 없습니다. 여러분은 녹색 버튼을 누르기만 하면 여러분의 모든 추억들을 쉽게 저장할 수 있습니다.

Solution

보이는 그대로의 세상을 보여 주는 자신들의 디지털 기술이라고 언급하는 것으로 보아 제품을 광고하고 있음을 추측할 수 있으며, 알맞은 크기에 조작이 간단한 카메라에 대해 언급했으므로 여자가 하는 말의 목적으로 가장 적절한 것은 ①이다.

Words

approach 접근법 pursue 추구하다 texture 질감
capture 포착; 포획 output 출력
last but not least 마지막으로 덧붙일 중요한 말은
operate 조작하다 store 저장하다

02 정답 ⑤

Script

M You look unhappy. What's the matter?
W I've been getting a lot of stress because of my studies.
M Well, how about laughing instead of making a face?
W Are you kidding? I don't feel like laughing at all.
M Just force yourself to laugh for one minute. According to a study, forced laughter helps improve your mood.

W Oh, really? I'm not sure it will work for me.
M In the study, most people reported feeling better after just 60 seconds of forced laughter.
W I don't understand how that would work.
M Our body releases hormones that make us happy because it doesn't know the laughter is fake.
W You mean just laughing can boost our mood?
M Yeah. It's worth trying.
W Okay. I'll give it a shot.

남 너 기분이 안 좋아 보이는구나. 무슨 일 있니?
여 학업 때문에 스트레스를 많이 받고 있어.
남 음, 얼굴을 찌푸리는 대신에 웃는 것은 어때?
여 농담하는 거야? 나는 전혀 웃고 싶은 기분이 아니야.
남 딱 1분 동안 억지로 웃도록 해 봐. 한 연구에 의하면 억지웃음이 기분을 좋게 하는 데 도움이 된대.
여 아, 정말? 그것이 내게도 효과가 있을지 모르겠어.
남 그 연구에서 대부분의 사람들이 단지 60초의 억지웃음 후에 기분이 나아졌다고 말했어.
여 그것이 어떻게 효과가 있는지 이해가 안 가.
남 우리 몸은 그 웃음이 가짜인지를 모르기 때문에 우리를 행복하게 하는 호르몬을 방출한대.
여 웃기만 해도 우리 기분이 좋아질 수 있다는 거니?
남 응. 그것은 해 볼 만한 가치가 있어.
여 좋아. 한번 해 볼게.

Solution

남자는 연구 결과를 토대로 억지웃음이 우리를 행복하게 하는 호르몬을 방출하여 기분을 나아지게 하는 데 도움이 된다고 여자에게 말하고 있으므로 남자의 의견으로 가장 적절한 것은 ⑤이다.

Words

make a face 얼굴을 찌푸리다 feel like -ing ~을 하고 싶다
force 억지로 ~시키다 improve 개선하다 mood 기분
release 방출하다 fake 가짜의 boost 증진하다, 돋우다
worth -ing ~할 가치가 있는 give it a shot 한번 해 보다

03 정답 ⑤

Script

M Good morning. How can I help you?
W Yes, I'd like to start an exercise program.
M Wonderful. Let me ask you a few questions first. Are you taking any medication?
W No, I'm not.
M Do you have any health conditions I should know about, such as shortness of breath or dizziness?
W No, I'm pretty healthy.
M Good. What is your goal in starting a fitness program? For example, are you trying to improve in a sport, such as tennis or golf?
W No, I'd just like to lose some weight. What kind of exercise do you recommend?
M You should do some aerobics. We have aerobics classes on Tuesdays and Fridays.
W Great. I'd like to get started as soon as possible.

남 안녕하세요. 무엇을 도와드릴까요?

여 네, 운동 프로그램을 시작하고 싶은데요.

남 좋습니다. 먼저 몇 가지 질문을 드리겠습니다. 복용하고 있는 약이 있습니까?

여 아니요, 없습니다.

남 숨가쁨이나 현기증 같은 제가 알고 있어야 할 건강상의 문제가 있습니까?

여 아니요, 꽤 건강한 편입니다.

남 좋습니다. 신체 단련 프로그램을 시작하시는 목표가 무엇입니까? 예를 들어, 테니스나 골프 같은 운동을 더 잘하려고 하시는 겁니까?

여 아니요, 그냥 체중을 좀 줄이고 싶어서요. 어떤 종류의 운동을 추천하시나요?

남 에어로빅을 좀 하셔야겠습니다. 매주 화요일과 금요일에 에어로빅 수업이 있습니다.

여 좋습니다. 저는 가능한 한 빨리 시작하고 싶습니다.

Solution

남자는 운동을 시작하려는 여자의 건강 상태와 동기에 대해 묻고 있으며 남자의 마지막 말 We have aerobics classes on Tuesdays and Fridays.로 보아 두 사람의 관계를 가장 잘 나타낸 것은 ⑤이다.

Words

medication 약, 약물 shortness of breath 숨가쁨
dizziness 현기증 fitness 신체 단련, 건강

04 정답 ⑤

Script

W Did you go to Michael's housewarming party?

M Yes. He moved to a new house with a large garden. I took a picture of the garden with my cellphone. Take a look.

W Wow! Michael has an outdoor table with a parasol.

M Yeah. We had lunch there.

W The big tree next to the table has many leaves. It goes well with the garden.

M What do you think about the swing that's hanging from the tree? Michael said he made it himself.

W It's great! And I like the pond in front of the tree.

M Me, too. There were many fish in the pond.

W The basketball hoop beside the swing is for his two sons, right?

M Yeah. They like to play basketball.

여 Michael의 집들이 파티에 갔니?

남 응. 그는 큰 정원이 있는 새집으로 이사했어. 내 휴대전화로 그 정원 사진을 찍었어. 한번 봐.

여 와! Michael은 파라솔이 있는 야외용 탁자가 있네.

남 응. 우리는 거기서 점심을 먹었어.

여 탁자 옆에 있는 커다란 나무는 잎이 무성하구나. 그것이 정원과 잘 어울려.

남 나무에 매달려 있는 그네는 어떻게 생각해? Michael이 자기가 직접 만들었다고 말했어.

여 훌륭한데! 그리고 나는 나무 앞의 연못이 마음에 들어.

남 나도 그래. 연못에 물고기가 많았어.

여 그네 옆의 농구 골대는 그의 두 아들을 위한 거구나, 그렇지?

남 응. 그들은 농구하는 것을 좋아해.

Solution

농구 골대가 그네 옆에 있다고 했지만 그림에서는 탁자 옆에 있으므로 대화

의 내용과 일치하지 않는 것은 ⑤이다.

Words

housewarming party 집들이 outdoor 야외의
go well with ~와 잘 어울리다 swing 그네 pond 연못
basketball hoop 농구 골대

05 정답 ⑤

Script

W Hi, David. Where are you going now?

M I'm going to a costume rental shop for the Halloween party.

W What costume do you have in mind this year?

M I'll borrow a vampire costume. What about you, Sharon?

W I'm going to be a witch. I've been working on making a witch costume.

M Wow! I didn't know you have talent for making clothes.

W I'm just trying. The problem is that I might not have enough time to make a witch's hat.

M Well, my little sister, Cindy, has a black one. If you want, I'll ask her if she'll lend it to you.

W Oh, thank you. A black hat will go well with my costume.

M She's not going to wear it because she wants to be a princess this time.

W That's good. I'm sure she'll make a beautiful princess.

여 안녕, David. 지금 어디 가니?

남 핼러윈 파티를 위해 의상 대여점에 가고 있어.

여 올해는 어떤 의상을 생각하고 있니?

남 나는 흡혈귀 복장을 빌릴 거야. 너는 어때, Sharon?

여 나는 마녀가 될 거야. 나는 마녀 의상을 만드는 작업을 해 오고 있어.

남 와! 네가 옷을 만드는 데 재능이 있는 줄 몰랐어.

여 그저 노력하고 있을 뿐이야. 문제는 마녀 모자를 만들 충분한 시간이 없을지도 모른다는 거야.

남 음, 내 여동생 Cindy가 검은색 모자를 가지고 있어. 네가 원하면 네게 그것을 빌려줄 것인지 그녀에게 물어볼게.

여 아, 고마워. 검은색 모자는 내 의상과 잘 어울릴 거야.

남 내 여동생은 이번에 공주가 되고 싶어 하기 때문에 그것을 쓰지 않을 거야.

여 잘됐네. 그녀가 아름다운 공주가 될 거라고 확신해.

Solution

핼러윈 파티를 위해 마녀 의상을 만들고 있는 여자가 마녀 모자를 만들 시간이 없다고 하자, 남자가 자신의 여동생이 검은색 모자를 가지고 있다고 하며 빌려줄 것인지 물어보겠다고 했으므로, 정답은 ⑤이다.

Words

costume 복장, 의상 rental 대여
have ~ in mind ~을 생각하다, ~을 염두에 두다
vampire 흡혈귀 witch 마녀 talent 재능 lend 빌려주다
go well with ~와 잘 어울리다

06 정답 ②

Script

M Good afternoon. How can I help you?

W I'd like to buy some roses for my husband. Tomorrow is

his 30th birthday.

M How many roses would you like to buy?

W I'd like 30 roses. What kinds of roses do you have?

M Take a look at our selection. We have red ones and yellow ones.

W How much are they?

M Red roses cost one dollar each, and yellow ones are one and a half dollars each.

W Then I'll take ten red ones and twenty yellow ones.

M Ten red ones and twenty yellow ones, right?

W Yes. Can you make a bouquet with a ribbon wrapped around it?

M Sure, but it'll cost an extra three dollars. Will that be okay?

W Yes, that's fine.

남 안녕하세요. 어떻게 도와드릴까요?

여 제 남편을 위해 장미를 좀 사려고 합니다. 내일은 제 남편의 서른 번째 생일입니다.

남 장미 몇 송이를 사시겠습니까?

여 장미 30송이를 사겠습니다. 어떤 종류의 장미가 있나요?

남 선택하실 수 있는 꽃들을 한번 보세요. 빨간색과 노란색 장미가 있습니다.

여 그것들은 얼마인가요?

남 빨간 장미는 한 송이에 1달러이고, 노란 장미는 한 송이에 1달러 50센트입니다.

여 그러면 빨간 장미 10송이와 노란 장미 20송이를 사겠습니다.

남 빨간 장미 10송이와 노란 장미 20송이 맞습니까?

여 네. 리본으로 꽃다발을 싸서 만들어 주실 수 있나요?

남 물론이죠. 그런데 추가로 3달러가 더 들 겁니다. 괜찮겠습니까?

여 네, 괜찮습니다.

Solution

한 송이에 1달러인 빨간 장미 10송이와 한 송이에 1달러 50센트인 노란 장미 20송이를 사기로 했고 꽃다발을 만드는 데 3달러의 비용이 추가되므로 여자가 지불할 금액은 ② '43달러'이다.

Words

selection 선택 가능한 것들(의 집합) bouquet 꽃다발 extra 추가의

07 정답 ⑤

Script

W Hi, Peter. Where are you going?

M Hi, Alice. I'm going to the school library. I have a part-time job there.

W What time do you finish work today?

M Four o'clock. Why?

W Listen, you know there is a soccer match between the LA Tigers and the Seattle Giants this evening, don't you?

M Yeah. The LA Tigers is my favorite soccer team.

W I have two free tickets for the match. Why don't you come to the game with me this evening?

M Oh, I'd love to go with you, but I can't. Today is my roommate's birthday, and there's no way I can miss his party.

W That's too bad. Well, I'll have to ask another friend.

여 안녕, Peter. 어디 가니?

남 안녕, Alice. 학교 도서관에 가. 거기서 시간제 일을 하거든.

여 오늘은 일이 몇 시에 끝나니?

남 4시. 왜?

여 있잖아, 오늘 저녁 LA Tigers와 Seattle Giants 사이에 축구 경기가 있는 거 알고 있지, 그렇지 않니?

남 알고 있어. LA Tigers는 내가 가장 좋아하는 축구팀이야.

여 나한테 그 경기 무료입장권이 두 장 있어. 오늘 저녁 나와 그 경기 보러 갈래?

남 오, 너와 가고 싶은데, 갈 수 없어. 오늘 내 룸메이트 생일이어서, 그의 생일 파티에 빠질 수 없어.

여 아쉽다. 음, 다른 친구에게 물어봐야겠어.

Solution

오늘 저녁 축구 경기 무료입장권을 가지고 있다고 하면서 함께 축구 경기를 보러 갈 것을 제안하는 여자에게 남자는 룸메이트 생일이어서 생일 파티에 참석해야 한다고 했으므로 정답은 ⑤이다.

Words

match 경기, 시합 free ticket 무료입장권 miss 빠지다, 놓치다

08 정답 ③

Script

W What are you reading, James?

M I'm reading an article from our school newspaper.

W What is it about?

M It's about a survey that asked students to rate the services provided by our school.

W Interesting! Tell me about the results.

M Eighty-five percent said our school gym was excellent and seventy-nine percent said we had good teachers.

W Was there anything the students were not satisfied with?

M Yes. Only twenty percent thought our school lunches were good, and twenty-five percent said the restrooms were not clean enough.

W I agree. I also think the restrooms are too dirty.

M Nevertheless, seventy-two percent of the students said they were proud of our school.

W That may be because our school has a longer history than other schools.

여 무엇을 읽고 있니, James?

남 우리 학교 신문 기사를 하나 읽고 있어.

여 무엇에 관한 것인데?

남 우리 학교에서 제공하는 서비스에 대해 학생들에게 평가하도록 한 설문 조사에 관한 거야.

여 재미있겠는데! 그 결과에 대해 내게 말해 줘.

남 85퍼센트가 학교 체육관이 훌륭하다고 말했고, 79퍼센트는 선생님이 훌륭하다고 말했어.

여 학생들이 만족하지 않은 것이 있었니?

남 응. 단지 20퍼센트가 교내 점심 식사가 좋다고 생각했고, 25퍼센트는 화장실이 충분히 깨끗하지 않다고 말했어.

여 나도 동의해. 나도 화장실이 너무 더럽다고 생각해.

남 그럼에도 불구하고, 72퍼센트의 학생들이 우리 학교가 자랑스럽다고 말했어.

여 그건 아마도 우리 학교가 다른 학교들보다 더 긴 역사를 가지고 있기 때문인지도 몰라.

09 정답 ⑤

Script

M Hi, everyone. Before you go back to your rooms, I'd like to tell you about the Wild Flower Tour the day after tomorrow. Tour participants will leave the hotel at 8 a.m. for Mount Green. There, they will experience beautiful nature and see about 100 beautiful wild flowers. The tour cost is $80 per person, and children under the age of 13 can join for half the price. Lunch and a bottle of water are included in the cost. If you want to join this tour, please sign up for it at the tour office next to the hotel front desk by 8 p.m. this evening. That's all. I hope all of you have a relaxing evening.

남 안녕하세요, 여러분. 객실로 돌아가시기 전에 모레 있을 Wild Flower Tour에 대해 말씀드리고 싶습니다. 투어 참가자는 오전 8시에 호텔을 출발해서 Green 산으로 갈 것입니다. 그곳에서 투어 참가자는 아름다운 자연을 경험하면서 약 100종의 아름다운 야생화를 볼 것입니다. 투어 비용은 1인당 80달러이고, 13세 미만의 어린이는 절반의 가격으로 참가할 수 있습니다. 점심 식사와 물 한 병이 비용에 포함되어 있습니다. 이 투어에 참가하기를 원하시면 오늘 저녁 8시까지 호텔 프런트 데스크 옆에 있는 여행사에서 참가 신청을 하십시오. 이상입니다. 모두들 편안한 저녁을 보내시기를 바랍니다.

Solution

남자는 호텔 프런트 데스크 옆에 있는 여행사에서 Wild Flower Tour 참가 신청을 하라고 했으므로 ⑤가 담화의 내용과 일치하지 않는다.

Words

wild flower 야생화 the day after tomorrow 모레
participant 참가자 be included in ~에 포함되다
sign up for ~을 신청하다, 등록하다 relaxing 편안한, 느긋한

10 정답 ⑤

Script

M There are lots of movies to choose from, honey.

W Anything is okay for me except for the horror movie.

M What do you think of seeing an action movie then?

W You mean *Rush in Time*? It's nine forty now.

M Oh, I didn't know that. Then how about watching a science fiction movie?

W It must be exciting, but our children won't be able to wait for over an hour to see the movie. What do you think of *Rainbow on the Hill*?

M Our daughter can't see the movie because she is only eight years old.

W I see. Then we have only one choice left.

M Okay. I think our children will also like it.

W Good. Let's watch that one.

남 선택할 영화들이 많네요, 여보.

여 난 공포 영화만 빼고는 어떤 것이든 좋아요.

남 그러면 액션 영화를 보는 건 어떻게 생각해요?

여 'Rush in Time' 말하는 거예요? 지금 9시 40분이에요.

남 아, 그걸 몰랐네요. 그러면 공상 과학 영화를 보는 건 어때요?

여 신나겠지만, 우리 아이들이 그 영화를 보려고 한 시간 넘게 기다릴 수는 없을 거예요. 'Rainbow on the Hill'은 어때요?

남 우리 딸은 겨우 8살이기 때문에 그 영화를 볼 수 없어요.

여 알겠어요. 그러면 딱 하나의 선택만 남았네요.

남 좋아요. 우리 아이들도 그것을 좋아할 거라고 생각해요.

여 좋아요. 그걸 봐요.

Solution

여자가 공포 영화는 싫다고 했고, 현재 시각이 9시 40분이므로 액션 영화는 볼 수 없다. 아이들이 영화를 보기 위해 한 시간 넘게 기다릴 수 없다고 했고, 딸이 8살이라고 했으므로, 두 사람이 볼 영화는 ⑤이다.

Words

except for ~을 제외하고 horror 공포 choice 선택

11 정답 ②

Script

W Tomorrow is our big math test. Are you ready for it?

M Yes! I'm sure I'll get a good grade this time.

W Are you? What makes you think so?

M I've studied really hard for the test.

여 내일이 중요한 수학 시험이야. 수학 시험 준비가 되어 있니?

남 그래! 난 이번에 좋은 점수를 받을 것이라고 확신해.

여 정말? 왜 그렇게 생각하니?

남 그 시험을 위해서 정말로 열심히 공부했거든.

Solution

수학 시험에서 좋은 점수를 받을 것이라고 확신하는 남자에게 여자가 그렇게 생각하는 이유를 물었으므로 이에 대한 남자의 응답으로 가장 적절한 것은 ② '그 시험을 위해서 정말로 열심히 공부했거든.'이다.

① 수학은 언제나 우리에게는 너무 어려워.
③ 너는 열심히 수학을 공부했어야 했어.
④ 나는 수학에 더 이상 관심이 없어.
⑤ 그것은 네가 수학을 잘하기 때문이었어.

Words

be ready for ~할 준비가 되다 grade 성적

12 정답 ②

Script

M What's up, Rachel? You look irritated.

W Well, I was pulled over by the police on my way to work.

M How come? What did you do?

W I went through a red light.

남 무슨 일이야, Rachel? 언짢아 보이는구나.

여 음, 출근길에 경찰이 내 차를 세웠어.

남 왜? 무슨 일을 했는데?
여 <u>나는 빨간 불을 지나쳤어.</u>

Solution

출근길에 경찰이 자신의 차를 세웠다는 여자에게 남자는 왜 그랬는지 이유를 묻고 있으므로 이에 대한 여자의 응답으로 가장 적절한 것은 ② '나는 빨간 불을 지나쳤어.'이다.

① 나는 어젯밤 늦게까지 일했어.
③ 나는 교통 혼잡에 갇혔어.
④ 나는 인터넷으로 표를 예약했어.
⑤ 나는 버스 대신에 지하철을 탔어.

Words

irritated 언짢은, 짜증 난 pull over (차를) 세우다
How come? 왜?, 어째서? go through ~을 통과하다, 지나다

13 정답 ①

Script

M Good afternoon. How can I help you?
W Can I exchange this brown shirt for a larger one?
M Sure. Do you have the receipt?
W Here it is. I bought this shirt for my son last Sunday, but it's a little bit tight on him.
M I see. Let me check for a moment. [Pause] Uh-oh, I'm afraid the larger ones in the same color are sold out.
W Would you check if any of your other locations have the size I need?
M Wait a second. [Typing Sound] Well, the shop in Kingstown has the size.
W Kingstown? That's too far.
M If it's okay with you, we can have the item delivered. It'll take three days.
W That would be great.
M <u>Okay. Just let me know your address.</u>

남 안녕하세요. 어떻게 도와드릴까요?
여 이 갈색 셔츠를 더 큰 것으로 교환할 수 있을까요?
남 물론이죠. 영수증을 가지고 계신가요?
여 여기 있습니다. 지난 일요일에 제 아들에게 주려고 이 셔츠를 구입했습니다만, 그 아이에게 약간 끼어서요.
남 알겠습니다. 잠깐 확인해 보겠습니다. [잠시 후] 아, 죄송합니다만 같은 색깔의 더 큰 셔츠가 품절되었습니다.
여 제가 필요한 사이즈가 다른 지점에 있는지 확인해 주시겠어요?
남 잠깐만 기다리세요. [자판 두드리는 소리] 음, Kingstown에 있는 상점에 그 사이즈가 있습니다.
여 Kingstown이요? 거긴 너무 멀어요.
남 괜찮으시다면 그 상품을 배달해 드릴 수 있습니다. 3일 걸릴 것입니다.
여 그게 좋겠네요.
남 <u>알겠습니다. 손님의 주소만 알려주세요.</u>

Solution

여자는 구입한 옷을 더 큰 사이즈로 교환하려 하는데, 그 상품이 품절되어 거리가 멀리 떨어져 있는 지점에 가야 하는 상황이 되자 남자는 그 상품을 배달해 주겠다고 제안하고 있으며, 여자는 이에 동의하고 있다. 따라서 이에 대한 남자의 응답으로 가장 적절한 것은 ① '알겠습니다. 손님의 주소만 알려주세요.'이다.

② 훌륭한 선택입니다! 당신의 아드님이 그 회색 셔츠를 좋아할 거예요.

③ 현금으로 지불하시겠습니까, 아니면 신용카드로 지불하시겠습니까?
④ 파란색 셔츠를 구입하셨으므로 회색 셔츠를 공짜로 드립니다.
⑤ 내일 다시 오시면 그것을 준비해 놓겠습니다.

Words

receipt 영수증 tight 꼭 끼는 location 지점, 위치

14 정답 ⑤

Script

W Okay, I've finished examining your eyes.
M Are my eyes infected?
W Yes, they are. But fortunately it's not that serious. Have you been to any crowded places recently?
M Well, I went to the movies a few days ago.
W You might have got infected there.
M Maybe, but I washed my hands before and after the show.
W I'll give you these eye drops. Put one or two drops into your eyes every two hours for the next three days.
M Okay. Is there anything else I should do?
W Well, it's important for you not to infect anyone else.
M Of course. What should I do then?
W <u>Please avoid sharing items with anyone until you're cured.</u>

여 좋아요, 눈 검사를 다 했습니다.
남 제가 눈병에 감염되었나요?
여 네, 그렇습니다. 하지만 다행히도 그렇게 심각하지는 않아요. 최근에 사람들로 붐비는 장소에 간 적이 있나요?
남 그게, 며칠 전에 극장에 갔다 왔습니다.
여 거기서 감염됐을지도 모르겠네요.
남 아마도요, 하지만 영화를 보기 전과 후에 손을 씻었어요.
여 이 안약을 드리겠습니다. 앞으로 3일 동안 두 시간마다 한두 방울씩 눈에 넣으세요.
남 알겠습니다. 제가 해야 할 또 다른 일이 있나요?
여 음, 환자분께서 다른 사람을 감염시키지 않는 것이 중요합니다.
남 물론이죠. 그럼 제가 무엇을 해야 하나요?
여 <u>다 나을 때까지 누구와도 물건을 공유하는 것을 피해 주세요.</u>

Solution

눈병에 걸린 남자에게 여자는 안약을 주면서 다른 사람을 감염시키지 않는 것이 중요하다고 말한다. 이에 남자가 무엇을 해야 할지 물었으므로, 여자의 응답으로 가장 적절한 것은 ⑤ '다 나을 때까지 누구와도 물건을 공유하는 것을 피해 주세요.'이다.

① 당신이 날마다 더 나아질 것이라고 확신해요.
② 감염된 것은 당신 잘못이 아니에요.
③ 그래서 제가 당신에게 그 영화를 가서 보라고 말한 것이었어요.
④ 당신은 지금 바로 안과에 가야 해요.

Words

examine 검사하다 infect 감염시키다 fortunately 다행히도
serious 심각한 recently 최근에
might have p.p. ~했을지도 모른다 eye drops 안약

15 정답 ③

Script

M Jenny gets homework to write a report on desert and

climates at geography class. Jenny goes to a study café with her classmate Robert and they write the report on their own notebook computers. About two hours later, they finish writing it and save the report files on their USB sticks. Now they only have to print out the files. But Jenny remembers that her printer is out of order. She wants Robert to print out her report file. In this situation, what would Jenny most likely say to Robert?

Jenny Can you print out my report file?

남 Jenny는 지리 시간에 사막과 기후에 관한 보고서를 쓰는 숙제를 받습니다. Jenny는 같은 반 친구인 Robert와 스터디 카페에 가서 자신들의 노트북 컴퓨터로 보고서를 씁니다. 약 두 시간이 흐른 후에, 그들은 보고서를 다 쓰고 보고서 파일을 USB 스틱에 저장합니다. 이제 그들은 파일을 출력하기만 하면 됩니다. 하지만 Jenny는 현재 자신의 프린터가 고장 난 것이 떠오릅니다. 그녀는 Robert가 자신의 보고서 파일을 출력해 주기를 원합니다. 이런 상황에서 Jenny는 Robert에게 뭐라고 말할 것 같은가요?

Jenny 내 보고서 파일을 출력해 줄 수 있니?

노트북 컴퓨터로 지리 보고서 작성을 끝낸 여자가 보고서 파일을 출력해야 하지만 자신의 프린터가 고장 난 것을 깨닫고, Robert가 자신의 보고서 파일을 출력해 주길 원하고 있으므로, 이러한 상황에서 Jenny가 Robert에게 할 말로 가장 적절한 것은 ③ '내 보고서 파일을 출력해 줄 수 있니?'이다.

① 네가 보고서 쓰는 것을 도와줄게.
② 너는 내 프린터를 언제든지 쓸 수 있어.
④ 프린터를 수리하는 게 어때?
⑤ 네 보고서를 언제 제출할 거니?

desert 사막 climate 기후 geography 지리, 지리학
USB stick USB 메모리 저장 장치 only have to ~하기만 하면 되다
print out 출력하다 be out of order 고장 나다

16 정답 ④   17 정답 ④

W Good morning, students. Yesterday, you learned about various plants living in the desert, remember? Let me start today's lesson by asking you a question. What animal do you think can go without water for a long time? Many of you probably guessed camels, and you are right. They can last for several weeks without water. But do you know there are other animals that can last longer without water than camels? They are giraffes, Fennec foxes and kangaroo rats. A giraffe eats about 75 pounds of leaves and fruit a day. Thanks to the high water content in them, giraffes can go several months without drinking water. Kangaroo rats are even more amazing. They can go up to 3 to 5 years without taking a single sip of water. They mainly eat seeds and they get enough water from them.

여 안녕하세요, 학생 여러분. 어제 여러분은 사막에 사는 다양한 식물에 대해 배웠습니다, 기억나죠? 여러분에게 질문 하나를 함으로써 오늘의 수업을 시작하겠습니다. 여러분은 어떤 동물이 오랫동안 물 없이 지낼 수 있다고 생각합니까? 많은 분들이 아마 낙타라고 추측할 것이고, 맞습니

다. 그것은 물 없이 몇 주 동안 견딜 수 있습니다. 하지만 낙타보다 물 없이 더 오래 견딜 수 있는 다른 동물이 있다는 것을 여러분은 알고 있나요? 그것들은 기린, 사막 여우와 캥거루쥐입니다. 기린 한 마리는 하루에 약 75파운드의 잎과 열매를 먹습니다. 그 안에 들어 있는 높은 수분 함유량 덕분에 기린은 물을 마시지 않고 몇 개월을 지낼 수 있습니다. 캥거루쥐는 훨씬 더 놀랍습니다. 그것은 물 한 모금도 먹지 않고 3년에서 5년까지 지낼 수 있습니다. 그것은 주로 씨를 먹으며, 그것들로부터 충분한 수분을 얻습니다.

16

물 없이 오래 견딜 수 있는 동물로 낙타, 기린, 사막 여우, 캥거루쥐를 소개하고 있으므로 여자가 하는 말의 주제로 가장 적절한 것은 ④ '오랫동안 물 없이 지낼 수 있는 동물들'이다.

① 긴 수명을 가진 사막 동물들
② 낙타가 물 없이 지낼 수 있는 이유
③ 사막 동물들의 수분 섭취량 측정하기
⑤ 기린이 수분 함유량이 높은 잎을 발견하는 방법

17

낙타, 기린, 사막 여우, 캥거루쥐는 언급되었지만, ④ '도마뱀'은 언급되지 않았다.

go without ~ 없이 지내다 thanks to ~ 덕분에 content 함유량
amazing 놀라운 up to ~까지 sip 한 모금 seed 씨, 종자

01 ②	02 ①	03 ②	04 ⑤	05 ①
06 ⑤	07 ③	08 ②	09 ②	10 ④
11 ③	12 ③	13 ②	14 ③	15 ⑤
16 ②	17 ①			

01 정답 ②

Script

W Good afternoon, everybody. Thank you for visiting Tailor's Mart. For better customer service, we've decided to start listening to your suggestions. Please let us know if you have any problems or inconveniences at any of our facilities including the sales sections, the lost and found centers, and the playrooms for children. You can text us at 1400–777 or post a message on our website at www.TailorsMart.com starting this Sunday. We'll select the best 10 customers and give a 100-dollar gift certificate to each of them at the end of this month. We're looking forward to your active participation. Thank you.

여 안녕하세요, 여러분. Tailor's Mart를 방문해 주셔서 감사합니다. 더 나은 고객 서비스를 위해서 저희는 여러분의 제안을 듣기 시작하기로 결정했습니다. 판매 코너, 분실물 보관소, 그리고 어린이 놀이방을 포함한 저희 시설 어디서든지 문제점이나 불편함을 겪으셨다면 저희에게 알려 주십시오. 이번 주 일요일부터 시작하여 1400–777로 문자 메시지를 보내주시거나, 저희 웹사이트 www.TailorsMart.com에 메시지를 올리실 수 있습니다. 저희는 이달 말에 최우수 고객 10명을 선정하여 각각 100달러의 상품권을 드릴 것입니다. 저희는 여러분의 적극적인 참여를 고대하고 있습니다. 감사합니다.

Solution

여자는 Tailor's Mart를 이용하는 고객들에게 매장 이용 시 문제점과, 불편 사항에 대해 알려 줄 것을 요청하며, 신고 방법과 상품에 관해 설명하고 있으므로 여자가 하는 말의 목적으로 가장 적절한 것은 ②이다.

Words

lost and found center 분실물 보관소   playroom 놀이방
gift certificate 상품권

02 정답 ①

Script

W I'm thirsty, Jeff.
M I have some water. Here you go.
W Thanks. *[Pause]* Wow! It tastes really good. Where did you buy this water?
M I didn't buy it. It's tap water. I'm just reusing the bottle.
W You drink tap water? Is it safe?
M Our tap water is strictly monitored, so it's clean enough to drink.
W Really? But I still don't feel like drinking tap water.
M Recently, I read a newspaper article that our city received an award for its water purification system.
W Did it? I didn't know that.
M The quality of our tap water is just as good as bottled water. You can count on it.
W I see. Thanks for letting me know.

여 나 목이 말라, Jeff.
남 내게 물이 좀 있어. 여기 있어.
여 고마워. *[잠시 후]* 와! 맛이 정말 좋네. 이 물 어디서 샀니?
남 산 것이 아니야. 그건 수돗물이야. 나는 단지 병을 재사용하고 있어.
여 수돗물을 마신다고? 그게 안전하니?
남 우리 수돗물은 엄격하게 관리되어서 마실 정도로 충분히 깨끗해.
여 정말? 하지만 여전히 수돗물을 마시고 싶은 기분이 들지는 않아.
남 최근에, 나는 우리 도시가 물 정화 시스템으로 상을 받았다는 신문 기사를 읽었어.
여 그랬니? 그건 몰랐어.
남 우리 수돗물의 품질은 생수만큼 좋아. 믿어도 돼.
여 알겠어. 내게 알려 줘서 고마워.

Solution

목이 말라 물을 달라는 여자에게 남자가 수돗물을 건네주며 수돗물 품질의 우수함을 이야기하고 있으므로 남자의 의견으로 가장 적절한 것은 ①이다.

Words

tap water 수돗물   reuse 재사용하다
purification 정화   quality 품질   bottled water 생수
count on ~을 믿다, ~에 의지하다

03 정답 ②

Script

W Good afternoon, Mr. Anderson. I really enjoyed your comedy show yesterday.
M Thank you for saying so.
W How do you feel today?
M I'm afraid I don't feel any better.
W Are you still busy then?
M Yes. I feel like I spend all day in front of cameras trying to make people laugh.
W I like your acting, but I want you to have enough rest.
M I try to, but it's easier said than done.
W I understand. Then, did you regularly take the medicine I prescribed?
M I couldn't. My busy schedule doesn't allow me to take it every eight hours.
W Oh, no! You should keep in mind that this is not a minor disease.
M I see.

여 안녕하세요, Anderson 씨. 어제 당신의 코미디 쇼 아주 잘 보았습니다.
남 그렇게 말씀해 주셔서 감사합니다.
여 오늘은 기분이 어떠세요?
남 더 나아진 것 같지 않아요.
여 그러면 아직도 바쁘세요?
남 네. 하루 종일 카메라 앞에서 사람들을 웃기려고 노력하면서 보내는 것 같아요.

여 저는 당신의 연기를 좋아합니다만, 충분한 휴식을 취하시면 좋겠습니다.
남 노력은 합니다만, 말처럼 쉽지 않네요.
여 이해합니다. 그러면 제가 처방해 드린 약은 규칙적으로 드셨어요?
남 그럴 수 없었어요. 바쁜 일정 때문에 8시간마다 먹는 게 불가능해요.
여 아, 안 돼요! 이것이 사소한 질병이 아니라는 것을 명심해야 합니다.
남 알겠습니다.

여자는 남자가 출연한 코미디 쇼를 잘 보았다고 말하며 몸 상태를 묻고, 남자는 자신의 상태를 말하며 여자가 처방해 준 약을 규칙적으로 먹지 못했다고 말하고 있으므로, 두 사람의 관계를 가장 잘 나타낸 것은 ②이다.

acting 연기 regularly 규칙적으로 keep in mind 명심하다, 유의하다
minor 사소한

04 정답 ⑤

[Cellphone rings.]

W Hey, Fred. Where are you now?
M I'm afraid I'll be a little bit late. Did you finish setting up the stage?
W Yeah. We're almost done. We put the banner on the stage wall.
M You mean the banner that says "10TH ANNIVERSARY"?
W Yeah. We placed it in the middle of the wall. And we made a rainbow out of colorful balloons.
M Good! Where did you put the chairs for the violinists?
W We put two chairs at the left side of the stage.
M Great! Where did you put the piano?
W We put it on the right side of the stage.
M How about microphones?
W We set up two microphones in the center of the stage.
M Thanks, Rachel.

[휴대전화가 울린다.]
여 이봐, Fred. 지금 어디야?
남 약간 늦을 것 같아. 무대 설치 끝마쳤어?
여 응. 거의 끝마쳤어. 현수막을 무대 벽에 붙였어.
남 '10번째 기념일'이라고 쓰인 현수막 말하는 거야?
여 응. 벽 중앙에 그것을 붙였어. 그리고 여러 가지 색깔의 풍선으로 무지개를 만들었어.
남 좋아! 바이올린 연주자들을 위한 의자는 어디에 두었어?
여 무대 왼쪽에 의자 두 개를 놓았어.
남 훌륭해! 피아노는 어디다 두었어?
여 무대 오른쪽에 놓았어.
남 마이크는 어때?
여 무대 가운데에 마이크 두 개를 설치했어.
남 고마워, Rachel.

무대의 중앙에 마이크를 설치했다고 했지만 그림에서는 무대 오른쪽의 피아노 옆에 마이크가 있으므로 대화의 내용과 일치하지 않는 것은 ⑤이다.

set up 설치하다 stage 무대 banner 현수막 microphone 마이크

05 정답 ①

W Excuse me, Professor Smith. Can I come in?
M Sure, Jane. What brings you here?
W Well, I'm here to ask you a favor.
M Tell me about it, Jane.
W I want to apply for the internship program at the City Museum.
M Good for you! It will give you precious experience. So, what do you want me to do?
W In order to apply, a résumé, a transcript, and a letter of recommendation are required.
M I see. Do you have everything ready?
W I only have to prepare a recommendation letter. Would you mind writing it for me by next Friday?
M Of course not. I'll have it ready no later than next Monday.
W Thank you, sir.

여 실례합니다. Smith 교수님. 들어가도 될까요?
남 물론이지, Jane. 여기는 무슨 일로 왔니?
여 음, 부탁을 드리려고 여기 왔어요.
남 말해 보렴, Jane.
여 시립 박물관의 인턴 연수 프로그램에 지원을 하고 싶어요.
남 잘됐구나! 그것은 네게 소중한 경험을 줄 거야. 그러면 내가 무엇을 해 주었으면 좋겠니?
여 지원하기 위해서는 이력서, 성적 증명서, 그리고 추천서가 필요해요.
남 알겠다. 모든 것이 준비되었니?
여 추천서를 준비하기만 하면 돼요. 다음 주 금요일까지 저를 위해 그것을 써 주실 수 있으실까요?
남 물론이지. 다음 주 월요일까지는 준비해 놓을게.
여 감사합니다, 교수님.

시립 박물관의 인턴 연수 프로그램에 지원하려는 여자가 교수에게 찾아가 추천서를 부탁하고 있으므로, 정답은 ①이다.

internship 인턴 연수 transcript 성적 증명서
a letter of recommendation 추천서 no later than ~까지는

06 정답 ⑤

M Hi, I'd like to buy dog shampoo.
W This way, please. How about this one made by Happy Pet? It's very effective for removing dirt and bacteria.
M How much is it?
W It's $20, and it's one of the most popular dog shampoos at the moment.
M I think the bottle is a bit small. Do you have a bigger one?
W Sure! This big one is $10 more expensive, but there's twice as much shampoo as in the small one.
M Okay. I'll buy this big one. I'd also like to buy dog toothpaste.
W I see. This one is also made by Happy Pet, and it's only $7 a tube.

M Then can I buy two dog toothpaste?
W So one big dog shampoo and two tubes of toothpaste, right?
M Yes. Here is my credit card.

남 안녕하세요, 애견 샴푸를 사고 싶은데요.
여 이쪽으로 오십시오. Happy Pet에서 나온 이것은 어떠세요? 때와 세균을 제거하는 데 매우 효과적입니다.
남 얼마죠?
여 20달러이고, 현재 가장 인기 있는 애견 샴푸 중의 하나입니다.
남 병이 약간 작은 것 같아요. 더 큰 것이 있나요?
여 그럼요! 이 큰 샴푸는 10달러가 더 비싸지만, 작은 것보다 용량이 두 배 더 많습니다.
남 좋아요. 이 큰 샴푸를 살게요. 애견 치약도 사고 싶어요.
여 알겠습니다. 이 치약 또한 Happy Pet에서 나온 것인데요, 한 통에 가격이 7달러밖에 하지 않습니다.
남 그러면 애견 치약은 두 통 살 수 있을까요?
여 그럼 큰 애견 샴푸 한 병과 치약 두 통, 맞죠?
남 네. 신용카드 여기 있습니다.

Solution

남자는 20달러인 작은 애견 샴푸보다 10달러 더 비싼 큰 애견 샴푸 한 병과 7달러인 애견 치약을 두 통 구입했으므로, 남자가 지불할 금액은 ⑤ '44달러'이다.

Words

effective 효과적인 remove 제거하다, 없애다 dirt 때, 먼지
bacteria 세균 toothpaste 치약 tube 통, 관

07 정답 ③

Script

M Sera, I heard that you quit working at the amusement park.
W Yeah, that's right. Working there was too demanding. I'm looking for a new part-time job.
M Then why don't you apply to the Taste of Sun Restaurant?
W The Taste of Sun Restaurant? It's located on Lincoln Street, isn't it?
M Right. It's close to your house. What's better, their hourly wage is $10.
W Ten dollars? That'd be great! What are the working hours?
M From 5 p.m. to 8 p.m. including weekends.
W Including weekends? Well, I guess I won't apply there.
M Why not? Don't your parents allow you to work part-time on weekends?
W They do, but I have to study on weekends.
M Well, then you'll have to find another one.

남 Sera, 네가 놀이공원에서 일하는 것을 그만두었다고 들었어.
여 그래, 맞아. 그곳에서 일하는 것이 너무 힘들었거든. 나는 새로운 시간제 일자리를 찾고 있어.
남 그러면 Taste of Sun 식당에 지원하는 게 어때?
여 Taste of Sun 식당? 그곳은 Lincoln 거리에 위치한 식당이지, 그렇지 않니?
남 맞아. 네 집에서 가까워. 게다가 시간당 임금이 10달러야.
여 10달러? 대단하다! 근무 시간은 어떻게 되니?
남 주말을 포함해서 오후 5시부터 8시까지야.

여 주말을 포함한다고? 음, 나는 그 식당에 지원하지 않을 것 같아.
남 왜? 부모님께서 주말에 시간제 일을 하는 것을 허락하지 않으시니?
여 부모님은 허락하셔. 하지만 난 주말에는 공부를 해야 하거든.
남 음, 그렇다면 너는 다른 일자리를 찾아야겠구나.

Solution

Taste of Sun 식당의 근무 시간이 주말을 포함해서 오후 5시부터 8시까지라는 남자의 말을 들은 여자는 거기에 지원하지 않을 것 같다고 하면서 주말에는 공부를 해야 한다고 말했으므로, 정답은 ③이다.

Words

quit 그만두다 amusement park 놀이공원 demanding 힘이 드는
apply to ~에 지원하다 what's better 게다가, 더욱이
hourly wage 시간당 임금 including ~을 포함하여 allow 허락하다

08 정답 ②

Script

[Telephone rings.]
W Hello?
M Hello. I'm calling about the apartment you're advertising.
W Okay. What would you like to know?
M Well, first I want to know how many bedrooms there are.
W There are three bedrooms.
M And is the apartment furnished?
W Yes. It has a refrigerator, an air conditioner, a new sofa and a set of reclining chairs in the living room.
M What about curtains?
W There are curtains on all the windows. They've just been dry cleaned.
M I see. And does the apartment have a nice view?
W Sure. It's on the 10th floor, so it has a fantastic view.
M I see. Would it be possible for me to stop by around 7 p.m. this evening?
W No problem.

[전화벨이 울린다.]
여 여보세요?
남 안녕하세요. 광고하고 계시는 아파트에 대해서 전화드립니다.
여 좋습니다. 무엇을 알고 싶으세요?
남 음, 우선 침실이 몇 개인지 알고 싶습니다.
여 침실은 세 개 있습니다.
남 그리고 아파트에 가구가 비치되어 있습니까?
여 네. 냉장고, 에어컨, 새 소파, 그리고 거실에 안락의자 세트가 있습니다.
남 커튼은 어떤가요?
여 모든 창문에 커튼이 있습니다. 이제 막 드라이클리닝 했습니다.
남 알겠습니다. 그리고 아파트는 경관이 멋집니까?
여 물론이죠. 10층에 있어서 경관이 환상적입니다.
남 알겠습니다. 제가 오늘 저녁 7시쯤에 들러도 될까요?
여 그럼요.

Solution

침실 개수, 가구 비치 여부, 커튼 유무 여부, 층수는 언급되었지만, ② '건축 연도'는 언급되지 않았다.

Words

advertise 광고하다 furnished 가구가 비치된 refrigerator 냉장고
reclining chair 안락의자 fantastic 환상적인

09 정답 ②

Script

M Hi, students. Let me tell you about our Water Rocket Competition. The school science club will hold a Water Rocket Competition on the first day of the school festival. The competition is open to first and second graders only. Applications will be made online on the science club website, and the application period is from this Monday until the end of this month. The first prize winner will be given a brand-new tablet PC along with a medal. I hope many of you will participate in this contest.

남 안녕하세요, 학생 여러분. 여러분에게 물 로켓 대회에 대해 말씀드리겠습니다. 교내 과학 동아리는 교내 축제 첫날에 물 로켓 대회를 개최할 예정입니다. 이 대회는 1학년과 2학년 학생들만 참가할 수 있습니다. 참가 신청은 과학 동아리 웹사이트에서 온라인으로 이루어질 것이고, 참가 신청 기간은 이번 주 월요일부터 이번 달 말일까지입니다. 1등 수상자에게는 메달과 함께 새 태블릿 PC가 주어질 것입니다. 많은 여러분들이 이 대회에 참여하기를 바랍니다.

Solution

1학년과 2학년 학생들만 대회에 참가할 수 있다고 했으므로, 담화의 내용과 일치하지 않는 것은 ②이다.

Words

brand-new 새것의 participate in ~에 참가하다

10 정답 ④

Script

W What are you doing on the computer, honey?

M I'm searching for a toy to give to Mary.

W Why don't you buy her a pretty doll?

M Girls don't have to play with dolls all the time.

W Oh, you're right. Then how about buying a baby drum for her?

M Mary is just 8 months old. I think we have to buy an appropriate toy for her age. What do you think of this color block?

W That looks nice. Which material do you think is okay for her?

M I think wood is safer than plastic. You know how she puts everything around her into her mouth.

W Yeah, I know. Well, this is made of wood and appropriate for her age.

M Great. I'll buy it for her.

여 컴퓨터로 뭐 하고 있어요, 여보?

남 Mary에게 줄 장난감을 검색하고 있어요.

여 예쁜 인형을 사 주지 그래요?

남 여자아이라고 항상 인형을 가지고 놀 필요는 없어요.

여 아, 당신 말이 맞아요. 그러면 아기 드럼을 사 주는 건 어때요?

남 Mary는 이제 8개월이에요. 나이에 맞는 장난감을 사야 할 것 같아요. 이 색깔 블록은 어떻게 생각해요?

여 괜찮아 보여요. 어떤 재료가 아기에게 좋을 것 같아요?

남 제 생각엔 나무가 플라스틱보다 더 안전한 것 같아요. 어떻게 아기가 근

처에 있는 것은 뭐든지 입 안으로 가져가는지 당신도 알잖아요.

여 네, 알아요. 음, 이건 나무로 만들어져 있고, 나이에도 적절하네요.

남 좋아요. 사 줄게요.

Solution

남자는 인형 구입에 대해 부정적이며, 8개월인 아기의 나이에 맞는 나무 재질의 색깔 블록을 구입하기로 결정했으므로, 남자가 구입할 장난감은 ④이다.

Words

appropriate 적당한, 적절한 material 재료, 원료

11 정답 ③

Script

W Why don't we go to lunch? It's already 12 o'clock.

M Why not? Is there anything in particular you want to eat for lunch?

W How about seafood spaghetti? I know a good spaghetti restaurant behind our office.

M Do you? Okay, let's go there for lunch.

여 점심 먹으러 갈래요? 벌써 12시예요.

남 좋죠! 점심으로 먹고 싶은 특별한 음식이 있나요?

여 해산물 스파게티 어때요? 우리 사무실 뒤에 좋은 스파게티 식당을 알고 있어요.

남 그래요? 좋아요, 그곳으로 점심 먹으러 가요.

Solution

점심으로 먹고 싶은 음식이 있는지 묻는 남자에게 여자는 해산물 스파게티를 제안하면서 사무실 뒤에 좋은 스파게티 식당이 있다고 말했으므로, 이에 대한 남자의 응답으로 가장 적절한 것은 ③ '그래요? 좋아요, 그곳으로 점심 먹으러 가요.'이다.

① 물론이죠! 그 식당에서 일할 거예요.

② 미안해요. 하지만 나는 이미 점심을 먹었어요.

④ 정말요? 당신이 만든 스파게티는 언제나 맛이 있어요.

⑤ 좋아요. 당신을 위해서 내가 해산물 스파게티를 만들어 줄게요.

Words

in particular 특별한 seafood 해산물

12 정답 ③

Script

M You always look lively and energetic, Mrs. Brown.

W Thank you for saying so, Mr. Anderson.

M I really envy you. Can you tell me the secret?

W Sure. I practice yoga every morning.

남 당신은 항상 활발하고 활기가 넘쳐 보여요, Brown 씨.

여 그렇게 말해 줘서 고마워요, Anderson 씨.

남 저는 당신이 정말 부러워요. 제게 그 비결을 말해 줄 수 있나요?

여 물론이죠, 저는 매일 아침 요가를 해요.

Solution

항상 활발하고 활기가 넘쳐 보이는 여자에게 남자가 그 비결을 알려 달라고 요청하고 있으므로, 이에 대한 여자의 응답으로 가장 적절한 것은 ③ '물론이죠. 저는 매일 아침 요가를 해요.'이다.

① 네. 저는 그것을 혼자서 했어요.

② 아니에요, 괜찮습니다. 저는 오늘 기분이 좋지 않아요.

④ 정말 미안합니다. 제시간에 맞춰 올 수 없었어요.
⑤ 정말요? 저도 라이브 음악을 좀 즐기고 싶어요.

Words

lively 활발한, 기운찬 energetic 활기가 넘치는 envy 부러워하다

13 정답 ②

Script

M Hi, Stella!
W Hi, David. How are you?
M Just existing. By the way, you look very happy now.
W Do I? Actually, I got a text message from ACE Company that I passed the written interview test.
M Really? Congratulations! When is the interview going to be held?
W Next Friday.
M And if you pass the interview, you'll be hired by ACE Company, right?
W Yes. Oh, I'm already quite nervous.
M Don't worry. With your ability and experience, you'll do great at the interview.
W Thank you. Well, I have to start preparing for the interview right away.
M You should. I really hope you get the job.

- -

남 안녕, Stella!
여 안녕, David. 잘 지내지?
남 겨우겨우 사는 거지. 그런데, 너 지금 매우 행복해 보여.
여 내가? 사실, ACE 회사로부터 내가 서면 인터뷰에 통과했다는 문자 메시지를 받았어.
남 정말? 축하해! 면접은 언제 실시될 예정이야?
여 다음 주 금요일이야.
남 그리고 그 면접을 통과하면, 너는 ACE 회사에 취직하는 거야, 그렇지?
여 그래. 오, 벌써 상당히 긴장이 돼.
남 걱정 마. 네 능력과 경험이면, 너는 면접을 잘할 거야.
여 고마워. 음, 지금 당장 면접 준비를 시작해야겠어.
남 그래야지. 네가 그 일자리를 얻기를 정말로 바라.

Solution

ACE 회사의 서면 인터뷰를 통과한 여자는 다음 주 금요일에 있는 면접을 잘하면 그 회사에 취직할 수 있다고 하면서 지금 당장 면접 준비를 시작하겠다고 말했으므로, 이에 대한 남자의 응답으로 가장 적절한 것은 ② '그래야지. 네가 그 일자리를 얻기를 정말로 바라.'이다.

① 아니. 그 면접은 그렇게 어렵지 않아.
③ 걱정 마. 너를 회사까지 차로 태워 줄게.
④ ACE 회사? 너는 거기서 일하길 원하니?
⑤ 그러면 내가 면접 준비하는 것을 도와줄래?

Words

Just existing. 겨우겨우 사는 거지. be hired 채용되다, 고용되다
prepare for ～을 준비하다

14 정답 ③

Script

M Hey, Anna. Let's get in the car and start our trip.

W Wait a minute, Henry! Did you check the oil?
M No, I didn't.
W What about the tire pressure?
M Well, I didn't check that, either. Why do you ask?
W You have to check every inch of the car before you drive a long distance.
M Don't worry. My car is as good as new. It's only two years old.
W I think we should get the car checked thoroughly before we set out.
M Come on, honey. We don't have enough time to do that. If we don't leave now, we may get caught in a traffic jam.
W But you should know safety is more important.
M It sounds like you don't trust me. I'm an experienced driver.
W I know, but it's better to be safe than sorry.

- -

남 이봐요, Anna. 이제 차에 타고 여행을 시작합시다.
여 잠깐만요, Henry! 엔진오일은 점검했나요?
남 아니, 안 했어요.
여 타이어 압력은요?
남 음, 그것도 점검하지 않았어요. 왜 묻는 거예요?
여 장거리 운전을 하기 전에는 차의 모든 구석구석을 점검해야 해요.
남 걱정 말아요. 내 차는 새것이나 다름없어요. 이제 2년밖에 안 된 걸요.
여 우리가 출발하기 전에 차를 철저하게 점검해야 한다고 생각해요.
남 그러지 말아요, 여보. 그렇게 할 시간이 충분하지 않아요. 지금 떠나지 않으면 교통 체증에 걸릴지도 몰라요.
여 하지만 안전이 더 중요하다는 것을 당신은 알아야 해요.
남 당신이 나를 믿지 않는 것처럼 들리는군요. 나는 숙련된 운전자라고요.
여 나도 알아요, 하지만 나중에 후회하는 것보다 안전한 게 더 나아요.

Solution

장거리 운전을 하기 전에 차를 철저하게 점검해야 한다는 여자의 말에 남자는 그럴 필요가 없으며 자신은 숙련된 운전자라고 말하고 있다. 이에 대한 여자의 응답으로 가장 적절한 것은 ③ '나도 알아요, 하지만 나중에 후회하는 것보다 안전한 게 더 나아요.'이다.

① 미안해요. 나는 운전하는 법을 몰라요.
② 나도 그래요. 나는 체크무늬를 더 좋아해요.
④ 나는 그렇게 생각하지 않아요. 당신이 비싸게 산 것 같네요.
⑤ 좋은 생각이에요. 그것이 어떻게 작동되는지 배우고 싶어요.

Words

get in ～에 타다 thoroughly 철저하게 set out 출발하다
leave 떠나다 get caught in a traffic jam 교통 체증에 걸리다
trust 믿다, 신뢰하다 experienced 숙련된, 노련한

15 정답 ⑤

Script

W Charlie flies to New York on a business trip for two days because he has a couple of important meetings. On the day of his arrival, he participates in a meeting. The meeting ends late at night, and he stays at a nearby hotel. The next morning, he gets up early and checks out. While he is on his way to the next meeting, however, he realizes that he left his wristwatch in the hotel room. Fortunately, he has enough time to get it back. He goes back to the desk clerk, and she asks how she can help him. In this situation, what would Charlie most likely say to the desk clerk?

Charlie I'm afraid I left my wristwatch in the room.

여 Charlie는 두서너 개의 중요한 회의가 있기 때문에 비행기를 타고 New York으로 이틀간 출장을 갑니다. 도착한 날, 그는 회의에 참석합니다. 그 회의는 밤늦게 끝나고, 그는 근처의 호텔에 머뭅니다. 다음 날 아침, 그는 일찍 일어나서 체크아웃을 합니다. 하지만 그는 다음 회의 장소로 가는 도중에, 자신의 손목시계를 호텔 방에 두고 온 것을 깨닫습니다. 다행히 그는 그것을 가지러 갈 충분한 시간이 있습니다. 그는 접수 담당자에게 돌아가고, 그녀는 어떻게 그를 도와줄 수 있는지 묻습니다. 이런 상황에서, Charlie는 접수 담당자에게 뭐라고 말할 것 같은가요?

Charlie 제가 방에 제 손목시계를 두고 온 것 같습니다.

체크아웃한 호텔 방에 두고 온 손목시계를 다시 찾으러 온 상황이므로, 이런 상황에서 Charlie가 호텔의 접수 담당자에게 할 말로 가장 적절한 것은 ⑤ '제가 방에 제 손목시계를 두고 온 것 같습니다.'이다.

① 제 방의 열쇠를 잃어버렸습니다.
② 하룻밤 더 묵고 싶습니다.
③ 내일 아침 모닝콜이 필요합니다.
④ 전 오늘밤 여기서 중요한 회의가 있습니다.

business trip 출장 a couple of 두서너 개의, 몇 개의
wristwatch 손목시계

---

16 정답 ②   **17** 정답 ①

M Good afternoon, everyone. What comes to your mind when you think of money? Bills or coins? In fact, many objects have been used as money throughout history. In the early days of America, tobacco was used as money, but so many people grew tobacco that it became worthless as a means of exchange. Roman soldiers once received part of their pay in salt, which is the origin of our word *salary*, or payment for one's work. Early Egyptians used grains of wheat and corn as money, while the native people on the island of Fiji used whale's teeth. Perhaps the most common object used as money was the seashell. Seashells were used in many parts of Africa, and American Indians had been using them as money before Columbus came to the continent.

남 안녕하세요, 여러분. 여러분은 돈을 생각하면 마음속에 무엇이 떠오릅니까? 지폐입니까, 또는 동전입니까? 사실, 역사를 통틀어 많은 사물들이 화폐로 사용되어 왔습니다. 미국의 초창기 시대에는 담배가 화폐로 사용되었지만, 아주 많은 사람들이 담배를 경작하면서 그것은 교환의 수단으로서의 가치를 잃게 되었습니다. 한때 로마의 군인들은 급여의 일부분을 소금으로 받았는데, 이는 직업에 대한 보수를 뜻하는 salary라는 단어의 기원입니다. 초기 이집트 사람들은 밀과 옥수수 낟알을 화폐로 사용했으며, 한편 피지 섬의 원주민들은 고래의 이빨을 사용했습니다. 아마도 화폐로 가장 흔하게 사용된 물건은 조개껍데기였을 것입니다. 조개껍데기는 아프리카의 많은 지역에서 사용되었고, 미국 인디언들은 Columbus가 그 대륙에 도착하기 전에 그것을 화폐로 사용하고 있었습니다.

16
역사적으로 돈의 역할을 했던 다양한 사물을 소개하고 있으므로, 남자가 하는 말의 주제로 가장 적절한 것은 ② '돈의 다양한 형태'이다.

① 돈의 새로운 사용법
③ 부의 불공평한 분배
④ 돈이 사회에 미치는 영향
⑤ 세계 경제의 진화

17
담배, 소금, 옥수수, 조개껍데기는 언급되었지만, ① '쌀'은 언급되지 않았다.

object 물건, 사물 worthless 가치 없는 means 수단
exchange 교환 salary 급여 grain (곡식의) 낟알, 곡물
continent 대륙

01 ④	02 ⑤	03 ④	04 ⑤	05 ④
06 ⑤	07 ①	08 ⑤	09 ④	10 ⑤
11 ⑤	12 ②	13 ⑤	14 ③	15 ②
16 ③	17 ③			

01 정답 ④

Script

W Attention, please. A disaster can happen anywhere and at any moment. That's why it is very important to know how to respond in disaster situations. As part of our office safety program, an emergency evacuation drill will be conducted in our company building on June 21st at 2 p.m. When the fire alarm sounds, all the workers will have to leave the building and move promptly to the outdoor parking lot. You must not use the elevators. The entire exercise will not take more than 30 minutes. We're sorry to cause any inconveniences, but the safety is most important. Thank you.

여 주목해 주십시오. 재난은 어느 곳에서든지 그리고 언제든지 일어날 수 있습니다. 그렇기에 재난 상황에서 대응하는 방법을 아는 것은 매우 중요합니다. 사무실 안전 계획 프로그램의 일환으로 비상 대피 훈련이 우리 회사 건물에서 6월 21일 오후 2시에 실시될 것입니다. 화재경보가 울리면 모든 직원들은 건물을 떠나 야외 주차장으로 신속히 이동해야 할 것입니다. 승강기를 이용해서는 안 됩니다. 전체 훈련은 30분이 넘지 않을 것입니다. 불편을 끼쳐 드려 죄송합니다만, 안전이 가장 중요합니다. 감사합니다.

Solution

비상 대피 훈련이 실시됨을 언급한 후, 구체적인 훈련 일자와 내용을 설명하고 있으므로 여자가 하는 말의 목적으로 가장 적절한 것은 ④이다.

Words

disaster 재난 emergency 비상 evacuation 대피 drill 훈련
conduct 실시하다 promptly 신속하게 inconvenience 불편

02 정답 ⑤

Script

M What are you looking at on the Internet, honey?
W I'm looking at some art lessons for our children.
M Are you going to sign Lucy up for one of them?
W Yeah. She's interested in fine art these days.
M Good. I heard children can develop their creativity through art.
W Right. This website says it helps children develop basic skills like reasoning, making decisions, and solving problems.
M One of my friends said his son showed less negative behavior after taking art lessons.
W I also heard that learning fine art can increase a child's

attention span.
M You mean it is also helpful for schoolwork?
W Yeah. According to a study, students who participated in art lessons got higher test scores in other subjects.

남 인터넷에서 무엇을 보고 있어요, 여보?
여 우리 아이들을 위한 미술 수업들을 좀 살펴보고 있어요.
남 Lucy를 그것들 중의 하나에 등록시킬 건가요?
여 네. 그 아이가 요즘 미술에 관심이 있어요.
남 좋아요. 미술을 통해서 아이들이 창의력을 계발할 수 있다고 들었어요.
여 맞아요. 이 웹사이트에서는 아이들이 추론하고, 의사 결정하고, 문제 해결을 하는 것과 같은 기본적인 기술을 계발하는 것에 그것이 도움이 된다고 해요.
남 내 친구 중의 한 명은 그의 아들이 미술 수업을 수강한 후에 부정적인 행동을 덜 보인다고 말했어요.
여 나도 미술을 배우는 것이 아이의 주의 집중 시간을 늘려 줄 수 있다고 들었어요.
남 학업에도 도움이 된다는 말인가요?
여 그럼요. 한 연구에 의하면 미술 수업에 참여한 학생들이 다른 과목에서 더 높은 시험 점수를 받았대요.

Solution

아이들을 위한 미술 수업을 살펴보며 미술을 통해 아이들이 창의력을 계발할 수 있고 주의 집중 시간을 늘릴 수 있으며 미술 수업에 참여한 학생들이 다른 과목에서 더 높은 점수를 받았다고 말하고 있으므로, 두 사람이 하는 말의 주제로 가장 적절한 것은 ⑤이다.

Words

sign up for ~을 등록하다 creativity 창의력 reasoning 추론
negative 부정적인 attention span 주의 집중 시간
schoolwork 학업

03 정답 ④

Script

M Hello. Could you introduce yourself?
W Sure. My name is Helen, and I'm from San Francisco.
M It's nice to talk to you, Helen. What do you do for a living?
W I'm a web designer.
M Good. What would you like to request?
W "My Heart Will Go On" by Celine Dion.
M Okay. Who do you want to dedicate the song to?
W My friend, Eric Baker. He is in the hospital. He was injured in an accident.
M Oh, I hope he'll get better soon. I bet you have something to tell him.
W Yeah. I want to tell him that my heart will go on forever.
M Wow, that's the name of the song you requested. I'll play the song for you. Thanks for calling.

남 안녕하세요. 자신을 소개해 주시겠어요?
여 네. 제 이름은 Helen이고, 저는 샌프란시스코에서 왔어요.
남 이야기하게 되어 반가워요, Helen. 무슨 일을 하세요?
여 저는 웹 디자이너예요.
남 좋습니다. 무엇을 신청하고 싶으세요?
여 Celine Dion이 부른 'My Heart Will Go On'이요.
남 좋습니다. 누구에게 이 노래를 바치고 싶으세요?
여 제 친구 Eric Baker요. 그는 병원에 입원해 있어요. 사고로 부상을 입

었거든요.

남 아, 빨리 쾌유하시길 빕니다. 그에게 할 말이 있을 것 같은데요.

여 네. 내 마음은 영원히 계속될 거라고 그에게 말해 주고 싶어요.

남 와, 바로 신청하신 노래 제목이군요. 노래 들려 드리겠습니다. 전화 주셔서 감사합니다.

Solution

남자가 여자의 이름과 직업을 물은 후 무엇을 신청할지 묻자, 여자는 듣고 싶은 노래를 신청하고 사연을 말하고 있으므로 두 사람의 관계를 가장 잘 나타낸 것은 ④이다.

Words

request 요청하다 dedicate 바치다, 헌정하다
get better (병·상황 등이) 좋아지다, 호전되다

04 정답 ⑤

Script

M What are you doing on the computer, honey?

W I'm getting some ideas about bathroom decorations from a website.

M Let me see. *[Pause]* Well, I like the three round lights.

W What do you think of the frog showerhead?

M I think our children will like it. And the toothbrush holder beside the mirror is practical, isn't it?

W Yeah. It saves space because it is attached to the wall.

M The shelf in the left corner is also a good idea.

W Right. We can put shampoo bottles on it. What do you think of the toilet seat?

M It doesn't have a pattern on it. Why don't we buy one with flowers?

W That sounds good.

남 컴퓨터로 무엇을 하고 있어요, 여보?

여 웹사이트에서 욕실 장식에 관한 아이디어를 좀 얻고 있어요.

남 어디 봐요. *[잠시 후]* 음, 세 개의 둥근 조명이 마음에 들어요.

여 개구리 샤워꼭지는 어떻게 생각해요?

남 우리 아이들이 그것을 좋아할 거라고 생각해요. 그리고 거울 옆의 칫솔 보관대는 실용적이군요, 그렇지 않나요?

여 네. 벽에 부착되기 때문에 공간이 절약되지요.

남 왼쪽 구석에 있는 선반 또한 좋은 아이디어네요.

여 맞아요. 그 위에 샴푸 병을 놓을 수 있어요. 변기 좌석은 어떻게 생각해요?

남 그 위에 아무런 무늬가 없네요. 우리는 꽃무늬가 있는 것을 사는 게 어떨까요?

여 좋은 생각이에요.

Solution

변기 좌석에 대한 의견을 묻는 여자에게 남자는 아무런 무늬가 없다고 했지만, 그림에서는 무늬가 있으므로 대화의 내용과 일치하지 않는 것은 ⑤이다.

Words

decoration 장식 showerhead 샤워꼭지 practical 실용적인
save 절약하다 attach 부착하다

05 정답 ④

Script

[Cellphone rings.]

W Hey, Jake. Where are you now?

M I'm on my way. I'll be there in fifteen minutes.

W Oh, no! We've got only thirty minutes before the presentation.

M That's why I called you. Can you set up the projector in the conference room?

W I already did. What about the presentation files? Don't you need to print them out?

M I'll take care of it as soon as I get there.

W Ah, there's one more thing! How about the microphones?

M Don't worry. I asked David to set them up.

W Good. Is there anything else I can help you with?

M Well, if you've got time, go to the conference room and help David, please.

W No problem.

- -

[휴대전화가 울린다.]

여 이봐, Jake. 지금 어디예요?

남 가고 있어요. 15분 후에 거기에 도착할 거예요.

여 아, 안 돼요! 발표까지 30분밖에 남지 않았어요.

남 그래서 제가 당신에게 전화한 거예요. 회의실에 프로젝터를 설치해 줄 수 있어요?

여 제가 이미 했어요. 발표 파일은요? 그것들을 출력할 필요는 없나요?

남 거기 도착하자마자 제가 처리할게요.

여 아, 한 가지가 더 있어요! 마이크는 어떤가요?

남 걱정하지 말아요. 그것들을 설치해 달라고 David에게 부탁했어요.

여 잘했어요. 제가 당신을 도와줄 수 있는 다른 것이 있을까요?

남 음, 시간이 있으면 회의실에 가서 David를 도와주세요.

여 문제없어요.

Solution

발표를 30분 남겨 둔 두 사람이 발표 준비를 위한 일들을 점검하는 대화로, 남자가 15분 후에 도착하자마자 자신이 발표 파일 자료를 출력하겠다고 했으므로 정답은 ④이다.

Words

presentation 발표 set up 설치하다 conference 회의

06 정답 ⑤

Script

M Cookies! Homemade cookies are on sale now!

W Excuse me. I'd like to buy some cookies for my son's birthday.

M Great! We have several kinds of cookies. Take a good look before you make a choice.

W He likes chocolate chip cookies and almond cookies.

M Those are many children's favorites, too. Chocolate chip cookies are one dollar and almond cookies are two dollars each.

W I'll take five chocolate chip cookies and four almond cookies, please.

M Five chocolate chip cookies and four almond cookies, right?

W Yes. And can you wrap them?

M No problem, ma'am. But it'll cost an extra three dollars.

W Okay. I'll take them wrapped, please.

M Thank you. Wait a minute, please.

남 쿠키요! 집에서 만든 쿠키가 지금 할인 판매 중입니다!
여 실례합니다. 제 아들 생일을 위한 쿠키를 좀 사고 싶은데요.
남 좋지요! 몇 가지 종류의 쿠키가 있습니다. 선택하시기 전에 잘 보세요.
여 그 애는 초콜릿 칩 쿠키와 아몬드 쿠키를 좋아해요.
남 그건 많은 아이들도 좋아하는 거지요. 초콜릿 칩 쿠키는 개당 1달러이고, 아몬드 쿠키는 개당 2달러입니다.
여 초콜릿 칩 쿠키 다섯 개와 아몬드 쿠키 네 개 주세요.
남 초콜릿 칩 쿠키 다섯 개와 아몬드 쿠키 네 개요, 맞습니까?
여 네. 그리고 그것들을 포장해 주실래요?
남 그렇게 하죠, 손님. 하지만 포장은 추가로 3달러가 더 들 겁니다.
여 좋습니다. 그것들을 포장해 주세요.
남 감사합니다. 잠깐만 기다려 주세요.

Solution

여자는 1달러짜리 초콜릿 칩 쿠키 5개와 2달러짜리 아몬드 쿠키 4 개를 구입하고, 포장비로 3달러를 지불했으므로 여자가 지불할 금액은 ⑤ '16달러' 이다.

Words

homemade 집에서 만든 extra 추가의, 별도의

07 정답 ①

Script

[Telephone rings.]
W This is Teddy's Toy Library. How can I help you?
M Hi. I checked out some toys for my son yesterday, but I have a problem with one of them.
W May I have your name, please?
M It's John Hamilton.
W Let me see. *[Typing Sound]* You checked out a toy car and a set of blocks, right?
M Yeah, but I'm afraid one wheel is missing from the car.
W You mean you lost it?
M I'm afraid so. My son must have put it somewhere. I'm wondering what I should do about that.
W You only have to pay the cost of the part when you return the toys.
M I see. The toys are due next Tuesday, right?
W That's right.

[전화벨이 울린다.]
여 Teddy의 장난감 도서관입니다. 어떻게 도와드릴까요?
남 안녕하세요. 어제 제 아들에게 줄 장난감을 좀 빌렸습니다만, 그것들 중 하나에 문제가 있습니다.
여 성함이 어떻게 되세요?
남 저는 John Hamilton입니다.
여 제가 살펴볼게요. *[자판 두드리는 소리]* 장난감 자동차와 블록 세트를 빌리셨군요, 맞으세요?
남 네, 하지만 자동차에서 바퀴 하나가 빠진 것 같습니다.
여 분실하셨다는 말씀이세요?
남 그런 것 같습니다. 제 아들이 어딘가에 놓아둔 것이 틀림없습니다. 그것에 관해 제가 어떻게 해야 할지 궁금합니다.
여 장난감들을 반납하실 때 그 부품의 비용을 지불하시기만 하면 됩니다.
남 알겠습니다. 장난감들은 다음 주 화요일이 반납일이죠, 그렇죠?
여 그렇습니다.

Solution

남자는 장난감 도서관에 전화를 걸어 빌린 장난감 자동차의 바퀴 하나를 잃어버렸다고 말하며 어떻게 처리해야 하는지 도서관 직원인 여자에게 묻고 있으므로 정답은 ①이다.

Words

check out 빌리다, 대출하다 wheel 바퀴 somewhere 어딘가에
only have to ~하기만 하면 되다 due ~하기로 되어 있는, 만기의

08 정답 ⑤

Script

M Laura, come here and look at these animals.
W Oh, they look weird, Dad. I've never seen them before.
M They're giant armadillos. They live in South America.
W They look like they're wearing armor over their necks and backs.
M Yeah. And they have large claws on their forefeet.
W Wow, the claws look powerful.
M They use them to dig burrows. And they also dig to find food or to escape from predators.
W What do they feed on?
M They prefer termites as prey, and they are known to live for 12 to 15 years.
W I see. Why don't we take some pictures? I want to show them to my friends.
M Okay.

남 Laura, 이리 와서 이 동물들을 보렴.
여 오, 신기하게 생겼어요, 아빠. 전에 그것들을 본 적이 없어요.
남 그것들은 왕아르마딜로(giant armadillo)란다. 남아메리카에 살지.
여 목과 등 위에 갑옷을 걸치고 있는 것처럼 보여요.
남 그렇구나. 그리고 그것들은 앞발에 커다란 갈고리 발톱이 있단다.
여 와, 그 갈고리 발톱이 강력해 보여요.
남 그것들을 이용해서 굴을 판단다. 그리고 먹이를 찾거나 포식자로부터 도망치기 위해서 땅을 파기도 하지.
여 무엇을 먹고 사나요?
남 먹이로 흰개미를 선호한단다. 그리고 12년에서 15년 동안 산다고 알려져 있지.
여 알겠어요. 우리 사진을 좀 찍는 것이 어때요? 그것들을 제 친구들에게 보여 주고 싶어요.
남 그래.

Solution

서식지, 생김새, 먹이, 수명은 언급되었지만, ⑤ '천적 종류'는 언급되지 않았다.

Words

weird 이상한, 신기한 armor 갑옷 claw 갈고리 발톱 forefeet 앞발
dig 파다 burrow 굴 predator 포식자 termite 흰개미

09 정답 ④

Script

M Good morning, students. I'm very happy to announce that the 5th Wilson High School Hiking Day will start soon. We are at the northern entrance of Hanes National

Park. Our hike will start here at 9 a.m. and it should take about three hours. We'll provide snacks and soft drinks for each of you at the rest area. And you will be given a chance to take group photos for each class at the rest area. The school buses will pick you up at 12:30 p.m. at the southern entrance. So be sure to arrive at the southern entrance before then. If you have any questions, ask your homeroom teacher.

남 안녕하세요, 학생 여러분. 제5회 Wilson High School Hiking Day 가 곧 시작할 것임을 알리게 되어 매우 기쁩니다. 우리는 Hanes 국립 공원의 북쪽 입구에 있습니다. 우리 도보 여행은 오전 9시에 여기에서 시작하여 약 세 시간이 걸릴 것입니다. 우리는 휴식 지역에서 여러분 각각에게 간식과 음료수를 제공할 것입니다. 그리고 여러분은 휴식 지역에서 학급별 단체 사진을 찍을 기회가 주어질 것입니다. 학교 버스는 남쪽 입구에서 오후 12시 30분에 여러분을 태울 것입니다. 그러므로 반드시 그 전에 남쪽 입구에 도착하도록 하십시오. 질문이 있으면 담임선생님께 질문하세요.

10 정답 ⑤

Script

W How many people applied for the security guard's job?
M There are five applicants. We have to choose one of them.
W Let me see. This applicant is the youngest, but he is not qualified.
M You're right. We need a security guard with at least five years of experience.
W What do you think of Paul Wilson? He has fifteen years of experience.
M I'm afraid he doesn't speak French. You know we have many visitors from France.
W Oh, right. Then, what do you think of this person? He has the most experience.
M Don't you think he is too old to be a security guard?
W I guess so. Well, this applicant satisfies all the qualifications, right?
M Yeah. Let's hire him.

여 보안 요원직에 몇 명이나 지원했죠?
남 지원자가 5명 있어요. 그들 중에서 한 명을 선택해야 해요.
여 어디 봅시다. 이 지원자는 가장 어리지만 자격이 안 되네요.
남 맞아요. 우리는 최소한 5년의 경력을 가진 보안 요원이 필요해요.
여 Paul Wilson은 어떻게 생각해요? 경력이 15년이에요.
남 그 사람은 불어를 구사하지 못하는 것이 유감이에요. 당신도 알다시피 우리는 프랑스에서 오는 방문객이 많아요.
여 아, 맞아요. 그러면 이 사람은 어떻게 생각해요? 그는 경력이 가장 많아요.
남 보안 요원을 하기에는 그가 너무 나이가 많다고 생각하지 않아요?
여 그런 것 같아요. 음. 이 지원자가 모든 자격 요건을 만족시키는군요. 그렇죠?

남 맞아요. 그를 고용합시다.

11 정답 ⑤

Script

W Dad, I feel a bit hungry. Is there anything to eat?
M Check in the refrigerator. There should be some leftover pizza.
W Leftover pizza? I already ate that in the afternoon.
M Really? Then let me cook something for you now.

여 아빠, 배가 좀 고파요. 먹을 게 있나요?
남 냉장고를 확인해 보렴. 남은 피자가 좀 있을 거야.
여 남은 피자라고요? 그것은 제가 오후에 이미 먹었어요.
남 정말? 그러면 지금 너를 위해 아빠가 먹을 것을 만들어 줄게.

12 정답 ②

Script

M It is getting hotter day by day, isn't it?
W You're right. Summer is coming. Do you like summer?
M No. I don't like it because I sweat too much. What about you?
W Summer is my favorite season.

남 나날이 더 더워지고 있어, 그렇지 않니?
여 맞아. 여름이 오고 있어. 너는 여름을 좋아하니?
남 아니. 나는 땀을 너무 많이 흘려서 여름을 좋아하지 않아. 너는 어때?
여 여름은 내가 가장 좋아하는 계절이야.

day by day 나날이 sweat 땀을 흘리다

13 정답 ⑤

Script

W Patrick, I heard that you'll go to Korea next year.

M Right. I have a plan to quit working here and start a new life in Korea.

W Wow, great! So what will you do for a living in Korea?

M A tour guide.

W Really? Since you're outgoing, working as a tour guide will be suitable for you.

M Absolutely! I'll be a good tour guide and have a more satisfying life in Korea.

W How about Korean? Won't you need Korean skills to work in Korea?

M Don't worry. I've been studying it at a language school for a few months.

W Have you? I think you are preparing well to be a tour guide.

M Sure! I'm looking forward to my new life in Korea.

여 Patrick, 네가 내년에 한국에 갈 거라고 들었어.

남 그래. 나는 여기서 일하는 것을 그만두고 한국에서 새로운 삶을 시작할 계획을 가지고 있어.

여 와, 멋지다! 그래서 한국에서는 무슨 일을 할 거니?

남 여행 가이드.

여 정말? 너는 외향적이니까, 여행 가이드로 일하는 것은 네게 적합할 거야.

남 당연하지! 나는 좋은 여행 가이드가 되어서 한국에서 더 만족스러운 삶을 살 거야.

여 한국어는 어때? 한국에서 일을 하려면 한국어 실력이 필요하지 않을까?

남 걱정 마. 몇 달 동안 어학원에서 한국어를 공부하고 있어.

여 그래? 네가 여행 가이드가 되기 위해서 준비를 잘 하고 있는 것 같아.

남 물론이지! 나는 한국에서의 새로운 생활을 고대하고 있어.

Solution

한국에 가서 여행 가이드로 일할 계획을 하고 있는 남자에게 여자는 한국에서 일하려면 한국어 실력이 필요할 것 같다고 말한다. 이에 남자가 몇 달 동안 한국어를 공부하고 있다고 말하자 여자는 남자가 준비를 잘 하고 있는 것 같다고 대답했으므로, 이에 대한 남자의 응답으로 가장 적절한 것은 ⑤ '물론이지! 나는 한국에서의 새로운 생활을 고대하고 있어.'이다.

① 좋은 생각이야. 다음 달에 같이 한국에 가자.

② 맞아. 너는 반드시 좋은 여행 가이드가 될 거야.

③ 네가 말한 대로, 여행은 언제나 우리를 행복하게 해 줘.

④ 미안. 나는 너와 함께 어학원에 갈 수 없어.

Words

outgoing 외향적인 suitable 적합한, 적절한 satisfying 만족스러운

14 정답 ③

Script

[Cellphone rings.]

W Hi, Raymond. What's up?

M Oh, Julia. Can you do me a favor?

W Sure. What is it?

M I'm afraid I can't make it to Jane's birthday party tomorrow. Can you deliver my gift to her?

W Of course I can. But do you have any other problems?

M Well, actually, I'm in the hospital. I broke my left anklebone a couple of days ago.

W Oh, my.... What happened?

M I was hit by a bicycle and fell to the ground. The doctor said I have to stay in the hospital for a week.

W Oh, that's too bad. What hospital are you in?

M I'm in Smith County Hospital on Franklin Avenue.

W Okay. I'll drop by the hospital on my way to the party.

[휴대전화가 울린다.]

여 안녕, Raymond. 무슨 일이야?

남 아, Julia. 부탁 좀 들어 줄래?

여 물론이지. 뭔데?

남 내일 Jane의 생일 파티에 갈 수 없을 것 같아. 그녀에게 내 선물 좀 전해 줄래?

여 물론 해 줄 수 있지. 그런데 무슨 다른 문제라도 있니?

남 음, 사실, 내가 입원했어. 며칠 전에 왼쪽 복사뼈가 부러졌어.

여 아, 저런…. 무슨 일이 있었는데?

남 자전거에 치여서 땅바닥에 넘어졌어. 의사가 일주일 동안 병원에 있어야 한다고 했어.

여 아, 참 안됐다. 어느 병원에 있니?

남 Franklin 거리에 있는 Smith County 병원에 있어.

여 알았어. 내가 파티 가는 길에 병원에 들를게.

Solution

병원에 입원하고 있어서 Jane의 생일 파티에 갈 수 없게 된 남자가 생일 선물을 대신 전해 달라고 여자에게 부탁하고 있는 상황이며, 마지막에 병원 위치를 알려 주고 있다. 이에 대한 여자의 응답으로 가장 적절한 것은 ③ '알았어. 내가 파티 가는 길에 병원에 들를게.'이다.

① 안 돼. 너는 휴식이 더 필요하다고 의사가 말했어.

② 늦지 마. 파티는 7시에 시작해.

④ 미안해. 네 생일 파티에 갈 수 없을 것 같아.

⑤ 문제없어. 내일 아침 너를 병원에 데려다줄 수 있어.

Words

make it (장소에) 나타나다 anklebone 복사뼈

15 정답 ②

Script

M Susan is a high school student. She is studying in the library to prepare for a midterm exam. While she is studying, she feels thirsty so she goes out and finds a vending machine in the lobby. She puts a one-dollar bill into the machine for a bottle of water, which costs 70 cents. She gets the water and she waits for the change to be returned. But nothing happens. She finds the phone number of the manager on the left side of the machine and calls him. The manager answers and asks her what the problem is. In this situation, what would Susan most likely say to the manager?

Susan I can't get my change from the machine.

남 Susan은 고등학생입니다. 그녀는 중간고사 준비를 위해 도서관에서 공부를 하고 있습니다. 공부를 하는 동안 그녀는 갈증을 느껴서 밖으로 나가 로비에 있는 자판기를 찾습니다. 그녀는 생수 한 병을 구입하려고 1달러 지폐를 자판기에 넣는데 그것은 70센트입니다. 그녀는 생수를 받고, 거스름돈이 반환되기를 기다립니다. 하지만 아무 일도 일어나지 않습니다. 그녀는 자판기의 왼쪽 면에 있는 관리자 전화번호를 찾아서 그에게 전화를 합니다. 관리자가 전화를 받고, 문제가 무엇인지 그녀에게 묻습니다. 이런 상황에서, Susan은 관리자에게 뭐라고 말할 것 같은가요?

Susan 기계에서 거스름돈을 받을 수 없어요.

Solution

Susan은 자판기에서 생수를 구입한 후 거스름돈이 반환되지 않아서 자판기 관리자에게 전화를 걸어 문제를 말하려는 상황이므로, 이러한 상황에서 Susan이 관리자에게 할 말로 가장 적절한 것은 ② '기계에서 거스름돈을 받을 수 없어요.'이다.

① 생수 한 병 더 마실 수 있을까요?
③ 1달러 지폐를 바꿀 잔돈을 가지고 있나요?
④ 이 생수를 환불받고 싶습니다.
⑤ 자판기가 어디에 있는지 말씀해 주시겠어요?

Words

midterm exam 중간고사 vending machine 자판기

16 정답 ③ 17 정답 ③

Script

W Hello, freshmen. I am Stella Brown, principal of Green High School. How was your first day of high school? I hope all of you will quickly adjust to high school life. To do that, I recommend you join a school club. Joining a school club will offer many benefits. First, you can meet seniors and make new friends. Take the classic guitar club for example. The club has many senior members, and they will help you make your school life more enjoyable. Second, you can improve your knowledge of the field you're interested in. If you are interested in computers, join the computer club. Finally, joining some clubs can actually help you pass the college entrance exam. If you join the math or science club, you will soon understand how helpful it can be.

여 안녕하세요, 신입생 여러분. 저는 Green 고등학교 교장 Stella Brown입니다. 고등학교 첫날이 어떤가요? 저는 여러분 모두가 빨리 고등학교 생활에 적응하길 바랍니다. 그렇게 하기 위해서, 저는 여러분에게 교내 동아리에 가입할 것을 추천합니다. 교내 동아리에 가입하는 것은 여러분에게 많은 이점을 가져다줄 것입니다. 먼저 여러분은 선배들을 만날 수 있고, 새로운 친구를 사귈 수 있습니다. 클래식 기타 동아리를 예로 들어 보겠습니다. 그 동아리에는 많은 선배 회원들이 있어서 그들이 여러분의 학교생활을 더욱 즐겁게 지내도록 도움을 줄 것입니다. 둘째, 여러분이 관심이 있는 분야의 지식이 향상될 수 있습니다. 여러분이 컴퓨터에 관심이 있다면 컴퓨터 동아리에 가입하십시오. 마지막으로 동아리에 가입하는 것은 대학 입학 시험에 합격하는 데 실질적으로 도움을 줄 수 있습니다. 수학 또는 과학 동아리에 가입한다면, 그것이 얼마나 도움이 될 수 있는지 곧 이해할 것입니다.

Solution

16
Green 고등학교 교장인 여자는 신입생들에게 교내 동아리에 가입하면 많은

이점이 있다고 하면서, 이러한 이점에 대해 구체적으로 언급했으므로 여자가 하는 말의 주제로 가장 적절한 것은 ③ '교내 동아리 가입의 이점'이다.

① 학교생활에 적응하는 방법
② 신입생들을 위한 동아리 선택 방법
④ 신입생들에게 동아리를 홍보하는 어려움
⑤ 고등학교 생활과 중학교 생활의 차이점

17
클래식 기타, 컴퓨터, 수학, 과학은 언급되었으나 ③ '미술'은 언급되지 않았다.

Words

principal 교장 adjust to ～에 적응하다
college entrance exam 대학 입학 시험

01 ①	02 ①	03 ③	04 ④	05 ②
06 ③	07 ①	08 ④	09 ④	10 ②
11 ⑤	12 ⑤	13 ④	14 ⑤	15 ⑤
16 ①	17 ③			

01 정답 ①

Script

M　Are you tired from taking care of your baby? Don't worry about it anymore! Modern electronics are here to help you. This new cradle automatically rocks when it hears a baby crying. The secret is the sensor hidden in the cradle. Combined with the voice-recognition technology, this sensor does not respond to everyday noises, but only recognizes the sound of a baby crying. In addition, the cradle can record your voice and replay it while it's rocking. At the same time, it can also play music babies feel comfortable with. Call us now for a free fifteen-day trial. For more information, visit our website at www.autocradle.co.uk.

남　아기를 돌보느라 지치셨나요? 더 이상 그것에 대해 걱정하지 마세요! 여러분을 돕기 위한 현대 전자 기술이 여기 있습니다. 이 새 요람은 아기가 우는 소리를 들으면 자동적으로 흔들립니다. 비밀은 요람에 숨겨져 있는 센서입니다. 음성 인식 기술과 결합된 이 센서는 일상적인 소음에는 반응하지 않으나, 아기의 울음소리만을 인식합니다. 게다가, 그 요람은 여러분의 목소리를 녹음할 수 있고, 흔들리면서 그 소리를 재생할 수 있습니다. 동시에, 그것은 또한 아기들이 편안함을 느끼는 음악을 재생할 수도 있습니다. 지금 전화하셔서 15일 무료 체험을 해 보세요. 정보를 더 원하시면 저희 웹사이트 www.autocradle.co.uk를 방문하세요.

Solution

아기의 울음소리를 인식하여 자동적으로 흔들리고 목소리나 음악을 재생하는 기능을 갖춘 요람을 광고하고 있으므로 남자가 하는 말의 목적으로 가장 적절한 것은 ①이다.

Words

cradle 요람　automatically 자동적으로　rock 흔들리다
combine 결합하다　recognition 인식　replay 재생하다
trial 시도, 시험

02 정답 ①

Script

M　What's wrong, Stella? You look upset.
W　I couldn't concentrate on the lecture because of some noisy students.
M　Really? Were they chatting during the lecture?
W　No. The problem was the typing and clicking sounds on their laptop.
M　Were the sounds really that loud?
W　They were loud enough to disturb other students.
M　But they were probably searching for information they didn't understand, weren't they?
W　You know what? Some students were just surfing the Internet for fun.
M　Oh, that's not good.
W　In addition, most of them rarely made eye contact with the professor. They just looked at their computer screens.
M　There seems to be many side effects of using laptops during the class.
W　You can say that again! Our professor should think twice before allowing laptops in class.

남　무슨 일 있니, Stella? 화나 보여.
여　몇몇 시끄러운 학생들 때문에 강의에 집중할 수 없었어.
남　정말? 강의 중에 잡담을 하고 있었니?
여　아니. 문제는 그들의 노트북 자판 두드리는 소리와 클릭하는 소리였어.
남　그 소리가 정말 그렇게 컸니?
여　다른 학생들을 방해할 정도로 충분히 컸어.
남　그런데 아마도 그들이 이해하지 못한 정보를 찾고 있었을 거야, 그렇지 않아?
여　그거 알아? 어떤 학생들은 재미 삼아 인터넷만 검색하고 있었어.
남　아, 그건 좋지 않은데.
여　게다가, 그들 대부분은 교수님과 시선을 거의 마주치지도 않았어. 그들은 컴퓨터 화면만 바라보았어.
남　수업 중에 노트북을 사용하는 데는 많은 부작용이 있어 보여.
여　바로 그거야! 우리 교수님은 강의실에 노트북을 허용하기 전에 재차 생각하셔야 해.

Solution

여자는 수업 중에 노트북을 사용하는 소리 때문에 수업에 집중할 수 없었고, 또한 학생들이 교수님과 시선을 거의 마주치지 않았다고 하면서 노트북 허용을 재고해야 한다고 말한다. 따라서 여자의 의견으로 가장 적절한 것은 ①이다.

Words

concentrate on ~에 집중하다　lecture 강의　chat 잡담하다
disturb 방해하다　for fun 재미 삼아　rarely 거의 ~ 않다
eye contact 시선을 마주침　side effect 부작용

03 정답 ③

Script

W　Excuse me. Aren't you Richard Taylor?
M　Yes, I am.
W　I'm a big fan of your work, Mr. Taylor. I've always wanted to meet you.
M　Thank you. It's always a pleasure to see people who appreciate my work.
W　The pictures at this exhibition are amazing. I think they're your best yet.
M　I'm glad you like them. I paid close attention to facial expressions of the Africans this time.
W　In what area of Africa did you take this picture?
M　I took this picture in Liberia, West Africa. I still cannot forget the pale black eyes of this boy.
W　When I paid the admission price, I was told that you donate all profits to African aid groups.

M Yes. I want to raise people's consciousness on Africa through my work.
W I'm really happy to contribute to the donation.
M Thank you very much. I hope you have a good time here.

여 실례합니다. Richard Taylor 씨 아니세요?
남 네, 그렇습니다.
여 당신 작품의 열혈 팬입니다. Taylor 작가님. 항상 뵙고 싶었습니다.
남 감사합니다. 제 작품을 인정해 주는 사람들을 만나는 것은 항상 기쁜 일이죠.
여 이번 전시회의 사진들은 정말 대단해요. 제 생각엔 지금까지 작가님의 작품들 중 최고인 것 같아요.
남 좋아해 주셔서 기쁘군요. 이번에는 아프리카인들의 얼굴 표정에 세심하게 주목했습니다.
여 이 사진은 아프리카의 어느 지역에서 찍으셨어요?
남 이 사진은 서아프리카의 라이베리아에서 찍었습니다. 이 소년의 창백한 검은 눈동자를 아직도 잊을 수가 없군요.
여 입장료를 낼 때, 작가님께서 모든 수익금을 아프리카 구호 단체에 기부하신다는 말을 들었어요.
남 네. 제 작품을 통해 아프리카에 대한 사람들의 의식을 높이고 싶거든요.
여 그 기부에 기여하게 되어서 정말 기뻐요.
남 대단히 감사합니다. 이곳에서 좋은 시간 되시길 바랍니다.

Solution
여자가 남자의 이름을 물으며 자신이 남자의 팬이라고 하면서 남자의 전시회 사진들에 관해 대화를 나누고 있으므로 두 사람의 관계를 가장 잘 나타낸 것은 ③이다.

Words
appreciate 인정하다, 진가를 알아보다
pay attention to ~에 주목하다 donate 기부하다, 기증하다
profit 수익금 aid group 구호 단체 raise 높이다, 올리다
consciousness 의식 contribute to ~에 기여하다

04 정답 ④

Script
W What's this picture, Minjun?
M That was taken at my son's first birthday party.
W Wow! This little child holding a pencil must be your son, right?
M Yeah. He is so cute, isn't he?
W He is adorable. And you also look great with a necktie on.
M Thank you. I wore a necktie like my son.
W Is this your wife lifting the teddy bear over her head?
M Yes, that's her. And the girl holding a balloon is Hana, my first daughter.
W She is so pretty. She has grown so much since I saw her last time.
M You know what? The cake on the table was made by my wife.
W Wow! She did a great job!

여 이 사진이 뭐예요, 민준 씨?
남 제 아들의 돌잔치에서 찍은 사진이에요.
여 와! 연필을 들고 있는 이 작은 아이가 당신의 아들이 틀림없군요, 그렇죠?
남 네. 아주 귀엽죠, 그렇지 않나요?

여 사랑스러워요. 그리고 넥타이를 매고 있는 당신도 멋져 보여요.
남 고마워요. 내 아들처럼 넥타이를 맸어요.
여 머리 위로 곰 인형을 들어 올리고 있는 이 분이 당신의 아내인가요?
남 네, 그녀예요. 그리고 풍선을 들고 있는 여자아이는 제 첫째 딸인 하나예요.
여 아주 예쁘네요. 제가 마지막으로 본 이후로 아주 많이 컸네요.
남 그거 알아요? 탁자 위의 케이크는 제 아내가 만들었어요.
여 와! 그녀가 정말 잘 만들었네요!

Solution
남자의 아들 돌잔치에서 찍은 사진을 보고 나누는 대화로, 여자아이가 풍선을 들고 있다고 했지만, 그림에서는 나팔을 불고 있으므로 대화의 내용과 일치하지 않는 것은 ④이다.

Words
adorable 사랑스러운, 귀여운 lift 들어 올리다

05 정답 ②

Script
M Mom, I'm home. Uh-oh, what's wrong with you?
W I think I caught a cold.
M Why don't you go see a doctor?
W Today is Sunday and all the hospitals are closed around our neighborhood.
M Then I'll go get some medicine. The pharmacy on May Street is open on Sundays.
W I've already taken some pills, but I don't feel any better.
M I heard vitamin C is good for a cold.
W Well, can you go and buy some juice? I'm feeling a little thirsty.
M I think fresh fruit would be better than juice.
W I feel like eating grapes, but they are out of season now.
M Then I'll go buy a bottle of grape juice. I'll be back in a minute.
W Thanks, James.

남 엄마, 다녀왔습니다. 어, 무슨 일 있으세요?
여 감기에 걸린 것 같구나.
남 의사의 진찰을 받지 그러세요?
여 오늘은 일요일이라서 인근의 병원들이 모두 문을 닫았구나.
남 그러면 약을 좀 사 올게요. May Street에 있는 약국은 일요일에 문을 열어요.
여 이미 약을 좀 먹었는데 더 나아지질 않네.
남 비타민 C가 감기에 좋다고 들었어요.
여 음, 가서 주스 좀 사 오겠니? 목이 좀 마르네.
남 신선한 과일이 주스보다 더 나을 것 같아요.
여 포도를 먹고 싶지만, 지금은 제철이 아니구나.
남 그러면 포도 주스 한 병을 사러 갈게요. 곧 돌아올게요.
여 고맙다. James.

Solution
감기에 걸린 여자에게 남자가 비타민 C 섭취를 권하자, 여자는 주스를 사다 달라고 부탁한다. 신선한 과일이 더 나을 것 같다는 남자의 말에 여자가 포도가 먹고 싶지만 제철이 아니라고 말하자, 남자는 포도 주스를 사러 가겠다고 했으므로 정답은 ②이다.

Words
neighborhood 인근, 근처 pharmacy 약국
out of season 제철이 아닌

06 정답 ③

M Hello. How may I help you?

W I'd like to rent a compact car for three days.

M We have a blue one and a gray one available now. They're both the latest model.

W Great. I'll take the blue one. How much is the rental fee?

M It's fifty dollars a day, but if you join our membership program, you can get a twenty-percent discount.

W Good. Then I'd like to become a member.

M Fill out this form, please. And I strongly recommend you get full-coverage insurance just in case. It's ten dollars per day.

W All right. I'll buy it. Oh, I need a GPS navigation system, too.

M No problem. The fee for that is five dollars a day.

W Okay. Here is my credit card.

M Thanks.

남 안녕하세요. 어떻게 도와드릴까요?

여 저는 소형차를 3일 동안 빌리고 싶습니다.

남 지금 파란색과 회색을 이용하실 수 있습니다. 그것들은 둘 다 최신 모델입니다.

여 좋습니다. 저는 파란색을 선택하겠습니다. 대여료가 얼마인가요?

남 하루에 50달러입니다만, 회원 프로그램에 가입하시면 20퍼센트 할인을 받으실 수 있습니다.

여 좋습니다. 그러면 회원이 되고 싶습니다.

남 이 서식을 작성해 주십시오. 그리고 만약을 위해서 종합 보험에도 가입하실 것을 강력히 추천합니다. 그것은 하루에 10달러입니다.

여 좋아요. 그것을 할게요. 아, 저는 GPS 내비게이션 장치도 필요합니다.

남 문제없습니다. 그것의 사용료는 하루에 5달러입니다.

여 좋습니다. 여기 제 신용카드가 있습니다.

남 감사합니다.

Solution

자동차 하루 대여료가 50달러이지만 회원에 가입해서 20퍼센트 할인을 받아 40달러이고, 종합 보험 10달러와 GPS 내비게이션 장치 5달러를 합하면 하루 총 비용은 55달러이다. 여자는 3일간 자동차를 빌리므로 여자가 지불할 금액은 ③ '165달러'이다.

Words

compact car 소형차   latest 최신의   rental fee 대여료
fill out ~을 작성하다   full-coverage insurance 종합 보험
just in case 만약을 위해서

07 정답 ①

Script

W Oh, at last the final exams are over!

M Right. Now we can enjoy summer vacation from next week.

W Great! By the way, will you take part in the swimming camp during the vacation?

M I'd love to, but I can't.

W Why not? Because of your part-time job?

M No. I'll go to Hawaii during the camp.

W Ah, your uncle is in Hawaii, running a guesthouse. You went there to help him on the winter vacation, didn't you?

M Right. But this time I'm not going to help him. I'm going to learn how to surf.

W Learn to surf? Sounds exciting.

M Yes! I'm really looking forward to my vacation in Hawaii.

여 오, 드디어 기말고사가 끝났어!

남 그래. 이제 우리는 다음 주부터 여름 방학을 즐길 수 있어.

여 멋져! 그런데 너 방학 동안에 수영 캠프에 참가할 거니?

남 그러고는 싶지만, 참가할 수 없어.

여 왜? 시간제 일자리 때문에?

남 아니. 나는 캠프 기간 동안에 하와이에 갈 거야.

여 아, 네 삼촌이 게스트하우스를 운영하시면서 하와이에 계시지. 네가 겨울 방학에 삼촌을 도우러 하와이에 갔었잖아, 그렇지 않니?

남 맞아. 하지만 이번에는 삼촌을 도우러 가는 것이 아니야. 나는 서핑하는 법을 배울 거야.

여 서핑을 배운다고? 흥미진진한데.

남 맞아! 하와이에서 보내는 내 방학을 정말로 고대하고 있어.

Solution

남자는 수영 캠프 기간 동안에 하와이에 가서 서핑을 배울 것이라고 했으므로 정답은 ①이다.

Words

be over 끝나다 take part in ~에 참가하다 run 운영하다
surf 서핑하다 look forward to ~을 고대하다

08 정답 ④

Script

W Well, Mr. Lee. I see from your résumé that you had a lot of experience working in a shoe store.

M Yes. My father runs a shoe store, and I helped him there after school.

W What kind of volunteer work have you done?

M I taught basketball at Wellington Orphanage.

W I see. Can I ask why you are thinking of leaving your present job?

M Well, I like counseling, but I miss sports. This job would give me a chance to do both of them.

W So you think you're ready to live in Chicago?

M Sure. I've been living in Columbus, but I've always wanted to live in a big city.

W Okay. I'll let you know the results in a few days or so.

M Thank you.

여 음. Lee 씨. 이력서에 보면 신발 가게에서 일한 많은 경력이 있다고 되어 있군요.

남 네. 아버지께서 신발 가게를 운영하셔서 방과 후에 거기에서 아버지를 도와드렸습니다.

여 어떤 종류의 자원봉사 활동을 했습니까?

남 Wellington 고아원에서 농구를 가르쳤습니다.

여 알겠습니다. 왜 현재의 직업을 떠날 생각이신지 물어봐도 될까요?

남 음, 저는 상담을 좋아합니다만, 스포츠가 그립습니다. 이 일은 두 가지를 모두 할 수 있는 기회를 줄 것입니다.

여 그래서 당신은 시카고에서 살 준비가 되어 있다고 생각하십니까?

남 물론이죠. 저는 Columbus에서 살아 왔습니다만, 항상 큰 도시에서 살고 싶었습니다.
여 좋습니다. 며칠 정도 후에 결과를 알려 드리겠습니다.
남 감사합니다.

Solution

경력, 자원봉사, 지원 동기, 사는 곳은 언급되었지만, ④ '자격증'은 언급되지 않았다.

Words

résumé 이력서 run 운영하다 volunteer 자원봉사 counseling 상담

09 정답 ④

Script

M Good morning, everyone. Have you ever heard of Komodo dragons? Look at this picture. They are the largest lizard in the world. As you see in this picture, they have powerful legs, sharp claws, and a long tail. Round, brownish-black scales cover their body, and their mouth has sharp teeth. Komodo dragons use their tongue to pick up chemical signals to locate injured prey. They lay around 20 to 30 eggs once a year. To avoid predators, the young spend much of their first few years in trees, but move to the ground once they've reached 30 inches in total length.

남 안녕하세요, 여러분. Komodo dragon에 대해 들어 본 적이 있습니까? 이 사진을 보십시오. 그것은 세계에서 가장 큰 도마뱀입니다. 이 사진에서 보시는 바와 같이, 그것은 강력한 다리, 날카로운 갈고리 발톱, 그리고 긴 꼬리를 가지고 있습니다. 둥글고 갈색이 도는 검은 비늘이 몸을 덮고 있고, 입에는 날카로운 이빨이 있습니다. Komodo dragon은 상처 입은 먹잇감의 위치를 알려 주는 화학적 신호를 포착하는 데 혀를 사용합니다. 그것은 1년에 한 번 약 20개에서 30개의 알을 낳습니다. 포식자를 피하기 위해 새끼는 첫 몇 해를 대부분 나무에서 보내지만, 총 길이가 30인치에 달하면 지상으로 내려옵니다.

Solution

1년에 한 번 약 20개에서 30개의 알을 낳는다고 했으므로 담화의 내용과 일치하지 않는 것은 ④이다.

Words

lizard 도마뱀 scale 비늘 signal 신호 injured 상처 입은, 부상당한
lay 알을 낳다 predator 포식자

10 정답 ②

Script

W What are you looking at on the computer, honey?
M I'm searching for a used car.
W Have you found any good ones?
M There are five that caught my attention. What color do you like?
W Well, any color is okay except black.
M Then how about this white one?
W Uh-oh, look at the mileage. It's well over one hundred thousand miles. That's a bad sign.
M Then I bet you'll like this green one. The mileage is the lowest among these five cars.

W Honey, have you forgotten that I can't drive cars with manual transmissions?
M Oh, I'm sorry. Then what do you think of this other white one?
W Well, I'm not satisfied with the price. I prefer this green one. I think its price is reasonable.
M That's good. Let's contact the dealer right now.

여 컴퓨터로 뭘 보고 있어요, 여보?
남 중고차를 살펴보고 있어요.
여 좋은 것을 발견했어요?
남 내 관심을 사로잡는 5대가 있어요. 어떤 색상이 좋아요?
여 음, 검은색 말고는 어떤 색이든지 좋아요.
남 그러면 이 흰색은 어때요?
여 어, 주행 거리 좀 보세요. 십만 마일이 훨씬 넘네요. 그건 안 좋은 징조예요.
남 그러면 이 녹색 차가 마음에 들 거라고 확신해요. 주행 거리가 이 다섯 자동차 중에서 가장 적어요.
여 여보, 내가 수동 변속기 차량을 운전하지 못한다는 걸 잊었어요?
남 아, 미안해요. 그러면 이 다른 흰색 차는 어떻게 생각해요?
여 음, 가격이 만족스럽지 않아요. 이 녹색 차가 더 낫겠어요. 그 가격이 적당하다고 생각해요.
남 좋아요. 판매업자에게 당장 연락합시다.

Solution

검은색이 아니고, 주행 거리가 십만 마일을 넘지 않으면서, 자동 변속기 차량이고, 가격이 적당한 중고차가 좋겠다고 했으므로, 두 사람이 구입할 자동차는 ②이다.

Words

mileage 주행 거리 manual transmission 수동 변속기
reasonable (가격이) 적당한, 비싸지 않은

11 정답 ⑤

Script

W Hi. I've got a flat tire. Can you fix it?
M Sure, but it'll take about 30 minutes. I have two bicycles to fix ahead of yours.
W No problem. I'll leave my bike with you and be back in 30 minutes.
M Okay. Then you will be able to ride your bike home.

여 안녕하세요. 타이어가 펑크 났는데요. 고칠 수 있나요?
남 물론이죠, 하지만 30분 정도 걸릴 거예요. 이것보다 앞서서 수리해야 할 자전거가 두 대 있거든요.
여 괜찮아요. 제 자전거를 맡기고 30분 후에 돌아올게요.
남 좋아요. 그러면 자전거를 타고 집에 갈 수 있을 거예요.

Solution

여자의 펑크 난 자전거를 수리하는 데 30분 정도 걸린다는 남자의 말에 여자는 자전거를 맡기고 30분 후에 돌아오겠다고 했으므로, 이에 대한 남자의 응답으로 가장 적절한 것은 ⑤ '좋아요. 그러면 자전거를 타고 집에 갈 수 있을 거예요.'이다.

① 아니요, 저는 검은색 자전거를 사고 싶지 않아요.
② 물론이죠. 당신이 원하는 아무 때나 제 자전거를 탈 수 있어요.
③ 당신 덕분에, 자전거 타는 법을 배울 수 있었어요.
④ 걱정 마세요. 자전거를 수리하기 위한 돈을 빌려줄게요.

flat tire 펑크 난 타이어   ahead of ~보다 앞서

12 정답 ⑤

Script

M Hey, Mary. Look at Jane standing over there. She looks really tired, doesn't she?

W Well, it's no wonder that she looks exhausted.

M Do you know the reason?

W Yeah. She's worked overtime for three days in a row.

남 이봐, Mary. 저쪽에 서 있는 Jane을 봐. 아주 피곤해 보이네, 그렇지 않아?

여 음, 그녀가 지쳐 보이는 것은 당연해.

남 너는 그 이유를 알고 있니?

여 응. 그녀는 3일 동안 연속해서 초과 근무를 했어.

Solution

Jane이 지쳐 보이는 것이 당연하다는 여자의 말에 남자는 그 이유를 알고 있는지 묻고 있으므로, 이에 대한 여자의 응답으로 가장 적절한 것은 ⑤ '응. 그녀는 3일 동안 연속해서 초과 근무를 했어.'이다.

① 아니. 나도 기분이 좋지 않아.

② 물론이지. 그녀는 그 가격이 합리적이라고 생각해.

③ 응. 신선한 과일을 좀 먹는 것은 좋은 생각이야.

④ 물론이지. 나도 그녀를 만나기를 고대하고 있어.

Words

exhausted 지친   in a row 잇달아, 연이어

13 정답 ④

Script

M Sarah, have you decided which course to take between chemistry and biology next semester?

W Not yet. What about you, John?

M I'll take the chemistry course. Why don't you take it with me?

W But don't you think chemistry is more difficult than biology?

M Not at all. Once you understand the basic concepts of chemistry, it'll be much easier to study than biology.

W Really? Who's the chemistry teacher?

M Patricia Jackson. Every student says she's one of the best science teachers in our school.

W That's right. I've heard that, too.

M Take chemistry, and you won't have any regrets.

남 Sarah, 다음 학기에 화학과 생물학 중에서 어떤 강의를 수강할지 결정했어?

여 아직 못 했어. 넌 어때, John?

남 난 화학 강의를 수강할 거야. 나랑 같이 화학을 수강하는 게 어때?

여 하지만 화학이 생물학보다 더 어렵다고 생각하지 않니?

남 결코 아니야. 일단 네가 화학에 대한 기본 개념을 이해하면, 생물학보다 공부하는 것이 훨씬 더 쉬울 거야.

여 정말? 화학 선생님은 누구시니?

남 Patricia Jackson. 그녀가 우리 학교 최고의 과학 선생님 중 한 분이라고 모든 학생들이 말해.

여 맞아. 나도 그것을 들었어.

남 화학을 수강하면, 너는 후회하지 않을 거야.

Solution

화학과 생물학 중에서 수강할 과목을 결정하지 못한 여자에게 남자는 자신과 함께 화학을 수강하자고 제안하면서 화학 선생님이 학교에서 가장 훌륭한 과학 선생님 중 한 분이라고 덧붙인다. 이에 여자가 자신도 그 이야기를 들었다고 했으므로, 이에 대한 남자의 응답으로 가장 적절한 것은 ④ '화학을 수강하면, 너는 후회하지 않을 거야.'이다.

① 음, 난 더 이상 화학에 관심이 없어.

② 좋아. 화학과 생물학 둘 다 공부하자.

③ 맞아. 너는 Patricia Jackson의 사무실에 가야 해.

⑤ 나도 그래. 생물학이 화학보다 공부하기 더 쉬워.

Words

chemistry 화학   biology 생물학   once 일단 ~하면   concept 개념
regret 후회

14 정답 ⑤

Script

W Hey, Stuart. You don't look very good. What's wrong with you?

M Well, I was fired from my job last week. That's why I'm in such a bad mood.

W I can't believe that. Why did they dismiss you?

M They said I wasn't performing my duties adequately.

W That's not true. I remember you won the top employee prize last year.

M That's right. I think my age is the real reason they fired me.

W They can't do that. It's totally unfair. I think you should file a lawsuit against the company.

M Do you really think I can win?

W Of course. Age discrimination is definitely against the law.

M I see. Then what should I do?

W I know a very competent lawyer. Let's contact him right away.

여 이봐요, Stuart. 그다지 좋아 보이지 않아요. 무슨 문제 있어요?

남 음, 저는 지난주에 해고당했어요. 그게 제가 지금 그렇게 기분이 나쁜 이유예요.

여 믿을 수 없어요. 왜 그들이 당신을 해고했죠?

남 제가 임무를 충분히 수행하지 못하고 있다고 하더군요.

여 그건 사실이 아니에요. 당신은 작년에 우수 직원상을 수상했던 걸로 기억하는데요.

남 맞아요. 제 생각엔 저를 해고한 진짜 이유는 제 나이인 것 같아요.

여 그들은 그럴 수 없어요. 그건 전적으로 부당해요. 회사에 대해 소송을 제기해야 한다고 저는 생각해요.

남 정말 제가 이길 수 있다고 생각하시나요?

여 물론이죠. 나이 차별은 명백히 불법이에요.

남 알겠어요. 그러면 제가 어떻게 해야 하죠?

여 제가 아주 유능한 변호사를 알고 있어요. 당장 그에게 연락합시다.

Solution

부당하게 해고를 당한 남자에게 여자는 회사를 상대로 소송을 제기해야 한다

고 말하고 있으며, 이에 남자는 어떻게 해야 하는지 여자에게 조언을 구하고 있으므로, 이에 대한 여자의 응답으로 가장 적절한 것은 ⑤ '제가 아주 유능한 변호사를 알고 있어요. 당장 그에게 연락합시다.'이다.

① 그 회사에 다시 한번 지원하는 게 어때요?
② 미안한 말씀이지만 당신은 그 일을 할 자격이 없습니다.
③ 그 회사와 계약을 하는 게 어때요?
④ 당신이 그 회사가 당신에게 요구하는 것은 무엇이든지 할 수 있다고 확신합니다.

fire 해고하다 dismiss 해고하다 duty 임무, 의무 adequately 충분히
unfair 부당한 file a lawsuit 고소하다, 소송을 제기하다
discrimination 차별 definitely 명백히

15 정답 ⑤

W Michael is an elementary school student. He likes to play computer games. His mother is very concerned about him because he is so hooked on computer games that he doesn't go outside to play with his friends. One day, Michael's mother gets a good idea. She decides to reward him for not playing computer games. She knows he also likes toy robots, so she tells him that if he doesn't play computer games for a week, she will buy him a toy robot. Michael agrees to her proposal and is excited about it. In this situation, what would Michael most likely say to his mother?

Michael I'm sure I can go without computer games for a while.

여 Michael은 초등학생입니다. 그는 컴퓨터 게임을 하는 것을 좋아합니다. 그가 컴퓨터 게임에 너무 푹 빠져서 밖에 나가 친구들과 놀지 않기 때문에 그의 어머니는 그를 매우 걱정합니다. 어느 날, Michael의 어머니는 좋은 아이디어가 떠오릅니다. 그녀는 컴퓨터 게임을 하지 않는 것에 대해 그에게 보상하기로 결심합니다. 그가 장난감 로봇 또한 좋아한다는 것을 알아서, 그녀는 그가 일주일 동안 컴퓨터 게임을 하지 않으면 장난감 로봇을 사 주겠다고 그에게 말합니다. Michael은 그녀의 제안에 동의하고, 그것에 대해 신이 납니다. 이런 상황에서, Michael은 그의 어머니에게 뭐라고 말할 것 같은가요?

Michael 한동안 컴퓨터 게임 없이 지낼 수 있다고 확신해요.

일주일 동안 컴퓨터 게임을 하지 않으면 장난감 로봇을 사 준다는 어머니의 제안에 대해 Michael이 동의하고 있는 상황이므로 Michael이 어머니에게 할 말로 가장 적절한 것은 ⑤ '한동안 컴퓨터 게임 없이 지낼 수 있다고 확신해요.'이다.

① 미안해요. 저는 이미 오늘 계획이 있어요.
② 좋은 생각이에요. 저는 컴퓨터 게임을 하고 싶어요.
③ 정말 그렇게 생각하세요? 저는 동의하지 않아요.
④ 아니요, 괜찮아요. 저는 장난감 로봇을 가지고 노는 것을 더 좋아해요.

be concerned about ~을 걱정하다 be hooked on ~에 푹 빠지다
reward 보상하다 proposal 제안 go without ~ 없이 지내다

16 정답 ①   ## 17 정답 ③

W Hello, everyone. It's nice to meet you again. Last week, I talked about how to communicate effectively to express feelings. Today I'd like to talk about communication through body gestures. Do you think communication is done only in language? I'm sure all of you don't think so. Your gestures can also convey as much meaning to the other as language. If you don't like an opinion, you will move your head sideways. Crossing your arms also means you're not satisfied with something. If you've done something you're proud of, you can shrug your shoulders. Do you want to know if someone is lying? Make sure that person touches his nose. Many people touch their noses while lying. Now watch the television in front. I'm going to show you a movie clip of various body languages from all over the world.

여 안녕하세요. 여러분. 다시 만나게 되어 반갑습니다. 지난주에 저는 감정을 효과적으로 전달할 수 있는 의사소통 방법에 대해 말씀드렸습니다. 오늘 저는 몸짓을 통한 의사소통에 대해 말씀드리고자 합니다. 여러분은 의사소통이 단지 언어로만 이루어진다고 생각하시나요? 여러분 모두는 그렇게 생각하지 않을 거라고 확신합니다. 여러분이 하는 몸짓 또한 언어만큼이나 많은 의미를 상대방에게 전달할 수 있습니다. 여러분이 어떤 의견이 마음에 들지 않는다면, 여러분은 머리를 양 옆으로 움직일 것입니다. 팔짱을 끼는 것 또한 여러분이 무언가에 만족하지 않는다는 뜻입니다. 만약 여러분이 자랑스러운 행동을 했다면, 여러분은 어깨를 으쓱할 수 있습니다. 상대방이 거짓말을 하는지 알고 싶은가요? 그 사람이 코를 만지는지 확인하십시오. 많은 사람이 거짓말을 하면서 자신의 코를 만진답니다. 이제 앞에 있는 텔레비전을 봐 주십시오. 전 세계의 다양한 신체 언어에 대한 동영상을 보여 드리겠습니다.

16

여자는 몸짓이 언어만큼이나 많은 의미를 상대방에게 전달할 수 있다고 하면서 다양한 몸짓에 대한 의미를 설명하고 있으므로 여자가 하는 말의 주제로 가장 적절한 것은 ① '언어로서의 몸짓'이다.

② 다른 문화에서의 몸짓
③ 감정을 효과적으로 전달하는 방법
④ 좋은 의사소통의 정의
⑤ 몸짓을 이해하는 것의 어려움

17

신체 부위로 머리, 팔, 어깨, 코는 언급되었으나 ③ '다리'는 언급되지 않았다.

effectively 효과적으로 express 표현하다 body gesture 몸짓
convey 전달하다 opinion 의견 cross one's arms 팔짱을 끼다
be satisfied with ~에 만족하다
shrug one's shoulder 어깨를 으쓱하다

01 ④	**02** ③	**03** ②	**04** ⑤	**05** ③
06 ③	**07** ②	**08** ⑤	**09** ⑤	**10** ④
11 ④	**12** ④	**13** ④	**14** ⑤	**15** ③
16 ⑤	**17** ⑤			

01 정답 ④

Script

W Hello, exercise lovers. As you've probably noticed, almost all gyms have mirrors of various sizes on the walls. Those mirrors help make the gym look bigger. But be careful! Mirrors can be one of the main reasons why you decide to stop going to the gym. You may not believe it, but it's true. If you look at your reflection during a workout, you feel more tired and less relaxed. It's because you are likely to have negative thoughts about yourself by looking at your reflection. So don't look at yourself in the mirror when you work out.

여 운동을 사랑하시는 여러분, 안녕하세요. 아마 여러분도 알아차리셨겠지만, 거의 모든 체육관은 다양한 크기의 거울이 벽에 있습니다. 그런 거울은 체육관이 더 크게 보이도록 하는 데 도움이 됩니다. 하지만 조심하십시오! 거울은 여러분이 체육관에 가는 것을 중단하는 결정을 내리는 주된 이유 중의 하나가 될 수 있습니다. 여러분이 믿지 않을지도 모르지만 그것은 사실입니다. 운동 중에 거울에 비친 자신의 모습을 보면 더욱 피곤함을 느끼게 되고 몸의 긴장이 덜 풀리게 됩니다. 이는 여러분이 거울 속 자신을 보는 것 때문에 자신에 대한 부정적 생각을 갖게 될 가능성이 높기 때문입니다. 따라서 운동할 때 거울 속 자신의 모습을 쳐다보지 마십시오.

Solution

운동 중에 거울에 비친 자신의 모습을 보는 것이 피곤하고 몸에 긴장이 덜 풀리며 스스로에 대한 부정적 생각을 만들어 내서 운동 중단 결정을 내리는 주된 이유가 될 수 있다고 지적하며 운동 중에 거울을 보지 말라고 하고 있으므로 여자가 하는 말의 목적으로 가장 적절한 것은 ④이다.

Words

notice 알아차리다 reflection (거울 등에 비친) 모습, 반사
workout 운동 negative 부정적인

02 정답 ③

Script

W Ross, have you decided on the topic for your social studies assignment?

M Yes. My topic is about the decrease in family size, especially single-person households in New York.

W Why did you choose New York?

M New York has the highest number of single-person households in the U.S.

W Why are there so many single-person households?

M Many divorced people remain in homes that they once shared with their spouses.

W I see. The divorce rate is very high these days. I think young people are waiting longer to get married and that may be another reason for the increase.

M Right. Besides, those who earn high incomes don't need to share their rooms with roommates.

W Are there any other factors?

M I haven't finished my assignment yet, but I'll let you know later.

여 Ross, 네 사회 과제 주제를 정했니?

남 응. 내 주제는 가족 규모의 축소, 특히 뉴욕의 1인 가구에 관한 거야.

여 왜 뉴욕을 선택했니?

남 뉴욕은 미국에서 1인 가구 수가 가장 많은 곳이야.

여 왜 거기에는 1인 가구가 그렇게 많은 거니?

남 이혼한 많은 사람들이 한때 배우자와 함께 살았던 집에 남아 있어.

여 그렇구나. 요즘 이혼율이 아주 높잖아. 젊은 사람들이 결혼을 미루고 있고 그것이 그 증가의 또 하나의 이유가 될 수도 있다고 생각해.

남 맞아. 게다가, 높은 소득을 버는 사람들은 룸메이트와 방을 함께 쓸 필요가 없지.

여 또 다른 요인이 있니?

남 아직 내 과제를 끝마치지 못했지만 나중에 알려줄게.

Solution

두 사람은 남자의 사회 과제 주제인 뉴욕의 1인 가구 증가에 대한 이유를 열거하고 있으므로 두 사람이 하는 말의 주제로 가장 적절한 것은 ③이다.

Words

assignment 과제 household 가구, 가정 spouse 배우자
income 소득 factor 요인

03 정답 ②

Script

M Excuse me.

W Yes? What can I do for you?

M I have a delivery for Alice Brewer.

W Alice Brewer? Wow! That must be the wedding gown.

M Really? Congratulations! I hope you have a great wedding.

W Oh, I wish it were for me.

M Then who's the lucky girl? I need her to come out and sign for this.

W She's my coworker, but she's not here right now. She won't be back for another hour.

M I'm afraid I can't wait that long. Could you receive it and sign for her?

W Sure. That won't be a problem.

M Thank you. I've got a lot of other deliveries to deal with.

W Where do I have to sign?

M Right here, please.

남 실례합니다.

여 네? 무엇을 도와드릴까요?

남 Alice Brewer란 분께 배달이 있습니다.

여 Alice Brewer요? 와! 웨딩드레스인가 보군요.

남 그래요? 축하드립니다! 멋진 결혼식이 되길 바랍니다.

여 오, 저에게 온 것이면 좋을 텐데요.

남 그럼 그 행운의 여성분은 누구시죠? 나오셔서 이것에 서명을 해 주셔야 해요.

여 그녀는 제 직장 동료인데 지금 여기에 없어요. 한 시간은 있어야 돌아올 거예요.

남 그렇게 오래 기다릴 수가 없을 것 같아요. 대신 수령하고 서명을 해 주실 수 있을까요?

여 물론이죠. 문제될 것 없을 거예요.

남 고맙습니다. 제가 처리해야 할 다른 배달이 많아서요.

여 어디에 서명하면 되나요?

남 바로 여기입니다.

Solution

남자는 물품을 배달하러 온 사람이고, 여자는 직장 동료 대신 물품을 수령하고 서명하고 있으므로 두 사람의 관계를 가장 잘 나타낸 것은 ②이다.

Words

delivery 배달 coworker 직장 동료 deal with ~을 처리하다

04 정답 ⑤

Script

W Hi, Tom. Thank you for sending me the picture yesterday.

M Hi, Grace. Did you have a look at it?

W Sure. I saved it in my cellphone here. Look, this wooden structure is really impressive.

M Yeah, it looks like an old pavilion, right?

W Yes. Where was the picture taken?

M On the top of a mountain in a suburban area.

W I guessed so, since you had a walking stick in your hand. The old pine tree behind the wooden building makes it look more attractive.

M Yeah. What's more interesting is that the structure was built on a rock.

W You must have been afraid when you were standing there.

M How did you know that?

W You were leaning against the wooden column.

여 안녕, Tom. 어제 사진 보내 주어서 고마워.

남 안녕, Grace. 그 사진 봤어?

여 물론이지. 여기 내 휴대전화에 저장해 두었어. 봐, 이 목조 건축물은 정말 인상적이야.

남 응, 오래된 정자처럼 보이지, 그렇지?

여 응. 사진은 어디서 찍었니?

남 교외 지역에 있는 산의 정상에서 찍었어.

여 네 손에 지팡이가 있어서 그럴 거라고 생각했어. 나무로 된 건물 뒤에 있는 노송이 건축물을 더욱 매력적으로 보이게 만들어 줘.

남 응. 더욱 흥미로운 점은 건축물이 바위 위에 지어졌다는 거야.

여 네가 그곳에 서 있을 때 무서웠나 보네.

남 어떻게 알았어?

여 네가 나무 기둥에 기대어 있잖아.

Solution

남자가 나무 기둥에 기대어 서 있다고 했는데, 그림에서는 정자에 걸터앉아 있으므로 대화의 내용과 일치하지 않는 것은 ⑤이다.

Words

pavilion 정자 suburban 교외의 walking stick 지팡이
pine tree 소나무 lean against ~에 기대다 column 기둥

05 정답 ③

Script

W Wow! You did a good job. The classroom is perfectly clean.

M Thanks. I'm good at cleaning.

W I see. Oh, look at the waste bin. It's almost full.

M Ted was supposed to empty that.

W Where is Ted?

M Maybe he already left. I saw him packing his school bag a while ago. Should I call him and tell him to come back?

W You don't have to do that. Maybe he forgot.

M Well, I can do his work for him.

W Will you do that? I'm sure Ted will do something to repay you later.

M Probably. But it doesn't really matter to me.

W You're such a nice boy!

여 와! 일을 아주 잘했구나. 교실이 흠잡을 데 없이 깨끗하네.

남 고맙습니다. 제가 청소를 잘해요.

여 그렇구나. 오, 쓰레기통을 보렴. 거의 꽉 찼네.

남 Ted가 쓰레기통을 비우기로 되어 있었어요.

여 Ted는 어디 있니?

남 아마 이미 갔을 거예요. 조금 전에 책가방을 싸는 것을 봤어요. 전화해서 다시 오라고 해야 할까요?

여 그럴 필요는 없단다. 아마 잊었겠지.

남 그럼, 제가 Ted 대신 그 일을 할게요.

여 그래 줄래? 나중에 Ted가 너에게 뭔가 보답해 줄 거라고 확신해.

남 아마도요. 하지만 그것은 제게는 정말로 중요하지 않아요.

여 착하기도 해라!

Solution

쓰레기통을 비우기로 되어 있던 Ted가 그것을 잊고 하교한 상황에서 남자가 그 일을 대신 하겠다고 했으므로 정답은 ③이다.

Words

waste bin 쓰레기통 repay 보답하다, 갚다 matter 중요하다

06 정답 ③

Script

W These pictures came out really well.

M Yes, they sure did. Why don't you frame some of them?

W That's exactly what I was thinking. I like those heart-shaped frames over there. How much are they?

M Normally they are ten dollars each, but I will give you ten percent off.

W That's still too expensive. Can you lower the price a little more? I had five rolls of film developed here.

M Well, that's why I offered you ten percent off. How many pictures are you going to frame?

W I'd like to frame two pictures from each roll of film.

M So a total of ten pictures, right? In that case, I will give you an extra one dollar off per frame.

W Okay. That sounds more reasonable. I'll pay by credit card.

여 이 사진들 정말 잘 나왔네요.

남 네, 정말 잘 나왔어요. 그것들 중 몇 장을 액자에 담아 보는게 어떠세요?

여 그게 바로 제가 생각하고 있었던 거예요. 저기 저 하트 모양의 액자들이 마음에 들어요. 그것들은 얼마예요?

남 원래는 액자 한 개당 10달러이지만 10퍼센트를 할인해 드릴게요.

여 여전히 너무 비싸네요. 가격을 조금 더 내려 주실 수 있나요? 제가 여기서 필름을 다섯 통이나 현상했어요.

남 음, 그래서 손님께 10퍼센트 할인을 제공해 드린 겁니다. 사진을 몇 장이나 액자에 넣으실 건가요?

여 각 필름에서 두 장씩을 액자에 넣고 싶어요.

남 그럼 총 10장이죠, 맞죠? 그렇다면 액자 한 개당 추가로 1달러씩 깎아 드릴게요.

여 좋아요. 한결 합당한 가격 같네요. 신용카드로 지불할게요.

Solution

원래 한 개당 10달러인 액자를 10퍼센트인 1달러씩 할인해 주겠다고 제안했다가 액자 한 개당 1달러를 추가로 할인해 주겠다고 했으므로 한 개당 가격은 8달러이다. 총 10장의 사진을 액자에 넣겠다고 했으므로 여자가 지불할 금액은 ③ '80달러'이다.

Words

come out really well (사진이) 아주 잘 나오다
frame 액자에 넣다; 액자 develop (필름을) 현상하다
in that case 그렇다면 extra 추가의

07 정답 ②

Script

M Ms. Donovan, can I talk to you for a second?

W Sure, Mr. Williams! Come on in and have a seat.

M Thank you.

W So, what's this about?

M Would you mind if I have the morning off tomorrow?

W Of course not. I hear the flu is going around. Are you feeling okay?

M I'm fine. It's just my mom. She is having an operation tomorrow morning.

W Oh, no! I'm sorry to hear that. I didn't know she was sick.

M Well, it's a fairly routine operation, but I think I have to be with her.

W I hope it isn't serious. And I think you should take the entire day off, not just the morning.

M Thanks a lot. You are so understanding.

W Don't mention it. That's how I should be.

- -

남 Donovan 씨, 잠시 말씀 좀 나눌 수 있을까요?

여 물론이죠, Williams 씨! 들어와서 앉으세요.

남 감사합니다.

여 그래서, 무슨 일이세요?

남 내일 오전에 휴가를 사용해도 괜찮을까요?

여 물론 괜찮지요. 독감이 돌고 있다던데. 오늘 기분 괜찮으세요?

남 저는 괜찮아요. 제 어머니 때문에요. 어머니께서 내일 아침에 수술을 받을 예정이세요.

여 오, 저런! 그것 안됐군요. 어머니께서 아프신지 모르고 있었어요.

남 음, 꽤 일상적인 수술입니다만, 어머니 옆에 있어 드려야 할 것 같아요.

여 심각한 것이 아니길 바래요. 그리고 단지 오전이 아니라 하루를 쉬셔야 할 것 같은데요.

남 정말 고맙습니다. 널리 헤아려 주시는군요.

여 천만에요. 당연히 그렇게 해야지요.

Solution

남자가 내일 오전에 휴가를 신청하며 자신의 어머니가 수술하게 되어 보살펴 드려야 한다고 이유를 말하고 있으므로, 정답은 ②이다.

Words

flu 독감 operation 수술 fairly 상당히, 꽤 routine 일상적인
understanding 이해심 있는

08 정답 ⑤

Script

W Kevin, look at the ad.

M Oh, a magic show will be held at the Royal Culture Center.

W Right. It says seven famous magicians will perform, including Jack Hunters.

M Jack Hunters is my favorite magician. Why don't we see this show?

W I'd like to, but the tickets are $20. Don't you think it's expensive?

M A bit. But I'm sure it'll be worth that much.

W Okay. Let's go. The show starts on May 10th and lasts 5 days. When do want to see the show?

M The earlier, the better. Let's see it on the first day.

W The first day? I love it. I can't wait to see the performance.

M Me, too.

- -

여 Kevin, 이 광고를 봐.

남 오, Royal 문화 센터에서 마술 쇼가 열리는구나.

여 그래. Jack Hunters를 포함해서 7명의 유명한 마술사들이 공연할 거라고 광고에 나와 있어.

남 Jack Hunters는 내가 가장 좋아하는 마술사야. 우리 이 쇼 보러 가는 게 어때?

여 그러고 싶은데, 입장료가 20달러야. 비싸다고 생각하지 않니?

남 약간은. 하지만 그만큼 가치가 있을 것이라고 확신해.

여 좋아. 같이 가자. 쇼는 5월 10일에 시작해서 5일간 지속돼. 언제 그 쇼를 보고 싶어?

남 빠르면 빠를수록 더 좋지. 첫날에 보자.

여 첫날? 아주 좋아. 공연을 빨리 보고 싶다.

남 나도 그래.

Solution

장소, 참가 마술사 수, 입장료, 공연 시작일은 언급되었으나 ⑤ '공연 시간'은 언급되지 않았다.

Words

the earlier, the better 빠르면 빠를수록, 더 좋다

09 정답 ⑤

Script

M Hello, students. Please give me your attention for a minute. Let me tell you about the Short Marathon, which will be held on the 1st of next month. The purpose of the marathon is to celebrate the school's 30th anniversary and the marathon is open to all students regardless of grade.

The marathon consists of three running courses: 5 km, 7 km, and 10 km, so you can sign up for the distance that is appropriate for your running ability. You can complete an entry form for the marathon on the school's website. Souvenirs will be offered to all participants, and those who complete their course will receive a medal. I hope many students who are interested in marathons participate.

- -

남 안녕하세요, 학생 여러분. 잠시만 저에게 집중해 주십시오. 다음 달 1일에 개최될 Short Marathon에 대해 말씀드리겠습니다. 이 마라톤의 목적은 개교 30주년을 축하하는 것으로, 마라톤은 학년에 관계없이 모든 학생이 참가할 수 있습니다. 마라톤은 5km, 7km, 10km인 세 개의 달리기 코스로 이루어져 있어서, 자신의 달리기 실력에 적합한 거리를 신청할 수 있습니다. 여러분은 학교 웹사이트에서 마라톤을 위한 참가 신청서를 작성할 수 있습니다. 모든 참가자에게 기념품이 제공될 것이고, 자신의 코스를 완주하는 참가자는 메달을 받을 것입니다. 마라톤에 관심 있는 많은 학생들이 참가하기를 바랍니다.

Solution

기념품은 모든 참가자에게 주어지고, 메달은 코스를 완주한 참가자에게만 주어진다고 했으므로, ⑤가 담화의 내용과 일치하지 않는다.

Words

regardless of ~에 관계없이 consist of ~로 구성되다
entry form 참가 신청서

10 정답 ④

Script

W What are you looking at?

M I'm looking for the best way to get to Holland Wedding Hall.

W Who's getting married?

M My cousin, Gerald. I'm going to accompany my parents to the wedding hall.

W Then you will drive your car there, won't you?

M I'd rather not. There's usually an awful traffic jam. Last time, it took me almost 3 hours to drive there, so I missed the wedding.

W Then are you going to take the subway?

M Not all the way there. Mom can't stand taking the subway for longer than one hour.

W Then the direct bus is a good option.

M Well, the fare is expensive for the amount of time we save, so I'd rather not ride it.

W Then you have two options, the one with a longer time and one transfer and the one with a shorter time and two transfers.

M I'll take the one with the shorter time.

- -

여 무엇을 보고 있어요?
남 Holland 결혼식장으로 가는 가장 좋은 방법을 찾고 있어요.
여 누가 결혼해요?
남 사촌 Gerald요. 부모님을 모시고 결혼식장에 갈 거예요.
여 그러면 거기에 차를 몰고 가겠네요. 아닌가요?
남 차를 몰고 가지 않는 편이 나아요. 보통 극심한 교통 체증이 있어요. 지난번에 거기까지 차를 몰고 가는 데 거의 3시간이 걸려서 결혼식을 놓쳤

어요.
여 그러면 지하철을 타고 가실 거예요?
남 내내 지하철을 타고 가지는 않을 거예요. 어머니께서 한 시간 넘게 지하철 타시는 것을 참을 수 없어 하세요.
여 그렇다면 직행버스가 좋은 선택이군요.
남 글쎄요, 절감되는 소요 시간에 비해서 요금이 비싸서 그것을 타고 싶지 않아요.
여 그러면 두 개의 선택권으로 시간이 더 오래 걸리는 한 번 환승과 시간은 덜 걸리는 두 번 환승이 있네요.
남 저는 시간이 덜 걸리는 것을 선택할 거예요.

Solution

교통 체증 때문에 차를 몰고 가지는 않을 것이고, 어머니 때문에 지하철을 1시간 이상 탈 수 없고, 직행버스는 절감되는 소요 시간에 비해 비싸다고 했다. 남자는 남은 두 가지 방법 중 시간이 덜 걸리는 것을 이용하겠다고 했으므로, 남자가 결혼식장으로 갈 방법은 ④이다.

Words

accompany ~와 함께 가다 stand 참다, 견디다 option 선택(권)
transfer 환승

11 정답 ④

Script

W Honey, how about booking the Rainbow Hotel for our trip to Jeju Island?

M I'd like to stay at a hotel near the beach. Is it located near the beach?

W Yes, it is. And it opened just last month, so all the facilities are in very good condition.

M I like it. Let's book the hotel right now.

- -

여 여보, 제주도 여행을 위해 Rainbow 호텔을 예약하는 게 어때요?
남 나는 해변 근처에 있는 호텔에 머물고 싶어요. 그 호텔이 해변 근처에 있나요?
여 네, 그래요. 그리고 이 호텔은 지난달에 막 개업해서, 모든 시설의 상태가 아주 좋아요.
남 마음에 들어요. 지금 바로 그 호텔을 예약합시다.

Solution

여자가 제주도 여행을 위해 Rainbow 호텔을 예약할 것을 제안하자, 남자는 그 호텔이 해변 근처에 있는지 물었고 여자는 그렇다고 하면서 시설 상태도 아주 좋다고 덧붙이고 있으므로, 이에 대한 남자의 응답으로 가장 적절한 것은 ④ '마음에 들어요. 지금 바로 그 호텔을 예약합시다.'이다.

① 걱정 마세요. 내가 좋은 호텔을 찾을게요.
② 아니요, 그 호텔은 어제 문을 열지 않았어요.
③ 그 해변에 가지 마세요. 여전히 추워요.
⑤ 물론이죠! 당신은 제주도 여행을 즐길 거예요.

Words

book 예약하다 be located 위치하다 facilities 시설, 설비

12 정답 ④

Script

M Hi! How much are the tickets?

W They're a dollar each, or fifteen tickets for ten dollars.

M Can you tell me how many tickets we have to spend for

each ride?

W Some cost two tickets, and others cost one.

남 안녕하세요! 티켓이 얼마죠?

여 한 장에 1달러 혹은 15장에 10달러입니다.

남 각각의 놀이기구를 타려면 티켓을 몇 장 써야 하는지 말씀해 주실 수 있나요?

여 어떤 놀이기구는 티켓 두 장을 쓰고, 나머지 놀이기구는 한 장을 씁니다.

남자는 여자에게 놀이기구를 타는 데 티켓을 몇 장 써야 하는지 수량에 관해 묻고 있으므로, 이에 대한 여자의 응답으로 가장 적절한 것은 ④ '어떤 놀이기구는 티켓 두 장을 쓰고, 나머지 놀이기구는 한 장을 씁니다.'이다.

① 당신이 원하는 놀이기구는 무엇이든 탈 수 있어요.

② 6세 미만의 어린이는 이것을 탈 수 없어요.

③ 이른 아침에는 덜 붐벼요.

⑤ 롤러코스터가 십 대들 사이에서 가장 인기가 있어요.

ride 놀이기구, 탈것; 타다 cost ~의 비용이 들다

13 정답 ④

M Hello, Mrs. Williams. You wanted to see me, right?

W Yes, Nick. Come on in and have a seat.

M Thank you.

W How's your school life?

M It's as good as ever.

W I'm glad to hear that. Actually, I hear you're doing very well.

M It's all thanks to you. I know what you've done to put me in the right direction.

W No, no. You made the choice to go in the right direction. By the way, have you seen Jack recently?

M No. We're not as close now.

W But you know where he lives, don't you?

M Yes, I do.

W So can you take me there this afternoon?

M Why not? I'll meet you here after school.

남 안녕하세요. Williams 선생님. 저를 보고 싶어 하셨죠, 그렇죠?

여 그래, Nick. 들어와서 앉으렴.

남 감사합니다.

여 학교 생활은 어떠니?

남 그 어느 때만큼이나 좋습니다.

여 그 말을 들으니 기분이 좋구나. 사실, 네가 아주 잘하고 있다는 것을 듣고 있단다.

남 모두 선생님 덕분입니다. 제가 올바른 방향으로 나아갈 수 있도록 선생님께서 애써 주신 것을 알고 있어요.

여 아냐, 아냐. 네가 올바른 방향으로 나아가기로 선택한 거야. 그건 그렇고, 최근에 Jack을 본 적이 있니?

남 아뇨. 저희는 이제 그렇게 친하지 않아요.

여 하지만 그가 살고 있는 곳을 알고는 있지, 그렇지 않니?

남 네, 알아요.

여 그럼 오늘 오후에 나를 그곳에 데려다줄 수 있니?

남 왜 안 되겠어요? 방과 후에 제가 선생님을 여기서 뵐게요.

여자는 남자에게 가정 방문을 하려고 하는 Jack의 집까지 데려다줄 수 있는지 도움을 요청하고 있다. 이에 대한 남자의 응답으로 가장 적절한 것은 ④ '왜 안 되겠어요? 방과 후에 제가 선생님을 여기서 뵐게요.'이다.

① 저는 지도를 잘 볼 줄 몰라요.

② 그는 지금 일주일째 결석하고 있어요.

③ 걱정 마세요. 선생님께서 너무 예민하세요.

⑤ 그는 엄마와 조부모님과 살고 있어요.

thanks to ~ 덕분에

go in the right direction 올바른 방향으로 나아가다

close 친한; 가까운

14 정답 ⑤

M Jenny, are you busy now?

W No. I'm just watching a movie on my smartphone. Why?

M Then will you stop watching it and help me for a minute?

W Sure! What should I do, Dad?

M You know your grandmother is coming this evening, don't you?

W Yes, I do. She will stay with us for about a week.

M That's right. So I'm thinking about making the seafood spaghetti that she likes.

W Great. I also like your seafood spaghetti.

M But the problem is that there's not enough seafood in the fridge.

W Don't worry. Let me go and buy some seafood right now.

남 Jenny, 지금 바쁘니?

여 아니요. 스마트폰으로 단지 영화를 보는 중이에요. 왜요?

남 그럼 영화 보는 것을 멈추고 잠시 나를 도와줄래?

여 물론이죠! 제가 무엇을 해야 하죠, 아빠?

남 오늘 저녁 할머니가 오시는 것을 알고 있지, 그렇지 않니?

여 네, 알아요. 할머니께서 일주일 정도 저희와 함께 계실 거잖아요.

남 맞아. 그래서 할머니께서 좋아하시는 해산물 스파게티를 아빠가 만들까 생각 중이야.

여 좋아요. 저도 아빠가 만든 해산물 스파게티를 좋아해요.

남 하지만 문제는 냉장고에 해산물이 충분하지 않다는 거야.

여 걱정 마세요. 제가 지금 바로 해산물을 좀 사러 갈게요.

남자는 여자에게 도움을 요청하면서 할머니를 위해 해산물 스파게티를 요리할 생각인데 냉장고에 해산물이 충분히 있지 않은 것이 문제라고 했으므로, 이에 대한 여자의 응답으로 가장 적절한 것은 ⑤ '걱정 마세요. 제가 지금 바로 해산물을 좀 사러 갈게요.'이다.

① 미안해요. 해산물 레스토랑 찾는 게 어려워요.

② 좋아요. 그녀와 함께 요리 수업에 가요.

③ 알겠어요. 영화 보고 난 후에 냉장고를 청소할게요.

④ 물론이죠! 할머니는 정말로 아빠의 스파게티를 좋아하셨어요.

for a minute 잠시 동안 fridge 냉장고

15 정답 ③

W Fred comes from a big family. His parents always put emphasis on honesty. To save his parents the burden of paying his tuition, Fred works part-time at a nearby supermarket. Yesterday, he failed to give change to a female customer. He only realized that after the customer had left, so he felt bad. Today, Fred sees the same customer waiting in line to pay for the groceries. He feels grateful that he can make up for his mistake. Right now she stands before the check-out counter, ready to pay. Fred wants to admit his mistake and give the change back to her. In this situation, what would Fred most likely say to the customer?

Fred I forgot to give you the change yesterday. Here it is.

여 Fred는 대가족 출신입니다. 그의 부모님은 항상 정직을 강조합니다. 부모님께서 자신의 학비를 지불하시는 부담을 덜어드리기 위해 Fred는 근처의 슈퍼마켓에서 아르바이트를 합니다. 어제 그는 한 여성 손님에게 거스름돈을 주지 못했습니다. 그는 그 손님이 떠나고 난 후에야 그 사실을 깨닫고는 기분이 좋지 않았습니다. 오늘, Fred는 같은 손님이 장을 보고 돈을 지불하려고 줄을 서 있는 모습을 봅니다. 그는 자신의 실수를 만회할 수 있어서 감사함을 느낍니다. 지금 막 그녀가 계산을 할 준비를 하려고 계산대 앞에 서 있습니다. Fred는 자신의 실수를 인정하고 거스름돈을 그녀에게 돌려주고 싶어 합니다. 이런 상황에서, Fred는 그 손님에게 뭐라고 말할 것 같은가요?

Fred 어제 제가 거스름돈을 드리는 것을 깜빡했습니다. 여기 있습니다.

Solution

슈퍼마켓에서 일하는 Fred가 어제 거스름돈을 주지 못한 손님을 우연히 만나 그 손님에게 실수를 인정하고 거스름돈을 돌려주려고 하는 상황이므로, 이러한 상황에서 Fred가 손님에게 할 말로 가장 적절한 것은 ③ '어제 제가 거스름돈을 드리는 것을 깜빡했습니다. 여기 있습니다.'이다.

① 당신 잘못이 아니에요. 그것에 대해 걱정하지 마세요.
② 여기에 또 오셨군요. 뵙게 되어 기쁩니다.
④ 줄을 서서 차례를 기다려 주세요. 오래 걸리지 않을 겁니다.
⑤ 여기에 지갑을 떨어뜨리셨어요. 좀 더 조심하도록 하세요.

Words

put emphasis on ~을 강조하다 burden 부담
tuition 학비 change 거스름돈 grateful 감사하는
make up for ~을 만회하다 admit 인정하다

16 정답 ⑤   17 정답 ⑤

M What kinds of television programs are popular varies depending on age, gender, region, and culture. However, global audiences gather to watch television for two reasons. They are huge news stories such as the explosion of an airplane by a missile and sporting events. Then which of the two attracts more advertisements? Needless to say, it's sporting events. Sports may be the best advertising vehicle ever invented. It fills much of the prime time when the highest advertisement rates are guaranteed. Other than hours of television time, you can create more profits by placing billboards around the grandstands, painting slogans on the fields, and getting the players to wear uniforms with corporate logos. Marketers realized that sports has generated and will continue to generate revenue. In fact, advertising during the 2020 Super Bowl is known to have cost $6,000,000 for a 30-second spot.

남 어떤 종류의 텔레비전 프로그램이 인기가 있는가는 연령, 성별, 지역, 그리고 문화에 따라 다릅니다. 하지만 전 세계 시청자들은 두 가지 이유로 모여서 텔레비전을 시청합니다. 미사일에 의한 항공기 폭발과 같은 대단한 뉴스거리와 스포츠 경기를 보기 위해서입니다. 그러면 그 두 가지 중 어느 것이 더 많은 광고를 이끌어 낼까요? 말할 것도 없이, 스포츠 경기입니다. 스포츠는 지금까지 만들어진 최고의 광고 수단일지도 모릅니다. 그것은 가장 높은 광고료가 보장된 황금 시간대의 대부분을 차지합니다. 텔레비전 시간 이외에도 관람석에 광고판을 배치하고, 경기장에 선전 문구를 장식하고, 선수들에게 회사 로고가 있는 유니폼을 입게 해서 더 많은 수익을 창출할 수도 있습니다. 마케팅 담당자는 스포츠가 수익을 창출해 왔으며 계속 창출해 나갈 것임을 깨달았습니다. 실제로, 2020년 Super Bowl 동안의 30초짜리 광고가 6백만 달러의 비용이 든 것으로 알려져 있습니다.

Solution

16

최고의 수익을 내는 광고 수단인 스포츠 경기에 대해 설명하고 있으므로 남자가 하는 말의 주제로 가장 적절한 것은 ⑤ '광고업 분야에서의 스포츠의 인기'이다.

① 시선을 사로잡는 일련의 국제 뉴스
② 텔레비전 뉴스가 인기가 있는 이유들
③ 세계에서 가장 인기 있는 스포츠 행사들
④ 광고가 시청률에 미치는 영향

17

텔레비전, 광고판, 선전 문구, 유니폼은 언급되었지만, ⑤ '후원'은 언급되지 않았다.

Words

needless to say 말할 필요 없이 vehicle 수단, 매개체
grandstand 관람석 generate 만들어 내다 revenue 수익, 수입

01 ⑤	02 ④	03 ②	04 ⑤	05 ①
06 ⑤	07 ④	08 ④	09 ③	10 ④
11 ③	12 ④	13 ⑤	14 ⑤	15 ⑤
16 ④	17 ③			

01 정답 ⑤

Script

W Are you looking for a place to spend your holiday? A place to provide you with a variety of water activities and a valuable experience with your family? Well, what about Paradise Springs? Paradise Springs is a fairly small town, but it offers much for your amusement. Water sports are by far the most popular. You can enjoy your day outside rafting or swimming in the sun. You can also try your luck at fishing in peaceful surroundings. Or maybe you would prefer to pick some wild strawberries that grow along the roadsides. Also, there are lovely campgrounds where you can share memorable experiences with your family. You can enjoy shopping at the open market where local folks sell produce grown in their gardens. If you want to have a nice holiday, you are welcome to visit Paradise Springs.

여 휴가를 보낼 곳을 찾고 있습니까? 다양한 수상 활동과 가족과의 소중한 경험을 제공해 줄 곳을 찾고 있습니까? 그럼, Paradise Springs는 어떻습니까? Paradise Springs는 아주 조그만 마을이지만 여러분을 즐겁게 해 줄 많은 것을 제공하고 있습니다. 수상 스포츠가 단연코 가장 인기가 있습니다. 여러분은 태양 아래 야외에서 여러분의 하루를 래프팅이나 수영으로 즐기실 수 있습니다. 또한 평화로운 환경에서 낚시를 하며 운수를 시험해 볼 수도 있습니다. 또는 길가를 따라 자라나는 산딸기를 따보는 것을 아마도 선호하실 것입니다. 또한 가족과 함께 기억에 남을 경험을 공유할 수 있는 아름다운 캠핑장도 있습니다. 마을 사람들이 텃밭에서 재배한 농산물을 판매하는 야외 시장에서 쇼핑을 즐기실 수 있습니다. 멋진 휴가를 보내길 원하시면 Paradise Springs를 방문하시는 것을 환영합니다.

Solution

다양한 수상 스포츠를 즐길 수 있고, 낚시나 산딸기를 따볼 수 있고, 가족들과 소중한 경험을 공유할 수 있는 캠핑장도 사용할 수 있는 조그마한 마을을 휴가를 보낼 장소로 추천하고 있으므로 여자가 하는 말의 목적으로 가장 적절한 것은 ⑤이다.

Words

amusement 즐거움 by far 단연코 roadside 길가
campground 캠핑장 memorable 기억할 만한 produce 농산물

02 정답 ④

Script

M Have you read *Captain Jackson's Destiny*?

W No, but I read about it in the paper. It said a movie will be made based on the book.

M I've heard that, too. Anyways, I'd like to recommend this book to you. It's really touching.

W Well, the title doesn't sound like my sort of thing.

M The story is different from what you would expect from the title. It's the best thing I've read in ages. I'm sure you'll like it.

W Really? Then when the movie comes out, I'll watch it.

M Well, I don't think that's a good idea.

W How come?

M The movie won't move you as much as the book.

W Do you really think so?

M Of course. Touching stories often fail to stir their intended emotions in the form of a movie.

남 'Captain Jackson's Destiny'를 읽어 봤니?

여 아니, 하지만 신문에서 그 책에 관해 읽기는 했어. 원작을 바탕으로 영화가 제작될 거라고 하던데.

남 나도 그것을 듣기는 했어. 어쨌든 난 네게 그 책을 권하고 싶어. 정말로 감동적이야.

여 글쎄, 제목을 보면 내가 좋아하는 종류의 것은 아닌 것 같아.

남 내용은 제목에서 네가 기대하는 것과는 달라. 그 책은 내가 오랫동안 읽어 본 최고의 것이야. 나는 네가 그것을 좋아할 거라고 확신해.

여 정말? 그렇다면 영화가 나오면 볼게.

남 글쎄, 그것은 좋은 생각은 아닌 것 같아.

여 어째서?

남 영화는 책만큼 너를 감동시키지는 못할 거야.

여 정말로 그렇게 생각해?

남 물론이지. 감동적인 이야기는 영화의 형태로는 의도된 감정을 불러일으키는 데 종종 실패하지.

Solution

남자는 책에 담긴 감동적인 줄거리는 원작으로 봐야하고 영화로 제작되면 책만큼의 감동을 주지 못한다며 책으로 읽을 것을 권하고 있으므로 남자의 의견으로 가장 적절한 것은 ④이다.

Words

my sort of thing 내가 좋아하는 종류의 것 in ages 오랫동안
stir (감정을) 일으키다, 감동시키다

03 정답 ②

Script

W Hi, Hank. You've been doing pretty well.

M Thank you, Lisa. Yeah, I'm satisfied with my recent performance. What's up, anyway?

W I have some good news and bad news for you.

M It's about my contract, right?

W Yes. The good news is that the Angels have offered you a three-year, 10 million dollar contract.

M A three-year, 10 million dollar contract? That's awesome. What's the bad news?

W You have to go through a special medical test, not just a routine physical exam. That is, you have to prove there is nothing wrong with your shoulder.

M Isn't my recent performance enough to prove that my shoulder is strong?

W I am afraid that they want to make sure about your

shoulder.

M Well, considering my injury history, it's understandable. I'll sleep on it. Thanks, Lisa.

여 안녕하세요, Hank. 아주 잘 해오고 있어요.

남 고마워요, Lisa. 그래요, 저의 최근 활약에 만족하고 있어요. 어쨌든, 무슨 일이에요?

여 당신에게 좋은 소식과 나쁜 소식이 있어요.

남 제 계약에 관한 것이죠, 맞죠?

여 네. 좋은 소식은 Angels 구단이 천만 달러의 3년 계약을 제안했다는 거예요.

남 천만 달러에 3년 계약이요? 그것 대단하군요. 안 좋은 소식은 뭐죠?

여 일상적인 건강 검진이 아닌 특별한 건강 검진을 받아야 한다는 거예요. 즉, 어깨에 이상이 없음을 증명해야 하는 거죠.

남 저의 최근 활약이 내 어깨가 튼튼하다는 것을 보여주기에 충분하지 않은가요?

여 그들이 당신의 어깨에 대해 확실하게 하고 싶어 하는 것 같아요.

남 사실, 부상 경력을 감안하면 이해는 돼요. 하룻밤 자며 생각해 볼게요. 고마워요, Lisa.

Solution

여자가 남자의 계약에 관한 소식을 전하는 상황으로, Angels 구단에서 3년간 천만 달러를 제시하며 특별한 건강 검진을 요구했다는 여자의 말에 남자가 생각해 보겠다며 감사의 말을 전하고 있으므로 두 사람의 관계를 가장 잘 나타낸 것은 ②이다.

Words

performance 활약, 실적 contract 계약
awesome 정말 대단한, 근사한 medical test 건강 검진
sleep on ~을 하룻밤 자며 생각하다

04 정답 ⑤

Script

W Look! I've finally finished decorating the living room for the Christmas party.

M Great! I like the Merry Christmas banner on the center wall.

W Thanks. And I placed the Christmas tree you bought next to the fireplace.

M I like it there. In particular, the star-shaped decoration on top of the tree looks very impressive.

W Thanks.

M Oh, you hung a big sock on each side of the fireplace.

W Yes. One is for our son, and the other is for our daughter.

M Good. What are the two square boxes on the round table?

W They are gift boxes. I'll put the kids' gifts there.

M They will be very happy to open them.

여 봐요! 크리스마스 파티를 위한 거실 꾸미는 것을 드디어 끝냈어요.

남 아주 좋아요! 벽 중앙에 있는 메리 크리스마스 현수막이 마음에 들어요.

여 고마워요. 그리고 당신이 산 크리스마스트리를 벽난로 옆에 두었어요.

남 나는 그것이 거기에 있는게 마음에 들어요. 특히, 크리스마스트리 꼭대기에 있는 별 모양의 장식이 매우 인상적이에요.

여 고마워요.

남 오, 벽난로의 양쪽에 큰 양말을 한 개씩 걸었군요.

여 그래요. 하나는 우리 아들, 다른 하나는 우리 딸을 위한 것이에요.

남 좋아요. 둥근 탁자 위에 있는 이 두 개의 네모난 상자는 무엇이죠?

여 선물 상자예요. 아이들의 선물을 그 안에 넣을 거예요.

남 그것들을 열면 아이들이 매우 행복해할 거예요.

Solution

둥근 탁자 위에 두 개의 네모난 상자가 놓여 있다고 했지만 그림에서는 둥근 상자가 있으므로 대화의 내용과 일치하지 않는 것은 ⑤이다.

Words

decorate 장식하다 banner 현수막 fireplace 벽난로
in particular 특히 star-shaped 별 모양의 impressive 인상적인

05 정답 ①

Script

M Linda, is that you?

W Oh, Mark. Hi.

M What are you doing outside your car in this hot weather?

W Can you believe this? I locked my keys in the car.

M Really? Did you call an insurance company?

W Yes. But the lines have been busy for the past ten minutes.

M It sounds like there's a high demand for their services right now.

W Mark, will you do me a favor?

M Sure. What is it?

W I have to go to the airport to pick up my cousin. He's supposed to arrive at 4 p.m.

M Sounds like you need to hurry.

W Yes. Can you drive me home right now? I have a spare key there.

M Sure. I can drive you back here again.

W Thanks a million.

남 Linda, 너니?

여 오, Mark. 안녕.

남 이 더운 날에 차 밖에서 뭐 하고 있는 거니?

여 너는 이것을 믿을 수 있겠니? 자동차 키를 차에 두고 문을 잠갔어.

남 정말? 보험 회사에 전화했니?

여 응. 하지만 10분째 통화 중이야.

남 지금 서비스 요구가 많아서인 것 같아.

여 Mark, 부탁 좀 하나 들어줄래?

남 물론이지. 뭔데?

여 공항에 사촌을 데리러 가야 해. 오후 4시에 도착하기로 되어 있어.

남 서둘러야 할 것 같은데.

여 응. 지금 나를 집까지 태워다 줄 수 있을까? 집에 여분의 키가 있어.

남 알았어. 내가 이곳으로 다시 태워다 줄 수 있어.

여 정말 고마워.

Solution

자동차 키를 차 안에 두고 문을 잠근 여자는 집에 여분의 키가 있다며 집까지 차로 데려다 달라고 남자에게 부탁하고 있으므로, 정답은 ①이다.

Words

insurance company 보험 회사 line 전화선; 전화 demand 요구
pick up 데리러 가다 spare 여분의

06 정답 ⑤

Script

M Excuse me.

W Yes. Is there anything you need?

M Yeah, I think there is something wrong with this check.

W Really? What is it, sir?

M Look at this. It says here the steak dinner costs $60, not $50.

W Oh, it was $50 up until the end of August. But because of the rising cost of beef, we raised the price by 20 percent at the beginning of September.

M Oh, you did? I didn't know that. What about the tax and service charges?

W The tax is included in the price of the meal and the service charge is 10 percent of the total. As you can see, your total is $60.

M I see. Here's my credit card.

W Thank you, sir.

남 실례합니다.

여 네. 필요하신 게 있나요?

남 네, 계산서에 잘못된 것이 있는 것 같아요.

여 그래요? 뭐가 말인가요, 손님?

남 여기 좀 보세요. 스테이크 저녁식사가 60달러라고 적혀 있어요. 50달러가 아니고요.

여 오, 8월 말까지는 50달러였습니다. 그런데 소고깃값 상승으로 9월 초에 가격을 20퍼센트 인상했습니다.

남 오, 그래요? 제가 몰랐군요. 세금과 봉사료는 어떻게 되죠?

여 세금은 식사 가격에 포함되어 있고, 봉사료는 총액의 10퍼센트입니다. 보시다시피 손님의 총액은 60달러입니다.

남 알겠습니다. 여기 제 신용카드가 있습니다.

여 고맙습니다, 손님.

Solution

소고깃값 상승으로 스테이크 가격이 50달러에서 20퍼센트 인상되어 60달러가 되었고, 10퍼센트의 봉사료(6달러)가 있으므로 남자가 지불할 금액은 ⑤ '66달러'이다.

Words

check 계산서 up until ~까지 charge 요금

07 정답 ④

Script

[Cellphone rings.]

M Hello, Laura! How are you?

W Hi, Jason. Fine, thanks. Listen! I'm going to make a weekly study group. Would you like to join us?

M A study group? Sure, I'd love to. Who else do you have in mind?

W Tony and Julia both said yes. Which time is good for you, Thursday evening or Friday evening?

M Thursday evening is better for me.

W Good. What's your e-mail address? I am going to send you the details.

M My e-mail address is Jason@naver.com.

W Okay. And I am trying to reach John, but I can't get a hold of him. You're in swimming class with him, aren't you?

M Yes. Is John going to be a member of the study group?

W That's what I want to ask him. Can you tell him to call me?

M No problem.

[휴대전화가 울린다.]

남 여보세요. Laura! 어떻게 지내?

여 안녕, Jason. 잘 지내, 고마워. 들어 봐! 주마다 하는 공부 모임을 만들려고 하고 있어. 우리와 같이 할래?

남 공부 모임? 물론, 하고 싶어. 달리 누구를 염두에 두고 있니?

여 Tony와 Julia 둘 다 좋다고 했어. 목요일 저녁과 금요일 저녁 중 어느 시간이 좋니?

남 목요일 저녁이 더 좋아.

여 잘됐다. 전자 우편 주소가 어떻게 되지? 내가 세부 사항을 보낼게.

남 내 전자 우편 주소는 Jason@naver.com이야.

여 알았어. 그리고 John하고 연락을 하려고 하는데, 연락이 안 돼. 그 애랑 같이 수영 수업 듣고 있지, 그렇지 않니?

남 응. John도 공부 모임 회원이 되는 거야?

여 그걸 그에게 물어보고 싶은 거야. 나에게 전화해 달라고 전해 줄래?

남 그럴게.

Solution

여자는 주마다 하는 공부 모임을 만들고 회원을 모으고 있으며, 연락이 되지 않는 John에게 모임 참석 여부를 묻기 위해 남자를 통해 John과 통화하려고 한다. 따라서 정답은 ④이다.

Words

have ~ in mind ~을 염두에 두다 details 세부 사항
get a hold of ~와 연락하다

08 정답 ④

Script

M Good morning, honey.

W Good morning. Did you sleep well last night?

M Yes, I did. When do you think breakfast will be ready?

W In half an hour.

M Then I'll trim the trees in the garden.

W Thanks. And can you feed Poppy? Our lovely dog needs some breakfast, too.

M Sure. I'll also water the flowers.

W Thank you, Ted. Oh, one more thing. I forgot to check the mailbox yesterday. Would you do that, too?

M No problem. I'm sure to work up an appetite doing all of those chores.

W Well, you'll be rewarded with a delicious breakfast.

남 좋은 아침이에요, 여보.

여 좋은 아침이에요. 지난밤에 잘 잤어요?

남 네, 그랬어요. 아침은 언제 준비가 될 것 같나요?

여 30분 후에요.

남 그러면 나는 정원의 나무들을 좀 다듬을게요.

여 고마워요. 그리고 Poppy에게 밥을 좀 줄래요? 우리의 사랑스러운 개도 아침식사가 좀 필요해요.

남 물론이죠. 꽃에 물도 줄게요.

여 고마워요, Ted. 오, 한 가지 더요. 어제 내가 우편함을 확인하는 것을 잊

었어요. 그것도 좀 해 줄래요?

남 문제없어요. 그 모든 일을 하면 식욕이 돋을 거라 확신해요.

여 음, 맛있는 아침식사로 보상받을 거예요.

Solution

남자가 할 일로 나무 손질하기, 개에게 밥 주기, 꽃에 물 주기, 우편물 확인하기는 언급되었으나 ④ '분리수거하기'는 언급되지 않았다.

Words

trim 손질하다, 다듬다 feed 먹이다 water 물을 주다 mailbox 우편함
work up ～을 불러일으키다

09 정답 ③

Script

M Welcome to the Jeju Teddy Bear Museum. Here you will find everything you want to know about teddy bears! The museum opened on April 24th, 2019. It has a history gallery and an art gallery. We are open from 9 a.m. to 7 p.m. throughout most of the year. But from July 16th to August 25th, we stay open until 10 p.m. Tickets are on sale until one hour before the closing time. No food or drinks may be brought into the museum. Our museum also has a gift shop, with over 1,000 products for sale. There you will find stuffed teddy bears of all sizes, jewelry, T-shirts, cups, and much more. During your visit, be sure to stop by the outside garden — it has a perfect view of Jeju Beach.

남 제주 테디베어 박물관에 오신 것을 환영합니다. 이곳에서 테디베어에 관해 여러분이 알고 싶어 하는 모든 것을 찾을 것입니다! 박물관은 2019년 4월 24일에 개관했습니다. 역사관과 미술관이 있습니다. 1년의 대부분은 오전 9시에서 오후 7시까지 개관합니다. 그러나 7월 16일부터 8월 25일까지는 오후 10시까지 개관합니다. 표는 폐관 시간 한 시간 전까지 판매합니다. 음식이나 음료는 박물관 안으로 가지고 들어갈 수 없습니다. 우리 박물관은 1,000개 이상의 상품을 구비한 선물 가게도 있습니다. 거기서 여러분은 모든 크기의 봉제 테디베어 인형, 보석, 티셔츠, 컵과 그밖에 더 많은 것들을 볼 것입니다. 방문 시에 야외 정원에 꼭 들르십시오. 그곳은 완벽한 제주 해변 전망을 갖추고 있습니다.

Solution

폐관 시간 한 시간 전까지 표를 판매한다고 했으므로 ③이 담화의 내용과 일치하지 않는다.

Words

gallery 미술관 gift shop 선물 가게

10 정답 ④

Script

M Honey, let's look at the Sun Star Hotel reservation site and decide which room to stay in for our trip next month.

W Okay. Is there any room type you'd prefer?

M Any room is okay, except for a standard room. It's our once-in-a-lifetime honeymoon.

W Yes. What about the view?

M I want to wake up in the morning and see the ocean.

W Me, too. An ocean view is better than a mountain view.

M Now we have to think about the room rate.

W Well, although it's our honeymoon, I think more than $300 a day is too expensive.

M I agree. Um... now there are two rooms left.

W Don't you think this room with breakfast is better than the cheaper one?

M Yes, I do. Okay, let's book this room.

남 여보, Sun Star 호텔 예약 사이트를 보고 다음 달 우리 여행에서 어느 객실에 투숙할지 결정해요.

여 좋아요. 당신이 선호하는 객실 유형이 있나요?

남 스탠더드 객실을 제외하면 모든 객실이 다 좋아요. 이것은 일생에 한 번 있는 우리 신혼여행이잖아요.

여 알았어요. 전망은요?

남 아침에 일어나서 바다를 보고 싶어요.

여 나도 그래요. 바다 전망이 산 전망보다 더 좋아요.

남 이제 객실 요금에 대해 생각해야 해요.

여 음, 비록 신혼여행이라 할지라도, 하루에 300달러 이상은 너무 비싼 것 같아요.

남 동의해요. 음… 이제 객실이 두 개 남았어요.

여 조식을 포함한 이 객실이 더 저렴한 객실보다 더 낫다고 생각하지 않으세요?

남 네, 그래요. 좋아요, 이 객실을 예약해요.

Solution

여자와 남자는 스탠더드 객실을 제외하고, 바다 전망을 가지고 있으면서 하루에 300달러가 넘지 않는 비용이고 조식을 제공하는 객실로 정했으므로 두 사람이 예약할 객실은 ④이다.

Words

except for ～을 제외하고 once-in-a-lifetime 일생에 한 번 있는
honeymoon 신혼여행 room rate 객실 요금

11 정답 ③

Script

W Oh, these yellow goldfish look really cute. I'll buy five of them.

M Thank you. That's $10 in total.

W Here's $10. Ah, how often do I have to feed the goldfish?

M Once a day. It's not difficult to raise them.

여 오, 이 노란 금붕어가 정말 귀엽네요. 노란 금붕어 다섯 마리 살게요.

남 고맙습니다. 모두 해서 10달러입니다.

여 10달러 여기 있습니다. 아, 금붕어에게 먹이를 얼마나 자주 주어야 하나요?

남 하루에 한 번이요. 금붕어를 키우는 것은 어렵지 않습니다.

Solution

금붕어를 구입한 여자가 먹이를 얼마나 자주 주어야 하는지 물었으므로, 이에 대한 남자의 응답으로 가장 적절한 것은 ③ '하루에 한 번이요. 금붕어를 키우는 것은 어렵지 않습니다.'이다.

① 맞아요. 그것들에게 먹이 주는 것을 멈추어야 해요.

② 내가 당신이라면, 그 금붕어를 살 거예요.

④ 내 생각도 그래요. 당신은 10달러를 지불하지 않았어야 했어요.

⑤ 걱정 마세요. 내가 금붕어를 돌볼게요.

Words

goldfish 금붕어 feed 먹이를 주다

12 정답 ④

M May I help you, ma'am?
W Yes. I'm looking for a present for my daughter.
M Okay. What do you have in mind?
W She really wants a new cellphone case.

남 도와드릴까요, 손님?
여 네. 딸에게 줄 선물을 찾고 있어요.
남 알겠습니다. 무엇을 염두에 두고 계시나요?
여 그녀는 새 휴대전화 케이스를 정말로 갖고 싶어 해요.

Solution

가게 직원인 남자가 손님인 여자에게 딸에게 줄 선물로 어떤 것을 마음에 두고 있는지 의견을 묻고 있으므로, 이에 대한 여자의 응답으로 가장 적절한 것은 ④ '그녀는 새 휴대전화 케이스를 정말로 갖고 싶어 해요.'이다.

① 이 치마를 환불받고 싶어요.
② 제 딸의 열한 번째 생일이에요.
③ 그것은 십 대 소녀에게는 너무 비싸요.
⑤ 그녀가 내 선물을 얼마나 좋아할지 궁금해요.

Words

have ~ in mind ~을 염두에 두다

13 정답 ⑤

Script

M Cindy, did you read the new post on our website's customer bulletin board?
W No, I didn't. What's it about?
M The shower room.
W The shower room? Is it about the water temperature?
M Yes, right. Someone complained that the water is not hot enough to take a shower after practicing yoga.
W I already fixed it last night. You don't have to worry about it.
M Oh, really? That was really fast.
W I also ordered the yoga mats you mentioned yesterday.
M Good. You always work hard.
W My pleasure. I'm just doing my job.
M I think you're the best worker at our yoga center.

남 Cindy, 우리 웹사이트 고객 게시판의 새 게시글을 읽었나요?
여 아니요, 읽지 않았습니다. 무엇에 관한 것이죠?
남 샤워룸이요.
여 샤워룸이요? 물 온도에 대한 것인가요?
남 그래요, 맞아요. 요가 수련을 한 후에 샤워를 하기에 물이 충분히 따뜻하지 않다고 누군가 항의했어요.
여 지난밤에 이것을 이미 수리했습니다. 이것에 대해서는 걱정하지 않으셔도 됩니다.
남 오, 정말이요? 정말로 빠르군요.
여 어제 말씀하신 요가 매트도 주문했습니다.
남 좋아요. 당신은 언제나 일을 열심히 해요.
여 천만에요. 저는 그저 제 일을 할 뿐입니다.
남 당신이 우리 요가 센터에서 최우수 직원이라고 생각해요.

Solution

샤워실의 물 온도에 대한 고객의 항의가 있다는 남자의 말에 여자는 이미 그것을 수리했으며 요가 매트도 주문했다고 말한다. 이에 남자가 여자에게 언제나 일을 열심히 한다는 칭찬을 하자, 여자는 그저 자신의 일을 할 뿐이라고 대답하고 있으므로, 이에 대한 남자의 응답으로 가장 적절한 것은 ⑤ '당신이 우리 요가 센터에서 최우수 직원이라고 생각해요.'이다.

① 당신은 요가 매트를 주문할 필요가 없어요.
② 당신은 이곳에서 요가를 연습하지 않았어야 했어요.
③ 제가 고객 게시판을 확인해 볼게요.
④ 요가 센터에서 일자리를 구하는 것은 어렵지 않아요.

Words

bulletin board 게시판 temperature 온도 complain 항의하다

14 정답 ⑤

Script

W Hi, Greg. Can you spare a few minutes to talk to me?
M Sure. What do you want to talk about?
W It's about Bob. I don't know whether to continue dating him or not.
M What happened? You've been seeing him for months.
W Do you remember the other day when his idea was turned down?
M Yes. He looked a bit disappointed.
W That evening, he said almost nothing.
M He might have been shocked. He had probably worked on his idea for days.
W Maybe, but he went too far. And the day before yesterday, his best friend fell off a bicycle. When he heard the news, guess what he said.
M Beats me. What did he say?
W He said it served him right.
M Well, Bob might have had a reason to be angry at him at that time.
W Well, I have no idea what kind of a person he is.

여 안녕, Greg. 나와 이야기할 시간 좀 잠시 내 줄 수 있을까?
남 물론이지. 무슨 이야기를 하고 싶은데?
여 Bob에 관한 거야. 그 사람하고 교제를 계속해야 할지 말아야 할지 모르겠어.
남 무슨 일이 있었니? 몇 달째 그를 만나고 있잖아.
여 일전에 그의 아이디어가 거절당했던 날 기억나지?
남 응. 좀 실망한 듯 보였어.
여 그날 저녁에, 그는 말을 거의 안 했어.
남 꽤나 충격을 받았나 보구나. 아마도 며칠 동안 그 아이디어에 매달렸을 테니까.
여 그럴지도 모르지만 그는 정도가 지나쳤어. 그리고 그저께는 그의 가장 친한 친구가 자전거에서 떨어졌어. 그 소식을 듣고 그가 뭐라고 했는지 맞혀 봐.
남 전혀 모르겠는데. 뭐라고 했는데?
여 그는 그 친구가 고소하다고 했어.
남 음. 그 당시에 Bob이 그에 관해서 화가 날 이유가 있었을 수도 있지.
여 글쎄. 그가 어떤 부류의 사람인지 모르겠어.

Solution

여자는 교제하고 있는 남자친구의 의외의 행동에 그를 계속 만나야 할지를

고민하며 남자에게 조언을 구하고 있고 남자는 여자의 남자친구를 이해하려는 방향으로 이야기를 하고 있다. 이에 대한 여자의 응답으로 가장 적절한 것은 ⑤ '글쎄, 그가 어떤 부류의 사람인지 모르겠어.'이다.

① 그때 이후로 나는 그로부터 아무것도 듣지 못했어.
② 그가 그렇게 반응하는 것도 당연해.
③ 난 그의 친구에 대해 좋게 말할 것이 없어.
④ 내가 너라면 그를 더 이상 만나지 않을 거야.

Words

spare 할애하다 turn down 거절하다, 퇴짜를 놓다
work on ~에 열심히 하다 (It) Beats me. 전혀 모르겠다.. 금시초문이다.
serve ~ right 고소하다, 인과응보다

15 정답 ⑤

Script

W Olivia and Dustin got married exactly one year ago, and today is their first wedding anniversary. Instead of eating out, they decide to have a small party at home. Olivia is now making hot chocolate. It's the drink she and Dustin had on their first date. Dustin is going to arrive about ten minutes later. Putting a cake with candles on the table, she speeds up to get the hot chocolate ready in time for his arrival. Now all she has to do is put chili pepper into the hot chocolate. She opens the cupboard and finds the chili pepper bottle almost empty. She wants to ask Dustin to pick up the ingredient. She calls Dustin on his cellphone and he answers it. In this situation, what would Olivia most likely say to Dustin?

Olivia Can you drop by the store and buy chili pepper?

여 Olivia와 Dustin은 정확하게 일 년 전에 결혼했으며, 오늘이 그들의 첫 번째 결혼기념일입니다. 외식 대신에 그들은 집에서 작은 파티를 하기로 결정합니다. Olivia는 지금 핫초코를 만들고 있습니다. 그것은 그녀와 Dustin이 첫 데이트 때 마셨던 음료입니다. Dustin은 10분쯤 후에 도착할 것입니다. 식탁에 초를 꽂은 케이크를 올려놓고 그녀는 그의 도착 시간에 맞추어 핫초코를 준비하려고 속도를 내고 있습니다. 이제 그녀는 핫초코에 칠리 페퍼만 넣으면 됩니다. 그녀는 찬장을 열고는 칠리 페퍼 병이 거의 비어 있음을 알게 됩니다. 그녀는 Dustin에게 그 재료를 사다 달라고 부탁하고 싶습니다. 그녀는 Dustin 휴대전화로 전화를 하고 그가 전화를 받습니다. 이런 상황에서, Olivia는 Dustin에게 뭐라고 말할 것 같은가요?

Olivia 가게에 들러 칠리 페퍼 좀 사 오겠어요?

Solution

Olivia는 결혼기념일을 맞아 칠리 페퍼를 곁들인 핫초코를 만들고자 하는데, 칠리 페퍼가 없어서 Dustin에게 이를 사다 달라고 부탁하고자 하는 상황이므로, 이러한 상황에서 Olivia가 Dustin에게 할 말로 가장 적절한 것은 ⑤ '가게에 들러 칠리 페퍼 좀 사 오겠어요?'이다.

① 늦게 귀가하지 말라고 부탁했잖아요.
② 초를 사는 것을 잊었어요. 어떻게 해야 하죠?
③ 서둘러요! 핫초코가 당신을 기다리고 있어요.
④ 칠리 페퍼 병이 어디 있는지 알아요?

Words

wedding anniversary 결혼기념일 speed up 속도를 높이다
in time for ~하는 시간에 맞춰 ingredient 재료 drop by ~에 들르다

16 정답 ④   17 정답 ③

Script

M Hello everyone and thanks for coming. I'm Jim Brown, a child education expert. Over the next three weeks, I will talk about various factors that affect children's emotions. Today, I'll start by talking about colors. As there are many colors in the world, each color affects children's emotions in many ways. First, red, the most intense color, can create a negative emotion such as anger in children, so red isn't a good color for children who get angry easily. On the other hand, a stressed or irritated child may feel calm and comfortable when they are exposed to green or blue. Does your child feel depressed? Then show your child yellow things such as yellow tulips. Yellow is the most joyful color on the color scale, so your child will feel much better after looking at yellow tulips. Are there any questions so far?

남 여러분 안녕하세요 그리고 와 주셔서 감사합니다. 저는 아동 교육 전문가, Jim Brown입니다. 앞으로 3주 동안 어린이의 감정에 미치는 다양한 요소들에 대해 말씀드리겠습니다. 색에 대한 내용으로 오늘 강연을 시작하겠습니다. 세상에는 여러 가지 색이 있는 만큼 각각의 색은 어린이들의 감정에 많은 방식으로 영향을 줍니다. 먼저, 가장 강렬한 색인 빨간색은 어린이에게 분노와 같은 부정적인 감정을 불러일으킬 수 있으므로, 쉽게 화를 내는 어린이에게 빨간색은 좋은 색이 아닙니다. 반면에 스트레스를 겪거나 짜증이 나 있는 어린이가 녹색 또는 파란색에 노출되면 차분해지고 편안해질 수도 있습니다. 여러분의 자녀가 우울해합니까? 그렇다면 자녀에게 노란 튤립 같은 노란색 사물을 보여 주세요. 노란색은 색도에서 가장 활기찬 색이어서, 노란 튤립을 본 후 여러분의 자녀는 기분이 훨씬 더 나아질 것입니다. 지금까지 질문이 있으십니까?

Solution

16
남자는 앞으로 3주 동안 어린이의 감정에 미치는 요소에 대해 말하겠다고 하면서 색이 어린이의 감정에 미치는 영향에 대해 다양한 색을 예로 들어 설명하고 있으므로, 남자가 하는 말의 주제로 가장 적절한 것은 ④ '색이 어린이의 감정에 미치는 영향'이다.

① 어린이를 키우는 것의 어려움
② 스트레스를 받는 어린이를 돌보는 방법
③ 감정을 표현하는 것의 중요성
⑤ 어린이가 그림 그리는 것을 좋아하는 이유

17
빨간색, 녹색, 파란색, 노란색은 언급되었지만, ③ '흰색'은 언급되지 않았다.

Words

expert 전문가 factor 요소 affect 영향을 미치다 intense 강렬한
negative 부정적인 on the other hand 반면에 irritated 짜증이 나는
be exposed to ~에 노출되다, ~을 접하다 depressed 우울한
color scale 색도

01 ⑤	02 ⑤	03 ①	04 ⑤	05 ⑤
06 ③	07 ⑤	08 ⑤	09 ⑤	10 ③
11 ⑤	12 ③	13 ④	14 ①	15 ①
16 ③	17 ④			

01 정답 ⑤

Script

M Hello, Grand City residents! We're here today to ask for your help. It's not for us, but for all of our residents, including our children and our grandchildren. Now, more than half of the rivers, lakes, and streams in our city are polluted. Doing water activities like swimming, rafting, and fishing in these polluted waters may entail serious health risks. At this moment, we need to strongly ask the government to do more to clean up our waterways and to improve water quality standards. We also need to urge big companies to stop dumping waste and polluting our waters. For all of these reasons, we need you to sign our petitions. Please take a little time and help save our bodies of water.

- - - - - - - - - -

남 안녕하세요, Grand City 주민 여러분! 저희는 오늘 여러분의 도움을 요청하기 위해 이곳에 왔습니다. 이것은 우리를 위한 것이 아니라 우리의 자녀들, 그리고 우리의 손주들을 포함한 우리 주민 모두를 위한 것입니다. 지금 우리 도시의 강, 호수, 개울의 절반 이상이 오염되어 있습니다. 이렇게 오염된 물에서 수영, 래프팅, 낚시와 같은 물놀이를 하는 것은 심각한 건강상의 위험을 수반할 수 있습니다. 지금 이 순간에, 우리는 정부에 수로를 청결하게 하고 수질 기준을 개선시키기 위해 더 많은 것을 하도록 강력하게 요구해야 합니다. 우리는 또한 대기업에 폐기물 투기와 수질을 오염시키는 것을 중단하라고 촉구해야 합니다. 이 모든 이유로 여러분은 저희의 탄원서에 서명할 필요가 있습니다. 시간을 조금만 내셔서 우리의 물줄기를 지키는 것을 도와주십시오.

Solution

남자는 수질 오염으로부터 도시를 지키기 위해 정부에 수질 개선을 위한 노력을 요구하고, 대기업에 폐기물 투기와 수질 오염 중지를 촉구하는 탄원서에 서명해 달라고 요청하고 있으므로 남자가 하는 말의 목적으로 가장 적절한 것은 ⑤이다.

Words

resident 주민　pollute 오염시키다　entail 수반하다, 일으키다
waterway 수로　urge 촉구하다　dump 버리다, 투기하다
petition 탄원서　body of water 물줄기

02 정답 ⑤

Script

W Hey, Henry. How's the Spanish course going?

M It's pretty tough.

W Tough? Why?

M Our teacher is using a lot of authentic material. He even tapes conversations with his friends and uses them in class.

W That sounds very helpful. So, what makes it difficult for you to learn Spanish?

M Well, the speed, for a start. They just talk so fast that I can't understand which word or phrase they use.

W Maybe you shouldn't try to understand every word and phrase in the initial stage of learning a foreign language.

M What do you mean?

W You should just listen for the key words. I mean the most important words.

M But how do I know what they are?

W They're usually the words with the most stress.

- - - - - - - - - -

여 이봐, Henry. 스페인어 수업은 잘 되어 가고 있니?

남 아주 힘들어.

여 힘들다고? 왜?

남 선생님이 실제적인 자료를 많이 사용하고 계셔. 그는 심지어 자신의 친구들과의 대화를 녹음해서 수업 시간에 사용하셔.

여 듣고 보니 도움이 될 것 같은데. 그래서 네가 스페인어를 배우는 것을 어렵게 만드는 게 뭐니?

남 음, 우선, 속도가 그래. 그들은 너무 빨리 말해서 나는 어떤 단어나 어떤 어구를 사용하는지 이해할 수가 없어.

여 외국어를 배우는 초기 단계에서는 모든 단어와 어구를 이해하려고 시도하지 말아야 할 거야.

남 무슨 말이야?

여 핵심어들만 귀담아 들어야 해. 가장 중요한 단어들 말이야.

남 그렇지만 가장 중요한 단어들이 뭔지 어떻게 알아?

여 그것들은 대개 가장 강한 강세가 들어가는 단어들이야.

Solution

여자는 스페인어를 배우는 데 어려움을 겪고 있는 남자에게 외국어를 배우는 초기 단계에서는 모든 단어와 어구를 이해하려고 하기보다는 핵심어를 귀담아 들어야 한다고 말하고 있으므로 여자의 의견으로 가장 적절한 것은 ⑤이다.

Words

authentic 진짜의; 믿을 만한　for a start 우선　initial 초기의
stress 강세

03 정답 ①

Script

M Hi! It's nice to see you.

W Hi! Have a seat here, please. Would you drink a cup of coffee?

M No thanks. First of all, congratulations on winning the Writer of the Month award.

W I really appreciate all the readers who love my new novel, *Police Life*.

M I also read it to write an article. It's really realistic.

W Well, I interviewed more than 100 policemen to write it.

M I heard that some movie directors want to make your novel into a movie.

W That's right. Once it's decided, I'll let you know first.

M Really? Then can I write an article about it?

W Of course, you can.

M Thank you. Your fans will be happy to read the news.

남 안녕하세요! 만나서 반가워요.
여 안녕하세요! 여기 앉으세요. 커피 한 잔 할래요?
남 아니요, 괜찮아요. 먼저, '이달의 작가' 상을 수상한 것 축하드려요.
여 제 신작 소설 'Police Life'를 사랑해 주시는 모든 독자들에게 진심으로 감사드려요.
남 저도 기사를 쓰기 위해서 소설을 읽었어요. 소설이 매우 사실적이에요.
여 음, 이 소설을 쓰기 위해 100명도 넘는 경찰들을 인터뷰했어요.
남 영화감독 몇 분이 당신의 소설을 영화로 만들고 싶어 한다는 것을 들었어요.
여 맞아요. 이것이 결정되면, 당신에게 먼저 알려 줄게요.
남 정말요? 그러면 이것에 대해 기사를 쓸 수 있을까요?
여 물론이죠.
남 고마워요. 이 뉴스를 읽으면 당신의 팬들이 좋아할 거예요.

Solution
남자는 여자에게 '이달의 작가' 상을 수상한 것을 축하한다고 말하고, 자신도 기사를 쓰기 위해 여자가 쓴 소설을 읽었다고 했다. 또한 여자가 쓴 소설이 영화화되는 것이 결정되면, 여자는 이를 남자에게 먼저 알려 주겠다고 했고 남자는 이것에 대해 기사를 써도 좋은지 물었으므로, 두 사람의 관계를 가장 잘 나타낸 것은 ①이다.

Words
appreciate 감사하다 article 기사 realistic 사실적인

04 정답 ⑤

Script

W At last, the Independence Day parade is starting.
M Look at the two girls playing drums in front.
W And the two boys are passing by waving the American flag just behind them.
M Both the girls and boys are very cute, aren't they?
W Yes, they are. Look behind them. Can you see the woman with a big hat waving a big American flag?
M That's a really big flag. What do you think about the old man with the beard?
W You mean the old man riding on a bicycle and waving?
M Yes. Let's wave at him, too.
W Why not? Look! There's a carriage drawn by two horses following the old man.
M Everyone in the carriage is really enjoying the parade.

여 마침내, 독립 기념일 행진이 시작되고 있어.
남 앞에서 드럼을 치고 있는 두 소녀를 봐.
여 그리고 소녀들 바로 뒤에서 두 소년들이 미국 국기를 흔들며 지나가고 있어.
남 소녀들과 소년들이 모두 정말로 귀엽다, 그렇지 않니?
여 그래, 귀여워. 그들 뒤를 봐. 큰 모자를 쓴 여자가 커다란 미국 국기를 흔들고 있는 거 보여?
남 저것은 정말로 큰 국기다. 턱수염을 기른 할아버지는 어떻게 생각해?
여 자전거를 타고 손을 흔드는 저 할아버지 말하는 거야?
남 맞아. 우리도 그에게 손을 흔들자.
여 좋지. 봐! 두 마리의 말이 끄는 마차가 할아버지 뒤를 따르고 있어.
남 마차에 있는 모든 사람들이 정말로 행진을 즐기고 있구나.

Solution
두 마리의 말이 끄는 마차가 할아버지 뒤를 따르고 있다고 했지만 그림에서는 한 마리의 말이 있으므로 대화의 내용과 일치하지 않는 것은 ⑤이다.

Words
Independence Day (미국의) 독립 기념일 parade 행진
wave 흔들다 flag 깃발 beard 턱수염 carriage 마차

05 정답 ⑤

Script

W Liam! Where are you?
M I'm in the yard. I just finished watering the plants. What's up?
W Where is the jacket I wore yesterday?
M It's in the washing machine. Why?
W Oh, my! I think my cellphone is in the pocket.
M No. I checked every pocket before putting it in.
W Then, where is my phone? I can't find it anywhere. I'm sure I put it in my jacket after I used it on the bus.
M Why don't you call your cellphone?
W I already did, but I just heard a recorded voice saying it's turned off.
M Maybe your cellphone dropped out of your jacket. What about calling the bus company?
W Okay. I really hope they have my phone.

여 Liam! 당신 어디에 있어요?
남 정원에 있어요. 나무에 물 주는 것을 막 끝냈어요. 무슨 일이에요?
여 어제 내가 입었던 재킷은 어디 있죠?
남 세탁기 속에요. 왜요?
여 오, 이런! 휴대전화가 주머니에 들어 있는 것 같아요.
남 아뇨. 세탁기에 넣기 전에 모든 주머니를 다 확인했어요.
여 그렇다면 내 전화기는 어디에 있죠? 어디에서도 찾을 수가 없어요. 버스에서 사용한 후에 분명히 재킷에 넣었어요.
남 휴대전화로 전화를 해 보지 그래요?
여 이미 해 봤는데, 꺼져 있다는 음성 메시지만 들렸어요.
남 아마도 휴대전화가 재킷에서 떨어졌을지도 몰라요. 버스 회사에 전화를 걸어 보는 것은 어때요?
여 알았어요. 그들이 내 전화를 가지고 있기를 정말 바라요.

Solution
여자는 휴대전화를 찾고 있는데, 버스에서 마지막으로 휴대전화를 사용했다는 여자의 말에 남자가 여자에게 버스 회사에 전화를 걸어 보라고 하자 여자는 그렇게 하겠다고 했으므로 정답은 ⑤이다.

Words
water 물을 주다 call one's cellphone 휴대전화에 전화하다
drop 떨어지다

06 정답 ③

Script

W What can I do for you?
M I'd like to sign up for flute lessons. How much are they per month?
W They're $120.

M Not too expensive. I'd also like my ten-year-old son to learn how to play the flute. How much are the lessons for him?

W They're $80 for children under 13.

M That's quite reasonable. Then can you sign both of us up for flute lessons?

W Sure. And since you and your son are family, we'll discount 10 percent off the total cost.

M Wow! That's a really good deal.

W That's not all. We'll give you both a cleaning set for free, which is a $20 value.

M Thank you. Here's my credit card.

W Hold on.

- -

여 무엇을 도와드릴까요?

남 플루트 강좌에 등록하고 싶습니다. 한 달에 얼마인가요?

여 120달러입니다.

남 그렇게 비싸지는 않군요. 10살짜리 아들에게도 플루트를 연주하는 법을 배우게 하고 싶습니다. 그 애를 위한 수업은 얼마인가요?

여 13세 이하의 어린이는 80달러입니다.

남 꽤 저렴하군요. 그럼 우리 둘 다를 플루트 강좌에 등록해 주실 수 있나요?

여 물론이지요. 그리고 손님과 아드님은 가족이므로 전체 금액의 10퍼센트를 할인해 드리겠습니다.

남 와! 그거 정말 좋군요.

여 그게 다가 아닙니다. 20달러 상당의 청소 세트를 두 분께 무료로 드리겠습니다.

남 감사합니다. 여기 제 신용카드가 있습니다.

여 잠시만 기다리세요.

Solution
남자의 수강료는 120달러이고 아들의 수강료는 80달러인데, 가족 할인으로 총액에서 10퍼센트가 할인되고 20달러 상당의 청소 세트는 무료로 준다고 했으므로 남자가 지불할 금액은 ③ '180달러'이다.

Words
sign up for ~에 등록하다 discount 할인하다 for free 무료로

07 정답 ⑤

Script

M Samantha, I think I found a good campsite for our camping trip next weekend.

W Did you? What's the name of the campsite?

M Forest Campsite near Wellington Mountain.

W Oh, then it's not that far from here.

M The fee is only $20 a day per tent. It's really cheap.

W Well, I think it must be popular with campers like us.

M For sure, so we have to hurry and book it.

W Um... I don't want to go camping in a crowded place.

M But it's also equipped with water play facilities. You said you wanted to play in the water.

W I do. But what I want more is to spend a peaceful time in nature.

M Well, then I'll look for another campsite.

- -

남 Samantha, 다음 주말 우리 캠핑 여행을 위한 좋은 캠핑장을 찾은 것 같아.

여 그래? 캠핑장 이름이 뭐야?

남 Wellington 산 근처에 있는 Forest Campsite야.

여 오, 그러면 여기서 그렇게 멀지는 않구나.

남 요금이 텐트 하나당 하루에 20달러에 불과해. 정말로 저렴해.

여 음, 우리 같은 캠핑객들에게 이곳이 인기가 많을 것 같아.

남 틀림없이, 그래서 서둘러서 이곳을 예약해야 해

여 음… 나는 사람들로 붐비는 장소에서 캠핑하고 싶지는 않아.

남 하지만 이곳은 물놀이 시설도 갖추고 있어. 네가 물놀이를 하고 싶다고 말했잖아.

여 물놀이를 하고 싶어. 하지만 내가 더 원하는 것은 자연 속에서 평화로운 시간을 보내는 거야.

남 음, 그렇다면 다른 캠핑장을 찾아볼게.

Solution
Forest Campsite가 캠핑객들에게 인기가 많을 것 같다는 여자의 말에 남자는 그렇다고 하면서 예약을 서둘러서 해야 한다고 덧붙인다. 이에 여자는 자연 속에서 평화로운 시간을 보내고 싶다고 하면서 사람들로 붐비는 장소에서는 캠핑을 하고 싶지 않다고 했으므로, 정답은 ⑤이다.

Words
campsite 캠핑장 fee 요금, 수수료
be equipped with ~을 갖추고 있다 facilities 시설, 설비
peaceful 평화로운

08 정답 ⑤

Script

M Stella, I heard that you're going to take a trip to Jeju Island this weekend.

W Yes. You know, it's my first trip since I started working here in Seoul.

M What are you going to do on Jeju Island?

W First, I'll visit Mara Island.

M Mara Island? Isn't that the smallest island in Korea?

W No, it isn't. It has an area of about 0.3 km^2.

M Ah, I must be confused with another island. It's located in the southernmost part of Korea, isn't it?

W That's right. I heard there are about 100 residents living on the island.

M How about the weather there?

W It should be good. Since the island has four distinct seasons just like Seoul, it's very sunny now.

M Great. I hope you'll have a wonderful trip.

- -

남 Stella, 네가 이번 주말에 제주도를 여행할 것이라고 들었어.

여 그래. 너도 알다시피 내가 이곳 서울에서 일하기 시작한 이래로 이번이 내 첫 번째 여행이야.

남 제주도에서는 무엇을 할 거니?

여 먼저, 나는 마라도를 방문할 거야.

남 마라도? 그 섬은 한국에서 가장 작은 섬이 아니야?

여 아니, 그렇지 않아. 마라도는 면적이 약 0.3제곱킬로미터 정도야.

남 아, 내가 다른 섬이랑 착각했나 봐. 마라도는 한국의 최남단에 위치해 있지, 그렇지 않니?

여 맞아. 그리고 이 섬에 약 100명의 주민이 살고 있다고 들었어.

남 그곳의 날씨는 어때?

여 좋을 거야. 꼭 서울처럼 이 섬이 네 개의 뚜렷한 계절을 가지고 있어서, 지금 매우 화창해.

남 멋지다. 네가 즐거운 여행을 하기를 바랄게.

09 정답 ⑤

Script

W Hi, Korean food lovers. I'm going to tell you some good news. The Korean Food Cooking Contest is going to be held at the Olympic Convention Center on Christmas Eve. Anyone who loves Korean food can participate in this contest. There are two different categories: amateur and professional chefs. The entry fee is $30 per person, and the winner of each category will receive a $1,000 prize and a round-trip ticket to Seoul, Korea. The contest is sponsored by Fact Newspaper and Star Department Store, and the entire event will be broadcast live on the Internet. Registration for participation is from December 5th to December 15th. I hope many of you who love Korean food participate.

여 안녕하세요, 한국 음식을 사랑하는 여러분. 여러분에게 좋은 소식을 전해 드리겠습니다. 한국 음식 요리 경연 대회가 크리스마스이브에 올림픽 컨벤션 센터에서 열릴 것입니다. 이 대회는 한국 음식을 사랑하는 사람이면 누구나 참가할 수 있습니다. 아마추어 부문과 직업 요리사 부문 이렇게 두 부문이 있습니다. 대회 참가비는 1인당 30달러이고, 각 부문의 우승자는 1,000달러의 상금과 한국의 서울행 왕복 티켓을 받게 될 것입니다. 이 대회는 Fact 신문사와 Star 백화점의 후원을 받고 있으며, 대회의 전 과정이 인터넷으로 생중계될 것입니다. 참가 등록은 12월 5일부터 12월 15일까지입니다. 한국 음식을 사랑하는 수많은 여러분의 참가를 바랍니다.

Solution

참가 등록은 12월 5일부터 12월 15일까지라고 했으므로, ⑤가 담화의 내용과 일치하지 않는다.

Words

round-trip ticket 왕복 티켓 sponsor (행사 등을) 후원하다
be broadcast live 생중계되다 registration 등록

10 정답 ③

Script

W Let's look at this pamphlet and choose a room for your father's seventieth birthday party.

M Okay. Wow! This restaurant is three stories tall.

W It specializes in family gatherings, company luncheons, and all kinds of group dining.

M I see. Which room do you think is the most suitable?

W Well, many guests are your father's age, so walking up to the third floor isn't easy for them.

M I agree.

W And almost one hundred friends of your parents' came to our wedding last year, right?

M Yes. We need a room that can hold at least 100 people.

W You're right. And you said most of them complained about the buffet.

M Yes, that's what I heard. Let's make the dinner a set menu.

W Then we have two choices left.

M Well, I think the second floor would be better, although it's a little more expensive.

W Then let's reserve that room.

여 이 책자를 보고 당신의 아버지 칠순 잔치를 위한 방을 정하죠.
남 좋아요. 와! 이 식당은 3층짜리 건물이네요.
여 여기는 가족 모임, 회사 오찬, 그리고 각종 단체 회식을 전문으로 하는 곳이에요.
남 그렇군요. 어느 방이 가장 적절할 것 같아요?
여 글쎄요. 많은 손님들이 아버님 연령대이시니까 3층까지 걸어 올라가는 것은 그분들에게 쉽지 않겠네요.
남 동의해요.
여 그리고 작년 우리 결혼식 때 당신 부모님의 친구분들이 거의 백 분정도 오셨죠, 맞죠?
남 맞아요. 적어도 백 명을 수용할 수 있는 방이 필요해요.
여 맞아요. 그리고 그들 대부분이 뷔페 음식에 대해 불만이 있으셨다고 당신이 말했어요.
남 그래요, 그렇게 들었어요. 저녁 식사는 세트 메뉴로 합시다.
여 그럼 이제 두 개의 선택권이 남았네요.
남 음, 조금 더 비싸기는 해도 2층이 더 나을 것 같아요.
여 그러면 그 방으로 예약하죠.

Solution

두 사람은 3층을 제외하고, 적어도 백 명을 수용하며, 세트 메뉴가 제공되고, 조금 더 비싸지만, 2층에 있는 방을 예약하고자 하므로 두 사람이 예약할 방은 ③이다.

Words

luncheon 오찬 suitable 적절한

11 정답 ⑤

Script

M Honey, look. More than half of the apples are rotten. Where did you buy them?

W At Green's Fruit Store. I can't understand how they sold such bad apples.

M Let's go there right now. We have to complain about it.

W Sure! We must ask them to exchange these for fresh ones.

남 여보, 봐요. 이 사과들 중 반 이상이 썩었어요. 이 사과를 어디서 샀나요?
여 Green's 과일 가게에서요. 그들이 어떻게 이런 상한 사과를 팔았는지 이해가 안 돼요.
남 지금 바로 그 가게에 가요. 이것에 대해서 항의해야 해요.
여 물론이죠! 우리는 이것들을 신선한 사과로 바꾸어 달라고 요청해야 해요.

Solution

남자가 상한 사과를 판매한 과일 가게에 가서 이에 대해 항의하자고 했으므로, 이에 대한 여자의 응답으로 가장 적절한 것은 ⑤ '물론이죠! 우리는 이것들을 신선한 사과로 바꾸어 달라고 요청해야 해요.'이다.

① 좋아요. 당신의 항의가 드디어 효과를 봤어요.
② 맞아요. 나는 그 과일 가게에서 일하고 싶지 않아요.
③ 네, 당신은 지금보다 사과를 더 많이 샀어야 했어요.

④ 물론이죠! 사과가 오렌지보다 더 맛있어요.

rotten 썩은, 부패한

12 정답 ③

Script

W I heard you do volunteer work every Sunday.
M Yeah, I go to the senior community and help bathe them.
W Oh, it must be hard work, right?
M Well, it's demanding but it's worth it.

─────────────────────────────

여 네가 매주 일요일에 자원봉사를 하고 있다고 들었어.
남 응, 나는 경로당에 가서 그분들을 목욕시키는 것을 도와드려.
여 오, 분명 힘든 일이겠다, 그렇지?
남 글쎄, 일이 벅차기는 하지만 할 만한 가치가 있어.

Solution

여자는 남자가 매주 일요일에 노인 복지관에 가서 목욕하는 것을 돕는 자원봉사를 한다는 말에 힘든 일일 것이라고 의견을 말하면서 동시에 묻고 있으므로, 이에 대한 남자의 응답으로 가장 적절한 것은 ③ '글쎄, 일이 벅차기는 하지만 할 만한 가치가 있어.'이다.

① 나의 할아버지가 그곳에 계셔.
② 그것은 내 생각이 아니야. 네 생각이었어.
④ 빨래하기, 말리기 등과 같은 일이야.
⑤ 오해하지 마. 나는 너를 돕고자 하는 거야.

Words

bathe 목욕시키다 demanding 벅찬, 힘든 worth ~의 가치가 있는

13 정답 ④

Script

W Hi, Austin. You look happy today.
M Hi, Molly. I have every reason to look so.
W Really? What happened?
M I got a hand-written letter from my mother.
W A hand-written letter? Why? Did she go somewhere?
M No, she's at home with us as usual.
W Then why did she send you a letter? What did she want to say?
M Nothing special. She just wanted me to know that she loves me.
W Doesn't she ever tell you that at home?
M Of course, she does.
W Then why did she send you a letter to tell you that?
M I have no idea, but I think the letter is very special. I had a totally different feeling than getting an ordinary text message.
W Well, I think I should write a letter to my dad.

─────────────────────────────

여 안녕, Austin. 오늘 기분이 좋아 보여.
남 안녕, Molly. 내가 그렇게 보이는 것도 당연해.
여 정말? 무슨 일이 있었니?
남 어머니에게 손으로 쓴 편지를 받았어.
여 손으로 쓴 편지라고? 왜? 어머니가 어디 가셨니?

남 아니, 어머니는 평소처럼 우리와 함께 집에 계셔.
여 그러면 왜 네 어머니께서 너에게 편지를 쓰신 거니? 무슨 말씀을 하고 싶으셨던 거니?
남 특별한 것은 없어. 단지 어머니가 나를 사랑한다는 것을 내가 알고 있기를 원했기 때문이야.
여 집에서 너에게 사랑한다고 말씀하지 않으시니?
남 당연히 말씀하시지.
여 그럼 왜 그것을 말하려고 너에게 편지를 쓰신 거니?
남 몰라, 하지만 그 편지가 매우 특별하다는 생각이 들어. 일상적인 문자 메시지를 받는 것과는 완전히 다른 느낌을 받았어.
여 음, 생각해 보니 나도 아버지께 편지를 써야겠어.

Solution

남자는 어머니에게 손 편지를 받고 아주 기뻐하며, 문자 메시지를 받는 것과는 완전히 다른 느낌이었다고 말하고 있으므로, 이에 대한 여자의 응답으로 가장 적절한 것은 ④ '음, 생각해 보니 나도 아버지께 편지를 써야겠어.'이다.

① 동의해. 그 편지에 대해 너무 기분 나빠 하지 마.
② 물론이지. 떠날 준비가 되면 전화 줘.
③ 쓸데없는 스팸 메일을 받는 것에 신물이 나.
⑤ 맞아. 나는 '사랑해.'라고 말하는 것에 익숙하지 않아.

Words

have every reason to do ~하는 것은 당연하다
hand-written 손으로 쓴 totally 완전히

14 정답 ①

Script

W Officer! Please help me.
M Calm down, please. What's the problem?
W Somebody just stole my bike.
M Did you lock it?
W Yes, I did. I think he broke my bike lock and took my bike.
M Where did you park your bike?
W In the public bike parking area in front of the post office on Lake Street.
M There's a CCTV nearby that shows that area. By checking it, we should be able to find out who took your bike.
W Really? I'm relieved to hear that.
M I'm sure you'll get your bike back soon.

─────────────────────────────

여 경찰관님! 저를 도와주세요.
남 진정하세요. 문제가 무엇이죠?
여 누군가 방금 전에 제 자전거를 훔쳐 갔어요.
남 자전거를 잠그셨나요?
여 네, 잠갔어요. 그 사람이 제 자전거 자물쇠를 부수고 자전거를 가지고 간 것 같아요.
남 자전거를 어디에 주차했죠?
여 Lake 거리에 있는 우체국 앞의 자전거 공용 주차 구역이에요.
남 그 구역을 보여 주는 CCTV가 주위에 있습니다. 우리가 그것을 확인하면, 누가 자전거를 가져갔는지 찾아낼 수 있을 거예요.
여 정말이요? 그 말을 들으니 안심이 돼요.
남 당신이 곧 자전거를 되찾을 것이라고 확신해요.

Solution

자전거 공용 주차 구역에서 자전거를 도난당한 여자에게 경찰관인 남자는 그곳 주변에 CCTV가 있다고 하면서 자전거를 훔친 사람을 찾을 수 있을 거라

고 말해 여자는 안심이 된다고 대답했으므로, 이에 대한 남자의 응답으로 가장 적절한 것은 ① '당신이 곧 자전거를 되찾을 것이라고 확신해요.'이다.

② 내 자전거를 훔쳐간 사람을 잡아 주세요.
③ 당신 덕분에 자전거 타는 법을 배웠어요.
④ 당신이 좋은 자전거를 구입했다는 소식을 들으니 나도 기뻐요.
⑤ 자전거 공용 주차 구역에 자전거를 주차할게요.

Words

officer 경찰관 calm down 진정하다 lock 잠그다; 자물쇠
public bike parking area 자전거 공용 주차 구역 relieved 안심하는

15 정답 ①

Script

M Nick is a high school teacher. Today is the first day he starts teaching at Winsley High School. Now he takes the subway to school. It's early in the morning, but all the seats are taken. A student wearing a high school uniform is reading a book in the seat in front of him. At the next stop, an old man gets on the subway. He looks like he's in his seventies. He searches for an empty seat. At that time, the student finds the old man, stands up, and yields his seat to him. Now the student is standing next to Nick. Feeling proud of him, Nick wants to praise him. In this situation, what would Nick most likely say to the student?

Nick It was nice of you to yield your seat to him.

남 Nick은 고등학교 교사입니다. 오늘은 그가 Winsley 고등학교에서 수업을 시작하는 첫날입니다. 이제 그는 학교로 가는 지하철을 탑니다. 이른 아침이지만 모든 좌석이 차 있습니다. 고등학교 교복을 입은 한 학생이 그의 앞에 있는 좌석에 앉아 책을 읽고 있습니다. 그 다음 역에서 한 어르신이 지하철을 탑니다. 그는 70대로 보입니다. 그는 빈 좌석을 찾습니다. 그때, 그 학생이 그 어르신을 발견하고는 일어나서 자신의 좌석을 그분에게 양보합니다. 지금 그 학생이 Nick의 옆에 서 있습니다. 그 학생이 자랑스럽게 느껴져서 Nick은 그를 칭찬해 주고 싶습니다. 이런 상황에서, Nick은 그 학생에게 뭐라고 말할 것 같은가요?

Nick 네가 그분께 자리를 양보해 드리다니 아주 잘했어.

Solution

Nick은 지하철에서 어르신에게 자리를 양보한 학생에게 칭찬해 주고자 하는 상황이므로, Nick이 학생에게 할 말로 가장 적절한 것은 ① '네가 그분께 자리를 양보해 드리다니 아주 잘했어.'이다.

② 고맙지만 이 가방이 보이는 것만큼 무겁지는 않단다.
③ 네 좌석을 그 어르신께 양보해 드리지 그러니?
④ 지하철에서 책을 읽는 것은 아주 좋은 습관이란다.
⑤ 이 좌석에 앉아도 돼. 나는 다음 역에서 내릴 거야.

Words

yield 양보하다 praise 칭찬하다

16 정답 ③   17 정답 ④

Script

W Hello, everyone. Welcome to my YouTube channel. I'm sports columnist Jane Fonda. Today, I'm going to talk about children and sports. Playing sports offers both adults and children many benefits. Playing team sports such as soccer and basketball can improve children's teamwork and communication skills. If your children enjoy individual sports such as swimming or marathon, it'll also have a positive effect on them. Studies show that children who participate in these sports have better endurance than those who don't. Do you think your children lack concentration? Then have them play table tennis or tennis. They will need to hit the ball accurately, and learning this skill will improve their concentration. That's all for today's video. See you next time.

여 안녕하세요, 여러분. 제 유튜브 채널에 오신 것을 환영합니다. 저는 스포츠 칼럼니스트 Jane Fonda입니다. 오늘은 어린이와 스포츠에 대해서 말씀드리겠습니다. 스포츠를 하는 것이 어른과 어린이 모두에게 많은 이점을 가져다줍니다. 축구와 농구 같은 단체 스포츠를 하는 것은 어린이의 협동심과 커뮤니케이션 능력을 향상시켜 줄 수 있습니다. 만약 여러분의 자녀가 수영이나 마라톤 같은 개인 스포츠를 즐긴다면, 이것 또한 어린이에게 긍정적인 효과를 줄 것입니다. 이러한 스포츠에 참여하는 어린이는 그렇지 않은 어린이보다 인내력이 더 낫다고 연구는 보여줍니다. 여러분의 자녀가 집중력이 부족하다고 생각하시나요? 그렇다면 자녀에게 탁구 또는 테니스를 하게 해 보십시오. 그들은 공을 정확하게 쳐야 할 것이고, 이러한 기술을 배우는 것은 그들의 집중력을 향상시킬 것입니다. 오늘의 영상은 여기까지입니다. 다음에 뵙겠습니다.

Solution

16

스포츠 칼럼니스트인 여자는 스포츠를 하는 것이 어른과 어린이 모두에게 이점을 가져다준다고 하면서, 어린이가 스포츠를 하면서 얻을 수 있는 이점에 대해 구체적으로 언급하고 있으므로, 여자가 하는 말의 주제로 가장 적절한 것은 ③ '스포츠가 어린이에게 미치는 긍정적인 효과'이다.

① 단체 스포츠를 하는 것의 어려움
② 개인 스포츠를 더 잘하는 방법
④ 어린이가 단체 경기를 하는 것을 좋아하는 이유
⑤ 스포츠를 할 때 어른과 어린이의 차이점

17

축구, 수영, 마라톤, 탁구는 언급되었지만, ④ '야구'는 언급되지 않았다.

Words

benefit 이점 improve 향상시키다 individual sports 개인 스포츠
endurance 인내(력), 참을성 concentration 집중(력), 정신 집중
accurately 정확하게

01 ⑤	**02** ①	**03** ②	**04** ⑤	**05** ①
06 ④	**07** ②	**08** ⑤	**09** ⑤	**10** ③
11 ⑤	**12** ③	**13** ④	**14** ⑤	**15** ③
16 ①	**17** ⑤			

01 정답 ⑤

Script

W What if you can save $100 a year simply by replacing your five most-used light bulbs? What if you can save another $100 by using a programmable thermostat? You can also save more if you keep window shades and curtains closed during summer and open in daylight hours during winter. And you can save money if you only run your bathroom fan for 15 minutes. These are just some of the tips you can find on our website, www.savebysmallthings.com. Together, these tips could cut hundreds of dollars from your annual household bills. Join our website and use it. The website is free, updated seasonally, so keep returning and saving.

여 단지 여러분이 가장 많이 사용하는 전구 5개를 교체하는 것으로 연간 100달러를 절약할 수 있다면 어떻게 하시겠습니까? 프로그램 작동이 가능한 온도 조절 장치를 사용해서 100달러를 더 절약할 수 있다면 어떻게 하시겠습니까? 여름철에는 창문 블라인드와 커튼을 닫아 놓고 겨울철에는 햇빛이 들어오는 시간에 열어 놓으면 여러분은 또한 더 절약할 수 있습니다. 그리고 화장실 환풍기를 15분만 작동시키면 여러분은 돈을 절약할 수 있습니다. 이것들은 여러분이 우리 웹사이트인 www.savebysmallthings.com에서 찾아보실 수 있는 정보 중 단지 일부입니다. 모두 합하면, 이런 정보들은 연간 가계비의 수백 달러를 줄여줄 수 있습니다. 우리 웹사이트에 가입하여 사용해보십시오. 웹사이트는 무료이며, 계절에 따라 새로운 정보로 채워지므로, 계속 들르셔서 절약하시기 바랍니다.

Solution

가계비를 줄일 수 있는 방법을 담고 있는 웹사이트를 소개하며 적극 이용할 것을 권하고 있으므로 여자가 하는 말의 목적으로 가장 적절한 것은 ⑤이다.

Words

replace 바꾸다, 대체하다 thermostat 온도 조절 장치
shade 블라인드 annual 연간의 bill 청구서 seasonally 계절에 따라

02 정답 ①

Script

M You have finally become an actress.
W It's all thanks to you.
M I don't think so. It's because of your constant effort. What's it like to live different lives in different movies?
W It's a lot of fun, but sometimes it's very tiring.
M What makes you so tired?
W Quite often I have to shoot through the night.

M Nothing in life is easy, especially if you want to make something special happen.
W I agree. And it's really hard to memorize all those lines. Sometimes I think I don't have a life of my own.
M Sounds like you're having a hard time now. But remember — those who deal with the hardest times wisely are successful.
W Yeah, that's what you used to say to us in my school days.
M I still say that. That's what matters in life.
W I'll keep that in mind and do my best. Thanks, Mr. Jeter.

남 마침내 네가 배우가 되었구나.
여 다 선생님 덕분이에요.
남 난 그렇게 생각하지 않아. 그건 너의 끊임없는 노력 때문이지. 영화마다 다른 삶을 살아 보니 어떠니?
여 아주 재미있지만 가끔씩 아주 피곤하기도 해요.
남 무엇 때문에 그렇게 피곤하니?
여 밤샘 촬영을 아주 빈번하게 해야 해요.
남 인생에서 쉬운 것은 아무것도 없단다. 특히 특별한 뭔가가 일어나게 하고 싶다면 말이지.
여 동의해요. 그리고 그 모든 대사를 암기하는 것이 정말로 힘들어요. 때로는 제 자신의 삶이 없다는 생각이 들어요.
남 지금 어려운 시기를 보내고 있는 것 같구나. 그러나 기억하렴. 가장 어려운 시기를 현명하게 대처하는 사람이 성공한다는 것을 말이야.
여 네, 학창 시절에 선생님께서 우리들에게 하셨던 말씀이에요.
남 아직도 그렇게 말한단다. 그것이 인생에서 중요한 것이거든.
여 그 말씀 명심하고 최선을 다할게요. 감사합니다. Jeter 선생님.

Solution

남자는 배우가 되어 힘든 생활을 하고 있는 여자에게 힘든 시기를 현명하게 대처하는 사람이 성공한다고 하면서 그것이 인생에서 가장 중요하다고 말하고 있으므로 남자의 의견으로 가장 적절한 것은 ①이다.

Words

shoot (영화를) 촬영하다
make something happen 뭔가를 이루어 내다 line 대사
wisely 현명하게 matter 중요하다

03 정답 ②

Script

M Good morning, Ms. Willson.
W Good morning, Mr. Jenkins.
M I'm happy to work with you again. Thank you for asking me.
W You deserve it. Furthermore, your voice is proper for the boy in my animation.
M Am I taking the role of a boy?
W Yes. A boy detective is the main character. He's solving a crime in the movie.
M I can't wait to read the whole script.
W Here's the script. After you read it, I'll explain my directing plan about the animation.
M Okay. While reading it, I'll practice voice acting for the boy.
W Please make your voice sound cheerful. The boy has a very positive personality.

M Okay. I'll be sure to do that.

- -

남 좋은 아침입니다, Willson 씨.
여 좋은 아침입니다, Jenkins 씨
남 당신과 다시 일하게 돼서 기뻐요. 저에게 요청해 줘서 고마워요.
여 당신은 그럴 자격이 있어요. 게다가 당신의 목소리는 제 만화 영화에 나오는 소년에게 적합해요.
남 제가 소년의 역할을 맡게 되나요?
여 네. 소년 탐정이 주인공이에요. 그가 영화에서 범죄를 해결할 거예요.
남 빨리 전체 대본을 읽고 싶어요.
여 여기 대본이 있어요. 당신이 이것을 읽은 후에, 만화 영화에 대한 저의 연출 계획에 대해 설명해 드릴게요.
남 알았어요. 이것을 읽으면서 그 소년의 목소리 연기하는 것을 연습할게요.
여 목소리를 쾌활하게 들리도록 해 주세요. 그 소년은 아주 긍정적인 성격을 가지고 있어요.
남 알겠어요. 반드시 그렇게 할게요.

Solution
남자는 만화 영화에서 소년의 목소리 연기를 하게 되었으며, 여자는 남자가 대본을 다 읽은 후에 자신의 연출 계획에 대해 설명해 주겠다고 했으므로, 두 사람의 관계를 가장 잘 나타낸 것은 ②이다.

Words
deserve ~을 받을 만하다 proper 적합한, 적절한
animation 만화 영화 main character 주인공 detective 탐정
crime 범죄 script 대본 direct 연출하다
voice act 목소리 연기를 하다 cheerful 쾌활한 positive 긍정적인
personality 성격

04 정답 ⑤

Script
M I heard you bought a computer and a computer desk.
W Yes. My parents bought them for me. Would you like to see the photo I took of my computer desk?
M Sure. Show me the picture.
W Hold on. Here it is.
M Wow! Your computer desk is quite simple. No bookshelves, and no drawers!
W Yes, the desk only has four legs.
M It looks good. I see you placed the monitor and keyboard in the middle of the desk.
W Yeah, and I put the desk lamp next to the monitor.
M That's a good idea. But don't turn it on for too long.
W Of course, I won't. What do you think about keeping the computer under the desk?
M Great. Mine is next to the monitor. I'd better move it under the desk, too. The wireless mouse in front of the monitor looks very convenient.

- -

남 네가 컴퓨터와 컴퓨터 책상을 샀다고 들었어.
여 응. 부모님께서 사 주셨어. 컴퓨터 책상을 찍은 사진을 보고 싶니?
남 물론이지. 사진을 보여 줘.
여 잠시만. 여기 있어.
남 와! 컴퓨터 책상이 아주 단순한데. 책꽂이도 없고, 서랍도 없네!
여 응, 단지 책상 다리만 네 개 있어.
남 좋아 보여. 모니터와 키보드는 책상 중앙에 두었네.
여 응, 그리고 책상 탁상용 스탠드를 모니터 옆에 두었어.

남 좋은 생각이야. 하지만 스탠드를 너무 오래 켜 두지는 마.
여 당연하지, 그러지는 않을 거야. 컴퓨터 본체를 책상 아래쪽에 둔 것에 대해서는 어떻게 생각하니?
남 좋아. 내 컴퓨터 본체는 모니터 옆에 있어. 나도 그걸 책상 아래로 옮기는 편이 낫겠어. 모니터 앞에 있는 무선 마우스는 아주 편리해 보여.

Solution
새로 산 컴퓨터와 컴퓨터 책상을 찍은 사진을 보며 나누는 대화로, 모니터 앞에 무선 마우스가 있다고 했지만, 그림에서는 유선 마우스가 있으므로 대화의 내용과 일치하지 않는 것은 ⑤이다.

Words
bookshelf 책꽂이 drawer 서랍 wireless 무선의

05 정답 ①

Script
W Welcome to YST English Institute. What can I do for you?
M I'm here to sign up for an English course.
W Okay. What's your name, please?
M Daniel Baggio.
W Sounds like you are from Italy.
M No, I'm Argentinian. But people always think I'm Italian because of my name.
W I see. What course are you thinking of taking?
M I'd like to take an advanced course. I took an intermediate course in Canada last year, so I think I'll be able to handle an advanced course here.
W You have to take a level test first to take an advanced course. It's our policy.
M Okay, I'll take the test. How long will it take?
W It takes about one hour to find out whether you're ready or not.
M All right.

- -

여 YST 영어 학원에 오신 것을 환영합니다. 무엇을 도와드릴까요?
남 영어 강좌를 등록하러 왔습니다.
여 알겠습니다. 성함이 어떻게 되시죠?
남 Daniel Baggio입니다.
여 이탈리아 출신처럼 들리네요.
남 아뇨, 아르헨티나인이에요. 하지만 제 이름 때문에 사람들이 항상 제가 이탈리아 사람일 거라고 추측해요.
여 그렇군요. 어느 강좌를 수강하실 생각인가요?
남 상급 강좌를 수강하고 싶어요. 제가 작년에 캐나다에서 중급 강좌를 들었기 때문에 여기에서는 상급 강좌를 감당해 낼 수 있을 거라고 생각해요.
여 상급 강좌를 듣기 위해서는 먼저 레벨 테스트를 보셔야 합니다. 그게 우리의 방침입니다.
남 알겠습니다. 시험을 보겠습니다. 얼마나 걸릴까요?
여 당신이 준비되어 있는지를 알아내는 데 한 시간 정도 걸립니다.
남 알겠습니다.

Solution
영어 상급 강좌를 수강하고 싶어 하는 남자에게 여자는 영어 상급 강좌를 수강하기 위해서는 레벨 테스트를 보는 것이 학원의 방침이라고 말하고 있고 남자는 이에 따르겠다고 했으므로 정답은 ①이다.

Words
institute 학원 advanced course 상급[고급] 강좌
intermediate 중급의 handle 감당하다, 취급하다 policy 방침

06 정답 ④

Script

M May I help you?

W Yes, please. I'm here to buy a dinner table.

M Great. How many people is the table for?

W I'd like to buy one for four people. *[Pause]* Oh, I like this table here.

M That's one of the most popular ones these days. That's $300, without the chairs.

W How much is it with the four chairs?

M It's $400.

W Hmm. Is there any way for me to get a discount? I really like the table, but it's quite expensive.

M Fortunately, we're celebrating our 10th anniversary. You can get a 10 percent discount on the total price.

W That sounds great. I'll buy the table and four chairs. Here's my credit card.

M Okay. Would you write down your home address?

W Sure.

남 도와드릴까요?

여 네. 식탁을 사러 이곳에 왔어요.

남 좋습니다. 몇 인용 식탁을 원하시나요?

여 4인용 식탁을 사고 싶어요. *[잠시 후]* 아, 여기 이 식탁이 마음에 드네요.

남 그건 요즘 가장 인기 있는 것들 중 하나예요. 의자를 빼고 300달러예요.

여 의자 네 개와 함께 하면 얼마죠?

남 400달러예요.

여 흠. 할인을 받을 수 있는 어떤 방법이 있을까요? 식탁이 정말 마음에 드는데, 꽤 비싸군요.

남 다행히도, 우리는 10주년 기념일을 축하하고 있어요. 손님은 총액에 대해 10퍼센트 할인을 받으실 수 있어요.

여 그것 좋네요. 식탁과 의자 네 개를 살게요. 여기 제 신용카드가 있어요.

남 알겠습니다. 집 주소를 적어 주시겠어요?

여 그럴게요.

Solution

여자는 의자 네 개를 포함한 식탁을 400달러에서 10퍼센트를 할인받아 구입했으므로 여자가 지불할 금액은 ④ '360달러'이다.

Words

dinner table 식탁

07 정답 ②

Script

[Telephone rings.]

W Hello. You've reached Morgan Bank. How may I help you?

M Yes, I'd like to talk to Ian Kennedy. Is he working there?

W Just a moment. I'm sorry he's on the line with another customer. Would you like to hold, or should I ask him to call you back?

M Could you ask him to call his cellphone?

W Call his cellphone? Do you have his phone?

M Yes. I found it on the subway. While I was looking for a way to return it, I pushed number one long enough to contact you.

W Okay. I'll tell him what you said. He'll probably give you useful advice in return about investments and savings accounts. That's his field of expertise.

M Good to hear that. I need that kind of advice.

W Oh, I think he can talk to you now. I'll put you right through to him.

M Thanks, and it was nice talking to you.

W You're welcome.

[전화벨이 울린다.]

여 여보세요. Morgan 은행에 전화하셨습니다. 어떻게 도와드릴까요?

남 네, Ian Kennedy와 통화하고 싶은데요. 그분이 그곳에서 일하고 있나요?

여 잠시만요. 죄송합니다만 그는 다른 고객과 통화하고 있어요. 잠시 기다리시겠습니까, 아니면 그에게 전화를 드리라고 할까요?

남 그의 휴대전화로 전화를 해 달라고 해 주시겠어요?

여 그의 휴대전화로 전화를 하라고요? 당신이 그의 전화기를 가지고 있나요?

남 네. 지하철에서 발견했어요. 휴대전화를 돌려줄 방법을 찾던 중에 1번을 충분히 길게 눌렀더니 당신과 통화가 되었네요.

여 알겠습니다. 말씀하신 그대로 그에게 전할게요. 아마도 그가 당신에게 투자와 예금 계좌에 관한 유용한 조언을 답례로 해 드릴 거예요. 그것이 그의 전문 분야거든요.

남 그 말을 들으니 좋군요. 저는 그런 조언이 필요해요.

여 아, 그가 지금 당신과 통화할 수 있을 것 같네요. 바로 연결해 드릴게요.

남 감사합니다, 그리고 대화 즐거웠습니다.

여 천만에요.

Solution

남자는 지하철에서 습득한 휴대전화를 돌려주기 위해 단축 번호를 눌러 휴대전화 소유자의 직장인 은행에 전화를 건 상황이므로 정답은 ②이다.

Words

contact 연락하다 saving account 예금 계좌 in return 답례로
put ~ through to ... ~을 …에게 연결하다

08 정답 ⑤

Script

M Welcome back from your business trip! Where did you go this time?

W I went to Hawaii, but I only stayed there for one night.

M How was it?

W The weather was great, and the beach was beautiful, but my schedule was too tight to enjoy either of them.

M Where did you go next?

W I flew to Tokyo, where I stayed for three nights.

M And you didn't have time to do anything else, right?

W Yes. Then I went to Bangkok, but I had a stopover in Taipei for three hours.

M How was Bangkok?

W Wonderful. I have a friend there, so we had dinner together.

M Great. Then you flew back to San Francisco from Bangkok?

W Right. I got home last night.

M So, where are you going next?

W I'm going to fly to Incheon next Monday.

남 출장에서 돌아온 것을 환영해요! 이번에는 어디에 갔어요?
여 하와이에 갔는데 하룻밤만 묵었어요.
남 그곳은 어땠어요?
여 날씨는 좋았고 해변이 아름다웠지만 그것들 중 어느 것을 즐기기에는 제 일정이 너무 빡빡했어요.
남 다음엔 어디에 갔는데요?
여 도쿄로 날아가서 거기서 3일밤을 묵었어요.
남 그리고 달리 뭔가를 할 시간은 없었지요, 그렇죠?
여 네. 그런 다음 방콕으로 갔는데, 도중에 타이베이에서 3시간 동안 머물렀어요.
남 방콕은 어땠어요?
여 멋졌어요. 거기에 친구가 있어서 함께 저녁을 먹었어요.
남 잘됐네요. 그런 다음 방콕에서 샌프란시스코로 날아왔군요?
여 맞아요. 어젯밤에 집에 왔어요.
남 그러면, 다음에는 어디로 갈 거예요?
여 다음 주 월요일에 인천으로 갈 거예요.

Solution

여자가 출장에서 경유한 곳으로 하와이, 도쿄, 방콕, 타이베이는 언급되었으나 ⑤ '부산'은 언급되지 않았다.

Words

business trip 출장 tight 빡빡한
stopover (여정의 두 지점 사이에 잠시) 머묾, 단기 체류

09 정답 ⑤

Script

M Why don't you spend your summer Saturday evenings attending Crystal Forest Concerts? These concerts will be held from six to nine in the evening every Saturday in July. Ten different bands will perform their beautiful songs. You can bring your own lawn chair or blanket to enjoy our live music under the forest trees. A food truck will be available throughout the concerts. The entrance fee is $10 per adult and it's free for youth under 18. We strongly recommend the whole family to come and enjoy the concerts. It's a great chance to make an unforgettable memory with your family.

남 당신의 토요일 여름 저녁을 Crystal Forest Concerts에 참석하면서 보내는 게 어떨까요? 이 콘서트는 7월 매주 토요일 저녁 6시부터 9시까지 열릴 것입니다. 10개의 다른 밴드들이 각자의 아름다운 노래를 공연할 것입니다. 여러분은 접이식 의자나 담요를 가져와 숲속 나무 밑에서 우리의 라이브 음악을 즐길 수 있습니다. 콘서트 내내 푸드 트럭을 이용할 수 있을 것입니다. 입장료는 성인은 1인당 10달러이며 18세 미만의 청소년은 무료입니다. 온 가족이 와서 콘서트를 즐기는 것을 강력히 추천합니다. 여러분의 가족과 잊을 수 없는 추억을 만들 멋진 기회입니다.

Solution

18세 미만 청소년의 입장료는 무료라고 했으므로, ⑤가 담화의 내용과 일치하지 않는다.

Words

unforgettable 잊을 수 없는 memory 추억

10 정답 ③

Script

M Now we have to decide on which auto camping site to reserve.
W I think we need a campsite bigger than 9 square meters. Anything else would be too small.
M You're right. What about electricity?
W I don't think we need electricity. It may disturb our view when we try to see stars in the sky.
M I agree. It won't be that uncomfortable to live without electricity for a couple of days.
W Do you think we need hot water?
M I don't care either way, but Jamie won't take a shower without hot water.
W I'm with him. I don't like to take showers with cold water, either.
M Now we have to decide on a deck.
W We definitely need one. With a deck, we don't have to worry about snakes or a little rain.
M You're right. Then let's reserve this auto camping site.

남 이제 어느 오토 캠핑장을 예약해야 할지를 결정해야 해요.
여 9제곱미터보다는 큰 캠핑장이 필요해요. 다른 것은 너무 좁을 거예요.
남 당신 말이 맞아요. 전기는 어때요?
여 전기는 필요하지 않다고 생각해요. 하늘에 있는 별을 보려고 할 때 우리의 시야를 방해할 수도 있어요.
남 동의해요. 이삼일 정도는 전기 없이 살아도 그다지 불편하지 않을 거예요.
여 온수가 필요하다고 생각해요?
남 나는 어느 쪽이든 신경 쓰지 않지만, Jamie는 온수 없이 샤워를 하지 않을 거예요.
여 나도 그와 같아요. 나도 찬물로 샤워하는 것을 좋아하지 않아요.
남 이제 갑판을 결정해야 해요.
여 그것은 절대적으로 필요해요. 갑판이 있으면 뱀이나 약간의 비도 걱정할 필요가 없어요.
남 맞아요. 그럼 이 오토 캠핑장을 예약합시다.

Solution

두 사람은 9제곱미터보다 크고, 전기는 필요 없으며, 온수가 나오고, 갑판이 있는 오토 캠핑장을 예약하기로 했으므로, 두 사람이 예약할 오토 캠핑장은 ③이다.

Words

disturb 방해하다 uncomfortable 불편한 deck 갑판, 데크
definitely 절대적으로

11 정답 ⑤

Script

W Honey, Henry is crying in his room.
M Okay. I'll go and check on him.
W He must be scared because he woke up alone in his room.
M I'll go and make him calm down right away.

여 여보, Henry가 자기 방에서 울고 있어요.
남 알았어요. 내가 가서 그를 확인해 볼게요.

여 자기 방에서 혼자 깨어나서 무서운 게 틀림없어요.
남 내가 바로 가서 그를 진정하도록 만들게요.

Solution

여자는 아들인 Henry가 방에서 우는 소리가 들리자 방에서 자다가 혼자 깨어나서 무서운 거라고 말하므로, 이에 대한 남자의 응답으로 가장 적절한 것은 ⑤ '내가 바로 가서 그를 진정하도록 만들게요.'이다.

① 그래요. 그는 혼자 잘 수 있을 만큼 충분히 나이가 들었어요.
② 그 애가 침대에서 떨어지지 않도록 해 주세요.
③ 당신 말이 맞아요. 그는 잠을 좀 잘 필요가 있어요.
④ 사실, 나는 하루 종일 그 애와 함께 있었어요.

Words

check on ~을 확인하다 scared 무서워하는 calm down 진정하다

12 정답 ③

Script

M Oh, dear. Are you okay?
W Yeah, I'm fine. The floor is very slippery.
M Yes, it really is. Can I help you up?
W Thanks. That's very kind of you.

- -

남 오, 이런. 괜찮아요?
여 네, 저는 괜찮아요. 바닥이 매우 미끄럽네요.
남 네, 정말로 그렇군요. 제가 일으켜 줄까요?
여 감사합니다. 매우 친절하시네요.

Solution

미끄러운 바닥에 넘어진 여자를 남자가 일으켜 주겠다고 도움을 제안하고 있으므로, 이에 대한 여자의 응답으로 가장 적절한 것은 ③ '감사합니다. 매우 친절하시네요.'이다.

① 스스로를 비난하지 마세요.
② 당신은 다음에 더 잘할 수 있어요.
④ 당신은 좀 더 주의했어야 했어요.
⑤ 오, 그것은 제 것이 아니에요. 어쨌든 감사합니다.

Words

slippery 미끄러운

13 정답 ④

Script

M Sophie, you don't look good today. What's wrong?
W Oh, Brian. I think I caught a cold.
M Then why don't you go see a doctor?
W No, I won't.
M Why not? The doctor will help you get over it faster.
W I'll just get some rest at home and drink lots of warm water.
M Is that all you do when you have a cold?
W Yes. Taking cold medicine doesn't make that much difference.
M What do you mean by that? The medicine will help you recover faster.
W Yes, but only a little bit faster.
M I see. You choose to relax enough without medicine.

- -

남 Sophie. 오늘 안 좋아 보여. 무슨 일이니?
여 오, Brian. 감기에 걸린 것 같아.
남 그럼 병원에 가 보는 게 어때?
여 아니, 안 갈 거야.
남 왜 가지 않겠다는 거지? 의사는 네가 더 빨리 회복하도록 도울 거야.
여 나는 그냥 집에서 좀 쉬고 따뜻한 물을 많이 마실 거야.
남 네가 감기에 걸렸을 때 그게 네가 하는 전부야?
여 응. 감기약을 먹는 것이 그리 많은 차이를 낳지 못해.
남 그게 무슨 뜻이야? 약은 네가 더 빨리 회복되는 것을 도울 거야.
여 그래. 하지만 단지 약간만 더 빠를 뿐이지.
남 알겠어. 너는 약 없이 충분히 휴식을 취하기를 선택한 거구나.

Solution

감기에 걸린 여자에게 남자는 의사에게 가 보라고 권유하지만, 여자는 그냥 집에서 쉬고 따뜻한 물을 많이 마시겠다고 하면서, 약을 먹는 것이 약간만 빠르게 감기를 낫게 하는 것일 뿐이라고 남자에게 말하므로, 이에 대한 남자의 응답으로 가장 적절한 것은 ④ '알겠어. 너는 약 없이 충분히 휴식을 취하기를 선택한 거구나.'이다.

① 알았어. 지금 바로 약을 좀 살게.
② 맞아. 나도 며칠 동안 감기로 고생했어.
③ 동의해. 감기를 빨리 치료하는 것이 가장 중요해.
⑤ 음, 네가 근처에 있는 병원을 추천해 주었으면 해.

Words

get over (병으로부터) 회복하다 make a difference 차이를 낳다
recover 회복되다

14 정답 ⑤

Script

W Hi, George! What a nice surprise to see you here!
M Oh, hi, Julie. What kind of greeting is that?
W You practice basketball every day at the gym and play baseball on the weekends, so I thought that you're only interested in sports.
M That's just one part of my life. Do you often come to this artist's exhibits?
W No, but it's not my first time to see his paintings in an art gallery.
M I see. Look at that painting. It's lovely, isn't it?
W You mean the one of the woman breast-feeding her baby?
M Yes. I can feel her love for her child.
W Well, I can't deny it's a nice drawing.
M It sounds like you don't like it.
W Actually, I don't like the way he depicts gender in his paintings.
M What do you mean?
W He seems to use fixed gender roles in his paintings.

- -

여 안녕, George! 여기서 너를 보니까 반갑고 놀랍기도 하네!
남 오, 안녕. Julie. 무슨 인사가 그래?
여 너는 매일 체육관에서 농구하고 주말에는 야구를 해서 오로지 스포츠에만 관심이 있을 거라고 생각했거든.
남 그것은 단지 내 삶의 일부일 뿐이야. 이 화가의 전시회에 종종 오니?
여 아니, 하지만 미술관에서 이 화가의 그림을 보는 것이 이번이 처음은 아니야.
남 그렇구나. 저 그림을 봐. 사랑스럽다, 그렇지 않니?

여 아기에게 모유 수유를 하는 여성의 그림 말이니?
남 응. 아기에 대한 엄마의 사랑을 느낄 수 있어.
여 글쎄, 그것이 멋진 그림이라는 것을 부인할 수는 없지.
남 너는 그 그림을 별로 좋아하지 않는 것 같은데.
여 사실, 난 그가 자신의 그림에서 성을 묘사하는 방식이 마음에 안 들어.
남 무슨 뜻이야?
여 그는 고정화된 성 역할을 그의 그림에서 이용하는 것 같아.

여자가 화가가 성을 묘사하는 방식이 마음에 들지 않는다는 자신의 의견을 표현하자 남자는 그에 대한 구체적인 의미를 질문하고 있으므로, 이에 대한 여자의 응답으로 가장 적절한 것은 ⑤ '그는 고정화된 성 역할을 그의 그림에서 이용하는 것 같아.'이다.

① 나는 그가 화가라는 것을 결코 짐작하지 못했을 거야.
② 그는 아기를 낳는다는 것이 어떤지 알지 못해.
③ 그는 그림을 명성을 얻는 수단으로 여겨.
④ 그는 어느 여성 화가보다도 더 많은 그림을 그려.

exhibit 전시회 breast-feed 모유를 먹이다 deny 부인하다
depict 묘사하다, 그리다 gender 성(性)

15 정답 ③

M Matt has been working for the same company for ten years since he graduated from college. He likes his job and coworkers, so he has never thought about leaving the company. But Matt has a father, who has owned a restaurant he inherited from his father for forty years. Matt gets a call saying that his father suddenly collapsed. He immediately goes to see his father. Still in the hospital bedroom, his father says it's time for Matt to take over the restaurant, adding that it would be his will. After sleeping on it, Matt finally decides to follow his father's decision. Now he knocks on the door and his boss says, "Come in." In this situation, what would Matt most likely say to his boss?
Matt Sorry to say this. I am afraid I have to quit.

남 Matt는 대학교를 졸업한 이래로 10년 동안 같은 회사에서 근무하고 있습니다. 그는 자신의 일과 동료들을 좋아하기 때문에 회사를 떠날 생각을 해 본 적이 없습니다. 하지만 Matt에게는 할아버지로부터 물려받은 식당을 40년 동안 운영해 오고 있는 아버지가 있습니다. Matt는 아버지가 갑작스럽게 쓰러지셨다는 전화를 받습니다. 그는 즉시 아버지를 뵈러 갑니다. 여전히 병실에 누워 계신 그의 아버지는 Matt가 식당을 물려받을 때가 되었다고 하며 그것이 그의 유언이 될 것이라고 덧붙입니다. 밤새 생각을 거듭한 끝에 Matt는 마침내 아버지의 결정을 따르기로 결심합니다. 이제 그는 문을 두드리고 사장은 "들어오세요."라고 말합니다. 이런 상황에서, Matt는 사장에게 뭐라고 말할 것 같은가요?
Matt 이런 말씀을 드리게 되어 죄송합니다. 회사를 그만두어야 할 것 같습니다.

Matt는 아버지의 식당을 물려받기로 결정해서 그 뜻을 회사에 전달해야 하는 상황이므로, 이러한 상황에서 Matt가 사장에게 할 말로 가장 적절한 것은 ③ '이런 말씀을 드리게 되어 죄송합니다. 회사를 그만두어야 할 것 같습니다.'이다.

① 휴대전화를 매너 모드로 해 놓았습니다.
② 음, 우선 저는 동료들이 마음에 듭니다.
④ 제 식당으로 오십시오. 점심을 대접하겠습니다.
⑤ 지금은 아버지가 괜찮습니다. 곧 업무에 복귀하겠습니다.

own 소유하다 inherit 물려받다, 상속받다 collapse 쓰러지다
immediately 즉시 take over 물려받다, 인수하다 will 유언
sleep on 밤새 생각하다

16 정답 ①   17 정답 ⑤

W Hello, this is Megan Lee, the music instructor from Sola Community Center. It is true that kids like music. Then why don't we help them make their own music by offering an opportunity to learn how to play musical instruments? But you might not know which instruments they like to learn. Here are some ideas. First, the piano is the musical instrument that kids want to learn the most. They are usually fascinated by its keyboard and put their hands on it automatically. Second, the flute is another musical instrument loved by most kids. I guess its shiny appearance attracts them. Next, the guitar is also a favorite. Almost every kid seems to want to play the guitar the moment he or she sees it, even though they can't play beautifully at all. Last, kids love to play the violin. The violin is played by rubbing the bow across the strings, which looks really fun to kids. There are many other instruments kids would love to learn. What others do you think they might enjoy?

여 안녕하세요, 저는 Sola 문화 센터의 음악 강사인 Megan Lee입니다. 아이들이 음악을 좋아한다는 것은 사실입니다. 그렇다면 악기 연주법을 배울 수 있는 기회를 제공함으로써 그들이 자기 자신의 음악을 만드는 것을 돕는 것은 어떨까요? 하지만 여러분은 그들이 어떤 악기를 배우기를 좋아하는지 모를 수도 있습니다. 여기 몇몇 아이디어가 있습니다. 첫째, 피아노는 아이들이 가장 배우고 싶어 하는 악기입니다. 그들은 보통 건반에 매료되어 건반에 자동적으로 손을 얹게 됩니다. 둘째, 플루트는 대부분의 아이들에게 사랑받는 또 다른 악기입니다. 그것의 빛나는 외양이 그들을 끌어당기는 것 같습니다. 다음으로, 기타 또한 아주 좋아하는 악기입니다. 거의 모든 아이가 비록 전혀 아름답게 연주할 순 없어도, 그것을 보는 순간 기타를 연주하고 싶어 하는 것 같습니다. 마지막으로, 아이들은 바이올린 연주하는 것을 좋아합니다. 바이올린은 활을 현에 가로질러 문지름으로써 연주되는데, 이것은 아이들에게 정말 재미있어 보입니다. 아이들이 배우고 싶어 할 많은 다른 악기들이 있습니다. 그들이 다른 어떤 것을 즐길 거라고 생각합니까?

16

아이들이 배우고 싶어 하는 악기와 그 이유를 설명하고 있으므로 여자가 하는 말의 주제로 가장 적절한 것은 ① '아이들이 배우고 싶어 하는 악기들'이다.

② 악기를 살 때 고려 사항들
③ 어릴 때부터 아이들에게 음악을 가르치는 것의 중요성
④ 현악기와 건반 악기의 다른 점
⑤ 아이들에게 악기 연주법을 가르치는 것의 이점

17

피아노, 플루트, 기타, 바이올린은 언급되었지만, ⑤ '첼로'는 언급되지 않았다.

Words

fascinate 매료시키다 automatically 자동적으로 attract 끌어당기다
rub 문지르다 bow 활 string (악기의) 현[줄]

01 ①	02 ②	03 ④	04 ⑤	05 ②
06 ③	07 ④	08 ⑤	09 ④	10 ③
11 ⑤	12 ③	13 ③	14 ③	15 ④
16 ②	17 ③			

01 정답 ①

Script

W Nowadays more and more people are realizing the importance of donating what they have in life to society. What a great spirit it is! To those who have the spirit, nothing is more important to their children than teaching them the value of sharing what they have with others. "I'd like to return to the world what I received from it." or "I am determined that my children should have no financial security." These are words from people who decided to donate what they earned to society. As a parent, nothing is a better gift to your children than letting them see you giving to others. Now spread your love to the world, and teach your children about the spirit of generosity.

여 요즘 점점 더 많은 사람들이 살면서 자신들이 가진 것들을 사회에 기부하는 것의 중요성을 깨닫고 있습니다. 이것은 얼마나 위대한 정신입니까! 이러한 정신을 가진 사람들에게 있어서 그들이 가진 것을 다른 사람과 공유하는 가치를 아이들에게 가르치는 것보다 더 중요한 것은 없습니다. "세상으로부터 받은 것을 세상에 돌려주고 싶습니다." 혹은 "아이들에게 재정적 안정을 물려주지 않기로 마음먹었습니다." 이것들은 자신들이 번 것을 사회에 기부하기로 결심한 사람들이 한 말입니다. 부모로서 타인에게 주는 모습을 자식들에게 보여 주는 것보다 더 나은 선물은 없습니다. 이제 여러분의 사랑을 세계에 펼치고 아이들에게 관대함의 정신을 가르쳐 주십시오.

Solution

여자는 자신이 가진 것을 사회에 기부하여 다른 사람과 나누는 것의 중요성을 강조하면서 아이들에게 이러한 관대한 행위의 정신을 가르쳐 달라고 말하고 있으므로, 여자가 하는 말의 목적으로 가장 적절한 것은 ①이다.

Words

donate 기부하다 spirit 정신 determined 단단히 결심한
financial 재정의 security 안정 spread 퍼뜨리다
generosity 관대(한 행위)

02 정답 ②

Script

M Jennifer, what happened? Brian is your best friend.
W It's all my fault.
M Don't blame yourself too much.
W I shouldn't have lost my temper. How's Brian?
M He's going to be fine. What happened?
W I told my classmates to close the door after they came in. They didn't seem to care, so I got angrier. Then I exploded

when Brian didn't close the door.

M I see. Things like that happen. The point is, never make the same mistake.

W I promise I won't.

M No one is perfect. We should learn from the mistakes we make.

W You're right, Mr. Reed. I'd like to apologize to him.

M Okay. Go ahead.

남 Jennifer, 무슨 일이 있었니? Brian은 너의 가장 친한 친구잖아.

여 다 제 잘못이에요.

남 너무 심하게 자책하지는 마.

여 제가 이성을 잃지 말았어야 했어요. Brian은 어때요?

남 그는 괜찮을 거야. 무슨 일이 있었니?

여 제가 반 친구들에게 교실에 들어온 후에 문을 닫으라고 말했어요. 반 친구들이 전혀 개의치 않는 것 같아서 더 화가 났어요. 그러다가 Brian이 문을 닫지 않았을 때 제가 폭발했어요.

남 그렇구나. 그런 일은 생기기 마련이니까. 중요한 것은 똑같은 실수를 절대 하지 않는 것이란다.

여 그렇지 않을 거라고 약속할게요.

남 완벽한 사람은 없어. 우리는 우리가 저지른 실수에서 배워야 해.

여 맞아요, Reed 선생님. 그에게 사과하고 싶어요.

남 그래. 가서 하렴.

Solution

여자는 Brian에게 화냈던 것을 자책하고 있고, 남자는 그런 일은 생기기 마련이고 같은 실수를 반복하지 않는 것이 중요하고 실수에서 배워야 한다고 했으므로 남자의 의견으로 가장 적절한 것은 ②이다.

Words

blame ~의 책임으로 돌리다; 비난하다
lose one's temper 이성을 잃다, 화를 내다   explode 폭발하다

03 정답 ④

Script

[Telephone rings.]

W Hello, how may I help you?

M Hi, Sally. I'm Mike Austin. I know it's short notice, but I need one actor and one actress for a film I'm directing this afternoon.

W This afternoon? It's so sudden.

M I know, but it's just one of those things. I never imagined this would happen, either.

W I understand, but all I can say is that I'll do my best. Tell me who you're looking for.

M The actor should play a rather tough role.

W Okay. What about the actress?

M She is a rather picky old lady.

W Okay. I'll start looking for people who fit your description.

M Thank you, Sally.

[전화벨이 울린다.]

여 안녕하세요, 어떻게 도와드릴까요?

남 안녕하세요, Sally. 저는 Mike Austin입니다. 촉박한 통보인 줄은 알지만, 오늘 오후에 내가 감독하고 있는 영화에 남자 배우 한 명과 여자 배우 한 명이 필요해요.

여 오늘 오후요? 너무 갑작스러워요.

남 알아요, 하지만 그건 흔히 있는 일이잖아요. 나도 이런 일이 일어나리라고는 전혀 생각도 못 했어요.

여 이해는 하지만 최선을 다해 보겠다고만 말씀드릴 수 있겠어요. 찾고 있는 사람을 말씀해 보세요.

남 남자 배우는 다소 강인한 역할을 해야 해요.

여 알겠어요. 여자 배우는요?

남 그녀는 다소 까다로운 노부인이에요.

여 알겠어요. 감독님이 묘사하는 것에 맞는 사람들을 찾아 보기 시작할게요.

남 고마워요, Sally.

Solution

남자가 여자에게 자신이 감독하고 있는 영화에 출연할 남자 배우와 여자 배우를 구해 달라고 하였고, 여자는 배우를 찾아보겠다고 하였으므로 두 사람의 관계를 가장 잘 나타낸 것은 ④이다.

Words

short notice 촉박한 통보   picky 까다로운   fit 어울리다
description 묘사, 서술

04 정답 ⑤

Script

W Tony, what are you looking at?

M I'm looking at the pictures I took last weekend.

W Let me see them. Oh, in this picture you're sitting on a mat on a big rock.

M Yes. See the tall boy, getting ready to dive? That's my son, Paul.

W He's in really good shape. Isn't it dangerous to dive there? Some kids are playing with a ball in the water.

M They know how to play safe. Can you recognize Jackie?

W Jackie is your daughter, right? Which one is she? The girl with the bucket?

M No, that's Jackie's friend. Jackie is trying to catch fish.

W You mean the girl with a dragonfly net?

M Yes. She tried to catch fish all day long, but caught none.

W What a pity! Where is Jennifer, your wife?

M She is over there, taking a picture of Jackie trying to catch a fish.

W I see. She is taking the picture with her cellphone.

여 Tony, 무엇을 보고 있어요?

남 지난 주말에 찍은 사진들을 보고 있어요.

여 저도 좀 봐요. 오, 이 사진에서 당신은 큰 바위 위 매트에 앉아 있네요.

남 네. 다이빙을 할 채비를 하고 있는 키 큰 남자애 보이죠? 제 아들 Paul이에요.

여 정말로 건강하네요. 저기서 다이빙하는 것은 위험하지 않나요? 물에서 공을 가지고 노는 아이들이 있는데.

남 그들은 안전하게 노는 법을 알아요. Jackie를 알아보실 수 있나요?

여 Jackie는 당신 딸이잖아요, 맞죠? 누구인가요? 양동이를 든 여자애인가요?

남 아뇨, 그 애는 Jackie의 친구예요. Jackie는 물고기를 잡으려고 하고 있어요.

여 잠자리채를 가지고 있는 여자애 말인가요?

남 네. 하루 종일 물고기를 잡으려고 시도했는데, 한 마리도 잡지 못했어요.

여 안됐네요! 당신의 아내, Jennifer는 어디 있죠?

남 그녀는 저쪽에서 Jackie가 물고기를 잡는 사진을 찍고 있어요.

여 알겠어요. 그녀가 휴대전화로 사진을 찍고 있군요.

남자의 아내는 휴대전화로 사진을 찍고 있다고 했지만 그림에서는 통화를 하고 있으므로, 대화의 내용과 일치하지 않는 것은 ⑤이다.

recognize 알아보다 bucket 양동이 dragonfly net 잠자리채

05 정답 ②

W Bob, can we talk for a second in the lounge?
M Yes. Let's go.
W Bob, I'm really sorry about last Saturday. Something urgent came up, so I couldn't keep my promise.
M That's okay. I understand.
W Thank you. What are you doing this Friday?
M Nothing special yet. Why?
W I think I can get two tickets to the Renegades concert. What do you think?
M Don't tell me it's just to make up for last Saturday.
W Not exactly. One of my cousins works at an entertainment agency. He said he would give me tickets if I want them. I need to call him to say yes or no this afternoon.
M Of course, I'd love to see the Renegades.
W Okay. Then I'll ask for the tickets.

여 Bob, 휴게실에서 잠시 이야기할 수 있을까요?
남 네. 가죠.
여 Bob, 지난 토요일 일은 정말 미안해요. 급한 일이 생겨서 약속을 지킬 수가 없었어요.
남 괜찮아요. 이해해요.
여 감사해요. 이번 금요일에 뭐 할 거예요?
남 아직 특별한 것은 없어요. 왜요?
여 Renegades 콘서트 표를 두 장 구할 수 있을 것 같아요. 어때요?
남 설마 단지 지난 토요일이 미안해서 그러는 것은 아니죠.
여 결코 아니에요. 사촌 한 명이 연예 기획사에서 일해요. 내가 원하면 표를 주겠다고 했어요. 그에게 오늘 오후에 전화해서 답을 줘야 하거든요.
남 당연히 Renegades 공연을 보고 싶죠.
여 좋아요. 그러면 표를 달라고 요청할게요.

여자는 오늘 오후에 연예 기획사에서 일하는 사촌에게 전화해 Renegades 콘서트에 갈 것인지에 대한 여부를 알려 줘야 하는 상황이다. 남자가 콘서트를 보고 싶다고 했고, 이에 여자가 표를 요청하겠다고 말했으므로, 정답은 ② 이다.

urgent 급박한 keep one's promise 약속을 지키다
make up for ~을 만회하다, ~을 보상하다
entertainment agency 연예 기획사

06 정답 ③

W Next, please!
M Yes, I received my telephone bill, and there's something wrong with it.
W Your total is $96. What's the problem?
M It says I accepted two collect calls last month. But, I never received any collect calls.
W Well, let me check. [Pause] Oh, I am sorry. You didn't accept a collect call from anyone.
M Could you take those charges off my bill?
W Sure. $16 will be deducted from your phone bill.
M And I'm supposed to get a 10 percent discount for the first three months. This was my third month and the 10 percent discount is not considered in the bill.
W You're right. We'll reissue your bill. We're terribly sorry for causing such an inconvenience.

여 다음 분이요!
남 네, 전화 청구서를 받았는데요. 잘못된 점이 있어요.
여 총액이 96달러네요. 무슨 문제인가요?
남 제가 지난달에 두 통의 수신자 비용 부담 전화를 받은 것으로 되어 있어요. 하지만, 저는 어떤 수신자 비용 부담 전화도 받지 않았어요.
여 음, 확인해 보죠. [잠시 후] 오, 죄송합니다. 누구한테서도 수신자 비용 부담 전화를 받지 않으셨군요.
남 청구서에서 그 요금들을 빼 줄 수 있나요?
여 물론이죠. 16달러가 전화 청구서에서 공제될 것입니다.
남 그리고 저는 처음 석 달간 10퍼센트의 할인을 받게 되어 있어요. 이번 달이 세 번째 달입니다만, 10퍼센트 할인이 청구서에 고려되지 않았습니다.
여 맞습니다. 청구서를 다시 발행해 드리겠습니다. 이런 불편을 끼쳐 드려서 대단히 죄송합니다.

96달러의 전화 청구서에서 16달러는 수신자 비용 부담 전화가 잘못 청구된 것이므로 이 비용을 빼고, 80달러의 10퍼센트인 8달러가 추가로 빼야 하므로, 남자가 지불할 금액은 ③ '72달러'이다.

bill 청구서 collect call 수신자 비용 부담 전화
take ~ off ~을 빼다[제거하다] charge 요금, 비용 deduct 공제하다

07 정답 ④

W Dad, I'm home.
M Emma, where have you been all afternoon?
W I was writing my social studies report at the Café Rose.
M Is that a good café for studying?
W Absolutely. The atmosphere is very quiet and there are many desks for using a laptop computer.
M The café is kind of a library to you.
W That's right. [Pause] Oh, no! I don't think I have my wallet with me.
M Did you have it at the café?
W Yes. I remember taking out some money from the wallet to pay for the coffee.
M Then you might have left it somewhere at the café. You'd better go check.
W You're right. I'll do that right away.

여 아빠, 저 왔어요.

남 Emma, 오후 내내 어디 있었니?

여 저는 Café Rose에서 사회 과목 보고서를 쓰고 있었어요.

남 그곳은 공부하기에 좋은 카페니?

여 그럼요. 분위기가 매우 조용하고 노트북 컴퓨터를 사용할 수 있는 책상이 많아요.

남 그 카페는 너에게는 일종의 도서관이구나.

여 맞아요. [잠시 후] 오, 이런! 지갑이 없는 것 같아요.

남 카페에서는 그것이 있었니?

여 네. 커피 값을 지불하기 위해 지갑에서 돈을 좀 꺼낸 게 기억이 나요.

남 그러면 카페 어딘가에 그것을 놓고 왔을지도 몰라. 가서 확인해 보는 게 좋을 거야.

여 아빠 말씀이 맞아요. 지금 바로 할게요.

여자는 카페에서 오는 길이라고 말하던 중 자신이 지갑을 분실한 것을 발견한다. 여자가 카페에서 지갑에서 돈을 꺼냈던 것이 기억난다고 하자 남자는 그곳에 그것을 놓고 왔을지 모르니 가서 확인해 보라고 한다. 이에 여자는 그러겠다고 했으므로, 정답은 ④이다.

social studies 사회 과목 atmosphere 분위기 wallet 지갑
leave 놓아 두다 check 확인하다

08 정답 ⑤

[Telephone rings.]

W Hello, this is Julia's Apple Farm. How can I help you?

M Hi. I heard you're having a harvest festival.

W That's right.

M Will you still be having it a week from tomorrow?

W Yes, till the end of September.

M Can you tell me what kinds of activities you provide?

W Certainly. First of all, you can pick as many apples as you can for an hour. For families with kids, there is a pony-riding event, an apple-peeling event, and an apple-pie baking contest.

M That sounds like fun. And can you tell me how much you're charging?

W It's $10 for adults and $5 for children under 12.

M Okay. How can I get to the farm? We live in Hills Village.

W It's very easy. We're just off the end of Highway 75.

M All right. Thanks for the information.

[전화벨이 울린다.]

여 안녕하세요. Julia 사과 농장입니다. 어떻게 도와드릴까요?

남 안녕하세요. 추수 축제를 연다고 들었습니다.

여 맞습니다.

남 내일부터 일주일 동안 여시는 거죠?

여 네, 9월말까지입니다.

남 어떤 활동들을 제공하는지 말씀해 주실 수 있나요?

여 물론이죠. 우선, 한 시간 동안 사과를 마음껏 딸실 수 있습니다. 아이들을 동반한 가족을 위해서는 조랑말 타기 행사, 사과 껍질 까기 행사, 애플파이 굽기 대회가 마련되어 있습니다.

남 재미있겠군요. 가격은 얼마인지 알려 주실 수 있나요?

여 성인은 10달러이고, 12세 미만의 아이들은 5달러입니다.

남 좋습니다. 농장에는 어떻게 찾아갈 수 있나요? 저희는 Hills Village에 살고 있어요.

여 아주 쉽습니다. 저희는 75번 고속도로의 끝을 막 벗어난 곳에 위치하고 있습니다.

남 알겠습니다. 정보 감사합니다.

행사 기간, 행사 내용, 입장료, 찾아가는 길은 언급되었으나, ⑤ '개장 시간'에 대해서는 언급되지 않았다.

harvest festival 추수 축제 provide 제공하다 first of all 우선
pony 조랑말 peel 껍질을 벗기다 charge 청구하다

09 정답 ④

M It was once considered a dream to spend a vacation in outer space. Not anymore. In 2019, 60-year-old Dennis Tito became the very first space tourist. Tito prepared for the trip by spending eight months at a Russian astronaut training facility. On April 28th, 2019, Tito and other astronauts blasted off from a launch pad in Kazakhstan. On April 30th, the spacecraft docked with the International Space Station. Tito spent most of his time gazing out the windows and taking photographs. On May 6th, Tito and the rest of the crew returned to Earth after spending 7 days, 22 hours, 4 minutes in space and orbiting Earth 128 times. Tito paid a reported $20 million for his trip.

남 우주에서 휴가를 보내는 것은 한때 꿈으로 여겨졌습니다. 더 이상 꿈이 아닙니다. 2019년에 60세의 Dennis Tito가 바로 최초의 우주 관광객이 되었습니다. Tito는 러시아의 우주 비행사 훈련 시설에서 8개월을 보내면서 여행 준비를 했습니다. 2019년 4월 28일에 Tito와 다른 우주 비행사들은 카자흐스탄에 있는 발사대에서 발사되었습니다. 4월 30일에 우주선은 국제 우주 정거장에 도킹했습니다. Tito는 시간의 대부분을 창밖을 내다보며 사진을 찍는 것으로 보냈습니다. 5월 6일에 Tito와 나머지 승무원들은 7일 22시간 4분을 우주에서 보내고 지구를 128차례 돈 후에 지구로 돌아왔습니다. Tito는 보도된 바에 의하면 여행 비용으로 2천만 달러를 지불했습니다.

우주에서 7일 22시간 4분을 보냈다고 했으므로, 담화의 내용과 일치하지 않는 것은 ④ '우주에서 6일동안 지구 궤도를 100회 이상 돌았다.'이다.

facility 시설 blast off 발사되다 launch pad 발사대
dock (우주선을) 도킹하다 gaze 바라보다
orbit (다른 천체의) 궤도를 돌다

10 정답 ③

W Honey, what are you doing on the Internet?

M I was shopping around for a new toolbox because ours is too worn-out.

W Let me help you choose one.

M Thank you. Well, I don't want to spend over $40 for the toolbox.

W Okay. What about the weight? I think a lighter one would be much better.

M Absolutely. So this one of almost 4 kg is out.

W Now we have to consider the warranty. Isn't it better to buy one with longer warranty?

M Of course. Now we have two options to choose from. I'll let you choose the color.

W Okay. Hmm... I'd like to take the green one.

M I see. Then I'll order this one.

여 여보, 인터넷에서 뭐 하고 있어요?

남 우리 공구 상자가 너무 낡아서 새 공구 상자를 둘러보고 있었어요.

여 내가 고르는 것을 도와줄게요.

남 고마워요. 음, 나는 공구 상자에 40달러 넘게 쓰고 싶지 않아요.

여 알았어요. 무게는 어때요? 내 생각에는 더 가벼운 게 훨씬 더 나을 것 같아요.

남 당연하죠. 그럼 거의 4킬로그램에 가까운 이것은 빠지는군요.

여 이제 우리는 보증 기간을 고려해야 해요. 보증 기간이 더 긴 것으로 사는 게 낫지 않아요?

남 물론이죠. 이제 우리는 고를 수 있는 두 가지 선택사항을 가지고 있어요. 당신이 색을 골라요.

여 알았어요. 흠… 난 초록색으로 하고 싶어요.

남 알겠어요. 그럼 이걸 내가 주문할게요.

두 사람은 40달러 미만이고, 거의 4킬로그램이 되는 것은 빼고, 보증 기간이 더 긴 초록색 공구 상자를 선택하였으므로, 남자가 주문할 공구 상자는 ③이다.

shop around for ~을 사러 둘러보다 toolbox 공구 상자
worn-out 낡은 warranty 보증 (기간) option 선택사항

11 정답 ⑤

M Ms. Peck, you're wearing glasses.

W These are reading glasses. I only wear them when I read.

M Actually, I need to get reading glasses. Would you recommend a good eyeglass shop?

W Sure. I'll let you know the one where I bought mine.

남 Peck 씨, 당신은 안경을 쓰고 있군요.

여 이것들은 돋보기안경이에요. 나는 읽을 때만 그것을 써요.

남 사실, 난 돋보기안경을 사야 해요. 좋은 안경점을 추천해 주시겠어요?

여 그러죠. 내가 내 것을 산 안경점을 알려 드릴게요.

남자는 돋보기안경을 쓰고 있는 여자에게 자신도 돋보기안경을 살 필요가 있다고 하면서 안경점을 추천해 달라고 부탁하고, 이에 대해 여자는 안경점에 대한 추천의 말을 하는 것이 자연스러우므로 ⑤ '그러죠. 내가 내 것을 산 안경점을 알려 드릴게요.'가 여자의 응답으로 가장 적절하다.

① 그래요. 나는 그 가게에서 안경을 이미 샀어요.

② 좋아요. 그 가게는 다양한 선글라스를 취급해요.

③ 미안해요. 당신이 안경을 살 때 같이 갈 수 없어요.

④ 고마워요. 그 가게 주인은 정말 따뜻하고 친절했어요.

reading glasses 돋보기안경 recommend 추천하다

12 정답 ③

W Frank! Here I am!

M Hi, Mom! Thanks for coming to meet me at the airport.

W You're welcome. How was the flight?

M Pretty good, but I'm a little tired.

여 Frank! 여기야!

남 안녕하세요, 엄마! 공항에 마중 나와 주셔서 감사해요.

여 천만에. 비행은 어땠어?

남 아주 좋았지만 조금 피곤해요.

비행기를 타고 공항에 도착한 남자를 맞이하면서 여자는 비행이 어땠는지 묻고 있으므로, ③ '아주 좋았지만 조금 피곤해요.'가 남자의 응답으로 가장 적절하다.

① 여기서부터 걸어가기에는 너무 멀어요.

② 예약을 취소하고 싶어요.

④ 조급하게 굴지 마세요. 공항에서는 시간이 걸려요.

⑤ 저는 높은 곳이 무서워요. 기차로 여행할게요.

flight 비행, (비행기) 여행

13 정답 ③

W Dave, how was your bike trip to Hola Island?

M Oh, Nancy. I had a great time at first.

W What do you mean by at first?

M My friends and I enjoyed the trip until we reached the middle point.

W What went wrong there?

M I got a flat tire.

W That's not a problem. You know how to fix a flat tire.

M Of course, I know. The problem was we forgot to bring any tools with us.

W Oh, my! So how did you handle the problem?

M Fortunately, there was a bike shop about 1 km away, and I took my bike there.

W That was lucky, or your trip could have been a disaster.

여 Dave, Hola 섬으로의 자전거 여행은 어땠어?

남 오, Nancy. 처음엔 정말 재미있었어.

여 '처음에'라는 것이 무슨 뜻이야?

남 내 친구들과 나는 중간 지점에 도착할 때까지는 그 여행을 즐겼어.

여 거기서 뭐가 잘못되었니?

남 타이어에 펑크가 났어.

여 그건 문제가 아니지. 넌 펑크 난 타이어 고치는 법을 알잖아.

남 물론 알아. 문제는 우리가 어떠한 도구도 가져오는 것을 잊었다는 것이었어.

여 아, 이런! 그래서 문제를 어떻게 처리했어?

남 다행히 1킬로미터쯤 떨어진 곳에 자전거 가게가 있어서, 자전거를 그곳

에 가져갔어.

여 그것은 운이 좋았던 거야. 그렇지 않았다면 네 여행은 엉망이 될 수도 있었어.

Solution

자전거 여행 중 타이어에 펑크가 난 남자는 그것을 고칠 도구를 가져가는 것을 잊었지만 다행히 1킬로미터 떨어진 곳에 자전거 가게가 있어서 그곳까지 자전거를 가져갔다고 말한다. 여자는 이에 대해 자신의 생각을 말하는 것이 자연스러우므로, ③ '그것은 운이 좋았던 거야. 그렇지 않았다면 네 여행은 엉망이 될 수도 있었어.'가 여자의 응답으로 가장 적절하다.

① 그 자전거 가게는 우리가 가기에는 너무 멀었어.
② 너는 떠나기 전에 어디로 갈지를 결정했어야 했어.
④ 그러니까 너는 친구로부터 도구들을 빌렸겠구나.
⑤ 다음번 자전거 여행에는 반드시 참가하겠다고 약속할게.

Words

get a flat tire 타이어에 펑크가 나다   handle 처리하다, 다루다

14 정답 ③

Script

W Bill, what are you doing on the Internet?
M Hi, Jean. I need to buy a present for Joe.
W What's the occasion?
M His birthday is coming.
W I see. What are you going to buy him?
M Well, I'm thinking about buying some tickets.
W That's a good idea. Since he's crazy about baseball, maybe tickets to the ballpark would be the best present.
M No. He's into jazz now.
W Jazz? That's incredible. I can't even imagine him listening to music, not to mention jazz.
M He even goes to jazz concerts. So I'm looking for tickets to one.
W Wow, is this the same Joe who used to play in the field all day long? What in the world has happened to him?
M Think about yourself when you were in love.
- -
여 Bill, 인터넷으로 뭘 하고 있어?
남 안녕, Jean. Joe에게 줄 선물을 사야 해.
여 무슨 중요한 일이 있는 거야?
남 그의 생일이 다가오거든.
여 그렇구나. 그에게 뭘 사 줄 건데?
남 글쎄, 입장권을 사 줄까 생각 중이야.
여 그거 좋은 생각이네. 그가 야구에 열광해 있으니까 아마 야구장 입장권은 가장 좋은 선물일 거야.
남 아니. 그는 지금 재즈에 푹 빠져 있어.
여 재즈라고? 믿을 수 없어. 재즈는 말할 것도 없고, 나는 심지어 그가 음악을 듣는 모습도 상상이 안 가는데.
남 그는 심지어 재즈 콘서트에도 다녀. 그래서 내가 재즈 콘서트 입장권을 찾고 있는 거야.
여 와, 하루 종일 운동장에서 경기를 하곤 했던 그 Joe와 같은 Joe야? 도대체 그에게 무슨 일이 벌어진 거야?
남 사랑에 빠졌을 때의 네 모습을 생각해 봐.

Solution

Joe의 생일 선물을 고르고 있는 남자에게 여자는 야구장 입장권을 추천하자 남자는 Joe가 재즈에 푹 빠져서 재즈 콘서트 입장권을 찾는 중이라고 말

한다. 여자는 예전과 완전히 달라진 Joe의 모습에 놀라움을 표현하고 있으므로, ③ '사랑에 빠졌을 때의 네 모습을 생각해 봐.'가 남자의 응답으로 가장 적절하다.

① 그러면 경기장에 가서 그를 응원하자.
② 그에게 콘서트 표를 사 준 것은 너였어.
④ 우리는 이번 토요일에 그에게 작은 파티를 열어 줄 거야.
⑤ 그는 단지 다른 유형의 음악에 식상해졌어.

Words

occasion (특정한) 때, 경우
be into ~에 심취해 있다   incredible 믿을 수 없는
not to mention ~은 말할 것도 없고   in the world 도대체
root for ~을 응원하다   be fed up with ~에 싫증이 나다

15 정답 ④

Script

W Chase is in his senior year of college. Three days before the mid-term examinations, he was so sick that he couldn't go to Dr. Sipp's biology class. Instead, he stayed in bed all day long. Dr. Sipp's class is very important to him since he majors in biology. Chase thinks that he needs to catch up with the class he missed. The best way to do that is to copy another student's lecture notes. He remembers that Jessica is good at note-taking. Chase calls Jessica and she answers the phone. In this situation, what would Chase most likely say to Jessica?
Chase Can I copy your notes from Dr. Sipp's lecture?
- -
여 Chase는 대학교 4학년 학생입니다. 중간고사 시험을 3일 앞두고 있는 가운데, 그는 너무 아파서 Sipp 교수님의 생물학 수업에 갈 수가 없었습니다. 대신 그는 하루 종일 침대에 누워 있었습니다. 그는 생물학을 전공하고 있기 때문에 Sipp 교수님의 수업은 그에게 아주 중요합니다. Chase는 놓친 수업을 따라잡아야 할 필요가 있다고 생각합니다. 그렇게 하는 가장 좋은 방법은 다른 학생의 강의 노트를 복사하는 것입니다. 그는 Jessica가 노트 필기를 잘한다는 것을 기억합니다. Chase는 Jessica에게 전화를 하고 그녀가 전화를 받습니다. 이런 상황에서, Chase는 Jessica에게 뭐라고 말할 것 같은가요?
Chase 내가 Sipp 교수님 강의의 네 노트를 복사할 수 있을까?

Solution

Chase는 몸이 아파서 강의를 듣지 못했지만 전공이라 중요한 Sipp 교수의 수업 내용을 필기한 것을 복사하고자 Jessica에게 전화를 건 상황이므로, 이러한 상황에서 Chase가 Jessica에게 할 말로 가장 적절한 것은 ④ 'Sipp 교수님 강의의 네 노트를 복사할 수 있을까?'이다.

① 너의 노트 필기 비결이 뭐니?
② Sipp 교수님의 강의는 너무 따분해, 그렇지 않니?
③ 네가 아팠다는 이야기 들었어. 지금은 괜찮니?
⑤ 생물학에 얼마나 오랫동안 관심이 있었던 거니?

Words

biology 생물학   all day long 하루 종일   catch up with ~을 따라잡다

16 정답 ②   17 정답 ③

Script

M Do you dream of harvesting your own homegrown foods,

but just don't know where to start? Actually, there are many vegetables that beginners can grow in containers at their verandas or in their gardens of any size. First, why don't you start growing lettuce? Lettuce doesn't require any special care. You just have to plant it, and then water it from time to time. Second, onions and garlic are crops that don't need special care either. Simply plant them on well-drained soil in spring, and then leave them to grow! In late summer, you can have the joy of harvesting them. What could be easier? Next, tomatoes are the ideal easy vegetable to grow. They can be grown in hanging baskets and window boxes. Last, try to grow beets, a root vegetable. Beets can be sown directly into the moist ground from March to July. With proper watering, you can look forward to harvesting your own colorful beets from May to September.

남 여러분은 자신의 집에서 기른 음식을 수확하는 꿈을 꾸고 있지만, 어디서부터 시작해야 할지 모르십니까? 사실, 초보자들이 그들의 베란다에서 용기에 또는 어떠한 크기의 정원에서든지 기를 수 있는 야채들이 많이 있습니다. 우선, 상추를 재배하기 시작하는 게 어떨까요? 상추는 어떠한 특별한 관리도 필요 없습니다. 여러분은 단지 그것을 심은 다음 가끔 물을 주면 됩니다. 둘째, 양파와 마늘도 역시 특별한 관리가 필요 없는 작물입니다. 봄에 물기가 잘 빠지는 토양에 심은 후 그것을 자라게 놔두십시오! 늦여름에는 그것들을 수확하는 즐거움을 얻을 수 있습니다. 무슨 작물이 더 쉬울 수 있을까요? 다음으로 토마토는 재배하기에 이상적으로 쉬운 야채입니다. 그것들은 매달린 바구니와 창가의 화단에서 재배될 수 있습니다. 마지막으로 뿌리채소인 비트를 재배해 보십시오. 비트는 3월부터 7월까지 촉촉한 땅에 직접 뿌릴 수 있습니다. 적절한 물 주기를 통해, 여러분은 5월부터 9월까지 자신만의 색이 다채로운 비트를 수확하는 것을 기대할 수 있습니다.

Solution

16
남자는 집의 베란다나 어떠한 크기의 정원에서 손쉽게 재배할 수 있는 야채들을 소개하고 있으므로, 남자가 하는 말의 주제로 가장 적절한 것은 ② '집에서 재배하기 쉬운 야채 식물'이다.
① 정원의 토양을 비옥하게 만드는 방법
③ 야채에 포함되어 있는 필수 영양소
④ 야채를 규칙적으로 먹는 것의 중요성
⑤ 특별한 물 주기를 필요로 하는 식물들

17
상추, 양파, 토마토, 비트는 언급되었지만, ③ '감자'는 언급되지 않았다.

Words
harvest 수확하다 from time to time 가끔
well-drained 배수가 잘 되는 sow (씨를) 뿌리다

---

01 ②	02 ⑤	03 ①	04 ⑤	05 ④
06 ③	07 ⑤	08 ④	09 ⑤	10 ⑤
11 ③	12 ③	13 ②	14 ④	15 ②
16 ④	17 ④			

01 정답 ②

Script

W Hello. I'm Bethany Peterson, the personnel manager at Zach Motors. As you know, Zach Motors is at the forefront of the automobile industry, and I'm sure all of you hope to work with us. This year, we are planning to recruit hundreds of new employees. If you have impressive school records and have participated in extra-curriculum activities, you are welcome to apply for a job at Zach Motors. Also, we put a lot of importance on hands-on experience. You will have the upper hand if you have interned at our company. If you think you meet our qualifications, please send us a school transcript and a résumé.

여 안녕하세요. 저는 Zach Motors의 인사 부장인 Bethany Peterson입니다. 여러분도 아시다시피, Zach Motors는 자동차 산업의 선두에 있으며, 저는 여러분 모두가 우리와 일하고 싶어 한다고 확신합니다. 올해, 우리는 수백 명의 신입 사원을 모집할 계획입니다. 여러분이 인상적인 학교 성적을 갖고 있고 방과 후 특별활동에 참여했다면, Zach Motors에 지원하는 것을 환영합니다. 또한, 우리는 실전 경험을 매우 중시합니다. 우리 회사에서 인턴사원으로 근무했다면 유리합니다. 여러분이 우리의 자격 요건에 충족된다고 생각한다면 학교 성적 증명서와 이력서를 보내 주시기 바랍니다.

Solution
여자는 Zach Motors에서 수백 명의 신입 사원을 모집하는데 학교 성적, 방과 후 특별활동, 실전 경험, 인턴 경험 등의 자격 요건을 설명하며 지원해 달라고 말하고 있으므로, 여자가 하는 말의 목적으로 가장 적절한 것은 ②이다.

Words
personnel (회사의) 인사과 at the forefront of ~의 선두에
recruit 모집하다 school record 학교 성적
extra-curriculum (교육과정 이외의) 특별활동
put importance on ~을 중요하게 여기다 hands-on 직접 해 보는
have the upper hand 유리하다, 우세하다 intern 인턴으로 근무하다
meet 충족시키다 qualification 자격 (요건)
school transcript 학교 성적 증명서

02 정답 ⑤

Script

M Lina, what are you still doing up? It's way past your bedtime.
W I'm brewing some coffee. I have to finish an assignment that's due tomorrow.

M Tomorrow? How come you didn't finish it earlier?

W I can concentrate better when I wait until the last minute.

M You're just saying that. I know you have a bad habit of putting important things off.

W I can't help it. Something always comes up when I try to do homework.

M That's because you don't have your priorities straight.

W You mean I have to put my schoolwork first and do other things later?

M Yes, no matter what happens.

W Okay, I'll try that from now on.

남 Lina, 아직까지 뭐 하고 있니? 취침 시간이 훨씬 지났잖아.

여 커피를 끓이고 있어요. 내일까지 제출할 과제를 끝내야 하거든요.

남 내일이라고? 어째서 미리 끝내지 않았니?

여 마지막까지 미룰 때 더 집중을 잘할 수 있거든요.

남 그냥 하는 말이잖아. 네가 중요한 일을 미루는 안 좋은 습관을 가지고 있다는 걸 알아.

여 어쩔 수 없어요. 숙제를 하려고 할 때 항상 뭔가 생겨요.

남 그건 네가 우선순위들을 제대로 세우지 않기 때문이야.

여 숙제를 가장 우선하고 다른 일들은 나중에 해야 한다는 말씀이세요?

남 응, 무슨 일이 있더라도 말이야.

여 좋아요, 앞으로는 그렇게 해 볼게요.

Solution

중요한 일을 미루는 습관이 있어서 내일 내야 할 과제를 오늘 밤에 하고 있는 여자에게 남자는 일의 우선순위를 제대로 정해서 중요한 일부터 해야 한다고 말하고 있으므로, 남자의 의견으로 가장 적절한 것은 ⑤이다.

Words

way 훨씬; 아주 멀리 brew 끓이다 assignment 과제
due ~하기로 되어 있는 concentrate 집중하다
wait until the last minute 마지막까지 미루다 put off ~을 미루다
come up 생기다 priority 우선순위, 우선 사항
put ~ first ~을 가장 우선하다

03 정답 ①

Script

M Good morning, ma'am. How may I help you?

W I have a terrible headache. Do you have anything to relieve the pain?

M Are you suffering from any other symptoms? Do you feel dizzy or nauseous?

W No, but both sides of my head hurt.

M Then take this. It will alleviate your pain.

W How often do I need to take it?

M Take two pills after each meal for three days.

W Okay. Do I have to keep away from alcohol?

M Yes. It can worsen your headache. And try to rest a lot.

W I understand. I'll be sure to follow your instructions.

M If your pain doesn't go away by the third day, you need to go see a specialist.

W I will. Thanks.

남 안녕하세요. 손님. 어떻게 도와드릴까요?

여 심한 두통이 있어요. 통증을 덜어 줄 만한 게 있나요?

남 또 다른 증상에 시달리고 계신가요? 어지럽거나 속이 메스꺼우신가요?

여 아니요. 하지만 양쪽 머리가 다 아파요.

남 그럼 이걸 드세요. 그것이 통증을 덜어 줄 거예요.

여 얼마나 자주 그것을 먹어야 하나요?

남 3일 동안 식사 후 두 알씩 드세요.

여 네. 술은 멀리해야 하나요?

남 네. 그것은 두통을 악화시킬 수 있어요. 그리고 휴식을 많이 취하도록 하세요.

여 알겠습니다. 지시 사항들을 꼭 따르겠습니다.

남 셋째 날까지 통증이 사라지지 않으면, 전문의를 찾아가 보셔야 해요.

여 그럴게요. 고맙습니다.

Solution

두통이 있다며 통증을 덜어 줄 약을 찾는 여자에게 남자는 약을 주며 얼마나 자주 먹어야 하고, 먹는 동안 어떻게 해야 하는지 알려 주고 있으며, 그래도 통증이 사라지지 않으면 전문의에게 가 보라고 이야기하고 있으므로, 두 사람의 관계를 가장 잘 나타낸 것은 ①이다.

Words

relieve (통증을) 덜어 주다 symptom 증상 nauseous 속이 메스꺼운
alleviate (고통을) 완화하다 pill 알약 keep away from ~을 멀리하다
worsen 악화시키다 instruction 지시, 설명 specialist 전문의, 전문가

04 정답 ⑤

Script

W Honey, Carl drew a picture for his grandmother's birthday. Here, take a look at it.

M Wow, it's a lovely drawing.

W It's amazing he remembers the armchair she used to sit on.

M She threw that away years ago. I see a kitten on her lap.

W That's one of the kittens her cat gave birth to last month.

M How cute! Look at this heart-shaped birthday cake.

W It looks yummy.

M The slippers under the table must be the ones you bought for her birthday.

W Yes. I asked him to draw them for me.

M What are these boxes next to her?

W The ones piled up on top of one another? I don't know.

M Let's ask him about them.

여 여보. Carl이 할머니 생신 선물로 그림을 그렸어요. 여기, 한번 보세요.

남 와, 사랑스러운 그림이군요.

여 그 애가 그녀가 앉곤 했던 안락의자를 기억하다니 놀라워요.

남 그녀는 수년 전에 그것을 버리셨죠. 무릎 위에 새끼 고양이가 보여요.

여 지난달 그녀의 고양이가 낳은 새끼 고양이들 중 한 마리예요.

남 정말 귀엽군요! 이 하트 모양의 생일 케이크를 보세요.

여 맛있어 보이는데요.

남 테이블 아래 슬리퍼는 당신이 그녀의 생신 선물로 사 드렸던 것이겠군요.

여 네. 그 애에게 저를 위해 그것들을 그려 달라고 부탁했죠.

남 그녀 옆에 있는 이 상자들은 뭔가요?

여 차곡차곡 쌓아 올려져 있는 것들이요? 모르겠어요.

남 그 애에게 그것들에 대해 물어봅시다.

Solution

할머니 옆에 놓인 상자들이 차곡차곡 쌓아 올려져 있다고 했지만, 그림에서는 바닥에 하나씩 놓여 있으므로, 대화의 내용과 일치하지 않는 것은 ⑤이다.

amazing 놀라운 throw away ~을 버리다 kitten 새끼 고양이
lap 무릎 yummy 아주 맛있는 pile up ~을 쌓아 올리다
on top of one another 차곡차곡

05 정답 ④

Script

M Joanne, you seem busy today. What's up?
W Well, today is my first day back from my week-long vacation.
M I know, but wasn't most of your work taken care of by others?
W It was. But I still have to check my e-mail messages and reply to some of them.
M I see. Aren't you hungry? Why don't you do that after lunch?
W I wish I could, but there is a delivery that's supposed to arrive in half an hour.
M Do you have to wait for it? I'd be happy to receive it.
W That's sweet of you, but I don't want to impose.
M You're not imposing. Go and grab a bite.
W Thank you so much.
M No worries.

남 Joanne, 오늘 바빠 보이는군요. 무슨 일이에요?
여 글쎄, 오늘이 제가 일주일간의 휴가를 마치고 온 첫날이잖아요.
남 알아요, 하지만 당신의 일 대부분을 다른 사람들이 처리한 거 아닌가요?
여 맞아요. 하지만 여전히 제 이메일 메시지를 확인하고 그것들 중 일부에는 답장을 해야 해요.
남 그렇군요. 배고프지 않으세요? 점심 드시고 나서 하는 게 어때요?
여 그러고 싶지만, 30분 뒤에 도착하기로 한 택배가 있어요.
남 그것을 기다려야 하나요? 제가 기꺼이 그것을 받아 놓을게요.
여 고맙지만, 부담 드리고 싶지 않아요.
남 부담 주시는 거 아니에요. 가서 뭐라도 좀 드세요.
여 정말 고맙습니다.
남 천만에요.

Solution

남자는 30분 뒤에 배달될 물건을 기다려야 하기 때문에 점심을 먹으러 가지 못한다는 여자의 말에 남자는 물건을 대신 받아 주겠다고 말하고 있으므로, 정답은 ④이다.

Words

reply 답장을 보내다 impose 부담을 주다 grab a bite 간단히 먹다

06 정답 ③

Script

M Welcome to Adventure Land!
W Hi, I'd like to buy two passes for adults and two for kids.
M Okay. Adult passes are $70 and for children from 4 to 12, they're $50.
W Our oldest child is 14, so I'm guessing he counts as an adult.
M That's correct. Also, if you are a member of our Adventure Club, you get a 10 percent discount.
W What is the Adventure Club?
M It is a membership service that provides you with various benefits at Adventure Land.
W How much do I have to pay to join the club?
M You can become a member for only $50 a year.
W Okay, I'd like to sign up. Will I get a discount on the passes I'm buying today?
M Sure. You get a 10 percent discount on both the adult and children's passes.
W Great. Here's my credit card.

남 Adventure Land에 오신 것을 환영합니다!
여 안녕하세요, 성인용 입장권 두 장과 어린이용 두 장을 사고 싶어요.
남 네. 성인용 입장권은 70달러이며 4세부터 12세까지의 어린이들은 50달러입니다.
여 저희 맏이가 14세이니 그 아이는 성인으로 간주해야겠네요.
남 맞습니다. 또한 저희 어드벤처 클럽 회원이면 10퍼센트 할인을 받습니다.
여 어드벤처 클럽이 뭐죠?
남 Adventure Land의 다양한 혜택들을 제공하는 멤버십 서비스입니다.
여 클럽에 가입하려면 얼마를 지불해야 하나요?
남 일 년에 50달러만으로 회원이 되실 수 있습니다.
여 좋아요, 가입하고 싶습니다. 오늘 제가 사는 입장권에 할인을 받을 수 있나요?
남 물론입니다. 성인용과 어린이용 입장권 둘 다에 대해 10퍼센트 할인을 받으실 수 있어요.
여 좋아요. 여기 제 신용카드입니다.

Solution

여자는 성인용 입장권 3장(210달러), 어린이용 입장권 1장(50달러)에, 가입비 50달러를 내고 어드벤처 클럽 회원이 되어 입장권에 대해 입장권에 대해 10퍼센트 할인을 받기로 했으므로, 여자가 지불할 금액은 ③ '284달러'이다.

Words

count as ~로 간주되다 benefit 혜택 discount 할인

07 정답 ⑤

Script

[Telephone rings.]
W Hi, Willy.
M Hi, Betty. How are you doing?
W I'm doing good. Are you available this weekend? I'm going to the nursing home to do volunteer work with Jack. Will you join us?
M If you're going on Saturday, I'm afraid I can't go.
W Do you have a family gathering on that day?
M No. We got together last Saturday.
W Then you have some assignment to finish soon, right?
M No. Actually, I started learning how to make bread at the community center. I have to go there on Saturday.
W I see. Next time I hope you make sure to join us.
M Of course. And I'd like to take some homemade bread to the nursing home someday.
W That's a fantastic idea.

[전화벨이 울린다.]

여 안녕, Willy.

남 안녕, Betty. 어떻게 지내니?

여 잘 지내고 있어. 이번 주말에 시간 있어? 나는 Jack과 함께 봉사 활동을 하러 양로원에 갈 거야. 우리와 함께 갈래?

남 토요일에 갈 거면, 나는 못 갈 것 같아.

여 그날 가족 모임이 있니?

남 아니. 우리는 지난 토요일에 모였어.

여 그럼 곧 끝내야 할 과제가 좀 있구나, 그렇지?

남 아니. 사실, 나는 문화 센터에서 빵 만드는 법을 배우기 시작했어. 나는 토요일에 그곳에 가야 해.

여 그렇구나. 다음번에는 꼭 우리와 함께 하길 바라.

남 물론이지. 그리고 언젠가 양로원에 집에서 만든 빵을 좀 가져 가고 싶어.

여 그건 정말 기막히게 좋은 생각이야.

08 정답 ④

W Brian! Why don't you focus on our homework instead of looking at your phone?

M But my friends keep posting messages on their blog.

W It seems like you're addicted to your phone.

M Well, that's probably true, but I can't help it.

W Why don't you set aside time for checking updates on your friends' blogs?

M I guess I should. And I ought to keep it in silent mode while I'm studying.

W Also, keep track of your cellphone use and try to limit the amount of time you use your phone.

M Okay, I'll try.

W One more thing — having a novel handy can keep you away from your phone when you get bored.

M Sounds good. I love to read books.

W You'll be just fine if you put these ideas into action.

여 Brian! 전화기를 보는 대신에 숙제에 집중하는 게 어때?

남 하지만 내 친구들이 계속 블로그에 메시지를 올리는걸.

여 넌 네 휴대전화에 중독된 것 같아.

남 음, 그게 사실일지도 모르지만, 어쩔 수 없어.

여 네 친구들의 블로그에 업데이트된 것들을 확인하는 시간을 따로 정해 두는 게 어때?

남 그래야겠어. 그리고 공부하는 중에는 그것을 무음으로 해 놓아야겠어.

여 또한, 네 휴대전화 사용 상태를 파악해서 휴대전화를 사용하는 시간의 양을 제한하도록 노력해 봐.

남 좋아. 시도해 볼게.

여 한 가지 더, 네가 지루해졌을 때 소설책을 휴대하고 있는 것도 휴대전화로부터 너를 멀리하게 해 줄 거야.

남 좋은 생각이야. 난 책 읽는 것을 좋아하거든.

여 이 생각들을 행동으로 옮긴다면 넌 괜찮을 거야.

09 정답 ⑤

M Good afternoon. I'm Tom Johnson, the vice principal of Benson High School. Today, I'm pleased to announce we're having the annual Benson Bake Sale on April 5th. The Benson Bake Sale has been a long-standing tradition in our 40 years of school history, and this year will mark the 26th time we're having this event. Besides baked goods such as bread and cookies, you can also prepare local foods to sell. The sale booths will be set up on the lawn between the athletic field and the auditorium. Not only are your parents invited, but local residents are encouraged to participate as well. All of the money raised will be donated to facilities for the disabled. I'm looking forward to your active participation.

남 안녕하세요. 저는 Benson 고등학교의 교감인 Tom Johnson입니다. 오늘, 우리 학교가 4월 5일에 연례 Benson Bake Sale을 열게 되었다는 것을 알리게 되어 기쁩니다. Benson Bake Sale은 40년의 우리 학교 역사의 오래된 전통이었으며, 올해는 이 행사를 개최하는 26번째를 기념합니다. 빵과 과자와 같은 구운 제품들 외에도, 여러분은 향토 음식을 준비해 판매할 수 있습니다. 판매 부스는 운동장과 강당 사이의 잔디밭에 설치될 것입니다. 여러분의 부모님이 초대될 뿐만 아니라 지역 주민들도 또한 참여하도록 권장되고 있습니다. 모금된 기금 전액은 장애인들을 위한 시설에 기부될 것입니다. 여러분의 적극적인 참여를 기대하겠습니다.

10 정답 ⑤

W Honey, I've just finished booking our flight tickets to Honolulu.

M Now let's decide where to stay. This is the website I like to use to reserve rooms at hotels.

W Okay, let's find out which hotel best suits us.

M We should choose one located in the downtown area to have easy access to tourist attractions.

W Yeah, we don't have to stay near the airport.

M Do you want to work out at a gym?

W No. I'd just like to relax. But we need free Wi-Fi.

M Yes, we do. Well, then we've got two choices left.

W Since we can have fun at the beach, I don't think a pool is necessary.

M You're right. Besides, the one without a pool is $10 cheaper per night.

W Great, let's stay at this hotel.

여 여보, 호놀룰루행 항공권 예약을 방금 마쳤어요.

남 이제 어디서 머무를지 정합시다. 이것이 호텔에서 방을 예약할 때 내가 즐겨 사용하는 웹사이트예요.

여 좋아요. 어느 호텔이 우리와 가장 맞는지 알아보죠.

남 관광지에 쉽게 가기 위해 시내 지역에 위치한 것을 골라야 해요.

여 네, 공항 근처에서 머무를 필요가 없어요.

남 헬스장에서 운동하고 싶어요?

여 아니요. 그냥 휴식을 취하고 싶어요. 하지만 무료 와이파이는 필요해요.

남 네, 맞아요. 음, 그럼 선택 가능한 두 곳이 남았어요.

여 해변에서 즐길 수 있으니, 수영장은 필요 없을 것 같아요.

남 당신 말이 맞아요. 게다가, 수영장이 없는 곳은 1박당 10달러 더 싸요.

여 좋아요, 이 호텔에서 머뭅시다.

Solution

시내 지역에 위치하고, 헬스장은 필요 없고, 무료 와이파이가 가능하며 수영장이 없는 1박당 10달러 더 싼 호텔에서 머물겠다고 했으므로, 두 사람이 선택한 호텔은 ⑤이다.

Words

suit ~에게 맞다 tourist attraction 관광지, 관광 명소
work out 운동하다

---

11 정답 ③

Script

M Mom, I'm very hungry. What's for dinner?

W I'm thinking of cooking some risotto. What do you think?

M I love it. My mouth is already watering, so please hurry.

W Okay. I'll make it for you as soon as I can.

남 엄마, 너무 배고파요. 저녁은 뭐예요?

여 리소토를 요리할까 생각 중이야. 어떻게 생각하니?

남 아주 좋아요. 벌써 입에 군침이 돌고 있으니 서둘러 주세요.

여 알겠어. 가능한 한 빨리 너를 위해 그것을 만들어 줄게.

Solution

배고파하는 남자에게 여자는 리소토를 만들 생각이라고 말하자 남자는 좋다는 의사를 밝히며 서둘러 달라고 말했으므로, ③ '알겠어. 가능한 한 빨리 너를 위해 그것을 만들어 줄게.'가 여자의 응답으로 가장 적절하다.

① 미안하구나. 하지만 난 이미 저녁을 먹었단다.

② 그래. 나는 너만큼 이탈리아 음식을 좋아한단다.

④ 좋은 생각이야. 그 이탈리아 음식점으로 가자.

⑤ 아니. 저녁식사 전에 간식을 먹지 않는 게 좋단다.

Words

watering 군침이 도는

---

12 정답 ③

Script

W I'm going to do some grocery shopping. Do you need anything?

M Could you pick up a bottle of shampoo? Ours is almost used up.

W Well, we still have some I got as a housewarming gift.

M Yeah, but it's not good for my oily hair.

여 장을 좀 보러 갈 거예요. 뭐 필요한 거 있나요?

남 샴푸 하나 사 올래요? 우리 것은 거의 다 썼어요.

여 음, 집들이 선물로 받은 것이 아직 몇 개 있어요.

남 네, 하지만 그것은 나의 지성 모발에 좋지 않아요.

Solution

장 보러 가는 여자에게 남자가 샴푸가 거의 다 떨어졌다며 하나 사 오라고 부탁하자 여자는 집들이 선물로 받은 게 몇 개 있다고 답하고 있다. 이에 대해 남자는 수긍하거나 다른 의견을 말하는 응답이 자연스러우므로 ③ '네, 하지만 그것은 나의 지성 모발에 좋지 않아요.'가 남자의 응답으로 가장 적절하다.

① 그들에게 집들이 선물을 사 줍시다.

② 헤어 컨디셔너도 사야 해요.

④ 머리를 어떻게 완벽하게 감는지 모르겠어요.

⑤ 와! 이 식료품 가게는 다양한 상품을 제공하는군요.

Words

housewarming gift 집들이 선물 cleanse 씻다, 세척하다
thoroughly 철저히

---

13 정답 ②

Script

W Mr. Choi, can I talk to you for a minute?

M Sure, Jane. What do you want to talk about?

W I was happy to find out that I made it into the advanced Chinese class.

M Yes, your grade on the test was very good.

W Today was my first time here but I had a problem following your lecture.

M So you're hoping to move to the intermediate class.

W Yes. I believe I can learn better there.

M Interestingly, I get this from a lot of students at the beginning of the semester.

W I thought it was only me who got discouraged.

M No, don't worry. I'll speak very slowly and explain things in more detail.

W Then I'll stay and focus really hard on your lecture.

여 최 선생님, 잠깐 이야기 나눌 수 있을까요?

남 물론이지, Jane. 무엇에 대해 이야기하고 싶은데?

여 제가 중국어 상급반에 들어갔다는 것을 알고서 행복했어요.

남 응, 네 시험 성적이 매우 좋았단다.

여 오늘이 이곳에서 첫 시간이었는데 선생님 강의를 따라가는 데 문제가 있

었어요.

남 그래서 중급반으로 옮기길 희망하는구나.

여 네. 전 거기서 더 잘 배울 수 있다고 믿어요.

남 흥미롭게도, 학기 초에 많은 학생들로부터 듣는 이야기야.

여 전 제가 유일하게 (수업이 어려워) 낙담한 줄 알았는데요.

남 아니야, 걱정하지 마. 매우 천천히 말하고 더 상세히 설명할 거야.

여 그러면 그대로 있고 선생님의 강의에 정말 열심히 집중할게요.

Solution

남자의 중국어 상급반 수업을 이해하기 힘들어서 중급반으로 옮기고 싶다는 여자에게 남자는 학기 초에 많은 학생들이 그런다며 앞으로 천천히 이야기하고 상세히 설명하겠다고 했으므로, 여자는 선생님의 조언을 받아들이는 것이 자연스러우므로 ② '그러면 그대로 있고 선생님의 강의에 정말 열심히 집중할게요.'가 여자의 응답으로 가장 적절하다.

① 제가 다른 반으로 옮길 수 있는지 알아볼게요.

③ 왜 그렇게 많은 학생들이 수업 시간에 졸려했는지 이제 알겠어요.

④ 공부를 열심히 해서 다음 시험에는 더 잘하겠다고 약속드려요.

⑤ 선생님께서 제 교과서 찾는 것을 도와주시면 감사하겠습니다.

Words

advanced 상급의 lecture 강의 intermediate 중급의
discouraged 낙담한 in detail 상세히

14 정답 ④

Script

W What are you reading, Daniel?

M I'm reading the novel, *We Are the One* by Cathy Nolans.

W Oh, I've heard of the novel. Isn't it based on the writer's real life?

M Yes. Cathy worked for the government for 10 years.

W She worked as an intelligence agent, didn't she?

M Yes. It seems like she had a variety of experiences.

W She must have written about many of them in her novel.

M Yes. That's why her novel is very interesting till the end.

W Isn't that the power from the true story?

M Right. A novel based on a true story is often much better.

- -

여 뭘 읽고 있니, Daniel?

남 나는 Cathy Nolans의 'We Are the One'이라는 소설을 읽고 있어.

여 아, 나는 그 소설에 대해 들어 본 적이 있어. 그것은 작가의 실생활에 바탕을 둔 것 아니니?

남 맞아. Cathy는 10년 동안 정부에서 일했어.

여 그녀는 정보 요원으로 일했지, 그렇지 않니?

남 응. 그녀는 다양한 경험을 했던 것 같아.

여 그녀는 자신의 소설 속에 그것 중 많은 것에 대해 분명 썼음이 틀림없어.

남 그래. 그래서 그녀의 소설이 끝까지 매우 흥미로운 거야.

여 그게 실화에서 나온 힘 아닐까?

남 맞아. 실화를 바탕으로 한 소설이 종종 훨씬 더 나아.

Solution

저자의 실제 경험을 기반으로 쓰인 소설을 읽고 있는 남자는 소설이 끝까지 흥미롭다고 말했고, 여자는 그것이 실화로부터 나온 힘이 아니겠냐고 했으므로, 남자는 이에 대해 여자의 의견에 동의하는 응답이 자연스러우므로 ④ '맞아. 실화를 바탕으로 한 소설이 종종 훨씬 더 나아.'가 남자의 응답으로 가장 적절하다.

① 아니. 내가 소설을 다 읽자마자 그것을 네게 빌려줄게.

② 맞아. 나는 쓰기 시작하기 전에 조사를 할 거야.

③ 물론이지. 그녀는 자신의 대단한 상상력을 사용하는 법을 알고 있어.

⑤ 좋은 작가가 되기 위해서는 가능한 한 많이 써 보려고 해야 해.

Words

intelligence agent 정보 요원 a variety of 다양한

15 정답 ②

Script

M Janice works for an oil company. Recently, her boss asked her to make a presentation on the project they've been working on. If she does a great job, her company could win a contract. Her boss said she might even get a promotion if things went well. Janice is thrilled to hear the news but she feels a lot of pressure. She has anxiety and doesn't know how to prepare the presentation. Then she remembers that her colleague, Richard, is well known for giving great presentations. She thinks it would be great if she gets some tips from him. In this situation, what would Janice most likely say to Richard?

Janice Could you lend me a hand with my presentation?

- -

남 Janice는 정유 회사에서 일하고 있습니다. 최근에, 그녀의 상사가 그들이 작업해 온 프로젝트에 대해 그녀가 발표할 것을 부탁했습니다. 만약 그녀가 잘해 낸다면, 그녀의 회사는 계약을 따낼 수 있을 것입니다. 그녀의 상사는 일이 잘 풀린다면 그녀가 승진까지도 할 수 있을 거라고 말했습니다. Janice는 그 소식을 듣고 매우 신이 나지만 많은 압박을 느낍니다. 그녀는 불안하고 발표를 어떻게 준비해야 할지 모릅니다. 그때 그녀는 그녀의 동료인 Richard가 훌륭한 발표를 하는 것으로 유명하다는 것을 기억해 냅니다. 그녀는 그에게서 약간의 조언을 얻는다면 좋을 것이라고 생각합니다. 이런 상황에서, Janice는 Richard에게 뭐라고 말할 것 같은가요?

Janice 제 발표를 좀 도와주시겠어요?

Solution

승진이 가능할지도 모를 중요한 발표를 앞둔 Janice는 압박을 느끼다가 동료인 Richard가 발표를 잘한다는 것을 기억해 내고 그에게 조언을 얻고자 하는 상황이므로, 이러한 상황에서 Janice가 Richard에게 할 말로 가장 적절한 것은 ② '제 발표를 좀 도와주시겠어요?'이다.

① 직장에서의 압박감을 대처하기 위해 무엇을 하나요?

③ 이 계약이 끝나면 당신은 확실히 승진할 거예요.

④ 발표를 연기해 주실 수 있다면 감사하겠어요.

⑤ 제가 출장 가 있는 동안 저 대신 일을 맡아 주시겠어요?

Words

make a presentation 발표를 하다 contract 계약 promotion 승진
thrilled 아주 신이 난 pressure 압박, 압력
lend ~ a hand ~에게 도움을 주다 cover for ~의 일을 대신해 주다

16 정답 ④   17 정답 ④

Script

W You definitely know how much healthier home-cooked meals are than ready-made meals. Well, the same goes for your dog. The less processed your dog's food is, the better it is for their health. If you've got the time, making dog food yourself is sure to benefit your dog. Then how should you make the food? Above all, proportions are important for the right nutrition. A healthy meal should contain 40% protein, 10% carbohydrates, and 50% vegetables. If you're going to prepare home-cooked food, mixing some ingredients will make your cooking much easier. For example, carrots, turkey thighs and peas can be cooked together in a delicious stew. You can also add brown rice in the stew afterwards. It will be a great meal for your dog. But you should avoid adding too much salt or sugar, which could raise a dog's cholesterol. Your dog will like your food. Why don't you try it?

여 집에서 요리된 식사가 기성품의 식사보다 얼마나 더 건강에 좋은지 여러분은 분명히 알고 있습니다. 음, 똑같은 내용이 여러분의 개에도 적용됩니다. 여러분의 개의 음식이 덜 가공되면 될수록 그것은 그들의 건강에 더 좋습니다. 여러분이 만약 시간이 있다면, 개의 음식을 직접 만드는 것이 여러분의 개에게 확실히 유익합니다. 그렇다면 여러분은 어떻게 음식을 만들어야 할까요? 무엇보다도 비율이 올바른 영양에 중요합니다. 건강에 좋은 식사는 단백질 40퍼센트, 탄수화물 10퍼센트, 야채 50퍼센트를 포함해야 합니다. 집에서 요리된 음식을 준비하려면, 일부 재료를 섞으면 요리가 훨씬 더 쉬워질 것입니다. 예를 들어, 당근, 칠면조 다리, 완두콩은 맛있는 스튜에서 함께 요리될 수 있습니다. 여러분은 또한 나중에 스튜에 현미를 첨가할 수 있습니다. 그것은 여러분의 개에게 훌륭한 식사가 될 것입니다. 하지만 개의 콜레스테롤을 높일 수 있는 너무 많은 소금이나 설탕을 첨가하는 것은 피해야 합니다. 여러분의 개는 여러분의 음식을 좋아할 겁니다. 한번 시도해 보는 게 어떨까요?

Solution

16

여자는 집에서 한 음식을 개에게 주는 것이 개의 건강을 위해 유익한 일로서, 개를 위해 집에서 요리하는 것과 관련된 사항에 대한 조언을 하고 있으므로, 여자가 하는 말의 주제로 가장 적절한 것은 ④ '개를 위해서 집에서 음식을 요리하는 것에 대한 조언'이다.

① 대부분의 개가 좋아하는 음식의 종류
② 개들의 건강을 위한 필수 영양소
③ 개가 먹는 음식을 살 때 고려 사항들
⑤ 개가 균형 잡힌 식사를 하는 것의 중요성

17

당근, 칠면조 다리, 완두콩, 현미는 언급되었지만, ④ '후추'는 언급되지 않았다.

Words

ready-made 기성품의, 이미 만들어진 go for ~에 적용되다 process 가공하다 proportion 비율 nutrition 영양 contain 포함하다 protein 단백질 carbohydrate 탄수화물 ingredient 재료

---

01 ⑤	02 ②	03 ①	04 ④	05 ③
06 ④	07 ④	08 ⑤	09 ⑤	10 ⑤
11 ②	12 ⑤	13 ⑤	14 ④	15 ①
16 ③	17 ④			

01 정답 ⑤

Script

M Hi, I'm Justin Smith from the Office of Education. Every year, colleges release new guidelines for applications, and it is quite difficult to keep track of them. This usually leads to teachers having difficulty giving advice to their students about which college to choose. To take the burden off teachers, we've prepared free lectures on college admission. They will introduce the features of this year's college admission process. In addition, teachers will get to learn how to write letters of recommendation. All of the lectures will be presented by experts in the field. If you're interested, please visit our homepage and sign up.

남 안녕하세요, 저는 교육청에서 나온 Justin Smith입니다. 매년, 대학은 새로운 입학 요강을 발표하는데 그것들을 계속 파악하기란 꽤 어렵습니다. 이것은 대개 교사들이 학생들에게 어떤 대학을 고를지에 대한 조언을 하는 데 어려움을 겪는 것으로 이어집니다. 교사들의 부담을 덜어 주기 위해, 저희는 대학 입학에 대한 무료 강의를 준비했습니다. 그 강의들은 올해 대학 입학 절차의 특징들을 소개해 줄 것입니다. 게다가, 교사들은 추천서를 쓰는 방법을 배우게 될 것입니다. 모든 강의는 그 분야의 전문가들에 의해 발표될 것입니다. 여러분이 관심이 있다면, 저희 홈페이지에 방문해 등록해주십시오.

Solution

학생들의 진학 지도에 어려움을 겪는 교사들을 위해 올해 대학 입학 절차의 특징 및 추천서 작성법을 설명하는 무료 강의가 있으니 신청할 것을 홍보하고 있으므로, 남자가 하는 말의 목적으로 가장 적절한 것은 ⑤이다.

Words

release 공개하다, 발표하다 guideline 지침, 요강
keep track of ~에 대해 계속 파악하고 있다 lead to ~에 이르다
burden 짐, 부담 admission 입학 feature 특징
letter of recommendation 추천서 present 발표하다
expert 전문가 sign up 등록하다

02 정답 ②

Script

W Good morning, Brad. Would you like a cup of coffee?
M No, thanks. I'm trying to avoid coffee these days.
W Why is that?
M I read an article that suggested coffee may raise our level of stress.
W That only happens when you drink too much coffee. I think a couple of cups a day are fine.

M I'm not so sure. Ever since I read the article, I've felt nervous having coffee.

W It must be a psychological thing. Coffee has certain health benefits, like different kinds of tea.

M Well, I've heard it helps increase concentration.

W That's right. As long as you don't have too much, coffee is good for you.

M I guess a cup a day isn't a bad idea.

W Then have some!

- -

여 안녕, Brad. 커피 한잔 마실래?

남 아니, 괜찮아. 요즘 커피를 피하려고 노력 중이야.

여 왜 그러는데?

남 커피가 스트레스 수준을 증가시킬지도 모른다고 말한 기사를 읽었거든.

여 그건 지나치게 많은 커피를 마셨을 때만 일어나는 거야. 하루에 두세 잔 정도는 괜찮다고 생각해.

남 그렇게 확신할 수 없어. 그 기사를 읽은 이후에는 커피를 마시는 것이 걱정이 돼.

여 그건 심리적인 것임이 틀림없어. 커피는 다른 종류의 차처럼 건강상의 어떤 이점을 가지고 있어.

남 음, 그것이 집중력을 향상시키는 걸 돕는다고 들었어.

여 맞아. 지나치게 마시지 않는 한, 커피는 너에게 도움이 돼.

남 하루에 한 잔은 나쁜 생각이 아닌 것 같아.

여 그럼 마시자!

커피가 스트레스 수준을 증가시킬 수도 있다는 생각에 커피 마시기를 꺼려하는 남자에게 여자는 그것은 지나치게 섭취할 때 일어나는 것이고, 하루 두세 잔의 커피는 몸에 이롭다고 말하고 있으므로, 여자의 의견으로 가장 적절한 것은 ②이다.

a couple of 두서너 개의 psychological 심리적인
benefit 이점, 혜택 concentration 집중력

03 정답 ①

W Here is the water you asked for.

M Great, thanks. Are any of the passengers feeling uncomfortable with the altitude?

W A few of them said they had headaches, so we provided them with painkillers.

M Good. And remember to keep an eye on the infants and the elderly.

W Of course. We'll check on them twice an hour to make sure they feel comfortable.

M By the way, we might experience some minor turbulence a little later.

W Okay, I'll tell the passengers to stay in their seats and fasten their seatbelts.

M Good. You're clear to start serving the meals once I turn off the seatbelt light.

W Okay. When would you like to have your meal?

M I'll let you know later, once all of the passengers have eaten.

여 요청하신 물 여기 있습니다.

남 좋아요, 고맙습니다. 고도로 인해 불편해 하는 승객들이 있나요?

여 몇 분이 두통이 있다고 말하셔서 진통제를 드렸습니다.

남 좋아요. 그리고 유아들과 노인분들을 계속 지켜보는 것 기억하세요.

여 물론이죠. 저희는 그들이 편안하다고 느끼는지 확인하기 위해 한 시간에 두 번씩 그들을 확인할 겁니다.

남 그건 그렇고, 잠시 뒤 약간의 난기류를 겪을지도 몰라요.

여 네, 승객들에게 자리에 남아서 좌석 벨트를 매라고 말해 두겠습니다.

남 좋아요. 그리고 제가 좌석 벨트 등을 끄고 나면 식사 제공을 시작하는 것을 확실히 하세요.

여 그러겠습니다. 식사는 언제 하고 싶으세요?

남 나중에 알려줄게요, 모든 승객들이 식사를 다하고 나면요.

남자는 고도로 불편해 하는 승객이 있는지 묻고, 노인과 유아들이 괜찮은지 지켜보라고 하면서 난기류가 있을 수 있으니 승객에게 이를 전달해 달라고 말하고 있다. 여자는 승객들이 편안한지 확인하고 있으며 좌석 벨트 등이 꺼진 후 식사를 제공하겠다고 말하고 있으므로, 두 사람의 관계를 가장 잘 나타낸 것은 ①이다.

passenger 승객 altitude 고도 painkiller 진통제
keep an eye on ~을 주시하다 turbulence 난기류
fasten 매다, 채우다

04 정답 ④

W So, this is one of the sets where you are shooting your film?

M Yes. Actually, many important incidents take place in this room.

W Why is the painting on the wall covered by cloth?

M It signifies something I cannot tell you now.

W I'm curious about that tall stack of books on the desk. What are they for?

M One of the characters in the movie is a scientist, so he constantly looks through them.

W How about this glass vase below the desk?

M I keep it down there so it doesn't fall off and break.

W Also I was wondering why there's nothing in the closet on the left.

M We're going to hang some clothes there later.

W This rectangular carpet on the floor is so unique!

M It is an important part of the movie, but I can't tell you more about it right now.

W I can't wait to watch it!

- -

여 그래서, 이곳이 당신이 영화를 찍고 있는 세트장 중 하나인가요?

남 네. 실제로, 많은 중요한 사건들이 이 방에서 발생하지요.

여 벽에 있는 그림이 왜 천으로 가려져 있나요?

남 지금은 이야기할 수 없는 뭔가를 나타내요.

여 책상 위에 있는 높은 책 더미가 궁금하군요. 무엇 때문에 있는 거죠?

남 영화 속 등장인물들 중 한 명이 과학자입니다. 그래서 그는 계속해서 책들을 보거든요.

여 책상 아래에 있는 이 유리 꽃병은요?

남 떨어져서 깨지지 않도록 거기에 내려놓은 거예요.

여 또 왼쪽에 있는 옷장 안에 왜 아무것도 없는지 궁금해요.

남 나중에 약간의 옷을 거기에 걸 거예요.

여 바닥에 있는 이 직사각형 카펫은 아주 독특해요!

남 그것은 영화의 중요한 한 부분이지만, 지금 당장은 그것에 대해 더 말할 수는 없어요.

여 어서 보고 싶은걸요!

옷장에는 아무것도 없다고 했지만 그림에서는 옷장 속에 옷이 몇 벌 걸려 있으므로, 대화의 내용과 일치하지 않는 것은 ④이다.

incident 사건 take place 발생하다
signify 나타내다, 의미하다 stack 더미

05 정답 ③

[Cellphone rings.]

M Hi. Honey, how did the meeting with your clients go?

W It went well. Did you have any trouble dropping off Karen at the daycare center?

M She didn't want to be separated from me at first, but it was alright.

W I'm sorry I made you do it. I know it was my turn to drop her off.

M I understand. By the way, can you get off work early today?

W Yes. Why do you ask?

M Could you drive to the daycare center and get Karen? I can't make it there before it closes.

W Sure. Are you going to finish work late tonight?

M I'm afraid so. There's a conference I need to prepare for.

W Okay, I'll do that. Don't worry about her.

M Thank you. I'll see you at home tonight.

[휴대전화가 울린다.]

남 여보세요. 여보, 고객들과의 회의는 어떻게 됐어요?

여 잘됐어요. Karen을 어린이집에 데려다주는 데 아무 문제 없었어요?

남 처음에는 나에게서 떨어지고 싶어 하지 않았는데, 괜찮았어요.

여 당신을 하게 만들어 미안해요. 내가 데려다줘야 할 차례인 줄 아는데.

남 괜찮아요. 그건 그렇고, 당신 오늘 일찍 퇴근할 수 있어요?

여 네. 왜 물어요?

남 어린이집에 운전해 가서 Karen을 데리고 올 수 있나요? 나는 어린이집이 문을 닫기 전에 도착하지 못할 것 같아요.

여 물론이죠. 오늘 밤 늦게 일을 마칠 건가요?

남 아마 그럴 것 같아요. 내가 준비해야 하는 회의가 있어요.

여 알았어요. 내가 데리러 갈게요. 그 애에 대해선 걱정하지 말아요.

남 고마워요. 오늘 밤 집에서 봐요.

남자는 준비해야 할 회의가 있어 늦게 일을 마치니 여자에게 딸 Karen을 어린이집에서 데려와 달라고 부탁하였으므로, 정답은 ③이다.

client 고객 drop off (차로) 데려다 주다
daycare center 어린이집, 탁아소 conference 회의, 학회

06 정답 ④

M Welcome to Oliver's Pizza. Are you ready to order?

W Yes, what special deals are you offering right now?

M You can upgrade the size of pizzas to go for only two extra dollars.

W Cool. How much is a medium pepperoni pizza?

M It's $20. Would you like one to go with the size upgrade?

W I'll take two, and both with the upgrade, please. And I'd like cheese sticks as a side dish.

M They are $10. How about a beverage? Coke is just a dollar a bottle.

W No, thanks. Are there any benefits for members here?

M Members who are celebrating birthdays this month can get a 20 percent discount on side dishes.

W Great, my birthday is this Friday. Here's my membership card.

남 Oliver's Pizza에 오신 것을 환영합니다. 주문할 준비되셨나요?

여 네, 지금 제공하는 특가가 무엇인가요?

남 추가로 2달러만 더 내시면 피자의 사이즈를 업그레이드하실 수 있습니다.

여 괜찮군요. 중간 크기의 페퍼로니 피자는 얼마인가요?

남 20달러입니다. 사이즈 업그레이드로 하나 포장해 가시겠어요?

여 두 개 사겠어요. 그리고 둘 다 업그레이드해서 주세요. 그리고 곁들임 요리로 치즈 스틱을 사고 싶어요.

남 그건 10달러입니다. 음료는 어떠세요? 콜라가 한 병에 딱 1달러예요.

여 아니요, 괜찮아요. 여기 회원이면 혜택이 있나요?

남 이번 달에 생일을 축하하는 회원들은 곁들임 요리에 한해 20퍼센트 할인을 받으실 수 있어요.

여 좋아요, 제 생일이 이번 주 금요일이에요. 여기 회원 카드요.

20달러인 피자를 추가 2달러를 내고 사이즈 업그레이드하여 두 판을 주문하고, 10달러인 치즈 스틱을 이번 달 생일 회원의 혜택으로 20퍼센트 할인된 8달러에 사기로 했으므로, 여자가 지불할 금액은 ④ '52달러'이다.

special deal 특가 (상품) medium 중간 크기의
side dish 곁들임 요리 bottle 병

07 정답 ④

M Hi, Sue. Where are you going?

W I'm on my way to the community center.

M Really? I'm going there too. You must be learning something there.

W Yes. I'm taking a cooking class there. I love it.

M It seems that you're using the center a lot. As I remember, you joined the center's volleyball club.

W Oh, you remember. I'm still a member of the club.

M You're leading a very active life.

W I am. By the way, what are you going there for?

M Actually, I joined the drama club there, and we will practice today.

W Sounds interesting. Can I see you perform on the stage

soon?

M Yes, you can, maybe in October.

남 안녕, Sue. 어디 가니?

여 지역 센터에 가는 길이야.

남 정말로? 나도 거기에 가고 있어. 넌 거기서 뭔가 배우고 있는 게 틀림없구나.

여 응. 거기서 요리 수업을 듣고 있어. 너무 좋아.

남 너는 그 센터를 많이 이용하는 것 같아. 내 기억으로는, 너는 그 센터의 배구 동아리에 가입했었어.

여 아, 기억하고 있구나. 나는 여전히 그 동아리의 회원이야.

남 넌 매우 활동적인 삶을 살고 있구나.

여 그래. 그건 그렇고, 너는 거기 무엇 때문에 가니?

남 사실, 난 그곳의 연극 동아리에 가입했고, 오늘 연습할 거야.

여 재미있겠다. 네가 곧 무대에서 공연하는 거 볼 수 있을까?

남 그래, 아마 10월에 볼 수 있을 거야.

08 정답 ⑤

Script

W Jake, are you available this weekend?

M Yes. Do you have any special plans?

W Yes. How about visiting the Orion Flower Fair together this Saturday? It's being held at Liberty Park.

M You like flowers very much, don't you?

W I do. The fair will be fun for you because there are many other activities, such as animation character parade and music concert, and more.

M That sounds fun. But what about going there together on Sunday?

W Actually, this Saturday is the last day of the fair. I don't want to miss it.

M Already? When did the fair start?

W It started in last Wednesday, May 9th.

M Will the fair be crowded?

W I guess so. About 20,000 visitors come to the fair every year. I'd like you to come with me.

M Okay. I'll make time for you.

여 Jake, 이번 주말에 시간 있니?

남 응. 너는 특별한 계획 있니?

여 응. 이번 주 토요일에 Orion 꽃 박람회에 방문하는 것은 어때? 그것은 Liberty 공원에서 열리고 있어.

남 넌 꽃을 무척 좋아하지, 그렇지 않니?

여 좋아해. 박람회는 만화영화 캐릭터 퍼레이드와 음악회 등의 많은 다른 활동들이 있어서 너에게 재미있을 거야.

남 재미있겠다. 하지만 일요일에 그곳에 함께 가는 건 어때?

여 사실, 이번 토요일이 박람회 마지막 날이야. 그것을 놓치고 싶지 않아.

남 벌써? 박람회는 언제 시작했지?

여 5월 9일인 지난 수요일에 시작했어.

남 그 박람회가 붐빌까?

여 그럴 것 같아. 매년 약 2만 명의 방문객들이 박람회에 와. 나는 네가 나와 함께 갔으면 좋겠어.

남 알았어. 내가 너를 위해 시간을 내 볼게.

09 정답 ⑤

Script

W Hello, students. I'm Lily Clyde, a faculty member at nearby Milton University. Today, I'd like to introduce one of our scholarships, Best Scholars. This program is for students who will be entering their first year of study at our university. To qualify for this scholarship, students must be in the top 20 percentile on the College Entrance Exam. Once selected as Best Scholars, they need to live on campus. Also, they should maintain a GPA of 3.4 or higher throughout their college years. When they meet these requirements, Best Scholars will receive $5,000 annually for four years. If you are interested in attending Milton University and you think you can become a Best Scholar, please apply for the program.

여 학생 여러분, 안녕하세요. 저는 인근의 Milton 대학교의 교수인 Lily Clyde입니다. 오늘, 우리 학교 장학금 중 하나인 Best Scholars를 소개하고자 합니다. 이 프로그램은 우리 대학에서 1학년으로 입학할 학생들을 위한 것입니다. 이 장학금에 대한 자격이 되기 위해서는, 학생들은 대학 입학 시험에서 상위 20퍼센트 안에 들어야 합니다. 일단 Best Scholars로 선발되면, 그들은 캠퍼스 안에서 지내야 합니다. 또한, 대학 기간 내내 평점 3.4 이상을 유지해야 합니다. 이 요구 조건에 부합하면, Best Scholar 장학생들은 4년 동안 매년 5천 달러를 받게 될 것입니다. 여러분이 Milton 대학교에 입학하는 것에 관심이 있고 여러분이 Best Scholar가 될 수 있다고 생각한다면, 이 프로그램을 신청하세요.

10 정답 ⑤

Script

W Honey, what are you doing?

M I'm browsing a website. I'd like to buy a speaker for our

smartphone.

W Sounds great. Which model do you have in mind?

M I haven't decided yet. Which one do you like?

W I'd prefer one with a built-in microphone. We can answer calls directly from the speaker.

M That sounds like it would be convenient. How about Bluetooth functionality?

W I think we need that fuction.

M I'd love to have that feature, too.

W All right. Then we've got two models to choose from.

M One of them costs $15 more because it has a longer warranty.

W Hmm. I think speakers should have more than a two-year warranty.

M I agree. The longer the warranty is, the better it is regardless of the price.

W Okay, then. Let's buy this one.

여 여보, 뭐 하고 있어요?

남 웹사이트를 둘러보고 있어요. 우리 스마트폰 스피커를 사고 싶어서요.

여 좋은 생각이네요. 어떤 모델을 염두에 두고 있나요?

남 아직 결정하지 못했어요. 어느 것이 좋아요?

여 난 마이크가 내장된 것을 선호해요. 스피커에서 바로 전화를 받을 수 있어요.

남 편리할 것 같군요. 블루투스 기능은 어때요?

여 우리는 그 기능이 필요한 것 같아요.

남 나도 그런 특징이 있으면 좋겠어요.

여 알겠어요. 그럼 선택할 수 있는 두 모델이 있네요.

남 둘 중 하나는 더 긴 품질 보증 기간 때문에 15달러가 더 들어요.

여 음. 난 스피커가 2년 이상의 품질 보증 기간을 가지고 있어야 한다고 생각해요.

남 나도 동의해요. 품질 보증 기간이 더 길수록, 가격에 상관없이 더 좋아요.

여 좋아요. 그럼. 이걸로 삽시다.

Solution

마이크가 내장되어 있고, 블루투스 기능이 있으며, 2년 이상의 품질 보증 기간을 가진 제품을 원하고 있으므로, 두 사람이 선택한 스마트폰 스피커는 ⑤이다.

Words

built-in 내장형의 directly 바로, 직접 functionality 기능
warranty 품질 보증 기간, 품질 보증서 regardless of ~와 상관없이

11 정답 ②

Script

M Honey, the sun is too strong. I think we need curtains.

W You're right. I'll buy some tomorrow.

M Okay. Do you want me to help you hang the curtains?

W I will do it on my own. Thanks anyway.

남 여보, 햇빛이 너무 강해요. 커튼이 필요한 것 같아요.

여 당신 말이 맞아요. 내일 내가 커튼을 좀 살게요.

남 알았어요. 내가 커튼을 거는 것을 도와줄까요?

여 그 일을 혼자서 할게요. 어쨌든 고마워요.

Solution

여자가 햇빛을 가릴 수 있는 커튼을 사겠다고 말하자 남자는 커튼을 거는 데

자신의 도움이 필요한지 묻고 있으므로, 이에 대해 여자는 수락하거나 거절하는 것이 자연스러우므로 ② '그 일을 혼자서 할게요. 어쨌든 고마워요.'가 여자의 응답으로 가장 적절하다.

① 커튼을 좀 사는 것에 대해 생각하고 있어요.

③ 고맙지만 사양할게요. 이미 커튼을 걸었거든요.

④ 음, 당신은 커튼을 정기적으로 세탁해야 해요.

⑤ 우리 집에 맞는 커튼을 고르는 것을 도와주세요.

Words

hang 걸다 on one's own 혼자서 regularly 정기적으로

12 정답 ⑤

Script

W Next Monday is our son's first day at school.

M Did you get him all of his school supplies?

W Not yet. I'll take him to the stationery store in town tomorrow.

M I'll drive you two there and we can shop together.

여 다음 주 월요일이 우리 아들의 학교 첫날이에요.

남 그 애의 학용품을 다 준비시켰나요?

여 아직이요. 내일 시내에 있는 문구점에 그 애를 데려갈 거예요.

남 내가 거기에 차로 둘을 데려다줄게요 그리고 우리 같이 쇼핑할 수 있어요.

Solution

여자는 아들이 아직 학용품을 다 준비하지 못해 내일 아들을 데리고 문구점에 가겠다고 했으므로, 이에 대해 도와주겠다고 말하는 것이 자연스러우므로 ⑤ '내가 거기에 차로 둘을 데려다줄게요 그리고 우리 같이 쇼핑할 수 있어요.'가 남자의 응답으로 가장 적절하다.

① 나는 그 가게에서 과자 사는 걸 즐겨요.

② 그 애에게 학교에서 예의 바르게 행동하라고 말해 둘게요.

③ 학교에서 그 애가 곤란에 처하지 않으면 좋겠어요.

④ 그 애가 시험에 제대로 준비되어 있지 않은 것 같아요.

Words

school supplies 학용품 stationery store 문구점
behave 행동하다, 처신하다

13 정답 ⑤

Script

W Dane, what are you doing?

M Mom, I'm doing my homework. It's about introducing a foreign country and its culture.

W That sounds interesting. Which country did you choose?

M I chose Korea because you took me to Seoul last year.

W Korea is a wonderful country and I'm glad you decided to write about its culture.

M The thing is there are so many things to write about that I can't pick just one.

W Hmm. Why don't you write about Korean food?

M I thought about it, but Korean food is already well-known.

W Do you want to write about less popular aspects of Korean culture?

M Yes, I do. I want to choose things that are unfamiliar to my classmates.

W Then think about what amazed you most when we visited there.

여 Dane, 뭐 하고 있니?
남 엄마, 숙제를 하고 있어요. 외국과 그 나라의 문화를 소개하는 것이에요.
여 흥미롭게 들리는구나. 어느 나라를 선택했니?
남 작년에 엄마가 절 서울로 데려가 주셔서 한국으로 골랐어요.
여 한국은 굉장한 나라이고 네가 그 나라의 문화에 대해 쓰기로 결정했다니 기쁘구나.
남 문제는 쓸 거리가 너무 많아서 하나만을 정하지 못하겠어요.
여 음. 한국 음식에 대해 쓰지 그러니?
남 그것에 대해 생각해 봤는데, 한국 음식은 이미 잘 알려져 있어요.
여 한국 문화의 덜 유명한 측면에 대해 쓰고 싶니?
남 네, 그래요. 전 제 학급 친구들에게 익숙하지 않은 것들을 고르고 싶어요.
여 그럼 우리가 거기를 방문했을 때 널 가장 놀라게 했던 것에 대해 생각해 봐.

Solution

남자는 한국 문화의 잘 알려지지 않은 부분에 대해 쓰고 싶어 하고 여자는 이에 대해 조언을 해 주는 것이 자연스러우므로, ⑤ '그럼 우리가 거기를 방문했을 때 널 가장 놀라게 했던 것에 대해 생각해 봐.'가 여자의 응답으로 가장 적절하다.

① 우리가 한국에 다시 여행갈 수 있으면 좋겠구나.
② 한국 음식에 대해 쓰는 것은 멋진 생각이야.
③ 한국은 너무나 인기 있어서 모두가 그곳에 대해 알고 있을 거야.
④ 서울을 방문하기 전에 한국 문화에 대한 책을 더 많이 읽으렴.

Words

aspect 측면, 양상 unfamiliar 익숙하지 않은

14 정답 ④

Script

W Honey, look at this picture.
M The girl in the picture looks just like our Sophie.
W Exactly. Sophie drew her portrait in her art class today. Isn't it surprising?
M Yeah. She must have artistic talent.
W You're right. In addition, she loves drawing very much.
M We must do something to help her develop her talent. What should we do?
W I think we should not push her into drawing a picture.
M That makes sense. Forcing her would not help her develop.
W If she were forced, she might even lose her interest in drawing. I think voluntary atmosphere is important.
M Right. We should let her draw because she wants to.

여 여보, 이 그림 좀 보세요.
남 그림 속의 소녀는 우리 Sophie와 똑같이 생겼네요.
여 맞아요. Sophie가 오늘 미술 시간에 자신의 초상화를 그렸어요. 놀랍지 않나요?
남 그래요. 그 애는 예술적 재능이 있는 게 틀림없어요.
여 당신 말이 맞아요. 게다가, 그 애는 그림 그리는 것을 매우 좋아해요.
남 우리는 그녀가 재능을 계발하는 것을 도울 무언가를 해야 해요. 우리는 무엇을 해야 할까요?
여 우리는 그 애가 그림을 그리도록 밀어붙여서 안 된다고 생각해요.

남 일리가 있는 말이에요. 그 애에게 강요하는 것은 그 애가 발전하는 것에 도움이 되지 않을 거예요.
여 강요당한다면, 그 애는 그림에 대한 흥미를 잃을 수도 있어요. 자발적인 분위기가 중요한 것 같아요.
남 맞아요. 그 애가 원하기 때문에 그리도록 해야 해요.

Solution

두 사람은 Sophie의 예술적 재능이 계발되도록 도와야 한다고 말하면서 그림 그리는 것을 강제해서는 안 된다는 것에 생각을 같이한다. 여자는 Sophie가 강요당한다면 그림에 대한 흥미를 잃을 수도 있으므로 자발적인 분위기가 중요하다고 했으므로, 이에 대해 동의하는 의견이 오는 것이 자연스러우므로 ④ '맞아요. 그 애가 원하기 때문에 그리도록 해야 해요.'가 남자의 응답으로 가장 적절하다.

① 그래요. 그 애의 흥미를 되찾기 위해 뭔가를 해야 해요.
② 음, 때때로 우리는 그 애가 자연을 그리게 해야 해요.
③ 물론이에요. 내가 그 애를 위한 미술 선생님을 찾아볼게요.
⑤ 알았어요. 사물을 다른 각도로 보라고 그 애에게 말할게요.

Words

portrait 초상화 artistic 예술적인 talent 재능 push 밀어붙이다
force 강요하다 voluntary 자발적인 atmosphere 분위기

15 정답 ①

Script

M Leonard is a college student. On campus, there are several dining establishments and his favorite one is a place that serves sandwiches. It is a type of restaurant where people have to place an order at the counter and take the food to their table by themselves. One day, after finishing his morning classes, Leonard feels hungry and goes to the restaurant. Placing an order, he looks around and notices that all the tables are already taken. Among them, there's one table where only one woman is having her meal. When his sandwich is ready, Leonard takes it and walks up to her. He wants to know if he can have a seat there and eat his sandwich. In this situation, what would Leonard most likely say to the woman?
Leonard Would you mind sharing your table with me?

남 Leonard는 대학생입니다. 캠퍼스에는 여러 개의 식당이 있는데 그가 가장 좋아하는 곳은 샌드위치를 제공하는 식당입니다. 그곳은 사람들이 카운터에서 주문을 하고 직접 음식을 본인의 테이블로 가져가야 하는 유형의 식당입니다. 어느 날, 오전 수업을 마친 후에, Leonard는 허기가 져 그 식당으로 갑니다. 주문을 한 뒤, 그는 주변을 둘러보고는 모든 테이블이 다 찼다는 것을 알아차립니다. 그것들 중에, 오직 한 여자만이 식사를 하고 있는 테이블이 있습니다. 자신의 샌드위치가 준비되자, Leonard는 그것을 들고 그녀에게 갑니다. 그는 그가 거기에 앉아 자신의 샌드위치를 먹을 수 있는지 알고 싶습니다. 이런 상황에서, Leonard는 그 여자에게 뭐라고 말할 것 같은가요?
Leonard 제가 합석해도 괜찮으시겠어요?

Solution

테이블이 다 차서 혼자 식사하는 여자와 합석을 원하고 있는 상황이므로, 이러한 상황에서 Leonard가 여자에게 할 말로 가장 적절한 것은 ① '제가 합석해도 괜찮으시겠어요?'이다.

② 제 샌드위치를 포장해 갈 수 있으면 고맙겠습니다.
③ 식사에 마실 것을 추가하시겠어요?

④ 카운터에서 샌드위치를 주문하셔야 해요.
⑤ 점심시간 동안 이 식당은 항상 붐비지는 않습니다.

Words

dine 식사를 하다 place an order 주문하다
to go 포장해서 가져가는

16 정답 ③　　17 정답 ④

Script

W Good morning, I'm Nora Dun from Happy Youth Center. You teenagers may want to take the financial responsibility in some parts of your life. How can you do it? As you already might have guessed, doing part-time jobs is one of the best ways to handle it. Let me share some good jobs for you to do. First, you can easily find a job as a babysitter because almost everyone in the neighborhood will need a babysitter. Second, grocery stores are always looking for cashiers and baggers. You can work after school and on weekends. Next, you can also work as a fast food server. Fast food restaurants usually want to hire teenagers. Last, a dog walker is another good job for teenagers because there must be some dog owners who need someone to walk their dogs. There are many other jobs. Let's talk about them.

여 좋은 아침입니다. 저는 Happy 청소년 센터의 Nora Dun입니다. 여러분 십 대들은 여러분의 삶의 일부 부분에서 재정적 책임을 지고 싶어 할지도 모릅니다. 여러분은 그것을 어떻게 할 수 있을까요? 여러분이 이미 짐작했던 것처럼, 시간제 일을 하는 것은 그 일을 처리하는 가장 좋은 방법 중 하나입니다. 제가 여러분이 할 수 있는 몇 가지 좋은 일을 말씀드리겠습니다. 첫째, 여러분은 이웃의 거의 모든 사람들이 보모를 필요로 할 것이기 때문에 보모로서의 일을 쉽게 찾을 수 있습니다. 둘째로, 식료품점들은 항상 계산원과 물건을 봉지에 담는 사람을 찾고 있습니다. 여러분은 방과 후와 주말에 일할 수 있습니다. 다음으로, 여러분은 패스트푸드점에서 서빙하는 사람으로도 일할 수 있습니다. 패스트푸드점들은 보통 십 대들을 고용하고 싶어 합니다. 마지막으로, 개를 산책시키는 사람은 십 대들에게 또 다른 좋은 일자리인데, 왜냐하면 자신들의 개를 산책시킬 사람이 필요한 일부 개 주인들도 분명 있을 것이기 때문입니다. 다른 많은 일자리들이 있습니다. 그것들에 대해 이야기해 보죠.

Solution

16
여자는 십 대들이 삶의 일부분에서 재정적 책임을 지고 싶어 하고 시간제 일을 하는 것이 이 문제를 해결할 좋은 방법 중 하나임을 말하면서 십 대들이 할 수 있는 좋은 시간제 일자리를 소개하고 있으므로 여자가 하는 말의 주제로 가장 적절한 것은 ③ '십 대에게 적합한 시간제 일자리들'이다.

① 십 대들에게 용돈을 주는 방법
② 십 대들이 선호하는 정규직
④ 십 대들이 경제적인 신념을 갖는 것의 중요성
⑤ 십 대들의 흥미에 근거해서 일자리를 선택하는 것에 대한 조언

17
보모, 계산원, 패스트푸드점의 서빙하는 사람, 개를 산책시키는 사람은 언급되었지만, ④ '잔디 깎는 사람'은 언급되지 않았다.

Words

financial 재정적인 handle 처리하다 cashier 계산원, 출납원
bagger 물건을 봉지[자루]에 담는 사람 hire 고용하다

● 실전 모의고사 13회　　본문 136쪽

01 ②	02 ②	03 ①	04 ④	05 ②
06 ③	07 ③	08 ④	09 ④	10 ②
11 ④	12 ⑤	13 ⑤	14 ②	15 ⑤
16 ④	17 ③			

01 정답 ②

Script

W Hi, I'm Kelly Howard from the maintenance office. I'd like to thank you all for being cooperative during the annual cleaning of the building last week. Now, let me make another announcement regarding our facilities. Starting June 1st, all the elevators in our company building will go through regular inspections for one week. The elevators that go to odd-numbered floors will be checked for the first two days, and the next two days are for the ones that stop at even-numbered floors. The elevators that have access to all floors will be examined for the rest of the week. During this period, those of you whose offices are located on lower levels are encouraged to take the stairs. Thank you in advance for your cooperation.

여 안녕하세요, 관리 사무소에서 나온 Kelly Howard입니다. 지난주 건물 연례 청소 동안 협조해 주신 여러분 모두에게 감사드립니다. 이제, 우리 시설과 관련해서 또 다른 공지를 하고자 합니다. 6월 1일부터, 우리 회사 건물의 모든 엘리베이터가 일주일 동안 정기 점검에 들어갈 것입니다. 첫 이틀 동안은 홀수 층에 가는 엘리베이터가 점검받을 것이고 그다음 이틀 동안은 짝수 층에 가는 엘리베이터가 점검받습니다. 모든 층에 가는 엘리베이터는 그 주 나머지 기간 동안 검사를 받을 것입니다. 이 기간 동안, 사무실이 저층에 위치한 분들은 계단을 사용하시길 권장합니다. 협조에 미리 감사드립니다.

Solution

6월 1일부터 일주일 동안 엘리베이터 정기 점검이 있을 예정이니 협조해 줄 것을 요청하고 있으므로, 여자가 하는 말의 목적으로 가장 적절한 것은 ②이다.

Words

maintenance office 관리 사무소 cooperative 협조적인
inspection 점검, 검사 odd 홀수의 even 짝수의 examine 검사하다
located 위치한 level 층 in advance 미리

02 정답 ②

Script

W Jack, do you have time to talk?
M Sure. What can I help you with?
W I need to ask about children's reading needs. You have experience of raising children.
M What's the matter? Hmm, your child is about nine, right?
W That's right. I want to do something to improve his reading. What should I do?

M I'd like you to recommend books so that he doesn't waste time reading.
W Waste time? I don't understand what you mean.
M You need to find books that are appropriate for his age.
W Yes, that is important.
M If he tries reading books that he can't understand, he's likely to lose interest in reading.
W Then he'll waste his time, right?
M That's right.
W Thank you. I'll follow your advice.

여 Jack, 이야기할 시간 있어요?
남 물론이지요. 무엇을 도와줄까요?
여 아이들의 독서 욕구에 대해 물어봐야겠어요. 당신은 아이들을 키운 경험이 있잖아요.
남 무엇이 문제죠? 흠, 당신의 아이는 대략 9살이죠, 맞죠?
여 맞아요. 나는 그의 독서를 향상할 뭔가를 하고 싶어요. 내가 무엇을 해야 되나요?
남 그 애가 독서하며 시간을 낭비하지 않도록 당신이 책을 추천하면 좋겠어요.
여 시간 낭비요? 무슨 말인지 이해가 안 가요.
남 그 애의 나이에 적합한 책들을 찾을 필요가 있어요.
여 그래요. 그것은 중요해요.
남 만약 그 애가 이해할 수 없는 책 읽기를 시도한다면, 그 애는 독서에 흥미를 잃을 가능성이 있어요.
여 그러면 그 애는 시간을 낭비하겠군요, 그렇죠?
남 맞아요.
여 고마워요. 당신의 충고를 따를게요.

Solution

자신의 아이의 독서를 향상시킬 방법을 묻는 여자에게 남자는 아이의 나이에 적합한 책이 있다고 하면서, 아이가 이해할 수 없는 책읽기를 시도한다면 독서에 흥미를 잃을 가능성이 있다고 말하고 있으므로, 남자의 의견으로 가장 적절한 것은 ②이다.

Words

raise 키우다 recommend 추천하다 appropriate 적합한

03 정답 ①

Script

M Good morning, Ms. Morton.
W Oh, you're Mr. Taylor, right?
M Yes. You gave me a call yesterday.
W The water in the kitchen sink doesn't drain. Come on in. [Pause] This sink is troubling me.
M Let me check pipes under the sink first.
W I hope it won't be a big problem.
M Don't worry, Ms. Morton. Usually, it's a simple problem caused by a blockage in the pipes.
W I hope so. Is there anything I can do while you are working at it?
M Well, would you bring me a glass of water?
W No problem.

남 좋은 아침입니다. Morton 씨.
여 아, 당신이 Taylor 씨군요, 맞죠?
남 네. 당신이 어제 제게 전화 주셨죠.
여 부엌 싱크대의 물이 빠지지 않아요. 어서 들어오세요. [잠시 후] 이 싱크대가 저를 괴롭히고 있어요.
남 제가 우선 싱크대 아래 파이프를 확인해 볼게요.
여 큰 문제가 아니기를 바라요.
남 걱정하지 마세요, Morton 씨. 보통은 파이프가 막혀서 생기는 간단한 문제예요.
여 그랬으면 좋겠어요. 당신이 일을 하는 동안 제가 할 수 있는 어떤 일이 있나요?
남 음. 물 한 잔 갖다 주시겠어요?
여 문제없어요.

Solution

여자는 자신의 부엌 싱크대의 물이 빠지지 않는다고 말하고 있으며 남자는 싱크대 아래의 파이프를 확인해 보겠다고 했으므로, 두 사람의 관계를 가장 잘 나타낸 것은 ①이다.

Words

sink 싱크대 drain (물이) 빠지다 trouble 괴롭히다 blockage 막힘

04 정답 ④

Script

M Mom, would you look at my poster? I'm going to submit it to the Environment Poster Contest.
W I like how you wrote 'Love Trees' in the middle at the top.
M Thanks. I tried to convey the message that we need to preserve trees.
W Okay. Two birds in the tree to the left look cute.
M The birds are there to show that if we preserve trees, birds will benefit as well.
W That's a good message. You did a good job with the man and the woman.
M See the potted plant the man is holding? That expresses the idea that we need to care for plants.
W The woman is watering a small plant. That means the same, right?
M Exactly. And what do you think of the message 'It's up to you.' at the bottom of the poster?
W That's a great way to tell everyone that they have a choice.
M Yeah. That's what I want everyone to think about.
W Your poster is very symbolic. I really like it.

남 엄마, 제 포스터 좀 봐 주시겠어요? 그것을 환경 포스터 대회에 제출할 거예요.
여 가운데 윗부분에 'Love Trees'라고 쓴 방식이 마음에 들어.
남 고마워요. 나무들을 보존할 필요가 있다는 메시지를 전하려고 했어요.
여 그렇구나. 왼쪽 나무에 새 두 마리가 귀여워 보이는구나.
남 우리가 나무를 보존하면 새들도 득을 볼 거라는 것을 보여 주기 위해 새들이 그곳에 있는 거예요.
여 좋은 메시지네. 남자와 여자도 잘 그렸구나.
남 남자가 들고 있는 화분 보이죠? 그것은 우리가 식물을 돌볼 필요가 있다는 생각을 표현해요.
여 여자는 작은 식물에 물을 주고 있네. 그것은 같은 뜻이지, 그렇지?
남 정확히 그래요. 그리고 포스터의 아래에 있는 'It's up to you.(그것은 당신에게 달려 있다.)'라는 말은 어떻게 생각하세요?
여 그것은 그들이 선택권이 있다는 것을 모두에게 말하는 멋진 방법이구나.
남 네. 그것이 제가 모두가 생각해 주기를 바라는 것이에요.

여 네 포스터는 매우 상징적이구나. 정말 마음에 들어.

Solution

여자가 작은 식물에 물을 주고 있다고 했지만, 그림에서는 여자가 무릎을 꿇고 작은 식물을 손으로 가리키고 있으므로 대화의 내용과 일치하지 않는 것은 ④이다.

Words

submit 제출하다 convey 전달하다 preserve 보존하다, 보호하다 benefit 득을 보다 water 물을 주다 symbolic 상징적인

05 정답 ②

Script

M Amelia, it's time for breakfast.
W Okay, Dad. Let me finish this first.
M What are you doing on your computer?
W I have to turn in my science assignment by email. It was due last night.
M How many times have I told you to finish things in time?
W I was trying to, but this one took longer than I thought.
M Hurry up or you'll be late for school.
W Okay, all I need to do is click the send button. *[Pause]* It's all done.
M Now get changed into your school uniform.
W Oh, I almost forgot. One of the buttons on my jacket is missing.
M And you're telling me that now? Okay, I'll quickly sew a new one on.
W Thank you so much, Dad.

여 Amelia, 아침 먹을 시간이야.
여 네, 아빠. 우선 이것부터 끝내고요.
남 컴퓨터로 뭘 하고 있는 거니?
여 이메일로 과학 과제를 제출해야 해요. 어젯밤이 마감 기한이었어요.
남 제때에 일을 끝내라고 얼마나 많이 말했니?
여 노력했지만, 이것은 제가 생각한 것보다 더 오래 걸렸어요.
남 서두르렴, 그렇지 않으면 학교에 늦을 거야.
여 네, 보내기 버튼을 누르기만 하면 돼요. *[잠시 후]* 다 끝났어요.
남 이제 교복으로 갈아입으렴.
여 아, 거의 잊어버릴 뻔했어요. 재킷에 달린 단추 중 하나가 없어졌어요.
남 그걸 이제 말하는 거야? 알았어, 빨리 새 단추를 달아 줄게.
여 정말 고마워요, 아빠.

Solution

여자가 교복 재킷에 단추 하나가 떨어져 없다고 말하자 남자가 달아 주겠다고 말했으므로, 정답은 ②이다.

Words

turn in ~을 제출하다 assignment 과제 due ~하기로 되어 있는 sew on (바느질로) ~을 달다

06 정답 ③

Script

M Hello, ma'am. How may I help you?
W I'd like to buy some clothes for my mother's birthday.
M Okay. Feel free to browse and tell me if you need any help.

W I like this brown skirt. I'm sure it would look great on her.
M This skirt is $150. It's one of our best-selling items.
W Great. I'll take it. And I'd like to buy something that goes well with it.
M We have a variety of blouses that will go great with the skirt.
W Let me take a look at them. Oh, these blouses are really pretty.
M Originally, they were $80, but they are 20 percent off now.
W Great. I'll take two of them — one in ivory and the other in sky blue.
M Okay. Would you like to pay by cash or credit card?
W I'll pay by credit card.

남 안녕하세요, 손님. 어떻게 도와드릴까요?
여 어머니 생신 선물로 옷을 좀 사고 싶어요.
남 네, 편히 둘러보시고 도움이 필요하시면 제게 말씀해 주세요.
여 이 갈색 치마가 좋은데요. 분명 어머니께 잘 어울릴 거예요.
남 이 치마는 150달러입니다. 가장 잘 팔리는 물건 중 하나예요.
여 좋아요. 그것을 살게요. 그리고 그것과 잘 어울리는 것을 사고 싶어요.
남 치마와 잘 어울릴 다양한 블라우스가 있어요.
여 제가 한번 볼게요. 오, 이 블라우스들은 정말 예쁘군요.
남 원래, 그것들은 80달러였지만, 지금 20퍼센트 할인 중이에요.
여 좋아요. 두 벌을 사겠습니다. 하나는 아이보리 색으로 또 다른 하나는 하늘색으로요.
남 네. 현금으로 지불하실 건가요, 혹은 신용카드로 지불하실 건가요?
여 신용카드로 지불할게요.

Solution

150달러인 치마 한 벌과 80달러인 블라우스를 20퍼센트 할인하여 두 벌 사기로 했으므로, 여자가 지불할 금액은 ③ '278달러'이다.

Words

browse (가게 안 물건들을) 둘러보다 go well with ~와 잘 어울리다 originally 원래 sky blue 하늘색

07 정답 ③

Script

W Tony, you look very busy.
M Oh, Mom. I'm editing a video clip for my movie club.
W What is it for?
M This is for advertising our club. I filmed it myself.
W Great. By the way, are you available tomorrow afternoon?
M No, I'm not. Why do you ask?
W Grandma will visit us for three days. She'll arrive at William Airport and I'd like you to join me for picking her up.
M I want to see Grandma as soon as possible. But I can't go there with you.
W Do you have an assignment to do or meet with your friend?
M No. I'm supposed to meet with my club teacher tomorrow.
W Okay.

여 Tony, 아주 바빠 보이는구나.
남 오, 엄마. 영화 동아리를 위한 비디오 클립을 편집하고 있어요.

여 그건 뭘 위한 거지?

남 이것은 우리 동아리를 홍보하기 위한 거예요. 제가 직접 촬영했어요.

여 멋지구나. 그건 그렇고, 내일 오후에 시간 있니?

남 아니요, 시간이 없어요. 왜 물어보세요?

여 할머니께서 3일 동안 우리를 방문하실 거야. 할머니는 William 공항에 도착하실 텐데, 나는 네가 나와 함께 할머니를 모시러 갔으면 좋겠어.

남 할머니를 가능한 한 빨리 보고 싶어요. 하지만 엄마와 함께 그곳에 갈 수 없어요.

여 할 숙제가 있거나 친구랑 만나니?

남 아니요. 내일 동아리 선생님과 만나기로 되어 있어요.

여 알겠어.

Solution

남자는 내일 동아리 담당 교사와 만나기로 해서 공항에 할머니를 모시러 가지 못한다고 말하고 있으므로, 정답은 ③이다.

Words

edit 편집하다 film 촬영하다 assignment 숙제

08 정답 ④

Script

W Honey, why don't we go to Willmar Family Day Event this Saturday?

M That's a good idea. Is it held in the Olsen Park as usual?

W Yes. And the Love Community Center will host the event this year. As you know, the hosting organization is different every year.

M I'd like to thank hosting organizations. We had fun there last year.

W Yes. Especially, our kids loved the games for kids.

M Are there new games for this year's event?

W According to this flyer, they prepared some games that parents and kids do together.

M Great. That'll be fun.

W Yes. The event starts at nine in the morning. Keep that in mind, honey.

M Okay. I'm sure our kids will enjoy it.

여 여보, 우리 이번 주 토요일에 Willmar 가족의 날 행사에 가는 게 어때요?

남 좋은 생각이에요. 평소처럼 Olsen 공원에서 열리나요?

여 네. 그리고 Love 문화 센터가 올해 그 행사를 주최할 거예요. 당신도 알다시피 주최 단체가 매년 달라요.

남 주최 단체들에 감사하고 싶어요. 우리는 작년에 그곳에서 재미있게 놀았어요.

여 그래요. 특히 우리 아이들은 아이들을 위한 게임을 좋아했어요.

남 올해의 행사를 위한 새로운 게임이 있나요?

여 이 전단지에 따르면, 주최 측은 부모와 아이들이 함께 하는 몇몇 게임을 준비했어요.

남 좋네요. 그거 재미있겠네요.

여 네. 그 행사는 오전 9시에 시작해요. 명심해요, 여보.

남 알았어요. 분명 우리 아이들이 좋아할 거예요.

Solution

행사 장소, 주최 단체, 새로운 게임, 개장 시간은 언급되었으나, ④ '참가자 기념품'에 대해서는 언급되지 않았다.

Words

as usual 평소처럼 host 주최하다 flyer 전단지
keep ~ in mind ~을 명심하다

09 정답 ④

Script

M Thomas Stearns Eliot was born into a middle-class family in the United States as the last of six children. He had to overcome physical limitations in his early years. This meant he could not participate in physical activities as a child. As he spent time alone reading, his love of literature deepened. He later studied philosophy at Harvard University and earned his bachelor's degree after three years. After that, he moved to France, where he continued to study philosophy. He later moved to the United Kingdom and became a British citizen at age 39. He received attention for his poem *The Love Song of J. Alfred Prufrock*, which was considered a modern masterpiece. In 1948, he was awarded the Nobel Prize in Literature.

남 Thomas Stearns Elliot은 미국 중산층 가정에서 여섯 자녀들 중 막내로 태어났습니다. 그는 어렸을 때에 신체적 제약을 극복해야만 했습니다. 이것은 어렸을 때 체육 활동에 참여할 수 없었음을 의미했습니다. 혼자서 독서를 하면서 시간을 보냄에 따라, 문학에 대한 그의 사랑은 깊어졌습니다. 그는 후에 하버드 대학교에서 철학을 공부했으며 3년 만에 학사 학위를 취득했습니다. 그 후에, 그는 프랑스로 건너가, 그곳에서 계속해서 철학을 공부했습니다. 그는 후에 영국으로 이주해 39세의 나이에 영국 시민이 되었습니다. 그는 자신의 시 'J. Alfred Prufrock의 사랑 노래'로 주목을 받았는데, 그것은 현대 걸작으로 여겨집니다. 1948년에, 그는 노벨 문학상을 수상했습니다.

Solution

프랑스에서 철학을 공부하고 그 뒤에 영국으로 이주해 영국 시민이 되었다고 했으므로, 담화의 내용과 일치하지 않는 것은 ④ '대학 졸업 후 프랑스로 가서 귀화하였다.'이다.

Words

physical 신체적인, 육체의 limitation 제약 literature 문학
philosophy 철학 earn 얻다 bachelor's degree 학사 학위
poem 시 masterpiece 걸작 award 수여하다

10 정답 ②

Script

W I think we're pretty much done purchasing home appliances.

M Yes, we bought a refrigerator, a laundry machine... Oh, how about an oven?

W I almost forgot. I brought a flyer back from the store. Ovens are on sale this week.

M Wonderful. Do you like this one with the microwave function?

W No, I don't think that would be useful.

M Okay, how about one with an auto-cooking menu?

W I would love that feature. You just press a button and the oven automatically cooks the food.

M I like that, too. Would you prefer an electric or steam oven?

W I heard steam-cooked foods maintain more of their flavor and fewer nutrients are lost.

M Steam ovens sound much better. Let's buy one.

W Good. And I'd like to spend less than $300.

M Okay. Well, there's only one model that's perfect for us.

W Great. Let's go to the store and buy it.

여 가전 기기 구입은 거의 다 끝낸 것 같아요.

남 네, 우리가 냉장고, 세탁기를 샀네요…. 아, 오븐은 어때요?

여 거의 잊어버릴 뻔했네요. 가게에서 전단을 가져왔어요. 이번 주에 오븐이 할인 중이에요.

남 좋아요. 전자레인지 기능을 가지고 있는 이것이 좋아요?

여 아니요, 그것은 유용할 것 같지 않아요.

남 알았어요, 자동 요리 메뉴가 있는 것은 어때요?

여 그 특징은 좋아요. 단지 버튼만 누르면 오븐이 자동으로 음식을 요리해 주잖아요.

남 나도 그건 좋아요. 전기 오븐이 좋아요, 스팀 오븐이 좋아요?

여 스팀으로 요리된 음식들이 풍미를 더 많이 유지하고 영양분이 더 적게 손실된다고 들었어요.

남 스팀 오븐이 훨씬 더 나은 것 같아요. 그것을 삽시다.

여 좋아요. 그리고 300달러 미만을 썼으면 좋겠어요.

남 알았어요. 그럼 우리한테 완벽한 모델이 하나 있어요.

여 좋아요. 가게에 가서 그것을 삽시다.

Solution

전자레인지 기능이 없고, 자동 요리 메뉴가 있는 스팀 오븐으로 300달러 미만인 것을 원하므로, 두 사람이 구입할 오븐은 ②이다.

Words

purchase 구입하다 home appliance 가전 기기 laundry machine 세탁기 flyer (광고, 안내용) 전단 microwave 전자레인지 function 기능 automatically 자동으로 maintain 유지하다 flavor 풍미, 맛 nutrient 영양분

11 정답 ④

Script

M Shelly, do you know a printer shop nearby?

W Yes. Actually there are two shops around here.

M Then would you tell me where the closer one is?

W It's located next to the gas station on King Street.

남 Shelly, 근처에 있는 인쇄소를 알고 있나요?

여 네. 사실 이 근처에 가게가 두 개 있어요.

남 그럼 더 가까운 게 어디 있는지 말해 줄래요?

여 그것은 King Street에 있는 주유소 옆에 있어요.

Solution

남자는 여자가 아는 인쇄소 두 곳 중에서 더 가까운 곳의 위치를 묻고 있으므로, ④ '그것은 King Street에 있는 주유소 옆에 있어요.'가 여자의 응답으로 가장 적절하다.

① 미안하지만 근처에 인쇄소가 없어요.

② 나는 내 발표 문서를 더 가까운 곳에 맡겼어요.

③ 그 인쇄소는 가까워서 거기에 걸어갈 수 있어요.

⑤ 그 인쇄소는 오전 10시에 문을 열어요.

Words

gas station 주유소

12 정답 ⑤

Script

W Do you have any special plans for winter vacation?

M I have poor eyesight, so I'm thinking about getting laser eye surgery.

W But I've never seen you wearing glasses.

M I always wear contact lenses when I go out.

여 겨울 방학에 특별한 계획이라도 있니?

남 시력이 나빠서, 레이저 눈 수술을 받을까 생각 중이야.

여 하지만 네가 안경을 쓰고 있는 걸 전혀 본 적이 없는데.

남 난 외출할 때 항상 콘택트렌즈를 착용해.

Solution

시력이 나빠서 겨울 방학 동안에 레이저 눈 수술을 받을 생각이라는 남자의 말에 여자는 남자의 안경 쓴 모습을 본 적이 없다고 했으므로, ⑤ '난 외출할 때 항상 콘택트렌즈를 착용해.'가 남자의 응답으로 가장 적절하다.

① 시력이 나빠지고 있어서 걱정이야.

② 난 항상 네가 시력이 좋다고 추측했어.

③ 눈을 검사받을 계획이야.

④ 수술을 받는 게 위험할지도 몰라.

Words

eyesight 시력 fail (시력이) 나빠지다 assume 추측하다 examine 검사하다

13 정답 ⑤

Script

W Hi. How may I help you?

M I'd like to know what your gym has to offer.

W We have yoga classes every day and boxing classes on Friday evenings.

M Are they all included in the gym membership?

W Yes. Is this your first time joining a gym?

M No, I joined two different gyms before, but I quit both after a couple of months.

W Could you tell me why you left?

M One had unsanitary shower facilities, and the other was much too crowded.

W We have clean facilities and our gym is never packed with people.

M Well, there was another reason. I wasn't determined enough to keep exercising.

W I see. That happens to many people.

M I'm afraid I might quit this gym after a few months, too.

W Don't worry. We'll motivate you to keep working out.

여 안녕하세요. 어떻게 도와드릴까요?

남 이 헬스장이 무엇을 제공하는지 알고 싶어요.

여 매일 요가 수업이 있고, 금요일 저녁에는 복싱 수업이 있습니다.

남 헬스장 멤버십에 그것들이 모두 포함되어 있나요?

여 네. 헬스장에 가입하는 게 이번이 처음이신가요?

남 아니요, 전에 두 곳의 다른 헬스장에 가입해 봤지만, 둘 다 두세 달 뒤에 그만두었어요.

여 왜 그만두었는지 알려 주시겠어요?

남 한 곳은 비위생적인 샤워 시설을 가지고 있었고, 다른 곳은 너무 많이 붐볐어요.

여 저희는 깨끗한 시설을 가지고 있고 절대로 사람들로 가득 차지 않습니다.

남 음, 한 가지 이유가 더 있었어요. 전 계속 운동할 만큼 단단히 결심하지 않았어요.

여 알겠습니다. 많은 사람들이 그렇죠.

남 이 헬스장도 몇 달 후에 그만둘까 봐 걱정이에요.

여 걱정하지 마세요. 저희가 계속 운동하시도록 동기 부여를 해 줄 거예요.

Solution

남자는 운동할 의지가 충분하지 않아 새로 등록할 헬스장도 곧 그만둘까 봐 걱정을 표현하고 있으므로, ⑤ '걱정하지 마세요. 저희가 계속 운동하시도록 동기 부여를 해 줄 거예요.'가 여자의 응답으로 가장 적절하다.

① 저도 동의해요. 이 헬스장은 항상 사람들로 가득해요.
② 그것은 제가 규칙적인 운동을 굳게 지킬 수 없었기 때문이에요.
③ 당신 말이 맞아요. 저희는 다양한 요가와 복싱 수업을 제공해요.
④ 저희가 다른 신체 단련 프로그램이 있는지 확인해 볼게요.

Words

unsanitary 비위생적인 packed with ~로 가득 찬
determined 단단히 결심한, 단호한
stick to (어려움을 참고) ~을 계속하다 workout 운동
fitness 신체 단련 motivate 동기를 부여하다

14 정답 ②

Script

M Alley, the news said the bridge will finally open.

W What bridge do you mean, Ryan?

M I mean the bridge over the Gen River. I've been waiting for it.

W You sound excited. When does it open?

M It'll open this Saturday. My commuting time will be much shorter with the bridge.

W Congratulations. You've been complaining about a long commuting time.

M Soon I'll just drive across the bridge to work.

W So how much time will it save you?

M My commute will be about 20 minutes shorter.

W 20 minutes? Now you won't be pressed for time.

M Right. I'll enjoy a leisurely commute.

남 Alley, 뉴스에서 다리가 드디어 개통될 거예요.

여 무슨 다리를 말하는 거예요, Ryan?

남 Gen 강의 다리를 말하는 거예요. 그것을 기다려 왔어요.

여 당신은 신나 보이네요. 그것이 언제 개통되나요?

남 이번 주 토요일에 개통될 거예요. 다리가 있으니까 제 통근 시간이 훨씬 더 짧아질 거예요.

여 축하해요. 통근 시간이 길다고 불평을 해왔잖아요.

남 곧 회사까지 차를 타고 다리를 건너기만 하면 될 거예요.

여 그렇게 하면 당신은 시간을 얼마나 절약하나요?

남 제 통근은 20분 정도 더 짧아질 거예요.

여 20분요? 이제 당신은 시간에 쫓기지 않겠네요.

남 맞아요. 여유로운 통근을 즐길 거예요.

Solution

다리가 생겨 출근 시간이 20분 정도 짧아질 거라는 남자의 말에 여자는 이제 시간에 쫓기지 않겠다고 말했으므로, ② '맞아요. 여유로운 통근을 즐길 거예요.'가 남자의 응답으로 가장 적절하다.

① 맞아요. 이제 회사까지 직접 운전할 거예요.
③ 당신 말이 맞아요. 이제는 더 일찍 집을 떠날게요.
④ 그래요. 그 아름다운 다리에 감명받았어요.
⑤ 물론이죠. 통근하면서 계속 독서를 해 왔어요.

Words

complain 불평하다 commuting time 통근 시간 commute 통근
pressed for ~에 쫓기는 leisurely 여유로운

15 정답 ⑤

Script

W Kevin is the starting quarterback on his school's football team. Everyone says he's an ace and talks about how great his play is. However, these days Kevin spends more time hanging out with his friends and less time practicing football. He's even skipped training sessions, where every member on the team is required to participate. His coach is concerned that Kevin believes in his abilities so much that he is neglecting his training. The coach thinks hard work is as important as talent and there won't be any growth when Kevin is content with his ability and does not make an effort to improve. In this situation, what would the coach most likely say to Kevin?

Coach If you don't train hard enough, you won't succeed.

여 Kevin은 자신의 학교 미식축구팀에서 주전 쿼터백입니다. 모두가 그를 에이스라고 말하며 그의 경기가 얼마나 훌륭한지 이야기합니다. 그러나 요즘 Kevin은 자신의 친구들과 노는 데 더 많은 시간을 보내고 미식축구 연습에는 시간을 덜 씁니다. 그는 심지어 훈련들을 건너뛰기도 했는데, 그것은 팀 멤버 모두가 참가하도록 요구되는 것이었습니다. 그의 감독은 Kevin이 자신의 능력을 너무나 믿어서 훈련을 등한시하는 것이 걱정입니다. 감독은 열심히 운동하는 것이 재능만큼이나 중요하고 Kevin이 자신의 능력에 만족해서 실력 향상을 위해 노력하지 않으면 그 어떤 성장도 없을 것이라고 생각합니다. 이런 상황에서, 감독은 Kevin에게 뭐라고 말할 것 같은가요?

Coach 충분히 열심히 훈련하지 않으면, 넌 성공하지 못할 거야.

Solution

자신의 능력만 믿고 훈련을 등한시하는 Kevin의 태도를 감독은 걱정하고 있는 상황이므로, 이러한 상황에서 감독이 Kevin에게 할 말로 가장 적절한 것은 ⑤ '충분히 열심히 훈련하지 않으면, 넌 성공하지 못할 거야.'이다.

① 너 같은 에이스 선수가 있었으면 좋겠구나.
② 네 가족과 더 많은 시간을 보낼 거니?
③ 너희 팀 멤버들에게 더 열심히 운동하라고 부탁해 주겠니?
④ 네가 이번 훈련 과정을 맡아 주기를 원해.

Words

hang out with ~와 놀다, ~와 시간을 보내다
be required to do ~하도록 요구되다 concerned 걱정하는
neglect 등한시하다 make an effort 노력하다
improve (실력이) 향상되다

16 정답 ④　　17 정답 ③

Script

M Hello, everyone. Have you ever heard that strange patterns of some animal behavior have been linked to the lunar cycle? For example, a full moon can scare normally night-active animals into the darkness. Here are some of the most unexpected ways the moon affects animal behavior. First, European badgers tend to raise their leg up as they pee more often when the moon is between the Earth and sun. The badgers use this move to mark their territory. Second, cats and dogs seem to get injured more often during the full moon. We don't know why they are less careful during this time. Next, lions usually hunt at night, but they will sometimes hunt during the day, especially after a full moon. For some reason, lions eat less food during moonlit nights. To make up for this less eating, they hunt during the following day. Last, the moonlight makes scorpions glow in the dark. The brighter they become, the deeper scorpions try to hide.

남 안녕하세요, 여러분. 몇몇 동물의 이상한 행동 패턴이 달의 주기와 연관되어 왔다는 것을 들어 본 적이 있습니까? 예를 들어, 보름달은 보통 야행성 동물들이 겁을 먹게 해 어둠 속으로 들어가게 할 수 있습니다. 여기달이 동물의 행동에 영향을 주는 가장 예기치 못한 방식 중 몇 가지가 있습니다. 첫째, 유럽 오소리들은 달이 지구와 태양 사이에 있을 때 오줌을 누면서 더 자주 다리를 들어 올리는 경향이 있습니다. 오소리들은 이 동작을 자신들의 영역을 표시하기 위해 사용합니다. 둘째로, 고양이와 개는 보름달이 떠 있는 동안 더 자주 다치는 것 같습니다. 우리는 왜 그것들이 이 기간 동안 덜 조심하는지 모릅니다. 다음으로, 사자들은 보통 밤에 사냥을 하지만, 그들은 때때로 낮 동안, 특히 보름달이 뜬 이후에 사냥을 할 것입니다. 어떤 이유에선지, 사자들은 달빛이 비치는 밤에 음식을 적게 먹습니다. 이렇게 적게 먹는 것을 보충하기 위해 그들은 다음날에 사냥을 합니다. 마지막으로, 달빛은 어둠 속에서 전갈이 빛나게 합니다. 전갈이 빛나면 빛날수록 그들은 더 깊이 숨으려고 합니다.

Solution

16
남자는 달의 주기 때문에 행동에 영향을 받는 몇몇 동물들의 예를 들고 있으므로, 남자가 하는 말의 주제로 가장 적절한 것은 ④ '달의 주기에 의해 영향을 받는 몇몇 동물들'이다.
① 야행성 동물의 독특한 습성
② 달이 동물들을 적게 먹도록 만드는 이유
③ 동물의 습성을 이해하는 것의 중요성
⑤ 몇몇 야행성 동물들이 생존을 위해 하는 노력

17
오소리, 고양이, 사자, 전갈은 언급되었지만, ③ '코요테'는 언급되지 않았다.

Words

link 연관시키다　lunar 달의　cycle 주기　scare 겁먹게 하다
pee 오줌을 누다　mark 표시하다　territory 영역, 영토
make up for ~을 보충하다　scorpion 전갈　glow 빛나다

---

01 ③	02 ①	03 ②	04 ⑤	05 ③
06 ②	07 ②	08 ⑤	09 ⑤	10 ④
11 ⑤	12 ⑤	13 ④	14 ④	15 ③
16 ⑤	17 ④			

01 정답 ③

Script

W Hello, students. This is the school librarian, Hannah Simpson. To help Africans living in extreme poverty, our school library is collecting old books and donating them to poor children in Africa. If you have books you don't feel like reading again, bring them to the school library. We'll wrap them with the help of student council members and send them to the African Librarian Council. If you want to donate your old books, you can bring them to the school library during lunch time. By participating in this book donation, you'll share the joy your beloved books have brought you with African children and help fight illiteracy in Africa.

여 안녕하세요, 학생 여러분. 학교 도서관 사서 Hannah Simpson입니다. 극심한 빈곤 속에서 살고 있는 아프리카 사람들을 돕기 위해서, 교내 도서관은 오래된 책을 모아서 아프리카의 가난한 아이들에게 기부하고 있습니다. 여러분이 다시 읽지 않을 것 같은 책이 있으면, 그 책들을 교내 도서관으로 가져오세요. 우리는 그것들을 학교 학생회 회원들의 도움을 받아 포장하고 아프리카 사서 협회로 보낼 것입니다. 여러분의 오래된 책들을 기부하고 싶다면, 점심시간에 그것들을 교내 도서관으로 가져올 수 있습니다. 이 도서 기부 행사에 참여하면, 여러분은 여러분이 사랑했던 책들이 여러분에게 가져다주었던 기쁨을 아프리카 어린이들과 나눌 수 있을 것이고, 아프리카의 문맹을 없애는 데 일조할 것입니다.

Solution

아프리카의 가난한 아이들을 돕기 위해서 교내 도서관에서 도서 기부 행사를 준비하고 있고 학생들에게 그 기부 행사에 참여할 것을 독려하고 있으므로, 여자가 하는 말의 목적으로 가장 적절한 것은 ③이다.

Words

poverty 빈곤, 가난　donate 기부하다　student council 학생회
illiteracy 문맹

02 정답 ①

Script

W Hey, John. What are you reading now?
M I'm reading a newspaper article about Himalayan expeditions.
W Is it about professional climbers who have conquered high peaks?
M No. It's about a cleanup expedition on Mt. Everest.
W Oh, I once heard about that. It's a kind of ecotourism, right?

M Yeah. Climbers gather trash on their way up to the peak.

W That's interesting. Tell me more about it.

M According to the article, they aim to remove 7 tons of trash this year.

W Wow! That'll help a lot to restore the environment.

M I agree. You know what? I'm going to write about the expeditions for my science class.

W That sounds like a great idea. Good luck!

여 이봐, John. 지금 무엇을 읽고 있니?

남 히말라야 원정대에 대한 신문 기사를 읽고 있어.

여 높은 봉우리들을 정복한 전문 산악인에 대한 것이니?

남 아니. 에베레스트산의 대청소 원정대에 대한 거야.

여 아, 그것에 대해 들어 본 적 있어. 일종의 생태 관광이지, 그렇지?

남 응. 산악인들이 높은 봉우리로 올라가는 도중에 쓰레기를 수거해.

여 흥미롭네. 그것에 대해 더 말해 줘.

남 그 기사에 의하면, 그들은 올해 7톤의 쓰레기를 없애는 것을 목표로 하고 있어.

여 와! 환경을 회복시키는 데 많은 도움이 되겠다.

남 나도 그렇게 생각해. 그거 알아? 나는 과학 수업 시간에 그 원정대에 대해서 글을 쓸 거야.

여 멋진 생각이야. 행운을 빌어!

에베레스트산을 올라가며 쓰레기를 수거하는 원정대에 대한 대화이므로 두 사람이 하는 말의 주제로 가장 적절한 것은 ①이다.

expedition 원정대, 원정 conquer 정복하다 peak 봉우리
cleanup 대청소 ecotourism 생태 관광(환경 훼손을 최소화하는 관광)
aim 목표로 하다 remove 없애다, 제거하다 restore 회복시키다

03 정답 ②

W Good morning, Leo.

M Good morning, Ms. Carter.

W We'll have a busy day because there's a festival nearby.

M A lot of people might visit us. How can we make use of this chance?

W We need to set up a stand outside of our store and display our bread on it.

M That's a good idea. The bakery might be too crowded for some customers to come in.

W Yes. Would you take care of the outside stand today?

M Sure. I'll set it up right away and move some bread outside.

W Thank you. It's been almost a year since you began to work for my bakery. You've worked very hard.

M Thank you for saying so. I enjoy working here.

W Thanks to you, sales have gone up a lot.

여 좋은 아침이에요, Leo.

남 좋은 아침이에요, Carter 사장님.

여 근처에서 축제가 있어서 우리는 바쁜 하루를 보낼 예정이에요.

남 많은 사람들이 우리를 방문할 수도 있겠네요. 이 기회를 어떻게 활용할 수 있을까요?

여 우리 가게 밖에 가판대를 설치하고 그 위에 빵을 진열해야 해요.

남 좋은 생각이에요. 빵집이 너무 붐벼서 일부 손님들이 들어올 수 없을지도 몰라요.

여 맞아요. 오늘 밖의 가판대를 맡아 줄래요?

남 그러죠. 지금 바로 그것을 설치하고 빵을 좀 밖으로 옮길게요.

여 고마워요. 당신이 내 빵집에서 일하기 시작한 지 거의 1년이 다 되었군요. 당신은 아주 열심히 일했어요.

남 그렇게 말해 줘서 고마워요. 나는 이곳에서 일하는 것이 즐거워요.

여 당신 덕분에 매출이 많이 올랐어요.

여자가 가게의 바깥에 가판대를 설치하고 그곳에 빵을 진열할 것을 제안하자 남자는 자신이 그것을 설치하고 빵을 옮기겠다고 말하고 여자는 남자가 자신의 제과점에서 일한 지가 거의 1년이 되었다고 하고 있으므로 두 사람의 관계를 잘 나타낸 것은 ②이다.

set up ~을 설치하다 go up 오르다

04 정답 ⑤

M Jessie, how was your family trip to the Bronx Castle?

W It was a new experience to me. Would you take a look at some photos?

M Sure.

W Here's my favorite. [Pause] The castle at the back is Bronx Castle.

M I see a flag on top of the castle, and it has a shield on it.

W That's the symbol of the Bronx family. And my family took this wagon drawn by two horses.

M That must have been a great experience.

W Yes. And this horseman with a beard was very kind.

M Was the sun very strong at that time? You're wearing a hat in the picture.

W Yes, it was. Thanks to the hat, I didn't get a sunburn.

남 Jessie. Bronx 성으로의 가족 여행은 어땠어?

여 그건 나에게 새로운 경험이었어. 이 사진들을 볼래?

남 물론이지.

여 여기 내가 가장 좋아하는 사진이 있어. [잠시 후] 뒤에 있는 성이 Bronx 성이야.

남 성의 꼭대기에 깃발이 보이는데, 그것에 방패가 있어.

여 그건 Bronx 가문의 상징이야. 그리고 우리 가족은 두 마리의 말이 끄는 이 마차를 탔어.

남 정말 멋진 경험이었겠구나.

여 응. 그리고 턱수염을 기른 이 마부는 매우 친절했어.

남 그때 태양은 아주 강했니? 사진 속에서 네가 모자를 쓰고 있네.

여 응, 그랬어. 모자 덕에 햇볕에 타지 않았어.

여자가 모자를 쓰고 있다고 했지만 그림에서는 모자를 두 손으로 들고 있으므로, 대화의 내용과 일치하지 않는 것은 ⑤이다.

flag 깃발 shield 방패 draw 끌다 beard 턱수염 sunburn 햇볕에 탐

05 정답 ③

W Dad, I'm home.

M Hi, Isabella. You don't seem to have any energy. Didn't you have anything to eat?

W No. I had a terrible stomachache, so I skipped lunch.

M My poor girl! Did you see the school nurse?

W I tried to. But there was a long line of students waiting in the nurse's office, so I went back to class.

M Why don't we see a doctor tomorrow? I'll call your homeroom teacher and tell her that you're sick.

W No, that's okay. Couldn't I just take some medicine instead?

M Sure, we have some in the first-aid kit. How about drinking some hot tea before you take the medicine?

W No, Dad. I don't really feel like having any.

M Alright. Go to your room and get some rest. I'll bring you some medicine in a few minutes.

W Thanks, Dad.

여 아빠, 저 왔어요.

남 안녕, Isabella. 너 힘이 없어 보인다. 아무것도 먹지 않았니?

여 네. 배가 몹시 아파서 점심을 걸렀어요.

남 불쌍해라! 학교 보건 선생님께는 가 봤니?

여 그러려고 했어요. 하지만 보건실에서 기다리는 학생들의 줄이 길어서, 교실로 돌아왔어요.

남 내일 병원에 가 보는 게 어떨까? 내가 네 담임 선생님께 전화해서 네가 아프다고 말할게.

여 아뇨, 괜찮아요. 대신 약을 좀 먹을 수 없을까요?

남 물론이지, 구급약 상자에 있어. 약을 먹기 전에 따뜻한 차를 마시는 게 어때?

여 아뇨, 아빠. 정말로 아무것도 먹고 싶지 않아요.

남 알았다. 네 방에 가서 좀 쉬거라. 곧 약을 좀 가져다 줄게.

여 감사해요, 아빠.

Solution

배가 아픈 여자가 학교 보건실에 기다리는 학생들이 많아서 진료를 받지 못하고 집에 돌아와 남자에게 약을 챙겨 달라고 하자 남자가 약을 가져다준다고 말했으므로, 정답은 ③이다.

Words

stomachache 복통 first-aid kit 구급약 상자

06 정답 ②

Script

[Telephone rings.]

M This is Albright Lighting. How may I help you?

W Hello, this is Serena Jones speaking. I'd like to place an order for some light bulbs.

M Okay. Which type of light bulbs do you need?

W Do you manufacture LED bulbs?

M Sure, we do. Our 5-watt LED bulbs cost $5 and our 7-watt bulbs cost $8.

W Great. I need some 5-watt and 7-watt bulbs. Ten of each, to be exact.

M We have enough 5-watt bulbs in stock, but I'm afraid we have just five 7-watt bulbs.

W Then I'll just order five of the 7-watt bulbs. And can I get them delivered by tomorrow afternoon?

M If you use an express delivery service, you can receive them by tomorrow morning. But you'll have to pay a charge of one dollar for each bulb.

W That's fine. I'll use the express delivery service.

M Alright. Please tell me your address.

[전화벨이 울린다.]

남 Albright 조명입니다. 어떻게 도와드릴까요?

여 안녕하세요, Serena Jones라고 합니다. 전구를 주문하려고요.

남 네. 어떤 종류의 전구가 필요하세요?

여 LED 전구 생산하시나요?

남 물론이죠. 5와트 LED 전구는 5달러, 7와트 전구는 8달러입니다.

여 좋아요. 저는 5와트, 7와트 전구가 필요해요. 정확하게 각각 10개씩이요.

남 5와트 전구는 충분히 재고가 있는데, 죄송하지만 7와트 전구는 5개밖에 없습니다.

여 그럼 7와트 전구는 5개만 주문할게요. 그리고 내일 오후까지 받을 수 있을까요?

남 특급 배달 서비스를 이용하시면, 내일 오전까지 받으실 수 있습니다. 그러나 각각의 전구에 대해 1달러를 지불하셔야 해요.

여 좋아요. 그 특급 배달 서비스를 이용하겠습니다.

남 알겠습니다. 주소를 알려 주세요.

Solution

5달러인 5와트 전구를 10개, 8달러인 7와트 전구를 5개 주문하기로 하고 각각의 전구(총 15개)에 대해 특급 배달 배송료로 1달러를 지불해야 하므로, 여자가 지불할 금액은 ② '105달러'이다.

Words

place an order for ~을 주문하다 light bulb 전구
manufacture 생산하다 delivery service 배달 서비스

07 정답 ②

Script

W Henry, you're going on the school camping trip this weekend, right?

M I'm sorry I can't.

W Why not? Do you have an assignment to finish?

M No, I don't.

W You were excited about it the other day, saying you had the camping gear ready.

M Right. But my mom is sick. She needs a helping hand.

W You're a good son. But your father can help her while you're at camp.

M Unfortunately, he is visiting my Grandma at her home. He'll be back next Monday.

W That's too bad. So you should take care of mom for the weekend.

M That's right.

W I hope your mom can get well soon.

M Thank you.

여 Henry, 너 이번 주말에 학교 캠핑 여행 갈 거지, 맞지?

남 미안하지만 갈 수 없어.

여 왜 못 가는 거야? 끝내야 할 과제가 있어?

남 아니, 그렇지 않아.

여 며칠 전에 캠핑 장비를 준비했다고 말하면서 신나 했었잖아.

남 맞아. 하지만 엄마가 편찮으셔. 엄마는 도움의 손길이 필요해.

여 넌 좋은 아들이구나. 하지만 네가 캠프에 있는 동안 네 아버지께서 어머니를 도울 수 있잖아.

남 유감스럽게도, 아빠는 우리 할머니 댁을 방문 중이야. 다음 주 월요일에 돌아오실 거야.

여 안됐구나. 그래서 너는 주말 동안 엄마를 돌봐 드려야 하는구나.

남 맞아.

여 너희 엄마가 빨리 나으셨으면 좋겠어.

남 고마워.

Solution

남자는 아버지가 할머니 댁에 가 계신 동안 아픈 어머니를 돌봐야 하기 때문에 캠핑 여행에 갈 수 없다고 말했으므로 정답은 ②이다.

Words

assignment 과제 the other day 며칠 전에, 요전날
camping gear 캠핑 장비 helping hand 도움의 손길
get well 회복되다

08 정답 ⑤

Script

W Joseph, do you know that Whitney Gym will open this Friday?

M Of course, Mom. I've been looking forward to it.

W It's on Cherry Street, so it's very close to our home. You can even walk there.

M Right. I'll play basketball with my friends at the gym this Friday.

W Then did you make a reservation already? I heard they have a reservation system.

M Sure. The reservation system is a first-come, first-served basis.

W How much is to play basketball?

M It's 10 dollars per hour. We rented a court for two hours.

W Does the fee include using the shower facilities?

M Of course. I saw pictures, and the shower facilities look great.

W I hope you have a good time at the new gym.

남 Joseph, Whitney 체육관이 이번 주 금요일에 문을 여는 거 아니?

남 물론이죠, 엄마. 저는 그것을 고대해 왔어요.

여 Cherry 거리에 있어서 그곳은 우리 집에서 아주 가까워. 너는 그곳에 걸어갈 수도 있어.

남 맞아요. 이번 주 금요일에 친구들과 체육관에서 농구를 할 거예요.

여 그럼 벌써 예약을 한 거니? 그곳은 예약 시스템이 있다고 들었어.

남 물론이죠. 예약 시스템은 선착순이에요.

여 농구를 하는 데 얼마니?

남 시간당 10달러예요. 우리는 코트를 두 시간 빌렸어요.

여 사용료에는 샤워 시설을 이용하는 것도 포함되어 있니?

남 물론이죠. 사진을 봤는데, 샤워 시설이 훌륭해 보여요.

여 새로운 체육관에서 좋은 시간 보내길 바란다.

Solution

위치, 예약 시스템, 사용료, 샤워 시설은 언급되었지만, ⑤ '운영 시간'에 대해서는 언급되지 않았다.

Words

first-come, first-served basis 선착순 fee 사용료

09 정답 ⑤

Script

M If you've always imagined running your own business someday, the One-Dollar Store can make your dreams a reality. The One-Dollar Store sells over 20,000 household items, including frozen foods and potted plants, all for a uniform price — just one dollar. And it retains over 900 franchises nationwide to provide easy access to customers. According to the latest US economic report, the One-Dollar Store currently holds a 60 percent market share of household items in the United States and continues to increase its competitive strength each year. If you want to become the owner of a One-Dollar Store franchise, you are required to make a minimum cash deposit of $60,000 in advance and submit the request form to our website, www.one-dollarstore.com.

남 여러분이 언젠가 자신의 사업체를 경영하는 것을 늘 상상해 왔다면, One-Dollar Store가 여러분의 꿈을 현실로 만들어 줄 수 있습니다. One-Dollar Store는 냉동식품과 화분에 심는 식물을 포함해서 20,000종 이상의 가정용품을 모두 균일 가격인 단 1달러에 판매합니다. 그리고 고객들이 쉽게 접근할 수 있게 하기 위해 전국에 900개 이상의 가맹점을 보유하고 있습니다. 최근의 미국 경제 보고서에 따르면, One-Dollar Store는 미국 내의 가정용품 분야에서 현재 60퍼센트의 시장 점유율을 차지하고 있으며 매년 계속해서 경쟁력이 강화되고 있습니다. One-Dollar Store의 가맹점의 경영주가 되기를 원하시면, 여러분은 최소 60,000달러의 예치금을 선불로 내야 하고, 우리 웹사이트인 www.one-dollarstore.com으로 신청서를 제출하셔야 합니다.

Solution

One-Dollar Store의 가맹점 가입을 원하면 최소 60,000달러의 예치금을 선불로 내야 한다고 했으므로, 담화의 내용과 일치하지 않는 것은 ⑤ '가맹점 가입을 위한 별도의 예치금은 없다.'이다.

Words

run 경영하다 household item 가정용품 uniform price 균일 가격
retain 보유[유지]하다 franchise 가맹점 access 접근
market share 시장 점유율 deposit 예치금 submit 제출하다

10 정답 ④

Script

M Honey, what are you looking at on the Internet?

W I'm shopping for a chair for Sue. Her chair is very worn-out.

M Let's pick one together. What price range do you have in mind?

W I don't want to spend more than $160 on the chair.

M Okay. What about an armrest? I think she needs one.

W Of course. And a headrest too?
M Well, I don't think so. It's necessary only for those who work at their desks for a long time.
W I see. Then we'd better choose one without a headrest.
M Yes. Now we have two options to choose from. What color would Sue like?
W She'd like red.
M Then this is the chair for Sue. Let's order it now.
W Okay.

남 여보, 인터넷에서 뭘 보고 있어요?
여 Sue를 위한 의자를 쇼핑하고 있어요. 그 애의 의자는 매우 낡았거든요.
남 하나를 같이 고르죠. 당신은 어떤 가격대를 생각하고 있나요?
여 그 의자에 160달러 넘게 쓰고 싶지 않아요.
남 알겠어요. 팔걸이는 어때요? 그 애가 그것을 필요로 할 것 같아요.
여 물론이죠. 그리고 머리 받침대도 필요하겠죠?
남 글쎄, 난 그렇게 생각하지 않아요. 그것은 책상에서 오래 일하는 사람들에게만 필요해요.
여 그렇군요. 그럼 머리 받침대 없는 걸로 골라야겠네요.
남 그래요. 이제 우리는 고를 수 있는 두 가지 선택 사항이 있어요. Sue는 어떤 색을 좋아할까요?
여 그 애는 빨간색을 좋아할 거예요.
남 그럼 이것이 Sue를 위한 의자네요. 그것을 지금 주문하죠.
여 알았어요.

Solution
160달러를 넘지 않으면서 팔걸이가 있고 머리 받침대는 없는 빨간색 의자를 주문하기로 했으므로, 두 사람이 주문할 의자는 ④이다.

Words
range 범위 armrest 팔걸이 headrest 머리 받침대

11 정답 ⑤

Script

M Do you have a dog?
W No, I don't. But I'd like to have one someday.
M Actually, my dog gave birth to two baby dogs. Do you want one?
W That'd be great. I finally have my own dog.

남 개를 키우고 있나요?
여 아니, 없어요. 하지만 언젠가 한 마리를 갖고 싶어요.
남 사실, 우리 개가 아기 강아지 두 마리를 낳았어요. 한 마리를 원하세요?
여 그거 좋겠네요. 내가 드디어 내 개를 키우는군요.

Solution
언젠가 개를 키우고 싶다고 말한 여자에게 남자는 자신의 개가 낳은 새끼 중 한 마리를 키우기 원하는지 묻고 있고, 이에 대한 수락이나 거절의 응답이 자연스러우므로, ⑤ '그거 좋겠네요. 내가 드디어 내 개를 키우는군요.'가 여자의 응답으로 가장 적절하다.
① 물론이죠. 개들은 친구를 갖는 것을 좋아해요.
② 아, 강아지들이 모두 똑같아 보이네요.
③ 네. 제가 강아지 돌보는 법을 가르쳐 줄게요.
④ 고마워요. 내 아기가 그 장난감 개를 좋아할 거예요.

Words
someday 언젠가 give birth to ~을 낳다

12 정답 ⑤

Script

W How are you doing on the sales report I asked for this morning?
M Oh, I'm really sorry, director. I forgot about it while I was doing other work.
W Richard, I'm disappointed in you. It seems like you didn't pay attention to what I said.
M I'll make sure a problem like this never happens again.

여 제가 오늘 아침에 요청한 판매 보고서는 어떻게 되어가고 있나요?
남 오, 정말 죄송합니다. 부장님. 다른 일을 하느라 그것을 잊어버렸어요.
여 Richard, 당신에게 실망했어요. 제 말에 주의를 기울이지 않은 것 같군요.
남 이런 문제가 다시는 일어나지 않도록 하겠습니다.

Solution
직장 상사인 여자는 자신이 요청한 판매 보고서를 잊고 하지 않은 남자에게 실망했음을 표현하고 있으므로, ⑤ '이런 문제가 다시는 일어나지 않도록 하겠습니다.'가 남자의 응답으로 가장 적절하다.
① 부장님께서 그에게 분명하고 큰 소리로 말씀하셔야 합니다.
② 저는 판매 보고서를 처리하느라 하루 종일 바빴습니다.
③ 짜증 내지 마세요. 제가 요청한 보고서 마무리만 해 주세요.
④ 부장님께서는 회계 보고서도 조만간 완성하셔야 합니다.

Words
sales report 판매 보고서 director (회사의) 부장, 관리자
disappointed 실망한
pay attention to ~에 주의를 기울이다, ~에 신경 쓰다

13 정답 ④

Script

M Alice, do you know the scope of the history mid-term exam?
W Yes. We should study from chapter 1 to 5.
M Thank you. I didn't hear it because I missed the previous class due to the flu.
W Are you okay now?
M Fortunately, yes. I think I need to study a lot more material than I expected.
W Yeah. We need to put a lot of time into preparing for the exam.
M I'm a little worried about studying five whole chapters.
W Don't worry. You can do it if you start preparing it right away.
M Do you really think so?
W Absolutely. Do you want me to lend you my notebook?
M Yes, please. Can I borrow it now?
W No problem. I'll go and get it from my locker.

남 Alice, 역사 과목 중간고사의 범위를 아니?
여 응. 1장부터 5장까지 공부해야 해.
남 고마워. 나는 독감으로 이전 수업을 놓쳐서 그것을 듣지 못했어.
여 이제 괜찮아?
남 다행히, 괜찮아. 내가 예상했던 것보다 훨씬 많은 내용을 공부해야 할 것

같아.

여 그래. 우리는 시험 준비에 많은 시간을 쏟아야 할 필요가 있어.

남 난 다섯 장 전체를 공부하는 것이 약간 걱정돼.

여 걱정하지 마. 네가 바로 그것을 준비하기 시작하면 그것을 할 수 있어.

남 정말 그렇게 생각해?

여 그렇고말고. 너는 내 공책을 빌리기 원하니?

남 응, 부탁해. 그것을 지금 빌릴 수 있을까?

여 그럼. 내가 가서 사물함에서 그것을 가져올게.

독감 때문에 이전 수업을 놓친 남자가 여자의 공책을 빌릴 수 있는지 묻고 있으므로, 이에 대한 수락 또는 거절의 대답이 자연스러우므로, ④ '그럼. 내가 가서 사물함에서 그것을 가져올게.'가 여자의 응답으로 가장 적절하다.

① 맞아. 그것은 내게 큰 도움이었어.
② 그래. 함께 가서 새 공책을 사자.
③ 미안해. 그것은 내가 빌리고 싶어 하는 게 아니야.
⑤ 물론이지. 내가 빌렸던 공책을 가져왔어.

scope 범위 mid-term exam 중간고사 chapter (책의) 장
previous 이전의 flu 독감 prepare 준비하다

14 정답 ④

M Good morning, Tina. You came to school early today.

W Good morning, Mr. Roberts. Actually, I usually get to school around 7 o'clock.

M Really? Is there any special reason you've become such an early bird?

W At the start of my senior year, I made up my mind to wake up early and study for an extra hour in the morning.

M It's nice to see a student with such a good work ethic.

W Thanks. By the way, could you do me a favor, Mr. Roberts?

M Sure. What can I do for you?

W Sometimes when I arrive at school early, I can't get inside.

M How come?

W If I get here too early, the front door is usually locked. Could you ask someone to open it before 7 o'clock?

M No problem. I'll talk about your situation to the school janitor.

남 안녕, Tina. 오늘 학교에 일찍 왔구나.

여 안녕하세요, Roberts 선생님. 사실 저는 보통 7시쯤에 학교에 와요.

남 정말? 이렇게 일찍 등교하는 사람이 된 특별한 이유가 있니?

여 3학년이 시작될 때, 일찍 일어나서 아침에 1시간 더 공부하겠다고 마음먹었어요.

남 아주 좋은 근면성을 가진 학생을 만나니 기쁘구나.

여 감사해요. 그런데 부탁 하나 들어 주시겠어요, Roberts 선생님?

남 물론이지. 뭘 도와줄까?

여 가끔 제가 학교에 일찍 오면, 전 안으로 들어갈 수 없어요.

남 왜지?

여 제가 너무 일찍 오면, 학교 정문이 보통 닫혀 있어요. 7시 전에 정문을 열도록 누군가에게 요청해 주실 수 있으세요?

남 문제없어. 너의 상황을 학교 관리인에게 말해 둘게.

여자는 아침 일찍 학교에 오면 보통 학교 정문이 닫혀 있어서 들어갈 수 없기 때문에 7시 이전에 문이 열릴 수 있게 요청해 달라고 남자에게 부탁하고 있으므로, ④ '문제없어. 너의 상황을 학교 관리인에게 말해 둘게.'가 남자의 응답으로 가장 적절하다.

① 미안하지만 오후 7시 이후론 학교에서 공부할 수 없단다.
② 나는 네가 좀 더 일찍 와서 더 열심히 공부하길 바란다.
③ 알겠어. 다른 학생들도 더 일찍 학교에 오도록 독려하게.
⑤ 부모님께 학교까지 너를 태워다 주시도록 요청하는 게 어떠니?

early bird 일찍 일어나는 사람, 정각보다 일찍 오는 사람
senior year 최고 학년
make up one's mind to do ~하기로 결심하다 work ethic 근면성
do ~ a favor ~의 부탁을 들어 주다 How come? 왜?
janitor 관리인, 수위

15 정답 ③

W Mr. Parker is staying at the Pacific Guam Hotel and is planning to go on a city tour today with his wife and little daughter. He expects to walk quite a distance around the city with his daughter, so he decides to use the baby carriage rental service, which is freely given to guests of the hotel. Dropping by the baby carriage rental office, he asks if there are any baby carriages available now. Luckily, the clerk says there are many carriages available to Mr. Parker and he can use one until 6 o'clock. But Mr. Parker is planning to come back after dinner and he thinks he won't be able to return the baby carriage on time. In this situation, what would Mr. Parker most likely say to the clerk?

Mr. Parker I'm sorry, but can I return this carriage after 6:00?

여 Mr. Parker는 Pacific Guam 호텔에 머물면서 그의 부인과 어린 딸과 함께 도시 관광을 가려고 계획하고 있습니다. 그의 딸과 도시 주변 상당한 거리를 걸어야 할 것을 예상해서, 그는 호텔 손님들에게 무료로 제공되는 유모차 대여 서비스를 이용하기로 결심합니다. 유모차 대여소에 잠깐 들러서 그는 현재 이용 가능한 유모차가 있는지 묻습니다. 운 좋게 대여소 직원은 Mr. Parker에게 이용 가능한 유모차가 많이 있고 그가 한 유모차를 6시까지 이용할 수 있다고 말합니다. 그러나 Mr. Parker는 저녁 식사 후에 돌아올 계획이고 그는 제시간에 유모차를 반납할 수 없을 것이라고 생각합니다. 이런 상황에서 Mr. Parker는 직원에게 뭐라고 말할 것 같은가요?

Mr. Parker 죄송하지만, 이 유모차를 6시 이후에 반납해도 될까요?

Mr. Parker는 유모차를 빌릴 수 있지만 6시까지 반납을 해야 하는데, 저녁 식사까지 하고 호텔로 돌아올 계획이어서 제시간에 유모차를 반납하지 못할 상황이므로, 이러한 상황에서 Mr. Parker가 직원에게 할 말로 가장 적절한 것은 ③ '죄송하지만, 이 유모차를 6시 이후에 반납해도 될까요?'이다.

① 도시 관광을 위한 시내 지도를 주시겠어요?
② 내일 사용할 유모차를 예약하고 싶습니다.
④ 한 시간 더 유모차를 이용하게 해 주셔서 감사합니다.
⑤ 두 대의 유모차를 사용하는 데 추가 요금이 있나요?

baby carriage 유모차 rental service 대여 서비스
drop by ~에 잠깐 들르다 on time 정시에, 제시간에

16 정답 ⑤   17 정답 ④

Script

M As many people are now suffering from headaches, skin problems, and various kinds of allergies inside buildings, they are gradually becoming more aware of sick building syndrome. So today I'd like to talk about what sick building syndrome is and how we should handle it. Sick building syndrome refers to a number of diseases that occur as a result of exposure to harmful air pollutants at a home or work building. Artificial pollutants such as dust, construction materials, chemical compounds, and toxic gases can all deteriorate indoor air quality. Bacteria and mold are "natural," but they are also major biological pollutants in the indoor air. If these indoor air pollutants are not carefully managed, they can cause sick building syndrome. To deal with this problem, you should improve the quality of air in your buildings by ventilating them well, using natural air fresheners and cleansers against indoor air pollutants, and growing live plants.

남 현재 많은 사람들이 건물 안에서 두통, 피부병, 다양한 종류의 알레르기 질환으로 고통받으면서 그들은 점차 새집증후군에 대해 더 많이 인식하게 되고 있습니다. 그래서 오늘 저는 새집증후군이 무엇인지 그리고 어떻게 대처해야 할지를 말씀드리겠습니다. 새집증후군은 가정이나 직장 건물에서 유해한 공기 오염 물질에 노출된 결과로 발생하는 많은 질병을 가리킵니다. 먼지, 건축 재료, 화학 화합물, 유독가스와 같은 인위적인 오염 물질들은 전부 실내 공기의 질을 악화시킬 수 있습니다. 박테리아와 곰팡이는 '자연적인' 것이지만 이것들 역시 실내 공기에서 주요한 생물학적인 오염 물질입니다. 이런 실내 공기 오염 물질이 주의 깊게 관리되지 않으면 그것들은 새집증후군을 일으킬 수 있습니다. 이 문제에 대처하기 위해서, 여러분은 건물을 잘 환기시키고, 실내 공기 오염 물질을 예방하는 천연 공기 방향제나 세제를 사용하고, 식물을 기르면서 실내 공기의 질을 높여야 합니다.

Solution

16
남자는 실내 공기가 오염되면서 발생하는 다양한 질병을 가리키는 새집증후군과 그것에 대처할 수 있는 방안에 대해서 말하고 있으므로, 남자가 하는 말의 주제로 가장 적절한 것은 ⑤ '실내 공기 오염 관련 질병과 대처법'이다.

① 실내 공기 오염의 원인
② 대기 오염이 인체에 미치는 영향
③ 실내 공기의 질을 측정하는 방법
④ 실내 공기 오염 물질과 질병의 상관관계

17
먼지, 유독가스, 박테리아, 곰팡이는 오염 물질로 언급되었지만, ④ '바이러스'는 언급되지 않았다.

Words

allergy 알레르기 sick building syndrome 새집증후군
refer to ~을 가리키다, ~을 나타내다 pollutant 오염 물질
deteriorate 악화시키다 mold 곰팡이 ventilate 환기시키다
air freshener 공기 방향제

● 실전 모의고사 15회   본문 148쪽

01 ④	02 ②	03 ⑤	04 ④	05 ⑤
06 ③	07 ③	08 ④	09 ⑤	10 ②
11 ④	12 ④	13 ④	14 ①	15 ⑤
16 ③	17 ③			

01 정답 ④

Script

W The most common saying about eating meals healthily is "Eat like a king at breakfast, a prince at lunch and a beggar at dinner." This saying may be based on the fact the amount of calories you consume from each meal should balance with the amount of your activity. In other words, because you become less active and burn fewer calories as the day goes by, you should control your weight by gradually lessening the intake of food. But unfortunately, that isn't true. Your body continuously burns calories day and night — even while you sleep. So I recommend you not to follow this common saying. You should eat the same amount of nutritionally dense foods at each meal in a balanced way.

여 건강하게 식사하는 것에 대한 가장 흔한 격언은 '아침은 왕처럼, 점심은 왕자처럼, 그리고 저녁은 거지처럼 먹으라.'는 것입니다. 이 격언은 여러분이 각각의 식사에서 먹는 칼로리의 양은 여러분의 활동량과 균형을 이뤄야 한다는 사실에 바탕을 둔 것인지도 모릅니다. 다시 말해 하루의 시간이 지나면서 여러분의 활동량은 줄어들고 더 적은 칼로리를 소비하기 때문에, 여러분은 음식의 섭취를 점차 줄이면서 여러분의 체중을 조절해야 한다는 것입니다. 그러나 불행히도, 이것은 사실이 아닙니다. 여러분의 몸은 밤낮으로 쉬지 않고, 심지어 자는 동안에도, 계속해서 칼로리를 태웁니다. 그래서 저는 여러분에게 이 속언을 따르지 말기를 권합니다. 여러분은 균형 있게 매 끼니마다 영양적으로 밀집된 동일한 양의 음식을 먹어야만 합니다.

Solution

여자는 아침은 왕처럼, 점심은 왕자처럼, 저녁은 거지처럼 먹어야 한다는 격언은 잘못된 것이며, 우리 몸은 밤낮으로 쉬지 않고 칼로리를 소비하고 있으므로 매 끼니 마다 영양가 많은 동일한 양의 균형 잡힌 식사를 해야 한다고 주장하고 있으므로, 여자가 하는 말의 목적으로 가장 적절한 것은 ④이다.

Words

consume 먹다 gradually 점차적으로 lessen 줄이다 intake 섭취
nutritionally 영양적으로 dense 밀도가 높은, 빽빽한

02 정답 ②

Script

M Oh, no. According to these figures, our company's going to be bankrupt soon.
W I think it's time to make a big decision.
M What decision are you talking about?
W We need to reduce the size of the company.

M Do you mean that we should lay off some of our employees to solve our financial problems?

W Unfortunately, yes. Because labor costs are so high, we need to cut down on them urgently.

M But the employees at this company are like a family. We should stay together.

W I know how you feel. But if our company goes bankrupt, they will all lose their jobs.

M What if all employees agree to a salary reduction to save the company?

W Isn't that too idealistic?

M I don't think so. If we share the burden of this financial crisis together, we can keep our company profitable.

남 오, 안 돼. 이 수치들에 의하면, 우리 회사는 곧 파산할 거예요.

여 제 생각에는 중요한 결정을 내려야 할 때인 것 같아요.

남 무슨 결정을 말씀하시는 거죠?

여 우리는 회사의 규모를 줄일 필요가 있어요.

남 재정적인 문제를 해결하기 위해서 직원들 중 일부를 해고해야 한다는 말씀이세요?

여 불행하지만, 그래요. 인건비가 너무 높아서 우리는 긴급하게 그것을 줄일 필요가 있어요.

남 그러나 이 회사의 직원들은 거의 가족이나 다름없어요. 우리는 함께 해야 해요.

여 어떤 마음인지 알겠어요. 하지만 회사가 파산하면 그들 모두가 직장을 잃을 거예요.

남 모든 직원들이 회사를 구하기 위해 감봉에 동의한다면요?

여 너무 이상적이지 않나요?

남 저는 그렇게 생각하지 않아요. 우리가 함께 이 재정 위기를 분담한다면, 우리는 우리 회사를 수익성 있게 유지할 수 있어요.

Solution

남자는 인건비를 절감하기 위해 일부 직원들을 해고하자는 여자의 의견에 반대하면서 회사의 자금난을 극복하기 위해서는 모두의 월급을 줄여서 재정 위기를 분담해야 한다고 주장하고 있으므로, 남자의 의견으로 가장 적절한 것은 ②이다.

Words

bankrupt 파산한 lay off ~을 해고하다 labor cost 인건비
cut down on ~을 줄이다 urgently 긴급하게
salary reduction 감봉, 임금 삭감
share the burden of ~을 분담하다

03 정답 ⑤

Script

[Knocking Sound]

W Come in. *[Pause]* Oh, you must be Mr. Cruise, Tom's father.

M That's right. Thank you for meeting with me.

W You're welcome. It's part of my job.

M Tom likes you a lot.

W Oh, really? I like him too. He's very funny.

M Thank you for saying so.

W His nurse said he doesn't cry any longer when he gets a shot.

M Good for him. Well, Tom said that he will be able to go

home soon. Is that right?

W That's right. He's much better. I think I can let him go home this Friday.

M Sounds great. I'd better get going now. Thanks for this good news.

W No problem. I'll see you again soon.

[노크 소리]

여 들어오세요. *[잠시 후]* 아, 당신은 Tom의 아버지인 Cruise 씨가 맞죠.

남 맞아요. 저를 만나 주셔서 고마워요.

여 천만에요. 이것은 제 일의 부분인걸요.

남 Tom이 선생님을 많이 좋아해요.

여 오, 정말요? 저도 그를 좋아해요. 그 애는 매우 재미있어요.

남 그렇게 말해 주셔서 고마워요.

여 그의 간호사가 말하길 그 애가 주사를 맞을 때 더 이상 울지 않는다고 하더군요.

남 그에게 잘된 일이죠. 음, Tom이 말하길 자신이 곧 집으로 갈 수 있을 거라고 말하더군요. 그게 맞나요?

여 맞아요. 그 애가 훨씬 좋아졌어요. 이번 주 금요일에 그를 집으로 가게 할 수 있다고 생각해요.

남 좋네요. 지금 전 가봐야겠어요. 이 좋은 소식 감사드려요.

여 고맙기는요. 조만간 다시 뵐게요.

Solution

남자가 자신의 아들인 Tom이 곧 퇴원할 수 있는지를 묻자 여자는 Tom이 이번 금요일에 퇴원할 수 있을 거라고 말하고 있으므로 두 사람의 관계를 가장 잘 나타낸 것은 ⑤이다.

Words

get a shot 주사를 맞다

04 정답 ④

Script

W Steve, I heard you spent a summer vacation at Pearl Island. How was it?

M It was great. Take a look at this picture. *[Pause]* Isn't it beautiful?

W The lighthouse on the hill is very tall.

M The lighthouse is a tourist attraction on the island.

W The seagulls in the sky are cute. The scenery looks very impressive.

M Right. Do you see the small house next to the lighthouse?

W Is it for the lighthouse worker?

M Yes. Look at the chairs down the hill. My wife and I spent so much time sitting on these two chairs.

W Sounds great. The tree next to the chairs makes the scenery look even better.

M I think so, too. I'll never forget the time on the island.

W I hope I can go there on vacation in the future.

여 Steve. 당신이 Pearl 섬에서 여름 휴가를 보냈다고 들었어요. 어땠어요?

남 정말 좋았어요. 이 사진 좀 봐요. *[잠시 후]* 아름답지 않나요?

여 언덕 위에 있는 등대가 매우 크군요.

남 그 등대는 그 섬에서 관광 명소예요.

여 하늘에 있는 갈매기가 귀엽네요. 풍경이 매우 인상적으로 보여요.

남 맞아요. 등대 옆에 있는 작은 집이 보이나요?
여 그것은 등대에서 일하는 근로자를 위한 건가요?
남 맞아요. 언덕 아래의 의자들을 보세요. 제 아내와 저는 이 두 의자에 앉아서 아주 많은 시간을 보냈어요.
여 멋지게 들리네요. 의자들 옆에 있는 나무가 경치를 훨씬 더 좋게 보이도록 만드네요.
남 저도 그렇게 생각해요. 저는 그 섬에서의 시간을 결코 잊지 않을 거예요.
여 저도 앞으로 휴가를 보내러 그곳에 갈 수 있었으면 좋겠어요.

언덕 아래 두 의자가 있다고 했지만 그림에서는 벤치가 하나 있으므로, 대화의 내용과 일치하지 않는 것은 ④이다.

lighthouse 등대 tourist attraction 관광 명소 seagull 갈매기
scenery 경치 impressive 인상적인

05 정답 ⑤

W Keith! Long time, no see.
M Hi, Jane. What are you doing in the library?
W I'm here to copy some pages from the history book I borrowed.
M Do you know you need a copy card to use the copy machine in this library?
W No, I didn't. Can I borrow yours if you have one?
M Sure, here it is. Anyway, what is the topic of the book you're studying?
W It's a collection of stories of those who fought for Korean independence from Japanese colonial rule.
M Sounds interesting. Can you make an extra copy of the stories for me?
W No problem. I'll have them ready for you in a few minutes.
M I appreciate it.

여 Keith! 오랜만이야.
남 안녕, Jane. 도서관에서 뭐 하고 있니?
여 대출한 역사책에서 몇 쪽 복사하려고 여기에 왔어.
남 이 도서관에서 복사기를 사용하려면 복사 카드가 필요한 거 알고 있니?
여 아니, 난 몰랐는데. 혹시 복사 카드 있으면 좀 빌릴 수 있을까?
남 그래, 여기에 있어. 그런데 네가 공부하고 있는 책의 주제가 뭐니?
여 그것은 일본의 식민지 지배하에서 대한민국 독립을 위해 싸웠던 분들에 대한 이야기 모음집이야.
남 흥미로운데. 나에게 그 이야기를 한 부 더 복사해서 나한테 줄 수 있어?
여 문제없어. 금방 너를 위해 그것들을 준비할게.
남 고마워.

여자는 남자에게 복사 카드를 빌려 달라고 했고, 남자는 여자에게, 여자가 대출한 이야기 모음집의 내용을 한 부 복사해 달라고 부탁했으므로 정답은 ⑤이다.

copy card 복사 카드 independence 독립
colonial rule 식민지 지배 appreciate 고마워하다, 감사하다

06 정답 ③

M Welcome to Hafa Tours. How may I help you?
W I'd like to reserve a hotel room on Emerald Island.
M Alright. When and how long are you going to stay?
W I'll arrive on August 15th and stay for two nights.
M Do you have a particular hotel in mind?
W No. I just want a hotel room with a nice ocean view.
M Then, the Keytings Hotel would be perfect for you. It's right on the beach.
W Good. How much is the nightly rate?
M A room with meals provided costs $300 a night. Without meals, it's just $250 a night.
W Please reserve a room without the meals. Here's my credit card.
M Oh, you have a card associated with our company. You can get a 10 percent discount off the total price.
W That's fantastic.

남 Hafa 여행사에 오신 것을 환영합니다. 어떻게 도와드릴까요?
여 Emerald 섬의 호텔 방을 예약하고 싶어요.
남 좋습니다. 언제 그리고 얼마 동안 머무르실 건가요?
여 8월 15일에 도착해서 이틀 밤을 묵을 예정이에요.
남 마음에 두신 특정한 호텔이 있으신가요?
여 아뇨. 그냥 멋진 바다 전망의 호텔 방을 원해요.
남 그러면, Keytings Hotel이 손님께 완벽하겠네요. 바로 해안에 있어요.
여 좋아요. 1박 숙박료가 어떻게 되나요?
남 식사가 제공되는 방은 1박에 300달러입니다. 식사가 제공되지 않는 방은 1박에 250달러입니다.
여 식사가 포함되지 않는 방으로 예약해 주세요. 여기 제 신용카드가 있습니다.
남 아, 저희 회사와 제휴된 카드를 가지고 계시는군요. 전체 금액에서 10퍼센트 할인을 받으실 수 있어요.
여 아주 좋네요.

여자는 식사가 포함되지 않은 1박 숙박료가 250달러인 호텔 방에서 이틀 밤을 머물기로 했는데, 여행사와 제휴된 카드가 있어 전체 가격에서 10퍼센트 할인되므로, 여자가 지불할 금액은 ③ '450달러'이다.

have ~ in mind ~을 염두에 두다 nightly rate 숙박료
associated with ~와 제휴된

07 정답 ③

M Mom, I'm home.
W Oh, Dave. You are home early. Didn't you say you'd be late because of your soccer club practice?
M I did. Unfortunately, it was cancelled.
W Oh, you must have been disappointed.
M Yes, I was.
W You were excited about practicing with the new soccer goalpost on the grass field.
M That's right. Furthermore, it's a perfect day for practice

today.

W Yes. So what was the matter?

M Our coach was absent today. He got the flu.

W That's too bad. I hope he'll get well soon.

M He will. He promised he'd make sure not to cancel next week's practice.

W I hope so.

남 엄마, 저 왔어요.

여 오, Dave. 집에 일찍 왔구나. 축구 동아리 연습 때문에 늦을 거라고 하지 않았어?

남 그랬죠. 아쉽게도 그게 취소되었어요.

여 아, 실망했겠구나.

남 네, 실망했어요.

여 잔디 구장에서 새 축구 골대를 가지고 연습하는 것에 대해 신나 있었잖아.

남 맞아요. 게다가, 오늘은 연습하기에 완벽한 날이에요.

여 그래. 그러면 뭐가 문제였니?

남 우리 코치 선생님이 오늘 결근하셨어요. 그 분이 독감에 걸렸거든요.

여 안됐구나. 그분이 빨리 완쾌되기를 바란다.

남 그럴 거예요. 선생님이 다음 주 연습은 반드시 취소하지 않겠다고 약속했어요.

여 그러길 바라.

Solution

남자는 축구 동아리 연습이 예정되어 있었지만 코치 선생님이 독감 때문에 결근해서 연습이 취소되었다고 말했으므로 정답은 ③이다.

Words

goalpost 골대 grass field 잔디 구장

08 정답 ④

Script

W Mark, have you seen the Wonder Circus?

M Several times. Actually, I'm a big fan of that circus.

W I heard they have a new theme every year.

M That's right. This year's theme is *The Sons of the Sun*.

W Then the circus will feature songs, dances, and performances based on that theme?

M Yes. The performance is incredible.

W I also heard that the circus is famous for its large scale of about 1,000 seats and a big stage.

M Yes. If you see it in person, you'll be impressed.

W I want to see it. Well, the tickets are a little expensive. It's 70 dollars for an adult.

M I agree with you, but it's worth seeing.

W Do you know the performance dates for this year?

M It'll start on June 10th and last for two months.

W I'll make sure to see the circus this year.

여 Mark, Wonder Circus 봤어?

남 몇 번 봤어. 사실, 난 그 서커스의 열렬한 팬이야.

여 그 서커스는 매년 새로운 주제가 있다고 들었어.

남 맞아. 올해의 주제는 '태양의 후예'야.

여 그럼 그 서커스가 그 주제에 맞게 노래, 춤, 공연을 특색있게 하는 거고?

남 그래. 공연은 정말 대단해.

여 그 서커스가 약 1,000석 정도의 큰 규모와 큰 무대로 유명하다고 또한

들었어.

남 맞아. 직접 그것을 보면 너는 감명을 받을 거야.

여 그것을 보고 싶어. 음, 표가 약간 비싸네. 성인 한 명당 70달러이니까.

남 나도 네 말에 동의하지만 그건 볼만해.

여 올해의 공연 날짜를 아니?

남 그건 6월 10일에 시작해서 두 달 동안 지속될 거야.

여 난 올해 서커스를 반드시 봐야겠어.

Solution

공연 주제, 객석 규모, 입장료, 공연 기간은 언급되었으나, ④ '공연장 위치'에 대해서는 언급되지 않았다.

Words

theme 주제 performance 공연 feature 특색을 이루다 scale 규모
impressed 감명을 받은 last 지속되다

09 정답 ⑤

Script

M Hello, I'm Harvey Smith, your science teacher. I'm going to make a brief announcement about the 18th annual Science Book Report Contest. Our high school holds this writing contest every year in celebration of Dr. Sparrow's birthday. I'm sure most of you have heard of Dr. Sparrow — he was one of the most influential physicists in the history of our country. All students except for 3rd graders can participate in the contest. Participants should read a science book in advance, and on the day of the contest they'll write a book report. Students will be unable to refer to the book while they are writing. The contest will be held on the morning of June 15th in the school library. After the contest we'll choose the winners and display their names on the school bulletin board on June 20th. If you want to take part in the contest, please come to my office and fill out the application form.

남 안녕하세요, 과학 교사 Harvey Smith입니다. 제18회 연례 과학 독후감 대회에 대한 간단한 안내를 해 드리겠습니다. 우리 고등학교는 Sparrow 박사의 탄생일을 기념하여 매년 이 독후감 쓰기 대회를 개최하고 있습니다. 저는 여러분 대부분이 Sparrow 박사에 대해 들어 보았다고 확신합니다. 그는 우리나라 역사에서 가장 영향력 있는 물리학자 중 한 분이셨습니다. 3학년을 제외한 모든 학생들은 이 대회에 참가할 수 있습니다. 참가자들은 미리 과학책을 읽어야 하고, 대회 당일에 독후감을 쓸 것입니다. 학생들은 독후감을 쓰는 동안 책을 참조할 수 없습니다. 대회는 학교 도서관에서 6월 15일 오전에 열릴 예정입니다. 대회 후에 우리는 수상자를 선정해서 6월 20일에 명단을 학교 게시판에 공지할 것입니다. 대회 참가를 원하면, 제 교무실로 와서 신청서를 작성하기 바랍니다.

Solution

대회 참가를 원하는 학생들은 직접 과학 교사의 교무실로 와서 신청서를 작성해 달라고 안내하고 있으므로, 담화의 내용과 일치하지 않는 것은 ⑤ '인터넷을 통해 참가 신청서를 작성해야 한다.'이다.

Words

brief 간단한; 짧은 announcement 공지
in celebration of ~을 기념하여 influential 영향력이 있는
physicist 물리학자 refer to ~을 참조하다 bulletin board 게시판

10 정답 ②

Script

W John, look at this schedule. Why don't we take an after-school class together?

M Okay. Do you have any class in mind?

W Well, I want to take a class to get a good workout.

M I heard Andrew gives wonderful lessons. He's well-liked by many students. What do you say to taking his class?

W Sorry, but I'm a little afraid of water.

M Then, what about the boxing class? I'm sure you would get a lot of exercise.

W It sounds interesting, but I can't attend a class that ends at 8 p.m.

M Why is that?

W I go to a math academy at 8 p.m. every day, and it takes me about fifteen minutes to walk there.

M Alright. But I have to do volunteer work at 6 p.m. every Wednesday.

W Then we have no other option but one. Let's sign up for it.

M Alright.

여 John, 이 스케줄 좀 봐. 우리 함께 방과 후 수업을 들으면 어떨까?

남 좋아. 마음에 두고 있는 수업 있니?

여 글쎄, 좋은 운동이 되는 수업을 듣고 싶어.

남 Andrew 선생님이 훌륭한 수업을 하신다고 들었어. 그는 많은 학생들이 좋아해. 그분 수업을 들어 보는 게 어때?

여 미안한데, 내가 물을 좀 무서워해.

남 그러면 복싱 수업은 어때? 네가 많은 운동을 하게 될 것이라고 확신해.

여 흥미롭기는 한데, 나는 오후 8시에 끝나는 수업은 참석할 수 없어.

남 왜 그런데?

여 난 매일 오후 8시에 수학 학원에 가야 하고 거기까지 걸어가는 데 약 15분이 걸려.

남 알겠어. 그런데 나는 매주 수요일 오후 6시에는 봉사 활동을 해야 해.

여 그러면 우리는 한 수업 외에는 선택의 여지가 없네. 그걸로 신청하자.

남 그래.

Solution

두 사람은 운동 수업이고, 물속에서 하지 않고 오후 8시에 끝나지 않으면서 수요일에 하지 않는 수업을 신청하기로 했으므로 두 사람이 선택한 수업은 ②이다.

Words

after-school class 방과 후 수업

11 정답 ④

Script

M Honey, it's hard for me to remember anniversaries.

W How about using an app on your cellphone?

M Sounds like a good way, but I don't know how to do it.

W Give me your cellphone, and I'll show you how.

남 여보, 내가 기념일을 기억하는 게 어려워요.

여 당신의 휴대전화에 있는 앱을 사용하는 건 어때요?

남 좋은 방법인 것 같은데, 그것을 어떻게 해야 할지 모르겠어요.

여 당신의 휴대전화를 내게 줘 봐요, 그러면 어떻게 하는지 보여 줄게요.

Solution

기념일을 기억하는 것을 어려워하는 남자에게 여자가 휴대전화 앱을 사용하라고 하자, 남자는 그것을 어떻게 하는지 모르겠다고 말하므로, ④ '당신의 휴대전화를 내게 줘 봐요, 그러면 어떻게 하는지 보여 줄게요.'가 여자의 응답으로 가장 적절하다.

① 당신의 탁상 달력에 기념일을 표시하세요.

② 당신이 그것들을 기억한다면, 다른 사람들이 고마워할 거예요.

③ 당신이 그것에 대해 알고 싶을 때 전화 주세요.

⑤ 천천히 하세요. 언젠가 당신은 그것들을 기억할 수 있어요.

Words

anniversary 기념일 Take your time. 천천히 하세요.

12 정답 ④

Script

W My watch has suddenly stopped. Can you fix it?

M No problem, ma'am. Please fill out this request form and leave your watch here with us.

W Okay. Then, when should I come back to get it?

M I'll give you a call when I'm done with it.

여 제 시계가 갑자기 멈췄어요. 고칠 수 있나요?

남 물론이죠, 손님. 이 신청서를 작성하시고 시계를 여기 저희에게 맡겨 주세요.

여 알겠어요. 그럼 그것을 언제쯤 찾으러 와야 하나요?

남 그것의 수리가 끝나면 전화드릴게요.

Solution

여자는 시계 수리를 맡기고 나서 언제쯤 찾으러 와야 하는지 질문하고 있으므로, ④ '그것의 수리가 끝나면 전화드릴게요.'가 남자의 응답으로 가장 적절하다.

① 당신은 조금 더 일찍 왔어야 해요.

② 죄송하지만, 그것을 수리할 수 없을 것 같아요.

③ 당신은 내일 새로운 시계를 사야 해요.

⑤ 서비스 센터에서 그것을 찾으실 수 있어요.

Words

request form 신청서

13 정답 ④

Script

W Nick, can I talk to you? It'll just take a moment.

M Sure, what's up?

W I found a hundred-dollar bill on my way to school.

M Really? What are you going to do with the money?

W I'd like to return it to the owner.

M If I were you, I would spend it all on myself.

W Wouldn't it be dishonest to use it like that?

M Haven't you ever heard the phrase "Finders keepers"?

W But my conscience tells me I should send the money back to where it came from.

M If your heart points you in that direction, just follow it.

W Okay. I'll go to the police station and ask if anyone is looking for it.

여 Nick, 이야기 좀 할 수 있을까? 조금밖에 안 걸릴 거야.
남 물론이지, 무슨 일이니?
여 학교 오는 길에 100달러짜리 지폐 한 장을 주웠어.
남 정말? 그 돈으로 뭘 할 거니?
여 주인에게 돌려주고 싶어.
남 내가 너라면, 그냥 나를 위해 쓸 텐데.
여 그렇게 사용하는 것은 정직하지 않은 것 아닐까?
남 '찾은 사람이 임자다'라는 말 들어 보지 못했니?
여 그렇지만 내 양심이 그 돈을 왔던 곳으로 돌려보내야 한다고 말해.
남 네 마음이 그 방향으로 지시하면, 그냥 그것을 따라.
여 알겠어. 경찰서에 가서 누가 그 돈을 찾고 있는지 물어볼게.

여자는 100달러를 주웠는데 자신을 위해서 쓰라는 남자의 의견과는 달리 그 돈을 꼭 주인에게 돌려줘야 한다고 말하고, 이에 남자는 마음 가는 대로 하라고 했으므로, ④ '알겠어. 경찰서에 가서 누가 그 돈을 찾고 있는지 물어볼게.'가 여자의 응답으로 가장 적절하다.
① 난 동의해. 너는 항상 올바른 일을 할 필요가 있어.
② 알았어. 그 돈을 뜻깊은 일에 기부하자.
③ 난 그렇게 생각하지 않아. 너는 나와 그 돈을 공유할 자격이 있어.
⑤ 결코 아니야. 난 도덕적 판단은 상황에 따라 달라진다고 생각해.

Finders keepers. 찾은 사람이 임자다. conscience 양심

14 정답 ①

M Honey, where are these vegetables from?
W Ms. Taylor gave them to me. She grew them in her garden.
M I think she's a good farmer. All her vegetables are very fresh.
W Yes. I'll make a salad with these for dinner.
M Sounds great.
W Why don't we have our own vegetable garden?
M I'd like to, but we need to realize that it's a lot of work.
W Still, I want to try it.
M Well, it would be good to grow and eat our own vegetables.
W Yeah. Ms. Taylor said that she'd give me many tips.
M It might be easier with her help.

남 여보, 이 채소들은 어디에서 온 거예요?
여 Taylor 씨가 그것을 줬어요. 그녀가 자신의 정원에서 그것들을 키웠어요.
남 나는 그녀가 훌륭한 농부라고 생각해요. 그녀의 모든 채소는 매우 신선하네요.
여 그래요. 저녁 식사로 이것들을 가지고 샐러드를 만들게요.
남 좋은 생각이네요.
여 우리도 우리의 채소 정원을 갖는 게 어때요?
남 그러고 싶지만, 그것은 일이 많다는 것을 알 필요가 있어요.
여 그래도 그 일을 해 보고 싶어요.
남 음, 우리 자신의 채소를 길러서 먹는 것은 좋은 일이겠지요.
여 그래요. Taylor 씨가 많은 조언을 해 주겠다고 말했어요.
남 그녀의 도움이 있으면 그 일은 더 쉬울 것 같네요.

자신의 정원에 채소를 기르고 싶다는 여자의 말에 남자도 동의하지만 그것은 일이 많다고 말한다. 이에 여자는 채소를 잘 기르는 Taylor 씨가 그것에 대

한 조언을 준다는 말을 했다고 했으므로, ① '그녀의 도움이 있으면 그 일은 더 쉬울 것 같네요.'가 남자의 응답으로 가장 적절하다.
② 당신의 도움 없이는 내가 그 일을 할 수 없을 거예요.
③ 그녀에게 채소를 좀 주는 게 어때요?
④ 좋은 농부가 되기는 어렵지만 당신은 할 수 있어요.
⑤ 정원에 있는 우리 채소들이 이미 많이 자랐어요.

realize 알다, 깨닫다 tip 조언

15 정답 ⑤

W Mr. Johnson is a teacher at Jimmy Carton High School. He and his students have planned a school picnic to Dream Land, the biggest amusement park in the state and have been eagerly looking forward to it for the past week. The picnic is scheduled for next Monday, but Mr. Johnson has just received some bad news. The principal mentioned that there was a big accident in that amusement park several days ago, and after a meeting with school board members, he decided to cancel the picnic to Dream Land. The principal now wants Mr. Johnson to announce the news to his class. In this situation, what would Mr. Johnson most likely say to the students?
Mr. Johnson Due to an accident at the amusement park, we should abandon our plan to go there.

여 Mr. Johnson은 Jimmy Carton 고등학교 교사입니다. 그와 그의 반 학생들은 주에서 가장 큰 놀이동산인 Dream Land로 학교 소풍을 가기로 계획하고 지난주 동안 그것을 굉장히 기대하고 있었습니다. 소풍은 다음 주 월요일로 예정되어 있지만, Mr. Johnson은 나쁜 소식을 막 들었습니다. 교장 선생님께서 며칠 전에 그 놀이동산에서 큰 사고가 있었고 학교 이사회 위원들과의 회의 후에 Dream Land로의 소풍을 취소하기로 결정했다고 했습니다. 교장 선생님은 이제 Mr. Johnson이 이 소식을 반 학생들에게 공지하기를 원합니다. 이런 상황에서, Mr. Johnson은 학생들에게 뭐라고 말할 것 같은가요?
Mr. Johnson 놀이동산에서의 사고 때문에 우리는 거기로 가는 우리 계획을 포기해야만 합니다.

며칠 전에 놀이동산에서 사고가 났기 때문에 교장 선생님은 이사회 위원들과의 회의를 통해 놀이동산으로의 소풍을 취소하기로 결정하였고, 이를 Mr. Johnson이 반 학생들에게 알리기를 원하는 상황이므로, 이러한 상황에서 Mr. Johnson이 학생들에게 할 말로 가장 적절한 것은 ⑤ '놀이동산에서의 사고 때문에 우리는 거기로 가는 우리 계획을 포기해야만 합니다.'이다.
① 안타깝게도 우리의 소풍은 다음 달로 연기되었습니다.
② 별도의 공지가 없으면 우리는 놀이동산으로 소풍을 갈 것입니다.
③ 교장 선생님께서 우리의 소풍에 대해 염려하고 계시니 여러분은 아주 조심해야 합니다.
④ 소풍을 가지 못하는 이유가 있으면 오늘까지 저에게 알려 주세요.

amusement park 놀이동산 eagerly 간절히
announce 공지하다, 알리다 postpone 미루다, 연기하다
abandon 포기하다, 버리다

16 정답 ③   17 정답 ③

Script

M We have a variety of beliefs about the common cold, but the fact is, most of them are wrong. So, today I'd like to talk about the myths relating to cold treatments and their real effects on a cold. Many people believe taking vitamins or drinking herbal tea will make a cold go away quicker. However, studies haven't proven either one to make an existing cold go away faster. What about steam? Although many think inhaling steam may temporarily relieve symptoms of a dry nose and sore throat, experts agree that this is not a cure. Another myth about the common cold is that antibiotics can be used as a treatment. Antibiotics kill bacteria, but the common cold is caused by a virus. Therefore, antibiotics will have no effect on viral organisms that cause the common cold.

남 우리는 보통 감기에 대한 다양한 믿음을 갖고 있지만, 실상은 그것들 중 대부분이 잘못된 것입니다. 그래서 오늘 저는 감기 치료에 관련된 근거 없는 믿음들과 그것들이 감기에 미치는 실질적인 영향에 대해 말씀드리고자 합니다. 많은 사람들은 비타민을 섭취하거나 허브 차를 마시면 감기를 더 빨리 낫게 할 것이라고 믿습니다. 그러나 (그 어떤) 연구도 둘 중 하나가 현존하는 감기를 더 빨리 낫게 한다는 것을 입증하지 못했습니다. 증기는 어떨까요? 많은 사람들이 증기를 들이마시면 코가 건조해지는 증상과 목이 아픈 증상을 일시적으로 완화시켜 줄 것이라고 생각하지만, 전문가들은 이것이 치료가 아니라는 것에 동의합니다. 보통 감기에 관한 또 다른 근거 없는 믿음은 항생제가 치료제로 사용될 수 있다는 것입니다. 항생제는 세균을 죽이지만, 보통 감기는 바이러스에 의해 발생합니다. 그러므로 항생제는 보통 감기를 일으키는 바이러스성 생물에는 효과가 없을 것입니다.

Solution

16
남자는 보통 감기 치료에 관한 다양한 근거 없는 믿음들을 소개하고 그것들이 실제로 감기를 낫게 하는 데 영향을 주지 않는다고 말하고 있으므로, 남자가 하는 말의 주제로 가장 적절한 것은 ③ '감기 치료에 관한 오해'이다.

① 다양한 보통 감기 증상
② 감기에 걸리는 다양한 원인
④ 보통 감기를 치료하는 효과적인 방법
⑤ 감기를 예방하는 민간요법

17
비타민, 허브 차, 증기, 항생제는 언급되었지만, ③ '꿀'은 언급되지 않았다.

Words

myth 근거 없는 믿음 inhale 흡입하다, 들이마시다
temporarily 일시적으로 relieve 완화하다, 덜어 주다
antibiotics 항생제 bacteria 세균, 박테리아 viral 바이러스성의
organism 생물, 유기체

● 실전 모의고사 16회   본문 154쪽

01 ④	02 ④	03 ①	04 ④	05 ③
06 ②	07 ⑤	08 ④	09 ⑤	10 ④
11 ⑤	12 ①	13 ①	14 ⑤	15 ⑤
16 ③	17 ③			

01 정답 ④

Script

W Hello, citizens. It's almost time to announce the fifth Sap Snow Festival. It's a festival of snow and ice held at Sap Park and other sites in the city of Sap. But first we need volunteers for various tasks. You can learn all the details on the different tasks by checking the Sap Snow Festival website. If you are interested in volunteering, please submit your application online. Your application will be viewed by the team leaders of the teams you wish to volunteer for. We can't have a successful festival without the volunteers like you. We're looking forward to hearing from you.

여 안녕하세요, 시민 여러분. 다섯 번째 Sap 눈 축제를 알릴 때가 거의 되었습니다. 그것은 Sap 공원과 Sap 시의 다른 장소에서 열리는 눈과 얼음 축제입니다. 그러나 저희는 먼저 다양한 일을 위한 자원봉사자가 필요합니다. Sap 눈 축제 웹사이트를 확인해 보시면 다양한 일에 대한 세부 사항들을 아실 수 있습니다. 자원봉사에 관심이 있으시다면 온라인으로 신청서를 제출해 주십시오. 신청서는 여러분이 자원봉사를 희망하는 팀의 팀장들에 의해 검토될 것입니다. 여러분과 같은 자원봉사자들 없이는 성공적인 축제를 치를 수가 없습니다. 저희는 여러분들로부터 소식이 오기를 고대합니다.

Solution

Sap 눈 축제를 위한 자원봉사를 신청해 달라고 말하고 있으므로, 여자가 하는 말의 목적으로 가장 적절한 것은 ④이다.

Words

detail 세부 사항 submit 제출하다

02 정답 ④

Script

M I know that you're busy today, but why are you eating while standing?

W I'm so busy that I don't have time to sit and eat properly.

M You know what? Posture is very important in order to properly taste food.

W In what posture should I eat?

M You have to sit and eat in a proper posture.

W Tell me in more detail.

M In a study, baked brownies were served to be eaten and then tasted. As a result, the group who sat down and ate brownies evaluated that they were more delicious than the group who ate them standing up.

W That sounds interesting.

M Yes. The research team recommended eating in a sitting position if you want to enjoy eating properly.

W I see. From now on, I should not eat while standing.

남 오늘 네가 바쁜 것은 아는데 왜 서 있는 채로 먹니?

여 너무 바빠서 제대로 앉아서 먹을 시간이 없어.

남 너 그거 아니? 음식 맛을 제대로 느끼려면 자세가 매우 중요해.

여 어떤 자세로 음식을 먹어야 하는데?

남 제대로 된 자세로 앉아서 먹어야 해.

여 좀 더 자세히 말해 봐.

남 한 연구에서는 구워진 브라우니를 제공해 먹게 한 뒤, 맛을 평가하도록 했어. 그 결과, 앉아서 브라우니를 먹은 그룹이 서서 그것을 먹은 그룹보다 브라우니가 더 맛있었다고 평가했어.

여 그거 흥미롭게 들리는구나.

남 그래. 그 연구팀은 식사를 제대로 즐기고 싶다면 앉은 자세로 먹을 것을 권장했어.

여 알았어. 이제부터는 서서 먹지 않아야겠네.

Solution

남자는 연구 결과를 통해 음식 맛을 제대로 느끼려면 앉아서 먹어야 한다고 했으므로, 남자의 의견으로 가장 적절한 것은 ④이다.

Words

properly 제대로 posture 자세 in detail 상세하게 serve 제공하다
evaluate 평가하다 recommend 권장하다

03 정답 ①

Script

M Wow, amazing! I bet you're really proud of yourself.

W Sure, I am.

M The works are really better than I expected.

W Thank you. Other visitors all agreed with that.

M Is there any reason you've been working with soap?

W It's a good material to express the passage of time.

M Now I understand why most of your works are reproductions of ancient remains.

W Right. Just like the ancient remains, my works won't lose their value even if they're damaged.

M You chose the right material. And I saw some people carrying around bars of soap. Are you selling them?

W Yes. You can buy them in the gift shop.

M Okay, great. I'll buy some on my way out. And once again, I love your works.

W Thanks so much.

남 와, 놀라워요! 틀림없이 스스로가 정말로 자랑스러우시겠어요.

여 물론, 그렇습니다.

남 작품들이 제가 예상했던 것보다 정말로 더 좋네요.

여 감사합니다. 다른 관람객들도 모두 그것에 동의했어요.

남 비누로 작업해 온 이유가 있나요?

여 시간의 흐름을 표현하기에 좋은 재료예요.

남 왜 선생님의 작품 대부분이 고대 유물의 재현인 것인지 이제 이해돼요.

여 맞아요. 고대 유물처럼 제 작품들도 손상은 될지언정 그것들의 가치를 잃지는 않을 거예요.

남 딱 맞는 재료를 선택하셨네요. 그리고 몇몇 사람들이 비누를 가지고 다니는 것을 봤어요. 그것들을 팔기도 하시나요?

여 네. 선물 가게에서 그것들을 사실 수 있습니다.

남 알겠습니다. 좋네요. 나가면서 몇 개 살게요. 그리고 선생님 작품이 너무 좋다는 말씀을 다시 한번 드립니다.

여 대단히 감사합니다.

Solution

남자는 여자의 비누 조각 작품이 훌륭하다고 감상을 말하면서 비누로 작업하게 된 이유를 물었고, 여자는 비누 조각을 하게 된 이유를 설명하고 있으므로 두 사람의 관계를 가장 잘 나타낸 것은 ①이다.

Words

material 재료 passage of time 시간의 흐름
reproduction 재현, 재생 remains 유물 damage 손상을 주다

04 정답 ④

Script

[Cellphone rings.]

W Oh, Mr. Smith. What's up?

M How's a next stage setting for the living room scene going?

W It's just finished. You can check it.

M Okay. Did you hang a picture of a sunflower on the wall?

W Of course. And I put a sofa under the picture.

M Good job. Is there a round table in front of the sofa?

W Yes. And I put a long, straight living room lamp on the left side of the sofa.

M I think it's not easy to get a lamp like that.

W No, it isn't.

M Finally, on the right side of the sofa, did you put a flower pot with a tree with many leaves?

W Of course.

[휴대전화가 울린다.]

여 오, Smith 감독님. 무슨 일이세요?

남 다음 거실 장면을 위한 무대 장치는 어떻게 되어 가고 있나요?

여 막 끝마쳤어요. 확인해 보셔도 됩니다.

남 좋아요. 벽에는 해바라기 그림을 걸어 놓으셨나요?

여 물론이지요. 그리고 그림 아래에는 소파를 놓았어요.

남 잘했어요. 소파 앞에는 원형 모양의 테이블이 있나요?

여 네. 그리고 소파 왼쪽 옆에는 길고 곧은 거실 램프를 놓았어요.

남 그와 같은 램프를 구하기가 쉽지 않은 것 같아요.

여 네, 그래요.

남 마지막으로 소파 오른쪽 옆에는 나뭇잎이 많은 나무가 있는 화분을 놓았나요?

여 물론입니다.

Solution

소파 왼쪽 옆에 길고 곧은 거실 램프를 놓았다고 했지만 그림에서는 휘어진 램프이므로, 대화의 내용과 일치하지 않는 것은 ④이다.

Words

straight 곧은 flower pot 화분

05 정답 ③

M Good morning. How can I help you?

W Good morning. I came here with a parking violation sticker on my car.

M It's our policy to attach a parking violation sticker on any unauthorized vehicles.

W Well, I just moved in 505 yesterday.

M You must not have received a parking permit sticker yet. You need to display that on your car.

W No, I have't gotten it yet. What should I do?

M First, we need a copy of your car registration.

W Hang on a second. I have my car registration in my car. I'll be right back.

M Okay.

남 안녕하세요. 어떻게 도와드릴까요?

여 안녕하세요. 제 차에 주차 위반 스티커가 붙어 있어서 왔어요.

남 모든 승인되지 않은 차량에는 주차 위반 스티커를 붙이는 것이 저희 규정입니다.

여 음, 전 어제 505호로 막 이사를 왔습니다.

남 아직 주차 허용 스티커를 발급받지 못하셨나 보군요. 그것이 차에 붙어 있다는 것을 보여 주셔야 합니다.

여 네, 아직 그것을 발급받지 못했습니다. 어떻게 해야 하나요?

남 우선, 자동차 등록증 사본이 필요합니다.

여 잠깐만요. 차 안에 제 자동차 등록증이 있어요. 지금 바로 가져올게요.

남 알겠습니다.

06 정답 ②

Script

W Hello. Can I help you?

M Yes. I'm looking for a cutting board to take camping.

W Let me see. *[Pause]* Yes, these wooden cutting board and plastic cutting board are suitable for camping.

M That's good. Oh, I like both. How much are they?

W The wooden cutting board is $40, and the plastic cutting board is $30.

M I'll buy the plastic cutting board. I think it's lighter than the wooden one. And I need a camping knife, too.

W Of course. For camping knives, this one is popular. What do you think?

M I like it. How much is it?

W It's $50, and since you're buying a cutting board, I can give you 10 percent off the knife.

M Really? That's great. Here's my credit card.

W Thank you.

여 안녕하세요. 도와드릴까요?

남 네. 저는 캠핑에서 쓸 도마를 찾고 있습니다.

여 어디 볼게요. *[잠시 후]* 네, 이 나무 도마와 플라스틱 도마가 캠핑용으로 적당한 것이에요.

남 좋군요. 오, 둘 다 마음에 드네요. 얼마인가요?

여 나무 도마는 40달러이고, 플라스틱 도마는 30달러입니다.

남 플라스틱 도마를 살게요. 그것이 나무 도마보다 더 가벼운 것 같아요. 그리고 캠핑용 칼도 필요해요.

여 당연하지요. 캠핑용 칼은 이것이 인기가 있어요. 어떠세요?

남 마음에 드네요. 그것은 얼마인가요?

여 50달러인데 도마를 구입하시니 칼 금액에서 10퍼센트 할인해 드릴 수 있어요.

남 그래요? 좋군요. 여기 신용카드가 있습니다.

여 감사합니다.

07 정답 ⑤

Script

M Where were you, Andrea? I called you several times, but you didn't answer the phone.

W Really? Sorry. Why did you call me?

M After class, I went to the library to borrow books.

W Did you borrow the books I asked for? *Musical History* and *Sound & Stage*.

M Actually, that's what I was calling about. I borrowed my books and went to borrow the ones you asked for, but I couldn't remember the title of one.

W Didn't I write them down on a Post-It?

M Yes, you did. But I left it at home because I thought I could remember them.

W So you were only able to borrow one of them? Which one?

M No. Surprisingly, I remembered the other before I left the library.

W What a relief! I couldn't answer the phone because I was giving a presentation during the class.

M I see. Well, I have your books here.

남 Andrea, 어디 있었어? 여러 번 전화했는데 전화를 받지 않던데.

여 그래? 미안해. 왜 전화했어?

남 수업이 끝나고 책을 빌리러 도서관에 갔어.

여 내가 부탁한 책들도 빌렸니? '뮤지컬의 역사'와 '소리와 무대' 말이야.

남 사실은 그것 때문에 전화한 거야. 내 책들을 빌리고 네가 부탁한 책들을 빌리려 했는데 한 권의 제목이 생각나지 않았어.

여 내가 포스트잇에 그것들을 적어 주지 않았니?

남 응, 그랬지. 하지만 기억할 수 있다고 생각하고 그것을 집에 두고 왔어.

여 그래서 그것들 중 한 권만 빌릴 수 있었어? 어느 것이니?

남 아니. 놀랍게도 도서관을 나오기 전에 나머지 한 권이 기억났어.

여 다행이다! 난 수업 시간에 발표를 하는 중이어서 전화를 받을 수가 없었어.

남 그랬구나. 자, 여기 네 책들이야.

ask for ~을 요청하다 relief 위안, 안도 presentation 발표

08 정답 ④

Script

[Telephone rings.]

W Good afternoon. This is Aram Gallery. How can I help you?

M Yes. I'd like to know about group visits.

W Okay. First of all, groups must have at least 20 people.

M I see. Can we get help from a docent?

W Yes, it's possible on request.

M What time is the museum open? Can we visit there at 10 a.m.?

W Sure. We are open between 10 a.m. to 3 p.m.

M Do I have to make a reservation in advance?

W Yes. Groups must make a reservation a week before your visit.

M I see. Thank you for your information.

[전화벨이 울린다.]

여 안녕하세요. Aram Gallery입니다. 어떻게 도와드릴까요?

남 네. 단체 관람에 관하여 알고 싶어요.

여 알겠습니다. 우선, 단체는 최소 20명이어야 합니다.

남 그렇군요. 해설사의 도움을 받을 수 있나요?

여 네. 요청하신다면 가능합니다.

남 박물관은 몇 시에 여나요? 오전 10시에 거기를 방문해도 될까요?

여 물론입니다. 오전 10시에서 오후 3시까지 엽니다.

남 미리 예약을 해야만 하나요?

여 네. 단체는 방문 일주일 전에는 예약을 하셔야 합니다.

남 알겠습니다. 정보 주셔서 감사합니다.

Solution

최소 인원, 해설사, 개장 시간, 사전 예약은 언급되었으나 ④ '관람 비용'에 대해서는 언급되지 않았다.

Words

docent (박물관 등의) 해설사, 안내원 on request 요청에 의하여
make a reservation 예약을 하다 in advance 미리, 사전에

09 정답 ⑤

Script

M Welcome to our 7th Sammamish Day Camp. As you know, our camp is open to all girls going into first through the sixth grades in the fall. The camp is run one hundred percent by volunteers from our community. The camp runs 9:00 a.m.–4:00 p.m., Monday through Friday for one week. It's filled with a wide range of great activities. Campers will also sing songs, create amazing crafts, participate in the community service projects and much more! Registration opens at 10 a.m. on July 5th. Thank you.

남 저희의 일곱번 째 Sammamish Day Camp에 오신 것을 환영합니

다. 아시다시피, 저희 캠프는 가을에 1학년부터 6학년에 들어가는 모든 여학생들이 참가 가능합니다. 캠프는 지역 사회로부터 모신 자원봉사자들에 의해 100퍼센트 운영됩니다. 그 캠프는 한 주 동안 월요일부터 금요일까지 오전 9시부터 오후 4시까지 운영됩니다. 다양하고 훌륭한 활동으로 가득 차 있습니다. 캠프 참가자들은 또한 노래를 부르고, 놀라운 공예품을 만들고, 지역 사회 서비스 프로젝트와 더 많은 것에 참여할 것입니다! 신청은 7월 5일 오전 10시에 시작됩니다. 감사합니다.

Solution

7월 5일 오전 10시에 신청이 시작된다고 했으므로, 담화의 내용과 일치하지 않는 것은 ⑤ '등록은 7월 5일 오전 9시부터 할 수 있다.'이다.

Words

craft 공예품

10 정답 ④

Script

W Good afternoon. Can I help you?

M Yes. I'm looking for a microphone for my son's birthday present.

W Okay. Please take a look at this brochure.

M Thanks. I think a wireless one would be better. That way he can be free to move around.

W Yes. What about the voice direction?

M Could you tell me more about it?

W Omnidirectional is best for group singing and unidirectional is great for singing alone.

M He likes to sing alone, so I'll take unidirectional.

W All right. Last, what about the battery life? Of course the longer, the better, right?

M You're right, but unfortunately, it's not within my $700 budget.

W I see. Then I think this one is also good.

M Okay. I'll take the cheaper one. Here's my credit card.

여 안녕하세요. 도와드릴까요?

남 네. 제 아들 생일 선물로 줄 마이크를 찾고 있어요.

여 알겠습니다. 이 책자를 봐 주세요.

남 감사합니다. 무선인 것이 더 좋을 것 같아요. 그러면 그 애가 움직이기에 자유로울 수 있어서요.

여 네. 소리 방향은요?

남 그것에 대해 더 말씀해 주실 수 있나요?

여 전 방향은 합창에 알맞고, 단일 방향은 독창에 적합해요.

남 그는 혼자 노래 부르는 것을 좋아하니 단일 방향을 살게요.

여 알겠습니다. 마지막으로 배터리 수명은요? 물론 길수록 좋겠지요?

남 맞아요. 하지만 불행히도 그것은 700달러의 제 예산 안에 있지 않네요.

여 알겠습니다. 그럼 이것도 좋을 것 같네요.

남 좋아요. 더 싼 것을 살게요. 여기 신용카드가 있습니다.

Solution

남자는 아들 생일 선물로 줄 마이크로 무선이고, 단일 반향이며, 700달러가 넘지 않는 범위 내에서 사겠다고 했으므로, 남자가 선택한 마이크는 ④이다.

Words

brochure (안내 · 광고용) 책자 wireless 무선의 direction 방향
omnidirectional 전 방향의 unidirectional 단일 방향의

11 정답 ⑤

Script

W Mike, are you ready for your interview tomorrow?
M I'm not sure. As you know, this is my first job interview, so I'm really nervous.
W Don't worry. You'll do fine. Oh, did you buy that suit for the interview?
M Yeah, it's important to make a good first impression.

여 Mike, 내일 면접 준비는 됐니?
남 잘 모르겠어. 알다시피 이번이 첫 면접이라서 정말 떨려.
여 걱정 마. 잘할 거야. 아, 면접을 위해 그 양복을 샀어?
남 그래, 좋은 첫인상을 남기는 것이 중요해.

Solution

여자는 남자에게 내일 면접 준비가 됐는지와 면접을 위해 양복을 샀느냐고 물었고 그에 대한 응답이 오는 것이 자연스러우므로, ⑤ '그래, 좋은 첫인상을 남기는 것이 중요해.'가 남자의 응답으로 가장 적절하다.

① 맞아. 친구에게서 그 양복을 빌렸어.
② 고마워. 넌 정말 내게 큰 도움이 되었어.
③ 실은 양복이 너에게 잘 어울리지 않는 것 같아.
④ 그래. 지금 당장 백화점에 가자.

Words

suit 양복 first impression 첫인상 match 어울리다

12 정답 ①

Script

M Congratulations on winning. It was a really cool dance.
W Thank you. It was a really tough competition. The opponent in the final was one of the best.
M I know. Now I see how hard you have been practicing.
W Right. I really practiced a lot.

남 우승한 것을 축하해. 정말 멋진 댄스였어.
여 고마워. 정말 힘든 대회였어. 결승전에서의 상대가 최고 중 하나였거든.
남 알아. 네가 그동안 얼마나 열심히 연습해 왔는지 이젠 알겠어.
여 그래. 나는 정말 많이 연습했어.

Solution

댄스 대회에서 우승한 여자가 정말 힘든 대회였다고 하자, 남자는 여자가 그동안 얼마나 열심히 연습했는지 알겠다고 말한다. 따라서 ① '그래. 나는 정말 많이 연습했어.'가 여자의 응답으로 가장 적절하다.

② 이번에는 경기에서 이기고 싶어.
③ 상대 팀에 대해 전혀 몰랐어.
④ 나와 함께 있어 준다고 하니 정말 기뻐.
⑤ 실수한 것에 대해 그렇게 많이 자책하지 마.

Words

tough 힘든 competition 대회 opponent 상대

13 정답 ①

Script

M Jessica, I heard that you were taking a computer programing class. Do you like it?

W At first, I was really excited to take it, but it's not what I expected.
M Really? How's that?
W Programing is way more difficult than I thought. I don't know how you're so good at it.
M You're right, it's difficult. It just requires a lot of patience and time.
W That's for sure. But I think it's too hard for me.
M It's brand-new to you right now. It'll get easier over time.
W That's what my instructor says.
M Come on! Give it time. You'll get really good at it!
W Do you really think so?
M Yeah. Practice makes perfect.

남 Jessica, 네가 컴퓨터 프로그래밍 수업을 받고 있다는 것을 들었어. 마음에 드니?
여 처음엔, 그것을 받는다는 것이 정말로 신났었는데, 내가 기대했던 것은 아니야.
남 그래? 그게 어떤데?
여 프로그래밍은 내가 생각했던 것보다 훨씬 더 어려워. 난 네가 어떻게 그것을 그렇게 잘하는지 모르겠어.
남 맞아, 그것은 어려워. 그저 많은 인내와 시간이 필요해.
여 확실히 그래. 하지만 내게는 아마도 너무 어려운 것 같아.
남 지금 당장은 그것이 네게는 매우 새로운 거잖아. 시간이 지나면 더 쉬워질 거야.
여 강사님도 그렇게 말씀하셔.
남 기운 내! 시간을 가져. 그것을 정말로 잘하게 될 거야!
여 정말 그렇게 생각하니?
남 그래. 연습이 완벽을 만들잖아.

Solution

프로그래밍 수업에 어려움을 느끼고 있는 여자에게 남자는 시간이 지나면 그것을 정말로 잘하게 될 거라고 격려하고, 이에 여자가 남자의 생각을 다시 묻고 있으므로 ① '그래. 연습이 완벽을 만들잖아.'가 남자의 응답으로 가장 적절하다.

② 고마워. 그 말을 들으니 정말 힘이 난다.
③ 그러고는 싶지만 그날은 너무 바빠.
④ 그 수업을 듣는다면 그것을 배울 수 있어.
⑤ 미안해. 프로그래밍을 해 본 적이 없어.

Words

require 필요로 하다 patience 인내 brand-new 아주 새로운
instructor 강사

14 정답 ⑤

Script

M It was a great presentation, Susan.
W Thank you. I sure hope the boss also liked it.
M I think he liked your idea. He took notes when you presented the part on company management.
W Really? That was an important part of my presentation. It took more than a month to prepare that part.
M I know. We went to visit some companies together. Don't you remember?
W Sure. How could I forget? I couldn't have done it without your help.

M I didn't do anything. I just went with you.
W I'd like to buy you dinner in return. How about this evening?
M All right. Do you have any restaurant in mind?
W How about the new Italian restaurant that opened downtown?

남 훌륭한 발표였어요, Susan
여 감사합니다. 사장님도 좋아하셨길 바라요.
남 당신 아이디어를 좋아하신 것 같아요. 당신이 회사 경영에 대한 부분을 발표할 때 메모를 하셨어요.
여 정말요? 그것은 제 발표에서 중요한 부분이었어요. 그 부분을 준비하는 데 한 달 이상이 걸렸어요.
남 저도 알아요. 몇몇 회사를 방문하러 같이 갔잖아요. 기억나지 않으세요?
여 그럼요. 제가 어떻게 잊을 수 있겠어요? 당신의 도움 없이는 못했을 거예요.
남 저는 아무것도 하지 않았어요. 단지 당신과 함께 갔을 뿐인걸요.
여 보답으로 저녁을 사고 싶어요. 오늘 저녁 어때요?
남 좋아요. 염두에 둔 식당이 있으세요?
여 시내에 새로 개업한 이탈리아 식당 어때요?

Solution

여자가 남자에게 도움에 대한 보답으로 저녁을 사고 싶다고 말하자 남자는 염두에 둔 식당이 있는 지를 물었고, 식당에 대해 구체적으로 언급하는 것이 자연스러우므로, ⑤ '시내에 새로 개업한 이탈리아 식당 어때요?'가 여자의 응답으로 가장 적절하다.

① 제가 당신 사장님을 만나볼 수 있게 도와주실 수 있나요?
② 언제 발표 준비를 시작했나요?
③ 제가 도움을 받을 사람들이 있나요?
④ 당신과 저희 사장님은 전에 함께 일해 본 적이 있나요?

Words

presentation 발표 management 경영 in return 답례로

15 정답 ⑤

Script

M One summer day, Dave goes to the local shopping mall to buy some summer clothes. After several hours of shopping, he feels tired. So he decides to take a coffee break at a café in the mall. While drinking his coffee, Dave sees a familiar face passing by in front of the café. Dave is sure it's James, a guy who was in his class in high school. They lost contact with each other over 5 years ago. Dave hurries out of the café and puts his hand on James' shoulder, and he looks back. At that moment, Dave realizes that the man is not James. In this situation, what would Dave most likely say to the man?
Dave I'm sorry. I took you for my friend.

남 어느 여름 날, Dave는 여름 옷 몇 벌을 사러 현지 쇼핑몰에 갑니다. 몇 시간 쇼핑 후 그는 피곤함을 느낍니다. 그래서 그는 쇼핑몰 안 카페에서 커피를 마시면서 쉬기로 결정합니다. 커피를 마시던 Dave는 카페 앞을 지나가는 낯익은 얼굴을 발견합니다. Dave는 그가 고등학교 때 같은 반이었던 친구 James라고 확신합니다. 그들은 서로 연락이 끊긴 지 5년이 넘습니다. Dave는 급히 카페 밖으로 나가 James의 어깨 위에 손을 올리고, 그는 뒤를 돌아봅니다. 그 순간 Dave는 그 남자가 James가

아니라는 것을 깨닫습니다. 이런 상황에서, Dave는 그 남자에게 뭐라고 말할 것 같은가요?
Dave 죄송합니다. 당신을 제 친구로 착각했어요.

Solution

Dave는 남자가 고등학교 동창 James인 줄 알고 어깨에 손을 올렸는데 다른 사람이라는 것을 알게 된 상황이므로, 이러한 상황에서 Dave가 남자에게 할 말로 가장 적절한 것은 ⑤ '죄송합니다. 당신을 제 친구로 착각했어요.'이다.

① 아니요. 괜찮아요. 제가 낼게요.
② 맞아. 내가 너와 같은 반이었어.
③ 괜찮아요. 신경 쓰지 마세요.
④ 정말 운이 좋다! 만나서 반가워.

Words

lose contact with ~와 연락이 끊기다
take ~ for ... ~을 …로 착각하다

16 정답 ③   17 정답 ③

Script

W Hello, everyone. When you eat fruits, do you eat even the skin? Most probably won't do that. However, various studies indicate that you need to eat fruit with its skin because it contains a lot of nutrients in it. Today, I'm going to give you some examples. First, banana peels are rich in dietary fiber and lutein, which is good for anti-aging of the eyes. Grape skin contains substances that activate the longevity gene. And it helps to keep blood sugar from rising after eating. Pineapple peel contains many minerals such as manganese and copper. Orange peel contains twice as much vitamins A and C than flesh, and apple peel contains 3 to 8 times more antioxidants than flesh, and kiwi peel contains hemocyanin, which helps sleep. What do you think? From now on, do you feel like eating the peels when you eat the fruits?

여 안녕하세요, 여러분. 여러분은 과일을 드실 때 껍질도 드시나요? 아마도 대부분은 그렇게 하지 않으실 겁니다. 그런데 여러 연구에서는 껍질에 많은 영양소가 함유되어 있기 때문에 과일을 껍질째 먹을 필요가 있다고 말합니다. 오늘 저는 몇 가지 예를 들어 보겠습니다. 우선, 바나나 껍질에는 식이섬유와 눈 노화 방지에 좋은 루테인이 풍부합니다. 포도 껍질에는 장수 유전자를 활성화하는 물질이 들어 있습니다. 그리고 그것은 식후에 혈당이 올라가는 것을 억제하는 데 도움이 됩니다. 파인애플 껍질에는 망간과 구리 같은 광물질이 많이 포함돼 있습니다. 오렌지 껍질은 과육보다 비타민 A와 C가 두 배나 많고, 사과 껍질에는 과육보다 3배에서 8배가 넘는 항산화 성분이, 키위 껍질에는 수면을 돕는 헤모시아닌(혈색소)이 포함돼 있습니다. 어때요? 지금부터는 과일을 드실 때 껍질까지 드시고 싶은 생각이 드시나요?

Solution

16

과일의 껍질에 들어 있는 영양소에 대해 예를 들어 설명하면서 과일을 먹을 때 껍질까지 먹는 게 좋은 이유에 대해 말하고 있다. 따라서 여자가 하는 말의 주제로 가장 적절한 것은 ③ '우리가 과일 껍질을 먹을 필요성'이다.

① 과일을 신선하게 유지하는 방법
② 과일 껍질을 재활용하는 법
④ 규칙적인 과일 섭취의 중요성

⑤ 여름 과일을 재배하는 것의 어려움

17
바나나, 포도, 오렌지, 키위는 언급되었지만, ③ '수박'은 언급되지 않았다.

---

01 ③	02 ⑤	03 ④	04 ④	05 ②
06 ④	07 ③	08 ⑤	09 ④	10 ④
11 ①	12 ②	13 ①	14 ④	15 ④
16 ④	17 ④			

01 정답 ③

Script

M Hello, students. I'm your school nurse Connor Evans. It's cold season again, so it's that time of year when it's important to protect yourself and the people around you. So I'd like to remind you of some simple tips to follow when you have to cough. First, make sure to cover your mouth and nose whenever you cough. If possible, use a tissue to cover your mouth or nose instead of handkerchief, and dispose of it immediately. If a cough suddenly sneaks up on you and no tissue is available, cough into your upper sleeve, not into your hands. This prevents spreading cold germs into the air. Please keep these tips in mind.

남 안녕하세요, 학생 여러분. 저는 보건 교사인 Connor Evans입니다. 다시 감기의 계절이므로, 여러분 자신과 여러분 주변 사람들을 보호하는 것이 중요한 연중 이맘때입니다. 그래서 저는 여러분에게 기침을 해야 할 때 따라야 할 몇 가지 간단한 조언을 상기시켜 드리고 싶습니다. 먼저, 기침할 때마다 반드시 입과 코를 가리도록 하세요. 가능하다면, 입이나 코를 가리기 위해 손수건 대신 티슈를 사용하고 그것을 즉시 버리세요. 만일 갑자기 기침이 나오려고 하는데 티슈가 없으면, 손에 하지 말고 소매 윗부분에 대고 기침하세요. 이렇게 하면 공중으로 감기 세균이 퍼지는 것을 막아 줍니다. 이 조언들을 명심하세요.

Solution

남자는 기침할 때 지켜야 할 간단한 팁을 상기시켜 주겠다고 하면서, 기침할 때 티슈를 사용하고 그것이 없다면 소매 윗부분을 사용함으로써 손에 감기 세균이 퍼지는 것을 막는 방법을 설명해 주고 있으므로, 남자가 하는 말의 목적으로 가장 적절한 것은 ③이다.

Words

protect 보호하다 remind ~ of ... ~에게 …을 상기시키다
make sure to *do* 반드시 ~하다 dispose of ~을 없애다[처분하다]
sneak up on ~에게 몰래 다가가다 available 이용 가능한
prevent 막다 germ 세균

02 정답 ⑤

Script

W Hi, Peter! It's been a while!
M Hello, Angela. Come on in. I'm cleaning the refrigerator.
W Oh, are you going to throw out those stuff over there?
M Yeah. I didn't realize that there was so much to throw away in there.
W You mean you can't use any of it?
M Everything is bad or expired. I forgot to check the dates

for a long time.

W I see. How about making a list of items in the refrigerator?

M A list of items?

W Yes. You can put the list of all the food on the refrigerator.

M I get it. That way I can easily see what's in the fridge and what I don't have.

W Right. Then you can also stop buying food you don't need.

M Okay. I'll try that. Thanks for the advice.

여 안녕하세요, Peter! 오랜만이에요!

남 안녕하세요, Angela. 들어오세요. 냉장고를 청소하고 있어요.

여 오, 저기 있는 것들은 모두 버릴 건가요?

남 맞아요. 저는 그곳에 버릴 물건이 이렇게 많다는 것을 깨닫지 못했어요.

여 그것 중 어느 것도 사용할 수 없다는 말이에요?

남 모든 것이 상하거나 유통 기한이 지났어요. 오랫동안 날짜를 확인하는 것을 잊어버렸어요.

여 그렇군요. 냉장고에 있는 품목의 목록을 작성하는 것은 어때요?

남 품목의 목록이요?

여 네. 당신은 모든 음식들의 목록을 냉장고에 붙여 놓을 수 있어요.

남 이해했어요. 그렇게 하면 냉장고 안에 무엇이 있고 무엇이 없는지를 쉽게 알 수 있겠네요.

여 맞아요. 그러면 필요하지 않은 음식을 사는 것을 막을 수도 있어요.

남 알겠어요. 그렇게 해 볼게요. 조언 고마워요.

냉장고에 보관된 상하거나 유통 기한이 지난 음식들을 버리려고 하는 남자에게 여자는 냉장고에 있는 품목들의 목록을 작성하여 붙여 두는 것이 냉장고 정리에 도움이 된다고 조언하고 있으므로, 여자의 의견으로 가장 적절한 것은 ⑤이다.

refrigerator 냉장고 throw out[away] ~을 버리다
expired 기한이 지난

03 정답 ④

M Hello in there! How are you doing?

W It couldn't be worse! Hey, please get me out quickly.

M Okay. We'll find the problem quickly and let you come out.

W Thank you, but please hurry. I can't stand being stuck in here anymore.

M I know. Just keep calm and be patient for another few minutes.

W But I am having trouble breathing. I am knocking myself out. You've got to get me out of here!

M Now, you'll be just fine. Try to relax.

W But what if this elevator crashes?

M You don't have to worry about that. That kind of thing will never happen. The cables are safe and secure.

W Okay. I'll trust you.

남 여보세요, 거기에 누구 있나요! 괜찮으세요?

여 최악이에요! 이봐요, 빨리 저를 꺼내 주세요.

남 알겠습니다. 빨리 문제를 찾아서 당신이 나올 수 있도록 해 드릴게요.

여 감사합니다. 하지만 서둘러 주세요. 더 이상 여기 갇혀 있는 것을 견딜 수

가 없어요.

남 알고 있습니다. 단지 진정하시고 몇 분만 더 참으세요.

여 하지만 숨쉬기가 어려워요. 이제 진이 다 빠지고 있어요. 여기서 저를 좀 꺼내 주세요!

남 이제, 괜찮아질 것입니다. 마음을 편하게 갖도록 하세요.

여 하지만 이 승강기가 추락하면 어떡하죠?

남 그것에 대해서는 걱정하실 필요 없으세요. 그런 일은 절대 일어나지 않을 겁니다. 케이블은 매우 안전합니다.

여 알겠어요. 당신을 믿을게요.

승강기에 갇혀 구조를 요청한 여자와 여자를 구조하기 위해 온 남자와의 대화이므로, 두 사람의 관계를 가장 잘 나타낸 것은 ④이다.

stand 참다 be stuck in ~에 갇혀 있다 patient 참을성 있는
breathe 숨쉬다 knock oneself out 녹초가 되다 crash 추락하다
secure 안전한

04 정답 ④

[Cellphone rings.]

W Hi, Justin. I texted you a picture of the poster I made for our concert a few minutes ago. Did you get it?

M Yeah. I like it.

W That's good. Should I keep the concert title, "Guitar & Songs," at the top?

M Yeah. It looks good there.

W Okay. What do you think of the girl playing the guitar?

M I think it's perfect. And I like the musical notes beside the guitar.

W Thanks. And I drew those three birds on the musical notes.

M That represents the songs in our concert, right?

W That's right.

M And I like how you put the time and place below the musical notes. Great job!

W Really? Thank you for saying so.

[휴대전화가 울린다.]

여 안녕, Justin. 몇 분 전에 우리 콘서트를 위해 만든 포스터 그림을 문자 메시지로 보냈어. 받았니?

남 그래. 마음에 들어.

여 다행이네. 'Guitar & Songs'라는 콘서트명을 맨 위에 두어도 될까?

남 그래. 거기가 좋아 보여.

여 알겠어. 기타를 치고 있는 소녀는 어때?

남 완벽하다고 생각해. 그리고 기타 옆에 있는 음표가 마음에 들어.

여 고마워, 그리고 음표 위에는 세 마리의 새를 그렸어.

남 그것은 우리 콘서트에서의 노래를 나타내는 거지?

여 맞아.

남 그리고 음표 아래에 시간과 장소를 넣은 방식이 마음에 들어. 잘했어!

여 정말? 그렇게 말해 줘서 고마워.

음표 위에 세 마리의 새를 그렸다고 했지만 그림에서는 한 마리만 그려져 있으므로, 대화의 내용과 일치하지 않는 것은 ④이다.

text 문자 메시지를 보내다 musical note 음표 represent 나타내다

05 정답 ②

Script

M Here we are. This is the restaurant I told you about.
W There are so many people in front of the restaurant!
M As far as I know, there's always a long line.
W Have you eaten here before?
M No, I haven't been there, but I wanted to come because I liked the reviews.
W I see. By the way, why is this restaurant so famous?
M I don't know, but they say there are special foods that are sold only at this restaurant.
W Okay. Why don't we wait in line over there?
M Oh, Look. It says that you have to get a waiting ticket at the counter first.
W Right. I'll go and pick up the ticket, so stay in line here.
M Okay.

남 다 왔어요. 여기가 제가 말했던 그 음식점이에요.
여 음식점 앞에 정말 사람이 많아요!
남 제가 알기로 항상 줄이 길어요.
여 당신은 전에 여기서 드셔 본 적이 있나요?
남 아니요. 거기에 가 본 적은 없지만, (이용) 후기가 마음에 들어서 와 보고 싶었어요.
여 그렇군요. 그건 그렇고 이 식당은 왜 그렇게 유명한가요?
남 잘은 모르지만, 이 식당에서만 파는 특별한 음식이 있다고 해요.
여 좋아요. 저기 줄을 서서 기다리는 게 어때요?
남 아, 보세요. 먼저 카운터에서 대기표를 받아야 한다고 쓰여 있어요.
여 그렇군요. 제가 가서 표를 받아 올 테니 여기 줄을 서 계세요.
남 알겠어요.

Solution

유명한 식당에 도착해서 줄을 서서 기다리려는 상황에서 남자가 카운터에서 먼저 대기표를 받아야 한다고 하자 여자는 자신이 가서 대기표를 받아 오겠다고 했으므로, 정답은 ②이다.

Words

as far as I know 내가 아는 한 review (이용) 후기, 평론
wait in line 줄 서서 기다리다 waiting ticket 대기표

06 정답 ④

Script

W Hi. Can I help you?
M Yes. I saw an advertisement for a discount sale on the door.
W Yeah, we're offering discounts of more than fifty percent.
M Great! [Pause] How much are these boots? I like their design.
W Their regular price is $100, but they're on sale for 50 percent off right now.
M Wow, I'll take them. And how about these sneakers?
W They're $20 at a discounted price.
M Wow, that's so cheap. I'll take them, too. And how about these shoes over here? Are they also on sale?
W Yes. They're $60.
M I'll have to buy them, too. Here's my credit card.

W Thanks.

여 안녕하세요. 도와드릴까요?
남 네. 문에 붙어 있는 할인 판매 광고를 봤어요.
여 네, 저희는 50퍼센트 이상의 할인을 제공하고 있습니다.
남 잘됐군요! [잠시 후] 이 부츠는 얼마인가요? 디자인이 마음에 들어요.
여 그것의 정가는 100달러지만 지금은 50퍼센트 할인 판매 중입니다.
남 와, 그것들을 살게요. 그리고 이 운동화는 얼마예요?
여 할인된 가격으로 20달러입니다.
남 와, 매우 싸네요. 그것들도 살게요. 그리고 이쪽에 있는 구두는 얼마인가요? 그것들도 할인 중인가요?
여 네. 그것들은 60달러입니다.
남 그것들도 사야겠네요. 여기 제 신용카드가 있습니다.
여 감사합니다.

Solution

100달러인 부츠를 50퍼센트 할인된 가격에 사고, 20달러인 운동화와 60달러인 구두를 사겠다고 했으므로, 남자가 지불할 금액은 ④ '130달러'이다.

Words

regular price 정가 on sale 할인 중인

07 정답 ③

Script

M How did the result come out? Were you accepted?
W No. Not yet. I didn't get a call from them.
M Why don't you call them first? They may let you know the result.
W No, I wasn't allowed to.
M Isn't it right that if you pass the exam, they will call you?
W Sure. I think it is about time they called me.
M If they don't call by 12 o'clock, what happens?
W It means I'm not hired.
M We've got just 30 minutes until 12 o'clock.
W Right. That's why I'm so anxious.
M What else can you do except waiting for the call?
W I never knew waiting could be so painful!

남 결과는 어떻게 됐니? 합격했니?
여 아니. 아직 안 나왔어. 전화를 받지 못했어.
남 네가 먼저 전화해 보는 게 어때? 그들이 결과를 알려 줄 수도 있잖아.
여 아니, 그렇게 하는 게 허용되지 않았어.
남 합격되면 분명 그들이 연락해 준다고 한 게 맞아?
여 틀림없어. 이 시간쯤이면 그들이 전화를 했을 거 같은데.
남 12시까지 전화가 안 오면 어떻게 돼?
여 채용되지 않은 것을 의미해.
남 12시까지는 30분밖에 남지 않았구나.
여 맞아. 그래서 나는 너무 불안해.
남 전화 기다리는 것 말고 무엇을 할 수 있겠니?
여 기다린다는 것이 이렇게 고통스러울 수 있을 줄은 몰랐어!

Solution

합격 여부를 통보하는 전화를 기다리고 있는 여자는 연락이 와야 될 시각이 다 되어도 전화가 오지 않아 불안하다고 했으므로, 정답은 ③이다.

Words

accept 받아들이다 allow 허용하다 hire 고용하다
anxious 불안해하는 painful 고통스러운

08 정답 ⑤

Script

M What are you going to do this weekend?

W I'm going to participate in the Milk Up Festival.

M Milk Up Festival? What is it?

W It's a festival held to save the declining dairy industry.

M I see. So what do you usually do at that festival?

W There are various programs such as exhibitions and performances, so I plan to take the kids.

M Who is sponsoring the program?

W It's run by the city hall.

M That sounds great. I'll also have to take my kids this weekend.

W You need to register first on their website.

M Okay. I'll access the website right now.

남 이번 주말에 뭐 할 거예요?

여 Milk Up Festival에 참가할 거예요.

남 Milk Up Festival이라고요? 그게 뭔데요?

여 위축되어 가는 낙농업을 살리기 위해 개최되는 축제예요.

남 그렇군요. 그럼 그 축제에서는 주로 무엇을 하나요?

여 전시와 공연 같은 다양한 프로그램이 있어서 아이들을 데리고 갈 계획이에요.

남 누가 그 프로그램을 후원하고 있나요?

여 시청에서 운영하는 거예요.

남 근사한 것 같네요. 저도 이번 주말에 아이들을 데리고 가 봐야겠어요.

여 먼저 웹사이트에서 등록해야 해요.

남 알겠어요. 지금 당장 웹사이트에 접속해야겠네요.

Solution

개최 목적, 프로그램, 후원, 신청 방법은 언급되었으나 ⑤ '참가 비용'에 대해서는 언급되지 않았다.

Words

participate in ~에 참가하다 decline 위축되다 dairy 낙농의
exhibition 전시 sponsor 후원하다 register 등록하다

09 정답 ④

Script

W Hello. We are proud to announce our 3rd Ballet Festival. The festival is scheduled to run from 11 a.m. to 4 p.m. on August 20th. The festival will be held in the main hall of the city hall, and the City Ballet will be invited to perform. Participants can take ballet class, and the cost of it is $25. Participants can audition for City Hall scholarships. The registration deadline is July 20th. We are extremely excited about the third annual Ballet Festival and look forward to seeing you there.

여 안녕하세요. 제3회 발레 축제를 발표하게 된 것을 자랑스럽게 생각합니다. 축제는 8월 20일 오전 11시부터 오후 4시까지 진행될 예정입니다. 축제는 시청 대강당에서 열리고, 시립 발레단이 초청되어 공연을 할 예정입니다. 참가자들은 발레 수업을 받을 수 있는데 그 비용은 25달러입니다. 참가자들은 시청 장학금을 위한 오디션을 볼 수 있습니다. 등록 마감일은 7월 20일입니다. 우리는 제3회 연례 발레 축제에 대해 매우 흥분

되며 그곳에서 여러분을 만나 뵙기를 기대합니다.

Solution

참가자는 시청 장학금을 위한 오디션을 볼 수 있다고 말했으므로, 담화의 내용과 일치하지 않는 것은 ④ '참가자 전원에게 장학금이 주어진다.'이다.

Words

announce 알리다, 발표하다 annual 연례의 ballet 발레, 발레단
perform 공연하다 participant 참가자 scholarship 장학금
registration 등록 deadline 마감일 extremely 매우

10 정답 ④

Script

M Honey, can you help me choose a summer kids programs for Josh?

W Sure.

M Which program are you thinking?

W Do you think he'd like to explore forests?

M Probably not. He never wants to go hiking.

W Ah, you're right. Then, how about computer coding? He's interested in computer programing.

M Sure, but he's got a full schedule in June. I think he'd like this program.

W Cooking? Yeah, he'd like that, but that's all the way on the east side.

M Right. That's too far away.

W But these two aren't far. I'm sure Josh would like both. Which of them do you think would be better?

M This one. It's cheaper. Spending $250 would be too much.

W Then let's sign him up for that program.

남 여보, Josh를 위한 여름 키즈 프로그램을 고르는 것을 도와줄 수 있어요?

여 그럼요.

남 어느 프로그램을 생각 중이에요?

여 그가 숲을 탐사하는 것을 좋아할 거라 생각해요?

남 아마도 아닐 것 같아요. 그는 절대 하이킹을 가고 싶어 하지 않아요.

여 아, 맞아요. 그럼, 컴퓨터 코딩은 어때요? 그는 컴퓨터 프로그래밍에 관심이 있어요.

남 그렇긴 한데, 6월에는 일정이 꽉 차 있어요. 그가 이 프로그램을 좋아할 것 같아요.

여 요리요? 네, 그는 그것을 좋아하겠지만 그곳은 완전 동쪽에 있어요.

남 맞아요. 너무 멀리 떨어져 있어요.

여 하지만 이 둘은 멀지 않아요. Josh는 분명 둘 다 좋아할 거예요. 그것들 중 어느 것이 더 낫다고 생각하나요?

남 이것이요. 더 싸네요. 250달러를 쓰는 것은 너무 많아요.

여 그럼 그를 그 프로그램에 등록시키죠.

Solution

두 사람은 Josh가 숲을 탐사하는 것을 좋아하지 않고, 6월에는 일정이 꽉 차 있어서 컴퓨터 코딩은 안 되고, 요리 프로그램은 거리가 너무 멀어서 안 된다고 말했다. 거리가 멀지 않은 것 중에서 더 저렴한 프로그램을 등록시켜 주기로 했으므로, 두 사람이 신청할 프로그램은 ④이다.

Words

explore 탐사하다, 탐험하다 all the way 완전히
sign ~ up for ... ~를 …에 등록시키다

11 정답 ①

Script

M Are you just getting back from your Taekwondo practice, Barbara? You look tired.

W Yes, Grandpa. I practiced longer today to get ready for my Taekwondo test next week.

M Oh, that's good. You've been practicing a lot for it.

W As you know, I really want to pass.

남 Barbara, 태권도 연습에서 막 돌아온 거니? 피곤해 보인다.

여 네, 할아버지. 다음 주 태권도 심사를 준비하기 위해 오늘 더 오래 연습했어요.

남 아, 잘했구나. 너는 그것을 위해 많이 연습해 왔지.

여 아시는 것처럼, 전 정말로 통과하고 싶어요.

Solution

남자는 다음 주에 있을 태권도 심사를 준비하기 위해 더 오래 연습하고 돌아온 여자에게 태권도 심사를 위해 많이 연습한 사실을 다시 언급하고 있으므로, ① '아시는 것처럼, 전 정말로 통과하고 싶어요.'가 여자의 응답으로 가장 적절하다.

② 연습 후에 그것을 하는 방법을 알려 드릴게요.

③ 사실, 제가 연습하는 것을 도와주세요.

④ 그래서 지금 심사 결과를 그저 기다리고 있어요.

⑤ 더 연습하는 것은 검은 띠를 따는 것을 도울 거예요.

Words

practice 연습; 연습하다 result 결과

12 정답 ②

Script

W Jacob, you're really good at playing the guitar.

M Thanks. Why don't you learn how to play the guitar? It can make you feel good.

W I'd love to, but I've never played it.

M Don't worry. I can teach you if you want.

여 Jacob, 정말로 기타를 잘 치시네요.

남 감사해요. 당신도 기타 치는 법을 배워 보는 것은 어때요? 그것은 당신을 기분 좋게 만들어 줄 수 있어요.

여 배우고 싶지만, 저는 그것을 쳐 본 적이 없어요.

남 걱정하지 말아요. 원한다면 내가 가르쳐 줄 수 있어요.

Solution

여자가 기타를 배우고 싶지만 한 번도 쳐 본 적이 없다고 했으므로, ② '걱정하지 말아요. 원한다면 내가 가르쳐 줄 수 있어요.'가 남자의 응답으로 가장 적절하다.

① 죄송해요. 지금은 너무 바빠서 당신을 가르쳐 드릴 수 없어요.

③ 고마워요. 당신은 항상 나를 기분 좋게 만들어 줘요.

④ 부탁해요. 당신이 기타 치는 것을 정말로 보고 싶어요.

⑤ 맞아요. 기타를 치는 것은 당신이 쉽게 배울 수 있는 것이 아니에요.

Words

be good at ~을 잘하다 too ~ to ... 너무나 ~해서 …할 수 없다

13 정답 ①

Script

M Is something wrong, Jennifer? You look upset.

W I am, Dad. I had an argument with my friend Linda.

M Really? Did you apologize to her first?

W Why me? She was at fault, too.

M I understand that. But it's always a good idea for you to apologize first.

W What do you mean?

M If both of you wait too long to apologize, you might never be able to recover your friendship.

W Oh, you think so?

M Yeah. If you value your friendship with her, you'd better act first.

W Okay, Dad. Thanks for your advice.

남 무슨 문제라도 있니, Jennifer? 화가 나 보여.

여 그래요, 아빠. 제 친구 Linda와 말다툼을 했어요.

남 그래? 그 애에게 사과했니?

여 왜 제가요? 그 애도 잘못했어요.

남 그것을 이해해. 하지만 네가 먼저 사과하는 것이 항상 좋은 생각이야.

여 무슨 말씀이세요?

남 너희 둘이 너무 오래 기다리다가 사과하지 못한다면, 너희들의 관계를 회복할 수 없을 수도 있단다.

여 아, 그렇게 생각하세요?

남 그래. 그 애와의 우정을 소중히 여긴다면, 먼저 행동하는 것이 좋아.

여 알겠어요, 아빠. 조언해 주셔서 감사해요.

Solution

친구와 말다툼을 한 여자에게 남자는 먼저 사과하는 것이 관계 회복에 도움이 된다는 말과 우정을 소중히 여긴다면 먼저 사과하라고 조언했으므로, ① '알겠어요, 아빠. 조언해 주셔서 감사해요.'가 여자의 응답으로 가장 적절하다.

② 정말요? 이제 왜 아빠가 속상하신지 알겠어요.

③ 죄송해요. 아빠 마음을 너무 아프게 했어요.

④ 좋은 지적이에요. 그녀는 사과하는 법을 배워야 해요.

⑤ 좋아요. 그럼 제가 그녀에게 사과한 것을 비밀로 해 주세요.

Words

argument 논쟁 apologize 사과하다 fault 잘못 recover 회복하다 value 소중히 여기다

14 정답 ④

Script

W Hello, Oliver. Where are you going?

M Hello, Margaret. I'm going to the community center.

W Why are you going there?

M Didn't I tell you about it? I've been volunteering there since last month.

W Really? What kind of volunteer work do you do?

M Well, I work for packing lunch boxes.

W You mean helping to prepare lunch boxes?

M Yeah, that's right.

W What do you do with the packed lunch boxes?

M We deliver them to the elderly living alone in the neighborhood.

W Really? Can I join you and do the work?
M Why not? Everyone in the center will welcome you.

여 안녕, Oliver. 어디 가는 중이야?
남 안녕, Margaret. 문화 센터에 가는 중이야.
여 왜 거기를 가는데?
남 그것에 대해 말해 주지 않았니? 지난달부터 거기에서 자원봉사를 해오고 있어.
여 그래? 무슨 자원봉사를 하는데?
남 음, 점심 도시락을 포장하는 일을 해.
여 점심 도시락을 준비하는 것을 돕는다는 말이니?
남 그래, 맞아.
여 포장된 점심 도시락으로 무엇을 하는데?
남 동네 독거 어르신들에게 그것들을 전달해.
여 정말? 나도 같이 가서 그 일을 할 수 있니?
남 왜 안 되겠어? 센터에 있는 모든 사람들이 너를 환영할 거야.

문화 센터에서 어르신들에게 드릴 점심 도시락을 포장하고 그것을 전해 드리는 자원봉사를 한다는 남자에게 여자는 자신도 그 일을 할 수 있는지를 묻고 있으므로, ④ '왜 안 되겠어? 센터에 있는 모든 사람들이 너를 환영할 거야.' 가 남자의 응답으로 가장 적절하다.

① 문제없어. 내가 그들을 돌볼 수 있어.
② 알고 있어. 네가 자원봉사를 하는 것을 좋아하지 않는다고 생각했어.
③ 미안해. 나는 그날 다른 약속이 있어.
⑤ 맞아. 우리는 어르신들에게 더 관심을 가져야 해.

pack 포장하다 deliver 배달하다 the elderly 어르신들

15 정답 ④

W Jenny is going to the local library to return the books she had checked out. She's going to come back home right after returning the books because her family is supposed to have dinner together. On the way to the library, she meets David by chance. Jenny asks him where he is going. He says he is going to the library to get some materials for the social assignment. Jenny asks him which library it is, and she learns he's going to the same library. Jenny wants to ask David if he can return her books for her. In this situation, what would Jenny most likely say to David?
Jenny Then, can you return my books to the library?

여 Jenny는 대출했던 책들을 반납하러 지역 도서관에 가고 있는 중입니다. 그녀는 그 책들만 반납하고 바로 집으로 돌아올 예정인데 왜냐하면 그녀의 가족이 다 함께 저녁을 먹기로 되어 있기 때문입니다. 도서관으로 가는 도중에, 그녀는 우연히 David를 만납니다. Jenny는 그에게 어디 가고 있냐고 묻습니다. 그는 사회 과제를 위한 자료를 좀 얻기 위해 도서관에 가고 있다고 말합니다. Jenny는 어느 도서관인지를 그에게 묻고, 그가 같은 도서관에 가고 있다는 것을 알게 됩니다. Jenny는 David에게 자신의 책들을 대신 반납해 줄 수 있는지 묻고자 합니다. 이런 상황에서 Jenny는 David에게 뭐라고 말할 것 같은가요?
Jenny 그럼, 내 책들을 도서관에 반납해 줄 수 있어?

책을 반납하러 도서관에 가던 Jenny가 같은 곳으로 가는 David를 만나 책

을 대신 반납해 줄 수 있는지를 묻고 싶어 하는 상황이므로, 이러한 상황에서 Jenny가 David에게 할 말로 가장 적절한 것은 ④ '그럼, 내 책들을 도서관에 반납해 줄 수 있어?'이다.

① 안됐구나. 그럼 내가 도와줄 수 있을 것 같아.
② 미안해. 지금은 너무 바빠서 도서관에 갈 수가 없어.
③ 음, 네가 그 책이 있는지를 확인해 주면 좋겠어.
⑤ 걱정 마. 네게 그 책들을 빌려줄 수 있을 거야.

return 반납하다 check out 대출하다
be supposed to do ~하기로 되어 있다 by chance 우연히
assignment 과제

16 정답 ④   17 정답 ④

M Hello, everybody. Perhaps many of you have struggled with being unable to sleep at night. Today I'm going to give you some tips for dealing with it. First of all, try to get enough sunlight during the day. If you get enough sunlight during the day, you can easily fall asleep because a large amount of melatonin is released at night. Try to walk for at least an hour a day right away. Never exercise at night. Exercising in the evening or late at night delays the time you fall asleep, so you should finish exercising 5-6 hours before bedtime. When you exercise, your blood pressure tends to rise. Also, do not try to force yourself to fall asleep. If you can't sleep after 20 minutes of lying down, sit on a sofa or chair and read a book or watch TV. Lastly, if you take a cool shower 2 hours before bed, it is good to sleep well. When your body temperature goes down, you can get a good night's sleep. Thank you for listening.

남 안녕하세요, 여러분. 아마도 여러분들 중 많은 분들은 밤에 잠을 잘 잘 수 없어 고생해 본 적이 있을 겁니다. 오늘은 그것을 다루기 위한 몇 가지 조언을 말씀해 드리겠습니다. 우선, 낮에 충분한 햇빛을 받도록 하십시오. 낮에 충분히 햇빛을 받으면 밤에 많은 양의 멜라토닌이 분비돼 쉽게 잠들 수 있습니다. 당장 하루에 적어도 1시간은 산책하려고 노력해 보십시오. 야간 운동은 절대 하지 마십시오. 저녁이나 밤늦게 운동하면 잠드는 시간을 늦추기 때문에 잠자기 5~6시간 전에 운동을 마쳐야 합니다. 운동을 하면 혈압이 올라가는 경향이 있습니다. 또한, 억지를 자려고 애쓰지 마십시오. 누워서 20분이 지났는데도 잠이 안 오면 소파나 의자에 앉아 책을 읽거나 TV를 보십시오. 마지막으로, 잠자기 2시간 전에 시원한 물로 샤워를 하면 숙면하기 .. 체온이 내려가면 밤에 숙면을 취할 수 있습니다. 들어 주셔서 감사합니다.

16

밤에 잠을 잘 잘 수 없을 때 그것을 다루기 위한 몇 가지 조언을 알려 주고 있으므로, 남자가 하는 말의 주제로 가장 적절한 것은 ④ '잠을 잘 수 없을 때의 효과적인 조치'이다.

① 건강하게 지내기 위한 간단한 습관
② 밤에 숙면을 취해야 하는 이유
③ 규칙적인 운동이 수면에 미치는 영향
⑤ 올바른 자세로 자는 것의 중요성

17

걷기, 운동, 독서, 샤워는 언급되었지만, ④ '낮잠'은 언급되지 않았다.

Words

struggle 고투하다, 해결하려고 애쓰다 fall asleep 잠들다
release 발산하다, 방출하다 delay 연기하다, 늦추다
blood pressure 혈압 body temperature 체온

MEMO

MEMO

MEMO

MEMO

MEMO

MEMO

Listening master

BASIC

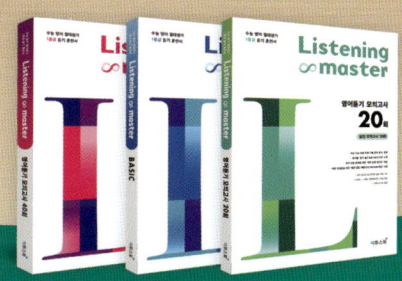

800문장으로 강화하는 **고등 필수 구문**

C.O.R.E 구문 800

✓ 우선 순위 빈출 구문 ✓ 고득점 대비 주요 구문

기본

워크북 제공

워크북 제공

핵심 800문장으로 완성하는 **고등 필수 구문**

C.O.R.E 구문 800 기본

이투스북

완성

워크북 제공

핵심 800문장으로 완성하는 **고등 필수 구문**

C.O.R.E 구문 800 완성

이투스북

❶ 필수 구문 포인트

도식화 설명으로
구문 패턴 학습 가능

PLUS코너를 통한
심화 내용 학습

❷ 대표&연습 문장

2~3개의 대표 문장으로
구문 패턴 연습 가능

직접 분석 및 해석 가능한
연습 문장 포함

❸ 고난도 문장

앞서 학습한 내용을
응용할 수 있는
고난도 문장 학습

이투스북